ADULT DEVELOPMENT AND AGING

Second Edition

Adult Development and Aging

Second Edition

John W. Rybash

Hamilton College
Mohawk Valley Community College

Paul A. Roodin

State University of New York, Oswego

John W. Santrock

University of Texas, Dallas

WCB Wm. C. Brown Publishers

Book Team

Editor *Michael Lange*
Developmental Editor *Carla J. Aspelmeier*
Production Editor *Harry Halloran*
Designer *David C. Lansdon*
Art Editor *Jess Schaal*
Photo Editor *Carol M. Smith*
Permissions Editor *Karen L. Storlie*
Visuals Processor *Andreá Lopez-Meyer*

WCB **Wm. C. Brown Publishers**

President *G. Franklin Lewis*
Vice President, Publisher *George Wm. Bergquist*
Vice President, Publisher *Thomas E. Doran*
Vice President, Operations and Production *Beverly Kolz*
National Sales Manager *Virginia S. Moffat*
Senior Marketing Manager *Kathy Law Laube*
Marketing Manager *George Chapin*
Executive Editor *Edgar J. Laube*
Managing Editor, Production *Colleen A. Yonda*
Production Editorial Manager *Julie A. Kennedy*
Production Editorial Manager *Ann Fuerste*
Publishing Services Manager *Karen J. Slaght*
Manager of Visuals and Design *Faye M. Schilling*

Cover: Charles Angrand, *Couple on the Street*. 1887. Oil on linen mounted on cardboard, 15 in. × 13 in. Giraudon/Art Resource, Inc. New York.

Interior design by Jeanne Marie Regan

Library of Congress Catalog Card Number: 90–80265

ISBN 0–697–03312–0

Printed in the United States of America by Wm. C. Brown Publishers, 2460 Kerper Boulevard, Dubuque, IA 52001

10 9 8 7 6 5 4 3 2 1

To my wife Vinnie, a continual source of encouragement, understanding, patience, and love.
J. R.

To my children Neal and Pamela whose constant love, joy, and thoughtfulness make each day of my life a delight.
P. R.

CONTENTS

PREFACE

TO THE STUDENT

The field of adult development and aging is an exciting one. For many years, the prevailing view of adult development was that the adult years were a time of steady decline and little, if any, positive psychological change. Many psychologists believed that an individual's intelligence, creativity, and personality were cast in stone by the end of adolescence. To be sure, childhood and adolescence have important effects on psychological makeup. But the next five, six, or seven decades are just as complex and just as important as the first two decades of life. They are important not only to the adults passing through them, but also to their children and grandchildren, who must live with and understand these adults.

As you read this book, you most likely will find yourself thinking about what the rest of your adult life holds in store for you. What will you be like at mid-life, at age seventy? By the time you have completed this book, you should have a much clearer picture of the awesome, complex unfolding of development during the adult years. Not only will you learn important facts about the nature of adult development, you should be able to use some of these facts to interpret your own life as you grow older. Our hope is that this book will leave something special with you, something that you will want to take with you after completing the class so that you can refer to it for the rest of your life. What you learn can be a guide to your future growth and development and make you aware of the significant challenges that all of us must face as we age.

TO THE INSTRUCTOR

An instructor faces a difficult task in deciding which textbook to adopt for a course in adult development and aging. The book you are about to read, *Adult Development and Aging*, presents a unique blend of up-to-date, cutting-edge research and theory; issue-focused discussion; and a writing style that will engage and motivate students. In this second edition, we offer you and your students a clear, comprehensive, and current account of the salient issues and concerns that dominate the field. After reading this text, your students will have a keen understanding of where the field of adult development and aging has been in the past, where it is right now, and where it will be headed in the future.

In *Adult Development and Aging,* we decided to adopt a *process* orientation. Through this orientation, your students will be able to see how different developmental *processes* produce fundamental changes in different dimensions of adult life. To this end, different chapters in the text focus on biological processes and physical development; cognitive processes and development; social processes, contexts, and development; and personality processes and development. In addition, the first two chapters of the text provide the most comprehensive and comprehensible discussion of developmental issues and developmental research methods available in any text on adult development and aging. The material contained in these chapters reflects a broad range of ideas that are too often written about in either too difficult or too simplistic a manner for most students to appreciate. We urge you to explore the two introductory chapters in *Adult Development and Aging;* we believe they are unsurpassed in terms of scientific accuracy, ease of understanding, completeness of coverage, and style of presentation. Also inspect our final chapter on death and dying. It emphasizes the psychological meanings of death, the coping processes of both the dying individual and his or her loved ones, and society's changing attitudes about death and dying.

Virtually all textbook authors try to accomplish the difficult task of maintaining academic excellence while avoiding a stuffy, didactic style that is likely to turn students off. We believe that the second edition of *Adult Development and Aging* accomplishes this task better than the dozen or so other adulthood and aging texts that are now on the market. First, the writing itself is clear, lively, logical, and communicative. Second, a number of pedagogical devices make the book interesting as well as informative. Each chapter opens with a chapter outline followed by an "Imagine" section, which stimulates students to think about a particular problem or crisis in adult development unique to the subject of the chapter. Each chapter also includes a number of boxed inserts containing supplementary, high-interest, discussion-provoking material. A comprehensive glossary appears at the end of the text; we have also made certain that all key terms are highlighted, defined, and thoroughly explained the first time they are mentioned in the text. These are just some of the pedagogical and organizational features that make the second edition of *Adult Development and Aging* not only the most current and informative text available but the most interesting and enjoyable to read as well.

AUDIENCE

This text is appropriate for students taking an introductory or advanced course in adult development and aging. Such courses may be titled Adult Development, Adult Development and Aging (or the Psychology of Adult Development and Aging), Adult Psychology, Psychology of Adulthood, or simply Aging. The typical student in such a course is likely to be a sophomore, junior, or senior undergraduate who has completed a general introductory-level psychology course. However, the text assumes no prior detailed knowledge of psychology and is written in a style that allows the student to build a conceptual structure of the field from the ground up.

Adult Development and Aging would also be useful to instructors who teach a course in life-span development and want to use two books—one on child and adolescent development and another on adult development and aging. The text is equally appropriate for faculty at two-year and four-year colleges and universities. Finally, *Adult Development and Aging* is most suitable for individuals teaching in the departments of Psychology, Human Services, Gerontology, Sociology, Social Work, Nursing, and Education.

CONTENT AND ORGANIZATION

Adult Development and Aging presents the basic views, principles, research findings, and ideas about adulthood from an interdisciplinary, process-oriented perspective. The adoption of such a perspective allows students to understand the psychology of the aging individual through an analysis of the biological, social, and cultural contexts in which aging occurs. The text consists of thirteen chapters, each concerned with a major theme or aspect of adult development and aging. (See the Contents for more detailed information.)

ADDITIONAL TEXTUAL LEARNING AIDS

This text has been written with the student in mind. We have already mentioned some of the unique pedagogical aids in the text, including the chapter outlines, "Imagine" sections, boxes, and extensive glossary. In addition, all of the terms contained in the glossary are printed in **boldface** type when they first appear in the text. This will alert your students to the importance of basic terms and provide them with a concise definition of each of these terms when needed. Graphs, tables, and figures illustrate the findings of important research studies, compare and contrast different theoretical perspectives, and summarize important issues. Photographs and line drawings give visual emphasis to key concepts and events and to those people, present and past, who have advanced our knowledge of adult development and aging. Finally, each chapter ends with a detailed summary, a list of review questions, and suggestions for further reading. Separate indexes for authors and subjects appear at the end of the book.

INSTRUCTOR'S MANUAL AND TEST BANK

An *Instructor's Manual and Test Bank* by Michael G. Walraven is available to adopters. This manual contains an introductory essay to the instructor for each chapter, followed by six to eight essay questions, twenty-five multiple-choice items, and a film/videotape list. The multiple-choice items are also available on *Testpak,* **WCB** 's computerized testing service.

ACKNOWLEDGMENTS

Special thanks go to Wm. C. Brown Publishers for the special attention given this book. Michael Lange and Carla Aspelmeier, Psychology Editors, have provided support and encouragement throughout this project. Production editor Harry Halloran has competently overseen the swift and accurate production of this book. David Lansdon, the designer, has made *Adult Development and Aging* very attractive and readable. And Carol Smith deserves credit for her work on the photographs, and Karen Storlie for her efforts in obtaining permissions. We also thank Anne Cody and Toni Michaels for their assistance in copyediting and photo research.

Michael Walraven deserves special thanks as well. He has prepared an *Instructor's Manual and Test Bank* that will greatly enhance the use of this text.

We owe special thanks to Dr. James C. Bartlett, Program in Psychology and Human Development, the University of Texas at Dallas. Dr. Bartlett's contributions to the chapters on Issues concerning the Nature of Adult Development and Aging and Methods in the first edition of *Adult Development and Aging* continued to serve as an important foundation for those chapters in the current edition.

The second edition of this text benefited greatly from the assistance provided by colleagues through user reviews of the first edition and in-depth reviews of the revised manuscript at various stages of development. For their countless good ideas and helpful suggestions, we would like to thank the following:

Frederic Agatstein, Rhode Island College
Denise R. Barnes, University of North Carolina–Chapel Hill
F. H. Blanchard-Fields, Louisiana State University
Dr. Philip Compton, Ohio Northern University
Elton C. Davis, Pasadena City College
Dr. Rodney Dennis, Kennesaw College
Joan T. Erber, Florida International University
Shirlee Fenwick, Augustana College
Robert J. Gregory, University of Idaho
Marcia Moshé, Ryerson Polytechnical Institute
Carmen H. Owen, York College of Pennsylvania
Suzanne Prescott, Governors State University
Robert F. Rycek, Kearney State College

We also remain indebted to the following individuals who reviewed the first edition and whose helpful guidance has been carried forward into the second edition:

Don C. Charles, Iowa State University
Ernest Furchtgott, University of South Carolina
Bert Hayslip, Jr., North Texas State University
Mary W. Lawrence, University of Toronto
Robert Bruce McLaren, California State University–Fullerton
Mary Jane S. Van Meter, Wayne State University

Finally, we would like to thank our wives, Vinnie Rybash, Marlene Roodin, and Mary Jo Santrock for their patient support and understanding during the long preparation of this manuscript.

CHAPTER 1

ISSUES CONCERNING THE NATURE OF ADULT DEVELOPMENT AND AGING

With James C. Bartlett

IMAGINE

Imagine All the Different Points of View You Have Had about Adulthood and Aging during the Course of Your Life Thus Far

As you approached elementary school age, you probably began to be aware of the concept of "age." You noticed that your life was divided into segments called "years." You realized that every year you had a birthday, and that the years of your life were measured by each new birthday. You probably found it easy to estimate the ages of the other children in your family and of some of your closest playmates. You could probably tell, for example, that if you were five years old, your little sister was three years old. On the other hand, estimating the ages of the grown-ups in your family and neighborhood was very difficult.

As you grew older, you probably began to notice differences between adults. You may have heard people call your grandparents "old" and your parents "young." You may have even heard people use negative-sounding words such as "sickness" and "death" when speaking of older people. Eventually you began to notice the physical differences between yourself, your parents, and your grandparents. Your grandparents looked different from your parents: they dressed differently, and they had gray hair and wrinkled skin. You may have also noticed that your grandparents were not able to engage in some of the strenuous physical activities you and your parents enjoyed. You may have concluded that older people sit a lot or never seem to have much energy. You probably loved and admired your grandparents a great deal because of the love they shared with you and because of the joyful times you spent with them. But you probably also began to realize that they were old and that, in the long run, young is better than old.

By the time you entered high school, you likely had developed a better understanding of the concept of age. You became capable of anticipating the differences that might exist between people who were twenty-five, forty-five, and sixty-five years old. Also, you began to understand the psychological as well as physical differences between adults of different ages. For example, you began to believe that individuals possess an array of permanent psychological traits (for example, open-mindedness) and abilities (for example, creativity). Most importantly, based on your observations of individuals of varied ages, you may well have begun to think that these traits and abilities grow and develop during the early part of a person's life, level off during young adulthood, and decrease during old age. At this time you most likely felt even more certain that young is better than old. You may have felt exceptionally happy that, for you, old age was a long way off.

At present, regardless of your age, you may still believe that you are quite a distance from "old age." But you certainly realize that with the passage of time you will become an older person. You may have already experienced the death of a grandparent, parent, or close relative. And you may see the first subtle signs of aging in your own parents or yourself. Suddenly you realize that aging affects everyone. As you enter adulthood, you may imagine what you or your parents will be like as you age. Will your earlier conceptions about growing old turn out to be true? Will you necessarily become less intelligent and less open-minded as you age? Will you be less active or more physically restricted? Or will you discover that development through adulthood and the later years is a much more challenging, multifaceted, and positive process than you ever imagined? Can growing older bring benefits? Can you become a different type of person as you age—more wise and kind? And to what extent will factors other than biological aging—personal life experiences, education, historical change, and so on—influence the pattern, rate, and direction of your own development?

INTRODUCTION

This chapter—indeed, this text—is concerned with the questions raised in the first "Imagine" section. The following pages will introduce a life-span perspective to the study of adulthood and aging. We will examine several characteristics of developmental change during the adult years and then explore some of the factors that enhance adult development. Finally, we will look at various models of adult development and relate these models to the different ways psychologists conceptualize developmental change.

A LIFE-SPAN PERSPECTIVE ON ADULTHOOD AND AGING

At first we want life to be romantic; later to be bearable; finally to be understandable.
—Louise Bogan

A book entitled *Adult Development and Aging* is obviously based on a premise; the premise that development is not restricted to children and adolescents but continues throughout the entire adult life span. Is this premise reasonable? Does it make sense to apply a single word—*development*—not only to the period between birth and twenty-one years of age, but also to the period between ages twenty-one and seventy, and even beyond to a hundred or more?

The vast majority of traditional approaches to the study of human development have been based on observations of the child. The developmental theories advocated by Jean Piaget and Sigmund Freud are exemplars of this child-focused approach. When major developmental theorists discussed adulthood, they viewed it as a period of stability and continuity; while old age, if they even addressed it, was characterized as a period of dramatic loss and decline. Aging, these theorists assumed, automatically is accompanied by deteriorating sensory capabilities (as evidenced by the need for bifocals, hearing aids, and canes); a loss in reaction speed (or reflex) and physical prowess; and even declines in intellectual capacities (Grandmother's memory is not what it used to be, is it?).

Given these widespread assumptions about the reality of age-related decline, it is hardly surprising that until recently no explicit developmental theory focused on adult development (Havighurst, 1973). Before the middle of the twentieth century, there was no systematic body of knowledge that encompassed the adult portion of an individual's lifetime, and there were no theories or models of adult psychological development. Scientists' neglect of the study of adulthood may be traced to two main factors. First, both common sense and scientific "wisdom" assumed that development ends in adolescence, typically at puberty. Second, many theorists viewed adulthood as a less salient part of the life span because of the shorter life expectancies of individuals who lived in earlier time periods.

Many of these earlier assumptions about adult development and aging are *not* supported by current scientific research. In fact, the **life-span approach** (Baltes, 1973; 1987; Baltes, Reese and Lipsitt, 1980) suggests that positive developmental change is likely to occur during all of the major epochs of the life span, especially adulthood. One of the major purposes of this text is to help you set aside preconceived notions about inevitable age-related declines and to replace such notions with more objective information about developmental change during the adult years—facts that have been derived from (1) careful observation, and (2) scientifically testable theories. These facts should help you attain a balanced and integrative view of adult development and aging—a view that considers the advances as well as the declines that occur over the course of adult life.

To achieve these goals, it is first necessary to understand the meaning of the term *development* from a life-span perspective and to distinguish between the concepts of **development** and **change.** Change involves a measurable alteration in a particular skill, ability, or function. For example, increasing age is accompanied by predictable changes in human learning ability. The ability to acquire new information becomes progressively more efficient from early childhood to early adulthood (a positive change), but seems to become less efficient from young adulthood to old age (a negative change). On the other hand, development refers to a form of change that is *organized* and *adaptive* (positive) in nature. For example, as we just indicated, learning efficiency seems to decrease with advancing age. At face value, this seems to be a purely negative change. Could there be anything remotely adaptive about an age-related decrement in learning efficiency? Yes, there could! Several psychologists (LaBouvie-Vief, 1985; Rozin 1976; Rybash, Hoyer, and Roodin, 1986) have suggested that the primary developmental goal of childhood and adolescence is to acquire new information from a large number of domains—children and adolescents are organized to be "ideal learning machines." It may be maladaptive in adulthood, however, to continually acquire new pieces of information. Perhaps adulthood is the time during the life span to develop an understanding or perspective on the information one has gained and to pass this information on to others. This may even be one of the primary goals of adulthood! The point is that adulthood may be viewed as a period of decay or decline when compared to the developmental tasks of childhood; but it may also be viewed as a period of adaptive developmental growth when considered on its own terms.

In essence, then, the life-span perspective suggests that development is not restricted to any one part of the life span: development is truly a lifelong process. It also suggests that development cannot be solely equated with steady incremental growth or change. Instead, development is characterized by the simultaneous appearance of gain and loss. Paul Baltes is considered one of the founders of the life-span perspective on adult development. Table 1.1 summarizes Baltes's general concepts and the specific propositions characteristic of the life-span approach. Some of these concepts have already been discussed. The remainder will be explored throughout the rest of this chapter.

Table 1.1

AN OVERVIEW OF THE GENERAL CONCEPTS AND SPECIFIC PROPOSITIONS THAT CHARACTERIZE LIFE-SPAN DEVELOPMENTAL PSYCHOLOGY

General Concepts	*Specific Propositions*
Life-span development	Development is a lifelong process. No age period holds supremacy in regulating the nature of development. During development, and at all stages of the life span, both continuous (cumulative) and discontinuous (innovative) processes are at work.
Multidirectionality	Considerable diversity or pluralism is found in the directionality of changes that constitute ontogenesis, even within the same domain. The direction of change varies by categories of behavior. In addition, during the same developmental periods, some systems of behavior show increases, whereas others evince decreases in level of functioning.
Development as gain/loss	The process of development is not a simple movement toward higher efficacy, such as incremental growth. Rather, throughout life, development always consists of the joint occurrence of gain (growth) and loss (decline).
Plasticity	Much intraindividual plasticity (within-person modifiability) is found in psychological development. Depending on the life conditions and experiences of a given individual, his or her developmental course can take many forms. The key developmental agenda is the search for the range of plasticity and its constraints.
Historical embeddedness	Development can also vary substantially in accordance with historical-cultural conditions. How ontogenetic (age-related) development proceeds is markedly influenced by the kind of sociocultural conditions existing in a given historical period, and by how these evolve over time.
Contextualism	Any particular course of individual development can be understood as the outcome of the interactions (dialectics) among three systems of developmental influences: age-graded, history-graded, and nonnormative. The operation of these systems can be characterized in terms of the metatheoretical principles associated with contextualism.
Field of development as multidisciplinary	Psychological development needs to be seen in the interdisciplinary context provided by other disciplines (for example, anthropology, biology, sociology) concerned with human development. The openness of the life-span perspective to interdisciplinary posture implies that a "purist"psychological view offers but a partial representation of behavioral development from conception to death.

From P. B. Baltes, "Theoretical Propositions of Life-Span Developmental Psychology: On the Dynamics Between Growth and Decline" in *Developmental Psychology*, 23:611–626. Copyright 1987 by the American Psychological Association. Reprinted by permission.

CHARACTERISTICS OF ADULT DEVELOPMENT

The life-span perspective raises several important issues that are beginning to guide research in adult development and aging. One such issue involves describing the basic characteristics of adult development. Is adult development characterized by qualitative or quantitative changes? Are these changes stagelike or nonstagelike? Is development continuous or discontinuous? Is it multidirectional or unidirectional? Are developmental changes reversible or irreversible? In the next section we'll examine each of these issues.

Qualitative versus Quantitative Change

Jean Piaget, the preeminent child psychologist, first made the provocative suggestion that it is inappropriate to evaluate children's intellectual abilities using the standards developed to assess adult intellect. Piaget argued that qualitative changes in intelligence occur between infancy and adolescence. This means that the basic manner in which individuals represent experience changes dramatically during the course of development. For example, Piaget suggested that infants can only represent objects by means of body movements, not by internal mental symbols (Flavell, 1985). Thus young infants do not possess *object permanence:* they do not conceive of objects as existing independently of themselves. Before infants fully develop object permanence, they may not realize that an object continues to exist when it is not in direct sight or when it is covered or partially hidden. At about two years of age, young children fully understand object permanence because of a qualitative shift in their intelligence—they become capable of representing objects by internal mental symbols rather than external body movement. Thus, development is characterized by a qualitative shift from one type of thinking to another. The development of object permanence serves as a prototype of qualitative change in development.

Does development in adulthood involve qualitative changes of the sort that Piaget claimed were a part of cognitive development in infancy and childhood? The answer, from the life-span perspective, is that qualitative changes are indeed possible. For example, several psychologists (Commons, Richards, and Armon, 1984; 1989) have extended Piaget's stage-structural theory of cognition into adulthood. They have found evidence suggesting that adulthood is marked by a qualitative change in thinking, especially about social/interpersonal relations. We will study more about the qualitatively distinct styles of adult intelligence in chapter 7.

Quantitative change refers to differences in amount rather than differences in kind. For example, throughout early childhood, the amount of information that individuals can hold in short-term memory increases. Many psychologists studying adult development emphasize the existence of quantitative changes in memory, attention, and reasoning ability. Similarly, many psychologists who are interested in the study of personality also view adulthood as a period of quantitative change.

For example, with increasing age, people may become more passive or active, masculine or feminine, and closed- or open-minded.

Whether adult development is essentially qualitative or quantitative in nature is both an empirical and theoretical issue. The life-span perspective simply *raises* the question of whether developmental change is qualitative or quantitative. It is certainly possible that developmental change may be *both* qualitative and quantitative (Lerner, 1984; Rybash, et al. 1986).

Stagelike versus Nonstagelike Change

Developmental theorists such as Freud and Piaget maintain that identifiable stages occur in the development of children. The notion of stagelike change is controversial; not only do researchers disagree about the existence of developmental stages, they also argue about the defining criteria which indicate the presence of stages.

Any conceptualization of developmental stages must incorporate the notion of qualitative change. Moreover, the stages-of-development concept implies that qualitative changes must occur in sequence (stage 1 must precede stage 2 and not vice versa). Many developmental psychologists (Flavell, 1985) go still further. They claim that the idea of stages implies that (1) each successive stage consists of the integration and extension of a previous stage, (2) the transition from one stage to another is marked by a certain degree of abruptness, and (3) each stage forms an organized whole (that is, there is a concurrence in the appearance of behaviors or competencies that are characteristic of a given stage). Thus, if an entire set of organized behaviors appeared rather suddenly in the course of development for most if not all individuals at a certain point in the life span, and if each new stage incorporated and extended the competencies of the previous stage, then we would have clear evidence for a developmental stage of some sort. Unfortunately, evidence for such occurrences is quite rare and unconvincing, leading some investigators to doubt the stage concept (Flavell, 1985) and others to want to redefine the concept (Fischer, 1988; Wohlwill, 1973). Despite these problems, the stage concept has an enduring appeal for many developmental psychologists, including those studying adult development and aging.

However, other developmental psychologists subscribe to the idea that the stage concept is excess baggage and serves little useful function (Kiel, 1986). For example, a great deal of research based on the administration of IQ tests has yielded invaluable evidence about the nature of adult intellectual change (Baltes, 1987; Schaie and Hertzog, 1985). But the measurement of intelligence using traditional IQ tests makes no reference whatsoever to *stages* in intellectual change.

Throughout this text, we will return to this point of tension in conceptualizing life-span development. The life-span perspective does not necessarily view development as *either* stagelike *or* nonstagelike. Instead, the life-span perspective suggests that some dimensions of the individual's development can be conceptualized as stagelike, while other dimensions do not lend themselves to the stage concept.

Continuity versus Discontinuity of Functioning

Nonstage theories imply that development is essentially *continuous*. This means that the same types of processes control psychological functioning over the entire life span. According to social learning theorists, an individual's behavior is continually shaped over the course of development through imitation, reward, and punishment. The influence of these mechanisms may result in an increase, a decrease, or stability in several different behaviors over the life span. For example, because of changes in certain reinforcement contingencies, we can expect that some adults will display increases in depressive symptomatology and feelings of helplessness as they age.

On the other hand, stage theories, because they imply an abruptness in development, also seem to imply a *discontinuity* of change. At another level, however, stage theories argue for continuity. Psychological functioning at one developmental stage is contingent upon functioning at a prior stage. Put simply, stage theories argue that the achievement of one stage depends upon the achievement of all prior stages; one cannot achieve stage 3 without going through stages 1 and 2 and so on.

Though change may be abrupt, stage theories assume a connection between functioning before and after the change (Kagan, 1980). This connective developmental thread is a type of continuity. Thus, while developmental change can be qualitative and even abrupt—as stage theories suggest—a clear sense of continuity can exist between stages.

Reversibility versus Irreversibility of Change

There is little doubt that many aspects of adult development appear unattractive. No one wants to experience a decline in visual acuity, physical prowess, or reaction speed. Yet some people do experience these changes as they grow older. As we will see, there is also some evidence, albeit controversial, for age-related declines in certain types of specific intellectual performance such as memory.

One exciting implication of a life-span perspective is that undesirable aspects of adult development may sometimes be reversible. That is, many age-related deficits may be altered through appropriate intervention, such as training and education programs or even changes in diet and life-style. Even biologically-based declines may someday prove reversible as we increase our understanding of the physiological mechanisms underlying behavior.

Although the reversibility of some aspects of adult development is an exciting possibility to explore, we have as yet very little scientific evidence on the magnitude and permanence of such reversibility. Moreover, many practical and ethical concerns crop up when considering the reversal of various aspects of adult development. Is the reversal of a developmental function always practical? Is it always in the individual's best interests?

To answer these questions, we must carefully consider the costs versus the benefits of altering these age-related declines. It may be possible to reverse a decline, but the high costs in terms of time, effort, and money may make the endeavor of questionable value. We must also be wary of imposing our own priorities and value systems upon those we presumably are serving. A rigorous educational program designed to improve certain aspects of social functioning in old age may simply fail to make sense within the context of an elderly person's life.

Multidirectional versus Unidirectional Change

A life-span perspective implies that development is multidirectional (Baltes, 1987). As we study adult human development, we may see stability in some types of functions, declines in others, and improvements in still others. Moreover, these patterns are not the same in all individuals. Consider, for instance, the range of individual differences in creative thought during adulthood. Creative thought may decline for some individuals, remain stable in others, and increase in still others.

Multidirectionality is a significant concept in understanding individual patterns in aging. One individual who displays an increase in creativity as he ages may also display a decrement in memory. Another individual may manifest an increase in creativity along with stability in the ability to remember. The life-span perspective suggests that individual differences in the course of adult development may help us understand the variety of patterns of intellectual, personality, and biological functioning in adulthood.

Put somewhat differently, the life-span perspective emphasizes the study of **intraindividual change** and **interindividual variability** over the adult years. Intraindividual change refers to the study of different patterns of developmental change *within* individual adults. The concept of interindividual variability refers to different patterns of developmental change *between* different adults. Thus, the life-span perspective suggests that various aspects of an individual develop in different ways and that different people show different overall patterns of development.

Earlier child-focused views of development, such as those advocated by Piaget and Freud, assumed a unidirectional view of developmental change. These theorists suggested that all individuals develop in the same predictable way. These non-life-span views attempted to explain psychological change by applying biological models. Human biological functions follow the same unidirectional path during development: rapid growth in infancy, childhood, and adolescence, stability during early adulthood, and decline in middle to later adulthood. Therefore, earlier theorists assumed that the entire range of human psychological functions followed the same pathway as well.

DETERMINANTS OF ADULT DEVELOPMENTAL CHANGE

Why do individuals change and develop as they do? In this section we will examine three different factors that promote developmental change: *normative age-graded factors, normative history-graded factors,* and *nonnormative life events.* We will see that development occurs as the result of the interaction of these factors. We shall also see how easy it is to mistakenly attribute developmental change to age-graded factors alone.

Normative Age-Graded Factors

When we study young children, it appears that development is *normative,* or similar across individuals and even cultures. It also appears that development is determined largely by a variety of **normative age-graded factors**—influences closely related to the individual's age. For example, the maturation and deterioration of the brain and nervous system occur at roughly the same ages in all individuals. Other life events are also closely related to age, such as obtaining our first "real" jobs or retiring from work. Such normative age-graded factors clearly have the potential to influence adult development. Thus it appears compelling, at first glance, to attribute developmental change solely to normative age-graded factors. For example, it seems intuitively true that older adults experience a generalized decline in their intellectual abilities and that this decline is entirely caused by the gradual deterioration of the nervous system that accompanies normal aging. It is inappropriate, however, to explain *all* developmental change during adulthood in terms of normative age-graded factors.

Nonnormative Life Events

Many influences on adult development are **nonnormative life events**—unique events not experienced by everyone. Some nonnormative life events are common to a small proportion of same-age individuals; others affect only a single individual. Furthermore, nonnormative life events do not happen at any predictable time in a person's life. For example, winning first prize in a multimillion-dollar state lottery is an event that would profoundly influence a person's behavior. However, it is only likely to happen to a small number of individuals and cannot be predicted to occur at any particular point in a person's life. Nonnormative life events, then, are usually chance occurrences.

Other typical examples of nonnormative events include accidents, illness, business failure, or the death of a loved one. Albert Bandura (1982) reminds us that nonnormative life events also include unintended meetings of people unfamiliar to one another. It is sobering to reflect that chance encounters may become critically important determinants of many aspects of our lives, including career choice and marriage. How many college students settle on an academic major because of an enthusiastic and inspiring professor they encounter by chance in an elective course? How many young men and women receive their first job offers through an unanticipated meeting at a party? These are important and interesting questions that have yet to be explored in the scientific literature. The role of scientific research in this area is probably not to predict the occurrence of chance encounters. Instead, we need to learn about different types of encounters, as well as related factors that determine the long-term effects of such encounters on life paths.

Winning a multimillion-dollar lottery is an example of a nonnormative life event.

Normative History-Graded Factors

Not only do nonnormative events influence adult development, but many normative influences are more closely related to specific historical eras or events rather than to age. These events, called **normative history-graded factors,** occur only at certain times in history. They produce dramatic effects on individuals who experience them—effects that may persist for a lifetime. Normative history-graded factors include the pervasive and enduring effects of societal events such as wars and economic depressions on individual lives. Think of the personality differences that may exist between different-aged adults—people in their thirties and forties generally seem much more liberal and open-minded than individuals in their seventies and eighties. Why do these differences exist? Is it simply because of the different ages of these two groups of adults? Or is it because today's middle-aged adults grew up in a period of economic prosperity and societal turmoil (the time of the Vietnam War and the civil rights movement) while today's older adults, when they were young, lived through a period of social stability but experienced economic turmoil (the Great Depression)? In other words, isn't it likely that the characteristics of

Events such as the Great Depression are called normative history-graded influences.

these different historical eras influenced today's middle-aged adults to be liberal and today's older adults to be rather conservative? It is easy to attribute differences between individuals to age-graded factors when, in fact, the differences may be due to history-graded factors! Box 1.1 reveals how growing up during the Great Depression may have influenced an individual's adult development.

What are some of the normative history-graded influences operating in today's society? Think, for example, of the AIDS epidemic. This history-graded event may have a huge impact on the sexual behaviors and attitudes of today's society.

Normative history-graded factors have been demonstrated to be very important in studies comparing the intellectual abilities of different-aged individuals. Consider a classic study by John Nesselroade, K. Warner Schaie, and Paul Baltes (1972) in which the intellectual performance of eight different age groups was compared. On the first test, the groups ranged in age from twenty-four to seventy years, and they differed dramatically in performance: intellectual performance dropped steadily from the youngest to the most elderly group. Taking these data by themselves, it might be concluded that cognitive ability declines sharply with age. However, participants in all age groups were tested again seven years later. Results from this second test showed that *there was no hint that intellectual performance declined between the first and second testing in any age group.* Indeed, performance in the second test was generally better than at the time of first testing. These results strongly suggest that the differences among age groups are not the sole result of age-related *changes* in intellectual ability. Rather, it appears that these group differences reflect **cohort effects**. Cohort effects are differences in behavior observed among individuals born at different times in history. For example, individuals born about 1900 may perform worse on measures of cognitive ability than individuals born about 1950 because of the greater educational opportunities available to the members of the 1950 birth cohort. The importance of cohort effects in developmental research cannot be overemphasized. We will consider cohort effects further in the subsequent chapter on methodological issues. For the present, note that history-graded factors can contribute to intellectual performance and doubtlessly to many other aspects of psychological functioning as well.

Finally, it may be of interest to consider the differential manner in which normative age-graded factors, normative history-graded factors, and nonnormative life events promote change across the life span. Figure 1.1 reveals that normative age-graded factors, for example, are most likely to influence development at the beginning and end of the life span. Most of the behavioral hallmarks of infancy (for example, crawling, walking, talking, and so forth) and very old age (for example, generalized decrements in vision and attention) are probably due, to a great extent, to age-related biomaturational changes. Normative history-graded factors are most likely to produce developmental change during adolescence and young adulthood. Adolescence and young adulthood are times when an individual first constructs an understanding of society and his or her relationship to it. It seems obvious, for example, that living through the Vietnam War and the civil rights movement in the United States would have the least effect on extremely young and old individuals and the greatest effect on adults entering the mainstream of societal life. Finally, nonnormative life events may take on a gradually more powerful role in promoting developmental changes as an individual ages. This idea may account for the observation that with increasing age, individual differences become progressively more identifiable. A group of sixty-year-olds, for example, is generally more heterogeneous among themselves than a group of forty-year-olds. As we grow older, the continued emergence and accumulation of unique nonnormative life events helps to shape our personal lives, making individual differences more and more apparent.

Thus, we can distinguish three types of influences on adult development. These include the normative age-graded factors that have been emphasized in traditional developmental research; nonnormative life-event influences (such as winning a lottery or being abducted by a terrorist); and normative history-graded factors (such as the Great Depression of the 1930s or the Vietnam War) (Baltes, Reese, and Lipsitt, 1980).

BOX 1.1

HOW HAVE HISTORICAL EVENTS AND LIFE EXPERIENCES INFLUENCED MIDDLE-AGED ADULTS?

One of the most elaborate longitudinal studies—the California Longitudinal Study—provides data on individual lives over a period of almost fifty years (Eichorn, Clausen, Haan, Honzik, and Mussen, 1981). The individuals in the California Longitudinal Study, who are now in later adulthood, were born in 1920–21 and 1928–29. Thus their birthdates preceded the depression. As Glenn Elder (1981) comments:

> . . . [the] forces set in motion by the swing of boom and bust—the economic growth and opportunity of the predepression era, the economic collapse of the 1930s, and recovery through wartime mobilization to unequaled prosperity during the 1940s and 1950s—influenced the life histories of these study members in ways that have yet to be fully understood. (p. 6)

Elder describes how individuals from these two cohorts (those born in 1920–21 and those born in 1928–29), although they experienced the same historical conditions of the 1920s and 1930s, underwent these experiences at different points of development and thus were affected in very different ways. The earlier-born subjects, those in the Oakland Growth Study, were children during the prospering 1920s. This was a time of unusual economic growth, particularly in the San Francisco area. The members of this cohort entered the depression after a reasonably secure early childhood, and they later avoided joblessness because of wartime mobilization. Most of them married and started families by the mid-1940s. This historical timetable minimized their exposure to the hardship of the depression.

For the group of adults born in 1928–29, the same historical events and circumstances occurred at a different point in their development as children. Members of this group, who formed the Guidance Study, grew up in Berkeley, California. During their early childhood years, they and their parents experienced the hardship of the depression; then again, during the pressured period of adolescence, they encountered the unsettling experience of World War II. According to Elder, the hardships they experienced increased their feelings of inadequacy during the war years and reduced their chances for higher education. Nonetheless, when they were studied at midlife, the disadvantages of deprivation had essentially disappeared, at least in terms of socioeconomic attainment.

Box table 1.1 shows the ages of the Oakland and Berkeley subjects at the time of various historical events. How might some of these events and circumstances influence the lives of people—in terms of generational differences, the employment of women, and childbearing, for example? As we consider such life events and circumstances, we can see how social history shapes the lives of adults.

Box Table 1.1

AGE OF OAKLAND GROWTH AND GUIDANCE STUDY MEMBERS BY HISTORICAL EVENTS

Date	Event	Age of Study Members	
		OGS*	GS**
1880–1900	Birth years of OGS parents		
1890–1910	Birth years of GS parents		
1921–22	Depression	Birth (1920–21)	
1923	Great Berkeley Fire	2–3	
1923–29	General economic boom; growth of "debt pattern" way of life; cultural change in sexual mores	1–9	Birth (1928–29)
1929–30	Onset of Great Depression	9–10	1–2
1932–33	Depth of Great Depression	11–13	3–5
1933–36	Partial recovery, increasing cost of living, labor strikes	12–16	4–8
1937–38	Economic slump	16–18	8–10
1939–40	Incipient stage of wartime mobilization	18–20	10–12
1941–43	Major growth of war industries (shipyards, munitions plants, etc.) and of military forces	20–23	12–15
1945	End of World War II	24–25	16–17
1950–53	Korean War	29–33	21–25

From G. Elder, "Social History & Life Experience" in *Present and Past in Middle Life.* Copyright © 1981 Academic Press. Reprinted by permission.
*OGS = Oakland Growth Study
**GS = Guidance Study

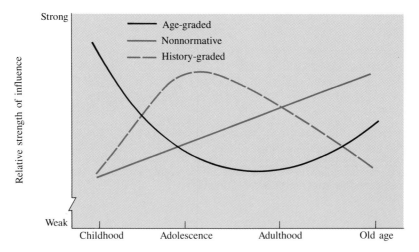

Figure 1.1   The relative influence of normative age-graded factors, normative history-graded factors, and nonnormative life-event factors in promoting developmental change at different times across the human life span.

Source: Data from P. B. Baltes, et al., *Annual Review of Psychology,* Volume 31. © 1980 by Annual Reviews, Inc.

THE CONCEPT OF AGE

A final issue raised by the life-span perspective is how to define the concept of age. What is age? Can it be considered a *cause* of development? Note that the concept of age is *multidimensional* in nature. In the following paragraphs we will describe the different meanings that Birren and Renner (1977) have attached to the concept of age.

Chronological Age

Chronological age refers to the number of years that have elapsed since a person's birth. Most individuals consider chronological age synonymous with the concept of age. Several psychologists (for example, Donald Baer, 1970) have argued that chronological age per se is *not* relevant to an understanding of psychological development. A person's age in and of itself does not cause development. Age is merely a marker of other processes that change over time and influence behavior. Jack Botwinick (1978), a prominent developmentalist, has offered the following analysis of the claim that chronological age is not relevant to an understanding of development:

> Age, as a concept, is synonymous with time, and time in itself cannot affect living function, behavior or otherwise. Time does not "cause" anything. . . . Time is a crude index of many events and experiences, and it is these indexed events which are "causal." If we study these events and experiences, we need not be concerned with the crude index

of time. We need not be concerned with age in order to understand that which has been "caused" by the time-indexed variables. These variables, unlike age itself, can be manipulated experimentally while holding related factors constant.

There is an important social reason, despite the foregoing arguments, for maintaining that age per se is germane to the purpose of studying developmental patterns. If age is regarded as irrelevant in studying developmental patterns, then the focus will be only on function, not the person. If focus is not upon the person as well as the function, then we are left with a cadre of cardiovascular specialists, for example, but few geriatricians. The problems of childhood require special focus and receive it in pediatrics; the problems of old age are too extensive and too important to negate a geriatric speciality. Our present knowledge of aging processes is too meager, and our social needs too great, to insist upon study of only what appears to be the more immediate, causative variables. (pp. 390–91)

Botwinick (1978) argues that we should adopt a two-stage strategy for researching developmental issues (see also Baltes and Goulet, 1971). The first stage involves *description:* one performs scientific studies to determine the developmental functions relating chronological age to some characteristic of interest (for example, reaction time). The second stage stresses *explanation:* one conducts experiments to test specific hypotheses regarding the *causes* of changes related to chronological age. For example, a researcher might test the hypothesis that age-related changes in reaction speed are caused by losses in sensory functioning.

Biological Age

The concept of **biological age** has been defined as "an estimate of the individual's present position with respect to his potential life span" (Birren and Renner, 1977, p. 4). This concept of age involves measuring the functional capacities of an individual's vital organ system. From this perspective, age can be viewed as an index of biological health. An individual's vital capacities may be better or worse than those of other persons of comparable chronological age. The younger a person's biological age, regardless of chronological age, the longer we would expect the individual to live.

Psychological Age

Psychological age refers to the adaptive capacities of an individual—that is, an individual's ability to adapt to changing environmental demands as compared to the adaptability of other individuals of identical chronological age. Individuals adapt to their environments by drawing on various psychological characteristics: learning, memory, intelligence, emotional control, motivational strengths, coping styles, and so on. Therefore, individuals who display more of such psychological characteristics than their chronological agemates are considered "psychologically young"; while those who possess such traits to a lesser degree are "psychologically old."

Two individuals of the same chronological age may be of vastly different biological ages.

Functional Age

A fourth aspect of age is a person's **functional age.** Measures of functional age gauge a person's ability to function effectively within a given environment or society. For example, an individual needs a number of skills and abilities (both psychological and physical) to function effectively as the sole occupant of an apartment—the individual has to be mobile and active to be able to shop, clean, cook, and wash as well as be able to efficiently plan and remember pertinent information. It is not surprising that some seventy-five-year-olds are more self-sufficient than some twenty-five-year-olds. Given the fact that chronological age is not perfectly related to functional age, psychologists find it increasingly important to develop valid and reliable measures of a person's functional abilities.

Social Age

Finally, it is necessary to consider the concept of **social age.** Social age refers to the social roles and expectations that people have for themselves as well as those imposed by other members of society. Consider the role of "mother" and the behaviors that accompany that role. Huyck and Hoyer (1982) have suggested that if one had to predict the behavior of an adult woman, it is probably more important to know that she is the mother of a three-year-old child than to know whether she was born twenty or thirty years ago. Furthermore, it is obvious that some individuals behave in a fashion considered either younger or older than their chronological age. Some older adults, for example, act like perpetual teenagers because they consider themselves "young."

From a life-span perspective, we see the need to develop an overall age profile for any individual. Only through such a profile can we be begin to apprehend the multifaceted nature of the concept of age. An age profile would consist of estimates for each of the different dimensions of age. For example, a seventy-year-old man (chronological age) might be in very good physical health (biological age), yet be experiencing a number of problems remembering and focusing attention (psychological age). The same man might be coping exceptionally well with the new demands placed on him by his wife's recent hospitalization (functional age) and might consider himself more a "retired businessman who likes to play golf" than a "grandfather" (social age).

MODELS OF ADULT DEVELOPMENT

Throughout this chapter we have focused on the basic question of how adults develop. It now is time to consider a different, though related, question: How has the science of adult development itself developed? As we shall see, the history of developmental psychology is not characterized by the steady collection and accumulation of "facts" concerning the "truth" of adult development. Everything we know about the history and philosophy of science suggests that such a process would never happen; and, in any case, researchers would not follow such a procedure. Rather, scientific research is directed by *models* that suggest important questions, define appropriate methodological approaches to answering these questions, and then try to determine answers to these questions. In other words, scientific activity is not a random process of collecting infinite numbers of observations. Rather, scientific activity is guided by certain presuppositions regarding what is important to study, how it should be studied, and what kinds of theoretical ideas can be advanced on the basis of such study (Kuhn, 1970).

A **model** is a highly metaphoric representation of some aspect of reality (Hultsch and Deutsch, 1981; Pepper, 1942; Reese and Overton, 1973). Models do not describe reality as it really "is." Instead, models employ metaphoric statements (as-if statements) to represent some perplexing aspect of reality in a form that is more familiar and knowable. Models are not directly testable; they incorporate assumptions that are too abstract to be objectively proved in the laboratory. Though models themselves are *not* testable, they serve to stimulate ideas, issues, and questions that *can* be tested. They also suggest the methodological approaches most appropriate for addressing these ideas, issues, and questions.

One very important aspect of models is that they cannot be disproved or rejected on the basis of scientific evidence. Each model can only be rejected in favor of another model that promises to serve as a better, or more encompassing, foundation for research. Thus, models are *not* to be equated with scientific theories.

Models lay the conceptual bases upon which theories are based. Theories are then used to make predictions that can be subjected to scientific tests. Put another way, models provide a framework in which to generate theories and conduct research. They can be judged (though perhaps only in hindsight) by how well they serve this purpose, not in terms of whether they are right or wrong.

There is no single framework or model that everyone in the field of life-span developmental psychology subscribes to. However, it is possible to conclude that the vast majority of research on adult development has its conceptual basis in one of three different models: the **mechanistic model,** the **organismic model,** and the **contextual model** (Hultsch and Deutsch, 1981; Pepper, 1942; Reese and Overton, 1970).

The best way to contrast these models is to examine the different metaphors upon which they are based. We will see that the metaphors associated with each model give rise to dramatically different conceptualizations of adult development.

The Mechanistic Model

The **mechanistic model** assumes that adults may be best thought of as if they were *machines.* Machines are complex entities that can be disassembled into a number of simple component parts. Furthermore, machines are inherently passive. They do not act on their own—they simply react to the environment. The mechanistic model thus envisions the adult as a passive organism that reacts to events but does not actively anticipate events, formulate goals, or engage in complex internal activity of any kind (in other words, emotions, thoughts, and ideas are absent). This model also suggests that complex adults can be broken down into a number of simple parts—with each part capable of being studied independently. For example, one could study intelligence without considering needs, aspirations, and desires. The mechanistic model serves as the foundation for various behavioristic theories of adult development. Behavioral theories focus on simple relationships between observable stimuli and observable responses rather than upon the hypothetical internal processes and structures we associate with the concept of mind. Also, behavioral theories focus attention on the quantitative, rather than qualitative, nature of developmental change.

The Organismic Model

The **organismic model** suggests that adults may be best conceptualized as if they were living biological systems—such as cells or embryos. A cell is more than the sum of its constituent parts. It is a complex, organized, and interrelated entity. Furthermore, the order and balance among the processes that take place within a cell are actively regulated by the cell itself, not by some outside agent; just as the orderly, universal transformations that take place during embryonic growth are regulated by mechanisms inside the embryo. The organismic model assumes that adults are active, planful, and inner-directed; that adults use self-initiated strategies to attain desirable end-states. It also assumes that adults are integrated organisms that defy being broken down into a number of independent parts.

The organismic model has laid the conceptual basis for cognitive-developmental (or structural) theories of development, most notably Piagetian theory. The important point of such theories is that cognitive developmentalists believe that human cognition is active, planful, and strategic. They also believe that cognitive development unfolds in a universal, orderly sequence of stages. The organismic model shifts the emphasis from the study of simple stimulus-response relationships and quantitative change to the study of internal processes and qualitative change.

A great deal of research in both cognitive psychology and artificial intelligence has its basis in the organismic model. For example, it is possible to develop a self-regulating, goal-directed computer program (Gardner, 1985; Johnson-Laird, 1988). The program determines the disparity between a goal-state (for example, the solution of a particular problem) and a current state. Then, the program engages in certain operations designed to systematically reduce the disparity. Once the disparity has been completely resolved (the problem has been solved), the program deactivates itself.

Finally, we should note that the organismic model is not simply restricted to the topic of cognition. Many theoretical ideas regarding personality, social processes, and human action also derive from this model (Chapman, 1984). The theories of Freud, Erikson, and Kohlberg, for example, may be linked to the organismic model.

The Contextual Model

The metaphor underlying the **contextual model** is the historical event. This model suggests that adults, like historical events, are ongoing, dynamic, and not directed toward an ideal goal or end-state. Furthermore, the meaning and interpretation of historical events may change, depending on the *context* or perspective from which such events are viewed. A war may be viewed as "moral" from one historical context and "immoral" from another. Similarly, the contextual model takes neither a purely passive nor a purely active view of the individual (Sameroff and Chandler, 1975). The basic conception of this model is that an adult individual continuously influences and is influenced by the different contexts of life.

It is important to understand that *context* is an open-ended term that may apply at different levels of analysis. For example, the environmental context pertains to one's physical environment. The social, historical, or cultural context pertains to influences such as societal norms and the expectations of friends and relatives. Further, the biological context pertains to an individual's health and physical skills. In all of these examples, not only do the contexts have an effect upon the individual, but also the individual has an effect upon the context. To take a simple example, one's family might make unreasonable demands. When the individual begins to refuse these demands more often, it might alter the family's subsequent demands, which in turn alters the individual's responsiveness to further demands.

Table 1.2

OVERVIEW OF THE THREE LIFE-SPAN MODELS OF ADULT DEVELOPMENT

Issues and Questions Surrounding the Models	*Models*		
	Mechanistic	Organismic	Contextual
What is the underlying metaphor?	machine	cell, embryo	historical event
What is the relationship between the person and the environment?	active environment; passive person	passive environment; active person	active environment; active person
What should be the focus of developmental psychology?	quantitative changes in observable behavior	qualitative changes in internal structures	person/environment transactions

The contextual model serves as the foundation for a broad range of theories that address various aspects of adult development. Hultsch and Deutsch (1981), for example, have suggested that an adult's ability to remember an event depends on (1) the psychological, social, and physical contexts in which the person initially experienced the event, (2) the unique skills, abilities, knowledge, and motivation that the individual brings to the context in which he must remember, and (3) the special characteristics of the context in which the person attempts to remember. As the individual changes, and as the contexts in which she is asked to remember change, we would expect the person's memory to change as well. Thus, we could say that memory is a dynamic process involving the continual *reconstruction* of past events and experiences. Adults, therefore, seem to serve as their own "historians." They constantly revise their pasts from the perspective of the present.

Sometimes the contextual model is referred to as the **dialectical view.** Klaus Riegel (1973, 1976), the developmentalist who championed the dialectic perspective, believes that individuals and the contexts of their lives are always in a state of flux: adults are constantly changing organisms in a constantly changing world. From Riegel's view, the individual and society are never at rest. Riegel also believed that contradiction and conflict are an inherent part of development and that no single goal or end point in development is ever reached. The dialectical perspective developed by Riegel has a great deal in common with the life-span perspective. Both stress the inherent multidirectionality of developmental change and the wide-reaching interindividual variability observed with increasing chronological age.

See table 1.2 for a summary of the three different models just discussed.

Table 1.3

MODELS AND CHARACTERISTICS OF ADULT DEVELOPMENT

Degree of Emphasis on Different Characteristics of Human Development	*Models*		
	Mechanistic	Organismic	Contextual
Qualitative change	Low	High	Medium
Stages of change	Low	High	Medium
Continuity of change	Low	High	Medium
Multidirectionality of change	Medium	Low	High
Reversibility of change	Medium	Low	Medium
Multiple determinants of change			
Normative age-graded factors	Low	High	Medium
Normative history-graded factors	Low	Low	High
Nonnormative life-event factors	High	Low	High
Chronological age as a useful variable	Low	High	Medium

Models and Issues in Adult Development

It is useful to compare the mechanistic, organismic, and contextual models with respect to the issues considered earlier in this chapter. Though this comparison is instructive, each of the models is abstract and tends to generalize a number of more specific ideas. Thus, we compare the models with respect to their emphases, realizing they cannot be held to black-and-white claims.

As table 1.3 shows, the organismic model is distinguished by the emphasis it places on qualitative change, distinctive stages of development, and continuity of change. It also is unique in emphasizing the importance of age-graded influences on development and of age as a variable in research (at least for purposes of describing change). The mechanistic and contextual models appear more similar to each other than to the organismic model. However, there are some very important differences. One of these is that the contextual model places greater emphasis on the multidirectional nature of developmental change. Another difference is the importance the contextual model places on history-graded influences on development. Put simply, the mechanistic model emphasizes nonnormative life-event influences at the expense of all other aspects of development. The contextual model also emphasizes nonnormative influences but not exclusively; it considers history-graded influences as well as individual differences. Indeed, as indicated in table 1.3, the contextual model stresses all aspects of development. The thrust of this model is the multifaceted and multidetermined nature of adult development. In a real sense, it incorporates the mechanistic and organismic models, but it goes further in its recognition of factors specific to individual people, individual cultures, and individual times in history.

OVERVIEW OF THE TEXT

Phases of Development

In this introductory chapter we have seen that there is disagreement about whether to approach adult development and aging from a stage perspective or from the perspective of chronological age. Nonetheless, theorists and researchers often use the labels of early, middle, and late adulthood to describe three different developmental periods.

Early adulthood usually signifies the time frame from the late teens or early twenties through the thirties. This time period often involves the establishment of personal and economic independence. Career development takes on an even more important role than in late adolescence. For many young adults, selecting a mate, learning to live with someone else in an intimate way, and starting a family and rearing children take up a great deal of time.

Middle adulthood characterizes the phase of the life cycle from between thirty-five and forty-five years of age to between fifty-five and sixty-five years of age. This is a time for expanding personal and social involvement and responsibility, for assisting teenagers to become responsible and happy adults, for adjusting to the physiological changes of middle age, and for finding and maintaining satisfaction in one's career.

Late adulthood extends from approximately sixty to seventy years of age until death. It is a time of adjustment to decreasing strength and health and to retirement and reduced income. Establishing affiliations with members of one's own age group and adapting to social roles are important during this period.

Not all individuals are characterized in the manner sketched here. As you read this text, you will find many more aspects of adult development and aging that characterize individuals in early, middle, and late adulthood; but you will see that not everyone agrees that these characteristics are universal.

Processes of Development

After you read about methods of studying adults in the next chapter, we'll discuss a number of processes of adult development and aging: biological processes, cognitive processes, social processes, and personality processes.

Biological processes and physical development refer to changes that range from simple alterations in size, weight, and other anatomical features, to the genetic blueprint that places constraints on our development from conception to death.

The genes we were born with still influence our adult development. Scientists are looking closely at the role genetics plays in such adult disorders as schizophrenia, dementia, alcoholism, and depression. Hormones are yet another aspect of biological makeup that play an important part in the understanding of adult development: for example, the onset of menopause in women is accompanied by significant hormonal change. Furthermore, we will pay close attention to age-related changes in the brain and nervous system. And we will describe how these changes influence psychological functioning.

Cognitive processes in adult development refer to the age-related series of changes that occur in mental activity—thought, memory, perception, and attention. As part of our study of cognitive development, we will explore how adults process information; how intelligence and creativity change over time; and how qualitatively new styles of thinking emerge during adulthood. We will look carefully at declines in memory during adulthood, paying special attention to the issue of how "normal" memory deficits may be distinguished from "pathological" memory deficits in older adults.

Social processes in adult development refer to the individual's interactions with other individuals in the environment. Two elderly people consoling each other, a mother hugging her daughter for bringing home a good report card, two sisters arguing, and a boss smiling at a secretary are all examples of interaction in the social world. Social development focuses on how these different aspects unfold as the individual grows. We also will study contexts in the section in which we discuss social processes and development. As we have seen in this chapter, the contexts in which adult development occurs are a very important factor in determining what people are like. Some of the most important social contexts of adult development are families, relationships, and work.

Personality processes in adult development usually refer to the properties distinguishing one individual from another individual. But as we will see, some experts believe that there are also commonalities that characterize individuals at particular points in adult development. One's sex-role orientation, perception of self, moral values, and sociability represent some of the aspects of personality we will discuss. You will find that it often is impossible to meaningfully present personality development in adulthood without frequently looking at the individual's interactions with and thoughts about the social world.

Indeed, although it is helpful to study the different processes of adult development in separate sections and chapters, keep in mind while reading this text that you are an integrated human being—you have only one mind and one body. Biological, physical, cognitive, social, and personality development are inextricably woven together. For example, in many chapters, you may read about how social experiences shape cognitive development, how cognitive development restricts or promotes social development, and how cognitive development is tied to physical development.

Summary

In this chapter we attempted to describe and characterize the life-span perspective of adult development. Beginning with a basic question—Do adults develop?—we presented a brief history and outline of the life-span developmental framework, stressing the notion of multidirectional trends in development and rejecting the older, unidirectional view of development.

We next turned to a discussion of a number of issues raised by the life-span perspective of development. The concept of qualitative change in adulthood derives from Piaget's basic insight that children's intelligence does not simply increase, but changes from one type to another. It is possible that similar sorts of qualitative changes occur during the adult years. Moreover, such changes need not be restricted to the intellectual sphere.

Though the issue of whether there are stages of adult development is an intriguing one, convincing evidence is sparse. Moreover, there is disagreement about the very nature of such stages.

Another issue in adult development is continuity versus discontinuity of change. Though change may be qualitative, and even abrupt, it still may be continuous in the sense that later achievements depend upon earlier achievements.

Multidirectional changes in adult development are widely acknowledged, and they clearly constitute an important issue facing life-span developmental psychologists. Nonetheless, the nature and causes of these differences remain obscure.

Although the issue of reversibility of change offers some exciting prospects, several practical and ethical issues have been raised. Some developmental processes can be reversed through specific intervention, education, or environmental modification. But whether such reversals are always desirable is another question yet to be explored.

A life-span perspective recognizes not only the multifaceted nature of change, but also the multiple influences affecting the nature of such change. In addition to the normative age-graded influences emphasized by traditional developmental theory, nonnormative life events (for example, accidents and chance encounters) and normative history-graded influences (for example, wars and depressions) also affect development. It is possible that many influences on adult development may be small, day-to-day events rather than the major events that make their marks in history or autobiography.

The issue of age as a concept in life-span developmental psychology deserves further investigation. While chronological age may not be useful in explaining change, age is an important descriptive variable in developmental research. Also, it is possible to construct a useful age profile based not only on chronological age, but on biological, psychological, functional, and social age.

Models, although not testable as scientific theories, are useful for generating ideas, issues, and questions for research. Models also suggest appropriate methodological approaches for exploring these ideas, issues, and questions. Three models of adult development include the mechanistic model, the organismic model, and the contextual model. The contextual model is unique in its broad attention to all types of change and all determinants of change. Indeed, the contextual model actually seems to encompass the mechanistic and organismic models.

Review Questions

1. Contrast the life-span perspective of adulthood with a traditional child-focused perspective.
2. Discuss the concept of qualitative change in adulthood.
3. Explain what is meant by intraindividual change and interindividual variability.
4. Describe the controversy over reversibility in developmental change.
5. Discuss the importance of nonnormative life events, normative history-graded factors, and normative age-graded factors in adult development.
6. Why is the concept of age a controversial variable in the study of adult development?
7. What are the purposes and functions of a model?
8. Describe the mechanistic, organismic, and contextual models of adult development.
9. Discuss the strengths and weaknesses of the mechanistic, organismic, and contextual models.
10. What are the differences and similarities between the contextual model and Riegel's dialectical position?

For Further Reading

Baltes, P. B. (1987). Theoretical propositions of life-span developmental psychology: On the dynamics between growth and decline. *Developmental Psychology, 23,* 611–626. This is an excellent overview of the key concepts that underlie the life-span perspective, especially with regard to adult intellectual development. Medium reading level.

Havighurst, R. J. (1973). History of developmental psychology: Socialization and personality development through the life span. In P. B. Baltes & K. W. Schaie (Eds.), *Life-span developmental psychology* (pp. 4–25). New York: Academic Press. Havighurst, a leading figure in the study of life-span development, presents a number of theoretical ideas that focus on life-span development. Reasonably easy to read.

Psychology and Aging, Developmental Psychology, Journal of Gerontology, and *The Gerontologist* These four leading journals will be referred to frequently in this text. To get a feel for the kinds of questions that interest people who study adulthood and aging, go to your library and browse through some issues of these journals published over the last four or five years. Reading level varies from medium to difficult.

Neugarten, B. L., & Datan, N. (1973). Sociological perspectives on the life cycle. In P. B. Baltes & K. W. Schaie (Eds.), *Life-span developmental psychology.* New York: Academic Press. Neugarten, one of the leading figures in the study of life-span development, describes her views of multiple-time perspectives and the changing rhythm of the life cycle. This well-written article stimulates thinking about the nature of life-span development. Moderate reading level.

CHAPTER 2

METHODS

with James C. Bartlett

IMAGINE

Imagine That You Are a Researcher Studying Whether Creativity Declines with Age

How Should You Proceed? You suspect that many opinions about aging and the decline of creativity are rooted in negative prejudices and stereotypes of the aged (*ageism*), or are based on socially accepted behavior standards for people of different ages. You are interested in obtaining objective, scientific evidence on creativity across the life span. How should you proceed?

One approach might be simply to ask people of different ages to rate their creativity (using a seven-point scale, for example). But your goal is to gather objective, scientific data on creativity, not subjective impressions that doubtlessly are influenced by conventional wisdom as well as the egos of your participants. Another approach might be to collect ratings on people's creativity from friends and relatives. This might solve the ego problem, but conventional wisdom and subjective judgments would remain troublesome factors. Moreover, how well can friends and relatives judge a person's creativity? (Do your friends and relatives know exactly how creative you are?) Another approach might be to use a questionnaire or structured interview. Rather than simply asking people about their creativity, you might ask them about a variety of items such as life-style (are they unconventional?), work habits (do they waste many idle hours until spurred by a creative burst?), and motivations (do they enjoy following orders and being told what to do, or do they prefer to set their own tasks and goals?). Responses could be scored or weighted for creativity, and a total creativity score derived. Unfortunately, participants might guess the purpose of your study and try to produce answers that appear creative.

Perhaps it would be better to test people's ability to find creative solutions to problems rather than to ask them about creativity. Indeed, it might be useful to find a standardized test of creative problem solving which many samples of people have taken. This approach seems promising, but you must ensure the reliability and validity of your creativity test. Does the test give consistent estimates of creativity if the same individual is tested twice? This demonstrates reliability. Does the test truly measure creativity, or simply intelligence? This question involves validity.

Even if a test shows high reliability and validity with young adults, the test might not be as reliable and valid for elderly people. Further, age differences in creative problem solving might not reflect age per se, but rather extraneous factors such as educational background or health. Some of these factors might be controlled by a longitudinal design, testing the same individuals every ten years from ages twenty to seventy. But do you have fifty years to complete your study? And how many of the participants you test today will still be available fifty years from now?

The problem of extraneous factors and the difficulty of conducting longitudinal designs might lead you to use archival or historical data. For example, you might investigate the typical ages at which people have produced great artistic or scientific achievements. Unfortunately, the evidence provided by archival investigations is highly indirect; many factors in addition to creativity determine at what age someone might produce a great artistic or scientific accomplishment. (Indeed, it is arguable that many social and cultural factors, including conventional wisdom about aging and creativity, may influence the time course of creative achievement in adults.) Further, the accuracy and completeness of archival data is always a concern.

Faced with all of these problems, you might wish to use animal models in your research. With animals, it is possible to control many factors (diet, experiences in infancy, and so forth) that cannot be controlled in humans. Also, many animals have a relatively brief life span, making longitudinal research more feasible. But how do you devise a creativity test that animals can complete? And can results obtained with animals be generalized to humans?

What, then, should you do to investigate aging and creativity? There is no one right answer—only alternative approaches with varying advantages and disadvantages. Furthermore, there is ample room for your own creativity in selecting, combining, and even modifying approaches to suit your own research goals. Indeed, the need for creativity in science is an integral part of its challenge and appeal.

INTRODUCTION

A major task of science is measurement (McCain and Segal, 1988; Shaughnessy and Zechmeister, 1990). We begin this chapter with a discussion of two basic issues involved in measurement: the reliability of measurements and the validity of measurements. Then we will discuss several basic techniques used for collecting observations: the structured interview and questionnaire, standardized tests, and behavioral research. Next, we'll consider some of the basic ways to describe and interpret measurements. Then we'll explore the topic of research design, considering first simple correlational designs and then more powerful experimental designs. We'll also discuss the role played by quasi-experimental designs in developmental research. The chapter closes with a section on sampling, a critical problem in all psychological research but particularly important in research on adult development and aging.

BASIC ISSUES OF MEASUREMENT

Measurement—a major task of science—sounds simple. However, to make accurate and meaningful measurements is far from simple. Let's look at two basic issues we must consider when making scientific measurements.

Reliability of Measures

Suppose you are assisting on a research project focusing on age changes in **reaction time,** the amount of time it takes to respond to a simple stimulus. You are asked to construct a task that will measure the reaction times of all the adults participating in this research study. After a great deal of thought, you develop the following reaction-time task. You ask participants to sit individually at tables and you place a set of earphones on each of their heads. Directly in front of each participant on the table is a telegraph key. You tell the participants that every now and then they will hear a beeping sound delivered to both ears via the earphones. You instruct the participants to press the telegraph key as quickly as possible whenever they hear a beep. Within this context, you define reaction time as the amount of time it takes a participant to press the key after the beep has initially sounded. Furthermore, you decide to measure the participants' reaction times by using a hand-held stopwatch that measures time in hundredths of seconds. You plan to start the watch when the participant hears the beep (you will also wear a pair of earphones connected to the same sound source as those worn by each participant). And you plan to stop the watch when the participant presses the key.

Suppose that you tell the principal investigator of the research project about your plan to measure reaction time. You assume that she will be very impressed with the task you have developed. However, she seems very concerned about the *reliability* of your measure. What exactly is the principal investigator worried about? How can you reassure her? Essentially, the concept of **reliability** refers to the degree to which measurement is consistent, stable, and accurate over time. Given your inexperience at measuring reaction time, there are many reasons why the measurements you collect might be inconsistent and unstable. For example, were all of the participants instructed to press the button by using the index finger on their preferred hand? Did some of the participants position their fingers directly on top of the telegraph key before some of the trials but place their fingers on the table before some of the other trials? If the participants positioned their fingers in different locations before each trial, you would collect very unreliable data. (Remember, you want to measure the time it takes to press the key—not the time it takes to move your finger to the key and *then* press the key!) Also, when did you plan to begin measuring the participants' response times—as soon as they begin to perform the reaction-time task or after several practice trials? Until a participant becomes familiar with the experimental task and apparatus, his or her reaction times could vary considerably from trial to trial. Finally, the principal investigator may wonder how accurately you can measure reaction time by using a hand-held stop watch. Is it possible for you to start your watch at the *exact* split-second the beep sounds and stop the watch at the *exact* instant the participant depresses the telegraph key? Even if you could accurately measure reaction time at the beginning of the experimental session (which is extremely doubtful), might you become increasingly tired, bored, and/or absent-minded as you measured more and more reaction times? As you can now see, there are a number of points to consider in measuring reaction time reliably. Other types of measurement can pose much greater problems of reliability. Suppose, for example, that you were asked to determine an adult's IQ to measure the life satisfaction of an elderly adult using some other instrument (standardized tests of life satisfaction do exist). How reliable would your estimations be? How many sources of measurement error would exist? Obviously, reliability of measurement can frequently be questioned in behavioral research.

Assessing Reliability

How can we assess the reliability of various measures? There are a variety of techniques, but all are based on the assumption that reliable observations are repeatable.

Test-retest reliability can be assessed by obtaining the same set of measurements on two different occasions. The question is whether measurements (frequently numerical scores of some kind) on occasion 2 are predictable from observations gathered on occasion 1. Thus, after a familiarization period, we could administer 100 reaction-time trials to participants on day 1 and 100 trials on day 2; if the test is reliable, we should be able to compute the reliability of the participants' reaction times. Of course, test-retest reliability is meaningful only when the variable we are measuring is assumed to be stable over time. Were we observing the momentary moods of individuals, we probably would not wish to assess test-retest reliability. For example, if a person were judged to be happy on day 1 and sad on day 2, this need not imply low test reliability. It could simply mean that the person's mood had changed.

Interrater reliability should be assessed whenever measurements involve a subjective, judgmental component. This is frequently the case in studies where observational data are collected. The technique is simply to use two or more observers independently, then assess the agreement among these observers. High agreement implies high reliability.

Interitem reliability can be examined whenever measurements entail multiple items. A common procedure for assessing interitem reliability is to divide the items into halves (for instance, the odd-numbered items versus the even-numbered items) and to determine the extent to which measurements (average scores) on one half are predictable from measurements on the other half. High predictability implies high reliability.

Improving Reliability

How do we improve the reliability of measurements? One method is to take many different measures of the same individual or behavior. However, an even better way is to refine and standardize the procedures and tools used for measurement. In our initial example of measuring reaction time, we could improve reliability by making multiple assessments of reaction time, particularly if the assessments were made by different research assistants. It obviously would also be helpful to use a carefully planned and standardized set of procedures for assessing reaction time (for example, instructing participants to place the index finger of their preferred hand on the telegraph key). Finally, the use of high-precision equipment would be beneficial (a computer with an internal clock could be programmed to record the exact time—in milliseconds—between the onset of the beep and the depression of the key). Future scientific advances should ultimately provide the refinements and standardization needed to produce truly reliable measures of physical, intellectual, and social behaviors.

Reliability is a concern in all psychological research. However, reliability problems are particularly bothersome in developmental research, especially when individual differences are at issue. If a group of people is given an IQ test at age eighteen and again at age forty-five, it is probable that some individuals will show gains from the first test to the second, whereas others will show losses. Are there true differences between the gainers and the losers in intelligence, or are we simply seeing the effects of an unreliable measuring instrument? Although statistical methods can be applied to this problem, reliability remains questionable. Furthermore, envision a situation where every person tested at age forty-five scores exactly ten points higher on the IQ test than they scored at age eighteen. Since we could exactly predict a person's IQ at age forty-five from their IQ at age eighteen, we would conclude that the test used to measure IQ is highly reliable—it possesses a perfect level of test-retest reliability. However, it is obvious that not one of our participants has the same IQ score at both times of testing, making the test's stability questionable. Therefore, since the concept of *reliability* entails both the predictability and the stability of measurements, separate measures of predictability and stability should be developed and used.

Validity of Measurement

In our example of measuring reaction time, the principal investigator questioned the reliability (essentially, the repeatability) of the measurement. What if she also doubted the **validity** of the measure itself? A measure is valid if it actually measures what it purports to measure. The measure of reaction time, therefore, is valid if it really measures the amount of time it takes adults to make a simple motor response once they hear a sound. The principal investigator might suggest that the task you developed to measure reaction time could actually measure how well participants can *hear* the beep rather than react to it. If older adults have trouble hearing, they will have difficulty reacting to the beep. Thus, in order to make certain that the measure of reaction time is valid, all of the prospective participants in the study will have to be screened for auditory sensitivity.

Although there are many different types of validity, the type we are currently addressing is **construct validity.** Constructs are abstract entities that cannot be directly observed but are presumed to influence observable phenomena. Intelligence is a construct; so are anxiety, creativity, memory, self-esteem, and other aspects of personality and cognition. We often attempt to observe phenomena that we believe might reflect these constructs. The question of whether the observed phenomena actually do reflect the constructs is the issue of construct validity.

Even when observations are highly reliable, they do not necessarily imply high construct validity. Were we to devise a test of creativity, we might be able to demonstrate high test-retest reliability as well as high interitem reliability. However, the test could still be vulnerable to the charge that it really measures intelligence, not creativity—or to the charge that creativity may not even truly exist.

Students of adult development and aging must consider whether a given test or measurement might have reasonable construct validity for young adults but not for elderly people. For example, a test of long-term memory might be reasonably valid for college students who are accustomed to memory tests. But the same test might be intimidating to elderly people who might not have taken a memory test for decades. Hence, the performance of elderly people might reflect anxiety more than memory per se.

BASIC TECHNIQUES USED FOR COLLECTING MEASUREMENTS

Interview and Questionnaire

Many inquiries on adult development have been based on the techniques of interview and questionnaire. An **interview** is a set of questions asked face-to-face. The interview can range from being very structured to very unstructured. For example, a very unstructured interview might include open-ended questions such as, "Tell me about some of the things you do with your friends," or "Tell me about yourself." On the other hand, a very structured interview might question whether the respondent highly approves, moderately approves, moderately disapproves, or highly disapproves of his friends' use of drugs. Highly unstructured interviews, while often yielding valuable clinical insights, usually do not yield information suitable for research purposes. However, unstructured interview questions can be helpful in developing more focused interview questions for future efforts.

Structured interviews conducted by an experienced researcher can produce valuable data. However, structured interviews are not without problems. Perhaps the most critical of these problems involves the response bias of social desirability. In a face-to-face situation, where anonymity is impossible, a person's responses may reflect social desirability rather than her actual feelings or actions. In other words, a person may respond to gain the approval of the interviewer rather than say what she actually thinks. When asked about sexual relationships, for example, a person may not want to admit having had sexual intercourse on a casual basis. Skilled interviewing techniques and built-in questions designed to help eliminate such defenses are critical in obtaining accurate information in an interview.

Researchers are also able to question adults through surveys or questionnaires. A **questionnaire** is similar to a highly structured interview except that adults read the questions and mark their answers on a sheet of paper rather than responding orally to the interviewer. One major advantage of questionnaires is that they can easily be given to a very large number of people. A sample of responses from five- to ten-thousand people is possible to obtain. However, a number of experts on measurement (for example, Bailey, 1987; Shaughnessy and Zechmeister, 1990; Simon and Burstein, 1985) have pointed out that surveys and questionnaires have been badly abused instruments of inquiry. For example, survey items should be concrete, specific, and unambiguous; often they are not.

Another problem with both interviews and surveys or questionnaires is that some questions may be retrospective in nature; that is, they may require the participant to recall events or feelings that occurred at some point in the past. It is not unusual, for example, to interview older adults about experiences they had during adolescence or young adulthood. Unfortunately, retrospective interviews may be seriously affected by distortions in memory. It is exceedingly difficult to glean accurate information about the past from verbal reports. However, because of the importance of understanding retrospective verbal reports, 1978 Nobel prize winner Herbert Simon and others are developing better ways to gain more accurate verbal assessments of the past (Ericsson and Simon, 1984).

Behavioral Research

Regardless of advances in our understanding of verbal reports, they probably will never be adequate, by themselves, as a basis for psychological research. Apart from problems of response set or memory, verbal reports obviously are dependent upon conscious awareness. Yet many aspects of cognition, personality, and social behavior apparently are subconscious. Thus we must go beyond what people tell us about themselves and examine how they behave.

Behavioral research does not depend upon participants' verbal reports regarding the issue under study. For example, a questionnaire might be based on verbal reports of memory problems as experienced by the elderly. In contrast, a behavioral study of memory might actually assess the accuracy of verbal recall by the elderly. (For instance, the researcher might present a list of words, followed by a test of verbal recall for these words.) Both approaches involve verbalization on the part of participants, but only the questionnaire involves verbalization *about* memory itself. Interestingly, evidence exists that indicates that reports of memory problems are not strongly associated with true deficits in performance on memory tasks. Marion Perlmutter (Perlmutter, 1978; Perlmutter, Metzger, Nezworski, and Miller, 1981) has collected both questionnaire and performance data on memory in young and elderly adults. Overall, she found that older adults report more memory problems on a questionnaire and that they also perform more poorly on some (but not all) memory tasks. But reported memory problems have proved to be a poor basis for predicting actual memory performance in this type of research (Perlmutter, 1986). For example, a person reporting many memory problems might actually perform very well on a memory test, and vice versa.

Behavioral Research in Laboratory versus Field Settings

In behavioral research, it is frequently necessary to control certain factors that might determine behavior but are not the focus of the inquiry. For example, if we are interested in studying long-term memory in different age groups, we might want to control motivation as well as the conditions of learning (study time, distracting noises, and so forth). Even extraneous factors such as temperature and time of day might be important. Laboratories are places that allow considerable control over many extraneous factors. For this reason, behavioral research is frequently conducted in laboratories.

However, costs are also involved in conducting laboratory research, and some of these costs are especially high when developmental issues are being addressed. First, it is impossible to conduct research in a laboratory without letting the participants know they are in an experiment. This creates problems of **reactivity.** Reactivity occurs when participants think they should behave in a specific manner because they are in an experimental setting. Second, the laboratory setting is unnatural and might cause unnatural behavior on the part of participants. This problem can be particularly severe with elderly participants, who may find the laboratory setting even more unnatural than young adults do. Finally, certain phenomena, particularly social phenomena, are difficult if not impossible to produce in the laboratory. The effects of "job-related stress on marital satisfaction," for example, might be difficult (and unethical) to investigate in a laboratory setting.

Because of these problems with laboratory research, many psychologists are beginning to conduct *field* or *observational* research in real-world settings. Such settings can include job sites, shopping malls, senior citizen centers, nursing homes, or any other place where appropriate observations can be made. The main drawback of field research is limited control over extraneous factors. However, this drawback is frequently outweighed by the benefits of low reactivity, natural contexts, and access to interesting phenomena that are difficult to observe in the laboratory.

Though they are often presented as dichotomous, laboratory and field research are really two points on a continuum, a continuum that can be labeled *naturalism versus control.* If some laboratory experiments employ conditions or tasks of a decidedly natural character, these experiments belong in the middle area of the continuum. For example, a laboratory study of memory might examine recall of events from one's past. A laboratory study of social behavior might bring middle-aged parents and their adolescent offspring together to discuss problems in their family. Researchers find that many benefits of field studies can be enjoyed in the laboratory *if* the activities of the participants are to some degree natural. This is an important lesson for psychologists interested in adult development and aging. It is frequently necessary to conduct developmental research within some form of laboratorylike context (perhaps a simple room with few distracting stimuli). This does not mean that the tasks performed by participants must be unnatural and uninteresting. Such tasks might put elderly people who are unaccustomed to performing artificial and irrelevant tasks at an unfair disadvantage.

Laboratory Research with Animal Models

Although laboratory and field research can be thought of as two points on a continuum, laboratory research with human participants is not the endpoint of this continuum. The endpoint is laboratory research with animal participants because such research allows far more control than is possible with humans. We can control an animal's genetic endowment, diet, experiences during infancy, and countless other factors that cannot be controlled when humans are studied. We can also investigate effects of treatments (brain lesions or restricted diet, for example) that would be unethical to attempt with humans. Moreover, with some animals it is possible to track the entire life course in a very short period of time. (Laboratory mice live at most a few years.)

A major disadvantage of animal research is, of course, that it may well not generalize to humans. Indeed, many aspects of human development—language, for example—are simply impossible to study except with humans. Nevertheless, some aspects of animal development do generalize to humans and promise to teach us much about development across the life span. For example, there is an amazing degree of similarity in the structure and function of the brain in humans and rats. Furthermore, a team of researchers (Selkoe, Bell, Podlisny, Price, Cork, 1987) have recently discovered that the same brain changes that accompany normal aging in humans (and abnormal aging such as Alzheimer's disease) occur in a wide variety of animals (for example, rats, dogs, and polar bears) as well. This suggests that researchers may be able to construct animal models which will shed a great deal of light on both normal and pathological age-related changes in the human nervous system.

Standardized Tests

Standardized tests attempt to measure an individual's characteristics or abilities *as compared to* those of a large group of similar individuals. Such tests may take the forms of questionnaires, interviews, or behavioral tests. To maximize reliability, a good test should have a reasonably large number of items and should be given in an objective, standardized manner. The **standardization** of tests actually refers to two different qualities: the establishment of fixed or standard procedures for administration and scoring, and the establishment of norms for age, grade, race, sex, and so on. Norms are patterns or representative values for a group. Hence, the performance of an individual can be assessed relative to that of a comparison group (people of the same age, sex, and so on).

Many standardized tests have good reliability but their construct validity can be questioned. IQ tests, for example, show impressive reliability, but there is considerable uncertainty about what such tests actually measure (Gardner, 1983, 1985; Sternberg, 1985). The problem is compounded by the possibility that a single test might measure different things at different ages—for example, an IQ test might measure intellectual ability in young adulthood, but anxiety in old age. This possibility is critical in interpreting developmental research that shows that IQ performance can change with age.

 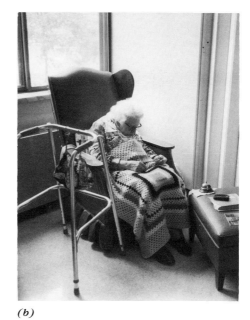

(a) *(b)*

(a) Older adults may be at a disadvantage when they take standardized psychometric tests.
(b) Environments with little stimulation may produce mental declines in older adults.

There are standardized tests for intellectual functioning, for psychopathology or mental illness, for life satisfaction, creativity, and many other aspects of personality and cognition. Such tests are used for a wide variety of purposes and are invaluable in developmental research. However, when using any test, it is important to consider construct validity. It is frequently questionable whether a standardized test for **x** truly measures **x**, or whether **x** even can serve as a scientifically useful concept (substitute intelligence, creativity, neuroticism, anxiety, self-concept, or whatever for **x**).

Physiological Research

There is no question that a biological level of analysis offers a great deal of information about adult development and aging. This is not to say that psychological and sociocultural factors are unimportant; indeed, there is good reason to believe that there are multiple determinants of adult development. Moreover, physiological factors and psychological-sociocultural factors *interact* during the course of adult development. Biological research frequently suggests strategies to remove or reverse certain types of behavioral change, which is sometimes desirable. Box 2.1 describes a study that tested one such strategy—administering a drug (propranolol) to reduce physiological manifestations of arousal.

BOX 2.1

PHYSIOLOGICAL AROUSAL AND LEARNING IN THE ELDERLY

Carl Eisdorfer and others established that young adults frequently outperform elderly subjects on some types of learning tasks, but that slowing the pace of the learning task can reduce this age-related difference. Further, evidence suggests that elderly subjects in learning experiments are more highly aroused physiologically than younger subjects (Powell, Eisdorfer, and Bogdonoff, 1964). Thus Eisdorfer and two colleagues, John Nowlin and Francis Wilkie, developed a hypothesis: perhaps we could improve learning performance in the elderly by reducing their physiological arousal.

In order to test their hypothesis, Eisdorfer, Nowlin, and Wilkie (1970) examined learning performance within two groups of elderly men whose average age was 68.6. One group was administered a drug—propranolol—prior to the learning test. Propranolol is known to reduce most physiological indicants of arousal, including heart rate and free fatty acid in the blood. The other group received a placebo (isotonic saline) known not to reduce indicants of arousal. Though each individual subject received either propranolol or the placebo, none of the subjects was told which he received. As a further control, the experimenters conducting the learning experiment did not know whether any individual subject had received propranolol or the placebo. (Only the physician who injected the substances had this information.) This double-blind procedure was used to help ensure the objectivity of the experimenters' observations.

The results of the experiment were clear: subjects in the propranolol group made fewer errors during learning. Three different measures—heart rate, free fatty acid in the blood, and galvanic skin response (GSR)—indicated that subjects in the propranolol group were physiologically less aroused. Thus the researchers' hypothesis was supported.

A single experiment like this is inadequate to support sweeping conclusions about arousal and learning in elderly people. There was no comparison group of young subjects, only one sort of learning task was employed, and it is always possible to speculate that a drug like propranolol affects more than just arousal. Nonetheless, the Eisdorfer experiment is instructive for two reasons. First, the study is an excellent example of how physiological measures can stimulate productive research on adult development and aging. Second, the study illustrates the importance of blind procedures in research. Without the double-blind procedure of the Eisdorfer experiment, it would be possible to argue that subjects in the propranolol group performed better because they were expected to perform better—that is, that demand characteristics of the situation increased motivation in this group. (This is the basic problem of reactivity.) Further, the experimenters might have let their biases and expectations affect their results by making inaccurate observations in favor of the propranolol group. (This is the problem of objectivity of measures.) Fortunately, because double-blind procedures were used by Eisdorfer and his colleagues, problems with demand characteristics and biased observations are unlikely. Rather, the results have interesting implications for the effects of arousal upon learning across the life span.

BASIC STRATEGIES FOR DESCRIBING AND INTERPRETING MEASUREMENTS

In most scientific studies, a vast number of measurements allow researchers to collect considerable amounts of raw data. For this data to be understood, they must be described and interpreted objectively. In this section we will summarize some of the statistical techniques that developmentalists use to make sense out of raw data.

Measures of Central Tendency and Variability

Most people are familiar with the procedure of averaging. Given a set of n scores (where n refers to the total number of scores in a data set), we add their values and divide by n. The result is called the **mean,** which is by far the most common—but not the only—measure of **central tendency.** Another such measure is the **median,** which is a value in the middle of the distribution of scores (so that as many scores fall above the median as fall below it). The **mode** is the most frequently appearing score in the set.

Measures of central tendency such as the mean provide important but incomplete information. Reporting the mean score is like telling another person that the score of a baseball game is 3–1 but failing to tell the person which team is ahead and which inning it is. For this reason, we often need information on the **variability** of scores as well as their mean.

The simplest measure of variability is the **range,** which is a comparison between the lowest and highest scores in a data set. A much more meaningful measure of variability is the **standard deviation.** The standard deviation is a mathematical index of the degree to which every score in a distribution of scores differs from the mean score. The more the scores in a distribution vary from the mean, the larger the standard deviation. The less the scores in a distribution differ from the mean, the smaller the standard deviation.

Means and standard deviations are reported frequently in research on adult development. There are several reasons for this, but none is more important than the relevance of these measures to individual differences in the course of adult development. For example, it is possible that a group of young adults and a group of older adults would both remember the same mean number of items on a test of memory ability (each group could recognize, on average, twenty words from a list of thirty-five). However, we might discover that the standard deviation for the older group was 7.4, while the standard deviation for the younger group was 3.1. These results would suggest that there is much more variability in the performance of older subjects than in that of the younger subjects. This important point would be obscured if the investigator only reported the mean score.

Correlation between Variables

To understand the concept of correlation, one must first understand the meaning of the term **variable.** A variable is something that can vary—that is, take on different levels or values. Age, for example, is a variable because it can take on values between 0 and 100 years or more. Other common variables are IQ, height, weight, and years of education. Some variables can take only two different values (biological sex, for example, can take on only male or female).

A **correlation** is a measure of the relationship or strength of association between two variables. During adulthood, for example, there is usually a correlation between a person's age and the number of grandchildren he has—generally, the older the adult, the greater the number of grandchildren.

Correlations can be either positive or negative. A **positive correlation** exists when high values of one variable are associated with high values of the other. During the adult years, the variables of age and onset of chronic illness are positively correlated—the older a person is, the more likely she is to develop a chronic illness such as arthritis. A **negative correlation** exists when high values of one variable are associated with low values of the other. In contemporary American society, there is a negative correlation between age and years of education—young adults in their thirties, on the average, have completed more years of formal education than older adults in their seventies and eighties. This is because of the relative lack of educational opportunity available to many individuals during the early part of the twentieth century. Remember that a positive correlation is not necessarily reflective of a "good" finding, nor is a negative correlation reflective of a "bad" finding. For example, there is obviously nothing "good" about the finding that as individuals grow older they are more likely to encounter a greater number of health problems.

Whether positive or negative, correlations can vary from weak to strong. A correlation is strong if the values of one variable are predictable from the values of the other. A perfect correlation exists when the values of one variable are perfectly predictable from the values of the other. The strength of a correlation can be measured quantitatively by computing the **Pearson product moment correlation coefficient,** which is abbreviated as r. A perfect correlation will yield an r of either $+1.0$ or -1.0, depending upon whether the association between the variables is positive or negative. As the association becomes weaker, the r score drops in absolute value from ± 1.0 to $\pm .90$, $\pm .60$, $\pm .40$, and so on, all the way down to 0.00, which is a noncorrelation. Perfect correlations (± 1.0) are seldom obtained, but even moderate correlations (say, those with r values of .30 to .60) can be very meaningful.

An example should help illustrate the importance of correlations and how they can be interpreted. One study involved measurement of IQ on individuals at two points in their lives, once in late adolescence and again in middle age (Eichorn et al., 1981). The striking result was that IQ in late adolescence and IQ in middle age were strongly correlated, with r values of about $+.80$. Despite these high correlations, it was also true that about half of the subjects showed changes of at least ten points in IQ between the two testings. These IQ changes are at least as important as the stability in IQ implied by the high correlation. To be sure, a strong correlation implies significant predictability of scores on one variable (IQ in middle age) from scores on another (IQ in adolescence). But significant predictability is not perfect stability. Even strong correlations allow for interesting discrepancies between the values on two variables.

One final point to make about correlations is that measures of correlation, such as Pearson's *r,* reflect the strength of the **linear** association between variables. This is fine in many cases, but sometimes there are **curvilinear** associations between variables. For example, it doubtlessly is true that most people have little personal income in childhood but that their income increases and then falls again as they grow older. Such a curvilinear association between age and income cannot be measured by Pearson's *r.*

Factor Analysis

To understand adult development, it is sometimes necessary to examine many variables and to assess the pattern of correlations between these variables. For example, we might be interested in examining the variables of age with mathematical ability, creativity, health, income, occupational status, and life satisfaction. That would give us seven variables in all, among which there are twenty-one possible correlations. How do we make sense of so many correlations? How do we get a view of the forest, not just the trees?

Factor analysis can be useful for producing a kind of summary of many correlations. The goal is simply to reduce a large number of correlations to a smaller number of independent sets called **factors.** Put somewhat differently, the purpose of this procedure is to discover what variables are significantly correlated with one another but totally uncorrelated with all the other variables. For example, if health, exercise, life satisfaction, and income all correlated with one another but were mathematically independent of all of the other variables, we might want to say that these variables make up a factor which we could label as "general well-being" or "vigor." Through this process, we would replace four original variables with a single derived factor.

A potential problem with factors derived from patterns of correlations is their meaning. Once we identify and label a factor as representing **x** (well-being or vigor, for example), there is a tendency to believe that **x** truly exists (that there is, in fact, a separate "trait" of well-being or vigor and that people differ on this trait). In reality, a factor is only a summary of a pattern of correlations among variables. Our label for a factor is just that, a label. It can be wrong or misleading.

Significance Tests

Suppose we conducted a study to determine if early retirement results in high levels of life satisfaction. We might ask a group of adults who opted for early retirement and a group of their agemates who are still working to complete a standardized measure of life satisfaction. After collecting the data, we discover that the mean scores for the early retirees versus the workers were 101 and 77, respectively. At this point we might wonder if there is a *significant* difference between the two groups on the measure of life satisfaction. Or we might wonder if there is a *significant* relationship between the participants' work status (working versus retired) and their scores on the measure of life satisfaction.

To determine the **statistical significance** of the results of a research study, it is first necessary to *determine the probability of obtaining the observed results by pure chance alone.* This is accomplished by employing any of a number of sophisticated statistical techniques. It is possible to determine mathematically the probability of getting the results we obtained in our study by chance. Although it is not within the scope of this text to show you how to obtain these probability estimates, you should know how these probability estimates are interpreted. If a researcher determined that the probability of obtaining the observed results by pure chance is 5/100 or less, she would conclude that the two groups in her study reflected differences so great that they are unlikely to have occurred by chance alone. Thus, differences this substantial would be viewed as "significant." Conversely, if the researcher determined that the probability of obtaining the observed results by chance is high (say 80/100 or more), she would conclude that the differences between the groups in her study were "not significant" and that the two groups responded in much the same way. Specifically, psychologists consider probabilities of 5/100 or less as indicative of statistical significance. To return to our original example, if we discovered that the probability of obtaining the observed differences between the workers and early retirees on the life satisfaction measure by pure chance was 1/100 or less, we would conclude that (1) the two groups differ significantly on their responses to the life satisfaction measure, and (2) there is a significant relationship between work status and life satisfaction.

BASIC STRATEGIES FOR RESEARCH DESIGN

In preparing to conduct a research project, it is especially important to consider design principles. The research design will determine the relationships assessed and/or the comparisons made. It will also determine how valid our conclusions can be. In general, there are two types of research designs: correlational and experimental designs.

Correlational versus Experimental Strategies

It often is said that the experiment is the principal tool of any research scientist. Yet the vast majority of studies on adult development and aging are not true experiments; rather, they are correlational studies. What is the difference between the two? Why are correlational strategies so often used to study development? Do developmental researchers pay a price for not performing true experiments?

A **correlational study** is one in which associations among variables are merely observed. An **experimental study** also assesses associations among variables; but, in an experiment, a distinction is made between **dependent variables,** which are measured or observed, and **independent variables,** which are manipulated by the experimenter. Thus, both the manipulation of independent variables and the observation of dependent variables are the critical features of experiments.

A concrete example may help to clarify the differences between a correlational versus an experimental study. Suppose we develop the hypothesis that living in a dull, nondemanding social environment causes a deterioration in the memories of older adults; while living in a stimulating, demanding social environment causes older adults to maintain their memories. We could investigate this hypothesis by conducting a correlational study. This might entail administering a standardized test of memory to two groups of older adults who live in two different types of environments: a nondemanding environment (perhaps a nursing home), and a demanding environment (living independently at home and being actively involved in a senior citizens center, doing volunteer work, and so forth). From this study we might discover that the demandingness of the social environment is positively correlated with memory performance—that is, as the demands of the environment increase, participants' scores on the memory test increase. Regardless of the strength of this correlation, however, we could *not* conclude that changes in the environment cause differences in memory. It may be that older people who remember and think well are likely to choose to live at home, while people who have more difficulty remembering and who are not self-sufficient wind up in nursing homes. Thus, it could be that the ability to remember determines the type of environment in which a person lives, rather than vice versa. The real purpose of a correlational study is to make accurate *predictions* (not to determine cause-effect relationships). For example, from this study we could predict that people who live in nursing homes often have poor memories, but we would not know why they have poor memories.

To determine cause-and-effect relationships, it is necessary to perform an *experimental study.* In order to conduct an experimental study, it is necessary to manipulate an independent variable. Ellen Langer and her associates (Langer, Rodin, Beck, Weinman, and Spitzer, 1979) conducted an experimental study that bears on the hypothesis described in the preceding paragraph. The investigators randomly divided a sample of the residents of a nursing home into different groups or conditions. In the *contingent condition,* residents were told that they would be visited several times during the next few weeks and would be asked a number of questions such as, "What did you have for breakfast two days ago?" These residents were given a poker chip for each memory question they answered correctly. The poker chips could be exchanged for gifts at a later date. The participants in the contingent condition thus lived in a demanding social environment. In the *noncontingent condition,* residents were asked the same memory questions over the same time period. At the end of each questioning session, these residents were given some poker chips as a "memento." (Care was taken to equate the number of chips given to members of the contingent and noncontingent groups.) Residents in the noncontingent group were told that the number of chips they received did *not* depend on the accuracy of their memory. They were also allowed to exchange their chips for gifts. The participants in the noncontingent condition, therefore, lived in a non-demanding social environment. After three weeks of treatment, all participants were administered a number of memory tests. Results indicated that the residents from the demanding environment (the contingent condition) performed significantly better on the memory tests than those from the nondemanding environment (the noncontingent condition). Thus, the initial hypothesis was confirmed. In this experiment the manipulated independent variable was whether participants received poker chips under contingent or noncontingent conditions. The observed or measured dependent variable was the way the participants scored on the memory tests.

But could other factors besides the conditions to which the participants were assigned account for the results of this experiment? How do we actually know that it was the independent variable that produced the differences between the participants in the two conditions?

One approach to this problem is to match the two groups on **extraneous variables** that are suspected to be important. For example, we could give IQ tests to all participants, making sure that the groups were matched with respect to IQ. Such matching can be useful; but **random assignment** is a much more powerful technique. In an experiment, individuals are always assigned to a specific group on a random basis. If assignment to groups is random and if the number of participants is reasonably large, we can assume that all extraneous factors will be randomly distributed in the two groups. This includes extraneous factors that we could never have thought of in advance, as well as the more obvious factors that might be handled through matching.

Manipulations between and within Subjects

Random assignment of participants to different groups is one way to manipulate an independent variable. Such manipulations are **between-subjects manipulations.** There are also **within-subject manipulations,** which involve observing each participant in an experiment under two or more conditions. For example, if we suspect that a certain drug improves memory in patients with Alzheimer's disease, we might measure memory ability in each individual after administration of this drug and also after administration of a placebo. Each individual then could be examined under the drug condition and later under the placebo condition to determine the effect of the drug. Counterbalancing would be advisable in such an experiment—we would test one half of the sample first in the drug condition and later in the placebo condition, and we would test the remaining sample first in the placebo condition and later in the drug condition. Counterbalancing controls the effects of the time at which variables are manipulated within subjects.

Quasi-Experimental Strategies in Developmental Research

All "true" experiments involve the manipulation of variables. Unfortunately, some variables are difficult if not impossible to manipulate. Age is one of these variables.

Since we cannot manipulate a person's age, we cannot perform true experiments to examine the effects of age on a person's behavior. Despite the fact that most studies involving age are not true experiments, they often resemble true experiments in the ways in which they are designed or analyzed; age is treated as an independent variable even though it is not actually manipulated. Thus, we look for *effects of age*—actually, *effects related to age*—on one or more dependent variables. Because they are similar to true experiments, but also because the independent variable—age—is not truly manipulated, such studies are called **quasi-experiments.**

Let's consider what it means to say that a person's age cannot be manipulated. Suppose we are conducting a study on adult development and succeed in finding individuals who are willing to serve as participants. We can observe their behavior under a variety of conditions that are under our control. For example, we might present one of several different types of instruction, or administer several different types of drugs. It is up to us, the experimenters, to decide which conditions or treatments each participant will receive. But we can't decide each participant's age; we cannot alter the number of years each person has lived.

Of course, we can assign any one participant to a group of similarly aged individuals and compare this group to another group of younger or older individuals. We can also plan to test our participants not only today but again several years from now. Using these strategies, we can compare functioning at different ages and gather evidence about effects and phenomena that are *related* to age. But clearly these strategies do *not* entail the actual manipulation of age. They simply allow us to take advantage of differences and changes in age that occur independently of our study and that are beyond our control.

The Problem of Internal Validity

Perhaps you feel that the difference between an experiment and a quasi-experiment is rather subtle and has no practical importance. If so, you are right about the subtlety but wrong about the importance. The difference is critical, and it is clarified by the concept of internal validity.

The concept of internal validity concerns the role played by an independent variable in an experiment (or quasi-experiment). An experiment possesses **internal validity** if the results of the experiment reflect the influence of the independent variable rather than the influence of any extraneous or uncontrolled variables.

Internal validity is a concept that was developed by Donald Campbell and Julian Stanley in their classic book, *Experimental and Quasi-Experimental Designs for Research* (1963). Campbell and Stanley enumerate several threats to internal validity and show that quasi-experimental studies, which include most studies of adult development and aging, are much more vulnerable to these threats than are true experiments.

One of the most serious threats to internal validity is **selection.** This threat is especially troublesome when different-aged groups are compared. In such cases, the procedures used to select groups can result in many extraneous differences among these groups, *differences that do not pertain to age per se.* For example, a young-adult group and an elderly group might differ with respect to years of education, health status, and so on. These differences between the members of these different cohorts may make the results of a research study very difficult to interpret.

A second threat to internal validity is **history.** This is especially serious when we test the same individuals at different ages. The problem is that between one time of testing and another, many events can have a profound affect on the person's behavior; also, of course, the person is growing older between testings. Possible historical effects include attitudinal changes (social attitudes toward aging, for example), economic events (increases in social security), and social changes (the development of new senior citizens centers), among others. These changes might have a positive effect on an aging population if, as individuals grow older, they (1) are looked upon more positively, (2) have more money to spend, and (3) have more opportunities for social and intellectual stimulation. Thus, these individuals are likely to function in a more adaptive psychological manner not because they are getting older, but because of positive sociohistorical changes.

A third threat to internal validity is **testing.** Taking a test on one occasion can affect test performance on a subsequent occasion. Obviously, the testing threat can accompany the history threat whenever we test the same individuals at different ages. However, the testing threat is especially serious when we are measuring some type of behavior that can change as an individual practices. (Many types of intellectual performance can change with practice.)

Suppose that we had a machine that could make someone twenty years old, or even ninety years old, by turning a switch (and that we could bring the person back to his or her original age with no harm done). We could take a sample of subjects and randomly assign half of them to a twenty-year-old condition and the other half to a ninety-year-old condition, and then compare them on many different dependent measures (for example, creativity). Random assignment would take care of all extraneous differences between the two age groups (the selection threat). History would not be a factor because we could test all subjects on the same day. Further, we would test each subject only once, thus avoiding the threat of testing. Under these ideal conditions, we could solve all problems of internal validity. Unfortunately, we have no ideal situation. In developmental research we must live with threats to internal validity and compensate for them as best we can.

Next we'll consider several different types of quasi-experimental designs that are used in research on adult development and aging. We will see that different designs compensate for different internal validity threats. We will also see that the time span of a research design is a critical factor in determining what kinds of threats it can handle.

QUASI-EXPERIMENTAL DESIGNS FOR THE STUDY OF ADULT DEVELOPMENT AND AGING

Discussion of quasi-experimental research designs can be complicated. Let's start with the simplest designs: the cross-sectional and longitudinal designs, which are the basis for all developmental research. Next, we'll describe more complex designs called sequential designs, which are actually further elaborations of the basic cross-sectional and simple longitudinal designs. There are ways in which all of these designs compensate, or fail to compensate, for the various threats to internal validity. Table 2.1 provides a summary of each design, its susceptibility to internal validity threats, and other distinguishing features. It may be helpful to consult this table throughout the discussion that follows.

Cross-Sectional and Longitudinal Designs

Consider two different ways in which we might attempt to examine the impact of aging on behavior. First, we might perform a **cross-sectional study,** comparing groups of people in different age ranges. A typical cross-sectional study might include a group of eighteen- to twenty-year-olds and a group of sixty-five- to seventy-year-olds. A more comprehensive cross-sectional study might include groups from every decade of life from the twenties through the nineties. The investigators could compare the different groups on a variety of dependent variables, such as IQ performance, memory, and creativity. They could collect data in a very short time; even a large study can be completed within a few months. The major purpose of a cross-sectional study is to measure *age-related differences.* As we shall see, a cross-sectional study allows us to determine if one age group of subjects differs from other age groups. Cross-sectional studies, however, do *not* allow us to measure age-related change (that is, the extent to which age-graded factors, by themselves, cause developmental change).

Another way we might explore the effects of aging on behavior is to perform a **longitudinal study.** In this case, we would take a single group of subjects, all the same age, and test them today and on one or more occasions in the future. For example, we might decide to examine creativity at ages fifty, fifty-seven, sixty-four, and seventy-one. Longitudinal studies clearly take a long time to complete. Furthermore, the purpose of a longitudinal study is to measure *age-related changes,* not age differences. As we shall see, simple longitudinal studies are not always successful in measuring such changes.

One advantage of cross-sectional designs, then, is time efficiency. Further, cross-sectional designs are virtually free of two important internal validity threats. There is no history threat because all subjects are tested at the same time. There is no testing threat because it is necessary to test each individual subject only once. For these reasons, cross-sectional designs are enormously popular. However, as mentioned earlier, cross-sectional designs are highly susceptible to the internal validity threat of *selection.* We often do not know the extent to which the results of a cross-sectional study reflect the effects of age versus the effects of countless extraneous factors.

Many extraneous factors involved in cross-sectional designs pertain to **cohort effects.** Cohort effects are caused by a subject's time of birth or generation but not actually to her or his age. For example, cohorts can differ with respect to years of education, child-rearing practices, health, and attitudes on topics such as sex and religion. These cohort effects are important because they can powerfully influence the dependent measures in a study concerned with age. Cohort effects can look like age effects, but they are not.

Since cross-sectional designs do not allow random assignment of individuals to age groups, there is no way to control cohort effects or other extraneous variables. Our only approach to controlling these variables is through *matching.* For example, if our young subjects are all college students, we might make sure that all our elderly subjects are also college students. Unfortunately, matching for extraneous variables is sometimes impossible. (We may be unable to find an adequate number of elderly college students who are willing to participate in our study.) Further, we can only match for the extraneous variables whose importance we recognize. Finally, matching can have the unwanted side effect of producing unusual or *non-representative* groups—elderly people in college may differ in many ways from the average person of their age. Selection poses a serious threat to cross-sectional studies, and matching is not truly adequate to remove it.

Figure 2.1 contains a diagram of a simple cross-sectional study that addresses the issue of whether IQ changes from fifty to sixty to seventy years of age. This study, if it were conducted in the year 1990, would employ participants of different ages (fifty, sixty, and seventy) representing different cohorts according to the year in which they were born (1920, 1930, and 1940). Interpreting the data obtained in this study would be impossible because changes in age are *confounded* (that is, confused with) changes in cohort. For example, we might find that seventy-year-olds have lower IQ scores than fifty-year-olds. But we would not know if this is because of the ages of the participants, the amount of education received by individuals born in 1920 versus those born in 1940, or some other extraneous factor.

Although longitudinal studies are time-consuming, they are valuable because they remove the threat of selection, or cohort effects. This is because individuals from a single cohort form the subject pool for a longitudinal study. Further, longitudinal studies have the great advantage of allowing us to track changes that take place within individual subjects over a long time interval. If one's primary concern is the study of intraindividual change over the course of development, longitudinal designs are indispensible.

Unfortunately, the threats of history, testing, and selective dropout are especially troublesome in longitudinal designs. **Selective dropout** refers to the possibility that over the course of a longitudinal study participants who either perform poorly on a particular test, or are unmotivated or ill, will be less likely to undergo repeated testing. To illustrate, consider the longitudinal study diagrammed in figure

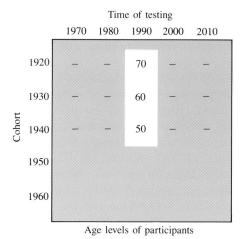

Figure 2.1 A cross-sectional design measures age-related differences between different cohorts.

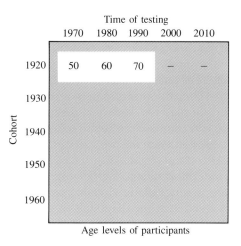

Figure 2.2 A longitudinal design measures age-related changes within a cohort.

2.2. This study measures IQ changes in individuals from the 1920 birth cohort as they move from fifty to sixty to seventy years of age. The study begins in the year 1970 and concludes in the year 1990. The same participants are retested at ten-year intervals. Interpreting the data obtained in this study would be very difficult. For example, we might find that the participants display higher IQ scores at age seventy than age fifty. This finding might be due to any number of facts; for example, it could be true that (1) people actually become more intelligent as they age; (2) between 1970 and 1990 our society has changed so that life has become more stimulating, enriching, and enjoyable for the typical older person; (3) the subjects became more familiar with the IQ test each time they were tested; or (4) at the end of the study in 1990, we were left with a very biased group of participants—those who were exceptionally bright, motivated, healthy, and so on.

It may be possible to remove the threats of testing and selective dropout by adding new or independent samples of participants at each testing. For example, we could collect data on a group of randomly selected sixty-year-olds in 1980 and compare their IQ performance to those participants tested for the second time in 1980. And we could also add another group of randomly selected seventy-year-olds in 1990. This procedure, however, would still not remove the history threat.

Cohort-Sequential Designs

Sequential research designs may be used to correct some of the inadequacies of cross-sectional and longitudinal research. A **cohort-sequential design** entails two or more longitudinal studies, each covering the same range of ages, conducted over differing lengths of time. An example of a simple cohort-sequential design is shown in figure 2.3. Three different cohorts are selected; a cohort born in 1920, a second cohort born in 1930, and a third born in 1940. A sample from each cohort is tested on three different occasions—first when the participants are fifty years old, again when they are sixty years old, and a third time when they are seventy years old. As in the simple longitudinal design, independent samples could also be drawn at the different times of testing to control the threats of testing and selective dropout.

The cohort-sequential design corrects for the major drawback associated with the simple cross-sectional design; that is, by conducting a cohort-sequential study we can estimate the relative importance of age effects in comparison to cohort effects. For example, we can compare performance by the 1920 versus 1930 versus 1940 cohorts by looking across the rows in figure 2.3. This tells us something about how cohort-related factors might influence our measure. We can also compare the performance of individuals from each of the three age groups. This is accomplished by looking at the diagonals in figure 2.3—we could calculate the average score of all of the fifty year olds and compare it to the average score for all groups of sixty year olds, and so on. This tells us how age influences our measure independently of cohort. Further, the design allows us to assess interactions between cohort and age. We can see if the age effect is constant across the two cohorts, or if it varies between the cohorts. This can obviously be very important if there are different rates of aging in different cohorts.

The main weakness of the cohort-sequential design is that it doesn't compensate for the history threat. We would have no understanding, in other words, of how the historical changes that occurred from 1970 to 2010 affected the behavior of our participants. Another weakness of the design is that it takes a great deal of time to complete. As you can see from figure 2.3, to study aging and cohort effects on IQ at fifty, sixty and seventy years of age, we need forty years to collect the data.

Time-Sequential Designs

The **time-sequential design** corrects for the major limitation of the longitudinal design. This design is capable of differentiating age effects from historical changes (or time-of-testing effects). Time-sequential designs involve two or more cross-sectional studies, each covering the same range of ages, conducted at different times. An example is shown in figure 2.4. According to this figure, in 1970, we examine performance of three age groups: fifty-, sixty-, and seventy-year-olds. In 1980 and also in 1990, we again examine the performance of individuals at these three age levels (these are, of course, entirely *new* samples of participants).

The strength of the time-sequential design is that history effects—or time-of-testing effects—can be examined explicitly, in addition to differences related to age. That is, looking at the columns in figure 2.4, we can examine differences between performance in 1970, 1980, and 1990; this tells us directly about history effects. Independent of history, we can look at the diagonals to examine differences between the fifty-, sixty-, and seventy-year-olds; this gives us information relevant to aging. Furthermore, we can examine the interactions between age and time of testing. If age-related differences in 1980 are smaller than age-related differences

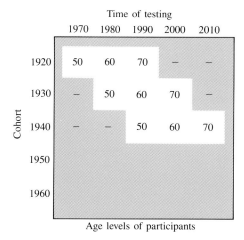

Figure 2.3 A cohort-sequential design involves two or more longitudinal studies covering the same age ranges over different time eras.

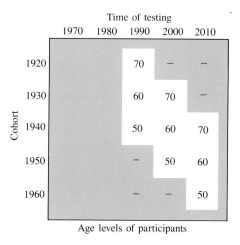

Figure 2.4 A time-sequential design differentiates age effects from historical changes.

in 1970 and 1990, it might support some interesting conclusions about history-related changes in the course of adult development.

Another advantage of the time-sequential design is that it is more time efficient than the cohort-sequential design. In our example (figure 2.4), age and history effects can be studied over a twenty-year span (compared to a forty-year span for the cohort-sequential design). Also, note that the time-sequential design (figure 2.4) takes the same length of time to conduct as the longitudinal design (figure 2.2)!

The disadvantage of the time-sequential design is that it does not consider cohort effects. At each time of measurement, we must be concerned with the possibility that differences between our age groups may, in part, reflect differences in their respective cohorts.

Cross-Sequential Designs

Cross-sequential designs are a kind of hybrid combination of cross-sectional and longitudinal designs. They are not fundamentally relevant to adult development and aging because they do not separate age effects from either cohort or history effects. Rather, cross-sequential designs separate cohort and history effects from each other.

The technique used in a cross-sequential design, illustrated in figure 2.5, is to examine two (or more) cohorts, covering different age ranges, at each of two (or more) times of testing. Differences among cohorts can be examined independently of differences among times of measurement. Unfortunately, neither of these differences can be separated from age. The cohorts differ on an age dimension, and subjects must obviously be older at the second testing than the first.

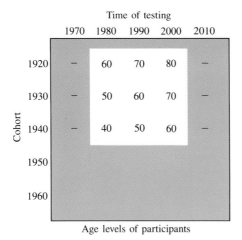

Figure 2.5   A cross-sequential design combines the cross-sectional and longitudinal designs.

Perhaps this is a good time for you to stop and review the various quasi-experimental designs in adult development and aging. Going over them once or even twice probably won't be enough. Take some time to study the material in table 2.1, which summarizes the main characteristics of each of these quasi-experimental designs.

Schaie's "Most Efficient" Design

We can summarize the preceeding discussion by saying that the cohort-sequential design is a useful extension of simple longitudinal designs and that the time-sequential design is a useful extension of cross-sectional designs. Furthermore, we could conclude that these sequential designs are far superior to the simple cross-sectional and longitudinal studies from which they are derived. However, the various sequential designs are still less than perfect. History or time-of-testing effects threaten the internal validity of cohort-sequential designs. Cohort effects threaten the internal validity of time-sequential designs. So what are we to do to ensure the internal validity of our research?

One answer is to use *both* the cohort-sequential and time-sequential designs, and then even to add the cross-sequential design for good measure. Incorporating all of these designs at once is more difficult than performing one of them alone. K. W. Schaie (1965, 1977), an authority on sequential designs, has developed the **most efficient design** to combine the best features of the other designs.

The "most efficient" design is illustrated in figure 2.6. Individuals in five different cohorts are studied: 1900, 1910, 1920, 1930, and 1940. Measurements are made at five different times: 1950, 1960, 1970, 1980, and 1990. Finally, it is necessary to collect data from new, independent samples of each cohort at each of the different

Table 2.1

SUMMARY OF QUASI-EXPERIMENTAL DESIGNS IN ADULT DEVELOPMENT AND AGING

Design	Description	Threats to Internal Validity	Other Properties
Simple Cross-Sectional	Two or more age groups are compared at one time of testing	Selection, especially cohort effects; differences between groups might reflect differences in time of birth	Easy to conduct; can be useful as a pilot study
Simple Longitudinal	A single group of subjects is tested repeatedly at different points in time	Time-of-testing (history) effects; historical changes might produce effects that appear to be age-related changes; repeated testing might influence measures (testing effects)	Time-consuming; subjects may drop out of study prior to completion—selective dropout (this threatens generalizability of findings); allows assessment of individual differences in developmental change
Cohort-Sequential	Two or more longitudinal comparisons are made on different cohorts	Time-of-testing and testing effects as for simple longitudinal (can remove testing effects with independent samples)	Extremely time-consuming; requires two time periods to examine change over one time period; allows separate examination of age-related effects and cohort effects
Time-Sequential	Two or more cross-sectional comparisons are made at different times of testing	Cohort effects, since every cross-sectional comparison is possibly influenced by cohort as well as age	Time-consuming, but not as time-consuming as cohort-sequential designs; allows separate examination of age effects and time-of-testing (history) effects
Cross-Sequential	Two or more cohorts are compared at two or more times of testing	Neither time-of-testing nor cohort effects are independent of age-related changes	Time-consuming; provides no clear information on age-related changes

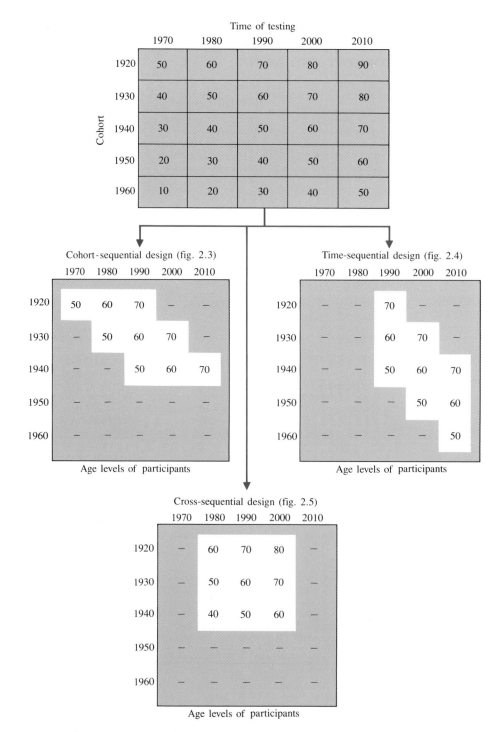

Figure 2.6   Schaie's "most efficient" design.

times of testing (though retesting of the original samples is also recommended). If all this is accomplished, it is possible to perform a cohort-sequential analysis, a time-sequential analysis, and a cross-sequential analysis all at once, as shown in figure 2.6.

Such analyses provide a wealth of interesting comparisons. Certain patterns can reveal strong evidence for age-related changes, cohort differences, and history effects. Consider the following possible outcome in a study of creativity: The cohort-sequential analysis may suggest a strong effect of cohort but only a weak effect of age. The time-sequential analysis supports only weak effects of time of testing and age. Finally, the cross-sequential analysis supports, again, a strong effect of cohort but only a weak effect of time of measurement. In this hypothetical case, we would have clear indications that cohort is an important variable but that age and time of measurement are not.

We must always be mindful of the tremendous difficulty of collecting the data that permit such complex analyses. Faced with this difficulty, it may frequently be advisable to first conduct simple cross-sectional studies, controlling as much as possible for extraneous, cohort-related variables known to be important. Examining the effects of different treatments in such designs can also help isolate the specific ways in which younger groups differ from older groups at a particular time in history. Subsequently, once important differences between younger and older groups have been isolated, longitudinal and even sequential strategies can be carried out, allowing a much more complete understanding of the causes of these differences.

Stated somewhat differently, cross-sectional studies seem to be the logical starting point in developmental research. If this type of research establishes reliable age differences in behavior, then other types of designs should be carried out to determine the underlying causes of the apparent age difference.

PROBLEMS OF SAMPLING IN DEVELOPMENTAL RESEARCH

When we decide to study a certain group of individuals (say, seventy-year-olds who have recently retired), we obviously cannot collect measurements on everyone in that group. Rather, we must study a sample of the entire population of individuals in the class. Although we study only a sample, we want to generalize our findings to the rest of the population. Thus, the sampling procedures form a very important aspect of research methodology.

A **representative sample** has the same characteristics as the larger population to which we want to generalize our findings. The best way to achieve a representative sample is through the technique of random sampling, a technique in which every member of the population has an equal chance of being in the sample that we study. For example, the ideal way to find a representative sample of recently retired seventy-year-olds would be to compile a list of every such individual in the world and then to pick randomly a number of these individuals to be in our study. Obviously, truly random sampling can rarely be employed. Indeed, we often must struggle to find people with certain characteristics who are willing to participate in our studies.

of adult development seldom can be sure that their samples are
s fact produces two consequences, one pertaining primarily to
igns and the other primarily to longitudinal designs.

ive Samples in Cross-Sectional Designs

signs, the problem of nonrepresentative samples adds to prob-
lity. Specifically, selection threats may be due partially to non-
ing. If we find differences between a group of young subjects
ly subjects but do not know whether either sample is repre-
to be sure if either age or cohort is responsible for the dif-
...ences. Perhaps these differences occurred because we selected a group of young
adults with below-average intelligence for individuals of their age and a group of
older persons with above-average intelligence for individuals of their age. The solution to this problem is to measure various extraneous variables (IQ, for example)
that are suspected to be important. We must measure the IQs of the two groups
and relate them to the norms for their age groups. Though not ideal, this approach
is much better than ignoring these issues.

Nonrepresentative Samples in Longitudinal Designs

The problem of sampling in longitudinal studies is not just a hypothetical problem;
it has been shown to occur. It frequently takes the form of selective dropout. As we
have already mentioned, selective dropout refers to the fact that some participants
drop out of a longitudinal study before all of the testings are complete. The problem
is that those who drop out of a study are likely to differ significantly from those who
continue until the end. Indeed, it has been shown that people who return for testing
in a longitudinal study often have greater intellectual abilities than those who do
not (Riegel and Riegel, 1972). Further, longitudinal declines in intellectual ability
are more likely to occur among those who drop out of a study after several testings
than among those who remain (Eisdorfer and Wilkie, 1973; Wilkie and Eisdorfer,1973). Finally, Cooney, Schaie, and Willis (1988) have shown that participants who leave a longitudinal study for health reasons are largely responsible for
producing the selective dropout effect. As a result, the data collected in a longitudinal study may reflect aging among adults of superior ability and good health,
not aging among adults of average or below-average ability and health.

At another level, sampling problems can threaten the external validity of longitudinal research (Campbell and Stanley, 1963). **External validity** refers to the
degree to which we may generalize the results of a scientific study. When we use
nonrepresentative samples, we often do not know whether age trends observed in
one longitudinal study are representative of age trends in the population at large.
The external validity of cross-sectional designs, of course, may be threatened for
the same reason.

Summary

Two basic problems of measurement are reliability and validity. Although the problem of reliability is serious, effective methods for assessing reliability (the test-retest method, for example) and for increasing reliability (collecting data on multiple items, for example) do exist. The problem of validity is more troublesome because many psychological concepts, such as creativity and self-concept, are highly abstract. When we attempt to evaluate such abstract concepts, it is often arguable that we are not truly measuring what we think we are measuring.

Among the basic measures used for collecting observations are the interview and questionnaire, behavioral research, standardized tests, and physiological research. Each has strengths and weaknesses. Interview and questionnaire studies can often be conducted when other sorts of studies are impossible or, at best, impractical. However, these types of studies are especially susceptible to the problem of reactivity, particularly the problem of response bias. Moreover, interviews and questionnaires are highly dependent upon the subjects' conscious impressions of themselves, and these impressions can be at variance with actual behavior.

Behavioral measures are many and varied. They can be collected in laboratory settings or in the field. Behavioral studies in the laboratory allow impressive control over many extraneous variables. However, they often can be artificial, even anxiety provoking, to subjects. Further, laboratory studies produce problems of reactivity, and they cannot be used to study certain kinds of real-world phenomena. Field studies allow fewer controls, but they can be very naturalistic, can reduce problems of reactivity, and can reveal real-life phenomena that are not reproducible in the laboratory. Standardized tests are useful for comparing a particular sample of subjects to representative samples of subjects tested previously. However, the validity of such tests is often questionable. Further, it is frequently the case that no previously developed test can measure exactly what we want to measure. Physiological measures can be invaluable for an increased understanding of behavioral data, and they can suggest ways to reduce or remove age-related differences in behavior when this is desirable.

Among the basic strategies for summarizing data are measures of central tendency and variability. Correlations are used to determine the degree to which two variables are related to each other. However, many studies produce so many correlations that interpretation is difficult. In these cases, factor analysis can be useful for reducing many correlations to a smaller number of factors. Significance tests are used to determine if the results of a study are due to chance.

In terms of research design, correlational studies must be distinguished from true experiments. Experiments involve the manipulation of independent variables and actually provide evidence for cause-effect relationships between independent and dependent variables. Quasi-experiments are similar to true experiments, but quasi-experiments do not involve the actual manipulation of independent variables. Since age cannot be manipulated, studies of this variable are considered to be quasi-experimental. Three threats to internal validity, threats that are problematic in such quasi-experimental studies, are selection, history, and testing.

Several types of quasi-experiments are used to study adult development and aging. Simple cross-sectional and longitudinal designs are limited in their usefulness. Cross-sectional designs suffer from cohort effects, whereas longitudinal designs suffer from both testing and history effects. Among the sequential designs, the cohort-sequential design allows independent assessment of age and cohort effects but does not solve the problem of history effects. The time-sequential design allows independent assessment of age and history effects but does not solve the problem of cohort effects. The use of both designs together, along with the cross-sequential design as well, can in principle allow us to distinguish age, cohort, and history effects. A greater investment of time and resources is necessary to use all these designs together, however.

Researchers must frequently sample their participants from different age groups (cohorts), and this sampling can introduce bias; samples may be nonrepresentative. The problem of sampling is unavoidable, but we must keep it in mind when we are interpreting the data in studies of adult development and aging. Particularly vexing is the problem of selective dropout or experimental mortality, which occurs when participants drop out of a longitudinal study. Those who drop out are likely to differ systematically from those who remain. This can threaten the generalizability of longitudinal studies.

Review Questions

1. How can we assess reliability? How can we improve the methods we use to assess reliability?
2. What are the central issues involved in the validity of measurement?
3. Describe the basic types of measures used for collecting information about adults. Include the advantages and disadvantages of each type.
4. What are the basic strategies for summarizing measurements?
5. Explain the logic behind the technique of factor analysis.
6. Provide an overview of correlational and experimental strategies in research design. Include in your answer information about manipulations between and within subjects.
7. Discuss quasi-experimental designs and the problem of internal validity.
8. Compare and contrast the simple quasi-experimental designs (cross-sectional and longitudinal) with the complex quasi-experimental designs (sequential designs) used to study adult development and aging.
9. What are some of the main sampling problems in conducting research with adults?

For Further Reading

Eichorn, D. M., et al. (1981). *Present and past in middle life.* New York: Academic Press.
   A longitudinal study that spans nearly fifty years. Includes information about physical, cognitive, emotional, social, and personality development. Reveals how a longitudinal study is conducted, as well as how factor analysis can be used effectively. Reading level: medium difficulty.

Neale, J. M., & Liebert, R. M. (1980). *Science and behavior: An introduction to methods of research* (2nd ed.). Englewood Cliffs, NJ: Prentice-Hall.
   An excellent introduction to scientific methodology, particularly issues related to reliability, validity, basic types of measures, basic strategies for summarizing measurements, and basic strategies for research design. Reading level: undergraduate.

Nesselroade, J. R., & Reese, H. W. (1973). *Life-span developmental psychology: Methodological issues.* New York: Academic Press.
   A series of articles by experts in life-span development. Articles focus on some of the issues discussed in this chapter, particularly the effective use of quasi-experimental designs in studying adult development and aging. Reading level: reasonably difficult.

CHAPTER 3

BIOLOGICAL PROCESSES: LONGEVITY, AGING, AND HEALTH

IMAGINE

Imagine That You Are 120 Years Old

Would you still be able to write your name? Could you think clearly? What would your body look like? Would you be able to walk? to run? Could you still have sex? Would you have an interest in sex? Would your eyes and ears still function? Could you work?

Has anyone ever lived to be 120 years old? Supposedly, one American, Charlie Smith (1842?–1979), lived to be 137 years old. In three areas of the world, not just a single person but many people have reportedly lived more than 130 years. These areas are the Republic of Georgia in the Soviet Union, the Vilcabamba valley in Ecuador, and the province of Hunza in Kashmir. In the United States, statistics tell us there are about 10 centenarians (people over 100 years old) per 100,000 people (Spencer, Goldstein, and Taeuber, 1987). But in the Republic of Georgia, these figures soar to approximately 400 centenarians per 100,000 people. Some of the Russians are reported to be 120 to 170 years old (Benet, 1976).

However, there is reason to believe that some of these claims about the longevity of people in Soviet Georgia are false (Medvedev, 1974). We really do not have sound documentation of anyone living more than approximately 115 to 120 years. In the case of the Soviets, birth registrations, as well as other documents such as marriage certificates and military registrations, are not available. In most instances, the ages of the Georgian centenarians have been based on the individuals' recall of important historical events and on interviews with other members of the village (Benet, 1976). In the Russian villages where people have been reported to live long lives, the elderly experience unparalleled esteem and honor. Centenarians are often given special positions in the community, such as the leader of social celebrations. Thus, these people have a strong incentive to claim to be older than they really are. One individual who claimed to be 130 years of age was found to have used his father's birth certificate during World War I to escape army duty. Later, it was discovered that he was only 78 years old (Hayflick, 1975).

What about Charlie Smith? Was he really 137 years old when he died? Charlie was very, very old, but no one could document that he was actually 137. In 1956, officials of the Social Security Administration began to collect information about American centenarians who were receiving benefits. They visited Charlie Smith in 1961. He gave his birthdate as July 4, 1842, and his place of birth as Liberia. On one occasion he said he had been bought at a slave auction in New Orleans in 1854. Charles Smith of Galveston, Texas, bought him and gave the young boy his own name. Charlie was 21 years of age in 1863 when he supposedly was freed under the Emancipation Proclamation, but he decided to stay with the Smiths. By the end of the nineteenth century, Charlie had settled in Florida. He worked in turpentine camps, and at one point owned a turpentine farm in Homeland, Florida. Smith's records at the Social Security Administration do not provide evidence of his birthdate, but they do mention that be began to receive benefits at age 113 based on Social Security credits earned from picking oranges (Freeman, 1982). Charlie Smith lived to be very old—exactly how old, we will never know.

There are more and more Americans living to be 100. It is expected that by the year 2080 there will be nearly 250 centenarians per 10,000 elderly (people over 65 years of age), compared to the 1986 figure of 1 per 10,000 (Spencer et al., 1987). Segerberg (1982) interviewed a number of centenarians about the physical, psychological, and social factors responsible for their longevity. Especially entertaining were some of the bizarre reasons several of the centenarians gave as to why they were able to live to 100: "Because I slept with my head to the north," "Because I ate a lot of fatty pork and salt," and "Because I don't believe in germs."

An examination of the scientific literature, on the other hand, reveals that a long life seems to be dependent on organized, purposeful behavior; discipline and hard work; freedom and independence; a balanced diet; a family orientation; good peer and friendship relations; and low to moderate ambition. We will learn more about the factors that promote long life in the following chapter.

INTRODUCTION

This is the first of two chapters that focus on the biological processes of development. We will begin this chapter with a discussion of the topic of longevity—a topic that likely makes each of us curious. We'll evaluate various demographic characteristics of the adult population, emphasizing the changing age structure of America. We'll discuss sex differences in longevity, and we'll take a fascinating journey through the reasons behind longevity. Next, we'll discuss a number of biological theories that have been developed to explain why people age, describing the possibility that humans have a biological clock that regulates the aging process. Then we'll address the topics of health and health care across the adult years. We'll focus on the peak of health and physical performance in early adulthood and the development of poor health habits when we are still physically competent. Our focus on health in the middle-adult years will emphasize weight control and cardiovascular disease. We'll describe the decline of health common in late adulthood and the beneficial effects of exercise on health and athletic performance.

LONGEVITY

How long do you think you will live? Do you think you have a shot at Charlie Smith's purported 137 years? Unfortunately, you probably do not. In this section, we'll look first at life expectancy in different historical periods, including projections of the number of people likely to be in different age ranges in the years 2030 and 2080. We'll make a distinction between *life expectancy* versus *life span,* and we'll discuss some of the reasons that life expectancy has undergone significant changes in recent times. We'll also explore the issue of sex differences in longevity. Finally, we'll discuss the social and economic impact of an aging population.

Life Expectancy versus Potential Life Span

It is only within the past thirty-five years that psychologists have paid serious attention to the developmental changes that occur during the adult years. There are several reasons why developmentalists took so long to become interested in adulthood and aging. First, as mentioned in chapter 1, psychologists assumed that development did not continue after adolescence. Second, only recently have we become an "aged" rather than a "young" society. Since 1900 the percentage of the American population aged sixty-five and over has increased substantially. In 1900, less than 5 percent of the United States population was sixty-five years of age or older. This rose to approximately 12 percent in the early 1980s and is projected to increase to 21 percent by the year 2030 (Kasper, 1988; U.S. Bureau of Census, 1982). The actual number of older people in the United States has increased more than eightfold this century—from 3 million in 1900 to 25.5 million in 1980 (U.S. Bureau of Census, 1983). The projected number of older adults by 2030 is 50 million, approximately twice the number alive at present (Schaie and Willis, 1986).

The population of the elderly (again, those sixty-five years of age and older) is itself aging. Those eighty-five years old and older now constitute nearly 10 percent of the population over age sixty-five, and by the year 2080 may represent as much as 25 percent of this population (Spencer et al., 1987). In fact, individuals eighty-five and older represent the most rapidly growing part of the American population. For example, between 1960 to 1980 the population of the United States 85 and over increased by 141 percent (Longino, 1988). Even more dramatic is the evidence of growth in the number of Americans who reach 100 or more years of age. Figure 3.1 shows that in 1990 there were 54,000 centenarians and that by the year 2000 this population will number over 100,000. By the year 2080, our society is projected to include more than 1,000,000 centenarians (Spencer et al., 1987).

The aging of our society is reflected in changes in **life expectancy.** Life expectancy refers to the age at which an individual born into a particular cohort is expected to die. By contrast, **longevity** refers to the number of years an individual actually lives. For example, a child born in 1900 had an average life expectancy of forty-eight years, whereas two of every three of you reading this book are likely to die at age seventy or older. In the past century, the average life expectancy in the United States increased by thirty years; a gain greater than that made during all of human history (Spencer et al., 1987)!

One of the best ways to see how we have become an older society is to examine changes in the **age structure** of our society. Age structure refers to the percentage of males and females within various age intervals. The first two graphs in figure 3.2 show the age structure of the United States in 1850 and 1950. The third graph indicates the projected age structure of the United States in the year 2030 (Bureau of the Census, 1977). As you can see, the shapes of these graphs change dramatically. The first graph looks like a pyramid. The last graph looks like a square. This means that between 1850 and 2030, there will be an increasing equalization of the percentage of Americans within various age intervals. By the year 2030, the number of individuals in each period of the life cycle will be approximately equal.

Until about 1970, most of the change in life expectancy came from improved health care in infancy and early childhood. Life expectancy for those who reached fifty years of age, by contrast, remained virtually unchanged for 150 years (Tanner, 1966). More recently, however, life expectancy at age fifty has witnessed some remarkable changes. This is primarily due to improvements in the health care available to today's adults. For example, during the last decade, fewer males in middle

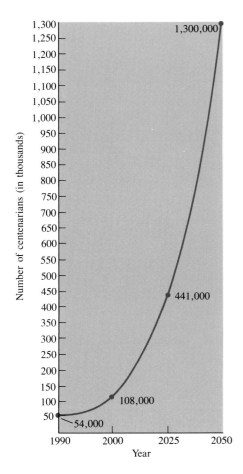

Figure 3.1   The projected increase of centenarians from the years 1990 to 2050.
Source: G. Spencer, A. A. Goldstein, and C. M. Taeuber, "America's Centenarians." Washington, DC: U.S. Government office, 1987.

adulthood and the early part of late adulthood seem to be dying because of heart attack or stroke (Longino, 1988; Rosenwaike and Dolinsky, 1987). However, projections about the future must be cautiously interpreted since changes in infant mortality, immigration, and social-environmental conditions will influence the life expectancy of tomorrow's adults (Spencer et al., 1987; U.S. Census Projections, 1984).

We have seen that life expectancy—the age at which an individual is expected to die—has undergone dramatic changes over time. However, the **potential life span** has remained virtually unchanged since the beginning of recorded history. Potential life span refers to ". . . the maximum age that could be attained if an individual were able to avoid or be successfully treated for all illness and accidents" (Schaie and Willis, 1986, pp. 368–389). It has been estimated that the maximum potential human life span is approximately 110 to 120 years of age (Cristofalo, 1986; Hayflick, 1980; Shock, 1975, 1986). This means that there is a limit to the effects of

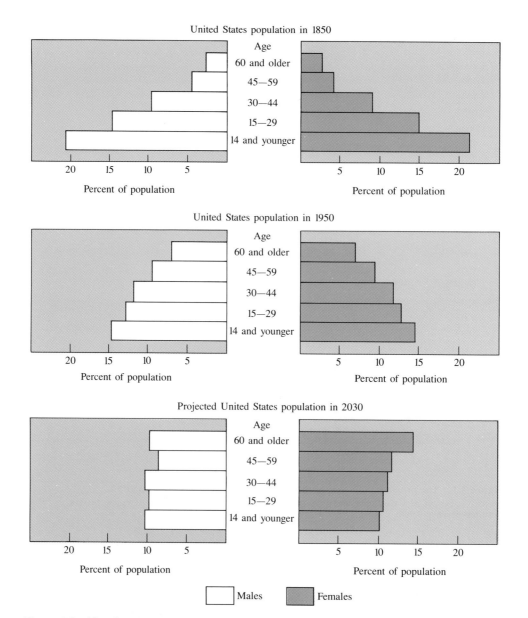

Figure 3.2   The changing age structure of the U.S. population.

Source: The 1850 and 1950 figures are from the United Nations Department of Economic and Social Affairs, *The Aging of Populations and It's Economic and Social Implications*. (Population Studies No. 26), 1956. New York: United Nations. The 2030 figures are from the U.S. Bureau of the Census, *Household and Family Characteristics*. (Current Population Reports, Series P-20, No. 326), 1977. Washington, DC: U.S. Government Printing Office.

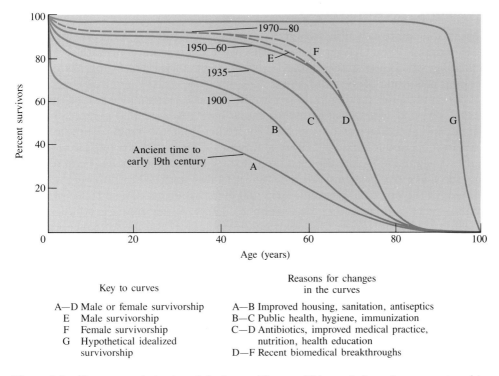

Key to curves

A—D Male or female survivorship
  E   Male survivorship
  F   Female survivorship
  G   Hypothetical idealized
      survivorship

Reasons for changes
in the curves

A—B Improved housing, sanitation, antiseptics
B—C Public health, hygiene, immunization
C—D Antibiotics, improved medical practice,
      nutrition, health education
D—F Recent biomedical breakthroughs

Figure 3.3   The rectangularization of the human life span. This graph shows human survivorship trends from ancient times to the present. These idealized curves illustrate the rapid approach to the rectangular survivorship curve that has occurred during the last 180 years. Note that since 1950 life expectancy for females has improved more than for males.
Source: Strehler, 1975; Hayflick, 1980; and Cote, 1981.

improved medicine, nutrition, and sanitation on our longevity. In the future, most of us may make it to the mid-seventies or eighties, and some of us will make it to 100, but none of us will live to 150 years of age.

The increase in life expectancy, coupled with a fixed upper limit on the potential human life span, has led to what has been termed the **rectangularization of the life span** (Cote, 1981; Hayflick, 1980; Strehler, 1975). This concept is most readily understood by looking at figure 3.3. As you can see, the survivorship curves become increasingly more rectangular as we move from ancient times to the present. Due to advances in sanitation, agriculture, medicine, and so on, more people have tended to live longer, fuller, more disease-free lives. However, once individuals reach the upper limit of the life span there is sharp increase in mortality.

Predicting Life Expectancy

What factors are responsible for life expectancy? We noted several possibilities at the beginning of the chapter when we discussed the reasons centenarians gave for their longevity. But contrary to the belief of one centenarian, facing north while sleeping is not one of the valid ones.

Just as actuaries predict longevity for the purpose of insurance risk on the basis of age, sex, and race, several investigations have revealed that certain physical, mental, and social factors can be used to predict life expectancy (Palmore, 1980, 1982; Palmore and Jeffers, 1971; Rose and Bell, 1971). One of the most well-known studies designed to isolate the best predictors of life expectancy has been referred to as the *Duke Longitudinal Study of Aging.* In this study, 270 volunteers were examined for the first time between 1955 and 1959 by means of a series of physical, mental, social, and laboratory tests (Palmore, 1970). At that time the adults ranged in age from sixty to ninety-four, with a median age of seventy. All were noninstitutionalized, and although they were not a random sample, the group was a mixture of males and females, blacks and whites, and different socioeconomic groups. The investigators analyzed these individuals again in 1981, some twenty-five years after their initial testing. Only 26 were still alive, and estimates of their life expectancy were made.

In the early analysis of the data collected in this study, the strongest predictors of life expectancy (when age, sex, and race were controlled) were physical function, being a nonsmoker, work satisfaction, and happiness (see, for example, Palmore, 1969). The most recent analysis of the Duke data (Palmore, 1982) allowed for a more precise determination of life expectancy because (1) some of the individuals alive in 1981 later died, so that their exact life span is now known, and (2) in addition to the original factors tested, a number of new ones were added to allow for more complex evaluation.

Palmore (1982) developed a mathematical model that predicted the **longevity difference** for the participants in the Duke study. The longevity difference is the difference between the number of years individuals live after initial testing and the actuarially expected number of years remaining in their lives based on age, sex, and race. Palmore's model took into consideration both the direct and indirect effects of the variables that influence life expectancy. The variables within this model include *parents' longevity, intelligence, activities, sexual relations, tobacco and alcohol abuse, life satisfaction,* and *health.* Parents' longevity was believed to have a direct effect on longevity through genetic transmission and an indirect effect through environmental experience. Intelligence was thought to have a direct effect on survival through problem-solving skills and adaptational ability. Activities were thought to have direct effect on longevity through increased physical, mental, and social stimulation and an indirect effect by means of their contribution to life satisfaction and improved health. Sexual relations were thought to have a direct effect through psychosomatic processes as well as an indirect effect through their influence on life satisfaction and health. Tobacco and alcohol abuse were predicted to have a direct effect on longevity through their effects on lung cancer, cardiovascular diseases, and other health problems and indirect effects through a reduction of life satisfaction and general health. Life satisfaction was also predicted to have a direct effect through psychosomatic processes and an indirect effect through its influence on general health. And finally, health factors were believed to have a direct effect on longevity.

Of the various predictors of longevity, the following were the most powerful:

1. In terms of parents' longevity: only the father's age at death was significant.
2. Two intelligence predictors were significant. But scores on the performance component of the Wechsler Adult Intelligence Scale were better predictors than were scores on the verbal part of this test.
3. Three socioeconomic predictors were significant: education, finances, and occupation.
4. Several activity factors were significant in predicting longevity: locomotor activities, which involved the number of activities requiring physical mobility; secondary activity, which was based on the number of organizations the individual belonged to, the number of meetings attended, the time spent reading, and the number of leisure activities mentioned; and a nongroup activity rating such as time filled with daily activities and hobbies.
5. Three indicators of sexual relations were significant predictors of longevity: frequency of intercourse per week, past enjoyment of intercourse in younger years, and present enjoyment of intercourse.
6. Tobacco use, as measured by the daily use of cigarettes, cigars, or pipes, was a significant negative predictor.
7. Four satisfaction factors predicted longevity: work satisfaction, religious satisfaction, usefulness, and happiness.
8. Three health predictors were significantly linked with longevity. A physical-function rating was based on the individual's medical history, physical and neurological examinations, audiogram, electroencephalogram, electrocardiogram, and laboratory evaluation of blood and urine. A health self-rating was based on each individual's *own* ratings of his or her health. And a health satisfaction score was determined by an individual's agreement or disagreement with six statements, including, "I feel just miserable most of the time" and "I am perfectly satisfied with my health."

Table 3.1 presents a summary of these eight factors. All of the correlations included in the table are statistically significant. Nevertheless, the magnitude of these correlations is, on the whole, quite small. Furthermore, it is interesting to note the sex differences listed in the table. Not only are some of the predictors for longevity different for men and women, but the age structure of our population and longevity itself are characterized by sex differences.

Table 3.1

SIGNIFICANT PREDICTORS OF LONGEVITY DIFFERENCE*

Predictors	Women (N = 130) r	Men (N = 122) r
1. Father's age at death	—	.15
2. Intelligence		
Performance	.21	.29
Verbal	.19	.22
3. Socioeconomic status		
Education	—	.14
Finances	—	.29
Occupation	—	.15
4. Activities		
Locomotor	.22	—
Secondary	.20	—
Clubs	.14	—
Secondary rating	.20	.19
Nongroup	.17	.22
5. Sexual relations		
Frequency of intercourse	—	.15
Past enjoyment of intercourse	.22	—
Present enjoyment of intercourse	.14	—
6. Tobacco use	−.17	−.15
7. Satisfaction		
Work	—	.28
Religious	—	.24
Usefulness	—	.16
Happiness	.17	.18
8. Health		
Physical function rating	.30	.31
Health self-rating	.21	.33
Health satisfaction	.36	—

*All values shown were statistically significant at the .05 level except for present enjoyment of intercourse, which had a p value of .12.

From E. B. Palmore et al., "Predictors of Retirement." Reprinted with permission of the *Journal of Gerontology,* Vol. 37, #6: 733–742, 1982.

Sex Differences in Longevity

Beginning at age twenty-five, as reported in the 1980 census data, females begin to outnumber males, a gap that widens through the remainder of the adult years. By the time people reach the age of seventy-five, slightly more than 61 percent of the population is female. For those eighty-five and over, the figure is almost 70 percent female (Longino, 1988).

Why might this be so? It has been argued that the sex difference in longevity may be due to social or biological factors. In regard to social factors, health attitudes, habits, life-styles, and occupational styles are thought to be important. For example, the major causes of death in the United States, such as cancer of the respiratory system, motor vehicle accidents, suicide, cirrhosis of the liver, emphysema, and coronary heart disease are more likely to strike men than women

Sex differences in longevity account for the increasingly higher percentage of females in the older population.

(Waldron, 1976). Such causes of death are often associated with habits or life-styles. For example, the sex difference in deaths caused by lung cancer and emphysema is probably linked to the fact that men have been reported to be heavier smokers than women.

However, if life expectancy is influenced strongly by stress at work, we would expect the sex difference in longevity to begin narrowing since so many more women have entered the work force in the last forty years. In reality, just the opposite has been occurring (Myers and Manton, 1984). Apparently the self-esteem and satisfaction that women derive from work actually outweighs the stress of holding a job and juggling family, marital, and parental demands when longevity is at issue.

There is good reason to believe that the sex difference in longevity is influenced by biological factors. In practically all animal species, females have a longer life span than males, even under laboratory conditions. Women have more resistance to infectious and degenerative diseases. For instance, the female's estrogen production helps to protect her from atherosclerosis (hardening of the arteries) (Retherford, 1975). Further, the two X chromosomes women carry may be linked with the production of more antibodies to fight disease (Waldron, 1976).

Women live longer than men. However, women may find older adulthood to be a more difficult period of life than men. See table 3.2 for information about some of the special problems faced by older women.

Table 3.2

PROBLEMS OF OLDER WOMEN

▶6.5 million or 77 percent of all elderly living alone are women.

▶72 percent of all poor over 65 are women. Two out of every five midlife and older women are poor or near poor.

▶In 1986, Medicare paid for 48 percent of the total healthcare expenditures for an unmarried man over 65, but only 33 percent for an unmarried elderly woman.

▶One-third of older single women rely on Social Security for at least 90 percent of their income. The average Social Security benefit for women is $440; for men it's $521.

▶The number of elderly women compared to men is growing. There are 68 men for every 100 women over the age of 65 and 40 men for every 100 women over 85.

Source: Data from Gannett News Service, 1989.

The Impact of an Aging Population

The aging of the population will have a significant impact on the United States and other countries. For example, the age structure of a society determines, in part, the allocation of its resources. This means that over the next several decades, the younger members of our society may be spending more and more money to meet the needs of a progressively more aged population. One way to understand how the young members of a society support the old members of a society is to calculate the **old-age dependency ratio.** The old-age dependency ratio is defined as the number of retired people sixty-five years and older for every 100 people of working age—that is, between eighteen and sixty-four. The **young-age dependency ratio,** on the other hand, is the number of individuals seventeen years of age and younger for every 100 people of working age. Table 3.3 shows how these dependency ratios are likely to change between the years 1960 and 2060. In 1960, the old-age dependency ratio was 16.4 (there were 16.4 retired adults for every 100 workers). The young-age dependency ratio was 65.1 (there were 65.1 youths for every 100 workers). By the year 2040, however, the old-age dependency ratio will have more than doubled to 38.7; and the young-age dependency ratio will be approximately cut in half to 38.1. Thus, from 1960 to 2040 we will be spending more money to support the needs of old people and less money to support the needs of young people. Also, 2040 will be the first time in history that we will likely be spending the same amount of money on young and old alike. This could lead to a situation in which the workers of the twenty-first century are torn between supporting the needs of the young and the needs of the old (Chen, 1987).

Beyond any doubt, we need to begin planning today for the significant impact that the aging population will have on society. Just think about health care issues alone. Eleven percent of our Gross National Product is spent on health care. Individuals over age sixty-five make up 11 percent of our national population, but they account for one-third of the money spent on health care (Longino, 1988). These figures will most certainly increase in the future. Similarly, consider retirement practices. Over the last few decades, individuals have been retiring earlier but living longer. If this trend continues in the future, what will happen to the relationship

Table 3.3

CHANGING DEPENDENCY RATIOS IN THE UNITED STATES BETWEEN 1960 AND 2060.

Year	Young-age dependency ratio	Old-age dependency ratio
1960	65.1	16.4
1970	60.7	17.1
1980	45.9	18.1
1990	41.0	20.2
2000	38.6	20.9
2020	37.1	29.5
2040	38.1	38.7
2060	38.3	38.9

Adapted from Chen, 1987.

Source: Data from Y. P. Chen, " Making Assets Out of Tommorow's Elderly" in *The Gerontologist,* 27: 410–416, 1987.

between old-age and young-age dependency ratios? Should we encourage individuals to retire at older ages? It may be that the seventy-year-old of 2020 will be much more fit for work than the seventy-year-old of the 1990s.

However, we should not necessarily look at older adults as "liabilities" who do nothing but consume the resources provided by the young. Social planners need to develop policies and programs that capitalize on the positive attributes of our growing population of elderly (Chen, 1987).

In this section we have looked extensively at the topics of life expectancy and potential life span. Next we'll look at some of the biological theories proposed to explain the aging process.

BIOLOGICAL THEORIES OF AGING

James Birren and Jan Renner (1977) define aging as "the regular changes that occur in mature, genetically representative organisms living under representative environmental conditions as they advance in chronological age." As we have indicated, the aging process includes biological, psychological, and social aspects. In this section, we will explore some of the biological theories proposed to explain aging.

In a very real way, the human body "wears out" as it ages. The problem, of course, is to determine what causes the body to wear out. Early theorists viewed the body as a type of machine. They assumed that the body aged because of overuse and repeated environmental stress. Such wear-and-tear theories led to several hypotheses—for example, the hypothesis that humans would *not* age if they did not engage in strenuous work and/or exercise or experience any biological and/or psychological stress. However, contrary to wear-and-tear theory, it has been observed that physical work and vigorous exercise are predictive of a long life (Schaie and Willis, 1986). Note that "exercise" and "work" are different from "labor." Hard physical labor is detrimental to longevity in that it repeatedly stresses joints, muscles, and various organ systems. Above and beyond normal wear and tear, physical stressors (such as radiation, alcohol, excessive sunlight, and so forth) and psychological stressors negatively affect longevity. We agree with Cristofalo (1986), Schaie and Willis (1986), and Shock (1977), who have concluded that wear-and-tear theory, by itself, is not an adequate explanation of the aging process.

At present, it seems safe to suggest that all biological theories must assign genetic mechanisms an important (if not the ultimate) role in the aging process. There are many different genetically based theories of aging (Shock, 1977). For the purpose of clarity, however, it may be useful to divide the various theories of aging into three categories: cellular, physiological, and macrobiological.

Cellular Theories

Cellular theories propose that aging is caused by various processes or malfunctions that take place within the cells of the body. For example, Leonard Hayflick's groundbreaking research has demonstrated that cells from specific species can divide only a limited number of times (Hayflick, 1965). This has been called the *Hayflick limit.* Prior to Hayflick's research, it was believed that cells could divide an unlimited number of times. Hayflick found that connective tissue cells extracted from human embryonic tissue double only about fifty times rather than an endless number of times. Also, cells taken from an older individual are likely to double fewer times than those obtained from a younger individual. Nonetheless, the cells of even elderly individuals are still likely to divide. This suggests that we rarely live to the end of our potential life span. Based on the manner in which human cells divide, the upper limit of human life has been estimated to be 110 to 120 years of age (Hayflick, 1980; Cristofalo, 1986).

Many theories suggest that aging is caused by damage to the genetic information that regulates cellular functioning. Genetic information is represented in the structure of a complex molecule called deoxyribonucleic acid (DNA). DNA controls the formation of life-sustaining proteins. The information contained in DNA must be transmitted to other locations within a cell where the formation of proteins actually occurs. The molecule that does this work is a second complex molecule called ribonucleic acid (RNA). RNA is sometimes called messenger-RNA because of its transportation function. Some scientists argue that aging is caused by some type of breakdown, or error, that develops in the DNA-RNA communication system.

There are a number of ways in which such errors could occur (Williamson, Munley, and Evans, 1980). According to the **mutation theory,** aging is caused by changes, or mutations, in the DNA of the cells in vital organs of the body. In cells that continue to divide throughout the life cycle, these mutations are likely to be passed on to new cells. Eventually, the number of mutated cells in a vital organ would increase to the point that the cell's functioning is significantly reduced. Possible sources for these mutations may be intrinsic factors in cell division, such as chance errors in DNA replication (Burnet, 1974) or genes that specifically cause mutations in other genes. These mutations may be beneficial in evolutionary terms but might also hasten the aging process (Spiegel, 1977). Other possible sources of mutations are extrinsic factors such as toxins in the air, in water, and in food.

According to the **genetic switching theory,** certain genes switch off, and this causes aging. Information needed to produce DNA is no longer available, and so the cells age (Strehler, 1973). Eventually, genetic switching leads to cell death and the loss of organ functioning. According to this theory, the biological aging clock is genetically programmed into each of the body's cells.

According to the **error catastrophe theory,** aging is caused by damage to RNA, enzymes, and certain other proteins rather than by errors in DNA. For example, if an error occurs in the RNA responsible for the production of an enzyme essential to cell metabolism, the result will be a marked reduction in cell functioning and possibly cell death. The escalating impact of the original error in the RNA is the "error catastrophe" (Orgel, 1973).

The **free-radical theory** was initially proposed by Harman (1968). *Free radicals* are chemical components of cell metabolism that exist for only one second or less before they react with other substances such as fats. Free radicals can damage cells through their reactions with other substances, and they can cause chromosome damage. It has been speculated that vitamins C and E reduce the collisions of free radicals with other cell substances and, as a consequence, may increase an individual's life span. Empirical evidence to support the vitamin hypothesis has not yet been obtained, however.

Physiological Theories

Many biological theories of aging focus on the breakdown in functioning of a particular organ system, or on the impairment of a particular physiological control mechanism (Shock, 1977). Two of the most important physiological control systems are the immune and endocrine systems.

Each of us has an immune system that protects our body from foreign substances such as viruses, bacteria, and mutant cells (for example, cancer). The immune system may generate antibodies that react with the proteins of foreign organisms, and it may form cells that literally eat up the invading cells. The efficacy of the immune system seems to peak in adolescence and gradually decline as the individual ages. Also as an individual ages, **autoimmunity** increases (Adler, 1974; Blumental, 1983). Autoimmunity occurs when the immune system actually attacks and destroys normal, healthy body cells, possibly because immune mechanisms mistakenly identify normal cells as pathological (Walford, 1969). Support for the **autoimmune theory** comes from the findings that diseases of the immune system such as rheumatoid arthritis and maturity-onset diabetes are age-related (Shock, 1977). Furthermore, recent evidence has shown that the disease of AIDS progresses more quickly in adults over forty years of age.

We also may age because the efficiency of our endocrine system declines. The glands of the endocrine system secrete hormones that travel to different points in the body. Hormonal changes are controlled by the brain, particularly by the pituitary gland and the hypothalamus. Finch (1976, 1988) believes that aging pacemakers in these control centers of the brain stimulate a series of hormonal changes that cause us to age. This is the basis of the **hormonal theory** of aging.

Another proponent of hormonal theory (Denckla, 1974) describes the developmental sequence of aging involving the hypothalamus and pituitary. The hypothalamus periodically stimulates the pituitary gland to release antithyroid or "blocking" hormones that travel in blood cells throughout the body. These blocking hormones begin releasing shortly after puberty. They keep the body's cells from absorbing an adequate supply of thyroxine, a hormone produced in the thyroid gland that is required for normal cell metabolism. A number of metabolic imbalances result when thyroxine is not available in adequate quantities. According to this view, it is these imbalances that produce an excess of free radicals, mutations, toxins, and autoimmunity, which together cause aging (Rosenfeld, 1976).

Macrobiological Theories

The biological theories outlined so far attempt to explain aging by looking at some part of the organism, either within a cell or within a particular organ of the body. Any theory that looks within a cell to explain the aging process is a microbiological theory. *Micro* refers to the fact that a cell is a very small unit of analysis. By contrast, some scientists believe that we ought to look at a more general, or *macro,* level when we attempt to explain the aging process. One such macrobiological perspective on aging is the **homeostatic imbalance theory.**

At the level of the organism, life may be defined as internal balance or homeostasis. The body's internal environment is adjusted within strict limits by compensating mechanisms in many organs, including the heart, lungs, kidneys, and liver. Various neural and endocrine systems help monitor and maintain this balance inside the body. In young adult life, the functional capacity of human organs is four to ten times that required to sustain life. The existence of this *organ reserve* enables the stressed organism to restore homeostasis, or balance, when it is damaged by external threat. Measurement of organ reserve over time shows an almost linear decline beginning at about the age of thirty (Shock, 1960). As organ reserve decreases, so does the ability to restore homeostasis. Eventually even the smallest external stress prevents the body from restoring homeostasis. The inevitable result is natural death, even without disease. Although a disease process may seem to be the cause of death, the actual cause may be the body's inability to maintain homeostasis. After the age of thirty an individual's mortality rate doubles every eight years (Upton, 1977). Proponents of the homeostatic imbalance theory link the linear decline in organ function to this increase in mortality rate.

Scientists acknowledge that a biological clock controls aging. Some scientists believe the clock resides in the cells of our bodies, others argue that it lies in the brain, still others search for it in genetic material, and yet others believe the ability to maintain homeostatic balance is a key to the aging process.

People have always been interested in preventing aging and extending the human life span. Some have looked for the fountain of youth; others have tried to find or develop a secret potion. Box 3.1 describes a number of research studies which have examined the role played by diet in the aging process. These studies have led to some provocative results.

HEALTH, HEALTH CARE, AND AGING

So far, we have discussed the progressive aging of the general population, and we have presented different biological theories of aging. In this section we will describe how healthy individuals function during early, middle, and late adulthood.

Health in Early Adulthood

Most people reach their level of peak physical performance during early adulthood. This is also the time within the life span when individuals are at their healthiest. According to data accumulated by the U.S. Department of Health, Education, and Welfare, more than nine out of ten people between the ages of seventeen and forty-four view their own health as good or excellent (1976). Few young adults have chronic health problems, and young adults have fewer colds and respiratory problems than children do. The most frequent reasons young adults are hospitalized are for childbirth, accidents, and digestive and genitourinary system problems (U.S. Department of Health, Education, and Welfare, 1976).

Physical Competence and Bad Health Habits

Young adults rarely recognize how much bad eating habits, heavy drinking, and extensive smoking can affect their physical status when they reach middle adulthood. For example, despite the warnings that cigarettes are hazardous to health, evidence suggests that as adolescents grow into early adulthood, there is actually an increase in their cigarette usage. In a longitudinal study, Bachman, O'Malley, and Johnson (1978) found that individuals who smoked increased their cigarette use in the five years following high school. They also increased their weekly use of alcohol, any use of marijuana, and any use of amphetamines, barbiturates, and hallucinogens.

Experts on health care suggest that it is important to begin preventive health care during early adulthood (Carroll and Nash, 1976). Recommended practices include proper nutrition, sleep, rest, and exercise. During early adulthood few individuals take the time to think about how their *present* life-styles will affect their health in middle and late adulthood. As young adults, many of us develop a pattern of poor eating habits. Furthermore, we fail to exercise regularly and we tend to smoke and drink to excess. Such poor practices were linked with poor health in one investigation of 7,000 individuals ranging in age from twenty to seventy (Belloc and Breslow, 1972). In the California Longitudinal Study, in which individuals were evaluated systematically over a period of forty years, physical health at age thirty was a significant predictor of life satisfaction at age seventy, especially for men (Mussen, Honzik, and Eichorn, 1982).

There are some hidden dangers in the fact that physical performance and health are at their peak in early adulthood. Though young adults can draw on their physical resources for a great deal of pleasure, the fact that they can bounce back so easily from physical stress, exertion, and abuse may lead young adults to push their

BOX 3.1

AGING AND DIET

How many times have you heard a parent, teacher, or nutritionist on a TV talk show say something such as: "Eat your spinach, or you won't grow up to be big and strong," "The key to good health is to eat a well-balanced diet," "Eat more, you'll have more energy," or "You are what you eat"? It seems obvious that a person's health and physical development are closely related to the quality of his or her diet. For example, nutritional deficiencies during the prenatal period have been found to prolong labor, delay maternal recovery time, and increase the probability of miscarriage, stillbirth, and prematurity (Alexander, Roodin, and Gorman, 1980). It has been proposed that dietary factors influence several indicators of physical development during adolescence, such as height and age of menarche (Tanner, 1961; 1973). Furthermore, it has been determined that diets lacking adequate amounts of such nutrients as vitamin B_{12}, folic acid, and niacin may cause significant mental impairment in elderly adults (Zarit, Eiler, and Hassinger, 1985). And a number of researchers have found that well-balanced diets lead to reductions in heart disease, hypertension, stroke, cancer, and pseudodementia during adulthood (Weg, 1983).

Given all this evidence, it would seem obvious that diet should be related to longevity. Well-fed individuals, whether animal or human, should live longer than poorly fed individuals. But do they?

There are many instances in science where experimental results fly in the face of common sense. One such instance is the observed relationship between diet and longevity! In the 1930s it was first discovered that moderate to severe *dietary restriction* initiated after weaning and continued throughout the rest of life drastically increased the longevity of the common laboratory rat (McCay and Crowell, 1934). This finding has been replicated a vast number of times. It has also been shown that dietary restriction, even if it is not begun until middle adulthood, can extend the longevity of animal subjects (Masoro, 1984). In these studies, dietary restriction is typically defined as reducing caloric intake by 25 to 60 percent from free feeding levels while providing an adequate intake of essential nutrients and vitamins.

It has been argued (Masoro, 1984) that dietary restriction increases the potential life span because it actually slows down the aging process. This position is based on several experimental findings. For example, it has been shown that reduced dietary intake can delay (or even prevent) age-related pathologies in the cardiovascular, renal, and central nervous systems (Masoro, 1984; Yu, Masoro, Murata, Bertrand, and Lynd, 1982; Levine, Janda, Joseph, Ingram, and Roth, 1981). Most interestingly, however, researchers still do not know *why* dietary restriction has this life-extending effect.

At present, several researchers are attempting to discover if reduced diets have beneficial psychological outcomes as well as beneficial physical outcomes. (It would not be beneficial for an aged animal to have a fit body but a declining mind.) Donald Ingram and his associates (Ingram, Weindruch, Spangler, Freeman, and Walford, 1987) have investigated the learning ability and motor performance of rats maintained on either standard or restricted diets. They reported that the restricted-diet group performed significantly better than the standard-diet group on a complex maze-learning task and on a task of motor coordination (balancing on a rotating rod). In fact, Ingram and his colleagues argued that the restricted diet *prevented* age-related declines in maze learning and motor coordination. They also discovered that dietary restriction increased the rats' performance in a runwheel activity test.

In a similar study, Byron Campbell and James Gaddy (1987) assessed the sensory motor abilities of underfed and normally fed rats ranging from maturity to old age. Undernourished rats performed better on three tasks of motor performance: balancing on a narrow, elevated plank; hanging from a wire; and descending a pole in a coordinated fashion. The differences between the two groups were observed after a few months of dietary restriction. This led Campbell and Gaddy to conclude that the reduced body weights of the underfed group enhanced their performance. Once these initial weight-related changes in performance were established, however, both groups of rats showed the same *rate* of progressive loss of behavioral ability.

Taken as a whole, the results of experiments on dietary restriction and aging are both important and interesting. Dietary restriction seems to produce beneficial effects with regard to life expectancy, biological integrity, and behavioral ability.

Before you begin your crash diet, or open a spa that features reduced-calorie dinners, remember that: (1) restricted diets have been found to have beneficial effects in *animals,* and (2) no one really understands why dietary restriction slows down the biological aging process—although Edward Masoro (1988), a leader in this type of research, believes that food restriction affects aging through its actions on the endocrine and/or neural regulatory systems. Also, you might wish to consider how researchers could investigate the effects of restricted diet on human longevity. Would it be possible, ethical, and/or legal to conduct a randomized experiment with humans on this topic? What would be the alternative to experimental research? Could experimental research on humans be conducted once we discover, through more animal studies, exactly how underfeeding influences longevity?

Poor health practices in early adulthood usually take their toll in middle and later adulthood.

bodies too far. Even if this pushing does not seem to cause any harm in early adulthood, its negative effects are bound to appear in middle or late adulthood.

An increasing health problem in adulthood is being overweight. Next we will examine one of the factors that contributes to the increase in obesity during the adult years, along with the decline that also appears in some aspects of physical functioning in early adulthood.

Obesity and Basal Metabolism Rate

In our society, there are relatively more overweight and obese young adults than adolescents or children. The most common definition of **obesity** is weighing more than 20 percent over ideal body weight (Epstein and Wing, 1987). Standards developed by the Metropolitan Insurance Company (1983) are typically employed to determine an adult's ideal weight. These standards are based on the statistically determined critical weight that increased longevity for each sex at various height levels (Weigly, 1984). This means that the percentage of obese adults is not based on the distribution of relative weight in the population. By these criteria, therefore, more than 50 percent of the adult population could be diagnosed as obese at any given time (Epstein and Wing, 1987).

Obesity is influenced by a number of factors, including diet, hormones, and exercise. One factor that we often fail to recognize is the biologial mechanism known as the **basal metabolism rate.** The basal metabolism rate (BMR) is defined as the minimum amount of energy a person uses in a state of rest. To a considerable extent,

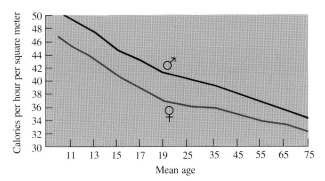

BMR varies with age and sex. Rates are usually higher for males and decline proportionally with age for both sexes.

Figure 3.4   **The decline of basal metabolism rate through the life cycle**.

BMR is genetically determined (although it can be regulated, within limits, through exercise or drugs, including nicotine). Young adults with high basal metabolism rates can eat almost anything and not get fat, whereas those with low BMRs must constantly monitor their food intake to keep from gaining weight.

As indicated in figure 3.4, an individual's BMR continuously drops from adolescence onward. Males usually have a slightly higher BMR than females. If young adults do not reduce their food intake or exercise more as they age, they are likely to gain weight because of the slowdown in BMR. In the middle to late twenties, the body also increases in fatty tissue. Early adulthood can be a particularly problematic time for individuals who exercised vigorously during adolescence and/or the first part of early adulthood and then took sedentary jobs that require them to sit for hours at a time. Individuals who were in athletic programs in high school or college are particularly prone to weight problems caused by the slowdown in BMR and in physical activity.

Around the age of thirty, muscle tone and strength often begin to show signs of decline—chins sag and abdomens may protrude. Thus, in the latter part of early adulthood, signs of decline in some aspects of health and physical development often begin to appear.

Health in Middle Adulthood

Health becomes a major concern in middle adulthood. Middle adulthood is characterized by a general decline in physical fitness, and some deterioration in health is to be expected. The three health concerns that have received the greatest attention in middle adulthood are heart disease, cancer, and obesity. Cardiovascular disease is the number one killer in the United States, followed by cancer (U.S. Department of Health, Education, and Welfare, 1979). Smoking-related cancer often surfaces for the first time in middle adulthood. A much more recent threat to the health of middle-aged individuals is AIDS. Box 3.2 contains some of the most current information available about AIDS and aging.

BOX 3.2

AIDS AND AGING

Health-care professionals are becoming increasingly concerned with the growing number of older individuals (fifty years of age and older) who suffer from AIDS. There is neither a vaccine nor a cure for AIDS. Therefore, preventing the transmission of the virus that causes AIDS, the Human Immunodeficiency Virus (HIV), is the primary goal of public health programs.

Joseph Catania and his associates (Catania et al., 1989) have noted three reasons why older adults may be more likely than younger adults to become infected with HIV and develop the symptoms of AIDS. First, the efficacy of the immune system declines with age. This would account for the finding that older adults have a shorter HIV incubation period than younger adults (5.8 years versus 7.3 years, respectively). Second, older adults—more so than younger adults—are likely to be the recipients of blood transfusions. This is important because HIV can be easily transmitted through contaminated blood. Third, postmenopausal women are likely to experience the thinning of the cells of the vaginal wall. Since AIDS is transmitted by sexual contact, the deteriorating vaginal wall of the older woman provides more potential sites for HIV infection.

Box table 3.1 summarizes our current knowledge of the relationship between AIDS and aging. It shows that between 1982 and 1987 the total number of AIDS cases among older adults rose from 76 to 1,450. It has been estimated, however, that as many as 125,000 older Americans may be infected with HIV (Stall et al., 1988)! Box table 3.1 also provides information about the different populations of older individuals who are at risk for AIDS. The highest-risk group consists of homosexual and/or bisexual men. The percentage of AIDs cases in this risk group, however, declined from 1982 to 1987. Catania et al. (1989) attach a great deal of significance to the finding that more older adults are becoming infected with HIV through blood transfusions as well as through heterosexual contact. Both Catania et al. (1989) and Peterman et al. (1988) suggested that older adults frequently come in contact with HIV through blood transfusions and then unwittingly infect their sex partners with this virus. It has been reported that older adults are more likely to receive blood transfusions than young adults and thus are more likely to become infected with HIV through such procedures.

The period from 1978 to 1985 is considered to be the time during which the blood supply of the United States was most highly contaminated with HIV. Since 1985, tremendous efforts have been made to make the blood supply safer for transfusion recipients. However, the risk of HIV infection through contaminated blood still remains. It has been estimated that 460 recipients of screened blood will become infected with HIV per year (Ward et al., 1988). Remember that there is a long time-lag (5.8 years) between initial HIV infection and the observable symptoms of AIDS in older adults. This suggests

Box Table 3.1

ANNUAL INCIDENT AIDS CASES AMONG ADULTS AGED FIFTY OR GREATER, BY RISK GROUP, 1982–1987, IN COLUMN PERCENTAGES

Risk Group	*Year of AIDS Diagnosis*						
	Pre-1982	1982	1983	1984	1985	1986	1987
Homosexual bisexual male	89.7	81.6	73.4	73.0	70.6	66.8	65.8
Transfusion	0.0	5.3	9.8	12.3	15.4	17.0	17.3
Intravenous Drug User (IVDU)	0.0	5.3	9.0	7.3	7.8	8.0	8.3
Heterosexual	0.0	1.3	2.7	2.6	1.9	3.6	4.6
Homosexual bisexual IVDU	6.9	1.3	3.9	2.8	1.9	2.6	1.9
Hemophiliac	3.4	5.3	1.2	2.0	2.4	2.1	2.0
N = (4752)	29	76	256	504	975	1462	1450

From J. A. Catania, et al., "Older Americans and AIDS Transmission Risks and Primary Research Needs" in *The Gerontologist*, 29: 373–381, 1989.

Note: 339 cases (6.7 percent) attributed to other categories of transmission have been omitted from this table.

that only about 50 percent of the older individuals infected with HIV in 1984 would be expected to display AIDS symptoms in 1990 (Kalbfliesch and Lawless, 1988), Thus, HIV-infected adults may unintentionally pass HIV onto their sex partners.

Traditionally, young homosexuals and bisexuals and intravenous drug users are the two AIDS risk groups that have been the focus of most media coverage. Catania et al. (1989) suggest that older adult transfusees should become the target of more media and public health efforts. For example, too many older transfusees (about 12 percent) do not even know they have received a blood transfusion. Also, older transfusees are often not aware of how their sexual behavior can transmit HIV. In one survey (Peterman et al., 1988), *none* of the older transfusees who sought testing for HIV infection used condoms during intercourse!

The Harvard Medical School Health Letter indicates that about 20 million Americans are on serious diets at any particular moment. Being overweight is a critical health problem in middle adulthood. For people who are 30 percent or more overweight, the probability of dying in middle adulthood increases by 40 percent. Furthermore, obesity increases the likelihood that an individual will suffer a number of other ailments, including hypertension and digestive disorders.

Women seem to show a much greater concern about weight than men do. Since our culture stresses a youthful appearance, many individuals with graying hair, wrinkled skin, and sagging bodies strive to make themselves look younger. Undergoing cosmetic surgery, dying the hair, enrolling in a weight-reduction program, participating in an exercise regimen, and taking heavy doses of vitamins are frequent practices of those in middle age. One investigation found that middle-aged women focus more attention on facial attractiveness than older or younger women do, and middle-aged women are more likely to perceive that the signs of aging have a negative effect on their physical appearances (Nowak, 1977).

In our culture, some aspects of aging in middle adulthood are viewed as attractive in men, whereas similar signs are viewed as disasters in women. Facial wrinkles and gray hair may symbolize strength, maturity, and character in men but be considered unattractive in women. This double standard of aging is particularly evident in our youth-oriented and sexist society.

Life-Style and Heart Disease

In the California Longitudinal Study (Livson and Peskin, 1981; Peskin and Livson, 1981), good health ratings at ages thirty-four to fifty were significantly and positively associated with several personality measures that reflect emotional stability and a controlled response to stress. Most strongly associated with health at middle age was a calm, self-controlled, and responsible personality; a pattern that appeared at least by early adolescence. Not only was health at mid-life linked with this personality pattern, but it also was associated with a number of similar personality characteristics during mid-life. Life-style has been specifically linked to cardiovascular problems as well.

The heart and coronary arteries undergo change in middle adulthood. Under comparable conditions of stress, the heart of a forty-year-old can pump a much smaller number of liters of blood per minute (twenty-three) than the heart of a twenty-year-old (forty). The coronary arteries that supply blood to the heart narrow during middle adulthood, and the level of cholesterol in the blood increases with age (average at age twenty: 180 milligrams; at age forty: 220 mg; at age sixty: 230 mg). The cholesterol begins to accumulate on the artery walls, which are themselves thickening. The net result is that arteries are more likely to clog, increasing the pressure on the arterial walls, which in turn pushes the heart to work harder to pump blood and makes a stroke or heart attack more likely. In fact, heart attacks are more common in middle adulthood than in old age (Schaie and Willis, 1986).

One intriguing theory relates individual behavior styles to either a high risk (Type A) or a low risk (Type B) of heart disease (Friedman and Rosenman, 1974). The **Type A behavior style** is excessively competitive, accelerates the pace of ordinary activities, is impatient with the rate at which most events occur, often thinks about doing several things at the same time, shows hostility, and cannot hide the fact that time is a struggle in his or her life. By contrast, the **Type B behavior style** is typified by the absence of these behavioral tendencies. About 10 percent of the subjects studied were clearly Type A or Type B styles, although most people were various mixtures of the two. It is interesting to note that high achievement and Type A behavior style seem also to be related (Friedman and Rosenman, 1974).

Stephanie Booth-Kewley and Howard Friedman (1987) reviewed 83 different studies conducted between 1945 and 1984 investigating the relationship between behavioral life-style (Type A versus Type B) and coronary heart disease. Their analysis revealed that Type A behavior is reliably related to the incidence of heart disease. Most interestingly, however, they discovered a somewhat different profile of the Type A behavioral style than the one originally outlined by Friedman and Rosenman (1974). Specifically, they concluded that

> "the picture of the coronary-prone personality emerging from this review does not appear to be that of the workaholic, hurried, impatient individual, which is probably the image most frequently associated with coronary proneness. Rather, the true picture seems to be one of a person with one or more negative emotions: perhaps someone who is depressed, aggressively competitive, easily frustrated, anxious, (or) angry . . ." (Booth-Kewley and Friedman, 1987, p. 358)

Similar findings have been reported by Wright (1988). Clearly, heart disease is influenced by many other factors such as diet, smoking, obesity, and family history. However, it also seems that behavioral life-style is significantly related to the incidence of coronary heart disease.

Health in Late Adulthood

As we age, the probability that we will contract some disease or illness increases. A majority of individuals who reach the age of eighty will likely have some type of health impairment; indeed, it is very rare to find anyone over the age of eighty who is free from disease or illness.

Perhaps the most significant change in late adulthood is that the entire cardiovascular system becomes less efficient. *Elastin,* made of molecules that determine the elasticity of heart and blood vessels, decreases, and *collagen,* the stiff protein that comprises about one-third of the body's protein, increases. An individual's heart rate does not rise as predictably in response to stress as it did during middle adulthood. Further, the heart muscle cannot contract and relax as fast, and the arteries are more resistant to the flow of blood (Weisfeldt, 1981). Heart output—about five quarts a minute at age fifty—subsequently drops about 1 percent a year. When the heart muscle is less efficient and the vessels are more resistant, heart rate and blood pressure both rise. Even for a healthy older person, blood pressure that was 100/ 75 at age twenty-five is likely to be about 160/90 in late adulthood. The blood also carries less oxygen to the brain and lungs. If elderly people rise too quickly, they may become dizzy; if they climb a set of stairs too rapidly, they may lost their breath.

Illness and Impairment

The two most common causes of death in elderly populations are heart disease and cancer. These diseases are chronic as well as deadly. They lead to long-term illness, both psychological and physical discomfort, and impairment. We usually equate these diseases with old age. However, it is possible that cancer and cardiovascular diseases may strike adults at any age. See box 3.3 for a discussion of how environmental and genetic factors may increase the risk of death from these diseases for young and middle-aged adults.

Other chronic conditions common to elderly populations, such as arthritis and hypertension, do not directly cause death but usually leave the afflicted person with some kind of physical impairment such as limited mobility. Almost two of every five people between the ages of sixty-five and seventy-five have some impairment of physical functioning. After age seventy-five, the rate rises to three of five (Riley and Foner, 1968). Some of the most prevalent chronic conditions that impair the health of the elderly are arthritis (38 percent), hearing impairment (29 percent), vision impairment (20 percent), and heart condition (20 percent) (Harris, 1978). Studies of sex differences in health indicate that elderly women are more likely to have a higher incidence of arthritis, hypertension, and visual problems but are less likely to have difficulty with hearing than men (Harris, 1978).

Although adults over the age of sixty-five often have a physical impairment, many can still carry on their everyday activities or work. Some of the chronic conditions linked with the greatest limitation of activity or work are heart disease, diabetes, asthma, and arthritis (Harris, 1978).

Low income is also strongly related to health problems, especially in late adulthood. Approximately three times as many poor as nonpoor people report that their activities are limited by chronic disease. In the elderly population, the health gap between low and middle income seems to continue (Wilson and White, 1977). This is especially true for the older members of various racial and minority groups. Ferraro (1987), for example, found that low-income elderly blacks are in poorer physical health, as measured by both objective and subjective criteria, than low-income elderly whites. However, among centenarians, blacks are more likely than whites to live to ages beyond 105. Moreover, black centenarians are typically poor, and are less likely to be living in institutions (Spencer et al., 1987).

Health Treatment

One important aspect of health is the interaction between people who seek health care and those who provide it. Unfortunately, research has revealed that physicians and other health-care personnel often share society's general stereotypes and negative attitudes toward the elderly. In a medical or health-care setting, such attitudes can result in avoidance, dislike, or pained tolerance rather than positive, hopeful care and treatment (Butler, 1975).

Several research studies have examined the relationship between elderly patients and their health-care providers. Greene, Hoffman, Charon, and Adelman (1987), for example, investigated how a group of middle-aged physicians responded to the psychosocial issues raised in treating young patients versus elderly patients. Psychosocial issues relate to the patients' general anxieties and worries, feelings of depression or bereavement, economic hardships, typical leisure activities, family relationships, and so on. Results indicated that physicians raised fewer psychosocial issues with older patients than younger patients and were less responsive to the psychosocial concerns raised by older patients. As an interesting corollary, patients are more satisfied with visits to their doctors and show more improvement in health status when physicians concern themselves with the patients' psychological problems (Ben-Sira, 1985).

Not only are physicians less responsive to older patients, older patients seem to take a less active role in medical encounters with health-care professionals. Woodward and Wallston (1987) have shown that individuals over sixty years of age are more likely, in comparison to young adults, to wish that health-care professionals would make decisions for them. Woodward and Wallston (1987) concluded that those individuals who are at the greatest risk for chronic disease and hospitalization (the elderly) are the most likely to take a passive role in their health care. Since this was a cross-sectional study, it is difficult to determine whether age or cohort factors were responsible for the observed results.

Another study (Pearlman and Uhlman, 1988) has shown that elderly individuals differ from physicians in their understanding of the relationship between health and quality of life. In this study, a number of elderly outpatients who suffered from several chronic diseases (for example, arthritis, heart disease, cancer, diabetes, and so on) and their physicians were interviewed about the quality of the patients' lives. Surprisingly, the patients rated the quality of their lives as just slightly worse than "good, no major complaints," while the physicians rated the elderly patients' quality of life in a much more negative manner. This discrepancy may have been due to the fact that the older patients were more likely to place a great deal of emphasis on factors such as financial status and interpersonal relationships in determining their quality-of-life ratings. The physicians seemed to have a much more narrow conceptualization of quality of life: they were more likely to equate it with health alone. These results suggest that quality of life for elderly patients is a multidimensional construct that may easily be misunderstood by physicians.

Finally, it has been documented that psychologists, like other health-care professionals, may also harbor negative attitudes towards older adults. Ray, McKinney, and Ford (1987) performed an experiment in which clinical psychologists were presented with several vignettes which described different types of mental disorders. In one version, all of the clients depicted in the vignettes were forty-five

BOX 3.3

GENETIC AND ENVIRONMENTAL INFLUENCES ON ADULT MORTALITY

As we have mentioned, a great many adults suffer from various forms of cancer and cardiovascular disease. One question it is obviously important to ask is, "What are the primary causes of these diseases?" We might further ask if these diseases are more likely to be caused by either genetic or environmental factors. Let's look at the results of a study that addressed this important topic.

The study was conducted by Thorkild Sorensen and his associates (Sorensen et al., 1988). The scientists employed a unique strategy to assess the role played by genetic and environmental factors on adult mortality. They obtained the medical records of 960 Danish adoptees who were born between 1924 and 1926. The vast majority of these individuals (93 percent) were adopted prior to the age of three years. Also, medical data was obtained for the biological and adoptive parents of these children. Until 1982, the investigators collected data from the medical records regarding time of death and cause of death of the adoptees, their biological parents, and their adoptive parents. The researchers sought to determine the adoptees' risk of dying from specific types of causes sometime between sixteen and fifty-eight years of age if their biological or adoptive parent died of the same cause before the age of either fifty or seventy.

When deaths from all natural causes (that is, deaths that resulted from biological illness rather than accidents, suicides, and so on) were examined, it was found that adoptees who had at least one biological parent who died before age fifty had a mortality rate 1.8 times greater than that of adoptees whose biological parents were both alive at this age. The time of death of adoptive parents had no significant effect on the adoptees' mortality.

Next, the researchers discovered that if a biological parent died of an infection before the age of fifty or seventy, the mortality rates for the adoptee increased by statistically significant factors of 5.8 and 5.1, respectively. The timing of the deaths of the adoptive parents from infections had no significant effect, however, on the adoptees' mortality rates.

Then, vascular diseases were considered. If a biological parent died before the age of fifty from a vascular disease, the adoptee's mortality rate increased by a statistically significant factor of 4.5. Deaths of the adoptive parents from vascular causes had no statistically significant effects on the adoptee's mortality.

Finally, when the researchers turned their attention to cancer, a very different picture came into focus. Deaths of adoptive parents from cancer prior to age fifty increased the mortality rate from cancer among the adoptees by a statistically significant factor of 5.2. Deaths of biological parents from cancer had no significant effect on the rate of mortality from cancer among the adoptees. Box table 3.2 summarizes Sorensen's results.

Box Table 3.2

THE EFFECT OF THE DEATH OF A BIOLOGICAL OR ADOPTIVE PARENT ON ADOPTEES' MORTALITY RATES

Cause of Death	Parent Dead Before the Age of 50		Parent Dead Before the Age of 70	
	Number#	Relative Risk##	Number	Relative Risk
Natural Causes				
Biological	739	1.9*	771	1.5
Adoptive	889	1.0	878	1.0
Infection				
Biological	641	5.8*	436	5.0*
Adoptive	840	0.7	537	1.0
Vascular Causes				
Biological	585	4.5*	464	1.9
Adoptive	822	3.0	627	1.5
Cancer				
Biological	593	1.2	463	0.9
Adoptive	818	5.2*	578	1.5

#This number refers to the *number* of parent-adoptee pairs in the analysis. A pair is included in the analysis only if a parent died of causes indicated in the table or if both parents were alive at the set age.
##*Relative Risk* of the adoptees' mortality represents the ratio of the mortality rate among adoptees with at least one parent who died of a specific cause before a particular age (fifty or seventy) to the mortality rate among adoptees whose parents were both alive at a particular age (fifty or seventy).
*indicates a statistically significant finding.

Source: Data from T. Sorensen, et al., "Genetic and Environmental Influences on Premature Death in Adult Adopties" in *New England Journal of Medicine*, 318: 727–732, 1988.

The researchers concluded that premature death in the adoptees (death between sixteen and fifty-eight years of age) has a strong genetic basis, especially for death due to infection or vascular causes. Alternatively, death from cancer appears to be influenced by one's family environment. Why do you think environmental factors are so heavily implicated in cancer-related deaths?

years of age or younger. In another version, the clients were portrayed as sixty-five years of age or older. Ray et al. found that the psychologists rated older clients in a more negative manner than a younger clients with identical symptoms and histories. Older clients were also given significantly poorer prognoses than younger clients.

We need to encourage older adults to take a more active role in their own health care. Furthermore, health-care professionals should recognize (and change) their negative stereotypes about the elderly. The data obtained in one recent study (Revenson, 1989) suggests that physicians who have a great deal of contact with the elderly may be beginning to adopt more compassionate stereotypes of this population. Specifically, it was found that elderly patients were judged as *less* adjusted and autonomous, but in *greater* need of support and encouragement than middle-aged patients.

The Benefits of Exercise

Thus far we may have presented a somewhat downbeat picture of the older adult. However, the majority of older adults are capable of functioning in everyday contexts and enjoying leisure time activities. In fact, many older adults are still capable of reaping the physical and psychological benefits of exercise. The body's capacity for exercise in late adulthood is influenced by the extent to which the individual has kept his or her body physically fit at earlier points in the life cycle. It is not uncommon to find that individuals who participate in the Senior Olympics have a greater capacity for exercise than some individuals much younger than themselves. See box 3.4 for more information on the relationship between age and peak athletic performance.

Early investigations demonstrated the physical benefits of exercise on men (deVries, 1970) and on women (Adams and deVries, 1973). When adults aged fifty to eighty-seven did calisthenics, ran, walked, and engaged in stretching exercises or swimming for forty-two weeks, researchers observed dramatic changes in the oxygen-transport capabilities of the adults' bodies. The improvements occurred regardless of the age of the individuals or their prior exercise history. More recent studies (Seals, Hagberg, Hurley, Ehsani, and Holloszy, 1984; Cunningham, Rechnitzer, Howard, and Donner, 1987) have shown that exercise training in the elderly may result in positive changes in both cardiovascular and respiratory functioning. It seems as if exercise and physical activity in late adulthood are capable of slowing down the rate of physical deterioration in an aging body.

Also, exercise seems to a have psychological benefits. In one study, Howard, Rechnitzer, Cunningham, and Donner (1986) discovered that a program of regular, vigorous exercise improved the cardiovascular fitness of a group of retired men. Significantly, the exercise program also produced a reduction in Type A behavior patterns in this sample.

Clarkson-Smith and Hartley (1989) investigated the relationship between vigorous physical exercise and cognitive ability in a large group of men and women

Many older adults still enjoy and benefit from exercise, especially if they were physically active earlier in life. Dr. Patricia Peterson, shown here, holds a number of world running records in her age group.

between fifty-five and ninety-one years of age. Vigorous exercisers were defined as those who (1) expended at least 3,100 kilocalories per week in exercise activities, and (2) engaged in at least one-and-a-quarter hours of strenuous exercise per week. Low exercisers were those who (1) expended less that 1,900 kilocalories per week in exercise, and (2) spent less than ten minutes per week exercising. Note that non-athletic pursuits such as gardening, climbing stairs, doing heavy housework, and so forth were included as exercise activities. Results showed that the men and women who exercised a great deal performed exceptionally well on tests of reasoning, working memory, and reaction time. These results held even when differences between the exercisers and nonexercisers in terms of age, educational levels, and health status were statistically controlled. Other researchers have also shown that exercise has beneficial effects on cognitive ability among the aged (Stones and Komza, 1989).

We end this chapter with table 3.4. It provides a summary of the major physiological changes that occur as a result of the aging process, along with the most likely effects these changes have on an individual's ability to perform physical exercise. Also, the table contains information about the possible beneficial effects of regular physical exercise.

BOX 3.4

AGING AND PEAK ATHLETIC PERFORMANCE

It seems obvious that individuals achieve their peak levels of athletic performance in young adulthood and that they display a significant, progressively steeper decrement in performance thereafter. The work of a number of scientists in a variety of disciplines (including sports psychology, gerontology, exercise physiology, and others) has made us rethink the validity of this claim. Age-related changes in athletic performance may be much smaller than most individuals imagine. Furthermore, continued training by older athletes may help them display high levels of athletic competence in the face of age-related declines in physiological functioning.

In a recent paper, K. Anders Ericsson (Ericsson, in press) reviewed a great deal of the research regarding age changes in swimming and running performance. These sports were chosen for analysis because (1) the distances of specific races within these sports have been fixed for approximately the last century, and (2) performance within these sports is measured objectively by specific units of time (minutes, seconds, and so on)—there is no subjective element in measuring performance in these sports, as there is in boxing or gymnastics. These attributes allowed researchers to make valid comparisons of changes in swimming and running performance from one historical era (the 1920s) to another (the 1980s).

Upon examining the world records and Olympic gold medal performances in these sports from 1896 (the year of the first modern-day Olympic games) to the present, Ericsson noted four major findings. First, over this time span, gold medalists and world record holders have generally achieved their feats during young adulthood, usually between 20 and 30 years of age. Second, world record and gold medal times have steadily and significantly decreased. Third, the shorter the distance of the race, the younger the age of the gold medalists and/or world record holders. Fourth, winners of shorter swimming events are becoming younger (in their early twenties); while the winners of longer running events such as the marathon are becoming older (in their late twenties to mid-thirties). For example, Carlos Lopes won the 1984 Olympic marathon at the age of thirty-seven.

The next task addressed by Ericsson was to determine how the maximum performance of well-trained athletes changes from early adulthood to old age. To accomplish this goal, he reviewed the results of a number of cross-sectional and longitudinal studies. Letzelter, Jungermann, and Freitag (1986), in a cross-sectional study, examined the mean race times in the German national masters swimming championships over a period of several years. Participants in these championships ranged from twenty-five to seventy years of age. Box figures 3.1 and 3.2 show the *best* times as well as the *average* times achieved by these swimmers. Both of these figures show a decrease in performance with age. This decrease becomes more rapid, however, when the average performance of swimmers over sixty years of age is examined. Also of interest was the finding that the best performance of the over-sixty-five-year-old group equalled the average performance of swimmers about forty years of age.

Letzelter, et al. (1986) also performed a longitudinal analysis on the same data. They selected swimmers in three age groups (thirty to thirty-four, thirty-five to thirty-nine, and forty to forty-four) in 1971 and recorded their performance at yearly intervals until 1983.

BOX 3.4 *Continued*

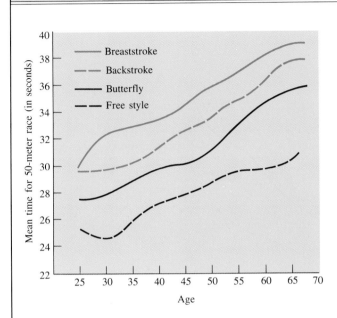

Box figure 3.1 Changes in the *best* race times for expert swimmers 25 to 70 years of age.

Source: Data from M. Letzelter, et al., '' Swimming Performance in Old Age'' in *Zeitschrift für Gerontologie*, 19: 389–395, 1986.

Analyses revealed that performances over this thirteen-year period did not show any significant decrements as a function of age! In a somewhat similar study, Hartley and Hartley (1984) showed that considerable declines in swimming performance occurred only after seventy years of age. When track performance was observed, a similar picture emerged. Stones and Kozma (1982) indicated, for example, that cross-sectional studies yield twice as steep a decline in performance as do longitudinal studies.

Overall, longitudinal studies suggest that athletes can maintain (and sometimes improve) their performance as they progress through middle adulthood and enter late adulthood. This occurs only if adults maintain (or increase) their levels of practice and training. Hagberg (1987) has argued that continued exercise is an important factor in miminizing the losses in *aerobic power* that are usually observed during adulthood. Aerobic power, which refers to the body's maximal ability to take in oxygen, is arguably the best predictor of performance in endurance events (long-distance running, for example). It has not been determined, however, if training can improve the aerobic power of individuals over seventy. And it is unclear if the age decline in aerobic power observed in the typical adult (one who is not involved in intense physical activity) is due to changes in age per se or to the progressively more sedentary life-style adopted by aging individuals. Finally, it seems as if the performance decrements reported in cross-sectional studies may be related to differences in training between members of different cohorts rather than to irreversible biological decline.

BOX **3.4** *Continued*

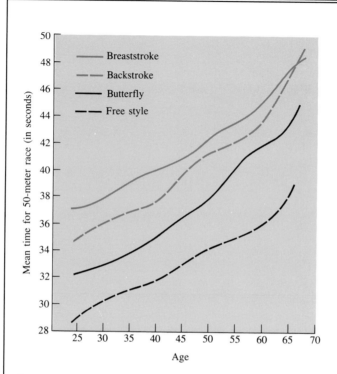

Box figure 3.2 Changes in the *average* race times for expert swimmers 25 to 70 years of age.

Source: Data from M. Letzelter, et al., "Swimming Performance in Old Age" in *Zeitschrift für Gerontologie*, 19: 389–395, 1986.

Changes in training also seem responsible for the steady decrease in world record times in running and swimming events over the last hundred years. In fact, the improvement in athletic performance over time may be used as a yardstick to judge the effects of aging. Box table 3.3 compares the winning times for several running events in the 1896 Olympics and the best performances of "master" athletes in 1979. As can be seen

---

BOX 3.4 *Continued*

Box Table 3.3

WINNING TIMES FOR OLYMPIC GOLD MEDALISTS IN 1896 AND
BEST TIMES FOR MASTER ATHLETES IN 1979

Event	Olympic Gold Medalists in 1896	Master Athletes in Different Age Groups in 1979			
		50–54	55–59	60–64	65–69
100 m *	12.0	11.4	11.6	12.0	13.2
200 m *	22.2	23.6	23.6	24.9	27.9
400 m *	54.2	52.9	54.6	59.1	65.1
800 m **	2:11	2:01	2:11	2:20	2:27
1,500 m **	4:33	4:14	4:20	4:53	4:59
Marathon ***	2:59	2:25	2:26	2:47	2:53

* event timed in seconds
** events timed in minutes and seconds
*** event timed in hours and minutes

Source: Data from K. A. Ericsson, "Peak Performance and Age: An Examination of Peak Performance in Sports" in *Successful Aging: Perspectives from the Behavioral Sciences* (P. B. Baltes and M. M. Baltes, eds.). New York: Cambridge University Press.

in box table 3.3 there are a number of performances by master athletes that surpass the performance of these earlier (and younger) gold medalists—even in the marathon, which covers a distance of twenty-six miles and 385 yards!!

Intensive training is necessary for peak performance. But, how long can this sort of training be maintained? As athletes become older there are many demands, pressures, and changes—psychological, social, and physical—that influence the quality and quantity of their training. It would seem impossible, therefore, to maintain an optimal level of training across the entire adult life span. This means, as Ericsson reminds us, that it is unlikely that adults ever reach the true limits of their performance.

Table 3.4

PHYSIOLOGICAL DECLINE ASSOCIATED WITH AGING AND THE POSSIBLE BENEFIT OF REGULAR STRENGTH AND ENDURANCE EXERCISE

Structural Changes	*Functional Effects*	*Effects of Exercise*
	Musculoskeletal System	

1. Muscular atrophy with decrease in both number and size of muscle fibers
2. Neuromuscular weakness
3. Demineralization of bones
4. Decline in joint function—loss of elasticity in ligaments and cartilage
5. Degeneration and calcification on articulating surface of joint
	1. Loss of muscle size
	2. Decline of strength
	3. Reduced range of motion
	4. Reduced speed of movement
	5. Joint stiffness
	6. Declining neuromotor performance
	7. Changes in posture
	8. Frequent cramping
	9. Gait characteristics affected:
	  a. Center of gravity
	  b. Span (height/arm length)
	  c. Stride length, speed
	  d. Width of stance
	10. Shrinkage in height
	11. Increased flexion at joints due to connective tissue change
		1. Increased strength of bone
		2. Increased thickness of articular cartilage
		3. Muscle hypertrophy
		4. Increased muscle strength
		5. Increased muscle capillary density
		6. Increased strength of ligaments and tendons

	Respiratory System	
1. Hardening of airways and support tissue 2. Degeneration of bronchi 3. Reduced elasticity and mobility of the intercostal cartilage	1. Reduced vital capacity with increased residual volume 2. Reduced O_2 diffusing capacity 3. Spinal changes lead to increased rigidity of the chest wall 4. Declining functional reserve capacity	1. Exercise has no chronic effect on lung volumes but may improve maximal ventilation during exercise and breathing mechanics
	Cardiovascular System	

1. Elastic changes in aorta and heart
2. Valvular degeneration and calcification
3. Changes in myocardium
  a. Delayed contractility and irritability
  b. Decline in oxygen consumption
  c. Increased fibrosis
  d. Appearance of lipofuscin
4. Increase in vagal control
	1. A diminished cardiac reserve
	2. Increased peripheral resistance
	3. Reduced exercise capacity
	4. Decrease in maximum coronary blood flow
	5. Elevated blood pressure
	6. Decreased maximal heart rate
		1. Increased heart volume and heart weight
		2. Increased blood volume
		3. Increase in maximal stroke volume and cardiac output
		4. Decreased arterial blood pressure
		5. Increase in maximal oxygen consumption
		6. Myocardial effects increased:
		  a. Mitochondrial size
		  b. Nuclei
		  c. Protein synthesis
		  d. Myosin synthesis
		  e. Capillary density
		7. Decreased resting heart rate

Robert A. Wiswell, ''Relaxation, Exercise, and Aging'' in *Handbook of Mental Health and Aging,* edited by Birren/Sloane, © 1980, p. 945. Reprinted by permission of Prentice-Hall, Inc., Englewood Cliffs, NJ.

Summary

This chapter focused on the biological aspects of adult development. While our life expectancy has increased substantially in recent years, the potential human life span has remained remarkably stable, with an upper limit of approximately 110 to 120 years. Though there have been reports of individuals living more than 120 years, none have been documented empirically. Until recently, the increase in life expectancy was mostly due to a reduction in deaths during infancy and early childhood. But in the last few decades, improved nutrition and health care have increased the chances that those reaching fifty or older will live longer. We find an increasingly larger segment of our population classified as elderly, with the greatest increase among those over 85 years of age.

People in future generations should live healthier, more productive, and longer lives until they reach the end of the potential life span. For reasons that are still unknown, women will probably continue to live longer than men. As our population ages and the old-age and young-age dependency ratios equalize, we will have to develop a system that equitably distributes the resources of our society to both young and old.

In the most comprehensive investigation exploring the factors contributing to longevity, the Duke Longitudinal Study followed individuals aged fifty-five to ninety-four over a twenty-five-year period. Of all of the predictors, none was better than health ratings. For men, the health self-rating was the best predictor of longevity, whereas for women the best predictor was satisfaction with their health. Not smoking, intelligence, education, work satisfaction, usefulness, secondary activities, and personal happiness contributed to the predictability of longevity. Other factors included finances and frequency and enjoyment of sexual intercourse.

A number of biological theories of aging have been proposed, several of which stress the role of genetics. There is considerable controversy about the biological causes of aging. Scientists argue as to whether the processes that control aging reside in the cells of our body, in the biochemical nature of genes, or at a more macrobiological level.

Most people reach their peak health in early adulthood. However, because young adults can bounce back readily from physical abuse of their bodies, it is easy for them to ignore bad health habits. Health becomes a major concern in middle adulthood. Heart disease, cancer, and obesity are the greatest health concerns of middle-aged adults. A pattern of emotional stability and controlled response to stress is associated with good health at mid-life. Coronary disease is influenced by many factors, including diet, smoking, obesity, and genetic predisposition. There is reason to believe that individuals who display Type A behavioral styles are more likely to develop coronary problems than those without these behavioral tendencies. At some point in late adulthood, biological deterioration is inevitable. The age and rate of decline varies considerably from one individual to another. Too often our research on individuals in late adulthood has focused not on healthy but on unhealthy individuals. By studying healthy older people, researchers hope to discover how the body can optimally age and to determine the factors that help maintain disease-free or disease-reduced aging.

Information about the type of health care the elderly receive suggests that some health-care providers, as well as older adults themselves, share some of society's negative stereotypes about the elderly. Changing these negative stereotypes into more compassionate stereotypes may improve health care for our older population. In searching for factors that will slow the rate of aging, the role of exercise has been accorded special attention. The evidence accumulates that a regular exercise program promotes both physical and mental health.

Review Questions

1. What is the difference between life expectancy and potential life span?
2. Outline the changing age structure of our population. What effects will the changing old-age and young-age dependency ratios have on our society?
3. What factors seem to contribute most to longevity?
4. Discuss the different biological theories of aging. Why is the wear-and-tear theory of aging the least acceptable?
5. What is the biggest threat to good health in early adulthood?
6. Compare the health statuses of middle-aged and older adults. Include in your answer suggestions about how illness, impairment, life-style, coronary disease, and exercise affect physical and mental health.
7. Discuss the factors that are responsible for peak athletic performance over the adult years.

For Further Reading

Hayflick, L. (1975). Why grow old? *The Stanford Magazine, 3,* 36–43.
> An easy-to-read overview of our aging population, biological theories of aging, and the limits of the life cycle.

Palmore, E. B. (1982). Predictors of the longevity difference: A twenty-five-year follow-up. *The Gerontologist, 22,* 513–518.
> The full report of Palmore's data analysis focused on the twenty-five-year longitudinal study of aging. Includes a detailed discussion of the factors that contribute to longevity. Moderately easy to read.

Rossman, I. (1980). Bodily changes with aging. In E. W. Busse & D. G. Blazer (Eds.), *Handbook of geriatric psychiatry.* New York: Van Nostrand Reinhold.
> Provides a comprehensive overview of bodily changes that occur during middle and late adulthood. Includes information about stature, contour, muscles, bones, joints and various organ systems, including the cardiovascular, pulmonary, renal excretory, reproductive, and digestive. Medium reading.

Segerberg, O. (1982). *Living to be 100: 1200 who did and how they did it.* New York: Charles Scribner's Sons.
> An easy-to-read, entertaining account of 1,200 people who became centenarians. Though written by a journalist, the conclusions seem intuitively on target. Easy reading.

Wiswell, R. A. (1980). Relaxation, exercise, and aging. In J. E. Birren & R. B. Sloane (Eds.), *Handbook of mental health and aging.* Englewood Cliffs, NJ: Prentice-Hall.
> A thorough overview of what we know and don't know about the role of exercise in adult development and aging. Moderately easy reading.

AGE CHANGES IN THE SENSORY, MOTOR, AND NERVOUS SYSTEMS

Imagine

Imagine That You Are an Aging Professional Baseball Player

You have been an exceptional outfielder for several years, winning several awards and have achieved a great deal of success. You are highly respected by both your peers and the general public. You are well known for possessing an unusual combination of power, speed, and agility. Unfortunately, you have noticed that you are a step or two slower than you were just a few years ago. Several times during the last season you were unable to run down fly balls that you would have caught easily when you were younger. Also, you have been striking out more often and your home run total is way down. Neither you nor your coaches believe you are experiencing a temporary slump. Instead, it seems you are undergoing a significant, steady, and progressive decline in your ability to perform as a professional baseball player, and this decline has occurred despite the fact that you have worked harder than ever during both the regular season and off-season to improve and maintain your skills. For example, during the last few years you have improved your diet and initiated a regular program of running, weight training, and flexibility exercises. Still, the decline continues. Rather than embarrass yourself before your fans and jeopardize your lifetime statistics, you are seriously considering retirement. *You are thirty-six years old.* You begin to wonder *why* your skills are declining. And you wonder if there really is life after sports.

The preceding story may seem very familiar. We are constantly reminded by the media that once the vast majority of athletes reach their mid-thirties, they are "over the hill." This seems equally true for exceptionally strenuous sports that demand power, speed, and agility (such as baseball, basketball, football, and tennis) as well as for sports that emphasize co-ordination and execution rather than power and speed (such as golf). Athletes who are able to continue after their contemporaries have retired are unusual, though not unheard of (remember Sugar Ray Leonard's third comeback to win the middleweight boxing championship).

Why does the performance of star athletes decline with age? In the previous chapter we discussed some information which might shed light on this matter. We noted, for example, the beneficial effects of exercise on the athletic performance of older adults. These beneficial features notwithstanding, it seems as if optimal performance in most sports is confined to individuals in their early twenties to the mid-thirties. This is because what seem to be very small decrements in a well-trained older athlete's ability to react to a stimulus may result in serious impairments in that individual's athletic performance. For example, a professional baseball player's ability to react to a fastball may decline by a fraction of a second as he ages. Yet this seemingly minute change in response time may mean the difference between a .300 and .200 batting average.

Furthermore, the age-related slowing of behavioral abilities is not confined to athletic endeavors. A significant slowing of nearly all behavioral skills seems to occur over the adult years (for example, reacting to an unanticipated event while driving a car). Even behaviors that do not demand strength, endurance, and cardiovascular integrity (the speed of signing a check or counting change in a supermarket check-out line) tend to slow as one ages.

Perhaps the major causes of performance decrements during the adult years can be traced to changes in the *sensorimotor* and *central nervous systems*. The sensory system transmits information from the environment via the senses to the brain. Could it be that the quality of the sensory information and the speed at which it is delivered to the brain diminishes with age? The motor system transmits information from the brain to the muscles which move our body parts. Could it be that the quality of the information and the speed at which it is delivered to our muscles diminishes with age? Finally, the most complex portion of the nervous system—the brain—is involved in interpreting incoming sensory information and deciding upon an appropriate motor response to that stimulation. Perhaps the quality (and the speed) of *interpreting* information in the brain, as well as *choosing* between response alternatives, declines with age. These possibilities, as well as a number of related issues, will be discussed in this chapter.

INTRODUCTION

In this, our second chapter on biological processes and physical development, we focus on sensorimotor development as well as developmental changes in the brain and nervous system. First we'll describe developmental changes in vision, hearing, and the other senses. Next we'll describe the developmental pattern of motor performance. Our discussion of the brain emphasizes its awesome complexity, power, and mystery. We'll pay special attention to various techniques that are used to measure the activity of the brain. We'll also describe some of the normal, as well as pathological, changes that occur in the brain as a function of the aging process, and we'll relate these brain changes to changes in psychological functioning. Next, we'll examine the primary building block of the brain, the neuron. We'll discuss the manner in which neurons function, and we'll also examine the neuron in search of substances that may be linked to the aging process. Finally, we'll link what we've learned about the nervous system to our current knowledge of Alzheimer's disease. We'll describe the symptoms, causes, and treatments for this devastating disease. Finally, we'll discuss the relationship between Alzheimer's disease and senescence—the normal aging processes.

SENSORIMOTOR DEVELOPMENT

We make contact with the world around us through our five primary senses—vision, hearing, touch, taste, and smell. Psychologists distinguish between sensation and perception. **Sensation** refers to the acquisition of information by our sensory receptors—the ears, skin, tongue, nostrils, and eyes. When we hear, for example, waves of pulsating air are sensed by the outer ear, transmitted through the bones of the middle ear to the cochlear nerve, and sent to the brain. When we see, sensation results when rays of light are collected by the eyes, focused on the retina, and travel along the optic nerve to the brain. **Perception** on the other hand, is the interpretation of what is sensed. The physical waves of air picked up by the ear may be interpreted by the brain as a musical sound or a human voice. The physical energy transmitted to the brain from the retina may be interpreted as a particular color, pattern, or shape.

Not only do we sense and perceive our environment through our five senses, but we must also move through the environment and react to it. For example, we walk, tap our feet to a catchy tune, and swat a pesky fly. The ways in which physical movements and actions change through the life cycle is called **motor development** and the growth and coordination of sensory and motor processes is described as **sensorimotor development.** These processes work together as incoming sensory information is carried to the brain through sensory pathways, and signals for motor performance are carried from the brain and spinal cord to various muscles in the body.

Sensation

What is the nature of the various sensory processes, and how well do they continue to function as we grow through the adult years? When does vision begin to decline? When does hearing begin to fail us?

Vision

Figure 4.1 shows a schematic diagram of the human eye. As light journeys from the environment to the brain, it must pass through several component parts of the eye. During the course of adult development there are a number of changes in the eye's ability to transmit sensory information to the brain. These age-related changes have profound effects on the visual abilities of different-aged adults.

Visual abilities seem to show little change during the early adult years. In the middle adult years, however, difficulties in vision become a problem for many people. **Accommodation** of the lens (the ability of the lens to focus and maintain an image on the retina) experiences its sharpest decline during the time an individual is between forty and fifty-nine years of age (Bruckner, 1967). In particular, it becomes difficult for individuals in middle adulthood to view objects at very close range (i.e., near vision); many middle-aged adults need special reading glasses or bifocals. As the lens gradually loses its capacity to accommodate to near and far objects, middle-aged adults may begin to hold their newspapers at progressively greater distances from their eyes to see the print more clearly. The reduction of near vision in middle adulthood is termed **presbyopia.** Another problem associated with the middle-aged years is an increased sensitivity to **glare.** This change in sensitivity is usually noticed after age forty-five. Age-related changes in glare sensitivity are largely due to changes in the lenses; and indeed, the lenses seem to become progressively thicker, less flexible, and more opaque with age (Weale, 1985). Also, the lenses take on a yellowish tint with increasing age. All of these changes in the lenses mean that less light reaches the retina of an older adult. It has also been shown that the number of cones (color receptors) on the fovea (the center of the retina) markedly decreases between forty and sixty years of age. Such a change has a negative influence on visual acuity (Kline and Schieber, 1985).

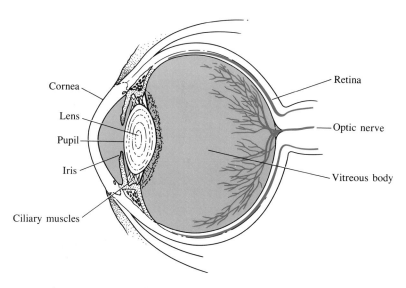

Figure 4.1 A side view of the human eye.

There is also evidence that the middle-aged adult will likely have trouble with **dark adaptation** (Weale, 1985). This means that middle-aged people have problems adjusting to changes in illumination—as when going from a brightly lit to a dimly lit environment. This explains why some adults have problems driving in the dark after leaving a well-lit environment.

As we move through the late adult years, the declines in vision that we first notice during middle adulthood become more pronounced and problematic. Night driving becomes very difficult for many individuals in the late adult years. This is because their tolerance for glare diminishes and because they are less able to react to reduced levels of illumination. Similarly, dark adaptation becomes even slower as one ages (McFarland, Domey, Warren, and Ward, 1960). Further, the area of the effective visual field becomes smaller with advancing age. This means that the size or intensity of stimuli in the peripheral area of the visual field must be increased if the stimuli are to be seen, and events occurring away from the center of the visual field may not be detected (Welford, 1980). Changes in the size of the visual field are due, in part, to an age-related reduction in the amount of blood reaching the eye (Weale, 1985).

Visual declines in late adulthood have also been traced to reductions in the quality or intensity of light reaching the retina. This is due to several factors, including the progressive yellowing of the lens, an increased waviness and irregularity of the cornea (Kuwabara, 1979), and a reduction in the diameter of the pupil (Weale, 1985). It has been determined that the retina of a sixty-year-old receives only approximately one-third of the light received by the retina of a twenty-year-old (Weale, 1985). These changes are often accompanied by degenerative changes in the retina, which can cause severe difficulties in vision (Corso, 1977). Consequently, older adults may need large-print books and magnifiers.

Blurred vision, glare sensitivity, and restricted vision are common problems for older adults. The photo on the left illustrates normal vision, while the photo on the right simulates the visual problems that might be experienced by an elderly person.

It has been well documented (Kline and Schieber, 1985) that the incidence of blindness is positively associated with age. Legal blindness is defined as corrected distance vision of 20/200 in the better eye, or a visual field restricted to 20 degrees at the largest diameter. Legal blindness occurs in less than 100 out of every 100,000 people under the age of twenty-one, but in people over the age of sixty-nine, it occurs in more than 1,400 cases per 100,000. Given these statistics, it is not surprising to discover that visual acuity also becomes less efficient as we age. If one's visual acuity is 20/50 or worse, such important activities as driving and reading are likely to be impaired. From the ages of sixty to sixty-nine, more than half of the 213 individuals tested in the Duke Longitudinal Study had good visual acuity, but for those aged seventy to seventy-nine, the figure dropped to almost one-fourth. It has been estimated that by the year 2000 there will be as many as 376,000 elderly people who are legally blind (20/200 or worse visual acuity) and that 1,760,000 older adults will suffer from severe visual impairment (Lowman and Kirchener, 1979). Not surprisingly, it has also been discovered that the loss of vision is, next to cancer, the most dreaded aspect of aging (Cogan, 1979).

Two of the most common pathologies of the aging eye that lead to blindness or severe visual impairment are **cataracts** and **glaucoma** (Kline and Schieber, 1985). A person with a cataract suffers from a lens that is completely opaque—light cannot travel through the lens to project onto the retina. Cataracts can be surgically treated by removing the damaged lens and inserting a special contact lens. Glaucoma results from increasing pressure inside the eye, which leads to irreparable damage to the retina and the optic nerve. Glaucoma affects 2 percent of individuals over the age of forty. It may be easily detected by a simple optometric test. Adults over the age of fifty should be routinely tested for glaucoma (Kline and Schieber, 1985).

The vast majority of vision research is carried out in the laboratory under highly controlled conditions. Participants are placed in an unfamiliar environment and are required to perform tasks that may have little, if anything, in common with their behavior in real-life contexts. In a recent study, Kosnik, Winslow, Kline, Rasinski, and Sekuler (1988) surveyed a large number of adults ranging from 18 to 100 years of age. These participants provided information about their ability to perform everyday visual tasks. The participants reported that five different aspects of vision declined with age: *visual processing speed* (the time necessary to read a passage or recognize an object); *light sensitivity* (trouble seeing at dusk or sorting dark colors); *near vision* (inability to read small print); *dynamic vision* (inability, for example, to read the moving credits at the end of a movie); and *visual search* (for example, difficulty in locating a particular type of cereal at the supermarket). These different dimensions of vision were found to decline in different ways. Dynamic vision, visual search, and the time necessary to adjust to dim environments declined very gradually with age; while visual processing speed, near vision, and the ability to see in dim environments declined very rapidly with age. Also of interest was the finding that adjusting to glare and brightly lit environments was a problem most commonly reported by middle-aged, not older adults.

Recently, psychologists have made an important distinction between changes in **visual acuity** and **contrast sensitivity** during the adult years. See box 4.1 for a discussion of this important issue.

Hearing

Hearing is usually at its peak in adolescence, remains fairly constant during much of early adulthood, and starts to decline upon entry into middle adulthood. By age forty, a specific decline in hearing can sometimes be detected. At about age fifty, we are likely to have problems hearing high-pitched sounds, such as those just below the pitch of a "silent" dog whistle. Why? The reduction in the ability to hear high-pitched sounds seems to be caused by a breakdown of cells in the **organ of corti,** the organ in the inner ear that transforms the vibrations picked up by the outer ear into nerve impulses. Sensitivity to low-pitched sounds, on the other hand, does not decline very much in middle adulthood. The need to increase the treble on stereo equipment is a subtle sign of this age-related hearing change. Men are more likely than women to lose their auditory acuity for high-pitched sounds (Farnsworth, McNemar, and McNemar, 1965). This sex difference may be due, in part, to the greater exposure of men to noise in occupations such as automobile work, construction work, and so forth.

Although hearing impairment may begin to occur during middle adulthood, it usually does not become much of an impediment until late adulthood. Only 19

BOX 4.1

AGE CHANGES IN CONTRAST SENSITIVITY

In recent years, a great deal of interest has developed in regard to the topic of **contrast sensitivity.** Contrast sensitivity refers to an individual's ability to perceive visual stimuli that differ in both contrast and spatial frequency. **Contrast** refers to the difference in brightness between adjacent areas of a visual stimulus. A black line on a white piece of paper possesses a great deal of contrast; a light grey line on a white piece of paper possesses a smaller amount of contrast. **Spatial frequency** refers to the number of cycles of bars of light (one cycle consisting of both a light bar and a dark bar of the same width) imaged within a specific area on the retina. This means that very wide bars of light have low spatial frequencies, while very narrow or fine bars of light have high spatial frequencies. Psychologists have constructed simple visual stimuli called **gratings** that differ in spatial frequency. See box figure 4.1 for an example of two simple gratings. If held at arm's length, grating A has a spatial frequency of 1 (each cycle of one light bar and one dark bar takes up one degree of visual angle on the retina); grating B has a spatial frequency of 3 (three cycles of light and dark bars are needed to take up one degree of visual angle). In other words, there are three times as many bars of light in grating B as in grating A.

It is possible to conduct an experiment in which we present adults of varying ages with a number of gratings differing in both contrast and spatial frequency. By doing such a study we can determine the **contrast threshold** for different-aged adults. This refers to the minimal amount of contrast needed to perceive gratings that differ in spatial frequency. Owsley, Sekuler, and Siemsen (1983) have discovered that the contrast threshold changes in a predictable manner from twenty to eighty years of age. Box figure 4.2 summarizes the results of this study as well as other research dealing with the topic of age-related changes in contrast sensitivity.

In a very real sense, it may be argued that box figure 4.2 indicates the "window of human visibility." The area below the curve represents combinations of contrast and spatial frequency that individuals can see. The area above the curve represents combinations of contrast and spatial frequency that are invisible to humans. In general, this figure shows that humans need a great deal of contrast to see gratings with very low or very high spatial frequencies, but relatively little contrast to see gratings of moderate spatial frequency. Furthermore, this figure also shows that, with increases in age, adults (1) need more and more contrast to see gratings with high spatial frequencies, (2) become progressively blind to higher spatial frequencies regardless of the amount of contrast inherent in a grating, and (3) display no alteration in their ability to see low spatial frequencies.

Why do you think that scientists are so concerned with the concept of contrast sensitivity in general and age-related changes in the contrast threshold in particular? To answer this question we need to consider the concept of **visual acuity.** When an adult goes to an optometrist for a routine eye exam she is typically given a test of visual acuity. Visual acuity refers to a person's ability to perceive objects under maximum amounts of contrast. When you take your eye exam, you are placed in a dark room and the

BOX 4.1 *Continued*

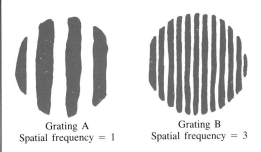

Grating A
Spatial frequency = 1

Grating B
Spatial frequency = 3

Box figure 4.1 Two gratings illustrate the concept of spatial frequency.

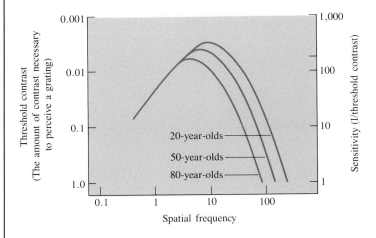

Box figure 4.2 Changes in human contrast sensitivity from 20 to 80 years of age.

Source: Data from C. Owsley, R. Sekuler, and D. Siemsen, "Contrast Sensitivity Throughout Adulthood" in *Vision Research*, 23: 689–699, 1983.

optometrist projects an eye chart consisting of black letters against a white background. Your task is to identify the letters. Alternatively, the contrast threshold is a measurement of the minimum amount of contrast necessary to see an object. This means that a test of visual acuity would be a very liberal estimate of an adult's visual ability— it would likely overestimate the individual's visual ability. For example, suppose that several older adults complain of poor vision. But when they are administered a test of

---

BOX 4.1 *Continued*

---

visual acuity, they appear to have normal vision. This does not mean that old people are "faking it" or that they are complaining because they want attention. Instead, it means that under conditions of reduced contrast (for example, driving at dusk or reading in a dimly lit room), older adults may experience a pronounced difficulty in seeing. But when high levels of contrast are available, as in a test of visual acuity, they experience less difficulty in seeing. Put somewhat differently, it is possible for two adults (one older and one younger) to test out at the same level of visual acuity while the contrast sensitivity of the younger adult greatly exceeds that of the older adult.

It has been suggested that contrast sensitivity is a more sensitive and more meaningful measure of a person's visual ability than is visual acuity. For example, a person's contrast sensitivity seems to be a better predictor of their ability to drive a car under conditions of reduced visibility (twilight, fog, and so forth) than a person's visual acuity. What are the implications of this conclusion? Does it mean that we, as a society, should use a test of contrast sensitivity (rather than visual acuity) to determine eligibility for a driver's license? If a test of contrast sensitivity was employed to determine a person's ability to drive, would this mean that more older adults would be denied a driver's license? Finally, it should be emphasized that corrective lenses (glasses and contact lenses) may be used to improve a person's visual acuity; however, there are no procedures or devices, as yet, that may be used to improve an individual's contrast sensitivity.

---

percent of people from forty-five to fifty-four years of age experience some hearing difficulty, but for those between seventy-five and seventy-nine, the percentage rises to 75 (Butler and Lewis, 1977). It has been estimated that 15 percent of the population over sixty-five is legally deaf (Corso, 1977). Such hearing loss is usually due to degeneration of the **cochlea,** the primary neural receptor for hearing. **Presbycusis** is the general term used to describe the most common age-related problems in hearing. It is a decline in the ability to hear high-pitched sounds. Another specific hearing disorder of late life is **tinnitus.** This is a constant high-pitched "ringing" or "whistling" sound in the ears. It has been reported in nearly 11 percent of those between sixty-five and seventy-four years of age (Rockstein and Sussman, 1979). While not unknown among middle-aged adults (9 percent) or younger adults (3 percent), tinnitus is a problem the elderly find most difficult to accept. It is distracting, virtually constant, and nearly impossible to "tune out."

With increasing age, adults find it more and more difficult to hear speech sounds. This effect becomes more powerful when adults (1) are exposed to sentences rather than single words, and (2) listen to speech sounds under noisy, adverse conditions. Furthermore, this finding is still obtained when researchers equate different-aged

Ronald Reagan, in order to compensate for his hearing loss, used a small, canal-style hearing aid while he was president.

adults for the degree of general hearing loss (Olson, Harkins, and Lenhardt, 1985). It is not clear why older adults have such difficulty processing speech sounds. John Corso, a noted sensory psychologist, has argued that the degeneration of certain areas within the brain, as well as within the ear, may be responsible for this phenomenon (Corso, 1981). Whatever the cause, it is certain that this deficit can have a negative effect on the older adult's ability to communicate with others (Huyck and Hoyer, 1982).

Hearing aids are used by many older adults. In fact, some older adults must wear two hearing aids to correct for different degrees of hearing loss in each ear. If the aids are not balanced or if only one is used, the subtle differences in phase and intensity at the two ears, which enable sounds to be localized and identified, are lost. Location of sounds helps us to attend to one conversation while ignoring another. When we don't do this well, both wanted and unwanted sounds combine and produce noise or confusion. Some adults who wear a single hearing aid complain that all it does is bring in noise. They may make other attempts to improve hearing, including such tricks as placing a hand to the ear (Welford, 1980).

Corso (1977) suggests that deficits in hearing often lead the elderly to choose patterns of physical and social isolation. This may contribute to reductions in intellectual enrichment, social functioning, and perhaps even life satisfaction.

The Other Senses

Not only do we experience declines in vision and hearing as we age, but we may also become less sensitive in our ability to *taste* (Engen, 1977; Schiffman, 1977). The declines observed in taste may not be as dramatic as those observed for vision and hearing. Nevertheless, the sense of taste is important enough to warrant close study. An older adult's sensitivity to taste may have a large bearing on his or her enjoyment and intake of food (Whitbourne, 1985). For example, Huyck and Hoyer (1982) suggest that some older adults suffer from nutritional deficiencies because of an increased desire for highly seasoned but nonnutritious "junk food." Craving junk food may be related to the fact that it is more highly flavored and "tastable" than nutritious food.

The human tongue contains specialized receptors that detect four different tastes: sweet, salty, bitter, and sour. Bartoshuk, Rifkin, Marks, and Bars (1986) found that older adults (averaging 82.8 years of age) were less sensitive than younger adults (24.4 years of age) to all of the basic tastes. Weiffenbach, Cowart, and Baum (1986) found no basic differences in taste sensitivity for those between forty and seventy years of age. However, the youngest age group (twenty-to thirty-nine-year-olds) in this study displayed greater taste sensitivity than the over-forty group. Other researchers have suggested that sensitivity to all tastes remains stable until the late fifties, when a steep decline in the ability to detect all tastes occurs (Whitbourne, 1985). As you can see, all researchers agree that age-related changes in taste sensitivity occur. But there seems to be some disagreement about when the changes first occur and how rapidly the changes occur.

Psychologists have come to realize that different medications influence taste during older adulthood. For example, Spitzer (1988) examined the taste sensitivity of young adults in comparison to groups of institutionalized and noninstitutionalized elderly. She discovered that all of the older participants were less sensitive to sour, salty, and bitter tastes. Sensitivity to sweet tastes, however, was not found to change with age. Furthermore, Spitzer reported that institutionalized elderly were less sensitive to sour tastes than noninstitutionalized elderly. This was probably due to the different types of drugs that were regularly administered to the institutionalized participants. Also, elderly subjects who were taking medication for hypertension were found to be relatively insensitive to the taste of salt. It is unclear, however, if this insensitivity was a result of the person's hypertension or a result of the medication taken for the hypertension. Insensitivity to the taste of salt could be a contributing cause of hypertension—it could make the older person ingest more heavily salted foods. Spitzer's study helps illustrate the important relationship between health and taste sensitivity. It also shows the serious problems involved in the interpretation of correlational findings.

Finally, it should be noted that changes in taste sensitivity may not be responsible for all changes in eating behavior during older adulthood. An older adult may eat less for a number of psychosocial reasons (such as loneliness) independent of his or her level of taste sensitivity (Hayslip and Panek, 1989).

Information about age-related changes in *smell* have been very difficult to reliably document (Engen, 1977; Whitbourne, 1985). This is because smell is one of the last senses to decline with age, and because smell is affected by a number of variables (for example, health) that are correlated with age. For example, Chalke, Dewhurst, and Ward (1958) examined how well two different groups of adults (a healthy group and a group of inpatients and outpatients in a hospital) could detect the smell of natural gas. Results showed that as many as 30 percent of adults over age sixty-five were not sensitive to lower concentrations of gas. However, these age-related differences tended to dissipate when the health status of the participants was taken into account.

Health may also influence smell preference as well as smell sensitivity. Springer and Dietzmann (1970) had younger and older participants rate the degree to which they found the smell of diesel exhaust fumes objectionable. Adults over age sixty-five found the odor less annoying than younger people. Interestingly, the ratings of these older adults were very similar to those participants, regardless of age, who described themselves as being in poor health.

Age-related changes have also been reported in *touch*. Verillo (1980), for example, examined vibrotactile sensitivity (that is, the ability to detect vibrations on the surface of the skin) in individuals between eight and seventy-four years of age. He found age-related declines for high-frequency but not low-frequency stimulation. Corso (1977) has observed that, with aging, the touch sensitivity of the lower extremities (ankles, knees, and so on) is more impaired than that of the upper extremities (wrists, shoulders, and so forth).

Hayslip and Panek (1989) summarize information that suggests that older adults are less sensitive to *temperature* changes than are young adults. Because older adults may not be able to detect changes in temperature, they are more susceptible to hypothermia, heatstroke, frostbite, and so on.

Ochs, Newberry, Lenhardt, and Harkins (1985) reviewed evidence that shows that the elderly are likely to have an impaired **kinesthetic** sense. Kinesthesis involves a person's ability to know where his or her body parts are as he or she moves through space. For example, being able to touch your nose when your eyes are closed. A reduced kinesthetic sense would make elderly adults more susceptible to falls.

One of the age-related losses in sensory sensitivity, the sensitivity to *pain,* may have an advantage. Earlier studies have shown that older people are less sensitive to and suffer less from pain than do their younger counterparts (see, for example, Harkins and Chapman, 1976; Kenshalo, 1977; Whitbourne, 1985). More recent research has revealed that older adults tend to underreport low levels of pain and overrate higher-intensity pain (Harkins, Price, and Martinelli, 1986). Nevertheless, Harkins, et al. (1986) reported that there were more similarities than differences when younger and older participants were compared. Although decreased sensitivity to pain may help the elderly cope with disease and injury, it can be harmful if it masks injuries and illnesses that need to be treated. Finally, it must be noted that a vast array of personality and cultural factors influence pain perception among the elderly.

Motor Development

The physical skills of an individual usually peak between the early twenties and the mid-thirties. Think about the football and basketball players as well as the boxers in the United States who are among the best in the world at their respective sports. By far, the majority of these athletes are in the early adult age bracket. It always is heartening, though, especially to middle-aged people, when "older" athletes such as Sugar Ray Leonard in boxing, Jack Nicklaus in golf, or Kareem Abdul Jabbar in basketball reach new heights of success in their sports. Jabbar, forty years old and the starting center, helped the Los Angeles Lakers to the 1988 world championship. Nolan Ryan pitched his sixth no-hitter when he was forty-three years old.

One of the major reasons for a decrease in athletic performance during adulthood is a reduction in strength and muscularity. Muscular strength and the ability to maintain maximum muscular effort have both been found to decline steadily during middle adulthood. At age thirty, about 70 of a man's 175 pounds are muscle. Over the next forty years, he loses ten pounds of that muscle as cells stop dividing and die. By age forty-five, the strength of a man's back muscles declines to approximately 96 percent of its maximum value, and by age fifty, it declines to 92 percent. Most men in their late fifties can only do physical work at about 60 percent of the rate achieved by men who are forty. Much of this decline appears to be linked with such physiological changes as the thickening of the walls of the air sacs in the lungs, which hinders breathing, and the hardening of connective sheaths that surround muscles, which is linked with decreases in both oxygen and blood supply (Marshall, 1973). All these age-related changes, because they have been identified for the most part by cross-sectional research, are hopelessly confounded with a variety of other potent variables, such as changes in life-style, cohort differences in exercise habits, and so on. Furthermore, we know that through repeated exercise, training, and physical activity, both men and women can reduce the rate of decline in a host of psychomotor and physical functions (Adrian, 1981; Eckert and Espenschade, 1980; Rikli and Busch, 1986). In general, lifelong patterns of physical activity, rather than age, are a better predictor of one's levels of physical performance (Rikli and Busch, 1986).

Very simple, unskilled behaviors that entail little, if any, strength and endurance are just as likely to slow down with aging as are complex behaviors that demand exceptional amounts of strength, endurance, and skill. For example, simple behaviors such as finger tapping and handwriting have been found to slow dramatically with age. Two leading developmentalists, James Birren (1974) and Timothy Salthouse (1985), have noted that the slowing of behavior (*psychomotor slowing*) is probably the most reliable finding obtained after decades of research on human aging.

Reaction time has been among the most widely studied aspects of psychomotor slowing during adulthood. **Reaction-time tasks** measure the time elapsed between the appearance of a signal and a person's response to that signal. In one study, Bleecker, Bolla-Wilson, Agnew, and Meyers (1987) gave a large group of males and females ranging from forty to ninety years of age a simple reaction-time task. Participants were required to press a button with the index finger of their preferred hand as soon as they saw a simple visual stimulus flashed on a screen. The stimuli were presented at random intervals so that anywhere from one to ten seconds elapsed between the occurrence of each stimulus. Forty-four measures of reaction time were collected from each participant. Results showed that reaction time significantly slowed down as the age of the participants increased. The males' reaction times increased by 33 percent, while the females' reaction times increased by 17 percent. Despite the fact that the males declined more than the females, the men were found to have consistently faster reaction times than the women. Most interestingly, the researchers discovered that the tendencies for reaction time to slow with age and for men to perform better than women were *not* related to participants' scores on several measures of personality, motivation, depression, fatigue, or practice.

Salthouse (1985) has argued that decrements in the speed of behavior during middle and older adulthood are of considerable importance. He maintains that the age-related slowing of behavior (that is, psychomotor slowing) is evident in several daily tasks: unwrapping a Band-Aid, dialing a telephone, using a knife, putting on a shirt, picking up coins, zipping a garment, and others. Older adults, because of the slowing of their motor performance, may be less able to adapt to the demands of a changing world than younger adults. According to Salthouse:

> If the external environment is rapidly changing, the conditions that lead to the initiation of a particular behavior may no longer be appropriate by the time the behavior is actually executed by older adults. This could lead to severe problems in operating vehicles, controlling equipment, or monitoring displays. Despite some claims to the contrary . . . it appears that the speed of decision and response can be quite important in our modern automated society, and, consequently, the slowness of older adults may place them at a great disadvantage relative to the younger members of the population. (1985, p. 401)

One way age-related behavioral slowing interacts with sensory loss to cause problems for older adults is in the incidence of falling. Box 4.2 discusses the sensorimotor causes of falling.

Salthouse (1985) has discovered three apparent exceptions to the overwhelming evidence suggesting an age-related slowing of behavior. First, physically

---

BOX 4.2

FALLING: THE LEADING CAUSE OF ACCIDENTAL INJURY AMONG THE ELDERLY

Among those over the age of sixty-five, falling is the leading cause of accidental injury. For example, of the 200,000 hip fractures each year in the United States, more than 170,000 occur to those over the age of sixty-five. The rate of mortality from falling increases directly with increased age and represents the seventh leading cause of death in those over seventy-five, surpassing even causes such as automobile accidents (Ochs, Newberry, Lenhardt, and Harkins, 1985). About 25 percent of older people require intensive medical intervention and hospitalization from falls. Severe falls are associated with broken bones (fractures of the hip, wrist, and vertebrae), head injury, and multiple facial, skin, and hand lacerations (Harvard Medical School Health Letter, 1989).

Most falls occur in the homes of older people (Ochs et al., 1985), especially in the living room or bedroom during the regular daytime routine. Stairs are also common places for falls, chiefly while descending (Harvard Medical School Health Letter, 1989). The institutionalized elderly are also at high risk of falling due to the many predisposing medical conditions that require institutional placement (Ochs et al., 1985). Institutional falls are more common at night, as older people perhaps become disoriented and confused in unfamiliar surroundings. Newly admitted patients in institutions are particularly vulnerable (Ochs et al., 1985).

The causes of falling among the elderly represent a burgeoning area of research. Many studies suggest that the elderly who are most likely to experience severe injury or death from a fall are those who are just beginning to undergo physical and psychological decline and have not yet recognized their limitations. On the other hand, those elderly who are frequent fallers and have identified their problem are less likely to be seriously injured in a fall. The risk of falling has been found to be related to poor illumination, dark staircases, and loose rugs. Some of the physical conditions that contribute to falling are arthritis, loss of balance and equilibrium (**presbystasis**), weakness in the muscles that control coordination of the knees and ankles, impaired vision, impaired hearing (hearing provides critical feedback for walking), and diabetes (leading

---

fit, active, and healthy older adults have not been found to differ in speed of performance from inactive, less healthy younger adults. However, physically fit, healthy older adults still react more slowly than young or middle-aged adults. This suggests that health and fitness can attenuate, but not eliminate, the age-related slowing of behavior. Second, reaction-time differences between younger and older adults have been found to diminish when research subjects are required to make a vocal rather than manual response. Salthouse notes, however, that the aforementioned finding has been very difficult to replicate on a consistent basis. Thus, until more reliable

to reduced sensation in the legs) (Harvard Medical School Health Letter, 1985). And of course, there are many neurological disorders that increase the likelihood of falling, including Parkinson's disease, stroke, and Alzheimer's disease. There are many drugs which can increase the risk of falling as well: tranquilizers, some antihistamines used for colds, antidepressants, and barbiturates. Common prescription drugs used to lower blood pressure can cause dizziness and light-headedness. Even large doses of aspirin (for example, for arthritis) can affect the inner ear and cause disturbance in balance (Harvard Medical School Health Letter, 1989). Physicians and pharmacists are increasingly aware of the problems associated with high drug dosages for the elderly and with drug interactions that may lead to an increased risk of falling.

Why do falls lead to such severe injury in the elderly? Two answers to this question have been suggested. First, because of the generalized age-related slowing of behavior, older people may not be as able as younger people to prepare themselves to break a fall. Second, the age-related phenomenon of **osteoporosis,** or thinning and weakening of the bones, may cause the spontaneous shattering of brittle, thinning bones (especially in the pelvis) in older people. This sudden breakage can actually cause a fall. Thus, falls can cause broken bones; and brittle or broken bones can cause falls.

One of the most profound consequences of falling is psychological—fear. Fear of falling may unnecessarily restrict the range of activities selected by an older person. This type of self-limiting life-style, focused on self-protection rather than freedom, may lead to isolation and depression.

How can advances in psychology, medicine, and even architecture decrease the likelihood of falling among the elderly?

data are obtained, developmentalists should be very cautious in interpreting the results of vocal reaction-time experiments. Third, it has been reported that with extensive practice, the reaction-time performance of older adults can be significantly improved (Clark, Lamphear, and Riddick, 1987). In fact, extensive practice may allow older adults to perform simple tasks as quickly and effectively as younger adults (see, for example, Murrell, 1970). Salthouse suggested that the latter results have been exceptionally difficult to replicate. Furthermore, most training studies do not include follow-up measures of extensive practice. Taking all of the pertinent studies into account, it seems reasonable to conclude that age-related differences in speeded performance are greatly reduced, not completely eliminated, by extensive practice. Small (but significant) differences remain favoring younger adults over older adults.

What accounts for age-related differences in motor performance? It is possible to explain these differences by referring to peripheral versus central processes. **Peripheral processes** are those that determine how (1) environmental information is registered at a sense organ and transmitted to the brain, and (2) information is relayed from the brain to the muscles, where a motor response is initiated. It is tempting to conclude that older adults are slower than younger adults because they (1) pick up less information via their senses and (2) transmit slow, poor-quality messages from their sensory systems to their brains and from their brains to their motor systems. This explanation seems both logical and rational. However, Salthouse (1985) has argued against this hypothesis. He maintains that the stimuli used in reaction-time studies are so intense (often, a loud noise), and the motor responses are so simple (pressing a button) that it is hard to envision how sensorimotor factors are the primary culprits responsible for age-related slowing.

Many psychologists seem to agree with the position taken by James Birren (1974). He suggested that **central processes** are responsible for the slowing of psychomotor performance. Central processes refer to the operations taking place within the brain. Specifically, Birren and his associates (Birren, Woods, and Williams, 1980) maintain that, due to the age-related, all-pervasive physical deterioration of the brain, it simply takes longer for an older brain to perform all mental operations. It is as if the older brain is in a continual state of electrical "brownout." Birren's position on this matter has come to be known as the **generalized slowing hypothesis.**

Other researchers (for example, Strayer, Wickens, and Braune, 1987) have argued against the generalized slowing hypothesis. More specifically, they maintain that reaction time is *not* a sensitive measure of how quickly mental (that is, central) processes occur in the brain. Reaction time is heavily influenced by the adoption of different response strategies or biases. For example, young adults are likely to adopt a liberal response bias (emphasizing speed over accuracy), while older adults adopt a conservative response bias (stressing accuracy over speed). Thus the selection of different response biases, not age per se, may account for the observed change in reaction time with age. Strayer et al. (1987) reported that an important sign of the brain's ability to process information, the P300 brain wave, is not affected by the selection of different biases (we'll explore the P300 brain wave further later in this chapter). Furthermore, these researchers showed that younger and older adults differ to a much greater extent on a measure of reaction time than on P300 activity. Based on these results, they concluded that reaction-time experiments overestimate the extent to which declining central processes are responsible for psychomotor slowing. Also, other investigators (Cerella, 1989; Johnson and Rybash, 1989) using reaction-time measures have suggested that different mental abilities slow at different rates. Thus, the validity of the generalized slowing hypothesis has been called into question.

In this section we have seen that sensorimotor development usually peaks during very late adolescence or early adulthood. By middle adulthood, a perceptible slowing or decline occurs in many aspects of sensorimotor development. By the time an individual reaches old age, the slowdown and decline are easily detected. We have also discussed the issue of whether the psychomotor slowing of behavior that accompanies aging may be traced to central or peripheral processes. In the next section, we will examine the human brain and the manner in which it changes with age. We will more closely examine the hypothesis that age-related changes in psychological functioning may be related to physical changes taking place in the brain.

THE BRAIN

The human brain is truly the most complex, intricate, and elegant system imaginable. The human brain can be considered the most advanced computer we know. Considering its capacity and power, the brain is exceptionally small. During adulthood the human brain weighs approximately three pounds (1400 g) and is only about the size of a large grapefruit.

Robert Ornstein and Richard Thompson, two leaders in the area of brain research, provide the following suggestions to help you visualize the brain:

> Place your fingers on both sides of your head beneath your earlobes. In the center of the space between your hands is the oldest part of the brain, the brainstem. Now, form your hands into fists. Each is about the size of one of the brain's hemispheres, and when both fists are joined at the heel of the hand they describe not only the approximate size and shape of the entire brain but also its symmetrical structure. Next, put on a pair of thick gloves—preferably light gray. These represent the cortex (Latin for *bark*)—the newest part of the brain whose functioning results in the most characteristically human creations, such as language and art. (Ornstein and Thompson, 1984, pp. 21–22)

Before we can describe how the brain changes with age, we need to know something about its basic makeup. Therefore, let's now turn our attention to a brief description of the major components of the brain.

Major Components of the Brain

The **brain stem** is, on an evolutionary basis, the oldest part of the brain. In fact, it is sometimes referred to as the "reptilian brain" because it resembles the entire brain of a typical reptile (Ornstein and Thompson, 1984). The brain stem begins as a swelling of the spinal cord and extends into the middle of the brain. It controls several basic biological functions such as breathing and heart rate. The **ascending reticular activation system (ARAS),** a structure which originates within the brain stem and extends to the other portions of the brain, regulates an individual's state of consciousness and level of arousal. Attached to the brain stem is the **cerebellum.** This structure helps maintain balance and posture and coordinate body movements. It has recently been discovered that memories for simple learned responses

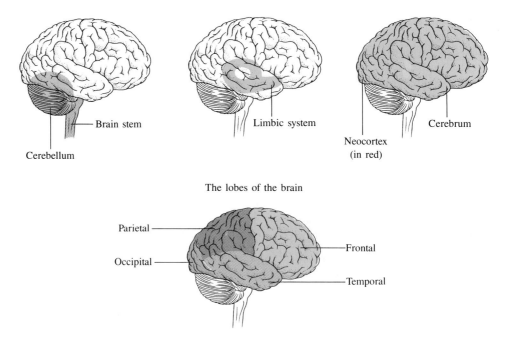

Figure 4.2   Relative sizes and locations of the brain stem and cerebellum, limbic system, and cerebrum and neocortex within the human brain.

are stored in the cerebellum (Thompson, 1985). In fact, age-related declines in the strength and ease of classical conditioning, both in humans and animals, may be affected by age-related changes in the cerebellum (Woodruff-Pak and Thompson, 1988). See figure 4.2 for an illustration of the relative sizes and locations of the brain stem and cerebellum.

The next major part of the brain is the **limbic system.** The term *limbic* comes from a Latin word that means *border.* Literally, then, the limbic system is a border area between the oldest part of the brain (the brain stem and cerebellum) and the newest part of the brain (the cerebrum). The limbic system is commonly called the "mammalian brain" because it seems to be most highly developed in mammals (Ornstein and Thompson, 1984). The limbic system contains a large number of separate components that control a vast number of basic biological processes. For example, a part of the limbic system called the hypothalamus, which is about the size of a pea in the adult brain, controls eating, drinking, body temperature, and sexual activity. It also regulates the activity of the master gland of the endocrine system, the pituitary gland. For many years, psychologists have known that the limbic system exerts a powerful influence on emotional behavior. Damage to certain areas of the limbic system can result in episodes of extreme rage or anger.

Of primary interest to developmental psychologists and gerontologists is a component of the limbic system called the **hippocampus.** Humans, as well as other mammals, have two hippocampi—one on each side of the brain. A great deal of evidence suggests that the hippocampus plays a crucial role in memory processes (Squire, 1987). Patients who suffer from amnesia and Alzheimer's disease, disorders in which memory failure is readily apparent, display significant damage to the hippocampus (Kolb and Whishaw, 1985; Scheibel and Wechsler, 1986; Cote, 1981). Furthermore, it has been suggested that biological changes in the hippocampus that accompany normal aging may be responsible, in part, for the declining memory abilities of older animals and humans (Moscovitch, 1982; Winocur, 1985, 1986). Finally, amnesia-like behavior patterns have been produced in animals by lesioning the hippocampus and surrounding tissue (Zola-Morgan and Squire, 1986). Refer to figure 4.2 for an illustration of the relative size and location of the limbic system.

The **cerebrum** is the largest—and evolutionarily the most recent—part of the brain. It totally covers the limbic system as well as significant portions of the brain stem and cerebellum. The cerebrum has several important features. First, it is divided down the middle into two halves or **hemispheres**—the right hemisphere and the left hemisphere. Second, the cerebral hemispheres are connected by a tract of nerve fibers called the **corpus callosum.** Third, the top covering of the cerebrum is called the **cortex.** Refer to figure 4.2 for an illustration of the relative size and location of the cerebrum and cortex.

The cortex, from the viewpoint of a psychologist, is one of the most important, if not *the* most important, part of the brain. In fact, it may be argued that it is the cortex which makes us "human" (Ornstein and Thompson, 1984). The cortex has been identified as the source of personality, cognition, perception, communication, and creativity (Bloom, Lazerson, and Hofstadter, 1985). Without a cortex we could still maintain our biological functions and perform simple movements, but the intrinsically human features of our existence would disappear. The cortex may be divided into four different regions called **lobes,** where various psychological functions are housed. In the **frontal lobe** are basic aspects of personality and social behaviors, planning and execution of complex behavioral sequences, and control of motor movements. In the **temporal lobe** we find consolidation of long-term memories, the assigning of emotional properties to incoming experiences, and simple auditory sensation. The **parietal lobe** controls processing of short-term memories and the construction of a spatial representation of one's body. Finally, the **occipital lobe** controls basic visual processing (Kolb and Whishaw, 1985).

Despite its importance in human psychological functioning, the cortex is amazingly delicate, fragile, and thin. In fact, the cortex only consists of the top *one-eighth inch* covering the cerebrum. Along with being very thin, the cortex is highly convoluted. This means that it appears as intricately folded or wavelike rather than smooth and flat. Convoluting the cortex increases its surface area. This is very important, since the power and humanity of the brain is derived from its large surface area.

The cortex can be envisioned as a device that symbolizes or represents experience. It has been concluded that the two hemispheres of the cortex are predisposed to symbolize information in very different ways (Springer and Deutsch, 1985). The left hemisphere seems to represent experience in a language-based, analytical manner; while the right hemisphere seems to symbolize events in a holistic, visually based manner. It should be recognized, however, that there are exceptions to this general rule. For example, Springer and Deutsch (1985) have noted that there seems to be a stronger division of labor in the male brain than the female brain and in right-handers than in left-handers.

As individuals age, they are more likely to suffer from damage or injury to the cortex. Also with aging, the brain becomes less plastic. This means that uninjured parts of the cortex are less likely to take over the functions of injured cortical areas. Therefore, an elderly adult, in comparison to either a young adult or a child, is less likely to recover from a brain injury. Damage to the elderly brain usually results from a stroke or a brain tumor. Strokes occur when brain tissue is deprived of oxygen. This deprivation may occur when a blood vessel in the brain becomes clogged, plugged, or broken. In general, damage to the left hemisphere results in **aphasia,** a breakdown or loss of an individual's language abilities. Damage to the right hemisphere, on the other hand, typically results in visual-spatial disorders (Damasio, 1985). Adults with right hemisphere damage may fail to recognize familiar objects or faces **(agnosia),** become lost in familiar environments (even their own homes or neighborhoods), and may not be able to form a visual representation of all of the objects (including their own bodies) in the left half of their visual field. Howard Gardner (1972) and Oliver Sacks (1985) have written fascinating accounts of the effects of brain damage on specific aspects of adult psychological functioning.

In the following section, we'll describe the methods used to observe and measure brain activity. We'll show how age-related changes in brain activity correspond to age-related changes in psychological functioning.

Observing the Brain and Measuring Its Activity

Going inside a human skull and physically observing the brain is usually the province only of surgeons faced with correcting serious problems. However, recent advances in the fields of computer technology and radiology allow us to take a noninvasive look at the human brain. For example, the technique of *computerized axial tomography,* or the **CT scan,** allows a scientist to view a two- or three-dimensional representation of the human brain. The CT scan has revealed that the ventricles—the four cavities within the brain containing cerebrospinal fluid—enlarge with normal aging. CT scans have shown that from the first through the seventh decades of life there is a gradual increase in the size of the ventricles and, importantly, in the eighth and ninth decades comes a sharper increase (Barron, Jacobs, and Kirkei, 1976). Whether the age-related changes observed in the CT scan data can actually cause cognitive deficits among the elderly is a matter of intense debate (Albert, et al., 1987; LaRue and Jarvik, 1982). For example, Albert, et al. (1987) have reported that CT changes are related to both changes in electroencephalogram recordings (EEGs) and decrements in cognitive abilities.

Somewhat similar to the CT scan, but much more powerful and safer, is the technique of *magnetic resonance imaging* or **MRI** (Cohen, 1988). In this procedure, various regions of the brain are surrounded by a strong magnetic field and exposed to a specific radio-frequency pulse. Under these circumstances the stimulated brain tissue emits a signal that is transformed into a two-dimensional image by a computer. The MRI technique is so powerful that it can identify structural abnormalities in the brain that are as small as 1 millimeter (Placa, 1990).

Unlike the CT scan and MRI, which reveal brain anatomy, the **PETT scan** (*positron emission transaxial tomography*) records the brain's actual metabolic activity (Cohen, 1988). PETT measures the radioactive emissions from the brain and produces an image revealing which regions are metabolizing the most glucose (in other words, which are the most active). Using the PETT scan, researchers have found different patterns of activity in the brains of individuals engaging in different mental activities (for example, reading versus solving math problems). PETT scans have shown that the metabolic activity of older healthy adults' brains is very similar to that of younger adults (deLeon, Ferris, and George, 1985). It has also been shown, however, that glucose metabolism is reduced in certain areas of the brains of Alzheimer's disease patients (Kuhl, 1986).

The CT scan, PETT scan, and MRI are remarkable breakthroughs in our ability to look inside the brain. They have allowed us to better understand age-related changes in the structure and activity of the human brain. However, none of these different methodologies can be used to make foolproof diagnoses of some of the serious neurological diseases (for example, Alzheimer's disease) that afflict older adults (Cohen 1988; National Institutes of Health, 1987). Until existing instruments are dramatically improved or new devices are invented, much of the research regarding brain changes in the elderly will continue to take place when an autopsy is performed (Bondareff, 1977).

It is also possible to measure the activity of the brain by means of an **electroencephalogram (EEG).** The EEG represents an amplification of the cortex's generalized electrical activity. Myers (1986) has suggested that determining the activity of the brain via the EEG is somewhat akin to studying a car engine by listening to the sound of its motor. Despite its apparent crudeness, research involving the EEG has yielded a number of important findings. For example, several different patterns of rhythmical electrical activity (that is, brain waves) have been detected in the brain by using the EEG. Each of these waves has been related to a particular level or state of consciousness. The **alpha rhythm** is the dominant rhythm displayed by the brain and is linked with alert wakefulness. The alpha rhythm contrasts with the faster **beta rhythm,** which characterizes an individual during a period of focused thinking and problem solving. The **delta rhythm** is the slowest of all of the different brain waves. It appears when individuals enter the deepest, most restful component of the sleep cycle. There are several important ways in which various brain rhythms, as measured by the EEG, change with age.

A number of researchers have focused their attention on how changes in EEG patterns are related to changes in the adult sleep cycle. Miles and Dement (1980) have argued that the most pronounced change in EEG during the aging process is the steady decrease in the amplitude of the **delta rhythm** during deep sleep. This is important because it has been discovered that with increasing age, adults seem to spend less and less time in deep sleep (Woodruff, 1985). This finding is consistent with one of the most universal complaints of older adults: "I don't seem to sleep as well as I did when I was young."

What can older adults do to get a better night's sleep? The results of a number of studies on sleep deprivation may help to answer this question. Carskadon (1982) found that after periods of sleep deprivation, elderly adults changed their patterns of sleep activity. They displayed a significant increase in deep sleep (high-amplitude, slow-frequency delta waves) and had fewer spontaneous awakenings from sleep. These results suggest that many older adults should rethink their sleep schedules and daily habits. For example, many older adults who complain of sleep problems spend more time in bed (ten to twelve hours) than younger adults. They are also more likely to take more afternoon naps and sleeping pills. Carskadon (1982) and Woodruff (1985) both suggested that these elderly individuals should discontinue their naps and sleeping pills. Also, they should spend a significantly shorter amount of time in bed each evening (about six hours). This would result in a beneficial form of sleep deprivation. It might help the elderly improve the quantity and quality of their daily sleep. By sleeping a smaller number of hours, older adults would be able to increase the time they spend in delta-wave sleep, which would produce a deeper, more satisfying sleep.

Another group of psychologists has examined age-related changes in alpha-wave activity. Davies (1941) was the first experimenter to show that the alpha rhythm is considerably slower in older adults. Several other investigators have replicated her original findings by conducting both longitudinal and cross-sectional studies (Woodruff, 1985). Diane Woodruff (1985), a noted neurophysiologist, has concluded that the most reliable age-related changes in EEG center around decrements in alpha activity. According to James Birren (1960), the age-related slowing of alpha activity makes the central nervous system physiologically less aroused by external stimuli.

There have been several attempts to link the slowing of the alpha rhythm with the age-related slowing of behavior. Surwillo (1960, 1961) discovered an exceptionally strong negative correlation between alpha activity and reaction time for participants ranging from eighteen to seventy-two years of age. On the basis of these results, he proposed that the alpha rhythm represents the primary "biological clock" or "timing mechanism" that regulates how rapidly and effectively information can be processed and behavior initiated. Surwillo further championed the hypothesis that the major purpose of the alpha rhythm is to arouse the cortex. The elderly, because they have slower alpha rhythms, may be in a constant state of **underarousal.** It is the underaroused state of the older adult, Surwillo suggested, that is responsible for the motor and cognitive deficits seen in this age group.

A major criticism of Surwillo's position is that it was based on correlational evidence (remember that correlation does not equal causation). Woodruff (1975) put Surwillo's hypothesis to an experimental test. Using biofeedback techniques, she trained groups of young and elderly adults to either increase or decrease their baseline levels of alpha activity. Then, she presented the participants with a reaction-time task. Results indicated that participants who were taught to increase alpha activity had significantly faster reaction times than participants who were trained to reduce alpha activity.

Woodruff (1985) has commented that it remains unclear exactly why the alpha rhythm slows down in late adulthood. Also, it is difficult to determine if the slowing of alpha activity represents a cause or an effect of aging. Obrist (1972) has suggested that the slowing of alpha activity results from reduced blood flow to the brain. The argument is that reduced blood flow causes reduced amounts of oxygen to reach the brain, reductions in oxygen result in the loss of brain cells, and reductions in brain cells cause the alpha activity to slow. Indeed, when adults with and without arteriosclerosis are compared, differences in cerebral blood flow and alpha frequency are usually detected, with the diseased adults showing a slowing in these areas (Obrist and Bissell, 1955).

Remember box 2.1? It described an experiment (Eisdorfer et al., 1970) which showed that the elderly may be in a perpetual state of *overarousal.* Carl Eisdorfer and his colleagues determined that older adults were overaroused by examining the biochemical content of their blood. In fact, most of the studies regarding the overarousal hypothesis employ biochemical measures of arousal level. On the other hand, proponents of the underarousal hypothesis have focused their attention on bioelectric measures of arousal, such as the EEG. In the future, psychologists may have to decide which is the more valid way to measure arousal. Or they may have to develop a more multidimensional understanding of this construct.

Rather than use the EEG, some researchers (for example, Bashore, Osman, and Heffley, 1989; Strayer, Wickens, and Braune, 1987) have attempted to examine age-related changes in the brain by measuring **event-related responses (ERPs).** Changes in ERPs have been linked to changes in basic perceptual and cognitive processes (Coles, Gratton, Bashore, Eriksen, and Donchin, 1985). A typical ERP experiment might involve embedding a novel stimulus in a series of common stimuli and determining the extent of electrical change in the brain when the infrequent stimulus is detected. For example, an individual might be presented with a series of similar tones in which a small number of extremely different tones is inserted on a random basis. The person's task is to count the irregular tones.

A late-occurring ERP is called the **P300** brain wave. This brain wave occurs somewhere between 300 to 500 milliseconds after a stimulus has been presented. The onset of the P300 seems to signify that the person has recognized a stimulus and has evaluated the psychological significance of the stimulus. A number of investigations have shown a shift toward longer latency (the amount of time it takes a person to respond) of the P300 brain wave with advancing age (see, for example, Brent, Smith, Michaelewski, and Thompson, 1976; Ford, et al., 1979; Miller, Bashore, Farwell, and Donchin, 1987; Picton, Stuss, Champagne, and Nelson, 1984).

Also, it has been discovered that reaction time, but *not* P300 latency, is related to the response strategies that participants employ in an experiential task. Remember that older adults adopt a more conservative response strategy than younger adults do. The adoption of a conservative strategy by older adults would lead them to show longer reaction times than younger adults. Bashore, et al. (1989) and Strayer, et al., (1987) have shown that older and younger groups of adults differ much more on measures of reaction time than on P300 latency. This means that reaction-time tasks may lead researchers to overestimate the extent to which behavioral slowing in late adulthood is caused by changes in central processes. An inspection of the P300 data suggests that the age-related slowing of reaction time is due to decrements in peripheral processes (for example, slower response output) in combination with the adoption of a conservative response bias (putting greater emphasis on accuracy than speed).

Until now we have focused our attention on the whole brain and the cortex in particular. In the next section we will examine the neuron—the special type of cell that makes up the brain as well as the rest of the nervous system.

THE NEURON

The brain consists of a vast number of highly specialized cells called **neurons.** It has been estimated that there are approximately 100 billion neurons in the typical human brain (Weiss, 1973). This is certainly a staggering number! The power of the brain, however, does *not* come from the sheer number of neurons it possesses. Instead, it derives from the complex manner by which the neurons connect with one another. Each neuron has the potential to interact with between five- and ten-thousand other neurons (Weiss, 1973). It has been calculated that the number of possible interconnections between the cells of the brain is greater than the number of atomic particles that make up the known universe (Thompson, 1986). Every instance of thinking, remembering, speaking, and creating represents the activity of an intricately connected network of neurons.

Major Components of the Neuron

There are several different types of neurons in the brain and nervous system. All of these different types of neurons, however, share the same three basic parts: the soma, the dendrites, and the axon. Each of these three structures may be seen in figure 4.3.

The **soma,** or cell body, may be thought of as the "brain" of the neuron. It contains the nucleus of the cell and directs the manufacture of the substances that are needed for growth, maintenance, and communication. The branchlike or tree-like structures to the left of the soma in figure 4.3 are the **dendrites.** The dendrites may be thought of as an extension of the soma. They are the receiving part of the neuron; they collect information and send it on to the cell body. In the cortex, the

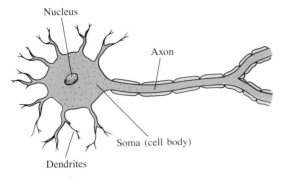

Figure 4.3   A typical neuron.

dendrites of many neurons are covered with thousands of tiny little extensions referred to as dendritic spines. The sprouting of dendritic spines over the course of development increases the receptive surface of the dendrite. This allows the neuron to receive information from an ever-expanding number of other neurons. The structure to the right of the soma in figure 4.3 is called the **axon.** Although a large number of dendrites may branch out from a soma, there is only one axon per neuron. The axon is much thinner and longer than a dendrite and resembles an ultrathin, long tube. The end portion of an axon usually branches into several individual terminals. These are either called synaptic terminals or synaptic knobs. Despite the minute size of most neurons, some axons are three feet in length—extending from the brain to the base of the spinal cord. The major function of the axon is to carry information away from the cell body to other neurons. Thus, within a typical nerve cell, information is received by the dendrites, monitored by the soma, and transmitted by the axon.

The information transmitted down the length of an axon takes the form of a brief electrical impulse or wave called an **action potential.** This is why axons are covered with a layer of fat called the **myelin sheath.** This fatty covering acts as an insulator so that a direct, efficient action potential may be transmitted. Action potentials obey what neuroscientists call the "all-or-none" law. This means that once a cell receives a critical level of stimulation, it initiates (or fires) the fastest, strongest action potential possible. A neuron either stays at rest or produces the most powerful action potential it can muster—it knows no in-between state. A runner, unlike a neuron, can run at different speeds from a light jog to an all-out sprint. A neuron knows only one speed.

Neural Communication and Neurotransmitters

Neurons do not form connections by physically touching one another. There is always an empty space or gap between the axon terminals of one cell and the dendritic spines of another cell. This space, called the synaptic cleft, is very, very small—

only about *20 billionths of a meter wide.* But, as Richard Thompson (1986) has stated, "It is always there." The more generic name for this small distance between neurons is the **synapse.**

How two nerve cells are functionally connected at a synapse is one of the most fascinating revelations of modern-day science. Once an electrical impulse or action potential reaches the end of an axon, a special chemical substance called a **neurotransmitter** is released from the axon terminal to flow across the synaptic cleft. These neurotransmitters, because they have a specific chemical structure, fit into specialized slots on the dendrites of the receptor cell—just as a key fits into a lock. Once the amount of neurotransmitter picked up by a receptor cell surpasses a critical threshold, an action potential is initiated. This cycle may repeat itself over and over again along a network of functionally interconnected neurons.

There are dozens of different neurotransmitters that cells in different areas of the brain use for communicative purposes. One of the most well-understood (and important) neurotransmitters is **acetylcholine** or **ACh.** ACh is manufactured within individual neurons out of a substance called choline. Choline is found in such common foods as egg yolks and several different vegetables. ACh is released from the synaptic knob of an axon, travels across the synaptic cleft, and stimulates the dendrites of another nerve cell. Once ACh reaches the dendritic spines on the receptor neuron, it is important that the ACh be immediately deactivated. Otherwise, it could continue to stimulate other neurons and the brain would go out of control, constantly firing burst after burst of activity. The deactivation of ACh is accomplished by an enzyme called **acetylcholinesterase** or **AchE.** Within a few microseconds, AchE deactivates ACh by transforming ACh back into choline. Then, the choline may reenter a neuron to be turned back into ACh.

ACh is an extremely important neurotransmitter for scientists interested in the aging process. The neurons in those parts of the brain responsible for memory (for example, the hippocampus) use ACh as a neurotransmitter. And, as we shall see in subsequent sections, there seems to be a significant reduction of ACh in the brain structures of adults who suffer from Alzheimer's disease.

Another important neurotransmitter is **dopamine** or **DA.** It is produced by a cluster of cells collectively called the **substantia nigra,** which is located in the innermost region of the brain. DA is transported from the substantia nigra to various cortical locations. There, specific groups of neurons use DA as their primary neurotransmitter. Some older persons (about 0.5 percent of the older population) suffer from a neurological disorder called **Parkinson's disease** (Kolb and Whishaw, 1985). This disorder, which is caused by a deterioration of the substantia nigra and a concommitant reduction in available DA, is marked by the presence of severe motor symptoms. These symptoms include constant stereotypical movements of the arms and/or legs, muscular rigidity, difficulty in initiating voluntary body movements, and difficulty in maintaining posture and walking. Initial treatment for Parkinson's disease involves the administration of **L-Dopa,** a drug that the brain converts into

DA. Unfortunately, as the disease progresses and the patient's symptoms become more debilitating, L-Dopa therapy becomes less and less effective. Recently, some scientists have begun to experiment with transplanting brain tissue as a means of treating patients with advanced Parkinson's disease. See box 4.3 for more information about this exciting line of research.

Age-Related Neuronal Changes

There are a number of changes in the neuronal structure of the brain that accompany normal aging. Overall, the brain loses neurons, and therefore loses weight, as it ages. Unlike other cells in the body, however, neurons do not have the capacity to divide and be replaced. It has been estimated that by age eighty, the brain has decreased in weight by nearly 15 percent (Cote, 1981). Anderson, Hubbard, Coghill, and Slidders (1983) as well as Henderson, Tomlinson, and Gibson (1980) have suggested that about 1 percent of the neurons in the human cortex are lost each year after age seventy. And as Bondareff (1985) has noted, the loss of neurons results in a loss of neuronal interconnections. It is the loss of these interconnections, not the loss of neurons per se, that is functionally important for the aging organism.

It should be emphasized that the brain has a great deal of reserve capacity. Thus, despite the inevitable neuronal loss that accompanies aging, the older brain may lose a rather small amount of functional ability (Labouvie-Vief, 1985). Moreover, Black et al. (1987) have suggested that through a variety of extrinsic factors such as cerebrovascular support (for example, increased transport of oxygen through the blood by the extra intake of sugar, physical exercise, improved nutrition, and so on) the functional capacity of the aging brain may be maintained or even enhanced.

Some scientists believe that the most significant aspects of the aging brain, as well as the processes of aging, may be discovered by examining the microscopic changes that take place within and between neurons. Researchers have discovered four prominent changes in the brains of aged humans: the accumulation of lipofuscin, granulovacuolar particles, neurofibrillary tangles, and senile plaques.

Lipofuscin is a yellowish or brownish pigment. As individuals age, more and more deposits of lipofuscin accumulate within the neurons of specific parts of the brain (Bondareff, 1977, 1985). However, there is no strong evidence to prove that an increase in lipofuscin impairs the functioning of the neurons in normal elderly adults (Cote, 1981; Petit, 1982). Interestingly, it has been shown that individuals who suffer from a vitamin E deficiency display above-average amounts of lipofuscin. However, vitamin E supplements have not been found to decrease the accumulation of lipofuscin or extend longevity (Hayflich, 1985; Cohen, 1988).

Granulovacuolar particles are small granules of matter in the soma and dendrites of degenerating neurons, especially in the hippocampus. The origin, effects, and functions of these particles are still unknown (Cote, 1981; Petit, 1982).

BOX 4.3

GRAFTING NEURAL TISSUE INTO THE AGING BRAIN

The thought of transplanting brain tissue conjures up visions of a horror film. Grafting brain tissue, however, is no longer science fiction. The results of experimental research on this topic may prove to have tremendously important ramifications for humans who suffer from a variety of neurological diseases. Research on neural transplantation took a giant step in 1979 when Perlow and his associates (Perlow et al., 1979) created a lesion in the substantia nigra of a healthy rat. Predictably, the animal displayed a number of motor abnormalities that were reminiscent of the symptoms of Parkinson's disease in humans. Next, Perlow et al. transplanted tissue from the substantia nigra of a donor fetal rat into the brain of the surgically diseased animal. Results indicated that the grafted neurons continued to live in the brain of the host animal. Furthermore, the transplanted cells produced dopamine. This led to a significant reduction in the rat's Parkinsonian-like symptoms.

In a somewhat similar line of research, Freed and his colleagues (Freed et al., 1981) surgically induced Parkinsonian symptoms in a rat by lesioning the substantia nigra. Next, they removed cells from the adrenal gland of the same rat and transplanted them into the rat's substantia nigra (cells in the adrenal gland, which is located above the kidney, also produce dopamine). This technique also resulted in a profound decrease in the animal's motor abnormalities.

In 1987, a team headed by Ignacio Madrazo (Madrazo et al., 1987) in Mexico City removed the right adrenal gland from a thirty-five-year-old man suffering from Parkinson's disease and transplanted some of this tissue into his brain. Before the surgery the man was confined to a wheelchair. After the operation, his condition steadily improved. Ten months after the surgery, he was able to play soccer with his son! Overall, 18 patients were treated by Madrazo and his colleagues. One of these patients was showing steady improvement but died unexpectedly of a heart attack forty-three days after his surgery. Interestingly, an autopsy revealed that the adrenal tissue never successfully grafted into this patient's brain. This led to the speculation that the improvement observed in all of Madrazo's patients may have been due to something other than (or in addition to) the grafting of adrenal cells (Lewin, 1987). Since the publication of

---

Neurofibrillary tangles are one of the most common and dramatic histological changes in the brains of the elderly. These tangles are most likely to appear in the cortex and the hippocampus (Reisberg, 1981). To understand the nature of neurofibrillary tangles, it is important to understand that long, straight, threadlike fibers or microtubules exist within neurons. The function of these fibers is to transport chemical substances between the distant parts of the neuron. With advanced age, the long, straight tubules become twisted and distorted. These tangles progres-

these results, over 180 Parkinson's patients in the United States and Canada were given adrenal transplants. Overall, these individuals only experienced modest benefits from the surgery (Marx, 1990). Furthermore, a significant number of these patients displayed profound side-effects (such as bladder infections) because of the surgery. Thus, the efficacy of adrenal transplants seems questionable.

More recently, a group of Swedish researchers headed by Olle Lindvall and Anders Bjorkland (Lindvall et al., 1990) provided conclusive proof that neural grafts may be used to treat Parkinson's disease. They transplanted dopamine-producing cells taken from four human fetuses (approximately eight to nine weeks gestational age) into the brain of a forty-nine-year-old patient who was severely affected by Parkinson's disease. For reasons still largely unknown, fetal transplantations have an unusually good chance of being accepted by the brain of a recipient (see Cohen, 1988). At the time of this writing, Lindvall and his associates have observed the patient for a period of five months after the surgery. They have seen a progressive and significant improvement in this man's condition. Most importantly, by the use of PETT scanning techniques, they have conclusively shown that the grafted fetal cells survived in the patient's brain! Thus, it seems as if fetal nerve grafts are superior to adrenal implants.

Lindvall et al. (1990) do not suggest that the transplantation of fetal neuronal tissue should immediately become the standard treatment for Parkinson's disease. There are obviously a number of important ethical issues involved in the grafting of fetal tissue. In fact, the U.S. government has banned the use of federal funds for this type of research.

Could there be alternatives to the use of fetal tissue for transplant surgery? Cohen (1988) has suggested that future researchers may use the principles of genetic engineering (recombinant DNA techniques) to produce cells that manufacture dopamine. These cells could then be transplanted into the brain of an afflicted person. Also, it has been suggested that damaged parts of the brain may be replaced with implanted computer microchips (Freed et al., 1985).

sively fill the soma and push the nucleus to one side. They also extend into the dendrite and axon. The presence of tangles may ultimately lead to the dysfunction and death of neurons. The growth of neurofibrillary tangles represents one of the most important features of the aging brain. It is hypothesized that the presence of these tangles may contribute to the slower responsiveness of the central nervous system (Cote, 1981; Reisberg, 1981; Damasio and Van Hoesen, 1986).

Senile plaques are spherical masses of a substance called **amyloid.** With aging, these plaques increasingly appear between neurons. The amyloid forms a core that is surrounded by degenerating axons and dendrites (Cote, 1981; Petit, 1982). Plaques are extracellular—they exist outside of neurons. They are frequently found at synapses and can certainly interfere with normal neuronal communication. Similar to neurofibrillary tangles, plaques are most likely to be found in the hippocampus and cortex. It has been suggested that the increased incidence of plaques and tangles may be related to memory loss among the elderly (Reisberg, 1981; Scheibel and Wechsler, 1986). Furthermore, it has been discovered that amyloid plaques increasingly occur in the brains of several different aging mammals, including monkeys, orangutans, polar bears, and dogs (Selkoe, Bell, Podlisny, Price, and Cork, 1987). Aged animals may help us form biochemical models of human aging. Finally, recent evidence (Whitson, Selkoe, and Cotman, 1989) suggests that the production of amyloid may represent a neuron's attempt to defend itself against the degenerative effects of aging. This defensive strategy ultimately backfires, and senile plaques form.

In the next section, we will describe the brain changes that take place in Alzheimer's disease, a debilitating and fatal neurological illness. We will contrast these brain changes with those that take place during the course of normal aging.

UNDERSTANDING ALZHEIMER'S DISEASE

The symptoms of **Alzheimer's disease** or **AD** were first described by a German physician, Alois Alzheimer, in 1907. Alzheimer's disease is a form of dementia; **dementia** is a global term for any neurological disorder whose primary symptomology is the deterioration of mental functioning. Dementia has often erroneously been referred to as senility. *Senility* is an overused and imprecise layperson's term that is used to summarize all of the debilitating personality and cognitive changes that may be observed in the elderly. To complicate things even further, several physicians and psychologists have begun to refer to Alzheimer's disease as *senile dementia of the Alzheimer's type* or *SDAT.* We have chosen to use the more general term *Alzheimer's disease* or *AD* in this text. In this section we will describe some of the most current research findings regarding AD, the disorder sometimes called the "disease of the century."

Description of Alzheimer's Disease

AD is arguably the most severe and devastating of all of the different types of dementia. It is a degenerative brain disease that is the most common cause of cognitive failure in older adulthood (Reisberg, Ferris, deLeon, and Crook, 1985; Selkoe, et al., 1987). The elderly person with AD loses the ability to remember, recognize,

Table 4.1

SOCIETAL COSTS OF ALZHEIMER'S DISEASE AND OTHER ILLNESSES

Disease	*Estimated Societal Cost*	*1989 Federal Funding*
Alzheimer's Disease	$51–$79 billion (1985)	$120 million
Heart Disease	$88 billion (1989)	$640 million
AIDS	$66 billion (1991)	$607 million
Cancer	$71.5 billion (1985)	$1.45 billion

Aging Research and Training News, March 27, 1989, p. 43, published by Business Publishers, Inc., 951 Pershing Dr., Silver Spring, MD 20910-4464.

and reason. In the final stages of the disease, the afflicted person develops profound physical as well as mental disabilities and typically needs institutional care. At present, there is no cure for this disease. Death usually occurs within five to ten years after the initial onset of symptoms, regardless of the age at which it strikes (Reisberg, 1987). It has been estimated that AD is the fourth leading cause of death for adults in the United States (Katzman, 1986) and that approximately 5 percent of the 30 million adults over sixty-five years of age suffer from AD (Reisberg, 1987; Thompson, 1986). Given the fact that the population of the United States, as well as most Westernized societies, is gradually aging, AD will become more prevalent in the future and the cost of caring for AD patients will rise dramatically. Currently, there are more elderly people in nursing homes than in hospitals (1.3 million versus 1 million). It has been estimated that 58 percent of the residents of nursing homes suffer from AD (Reisberg, 1987).

Several health economists have tried to calculate the monetary impact of AD. It was estimated that in 1985, approximately 80 billion dollars were lost due to AD and related dementias. This estimate includes 13.3 billion dollars spent on direct patient care (Cartwright, Haung, and Hu, 1988). See table 4.1 for information concerning the societal costs of caring for AD patients as well as those with other life-threatening disorders. The table also contains information about the extent to which the federal government funds research projects designed to find the causes and cures for these disorders. Based on the data in table 4.1, it would seem as if research on AD is dramatically underfunded.

In the past, AD was defined as a type of dementia not associated with old age. AD was thought to be a neurological disease that occurred during middle age and was thus viewed as a type of "presenile dementia." Furthermore, it was discovered that AD only afflicted an exceptionally small number of middle-aged adults. Thus, AD was thought of as a very rare disorder that the typical older person had little need to worry about. It was believed that true senility or dementia was a totally different disease. Senility was thought to be a disorder of old age, and it was believed to be caused by vascular disorders such as cerebral arteriosclerosis (that is, a hardening of the arteries that feed the brain). In the late 1960s and early 1970s, however, it was discovered that the symptoms and causes of dementia in both middle-aged and elderly adults were identical (Petit, 1982; Wurtman, 1985)! This

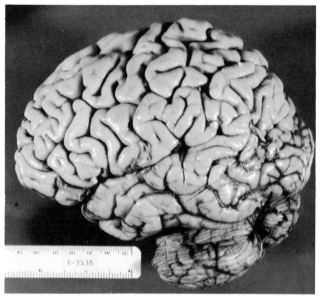

(a)

Examples of (a) a normal human brain and (b) the brain of a patient with Alzheimer's disease. Note the widening of the sulci and shrinkage of the gyri of the cortex in the case of Alzheimer's disease. The motor cortex and visual cortex are less affected than the rest. (c) Light microscopic images of senile plaques (SP) and neurofibrillary tangles (NFT) from the brain of a patient with Alzheimer's disease.

finding revolutionized our ideas about the prevalence and seriousness of AD. Scientists began to realize that AD in old age had been misdiagnosed and misunderstood for an extremely long time.

To gain a general understanding of AD, read box 4.4—a reproduction of a fact sheet recently prepared by the National Association of Alzheimer's Disease and Related Disorders.

Some of the most interesting and important findings about AD are the types of brain changes that appear in patients with this disorder. Specifically, AD patients have an excessive number of senile plaques and neurofibrillary tangles. These plaques and tangles are spread throughout the brain, but they are most concentrated in the hippocampus and the cortex (Petit, 1982; Reisberg, 1981; Cote, 1981; Scheibel and Wechsler, 1986). Remember that the presence of plaques and tangles are two of the prominent features of normal aging. This suggests that there is a quantitative, rather than a qualitative, difference between the brains of the healthy elderly and those with AD—the brains of AD patients have *more* plaques and tangles than those contained in normal, aged brains. This has led to the speculation (Cote, 1981) that AD may really be "accelerated, normal aging"! Think about the implication of this statement. If we live long enough—if we begin to approach the

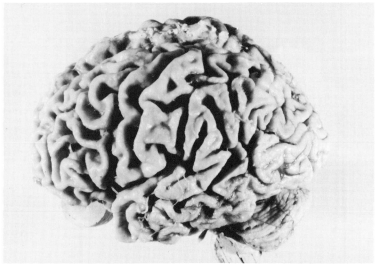

(*b*)

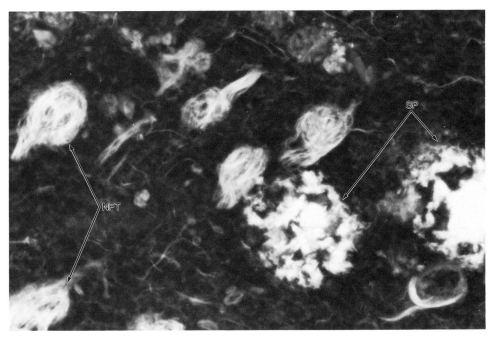

(*c*)

BOX 4.4

FACTS ABOUT ALZHEIMER'S DISEASE

DEFINITION AND SCOPE

Alzheimer's disease (pronounced Altz-hi-merz) is a progressive, degenerative disease that attacks the brain and results in impaired memory, thinking, and behavior. It affects an estimated four million American adults. It is the most common form of dementing illness. More than 100,000 people die of Alzheimer's disease annually in the U.S., which makes it the fourth leading cause of death in American adults, after heart disease, cancer, and stroke.

The disease, first described by Alois Alzheimer in 1907, knows no social or economic boundaries and affects men and women almost equally. Most victims are over 65; however, Alzheimer's disease can strike in the forties and fifties. Most Alzheimer's disease victims are cared for at home, although many persons in nursing homes have dementia. Alzheimer's disease is devastating for both victims and their families and has been called "the disease of the century."

SYMPTOMS

Symptoms of Alzheimer's disease include a gradual memory loss, decline in ability to perform routine tasks, impairment of judgment, disorientation, personality change, difficulty in learning, and loss of language skills. There is variation in the rate of change from person to person. The disease eventually renders its victims totally incapable of caring for themselves.

CAUSE(S) AND RESEARCH

The cause of Alzheimer's disease is not known and is currently receiving intensive scientific investigation. Suspected causes include a genetic predisposition, a slow virus or other infectious agents, environmental toxins, and immunologic changes. Other factors also are under investigation.

Scientists are applying the newest knowledge and research techniques in molecular genetics, pathology, virology, immunology, toxicology, neurology, psychiatry, pharmacology, biochemistry, and epidemiology to find the cause, treatment, and cure for Alzheimer's disease and related disorders.

DIAGNOSIS

There is no single clinical test to identify Alzheimer's disease. Before diagnosis of the disease is made, other conditions must be excluded. These include potentially reversible conditions such as depression, adverse drug reactions, metabolic changes, nutritional deficiencies, head injuries, and stroke.

Each person with possible Alzheimer's disease symptoms should have a thorough evaluation. The evaluation should include a complete health history, thorough physical examination, neurological and mental status assessments, and diagnostic tests including blood studies, urinalysis, electrocardiogram, and chest Xrays. Other studies often recommended include computerized tomography (CT Scan), electroencephalography (EEG), removal from medication, formal psychiatric assessment, neuropsychological testing, and, occasionally, examination of the cerebrospinal fluid by spinal tap. While this evaluation may provide a clinical diagnosis, confirmation of Alzheimer's disease requires examination of brain tissue, which is usually performed at autopsy.

TREATMENT

Although no cure for Alzheimer's disease is available at present, good planning and medical and social management can ease the burdens on the patient and family. Appropriate medication can lessen agitation, anxiety, and unpredictable behavior, improve sleeping patterns, and treat depression. Physical exercise and social activity are important, as are proper nutrition and health maintenance. A calm and well-structured environment may help the afflicted person to maintain as much comfort and dignity as possible.

ECONOMIC IMPACT

The course of the disease usually runs from two to ten years, but can take as long as twenty years. During the latter stages of the disease, twenty-four hour care is required with regard to daily activities such as eating, grooming, and toileting. The financing of care for Alzheimer's disease—including costs of diagnosis, treatment, nursing home care, informal care, and lost wages—is estimated to be more than $80 billion each year. The federal government covers $4.4 billion and the states cover another $4.1 billion. Much of the remaining costs are borne by patients and their families.

A nationwide twenty-four hour information and referral line links families who need assistance with nearby Alzheimer's Association chapters. Those interested in help may call the Alzheimer's Association at 800–621–0379 (Illinois residents call 800-572-6037).

upper end of the potential human life span—we may face an ever-increasing risk of suffering from AD.

Furthermore, AD is difficult to diagnose. There are a number of other biological and psychological disorders which closely imitate the symptoms of AD. For example, individuals who are clinically depressed or who suffer from curable dementias display some of the same behavioral symptoms as AD patients (Heston and White, 1983; Zarit and Zarit, 1983). (We will provide a description of a number of different dementias, besides AD, that commonly afflict older adults in chapter 12 of this text.) The only way to make a certain diagnosis of AD is by an autopsy (Heston and White, 1983). In this procedure, brain tissue is analyzed to determine the presence and location of excessive plaques, tangles, and cell loss. Prior to a patient's death and autopsy, Reisberg (1987) notes, clinicians make the diagnosis of AD by exclusion of other causes (that is, all other diagnoses are ruled out and nothing else is known that could explain the symptoms). As yet, there is no clear diagnosis by inclusion, or by a listing of the physical and behavioral symptoms that must be present if AD is to be diagnosed.

The Stages of Alzheimer's Disease

In AD there seems to be a predictable, progressive decline in specific areas of psychological, physiological, and social functioning. Reisberg and his colleagues (Reisberg, Ferris, and Franssen, 1985; Reisberg and Bornstein, 1986) have developed a **Functional Assessment Staging system** (FAST staging system) to categorize these losses. The advantage of such an approach is that it provides clinicians and family members with the information necessary to provide appropriate intervention and to identify the projected course of the disease. Table 4.2 contains a description of the FAST staging system. This table lists the approximate time spent in each stage, the functional loss associated with each stage, and the mean duration of each stage. The early stages (1, 2, and 3) are *not* specifically descriptive of AD. For example, stages 1 and 2 are included to inform professionals of the typical patterns seen in normal aging. Stage 3 describes an early confused state that may be characteristic of a number of possible disorders. The patterns emergent in the remaining four stages clearly reflect AD.

A more in-depth description of the clinical manifestations of AD may be found by examining the *Global Deterioration Scale* (table 4.3). The numbers on the far left of the table refer to the FAST stages described in table 4.2.

Causes and Treatments of Alzheimer's Disease

At present, no one knows the actual cause of AD. Researchers know that there are excessive amounts of plaques and tangles found in the brains of AD patients. But they are still uncertain as to whether plaques and tangles are a cause or an effect of AD. Nevertheless, a number of different theories have been advanced to explain the development of this disease. McLachlan (1982) has suggested AD is caused by

As Alzheimer's disease progresses, the person needs help performing even the simplest daily function.

Table 4.2

FUNCTIONAL ASSESSMENT STAGING (FAST STAGING) OF ALZHEIMER'S DISEASE: CORRESPONDENCE OF FAST STAGES WITH NORMAL HUMAN DEVELOPMENT AND ESTIMATED TIME COURSE OF PROGRESSION

FAST Stage and Characteristics	Clinical Diagnosis	Approximate Age at Which Function Is Acquired	Estimated Mean Duration in Survivors
1. No functional decrement	Normal adult	Adult	50 years
2. Subjective word difficulties	Normal aged adult	—	15 years
3. Decreased function in demanding employment settings	Compatible with possible incipient Alzheimer's disease in minority of cases	Young adult	7 years
4. Decreased ability to perform complex tasks such as handling finances or planning dinner for guests	Mild Alzheimer's disease	8 years to adolescence	2 years
5. Requires assistance in choosing proper clothing	Moderate Alzheimer's disease	5–7 years	18 months
6. (a) Difficulty putting on clothing properly	Moderately severe Alzheimer's disease	5 years	5 months
(b) Requires assistance bathing		4 years	5 months
(c) Inability to handle mechanics of toileting		48 months	5 months
(d) Urinary incontinence		36–54 months	4 months
(e) Fecal incontinence		24–36 months	10 months
7. (a) Ability to speak limited to about six words	Severe Alzheimer's disease	15 months	12 months
(b) Intelligible vocabulary limited to a single word		12 months	18 months
(c) Ambulatory ability lost		12 months	12 months
(d) Ability to sit up lost		24–40 weeks	12 months
(e) Ability to smile lost		8–16 weeks	18 months
(f) Ability to hold up head lost		4–12 weeks	Not applicable

From B. Reisberg and J. Borenstein, "Clinical Diagnosis of Alzheimer's Disease" in *Drug Therapy*, 16:43–59. Copyright © 1986 BMI/McGraw-Hill, Inc., New York, NY.

a slow virus that infects the brain. Other researchers have discovered that one type of AD runs in families. They have developed a genetic model to explain the cause of the *early-onset familial* form of AD. However, this variation of AD may account for only about 10 percent of the total cases (Jarvik, 1987). In a tremendously important study, Peter St. George-Hyslop and his associates (St. George-Hyslop, et al., 1987) discovered that the familial type of AD is associated with a defective gene located on chromosome 21. Furthermore, Rudolph Tanzi and his colleagues (Tanzi, et al., 1987) found that the gene responsible for the production of amyloid (the core material of senile plaques) is also located on chromosome 21! This is most interesting since it has been well documented that nearly every individual suffering from Down syndrome (most frequently related to extra chromosome material on the 21st pair) begins to develop the biochemical and psychological symptoms of AD by about age forty (Kolata, 1985; Wurtman, 1985). Thus, the excessive amyloid in both AD and Down syndrome patients may have a common origin—chromosome 21. However, as Jarvik (1987) has noted, the genes responsible for amyloid production, early-onset familial AD, and Down syndrome are positioned in very different locations on chromosome 21. Thus, the specific relationship between AD, amyloid production, and Down syndrome is still a genetic mystery.

Another interesting finding is that the neurons in the hippocampus and particular areas of the neocortex (for example, the temporal lobe) are among the most negatively affected parts of the brain in AD patients. These portions of the brain play a crucial role in memory. Furthermore, these brain structures employ ACh as a neurotransmitter. It has been documented that the brains of individuals with AD contain significantly less ACh than those of normal individuals. This has led to the hypothesis that a reduction in the ability to produce ACh may cause AD (Butcher and Woolf, 1986; Coyle, Price, and DeLong, 1983; Wurtman, 1985). Again, however, it is difficult to tell if a decrement in ACh is a cause or an effect of AD.

Because we don't know the specific cause of Alzheimer's disease, it has been difficult to develop effective treatments that cure or prevent it. There is one promising approach, however, as to how some of the cognitive symptoms of AD (memory loss, confusion, and so on) may be relieved or greatly reduced. Initially, there were two variations to this approach. The first variation was based on the idea that the symptoms of AD should lessen if patients could produce more ACh. This led physicians to advise patients with AD to eat foods rich in choline. (Remember that choline is a food substance that the brain transforms into ACh.) Unfortunately, this approach has not produced any significant changes in patients' functioning. There are a number of drugs that can also increase ACh levels in the brain. But these drugs are dangerous, and it is not advisable to administer them to humans (Thompson, 1986). The second variation of the ACh approach was based on the theory that patients' AD symptoms should dissipate if they are given a drug that inhibits the activity of AChE. (Remember that AChE is the chemical responsible for the synaptic absorption and deactivation of ACh.) The inhibition of AChE should allow small amounts of ACh to gradually accumulate on the receptor sites of neurons. These small amounts of ACh would be quickly deactivated if AChE production was at its

Table 4.3

GLOBAL DETERIORATION SCALE FOR AGE-ASSOCIATED COGNITIVE DECLINE AND ALZHEIMER'S DISEASE

GDS Stage	Clinical Phase	Clinical Characteristics	Diagnosis
1. No cognitive decline	Normal	No subjective complaints of memory deficit; no memory deficit evident on clinical interview.	Normal
2. Very mild cognitive decline	Forgetfulness	Subjective complaints of memory deficit, most frequently in the following areas: (a) forgetting where one has placed familiar objects; (b) forgetting names one formerly knew well. No objective evidence of memory deficit on clinical interview; no objective deficits in employment or social situations; appropriate concern with respect to symptomatology.	Normal for age
3. Mild cognitive decline	Early confusional	Earliest clear-cut deficits; manifestations in more than one of the following areas: (a) patient may have gotten lost when traveling to an unfamiliar location; (b) coworkers become aware of patient's relatively poor performance; (c) word- and name-finding deficits become evident to intimates; (d) patient may read a passage or a book and retain relatively little material; (e) patient may demonstrate decreased facility in remembering names upon introduction to new people; (f) patient may have lost or misplaced an object of value; (g) concentration deficit may be evident on clinical testing. Objective evidence of memory deficit obtained only with an intensive interview conducted by a trained diagnostician; decreased performance in demanding employment and social settings; denial begins to become manifest in patient; mild to moderate anxiety accompanies symptoms.	Compatible with possible incipient Alzheimer's disease in a minority of cases
4. Moderate cognitive decline	Late confusional	Clear-cut deficit on careful clinical interview; deficit manifest in the following areas: (a) decreased knowledge of current and recent events; (b) may exhibit some deficit in memory of personal history; (c) concentration deficit elicited on serial subtractions; (d) decreased ability to travel, handle finances, and so on.	Mild Alzheimer's disease

| 5. Moderately severe cognitive decline | Early dementia | Frequently no deficit in the following areas: (a) orientation to time and person; (b) recognition of familiar persons and faces; (c) ability to travel to familiar locations. Inability to perform complex tasks; denial is dominant defense mechanism; flattening of affect and withdrawal from challenging situations.

Patients can no longer survive without some assistance; patients are unable during interview to recall a major relevant aspect of their current lives: for example, their address or telephone number of many years, the names of close members of their family (such as grandchildren), the name of the high school or college they attended.

Frequently some disorientation to time (date, day of week, season) or to place; an educated person may have difficulty counting backward from forty by fours or from twenty by twos.

Persons at this stage retain knowledge of many major facts regarding themselves and others; they invariably know their own name and generally know their spouse's and children's names; they require no assistance with toileting or eating, but may have some difficulty choosing the proper clothing to wear. | Moderate Alzheimer's disease |
| 6. Severe cognitive decline | Middle dementia | May occasionally forget the name of the spouse upon whom they are entirely dependent for survival; are largely unaware of all recent events and experiences in their lives; retain some knowledge of their past lives, but this is very sketchy. Generally unaware of their surroundings, the year, the season, and so on; may have difficulty counting from ten backward and, sometimes, forward; require some assistance with activities of daily living, for example, may become incontinent, require travel assistance but occasionally display ability to travel to familiar locations; diurnal rhythm frequently disturbed; almost always recall their own name; frequently continue to be able to distinguish familiar from unfamiliar persons in their environment. | Moderately severe Alzheimer's disease |

Table 4.3 *Continued*

GOS Stage	Clinical Phase	Clinical Characteristics	Diagnosis
		Personality and emotional changes occur; these are quite variable and include: (a) delusional behavior (for example, patients may accuse their spouse of being an impostor, may talk to imaginary figures in the environment, or to their own reflections in the mirror); (b) obsessive symptoms (for example, person may continually repeat simple cleaning activities); (c) anxiety symptoms, agitation, and even previously nonexistent violent behavior may occur; (d) cognitive abulia (that is, loss of willpower because individual cannot carry a thought long enough to determine a purposeful course of action).	
7. Very severe cognitive decline	Late dementia	All verbal abilities are lost; frequently there is no speech at all—only grunting; incontinent of urine; requires assistance toileting and feeding; loses basic psychomotor skills (for example, ability to walk); it appears the brain no longer is able to tell the body what to do.	Severe Alzheimer's disease

From B. Reisberg and J. Borenstein, "Clinical Diagnosis of Alzheimer's Disease" in *Drug Therapy*, 16:43–59. Copyright © 1986 BMI/McGraw-Hill, Inc., New York, NY.

normal level. Once Ach levels reach a critical threshold, the receptor cell fires—and the person remembers, thinks, and reasons. William Summers and his colleagues (Summers et al., 1986) have gathered impressive results using this strategy. They administered THA (tetrahydroaminoacridine), a drug that inhibits AChE, to a group of AD patients. Compared to a control group, the patients administered THA showed significant improvement on a number of cognitive measures. Furthermore, some of the members of the treatment group were even capable of resuming normal activities such as homemaking, golfing, holding down a part-time job, and so on. THA, like other **palliative** treatments, only treats the symptoms, not the causes, of AD. It helps patients function in a more effective manner. But unfortunately, as with all palliative treatments, the underlying disease progresses and the AD patient ultimately dies. Moreover, despite the promise of THA, recent clinical trials have revealed an unacceptable incidence of liver damage in patients who have received this drug. Quite clearly, a great deal of work must be done before we can cure AD or even treat its cognitive symptoms.

The picture is somewhat brighter when one considers the noncognitive symptoms associated with AD, such as paranoia. Reisberg (1986, 1987) suggests that these symptoms may be treated by using various drugs that have proven effective in psychiatric settings.

Most assuredly, a diagnosis of Alzheimer's disease spells a number of significant problems for the victim's spouse, family, and friends. Therefore, psychologists are concerned with providing care and support for the individuals who will survive the patient (Zarit, Anthony, and Boutselis, 1987). It has been well documented that there are profound physical, emotional, and financial costs to the family members of AD patients (Brody, 1985; Zarit, Todd, and Zarit, 1986). It has even been suggested that families are the "hidden victims" of AD (Zarit, Orr, and Zarit, 1985). Increasing awareness of AD and the availability of community support groups help provide for the needs of concerned relatives. Table 4.4 provides a description of some of the management strategies that may be considered for patients in the different FAST stages.

This concludes our second chapter exploring the biological aspects of adult development and aging. Most certainly, there is a great deal to learn about adult behavior by studying the biological processes that sustain it. However, we do not wish to reduce all psychological functioning to biological or biochemical processes. In the remainder of this text, therefore, we will focus more attention on the psychological dimensions of adult development and aging.

Summary

The term *sensorimotor development* refers to the sensory systems that input information from the environment and the motor systems that enable us to perform physical actions in the environment. Vision and hearing are the two most important sensory systems in adulthood. Some decline in vision is characteristic during the middle adult years. Visual decline in late adulthood is characteristic of most individuals and can be traced to physiological

Table 4.4

TREATMENT IMPLICATIONS FOR AD PATIENTS IN FAST STAGES

Stage 1: No treatment necessary.

Stage 2: No treatment necessary.

Stage 3: Advise a withdrawal from overly complex and anxiety-arousing situations; basic living skills remain functionally adaptive.

Stage 4: Maximize personally adaptive functional skills, and monitor areas in which concerns arise such as structured travel and leisure activities and wearing identification bracelets and name tags in clothes. Provide financial supervision.

Stage 5: Independent living in the community a great risk; need for home monitoring (night and day) and direct supervision such as Adult Day Care. Provide continuous support groups and time off for the caregiver(s).

Stage 6: Full-time home health care required to assist in management of bathing and toileting needs. Possible need for psychiatric drugs to combat agitation, paranoia, delusions, and so on. Develop strategies to minimize emotional stress in caregiver(s).

Stage 7: Full enrollment in community or institutional setting is mandatory to cope with fundamental loss in daily living skills: self-feeding, swallowing, comprehension and production of language, ambulation, sitting up, smiling. Encouragement to caregivers arriving at this decision.

From B. Reisberg, et al., ''Patient and Caregiver Management'' in *Drug Therapy,* 16:65–93. Copyright © 1986 BMI/McGraw-Hill, Inc., New York, NY.

changes in the visual system, including changes which limit the quality and intensity of light reaching the retina. It is important to make a distinction between visual acuity and contrast sensitivity. With increasing age, important changes take place in both contrast sensitivity and visual acuity.

Hearing usually reaches its peak in adolescence and remains reasonably stable during early adulthood, but in middle adulthood it may start to decline. Less than 20 percent of individuals between forty-five and fifty-four years of age have a hearing problem, but for those between seventy-five and seventy-nine, the figure rises to 75 percent. We also become less sensitive to taste, smell, and pain as we age.

Motor skills usually peak during young adulthood. One of the most common measures of motor performance is reaction time. Many studies have shown that reaction time becomes gradually slower as we approach older adulthood. Decrements in reaction time may have potentially significant effects on the ability of older adults to function effectively in our complex, modern society. Experts disagree over the extent to which age-related psychomotor slowing is due to the deterioration of central rather than peripheral processes.

The human brain is a most complex, elegant, and intricate system. The brain has three major components: the brain stem (including the cerebellum), the limbic system, and the cerebrum. The hippocampus, a structure within the limbic system, seems to be involved in the process of remembering and storing information. The cortex, the top covering of the cerebrum, is responsible for all higher-order psychological functioning. The cortex may undergo widespread or localized damage in aged individuals. In many instances, damage to the cortex may have far-reaching effects on adults' psychological abilities.

It is possible to observe the brain in a noninvasive manner by the use of the CT scan, PETT scan, or MRI. The electroencephalogram (EEG) has been used to measure the electrical output of the brain in general, and the cortex in particular. The alpha rhythm, as measured by the EEG, begins to slow as we approach older adulthood. Some psychologists have linked the slowing of alpha activity to the generalized pattern of psychomotor slowing. It has also been proposed that the slowing of the alpha rhythm causes the older adult to be chronically underaroused. The delta rhythm also changes with age. Alterations in delta activity have been linked to changes in sleep patterns and sleep satisfaction among the elderly. Age-related changes in evoked brain potentials are also of interest to gerontologists. Of particular importance is the latency of the P300 brain wave.

The brain is composed of specialized cells called neurons. Neurons have three different component parts: the soma, the dendrites, and the axon. Neurons communicate by releasing special chemical substances called neurotransmitters. ACh is one of the most important neurotransmitters employed in neuronal communication. It is generally agreed that we lose a large number of neurons as we grow old, but there are few precise conclusions about the psychological effects of neuronal loss. With increasing age comes an increase in the amount of lipofuscin, the number of granulovacuolar particles, and the number of neurofibrillary tangles inside the neurons. Senile plaques have also been found to increase in the synaptic area between neurons.

Alzheimer's disease is the most common and most devastating type of dementia. It is characterized by an excessive number of tangles and plaques within the hippocampus and cortex. This finding has led to the suggestion that Alzheimer's disease may represent accelerated normal aging. Genetic factors seem to be responsible for a small percentage of the total number of cases of Alzheimer's disease. At present, there is no cure for this disease. The FAST staging system provides professionals with a convenient way to understand the general course of Alzheimer's disease. It is also important to recognize the psychosocial problems encountered by spouses and loved ones when Alzheimer's disease strikes a family member.

Review Questions

1. Discuss the development of sensory systems during the adult years, focusing especially on vision and hearing.
2. Explain the difference between visual acuity and contrast sensitivity.
3. Describe the significant changes that take place in motor performance during adulthood.
4. Are changes in reaction time most likely due to age-related changes in peripheral or central processes?
5. Describe the major components of the brain as well as the major components of the neuron.
6. Describe the age-related changes in the electrical activity of the brain. How do these changes in brain activity influence the behavioral abilities and sleep patterns of older adults?
7. What do the major functions of the hippocampus and cortex seem to be?
8. What are the major changes that take place at the neuronal level as we age? Compare and contrast the neuronal changes that take place during normal aging with those that occur in Alzheimer's disease.
9. Describe the symptoms and hypothesized causes of Alzheimer's disease.
10. Describe the FAST staging system of AD. What are the potential benefits of using this system?
11. Discuss the potential links between AD and normal aging and between AD and Down syndrome.

For Further Reading

Birren, J. E., & Schaie, K. W. (Eds.). (1985). *Handbook of the psychology of aging.* New York: Van Nostrand Reinhold.

An authoritative volume containing thirty-two chapters by various contributors, including chapters on motor performance, vision, hearing, arousal and sleep, and the intervention, treatment, and rehabilitation of psychiatric disorders. Medium to difficult reading.

Gardner, H. (1975). *The shattered mind: The person after brain damage.* New York: Alfred A. Knopf.

An excellent account of the impact of brain damage on the psychological functions of the developing and aging brain. Of special interest is Gardner's lucid account of various aphasias—breakdowns in language. In many ways, this book is a classic. Very easy reading.

Heston, L. L., & White, J. A. (1983). *Dementia: A practical guide to Alzheimer's disease and related illnesses.* New York: W. H. Freeman.

This short book, written for the lay reader, provides a number of basic facts about dementia. It addresses in a positive manner the question of how family members can cope with the affected person's deteriorating behavior. Also discussed are the financial and social consequences of the dementing illnesses. Very easy reading.

Scheibel, A. B., Wechsler, A. F., & Brazier, M. A. B. (Eds.). (1986). *The biological substrates of Alzheimer's disease.* New York: Academic Press.

This edited volume represents one of the most comprehensive and up-to-date books on the biological aspects of Alzheimer's disease. New ideas concerning the diagnosis, cause, and treatment of AD are presented. The book also includes edited transcripts of round-table discussions about the relationship between normal aging and AD. Moderately difficult to very difficult reading.

Thompson, R. F. (1986). *The brain: An introduction to neuroscience.* New York: W. H. Freeman.

One of the most elegant, comprehensible, and well-illustrated texts written about the brain and the neuron. A special section is devoted to the life cycle of the brain (its development, plasticity, and aging). Richard Thompson is one of the world's most distinguished brain researchers. Easy to medium reading.

Zarit, S. H., Orr, N. K., & Zarit, J. M. (1985). *The hidden victims of Alzheimer's disease: Families under stress.* New York: New York University Press.

This important book describes the different problems and burdens encountered by the families of Alzheimer's patients. It gives insight into the different intervention programs that may be used to relieve the stress faced by those who care for terminally ill, demented family members. Moderate reading level.

CHAPTER 5

INTELLIGENCE, CREATIVITY, AND ADULT DEVELOPMENT

Imagine That You Are an Executive in a Large Company Who Has to Make a Decision about the Status of an Older Worker

You are considering one of your employees for an important promotion. At present, this employee has a middle-management position in your marketing department. You are thinking of making her head of the entire marketing department. In this position, she would exercise direct control over a large number of employees and would exert a powerful influence over the future of your company.

There are a number of reasons for giving this person a promotion. First, she has worked for your organization for fifteen years. During this time she has performed exceptionally well on every task assigned her. In fact, she has initiated a number of changes which have made your company's marketing approach far more effective, resulting in great financial benefits for your company. Second, this person is well liked. She treats everyone in your organization—from the janitors to the members of the board of directors—with a great deal of friendliness, warmth, and respect. Third, this employee has had a distinguished academic career. She was an honors student at a prestigious Ivy League university and received an M.B.A. from a well-known business school. Fourth, she is a tireless worker, devoting long, hard hours to advance your company's goals. Fifth, despite this commitment to the company, this employee is not a one-dimensional person. She has several interesting hobbies and is actively involved in a variety of community organizations. Finally, you have learned that this employee wants to become director of marketing. She views this new position as challenging and rewarding. In sum, she seems to be the perfect person for this position.

However, there is one consideration gnawing at you, making you think that this employee may not be the ideal candidate—*age*. The person you are considering for this position is fifty-eight years old. Because of her age you wonder if it is wise to promote her to such a key position. You know that she has done a tremendous job in the past. But are her most productive years behind her? Should you hire on the basis of her past performance or her potential for future performance? Specific questions about that future performance concern you. Will this person's ability to make good, intelligent decisions decline with age? And what about this person's ability to develop creative solutions to your company's problems? Along with solving problems, a good executive must call upon her creativity to invent new strategies that will move your company ahead of the competition. Will this person's creative ability decline with age? What about her health? Right now she is mildly overweight and her blood pressure is slightly elevated. If she does fall into ill health as she gets older, what will happen to her critical thinking ability and her creativity? What about this person's ability to learn new information and technologies? A productive executive cannot rely on what she has learned in the past to help her in the present. She must be able to acquire new skills and abilities—like learning how to use the latest computer programs to boost your company's productivity. Will this person's ability to learn new skills decrease with age? What *should* your decision be? What *will* your actual decision be? If you were the older worker, what decision would you expect? Will this employee receive the promotion?

In this chapter, we will explore how intelligence and creativity change during adulthood. After reading this chapter you should be in a much better position to make a sound decision about the fate of this older worker.

INTRODUCTION

This is the first of three chapters that focus on adult cognitive development. Cognitive change is one of the key features of adult development. In fact, more research has been conducted on cognitive functioning than any other aspect of adult development (Baltes, 1987). There are several different perspectives from which to study adult cognition. In this chapter we will center our attention on the psychometric approach, a measurement-based view that has sparked considerable debate on the very nature of intelligence, the way it is assessed, and its development (and possible decline) during adulthood. We'll examine the roles of physical health and generational (or cohort) influences in adult intellectual change. Furthermore, we'll discuss the relationship between adult scores on psychometric intelligence tests and the ability of those adults to solve real-life problems. Next, we'll examine the issue of creativity. We'll distinguish between creativity and intelligence and chart the developmental course of creativity over the adult years. Finally, we'll examine the topic of adult education, discussing the many benefits adults derive from life-long learning.

THE PSYCHOMETRIC APPROACH TO THE STUDY OF INTELLIGENCE

The term **psychometric** literally means "the measurement of the mind." More specifically, psychometricians construct and validate various tests that measure a number of relatively enduring characteristics of the individual. It seems safe to say that the greatest emphasis in psychometric research has been placed on the measurement of human intelligence. In this chapter, we'll present information about age-related changes in psychometrically measured intelligence. But before we can determine the changes that take place in intelligence during adulthood, we need to determine what, exactly, intelligence *is*.

The Nature of Intelligence

Intelligence is a concept that is easy to understand but hard to define. The word *intelligence* is derived from the Latin words that mean "to choose between" and "to make wise choices" (Rebok, 1987; Schaie and Willis, 1986). These literal meanings of intelligence are, at best, vague. How can we determine if an individual has made a truly wise choice?

Are psychologists capable of developing a precise, meaningful definition of intelligence? In a well-known symposium sponsored by the *Journal of Educational Psychology* in 1921, a number of expert psychologists gave the following definitions of intelligence:

1. The ability to carry on abstract thinking (Louis Terman)
2. The ability to give true or factual responses (Edward Thorndike)
3. The ability to learn to adjust oneself to the environment (S. S. Colvin)

4. The ability to adapt to new situations, which reflects the general modifiability of the nervous system (Rudolf Pinter)
5. The capacity to acquire new abilities (Herbert Woodrow)
6. A group of complex mental processes traditionally defined as sensation, perception, association, memory, imagination, discrimination, judgment, and reasoning (M. E. Haggerty)

These definitions seem to possess as much generality and tenuousness as you would expect from the proverbial man on the street! However, if we analyze each of the definitions, an important issue emerges: is intelligence a general, single, or unitary process? Or does intelligence consist of a number of different, independent, or separate mental abilities? Charles Spearman (1927), a well-known English psychologist in the earlier part of this century, argued that intelligence consisted primarily of a single ability that an individual could apply to any task. Spearman called this unitary ability the **g factor**—"g" for "general capacity." Spearman assumed that because of the g factor, an individual should perform at the same level of proficiency regardless of the type of task he or she had to solve. The notion that intelligence is best conceptualized as a single, general ability was also held by Alfred Binet. Binet was the French psychologist who developed the first intelligence assessment in 1906. Today, Spearman and Binet would be likely to conceptualize intelligence as a very general and abstract computer program. This program would be so general that it could be applied, with the same degree of success, to any problem it was called upon to solve.

Several other psychologists have suggested that intelligence consists of a number of separate, independent mental abilities. This position was originally advocated by Thurstone (1938), who proposed that there are a small number of **primary mental abilities.** These primary mental abilities include verbal comprehension, word fluency, number, space, associative memory, perceptual speed, and induction. Table 5.1 describes each of these abilities. K. Warner Schaie, a well-known advocate of the psychometric approach, has recently developed an adult intelligence test based on Thurstone's research. This test is called the **Schaie-Thurstone Adult Mental Abilities Test** (Schaie, 1985). To continue our computer analogy, Thurstone and his associates would likely argue that intelligence consists of a number of separate, specialized computer programs. Each program would be designed to solve a particular type of task.

Some psychometricians have even gone a step further than Thurstone. They believe there are more basic components of intelligence than Thurstone originally envisioned. Ekstrom, French, and Harman (1979) have isolated 29 separate mental abilities. Guilford (1959a, 1959b, 1967) has argued for the existence of an astonishing 120 independent components of intelligence!

Raymond Cattell (1971) and John Horn (1970, 1982a, 1982b) have pointed out that a model based on a large number of mental abilities (for example, 29 or 120) is too unwieldy. They suggest that it is difficult, if not impossible, to represent a large number of mental abilities in an internally consistent, parsimonious, coherent, and empirically sound fashion. For this reason, Horn (1970) has argued for

Table 5.1

THE PRIMARY MENTAL ABILITIES

V.	**Verbal comprehension:** The principal factor in such tests as reading comprehension, verbal analogies, disarranged sentences, verbal reasoning, and proverb matching. It is most adequately measured by vocabulary tests.
W.	**Word fluency:** Found in such tests as anagrams, rhyming, or naming words in a given category (for example, boys' names or words beginning with the letter T).
N.	**Number:** Most closely identified with speed and accuracy of simple arithmetic computation.
S.	**Space (or spatial orientation):** May represent two distinct factors, one covering perception of fixed spatial or geometric relations, the other manipulatory visualizations in which changed positions or transformations must be visualized.
M.	**Associative memory:** Found principally in tests demanding rote memory for paired associates. There is some evidence to suggest that this factor may reflect the extent to which memory crutches are utilized. The evidence is against the presence of a broader factor through all memory tests. Other restricted memory factors, such as memory for temporal sequences and for spatial position, have been suggested by some investigations.
P.	**Perceptual speed:** Quick and accurate grasping of visual details, similarities, and differences.
I (or R).	**Induction (or general reasoning):** Early researchers proposed an inductive and a deductive factor. The latter was best measured by tests of syllogistic reasoning and the former by tests requiring the subject to find a rule, as in a number series completion test. Evidence for the deductive factor, however, was much weaker than for the inductive. Moreover, other investigators suggested a general reasoning factor, best measured by arithmetic reasoning tests.

Reprinted with permission of Macmillan Publishing Company from *Psychological Testing,* 6th ed., by Anne Anastasi. Copyright © 1988 by Anne Anastasi.

the existence of two highly abstract components of intelligence that subsume the various primary mental abilities. These two abstract components are **crystallized intelligence** and **fluid intelligence.** Crystallized intelligence roughly represents the extent to which individuals have incorporated the valued knowledge of their culture. It is measured by a large inventory of behaviors that reflect the breadth of culturally valued knowledge and experience, the comprehension of communications, and the development of judgment, understanding, and reasonable thinking in everyday affairs. Some of the primary mental abilities associated with crystallized intelligence are verbal comprehension, concept formation, logical reasoning, and induction. Tests used to measure the crystallized factor include vocabulary, simple analogies, remote associations, and social judgment.

Fluid intelligence represents an individual's "pure" ability to perceive, remember and think about a wide variety of basic information. In other words, fluid intelligence involves mental abilities that are *not* imparted by one's culture. Abilities included under the heading of fluid intelligence are seeing relationships among patterns, drawing inferences from relationships, and comprehending implications. Some of the primary mental abilities that best reflect this factor are number, space, and perceptual speed. Tasks measuring fluid intelligence include letter series, matrices, and spatial orientation. It has been suggested that fluid intelligence represents the integrity of the central nervous system (Horn, 1982b). See figure 5.1 to

Figure 5.1 contents:

Fluid intelligence

Matrices Indicate the figure that completes the matrix.

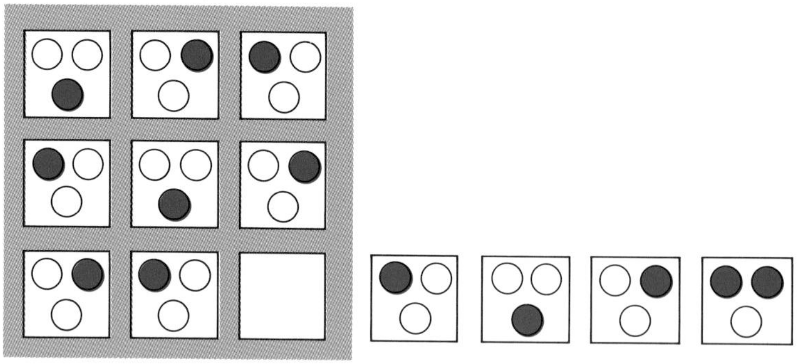

Letter series Decide which letter comes next in the series.
A   D   G   J   M   P   ?

Topology Find the figure on the right where the dot can be placed in the same relation to the triangle, square, and circle as in the example on the left.

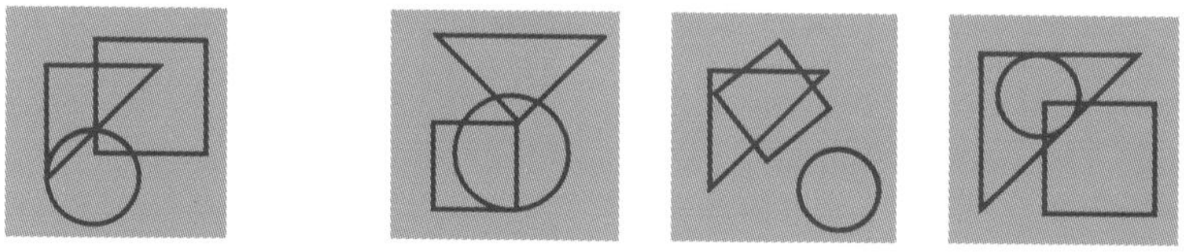

Crystallized intelligence

Esoteric analogies Fill in the blank.
Socrates is to Aristotle as Sophicles is to _____ .

Remote associations What one word is well associated with the words *bathtub, prizefighting,* and *wedding*?

Judgment You notice that a fire has just started in a crowded cafe. What should one do to prevent death and injury?

Figure 5.1 **Examples of test items that measure fluid and crystallized intelligence.**

gain a better understanding of the differences between crystallized and fluid intelligence. This figure contains a number of sample tasks that measure both of these types of intelligence.

Paul Baltes and his associates (Baltes, 1987; Dixon and Baltes, 1986) have provided psychologists with a useful way to distinguish crystallized intelligence from fluid intelligence. They regard fluid intelligence as the *mechanics of intelligence*. Fluid intelligence, in other words, involves the raw, basic operations of our human information-processing systems. The mechanics of intelligence allow us to perceive the environment and to classify and remember our perceptions. On the other hand, crystallized intelligence may be defined as the *pragmatics of intelligence.* This form of intelligence concerns the context- and experience-related applications of the mechanics of intelligence. The pragmatic component of intelligence involves (1) the general system of factual knowledge accessible to members of a particular culture, (2) specialized systems of knowledge available to individuals within particular occupations and avocations, and (3) an understanding of how to effectively activate different types of knowledge within particular contexts to aid problem solving.

The Measurement of Intelligence

It is one thing to develop a theory of intelligence and another thing to develop a valid and reliable test or measure of intelligence. A psychometrician must take a number of factors into account in developing an intelligence test. First, it is important to realize that intelligence does not really exist! Intelligence is a **hypothetical construct** rather than a real entity. It is not possible, for example, to look inside the brain of an individual and see the amount of intelligence she possesses in the same way that one can look inside a refrigerator to see the amount of food stored there. This means that psychometric tests must measure intelligence *indirectly* by examining performance on tasks that depend on the generation and application of intelligent behavior.

A second factor psychometricians must consider, since intelligence cannot be directly measured by any psychometric test, is that intelligence test performance is influenced by many factors other than intelligence. These factors include personality characteristics, motivation, educational background, anxiety, fatigue, and so on (Schaie and Willis, 1986). Despite the influence of these extraneous factors, however, psychometricians still assume that intelligence tests primarily measure intelligence.

A third consideration for psychometricians to remember in developing an intelligence test is that it is necessary to present individuals with a wide variety of tasks to evaluate whether intelligence is a single ability such as a g factor or a number of independent abilities. This is why contemporary intelligence tests consist of a number of different *scales* or minitests or subtests. One of the most commonly used tests to measure adult intelligence is the **Wechsler Adult Intelligence Scale (WAIS).** This test consists of eleven subtests. Six of the subtests comprise a *verbal scale.* These subtests include general information, digit span, vocabulary, arithmetic, comprehension, and similarities. The items on this scale require a strong language component. The remaining five subtests make up a *performance scale.* The subtests on this scale include picture completion, picture arrangement, block design, object assembly, and digit symbol. On this scale, a person is required to make a nonverbal response (for example, arranging a number of pictures in a logical sequence so as to tell a story) after a careful appraisal of each problem. Table

Table 5.2

SUBTESTS OF THE WAIS

Verbal Scale
1. *Information:* Twenty-nine questions covering a wide variety of information that adults have presumably had an opportunity to acquire in our culture. An effort was made to avoid specialized or academic knowledge.
2. *Comprehension:* Fourteen items, in each of which the examinee explains what should be done under certain circumstances, why certain practices are followed, the meaning of proverbs, and so forth. Designed to measure practical judgment and common sense.
3. *Arithmetic:* Fourteen problems similar to those encountered in elementary school arithmetic. Each problem is orally presented and is to be solved without the use of paper and pencil.
4. *Similarities:* Thirteen items requiring the subject to say in what way two things are alike.
5. *Digit span:* Orally presented lists of three to nine digits to be orally reproduced. In the second part, the examinee must reproduce lists of two to eight digits backwards.
6. *Vocabulary:* Forty words of increasing difficulty presented both orally and visually. The examinee is asked what each word means.

Performance Scale
7. *Digit symbol:* A version of the familiar code-substitution test, which has often been included in nonlanguage intelligence scales. The key contains nine symbols paired with the nine digits. With this key before him, the examinee has one and a half minutes to fill in as many symbols as he can under the numbers on the answer sheet.
8. *Picture completion:* Twenty-one cards, each containing a picture from which some part is missing. Examinee must tell what is missing from each picture.
9. *Block design:* A set of cards containing designs in red and white and a set of identical one-inch blocks whose sides are painted red, white, and half red and half white. The examinee is shown one design at a time, which he or she must reproduce by choosing and assembling the proper blocks.
10. *Picture arrangement:* Each item consists of a set of cards containing pictures to be rearranged in the proper sequence so as to tell a story.
11. *Object assembly:* In each of the four parts of this subtest, cutouts are to be assembled to make a flat picture of a familiar object.

Reprinted with permission of Macmillan Publishing Company from *Psychological Testing,* 6th ed., by Anne Anastasi. Copyright © 1988 by Anne Anastasi.

5.2 contains a brief description of all of the subtests on both the verbal and performance scales of the WAIS.

Another factor to consider in developing intelligence tests is that although we can construct tests that possess a large number of subtests, this does not necessarily mean that each subtest measures a different aspect of intelligence (Schaie and Willis, 1986). Each subtest might measure the same mental ability, the g factor for example, but in a different way. To determine whether the various subtests of an intelligence test are measuring a single ability or a number of special abilities, researchers developed the technique of **factor analysis.** As you remember from chapter 2, factor analysis is a statistical procedure used to determine how scores on a large number of tasks intercorrelate (or fail to intercorrelate) with one another. Using the method of factor analysis, Thurstone developed the different primary mental abilities. Cattell and Horn also used factor analytic procedures to discern the difference between crystallized and fluid intelligence.

Finally, it is important to understand how a person's IQ score is calculated. The first intelligence tests were constructed solely for children and young adolescents. On these tests, IQ was computed by multiplying the ratio of mental age to chronological age by 100 ($IQ = MA/CA \times 100$). A child's mental age was measured by the items passed on the IQ test. For example, if a child passed all of the items that a typical six-year-old could pass but could not pass any of the items solved by children seven years of age and above, a mental age of six years was assigned to that child. Then the child's IQ could be computed by determining the ratio between mental age and chronological age and multiplying by 100. For example, if the child with a mental age of six is six years old chronologically, the child's IQ is 100 ($IQ = 6/6 \times 100$). Thus, an average IQ, regardless of the age of the person tested, is always 100.

Psychometricians discovered that it was very easy to classify the mental ages of children. However, the concept of mental age broke down when applied to adults. It is relatively easy to develop questions that distinguish between children with mental ages of six and seven; but it is impossible to develop questions that distinguish between adults with mental ages of sixty-six and sixty-seven. The IQ formula used for children could thus not be used to determine adult intelligence. To resolve this problem two approaches were taken. The first approach, which is no longer used today, was to assign a mental age of no greater than sixteen to adults' IQ test items. This approach wrongly assumed that little, if any, development in intelligence occurs beyond mid-adolescence. The second approach, the one adopted by contemporary psychologists, is to determine an adult's IQ by comparing the number of correct answers a person achieves on the whole test to people of the same chronological age. A score of 100 is arbitrarily assigned to those performing at the average for their age group, while IQs greater or lesser than 100 are assigned according to the degree of statistical deviation from this average.

Using this scoring system, it is possible for different-aged adults to perform in a manner identical to one another yet receive radically different IQ scores. To take a simple example, suppose that the average twenty-five-year-old can pass sixty-five questions on an IQ test while the average seventy-five-year-old can pass forty-five questions on the same test. Thus, a twenty-five-year-old who passed fifty-five questions would be assessed to have a below-average IQ, while a seventy-five-year-old who passed fifty-five questions would be assessed as having an above-average IQ. This discovery leads to an interesting question. What should we pay closest attention to when we conduct research on developmental changes in adult intelligence? Should we focus on the raw scores (the total number of questions correctly answered) obtained by different-aged adults or on the adjusted IQ scores (the comparison of the raw score to the average score for a particular age group) for different-aged adults? It seems that examining raw scores would provide more valuable information about developmental changes in test performance than examining the adjusted scores (the IQ scores). Significant changes in test performance would most certainly be obscured if we focused attention on the IQ scores alone.

DEVELOPMENTAL CHANGES IN INTELLIGENCE

There is no doubt that the raw scores that adults obtain on intelligence tests decline with age. However, the age at which decrements in IQ test performance first begin, as well as the magnitude of the decline, depends on the research design employed to measure developmental change. In this section we'll compare the results of various cross-sectional and longitudinal studies of adult intellectual development. Overall, we will see that declines in intelligence (1) occur much later than was earlier thought, (2) affect a smaller number of individuals than was earlier thought, and (3) affect a smaller number of intellectual abilities than was earlier thought.

Cross-Sectional Studies

Initially, a number of cross-sectional studies (Garret, 1957; Jones and Conrad, 1933; Wechsler, 1939) showed that raw or unadjusted scores on intelligence tests decreased with age. Decrements in test scores began in late adolescence and early adulthood (at about twenty years of age) and steadily continued over the remainder of the life span. These results suggested that intelligence peaked in early life, and this conclusion was not at all surprising to the psychologists of this era. At this point in time, you will remember, psychologists held a child-focused perspective on developmental change. A child-focused approach assumes that adulthood can only be characterized by the decline of intellectual abilities.

A few researchers began to notice that adults displayed a steeper rate of decline on some types of intellectual tasks in comparison to others. For example, Wechsler (1958, 1972) and Siegler (1983) reported that with increasing age, the scores on performance subtests of the WAIS declined more rapidly than the scores on the verbal subtests. It should be noted, however, that performance subtests are speeded while verbal subtests are nonspeeded. A speeded subtest is one in which individuals must make their responses as quickly as possible, while in a nonspeeded test, individuals are allowed to take their time answering items. These data suggest that speed of responding may underlie the poor performance of the elderly on nonverbal tasks. However, many older adults continue to perform poorly on the performance subtests of the WAIS even if given unlimited time to respond (Botwinick, 1978). See figure 5.2 for a graphic illustration of the developmental changes in performance on the WAIS. Remember that the data in the figure are based on cross-sectional research.

When the developmental changes in crystallized and fluid intelligence are analyzed in a cross-sectional manner, an interesting pattern emerges. With advancing age, crystallized intelligence shows increases up until the sixth decade of life (Horn, 1970, 1982a, 1982b; Horn and Donaldson, 1976). On the other hand, fluid intelligence exhibits a steady decline beginning in early adulthood. The net effect is that the increases in crystallized intelligence tend to cancel out the decreases in fluid intelligence. Therefore, if one did not make a distinction between crystallized and

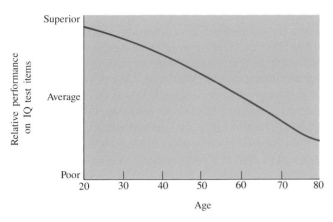

Figure 5.2 An illustration of the results of cross-sectional studies investigating the relationship between age and intelligence.

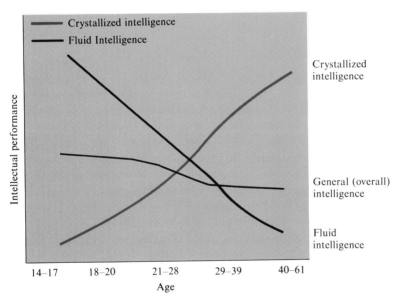

Figure 5.3 Age-related changes in crystallized intelligence, fluid intelligence, and general intelligence from adolescence to older adulthood.

fluid abilities, one would conclude that intelligence, as a general ability, remains relatively stable until the onset of late adulthood. Figure 5.3 contains a schematic representation of the relationship between crystallized intelligence, fluid intelligence, and general intelligence.

In summary, early cross-sectional research painted a simple picture of adult intellectual development. IQ test scores peaked in very young adulthood and significantly decreased with age. It seemed as if intellectual development and physical development followed the same pattern of steady decline—a pattern of irreversible decrement. More recent cross-sectional studies, however, have revealed a more complex pattern of intellectual change during adulthood. Scores on the performance subtests on the WAIS show a significantly greater rate of decline than scores on the verbal subtests of the WAIS. The tendency for nonverbal abilities to deteriorate more rapidly than verbal abilities has been referred to as "the classic aging pattern" (Botwinick, 1977). Consistent with this pattern, fluid intelligence has been found to decrease with age, while crystallized intelligence has been found to increase with age. How can we understand these different patterns of performance? John Horn and colleagues (Horn, 1982a; Horn and Donaldson, 1976) have proposed that crystallized intelligence increases with age because it reflects the cumulative effects of experience, education, and acculturation over a lifetime. They also suggest that fluid intelligence decreases with age because of a gradual age-related deterioration of the physiological and neurological mechanisms necessary for basic intellectual functioning.

Longitudinal Studies

Longitudinal studies offer a very different impression of adult intellectual development than cross-sectional studies. Schaie and Willis (1986) have observed that a number of longitudinal studies were initiated during the early 1920s. It was at this time that incoming groups of college freshmen in the United States were administered intelligence tests on a routine basis. Psychologists kept track of these individuals as they grew older, retesting them at different intervals during adulthood. To the amazement of many developmentalists, the participants in these longitudinal studies showed an increase in IQ test performance up to approximately age fifty (Owens, 1966). After age fifty, these gains were usually maintained or sometimes evidenced a small decline (Cunningham and Owens, 1983).

In one longitudinal study, Schwartzman, Gold, Andres, Arbuckle, and Chiakelson (1987) analyzed the intelligence test scores of a group of 260 men. These men were first administered intelligence tests when they were army recruits during World War II. Forty years later, the men were retested. At the second testing, the men were approximately sixty-five years of age. They had completed, on average, nine years of formal education. One of the interesting twists of this study was that at the forty-year retesting, the men were given the intelligence test under two different conditions: a normal-time condition in which participants were given the standard amount of time to answer the test questions, and a double-time condition in which participants were given twice as much time to answer the test questions. Overall results showed a slight decline in test scores under the normal-time condition but a reliable and significant improvement in scores in the double-time condition. IQ gains were most likely to occur in those portions of the test that measured

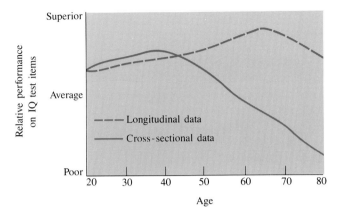

Figure 5.4   A comparison of the results of cross-sectional and longitudinal studies investigating the relationship between age and verbal intelligence.
Source: Data from K. W. Schaie and S. L. Willis, 1986.

verbal abilities (for example, vocabulary), while losses in IQ appeared in essentially nonverbal abilities (for example, spatial problem solving). Three other findings are especially noteworthy. First, individual differences in IQ scores remained very stable over the forty-year time span. Second, gains in IQ were more highly associated with the number of years of formal education the men had attained than with their ages at the retesting. Third, self-reported activity levels and personal lifestyle differences were related to IQ scores at both times of testing.

One way to compare the results of cross-sectional and longitudinal studies of adult intellectual change is to examine the information illustrated in figure 5.4. The cross-sectional data indicate that adults show a peak in verbal ability at thirty-five years of age, followed by a significant decline thereafter. The longitudinal data, on the other hand, show that verbal ability peaks at about age fifty-five. In addition, the longitudinal data exhibit only a very small decline up until seventy years of age, while the cross-sectional data show a more dramatic and earlier rate of decline.

One of the most detailed investigations of adult intelligence was carried out by K. Warner Schaie and his associates. This investigation, called the *Seattle Longitudinal Study* or *SLS,* employed a sequential research design (that is, a combination of both cross-sectional and longitudinal methods of data collection). The study began in 1956 when 500 participants between twenty-two and seventy years of age were administered the Primary Mental Abilities Test. These subjects were retested at seven-year intervals in 1963, 1970, 1977, and 1984. Thus, this research project consisted of five cross-sectional studies and one longitudinal study covering a twenty-one-year period.

There have been a large number of published reports summarizing the outcomes of the SLS (Schaie and Labouvie-Vief, 1974; Schaie, 1979, 1983; Schaie and Hertzog, 1983, 1985). Generally, the cross-sectional comparison exhibited the typical pattern of decline across all of the different primary mental abilities. These

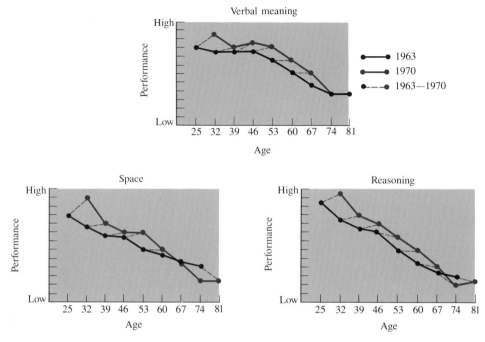

Figure 5.5   A comparison of cross-sectional and longitudinal findings concerning the relationship between age and intelligence based on the data obtained by Schaie and Labouvie-Vief (1974).

Source: Data from K. W. Schaie and G. Labouvie-Vief, "Generational Versus Ontogenetic Components of Change in Adult Cognitive Behavior: A Fourteen-Year Cross-Sequential Study" in *Developmental Psychology,* 10:305–320, 1974.

comparisons support the irreversible decrement model of intellectual aging. The longitudinal findings, however, tell a different story. They indicate that intelligence test scores either increase or remain stable until approximately age sixty, when a small decline becomes evident. The results from one of the first reports of this investigation are illustrated in figure 5.5. This figure, based on the findings of Schaie and Labouvie-Vief (1974), compares the cross-sectional data collected in 1963 (black lines) with the cross-sectional data collected in 1970 (colored lines). The longitudinal data is signified by the dashed lines connecting the black and colored lines.

Two of the more recent reports (Schaie, in press; Hertzog and Schaie, 1988) based on the SLS are especially important. Schaie and Hertzog (1988) examined the relationship between the *mean stability* of intelligence (for example, the extent to which the average intellectual performance of a group of seventy-year-olds differs from the average performance of a group of fifty-year-olds) and the *covariance stability* in intelligence (for example, how individuals perform compared to their age-mates at fifty versus seventy years of age). Participants were between twenty-two and seventy years of age at the beginning of the study. They were tested three times over a fourteen-year period on five different primary mental abilities. Results showed that the mean stability of the participants' performance was affected by age. The youngest participants displayed progressively higher levels of performance, middle-aged adults showed stability of performance, and older adults displayed a significant linear decline in performance—a decline that seems to take place for the majority of individuals somewhere between fifty-five and seventy years of age. On the other hand, all of the participants displayed exceptionally high levels of covariance stability across the fourteen-year period during which they were tested. These data provide substantial evidence for normative age-related changes in the mean stability of intelligence and the maintenance of individual differences in intellectual performance throughout the adult years.

Schaie (1989, in press) also reported that significant intellectual decline in the participants in the SLS began at about sixty years of age and became more pronounced thereafter. Most interestingly, Schaie (in press) discovered that significant decline was exhibited by only one-third of the participants at age seventy-four. Furthermore, he found that very few individuals showed global intellectual decline. For example, at age sixty, 75 percent of the participants maintained their performance on at least four out of five primary mental abilities. This level of maintenance was also found for slightly more than half of the eighty-one-year-olds in the sample. Finally, it was noted that there were no participants who displayed constant intellectual decline on all five primary mental abilities over the twenty-eight years during which data was collected! Overall, these results suggest that constant, linear, and all-pervasive intellectual decline is more mythical than real. More positively stated, these data show that a significant percentage of individuals maintain most of their intellectual abilities well into old age.

FACTORS RESPONSIBLE FOR DEVELOPMENTAL CHANGES IN INTELLIGENCE

Several investigators (for example, Horn, 1982b) have suggested that intellectual decline results from the deterioration of the central nervous system. Without doubt, age-related changes in the brain have a significant impact on adult intellectual functioning. However, these changes alone cannot account for the pattern of results researchers found, nor can they adequately explain the individual differences that dispute the claim of universal biologically-based loss. In this section, we'll discuss a variety of factors that may have a profound impact on intellectual performance during adulthood.

Cohort Effects

Why do cross-sectional studies paint a more pessimistic picture of adult intellectual change than longitudinal studies? The answer may be that in cross-sectional studies age-related differences are confounded with **cohort** differences. As you remember from chapter 2, *cohort* means the generation one is born into, or the year of one's birth.

In a cohort-sequential analysis of the data from the Seattle Longitudinal Study, Schaie (1979, 1983) discovered that adults' intellectual performance changed as a function of both age and cohort. Figure 5.6, adapted from Schaie's (1979) data, illustrates the profound influence of cohort effects on five different primary mental abilities. This graph represents the IQ test performance of individuals from ten successive birth cohorts (1889 to 1952). Notice the multidirectional manner in which the abilities change. The graph shows that space and reasoning abilities increased until the 1938 birth cohort, at which time the abilities either declined or leveled off. Verbal meaning displays a progressive increase over all cohorts measured. Number ability seems to have peaked with the 1924 cohort and declined since then. Finally, word fluency declined steadily until the 1938 cohort; since then it has displayed upward movement.

Gisela Labouvie-Vief (1985) has called attention to the fact that performance on tasks of fluid intelligence (for example, space) is not immune to cohort effects. Even measures of fluid intelligence do not assess the pure information-processing abilities of the human mind; they are influenced by socioenvironmental forces such as cohort.

Cohort effects do not necessarily affect intellectual development negatively. Paul Baltes (1987) has described three different ways in which cohort differences can boost intellectual performance: in terms of education, health, and work. First, successive generations have received increasingly more formal education. Educational experience has been positively correlated with IQ scores. Second, each succeeding generation has been treated more effectively for a variety of illnesses (for example, hypertension) that are known to have a negative impact on intellectual performance. Third, changes in the work life of more recent generations have placed a much stronger focus on cognitively oriented labor. Many of our grandfathers or great-grandfathers may have been farmers or manual laborers. Today, we are more likely to find jobs in service fields, such as emergency medical assistants, paralegal aides, or computer operators. This increased emphasis on cognitively oriented occupations most assuredly modifies and enhances intellectual abilities.

Selective Dropout

The **selective dropout** of participants may mean that longitudinal studies provide an overly optimistic view of adult intellectual change. The concept of selective dropout (already discussed in chapter 2) is based on the idea that as information is gathered during a longitudinal study it becomes harder and harder to keep one's original sample of participants intact. Specifically, participants who are unhealthy, unmotivated, or who consider themselves to be performing poorly on an intelligence test are not likely to return for repeated testing. As a longitudinal study progresses, a positively biased sample of participants is thus likely to evolve. This biased sample consists of adults who tend to do well on measures of intellectual functioning—that is, those who are highly educated, successful, motivated, and healthy.

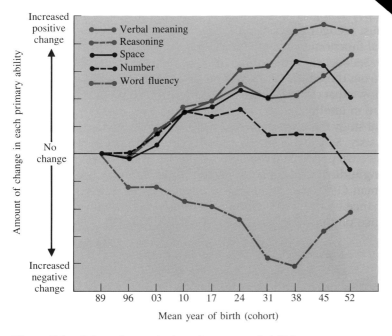

Figure 5.6 Cohort changes in the primary mental abilities.

There is another point of view from which to interpret the results of longitudinal studies of intelligence. This perspective maintains that longitudinal data, despite its inherent bias, may be extremely valuable because they show that certain populations of older adults (the educated, the healthy, and so on)—those who form the backbone of any society—show positive developmental changes in intelligence during adulthood (Schaie and Willis, 1986). Furthermore, one could argue that the psychometric evaluation of intelligence is least valid for those individuals who tend to drop out of longitudinal studies (the unhealthy, the uneducated, and so on).

Health

It seems obvious that individuals who are in good physical health can think, reason, and remember better than those in ill health. Even twenty-year-old college students may find it difficult to concentrate during an exam if they are ill with the flu or some other illness. The problem for developmental researchers, of course, is that older adults are much more likely to suffer from chronic illness than younger people are. The relatively poor health of the elderly population can bias both cross-sectional and longitudinal studies. The older the population studied, the greater the number of persons with limiting health problems (Siegler and Costa, 1985).

is must concern themselves with two interrelated
e that health may become much more of a deter-
ng as individuals move through the life span (Sieg-
ey must try to develop methodologies that separate
fects of disease on psychological abilities.

he incidence of hypertension (high blood pressure)
lectual abilities. Wilkie and Eisdorfer (1971) discov-
at hypertension was linked to decreases on the WAIS
aie (in press) found that hypertension was a better
erformance of older adults than was a measure of overall
al study of middle-aged adults, Schultz, Elias, Robbins,
)86) reported that nonhypertensive subjects displayed
n the WAIS, while hypertensives showed no significant
the WAIS.

Termin...

Closely associated with selective dropout and health status is the notion of **terminal drop.** Terminal drop refers to the tendency for an individual's psychological and biological abilities to exhibit a dramatic decrease in the last few years prior to death. Terminal drop occurs when individuals die of chronic illnesses which drain them of their strength, energy, and motivation. Most older people die of chronic diseases rather than accidents or injuries. Chronic diseases reduce older adults' capacities for clear thinking, undivided attention, and mental effort. As a result, their scores on cognitive tasks drop off dramatically (Kleemeier, 1962; Riegel and Riegel, 1972). Given the greater number of older versus younger adults being tested near their deaths, the intelligence test scores of older adults are much more likely to reflect terminal drop than the test scores of younger adults. Thus, the declines in intelligence revealed in cross-sectional and longitudinal studies may be, at least in part, a statistical artifact caused by terminal drop.

More recently, White and Cunningham (1988) have examined the relationship between distance from death and adults' scores on tests of vocabulary, numerical facility, and perceptual speed. They found that vocabulary scores were most likely to decline in the years just prior to a person's death. Thus, terminal drop may be limited to those abilities (such as vocabulary and other verbal abilities) that are usually the least affected by age.

Mental Exercise and Training

The idea that mental abilities can be improved by training, experience, or exercise has intrigued psychologists for many years. The enhancement of mental abilities via training is consistent with Baltes's (1987) notion of the **plasticity** of adult intellectual development. The concept of plasticity suggests that older adults have

Individuals such as Georgia O'Keefe may well maintain their creativity in older adulthood.

substantial cognitive reserve capacity and that training makes use of untapped reserve (Baltes, Sowarka, and Kliegel, 1989, Kliegel, 1990). Baltes and Kliegel (1986) and Willis (1985) hypothesized, for example, that older adults have little everyday experience with test items that measure fluid intelligence. But they also assumed that older adults possess the reserve capacity to raise their levels of performance on fluid-intelligence tasks. These researchers found that older adults between sixty and eighty years old who were exposed to a program of cognitive training exhibited performance levels on fluid tasks that were comparable to the performance levels of a group of untreated younger adults. Baltes, et al. (1989) have even shown that older adults can train themselves to become more proficient in tasks of fluid intelligence.

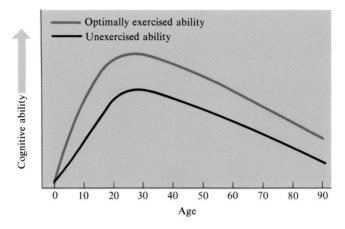

Figure 5.7   The hypothesized relationship between age and both unexercised ability and optimally exercised ability.

Nancy Wadsworth Denney, "Aging and Cognitive Changes" in *Handbook of Developmental Psychology,* edited by B. J. Wolman, © 1982, p. 819. Prentice-Hall, Inc., Englewood Cliffs, N.J.

Nancy Denney (1984) believes that to better understand intellectual change over the adult life span we should distinguish between *unexercised* ability (the level of performance that can be expected if the individual has had no exercise and/or training on a specific ability) and *optimally exercised* ability (the level of performance expected if the individual has received optimal exercise and/or training). The proposed developmental levels for these two types of ability are shown in figure 5.7.

The region between the two abilities in the figure represents the degree to which mental exercise and/or training can affect abilities. Of course, exercise or training can accumulate over a long period of time, even years or decades. Thus some types of ability might be essentially unexercised for many young adults but optimally exercised for middle-aged adults. Such abilities should not decline from young adulthood to middle adulthood. Indeed, they might even improve.

Willis and Schaie (1986), along with Schaie, Willis, Hertzog, and Schulenberg (1987), have found that older adults can, with training, show significant gains on different primary mental abilities. Moreover, gains in specific primary abilities derived from the training programs were found to generalize to other tasks measuring the same mental ability. These researchers discovered, therefore, that increases in intellectual ability associated with training studies go beyond merely teaching the test or changing the ability that is trained.

These results are especially significant in light of the criticisms leveled at training studies by Donaldson (1981). He suggested that training programs designed to improve fluid intelligence may provide misleading results. More specifically, he argued that fluid abilities themselves become "crystallized" with extensive training. Thus, successful intervention programs transform a fluid ability into a crystallized ability. This speculation seems less credible given the results obtained by Schaie and his associates.

INTELLIGENCE AND EVERYDAY LIFE

We have described the developmental changes in intelligence that take place over the adult years. In this section, we'll discuss the relationship between adults' scores on intelligence tests and their ability to solve real-life problems.

At first glance, there seem to be a number of reasons why IQ test scores are poor indicators of everyday problem-solving abilities (Rebok, 1987; Schaie and Willis, 1986). First, several of the items in IQ tests—such as defining unusual words, solving arithmetic problems, arranging pictures in a particular sequence, and so on—have little in common with the problems adults face in real life. Second, many of the performance items on IQ tests are speeded in nature. This puts older adults at a disadvantage given the phenomenon of psychomotor slowing. Their responses are slower than those of the typical younger adult. Third, older adults are not as accustomed as younger adults to taking tests and as a result may be more anxious and/or cautious. Fourth, older adults seem to be less motivated than younger adults to take IQ tests seriously and to perform at their optimal levels. Fifth, the original goal of IQ tests was to predict school success or failure among groups of children and adolescents. This goal seems to possess little meaning when applied to older adults.

Despite the above-mentioned factors, many psychologists have found that scores on various psychometric intelligence tests are somewhat predictive to real-life problem solving. Willis and Schaie (1985), for example, administered a test of the seven primary mental abilities to a group of eighty-year-olds along with a variety of everyday intellectual tasks: reading street maps, interpreting the information found on medicine bottles, filling out forms, comprehending Yellow Page advertisements, and so forth. Willis and Schaie found that performance across all of the everyday tasks was related to several of the primary abilities, especially reasoning.

In a more recent study, Cornelius and Capsi (1987) investigated the relationship between aging and the *implicit* and *explicit* dimensions of intelligence. Implicit theories of intelligence (Sternberg, 1985) refer to people's commonsense beliefs about intelligence and how it develops. Explicit theories, in contrast, are concerned with formalized psychometric notions about what intelligence is and how it is best measured. It has been found that implicit views place a heavy emphasis on the practical or social aspect of intelligence. Practical or social intelligence involves sizing up situations, admitting mistakes, determining how to achieve goals, and so on. These types of abilities are *not* measured by the items found on traditional IQ tests.

Cornelius and Capsi's (1987) study assessed the relationship between practical intelligence and measures of crystallized and fluid intelligence. Their study consisted of two phases. In phase 1, these researchers developed a measure of practical

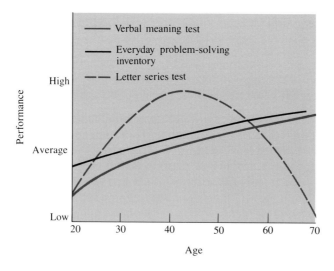

Figure 5.8   An illustration of age-related changes on the Everyday Problem-Solving Inventory, the Verbal Meaning Test, and the Letter Series Test.
Source: Data from S. W. Cornelius and A. Capsi, "Everyday Problem Solving in Adulthood and Old Age" in *Psychology and Aging,* 2:144–153. Copyright © 1987 by American Psychological Association, Arlington, VA.

intelligence called the *Everyday Problem-Solving Inventory.* This test consisted of forty-eight problems within six different social areas such as managing domestic issues and resolving interpersonal conflicts between family members, friends, and coworkers. Phase 2 involved the administration of the Everyday Problem-Solving Inventory along with measures of crystallized intelligence (the *Verbal Meaning Test)* and fluid intelligence (the *Letter Series Test)* to groups of young, middle-aged, and older adults. The results of this study, illustrated in figure 5.8, indicate that performance on the Everyday Problem-Solving Inventory and the Verbal Meaning Test increased with age, while performance on the Letter Series Test decreased with age. Furthermore, a modest correlation was found between scores on the Problem-Solving Inventory and both the Verbal Meaning Test and the Letter Series Test. Finally, it was discovered that familiarity with problems on the Everyday Problem-Solving Inventory was not related to scores on this measure.

These results suggest that practical problem solving, an important component of people's implicit view of intelligence, may be somewhat distinct from traditional measures of fluid and crystallized intelligence. The results also seem contrary to Denney's (1984) position that older adults perform better on measures of practical intelligence since they have much more experience in solving these problems. More positively, the results of this study support the viewpoint advocated by Paul Baltes and his associates (Baltes, 1990; Dixon and Baltes, 1986; Dittmann-Kohli and Baltes, 1988). These investigators suggested that practical or social intelligence increases with age and has little in common with traditional psychometric measures of intelligence.

CONCLUSIONS ABOUT ADULT INTELLECTUAL CHANGE

One of the major goals of this chapter was to answer what seems to be a relatively simple question: What happens to intelligence as one ages? As we have seen, however, this is not a simple question with any simple answers. Cross-sectional studies show a more dramatic and steeper rate of intellectual decline than longitudinal studies. Cross-sectional studies, because they are likely to be contaminated by cohort effects and terminal drop, are likely to paint an overly pessimistic picture of adult intellectual change. Longitudinal and sequential studies indicate that intelligence remains stable (or actually increases) until approximately sixty years of age, after which a slight decline may be observed. This conclusion seems most valid, however, for healthy, well-educated adults. Furthermore, the findings of longitudinal studies may be contaminated by selective dropout.

We have also seen that different types of intelligence show different patterns of change over age. Crystallized and verbal components of intelligence seem to increase with age, while fluid intelligence as well as performance measures of intelligence decline with age. Despite these predictable patterns of age-related change, there is a great deal of plasticity in adult intelligence. It is possible to train adults to increase their scores on intelligence tests, even on tasks that measure fluid abilities.

Finally, we discovered that traditional measures of intelligence are modestly related to measures of practical or social intelligence during adulthood. This finding does *not* mean that traditional tests are invalid measures of intelligence. Rather it suggests that psychometricians need to develop a more differentiated theory (and tests) of intelligence—a theory that does full justice to the broad array of intellectual abilities manifested by adults as they age. Two of the more recent theories of the nature and meaning of intelligence are discussed in box 5.1. The theories presented in box 5.1 may help lay the basis for the development of more meaningful measures of adult intelligence.

Adults are not only intelligent, they are creative as well. In the next section we'll examine the differences between intelligence and creativity, and we'll look at the course creative thinking takes during the adult years.

THE PSYCHOMETRIC APPROACH
TO THE STUDY OF CREATIVITY

Psychologists have assigned an important role to the study of creativity. David Wechsler, who developed the WAIS, suggested that, "Wisdom and experience are necessary to make the world go round; creative ability to make it go forward." (1958, p. 143)

What is it about someone like Thomas Edison that made him able to create so many inventions? Was he simply more intelligent than most people? Did he spend long hours toiling away in private? Surprisingly, when Edison was a young boy, his teacher told him he was too dumb to learn anything! There are other examples of

---

BOX 5.1

NEW VIEWS OF INTELLIGENCE

Two prominent psychologists of the 1990s are Howard Gardner and Robert Sternberg. They have developed unique theories that challenge the traditional psychometric views concerning the measurement and meaning of intelligence.

Howard Gardner (1983), in a controversial book entitled *Frames of Mind,* proposed a theory of multiple intelligences. This theory suggests that there are seven different human intelligences, each of which is localized in a different area in the brain. The different intelligences identified by Gardner are *linguistic intelligence, logical-mathematical intelligence, spatial intelligence, musical intelligence, bodily-kinesthetic intelligence, interpersonal intelligence,* and *intrapersonal intelligence.* Each of these different intelligences makes use of a different symbol system through which individuals represent or structure experience. For example, experience can be symbolized through words; logical-numerical relationships; visual images; tones, pitches, or rhythms; body movements; and so forth. Furthermore, Gardner maintains that only the first three of the above-mentioned intelligences are measured on traditional IQ tests.

Gardner's criteria for identifying specific types of intelligences include: (1) each intelligence can be independently represented in the brain and destroyed by damage or injury to a localized brain site; (2) exceptional individuals, child prodigies, and idiot savants may exhibit extraordinary performance in one form of intelligence but moderate or poor performance in other forms of intelligence; (3) each intelligence has a unique developmental history; (4) each intelligence consists of a core set of operations which are automatically triggered by particular types of experiences or information; (5) each intelligence has an evolutionary history; (6) the existence of each intelligence can be demonstrated by laboratory experiments and psychometric research; and (7) each intelligence possesses its own unique symbol system.

---

famous individuals whose creative genius went unnoticed when they were younger (Larson, 1973): Walt Disney was fired from a newspaper job because he didn't have any good ideas; Enrico Caruso's music teacher informed him that he could not sing and that his voice was terrible; Winston Churchill failed one year of secondary school; John Lennon was not viewed as especially bright by his teachers. One of the reasons that creative ability is overlooked is because we have such difficulty in defining and measuring creativity.

Definition and Measurement of Creativity

The prevailing belief of experts who study creativity is that intelligence and creativity are not the same (see, for example, Getzel, 1975; Richards, 1976; Wallach,

Gardner's theory is new enough that it has not been assessed fully in adult and/or aged populations. It would certainly be interesting, however, to determine what types of intelligence are likely to remain stable, decline, or increase with age.

Robert Sternberg (1985) has developed a triarchic theory of intelligence. According to Sternberg's viewpoint, intelligence can be described in terms of three different subtheories. The *contextual subtheory* describes a type of intelligence that helps individuals adapt to the changing circumstances (or contexts) of life. The *componential subtheory* involves a set of basic mental processes or subcomponents used to encode and organize relevant information, allocate attention, plan a strategy, monitor the effectiveness of the strategy, and modify the strategy in light of external feedback. The *experiential subtheory* describes how the internal component processes of intelligence are used to meet the demands of the changing external world. This subtheory focuses on two related phenomena—novelty and automatization.

According to this subtheory, individuals who can rapidly react to novel circumstances and who can quickly automate a newly learned skill are highly intelligent. As individuals develop a larger repertoire of automatized skills, they can adapt to a larger range of familiar environmental events while at the same time freeing basic cognitive resources for the demands of new, more novel challenges.

As with Gardner's theory, there is as yet little, if any, solid research relating Sternberg's triarchic theory to adulthood intellectual change. It might be proposed, however, that in the face of dwindling information-processing abilities (the componential subtheory), older adults will select environments in which they can maximize their intellectual performance (the contextual subtheory) through the application of highly practiced, automatized intellectual skills (the experiential subtheory).

1973; Wallach and Kogan, 1965; Weisberg, 1986). Just think about it: if intelligence and creativity were identical, there would be no reason to make a distinction between them! We could choose one of these terms—intelligence or creativity—to describe the same phenomenon.

Distinguishing between creativity and intelligence is a difficult task. David Ausubel (1968) has emphasized that creativity is one of the most ambiguous and confusing terms in psychology. He believes the term *creative* should be reserved for people who make unique and original contributions to society. Surely a list of creative individuals, from this point of view, would include Marie Curie, Charles Darwin, Thomas Edison, Georgia O'Keefe, Pablo Picasso, and William Shakespeare—they possessed creative genius, or **exceptional creativity.** The world we live in has been shaped and influenced by the creative acts of these individuals. Several other researchers (for example, Mumford and Gustafson, 1988; Simonton, 1988) have also agreed that psychologists should focus their attention on the study of "exceptional creativity."

Simonton (1988) has noted that a thorough understanding of the relationship between age and exceptional creativity is by no means a purely academic issue. For example, because of the aging of the baby-boom generation, the mean age of the typical U.S. scientist will be fifty by the year 2000. If exceptional creativity peaks in early adulthood (and many researchers believe that this is the case), then, as a nation, we may be only a short time away from an era when other nations with a younger age-structure begin to surpass us in scientific accomplishment. What would be the ramifications of this on our economy, national security, medical care, and so on?

Robert Weisberg (1986) has argued for the existence of what may be called **ordinary creativity.** Ordinary creativity is exhibited in the behavior of "ordinary" adults who find themselves in "ordinary" real-life situations. George Rebok (1987) also describes a kind of ordinary or everyday creativity in which we respond in give-and-take banter with friends, add new spices as we cook old family recipes, or create new outfits from our staid wardrobes.

J. P. Guilford's model of intelligence (1967) has important implications for creative thinking. The aspect of his model most closely related to creativity is what he calls **divergent thinking,** a type of thinking that produces many different answers to a single question. Divergent thinking is distinguished from **convergent thinking,** a type of thinking that moves toward one correct answer. For example, there is one correct answer to the question, How many quarters can you trade for sixty dimes? This question calls for convergent thinking. But there are many possible answers to the question, What are some uses for a coat hanger? This question requires divergent thinking. Examples of what Guilford means by divergent thinking (his term for creativity) and ways of measuring it are shown in table 5.3. Guilford's model has been useful in the development of standardized, psychometric measures of ordinary creativity.

Rebok (1987), while in general agreement with the position advocated by Guilford (1967), has suggested that the generation of novel ideas (divergent thinking) should be viewed as a necessary but not sufficient condition for creativity. Rebok points out that creativity is dependent on possessing a great deal of knowledge within a particular area of interest. For example, it would be very difficult to be a creative composer if one did not know much about musical composition. Researchers interested in creativity should simultaneously assess an individual's thinking style and the degree of knowledge he or she possesses within a particular domain. This suggestion may be especially important when we examine creativity in older adults. As individuals age, they may be more likely to develop a sophisticated knowledge base within a particular area.

Table 5.3

GUILFORD'S COMPONENTS OF DIVERGENT (CREATIVE) THINKING

1. *Word fluency:* How facile are you with words? For example, name as many words as you can as fast as possible that contain the letter *z*.

2. *Ideational fluency:* Name words that belong to a particular class. For example, name as many objects as you can that weigh less than one pound.

3. *Associational fluency:* In this type of divergent thinking you name words that are associated with other words, such as by similarity of meaning. For example, name as many words as possible that mean "easy."

4. *Expressional fluency:* Put words together to meet the requirements of sentence structure. For example, write as many sentences as you can that have four words, each word starting with these letters: *T, a, s, a.* (One sentence using these letters might be: *Tomorrow a salesman arrives.*)

5. *Spontaneous flexibility:* Even when you are not asked to give divergent answers, do you give unique as well as common answers? For example, if you are asked what a paper clip can be used for, do you spontaneously generate different categories of use for the paper clip?

6. *Adaptive flexibility:* In this type of divergent thinking you must be able to vary your ideas widely when this is called for. For example, if you are shown a series of matchsticks lined up on a table, you may be asked to put them together to form four triangles.

7. *Redefinition:* You might be asked to say how specific common objects can be used for new purposes.

8. *Originality:* Name some unique ways to use an object. For example, what are some unusual ways to use hairpins?

From J. P. Guilford, *The Nature of Human Intelligence.* Copyright © 1967 McGraw-Hill, Inc., New York, NY. Reprinted by permission.

Developmental Changes in Creativity

Because of the different conceptualizations of creativity, we'll divide this section into two parts. First, we'll discuss age-related trends in exceptional creativity—the important, creative accomplishments of well-known people within various fields of specialization. Second, we'll discuss age-related differences in ordinary creativity. This form of creativity has been measured by administering psychometric tests of creativity to typical as opposed to exceptional individuals.

Harvey Lehman (1953, 1960) and Wayne Dennis (1966, 1968) conducted some of the earliest and most influential research on age-related changes in exceptional creativity in adulthood. Lehman (1953) charted the ages at which adults produced highly creative works that had a significant impact on their fields. The quality of productivity was highest when such individuals were in their thirties and then gradually declined. Lehman argued that approximately 80 percent of the most important creative contributions are completed by age fifty. Lehman concluded that "genius does not function equally throughout the years of adulthood. Superior creativity rises rapidly to a maximum which occurs usually in the thirties and then falls off slowly." (Lehman, 1953, pp. 330–331)

Unlike Lehman (1953), Wayne Dennis (1966) studied the *total* productivity, not just the superior works, of creative people in the arts, sciences, and humanities who lived long lives. He discovered that the point at which creative production peaked in adult life varied from one discipline to another. For example, in the humanities, people in their seventies appeared equally creative as people in their forties. Artists and scientists, however, began to show a decline in creative productivity in their fifties. In all instances, the twenties was the least productive age period in terms of creativity.

Dennis (1968) also examined the creative output of famous scholars, scientists, and artists who lived until at least eighty years of age. Dennis discovered that, on the average, the sixties was the most creative decade in the lives of these individuals! Thirty-five percent of the total output of scientists was produced after age sixty— 20 percent while they were in their sixties and 15 percent while they were in their seventies. Famous inventors produced more than half of their lives' work after age sixty. Approximately 20 percent of the total output of artists was achieved after age sixty. In a study of Nobel laureates in science, it was found that the average age at which they published their first major paper was twenty-five. Furthermore, all of the laureates in this study who were past seventy continued to publish scholarly papers in scientific journals. Therefore, by relaxing the criteria for defining exceptional creativity (that is, by examining the total creative output of individuals, not just their best work), we see that creativity may not decline as early as Lehman (1953) suggested. It seems as if individuals who are bright and productive in early and middle adulthood have a good chance of maintaining their creativity in older adulthood. This conclusion is consistent with Simonton's statement that the most creative individuals "tend to start early, end late, and produce at above-average rates . . ." (1988, p. 253).

See figure 5.9 for an illustration of the data obtained by both Lehman and Dennis. Also, see table 5.4 for a list of some creative accomplishments that have been produced by older adults. These two illustrations summarize the conclusions of the early studies by Lehman and Dennis.

More recently, Raymond Over (1989) examined the relationship between age and exceptional creativity by using a novel methodology. He analyzed the percentage of both high- and low-impact articles published by scientists at different ages. Over discovered that young scientists published more high-impact articles than older scientists. This finding was consistent with Lehman's (1953) research. However, Over also found that younger scientists published substantially more low-impact articles than older scientists. He concluded that older and younger scientists do not differ in their probability of producing high- versus low-impact contributions (1989). At the same time, however, he found that as scientists age, they produce less high- *and* low-impact work. Thus, Over suggested that we need to determine what, if any, interventions will increase the research output of older scientists.

Without relying on scientific studies, think of all the older individuals around the world who employ their creativity, intelligence, and leadership skills to shape events and change the course of history. For example, as Lehman (1953) observed,

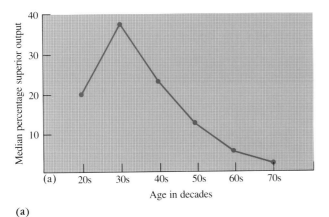

(a)

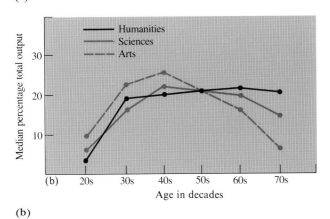

(b)

Figure 5.9   (a) The percentage of superior output as a function of age. This generalized curve represents a combination of various fields of endeavor and various estimates of quality. Data are from Lehman, 1953, table 34. (b) The percentage of total output as a function of age. The humanities, sciences, and arts are represented by the means of several specific disciplines. Data are from Dennis, 1966, table 1.

most of the presidents and prime ministers of the major countries of the world, chief justices in most of the world's courts, the world's religious leaders, and so on are over sixty years of age. Most interesting, however, is Simonton's (1988) observation that older individuals occupy positions of power and leadership within a number of social, political, and religious institutions, while younger adults are more likely to create new institutions and/or revolutionize existing ones. For example, a typical Pope of the Roman Catholic Church assumes his position at approximately double the age at which Jesus of Nazareth ended his ministry (Simonton, 1988). This seems to support Hall's (1922) position that "men in their prime conceived the great religions, the old made them prevail." (p. 420)

Table 5.4

SOME CREATIVE ACCOMPLISHMENTS OF OLDER ADULTS

Accomplishment	*Age*
George Bernard Shaw writes his first play	48
Sophocles writes *Oedipus Rex*	75
Sigmund Freud writes last book	83
Benjamin Franklin invents the bifocal lens	78
Claude Monet begins the Water Lily series	73
Michelangelo creates St. Peter's and frescoes the Pauline Chapel	71–89
Mahatma Gandhi launches the Indian Independence Movement	72
DeGaulle returns to power in France	68
Frank Lloyd Wright completes the Guggenheim Museum	91

What happens when we administer psychometric tests of creativity to "typical" as opposed to "exceptional" groups of aging individuals? Does ordinary creativity show a pattern of age-related change? One of the first scientific studies on this topic was conducted by Alpaugh and Birren (1977). Their cross-sectional sample consisted of 111 teachers between twenty and eighty-four years of age. These subjects were administered the WAIS as well as a battery of psychometric tasks that measure creativity. Within this well-educated sample, scores on the WAIS remained stable across adulthood. However, scores on the measures of creativity were found to peak at thirty and decline thereafter.

In a more recent study, Ruth and Birren (1985) tested 150 persons enrolled in adult education classes in Finland with several psychometric tests of creativity as well as measures of crystallized and fluid intelligence. The adults ranged from twenty-five to seventy-five years old. Results indicated that performance on the creativity measures declined with age. The great majority of this decline, however, was found to occur between young and middle adulthood. No age-related differences were found on the measure of crystallized intelligence; but scores on the fluid task were found to decline with age. Ruth and Birren offered three possible explanations for the age-related declines in both fluid intelligence and creativity. First, the age-related slowing of the central nervous system may reduce the amount of information that older adults can process as well as the speed at which they process it. Second, the cognitive changes that accompany aging may reduce the complexity of the information that adults can process. Third, because of the way older adults are socialized, it may be that they are less willing to risk novel solutions to problems. As adults age, they may become more risk-aversive, fearful, and cautious.

One of the major problems associated with the Alpaugh and Birren (1977) and Ruth and Birren (1985) studies is the use of a cross-sectional methodology. In comparison, Schaie and Hertzog (1983), in a longitudinal study on aging and creativity, discovered that only one aspect of divergent thinking (word fluency) declined with age. Unfortunately, the results of this study are clouded by the fact that the word fluency task was highly speeded. This may have placed the older adults at a greater disadvantage than the younger adults.

In one of the most comprehensive studies of aging and creativity, McCrae, Arenberg, and Costa (1987) combined cross-sectional, longitudinal, and cross-sequential methods of data collection. Their research, a component of the Baltimore Longitudinal Study of Aging, involved testing 825 well-educated men at regular intervals between 1959 and 1972. The men ranged from 17 to 101 years old. All of the participants were administered several different divergent-thinking tasks. These tasks involved (1) *associational fluency*—the ability to provide synonyms for specific words; (2) *expressional fluency*—the ability to write sentences with words beginning with certain letters; (3) *ideational fluency*—the ability to name objects in specific classes; (4) *word fluency*—the ability to write words containing a designated letter; and (5) *consequences*—the ability to imagine unusual, novel outcomes for particular situations. The participants were also administered the vocabulary test from the WAIS. Results indicated that scores on the measures of creativity and the WAIS were distinct from each other. This is surprising, given the fact that the vocabulary test and all of the measures of creativity were verbal in nature. Furthermore, all the different methods of data collection and analysis (cross-sectional, longitudinal, and cross-sequential) revealed that scores on the measures of creativity declined with age. Based on these results, McCrae, et al. (1987) concluded that creativity, like fluid intelligence, declines with age. However, the correlations between age and performance on the measures of creativity, although statistically significant, were in the modest range ($-.10$ to $-.30$). Also McCrae and his colleagues administered the tests of creativity under standardized conditions with strict time limits, a procedure that may be especially disadvantageous to older participants.

Perhaps the complex and somewhat confusing nature of developmental changes in creativity may be best understood by approaching creativity from a contextual perspective. A contextual view suggests that a number of psychological and social changes may influence creativity during adulthood. In a discussion of life-span creativity, Jean and Michael Romaniuk (1981) provide an example from the academic world of how incentives for productivity may influence an individual's creativity. Tenure and the pressure to publish may affect creative accomplishment. Shifts in career interests and activities, such as transferring from research to administrative activity, individual shifts in priorities concerning career goals and job security, and attention to refining earlier creative accomplishments may influence creativity. And the opening of new research fields, along with the saturation of existing fields, may also influence creative accomplishments.

In addition to the environmental circumstances that may influence creativity, one model of creativity attempts to delineate qualitatively different stages of creative development during the adult years (Taylor, 1974). Taylor believes that creative ability undergoes five sequential stages: expressive spontaneity, technical proficiency, inventive ingenuity, innovative flexibility, and emergentive originality. See table 5.5 for an explanation of these forms of creativity that seem to appear at different points in the adult years.

Table 5.5

HYPOTHESIZED STAGE OF CREATIVITY IN ADULTHOOD

Type of Creativity	*Age Range*
Expressive spontaneity: Creativity that may have a biological base and may be suppressed by formal education; shows up in children's games, dances, drawings	Childhood, appearing again in the late thirties
Technical proficiency: Creativity that is a function of the refinement of skills, as in concert instrumental work, dance	Typical of the twenties and forties
Inventive ingenuity: Creativity as it is expressed in idealized drawing, gadgetry, tinkering	Typical of the thirties and fifties
Innovative flexibility: Creativity that allows one to modify and adapt basic ideas, systems, and organizations for new purposes	Ages twenty-five to fifty
Emergentive originality: Creation of totally new or original ideas	After fifty

From E. Taylor, "Creativity and Aging" in *Successful Aging: A Conference Report* (E. Pfeiffer, ed.). Copyright © 1974 North Carolina Central University Center for the Study of Aging and Human Development, Durham, NC. Reprinted by permission.

In summary, we have seen that creativity is an elusive concept, one that is difficult to define, measure, and chart. It seems as if exceptionally creative individuals may continue to function in a creative manner well into middle and late adulthood. In fact, many creative people do some of their best work late in life. When we study ordinary creativity in typical individuals, we usually observe a gradual decline in divergent-thinking skills as measured by standard psychometric tests. However, studies in this area have found relatively modest correlations between age and various components of divergent thinking. Standardized tests of divergent thinking (because they are speeded) may place older adults at a distinct disadvantage.

ADULT EDUCATION

In recent years, there has been a tremendous increase in adult education—both formal and informal. Adults today constitute more than half of all full- and part-time college students. More than 50 million adults are learning at their places of employment as American industries mandate skill enhancement and retraining programs. Through private instruction, in local school districts, in synagogues and churches, through professional associations, and in voluntary community organizations, adults continue their lifelong learning. Adults also continue learning on their own through television, libraries, museums, correspondence courses, and other sources (Aslanian and Brickell, 1980).

In the past, most of our society's educational efforts were focused on children and adolescents. As Sherry Willis (1985) commented, in today's complex, fast-paced, and changing world, the education children receive will simply not last a lifetime. Our society needs to re-educate and re-socialize adults into roles they were not prepared for in their youths. We must view education as a lifelong process that helps maximize the development of individuals across the entire human life span.

Adults constitute over half of all full- and part-time college students in the United States today.

Why Adults Initiate or Continue Their Education

Willis (1985), after a careful review of all the available research, identified five possible goals associated with the initiation of an adult education program:

1. *Education as a means of comprehending one's own aging.* As individuals grow older, they feel a greater need to seek information about the direction and meaning of the aging process.

2. *Education as a means of comprehending sociocultural change.* Older adults need to understand the social and technological changes that have produced dramatic changes in their personal behavior. Several studies (Daniel, Templin, and Shearon, 1977; Romaniuk and Romaniuk, 1982) have shown that adults enroll in education programs because they want to learn new things and continue to be contributing members of society.

3. *Education as a means of combatting technological and sociocultural obsolescence.* The education most older adults obtained in their youth does not allow them to cope with societal and career demands many decades later. Education becomes a means, therefore, of overcoming generational differences in both relevant knowledge and relevant skills. Given the rapid changes occurring in our society, perhaps we need another period of compulsory education in middle or late adulthood.

4. *Second-career education.* Middle-aged to older workers who seek to remain competitive in the work force may have to undergo routine boosts or changes in their education. In the past, individuals made career choices in adolescence and young adulthood and stuck with those choices throughout life. Today, this pattern has dramatically changed. Because of technological change, several occupations that existed fifteen years ago no longer exist today. Conversely, several of today's occupations were not even identifiable fifteen years ago.

5. *Education as a source of satisfactory retirement roles.* Much of our adult work life does not provide us with the skills we need to adapt to retirement. Educational programs focusing on self-discovery and leisure-time activities may aid individuals making the transition into retirement.

Transitions and Triggers As Instigators of Adult Education

In the book *Americans in Transition,* Aslanian and Brickell (1980) describe a number of life changes as possible reasons for initiating adult learning. Changes in population, mobility, technology, occupation, housing, income, inflation, government, family life, politics, minority affairs, and leisure will trigger an even faster rate of change in adult life than ever before. Career changes also trigger the need for adult education as people enter, progress through, and exit various fields. Aslanian and Brickell (1980) estimated that at the time of their study some 40 million adults in the United States anticipated making a job or career change.

Transitions are triggered by many life events besides career and job changes. These life events, which may serve as triggers for continued education, include giving birth, joining the armed services, suffering a heart attack, divorcing, having a loved-one contract a deadly disease, seeing the youngest of your children leave for college, retiring, and others.

Aslanian and Brickell (1980) have raised some important questions about adult education. Some of the most provocative of these questions are:

1. Presumably a large number of adults experience major transitions in their lives. Why do some adults choose learning as a means to cope with these transitions, while others do not?
2. Why do the advantaged seek learning more often than the disadvantaged? Do the disadvantaged experience fewer life transitions, or do they overlook the value of education in making those transitions?
3. Is there some optimum match between a given type of transition and a given provider of learning? For example, are employers the best providers of education for those in career transition?
4. Adult participation in learning is increasing, but at a slower rate than in earlier years. If social and economic changes are taking place at an ever-increasing pace, why isn't adult participation in learning taking place at an ever-increasing rate?

Why Adults Discontinue Their Education

Patricia Cross (1978) examined the possible barriers that have kept some adults from continuing their education. She concluded that three such barriers exist:

1. *Situational barriers.* Such barriers arise for individuals in particular situations. Perhaps they lack the time to continue their education due to home or job responsibilities. Other barriers might include lack of transportation, geographical isolation, lack of child care, and so forth.
2. *Dispositional barriers.* One's attitudes about learning and perceptions of oneself as a learner may create barriers. Individuals may feel too old to learn, may lack confidence, or be bored with school.
3. *Institutional barriers.* Learning institutions or agencies may erect barriers that exclude or discourage certain groups of learners. Such barriers include inconvenient schedules, full-time fees for part-time study, or restrictive locations.

One investigation undertaken by the College Entrance Examination Board (Brickell, 1979) analyzed the role played by economic factors in adults' decisions to continue their education. Investigators collected information from 3,500 workers in a truck assembly plant to find out why 99.5 percent did not use the tuition reimbursement plan their union leaders won in their current contract. The tuition reimbursement plan is one method designed to remove economic barriers to learning. In such a plan, the company pays for any job-related training—training that can even include earning college degrees. But although in this case, the company had removed the economic barriers, the workers themselves were never motivated to go to school, to take television or correspondence courses, or to undertake independent study. The economic barriers seem to have been less important than other factors. Perhaps the workers used the economic argument to rationalize their anxiety about embarking on new educational careers.

Intelligence, Creativity, and Adult Education

Does the information we have explored about age-related changes in intelligence and creativity have a bearing on adult education? Most certainly it does! If you remember, most of the longitudinal studies of intelligence revealed that mental abilities actually increase until mid-adulthood, after which they either remain stable or show a small decline. Findings such as these have led Willis (1985) to suggest that individuals in their thirties, forties, and fifties may be particularly suited for higher educational pursuits—rather than people in their twenties, as we have come to expect. Furthermore, longitudinal studies suggest that adult education may have different functions at different times in the adult life span. The acquisition of new information and the sharpening of basic abilities may be the wisest goal of education until individuals reach their fifties. During the sixties and beyond, because of the declines seen in some intellectual abilities, the basic goal of education should probably be to maintain and support established abilities. The results of several cognitive and intellectual training studies seem to suggest that observed declines in mental abilities, even fluid abilities, may be reversible. These studies have given support to a **decrement with compensation model** of intellectual aging. This model suggests that declines in intellectual abilities occur during the course of aging, but that these declines may be reversed (or compensated for) by appropriate educational intervention.

The importance attached to cohort effects in the study of intellectual aging has important implications for adult education programs. The goals of an education program aimed at older adults should be the remediation of intellectual deficits due to cohort and/or age. Older adults, in other words, may have two strikes against them when entering an educational program. First, coming from an earlier birth cohort, they may lack a number of the basic skills and areas of knowledge possessed by younger persons. Second, older adults may experience a decline in some (but not all) of their basic intellectual abilities.

Developmental changes in creativity suggest that older adults possess the abilities necessary for creative accomplishment. Studies within this area suggest that adult education programs should help adults mobilize the best aspects of their intellectual abilities and creative talents.

Future studies should examine the specific characteristics of adult learners, the intellectual and creative activities that are most likely to change, and the environments within which adult learning best proceeds.

Summary

The psychometric approach emphasizes a measurement-based orientation to the study of adult intellectual change. Psychometricians differ on the issue of whether intelligence is a general ability or a constellation of separate abilities. Intelligence, from the psychometric perspective, is assessed by the use of standardized tests. One of the most widely used tests to assess adult intelligence is the Wechsler Adult Intelligence Scale (WAIS). This test contains both verbal and performance scales.

Different types of developmental studies have reflected different patterns of age-related changes in intelligence. Cross-sectional studies show that intelligence declines sharply from early adulthood onwards. Longitudinal studies, on the other hand, indicate that intelligence remains stable until late adulthood, when it may undergo a slight decline. Verbal intelligence is likely to improve with age, while nonverbal or performance components of intelligence are likely to decline with age. Put somewhat differently, crystallized intelligence has been found to increase with age, but fluid intelligence seems to decrease with age. Several factors appear to contribute to the observed age-related changes in intelligence. These factors include cohort effects, selective dropout, health status, and terminal drop. It has been shown that adults who actively exercise specific mental abilities, or who receive special training in specific abilities, do not display significant age-related decrements in those abilities.

As adults we not only think, but we think creatively as well. Definition and measurement problems have always plagued research on creative thought. Research on developmental changes in exceptional creativity suggests that in the arts and sciences creative thought may peak in the forties, while in the humanities creativity maintains itself well into the early part of late adulthood. Regardless of when creativity reaches its peak, research shows that for the majority of individuals creative output continues throughout mid-adulthood to later life. Research designed to study everyday creativity in typical individuals has shown a modest, but statistically significant, decline in divergent thinking over the adult life span. This research, however, may be marred by various methodological problems (including the speeded nature of standardized tests of creativity).

Adult education is and will continue to be a significant phenomenon for years to come. Adults initiate or continue their education for many reasons: to advance careers, to prepare for retirement, to understand themselves better, and to keep up with social and technical changes, to name a few. Based on the results of various psychometric studies of intelligence and creativity, it seems clear that middle-aged adults have the capacity to be competent and capable learners. In the future, more researchers will need to determine how to challenge adult learners and develop effective, practical, and efficient educational techniques and environments to fit our society's need for lifelong learning.

Review Questions

1. What does the term *psychometric* mean?
2. Explain how psychometricians determine the IQs of different-aged adults.
3. What does it mean to say that intelligence reflects the operation of a single g factor? Have researchers obtained data supporting the g factor theory?
4. Explain the difference between crystallized and fluid intelligence. How do these different forms of intelligence change over time?
5. Explain the different results obtained by cross-sectional versus longitudinal studies of adult intellectual change.

6. Explain how cohort effects, selective dropout, health status, and terminal drop influence IQ test scores.
7. Discuss the concepts of mental exercise, plasticity, and cognitive intervention in late adulthood.
8. Describe two different approaches to the study of creativity and explain what you think is the best way to measure it.
9. Trace the developmental course of creativity during adulthood. How do developmental changes in "exceptional" creativity differ from those in "ordinary" creativity?
10. What factors cause adults to initiate or continue their education? What factors influence the decision to terminate education?
11. What are some of the transitions and triggers related to adult education?
12. Given the observed age-related changes in intelligence and creativity discussed in this chapter, at what age do you believe it is best to begin (and end) one's education?

For Further Reading

Baltes, P. B. (1987). Theoretical propositions of life-span developmental psychology: On the dynamics between growth and decline. *Developmental Psychology, 23,* 611–626. An excellent article focusing on the basic tenets of life span developmental psychology and how these principles may be best understood by studying intellectual change during adulthood. Moderate reading level.

Gardner, H. (1983). *Frames of mind: The theory of multiple intelligences.* New York: Basic Books.
In this fascinating and award-winning book, Howard Gardner outlines his provocative theory of multiple intelligences. Moderate reading level.

Rebok, G. W. (1987). *Life-span cognitive development.* New York: Holt, Rinehart, and Winston.
In this comprehensive book, George Rebok describes how intelligence, creativity, and other cognitive functions change over the entire human life span. Moderate reading level.

Schaie, K. W., and Willis, S. L. (1986). Intellectual development: The display of competence. In K. W. Schaie and S. L. Willis (Eds.), *Adult development and aging.* 2nd ed. Boston: Little, Brown.
Schaie and Willis are two of the foremost researchers on the topic of intellectual change during adulthood. In this chapter they outline some of the most important empirical findings in this area. Easy reading.

Weisberg, R. W. (1986). *Creativity: Genius and other myths.* New York: W. H. Freeman.
This book, although it does not directly address the developmental course of creativity, provides a good overview of some of the myths and misunderstandings that surround the topic of creativity. Easy reading.

Willis, S. L. (1985). Towards an educational psychology of the older learner: Intellectual and cognitive bases. In J. E. Birren and K. Warner Schaie (Eds.), *Handbook of the psychology of aging.* New York: Van Nostrand Reinhold.
This chapter points out the important implications of research findings concerning intellectual change during adulthood for formulating an educational psychology of the adult learner. Moderate reading level.

CHAPTER 6

INFORMATION PROCESSING
AND ADULT COGNITION

IMAGINE

Imagine That a Computer Could Age in the Same Way a Human Mind Ages

To comprehend what would happen to a computer as it "ages," we need to describe the different components of a computer and how these components function.

At the most general level, a computer consists of two different components: a *hardware* component, and a *software* component. The hardware component consists of the actual physical pieces of the computer as well as the type of material it is constructed from (metal, silicon, and so forth). The software component consists of the different *programs* used to perform particular operations on information. Some programs might perform mathematical operations. A program of this sort could, for example, find the sum of a series of numbers and then divide the sum by the number of figures in the series (in other words, this simple program could be used to find the mean of a distribution of numbers). Other programs might be used to perform logical operations. This type of program might determine that if $A > B$ and $B > C$, then $A > C$ (or, the computer could infer that if Sally is older than Jane and Jane is older than Mary, Sally is older than Mary).

The major function of a computer is to process information. In fact, a computer is an information-processing device that encodes, stores, and retrieves information as well as performs operations on information. The process of *encoding* refers to how the computer represents or symbolizes incoming information. Computers usually symbolize information in a binary fashion by a long series of 0s and 1s. The process of *storing* refers to how the computer copies encoded information. Some information may be placed in a temporary short-term memory, or working memory. Other information may be permanently copied by the computer. Permanent copies of information are stored in long-term memory. The process of *retrieving* refers to how the computer locates information stored in long-term memory and places it back in working memory. Once information is placed in working memory, different types of programs may be used to perform different types of operations on the information. Of course, a number of specific programs may be used by a computer to help it encode, store, and retrieve information.

If you think about it, the human mind is one type of information-processing device. The human mind encodes, stores, and, retrieves information through specific "programs." Furthermore, the mind, like a computer, uses programs (or rule systems) to perform operations on information.

If computers could age, how might young adult computers differ from elderly computers? Would young computers use more efficient programs to help them acquire and remember information? Or would younger and older computers use the same programs but work at different processing speeds? Would older computers take significantly longer to perform the same operations as younger computers? Or would older computers experience a reduced capacity to store information, or to move information into memory?

If the human brain is like a computer, we might hypothesize that older individuals exhibit a decline in their mental abilities because (1) they use less efficient programs or strategies for processing information, (2) they process information in a progressively slower manner, and (3) they experience a reduction in the amount of information that their cognitive systems can store. Psychologists interested in information processing during the adult years have, in fact, considered these and other possibilities.

INTRODUCTION

In chapter 5 we discussed how systematic changes in adult cognition can be understood within the framework of the psychometric perspective. In this chapter, we'll consider the information-processing approach to the study of adult cognition. We'll begin by briefly tracing the history of this approach and describing its essential characteristics. Then we'll consider how the information-processing approach might apply to age-related changes in the areas of perception, attention, and memory. Despite its current appeal, the information-processing approach has two main limitations. First, the great majority of information-processing research is cross-sectional in nature, so that it is hard to distinguish between the effects of age and cohort (see chapter 2). Second, most of this research involves comparisons between young adults and elderly adults, so that we know relatively little about information processing in middle adulthood. These limitations will no doubt eventually be corrected; meanwhile, we have made tremendous progress in our understanding of information-processing differences between younger and older adults.

THE INFORMATION-PROCESSING APPROACH

According to the **information-processing approach,** mental activity is the processing of incoming information from the world. This processing underlies such phenomena as **perception,** which is conceptualized as the encoding of information; **attention,** which controls what and how much information is encoded; and **memory,** which involves the encoding of information as well as the storage and retrieval of encoded information for later use. Perception, attention, and memory are *not* considered unitary processes; they are best considered *functions* or *capacities,* each based on many different processes. In other words, many processes contribute to perception, attention, and memory. The goal of scientists in this area is to study and understand the elementary processes that determine how perception, attention, and memory work, as well as how all of these functions may work differently at different points in the life span. Such differences are the focus of the information-processing approach to adult development and aging.

The Roots of Information-Processing Theory

The information-processing approach has its historical roots in the growth of computer science and the development of artificial intelligence (see, for example, Churchland and Churchland, 1990; Klahr and Wallace, 1975; Gardner, 1985; Newell and Simon, 1972; Siegler, 1982; Stillings, et al., 1987). Computers are essentially high-speed information-processing systems. Advocates of the information-processing approach reason that the computer serves as a viable model of how information might be processed in the human mind. For example, both the computer and the human mind employ *logic* and *rules* (Belmont and Butterfield, 1971; Gardner, 1985; Wallace, 1977). Both have limits on their capabilities to handle and process certain

The information-processing theory holds that the computer offers a viable model of how information might be processed in the human mind.

types of information. Some of these limitations have to do with physical **hardware**—for the computer, the physical machinery; for the human mind, the limits of the brain and sensory systems. Other limitations are imposed by the **software**—for the computer, the programming; for the human, past learning and current developmental level. Many experts believe that as we make progress in understanding computers, we will gain an increased understanding of how the human mind works. Some go so far as to claim that unless we have a working computer program that delineates the steps needed to complete human cognitive tasks, we will not really understand how the human mind works at all (Gardner, 1985; Simon, 1980).

PERCEPTION AND AGING

Donald Kline and Frank Schieber (1985) reviewed scientific research about the nature of perceptual change within the domain of vision in late adulthood. One aspect of visual perception that appears to undergo a decline as people get older is the ability to discriminate relevant from irrelevant information. For example, investigators have found that individuals in late adulthood have more difficulty than young adults detecting figures embedded in complex target designs (Crook, et al., 1962; Panek, 1982). This difficulty may reflect age-related differences in attention, which we will consider later.

Another area of perception that presents difficulties for the aged is perceptual flexibility. Older adults are slower to modify a perception once they form it. For example, older adults report less reversals while looking at a Necker cube such as the one in figure 6.1 (c) (Heath and Orbach, 1963). Also, older adults are less likely to report seeing reversals while looking at other types of ambiguous figures (Botwinick, Robbin, and Brinley, 1959).

Older adults also find it difficult to identify incomplete figures. An incomplete figure consists of a drawing of an object in which several components have been removed (Biederman, 1987). Imagine a drawing of a coffee cup in which a number of the lines, angles, and curves that constitute the drawing were erased. Older adults would have more difficulty than younger adults recognizing the object portrayed in the drawing. Some examples of incomplete figures are contained in figure 6.1, along with several ambiguous or reversible figures.

A fourth type of perceptual deficit that can occur in old age has been detected in laboratory experiments in which **masking techniques** are used. If a visual pattern is presented briefly and then, after a very short time interval, is replaced by another visual stimulus, the individual's perception of the first pattern may be impaired—the second stimulus has *masked* the first. Presumably, it takes time for the data from the initial pattern to build up to a critical perception level and thus become relatively immune to interference by further stimulation. In the absence of a masking stimulus, data from the initial pattern can continue to accumulate in some kind of perceptual image up to one-half second or so after the initial stimulus has been removed. It has been found that older adults are more susceptible to masking effects (Byrd and Moscovitch, 1984; DiLollo, Arnett, and Kruk, 1982; Kline and Szafran, 1975; Walsh, 1976). To perceive a stimulus, older adults seem to require either a longer exposure of the original visual stimulus or a longer time interval between the onset of the original stimulus and the masking stimulus (Poon, 1985).

A plausible interpretation of all these results is that the rate of visual information processing slows with age. However, we still need to determine more precisely the mechanisms and locus of perceptual differences between young and elderly adults (Kline and Schieber, 1985). Is age-related visual slowing caused by changes in the photoreceptors of the retina (Pollack, 1978)—a more peripheral explanation—or by changes in more central structures such as the visual cortex of the brain (Botwinick, 1978; Hoyer and Plude, 1980)? Researchers are actively involved in attempting to answer such questions.

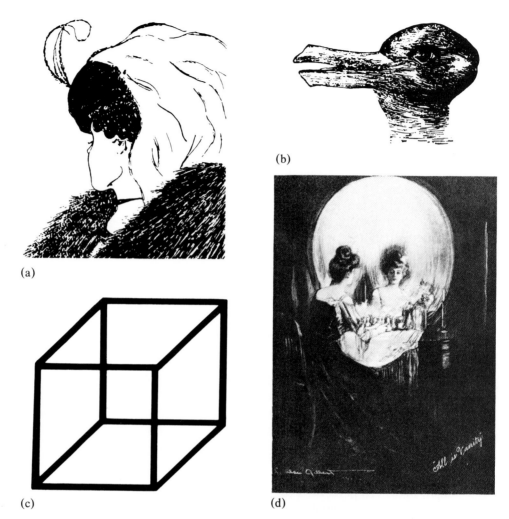

(a)

(b)

(c)

(d)

Figure 6.1 Ambiguous or "reversible" figures and incomplete figures. In (a)-(d), at least two scenes can arise from the same sensory pattern. (c) This person can either be seen as a beautiful young woman or and unattractive old one. (b) Is this figure a rabbit or a duck? (c) The Necker Cube. Stare at the interior corner that you think is nearest to you, and you will suddenly discover that it has become the farthest corner. The cube spontaneously reverses in depth. (d) Viewed up close, this scene reveals to most people a woman examining herself in the mirror; at a distance, the same scene reveals a skull. (e) & (f) Incomplete figures. Older adults find it more difficult to identify the content of such drawings. They also have difficulty reversing ambiguous figures once they have formed a perception.

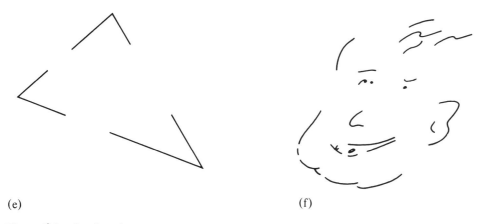

(e)   (f)

Figure 6.1   Continued

Practice Effects

If there are differences between young and elderly adults in various aspects of perception, to what extent can these differences be eliminated through practice? This was one of the questions raised by Timothy Salthouse and Benjamin Somberg (1982). They examined the performance of young and elderly adults on a visual-detection task over a period of fifty experimental sessions. Participants viewed a screen on which a pattern of sixty dots appeared. The dots were displayed for one-quarter of a second (250 milleseconds). The participants' task was to judge whether any of the dots were in motion. During half of the trials, a pattern of five dots was in motion. On the remaining trials, all of the dots were stationary.

The detection task devised by Salthouse and Somberg was difficult and demanded very rapid perceptual processing. For this reason, we would expect young adults to outperform elderly adults. Indeed, this is precisely what Salthouse and Somberg observed. Of greater interest, however, was the fact that the difference between young and elderly adults persisted over fifty days of practice.

The results of the Salthouse and Somberg experiment are shown in figure 6.2. The graph shows clearly that performance improved with practice and that this practice effect was perhaps slightly larger among elderly participants than young adults. It also shows that, with a moderate amount of training, older adults can perform better than untrained younger adults. However, the graph also shows a performance difference between young and elderly participants—a difference that does not disappear after extensive practice. In response to these data and other experiments, Salthouse and Somberg concluded that "older adults go through essentially the same processing operations as young adults but merely at a slower rate." They attribute this reduced rate of processing to a "fundamental physiological change in the nervous system." (1982, p. 203)

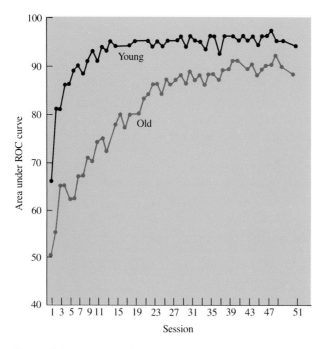

Figure 6.2   Mean signal-detection performance for young and old adults as a function of extended practice.

ATTENTION AND AGING

Attention is a multifaceted phenomenon (Stankov, 1988). The vast majority of the research on attention, however, has focused on two different ways in which attention may fail as we age. First are failures of **selective attention.** These occur when we have difficulty ignoring material that is irrelevant to our interests or goals (for example, try reading difficult material while ignoring a television set going full blast in the same room). Second, there are failures of **divided attention.** These occur when we have problems processing all of the information in a situation that is of importance to us (for example, try listening to two or more important conversations simultaneously).

Selective Attention

The research conducted by David Madden and Robert Nebes (1981) argues *against* the existence of important age-related differences in selective attention. In one of their experiments, individuals were assigned two target items (letters of the alphabet) to keep in memory. On each trial of the experiment, they were instructed to respond "yes" or "no" as to whether one of these targets appeared in a display of six letters. The display was composed of three red and three black letters. One half of the trials were *cued,* meaning that before the visual display appeared, participants were shown either a black dot or a red dot. If the dot was black, the participants were told that the target (if present) would be one of the three black letters. If the dot was red, the participants were told that the target (if present) would be one of the three red items. The presence of the cue effectively indicated which three letters of the display were relevant (and therefore should be attended to) and which three were irrelevant (and therefore should be ignored). The other half of the trials were *noncued.* These trials were preceded by a green dot that gave no information regarding the target item's potential color. Thus, on the noncued trials, all six display items were relevant and attention was directed at them all.

On each trial, the cue was presented for 100 msec, followed by a 900 msec delay interval, followed by the visual display. The display remained in view until the individual responded. If an age-related deficit in selective attention existed, it should create greater age-related differences on the cued trials than on the noncued trials. This finding would mean that older adults did not benefit from the cue. But analysis of reaction times failed to reveal an age-related impairment in selective attention. The older adults were found to benefit from the cue as much as the younger adults did. This does not mean that the elderly adults performed as well as the younger adults. The elderly adults, in fact, performed more poorly on both the cued and noncued trials than the younger participants. But the results did show that the elderly adults did not perform disproportionally worse on the cued trials than they did on the noncued trials. Generally, age-related differences in selective attention are not well supported by research evidence.

Divided Attention

The topic of age-related differences in divided attention is very controversial. Divided-attention tasks require processing two or more different tasks or problems at once. For example, driving a car in heavy traffic while looking for a specific road sign is an example of a real-life divided-attention task (Ponds, Brouwer, and Van Wolffelaar, 1988). Somberg and Salthouse (1982) have noted that previous studies (see Craik, 1977) that revealed age-related changes in divided attention suffered from several methodological problems. First, previous researchers examined developmental changes in divided attention by measuring **dual-task performance** without taking **single-task performance** into account. Dual-task performance refers to a person's ability to perform two different tasks at once (for example, learning a poem while pressing a button every time a light goes on). Single-task performance refers to the ability to perform just one task at a time (the ability to either learn a poem *or* press a button in response to a light). The distinction is important because older adults may perform poorly on a dual-performance task *not* because they have problems dividing attention between the tasks, but because they cannot perform either of the two individual tasks very well.

Another issue raised by Somberg and Salthouse is that measures of dual-task performance have not adequately accounted for **resource allocation** strategies.

Driving a car is an example of a divided-attention task—a task that requires processing two or more different problems at once.

That is, when placed in a dual-task situation, young and elderly adults may differ in their strategies for trading off one task against the other. For example, younger adults may give equal attention to the two different tasks, whereas elderly adults may simply concentrate on one task alone.

To deal with these issues, Somberg and Salthouse devised a dual-task experiment in which single-task performance was controlled. In this experiment, participants were asked to view a computer monitor. On each trial, a pattern consisting of four X symbols (forming a rectangle) and four + symbols (forming a smaller rectangle) were presented for less than a second. The participants' task was to judge whether one of the four Xs contained a target (a small vertical or horizontal line extending from one of the Xs) and also to judge whether one of the four + signs contained a target (a small diagonal line extending from one of them). Since the Xs and + signs were presented simultaneously, the participants' task was one of divided attention.

The experiment included two important innovations. First, Somberg and Salthouse controlled for single-task performance by young and elderly participants. Prior to the divided-attention trials, each participant was tested on his or her ability to perform under single-task conditions (with Xs only and with + signs only). The duration of the displays was then adjusted for each young and elderly participant.

Specifically, the duration of the displays was matched to the exposure time under which each participant responded correctly between 80 and 90 percent of the time under single-task conditions. Second, the investigators systematically varied the resource allocation strategies of their participants. They did this by providing financial rewards for accurate performance and by giving varying rewards in different conditions (for example, rewarding more for the × task than for the + task or vice versa, or by making rewards equal for the × and the + tasks).

The results of the experiment were straightforward. Both age groups showed lower performance under dual-task (divided-attention) conditions than under single-task conditions. Of greater importance, however, was that the authors found *no* evidence that elderly participants performed disproportionally poorer in the dual-task condition than younger individuals. Further, both age groups were able to trade off one task against the other in accordance with the rewards they were offered.

Other researchers have found results consistent with the results obtained by Somberg and Salthouse. Wickens, Braune, and Stokes (1987) had four groups of participants ranging from twenty to sixty-five years of age perform a perceptual-motor stability test (a task similar to balancing a stick on the end of one's finger). Participants performed the task either alone or concurrently with a memory-search task (for example, searching a visual display to determine if it contains a previously targeted letter of the alphabet). When both types of tasks were performed separately, results indicated that older participants (1) took a longer amount of time to perform the memory-search task and (2) made more errors on the perceptual-motor stability task. When both tasks were performed concurrently (a divided-attention task), the older participants displayed a greater decrement in performance on both tasks than the younger participants. Like Somberg and Salthouse, Wickens et al. (1987) took into account age-related differences in single-task performance when evaluating performance on the divided-attention task. This analysis indicated that older participants did not perform disproportionally poorer when performing the tasks concurrently. Wickens et al. (1987) concluded that although information-processing speed significantly decreases with age, the ability to divide attention does not change with age.

Although the research conducted by Somberg and Salthouse (1982) and Wickens et al. (1982) seems convincing, it may be premature to conclude that the ability to divide attention does not change with age. Wickens et al. (1987) have cautioned that (1) not all of the different circumstances under which divided attention could decline in elderly individuals have been explored, and (2) on logical grounds it is impossible to prove the null hypothesis (that is, the hypothesis that differences between participants do *not* exist on a particular task). Furthermore, other researchers (Madden, 1987; McDowd and Craik, 1988), using methodologies different from both Somberg and Salthouse (1982) and Wickens et al. (1987), have obtained evidence suggesting an age-related decrease in divided attention. Specifically, McDowd and Craik (1988) found that age-related differences in divided attention emerge when complex tasks are given to participants, but age-related decrements are negligible when simple and relatively automatic tasks (such as those employed by Somberg and Salthouse) are used. In fact, McDowd and Craik suggested that overall task complexity, rather than the requirement to divide attention per se, may account for age-related performance decrements on divided-attention tasks.

Limited Attentional Capacity

The existence of age-related differences in attention may be better understood by considering the concept of **limited attentional capacity** (Hasher and Zacks, 1979; Kahneman, 1973). Attentional capacity is a type of psychological energy needed to perform mental work. This capacity can vary depending upon a person's level of arousal and other factors; at any one moment, attentional capacity is, at least to some degree, limited. Further, attentional capacity is thought to decline with age (Craik and Simon, 1980; Hasher and Zacks, 1979).

Several kinds of evidence point to a decline in attentional capacity in late adulthood. Perhaps the strongest evidence comes from comparisons of **effortful information processing,** which is thought to draw on limited attentional capacity, and **automatic information processing,** which presumably does not draw on limited attentional capacity. In one of William Hoyer's experiments (Plude and Hoyer, 1981), young and elderly women searched for two or four target letters in computer displays composed of one, four, or nine letter arrays. Half of the women in each age group were placed in a *varied-mapping condition;* they looked for different target letters on different trials. The remaining women were included in a *constant-mapping condition;* they looked for the same letters on all trials. There is good evidence (Schneider and Shiffrin, 1977) that practice on the constant-mapping procedure results in automatic processing, or processing that is independent of other demands on limited attentional capacity. Interestingly, Plude and Hoyer found only very small age-related differences in the constant-mapping condition. In contrast, the varied-mapping condition, which demanded effortful processing, produced a large deficit in the elderly participants. The results support the contention that there are age-related differences in effortful processing (which draws on limited attentional capacity), but not in automatic processing (which does not draw on limited attentional capacity). A more recent study conducted by Plude and Hoyer (1986) has yielded results consistent with those from the first. Taken as a whole, these findings suggest important practical implications. For instance, although elderly people may suffer processing deficits, these deficits can be overcome, to some extent, if processing becomes automatic.

Dana Plude and Lisa Murphy (in press) have called attention to the costs as well as the benefits of automatic information processing. For example, because attention is not allocated to the performance of highly automated, habitual acts (such as turning off the burner on a stove or taking medication for hypertension) older individuals may have a difficult time remembering whether they performed these behaviors. Poor memory for habitual actions may lead to disastrous consequences (such as taking a double dose of medication). Plude and Murphy suggest that older adults may improve their memories for habitual acts by trying to deautomatize these activities. For example, when taking a pill for high blood pressure, an older person might say aloud: "I'm taking my pill now, it's one o'clock in the afternoon."

MEMORY AND AGING

The experimental psychology of memory is approximately 100 years old, originating with the research of Herrmann Ebbinghaus (1885). The vast majority of this work has been carried out with young adults, usually college students, and has added little to our knowledge of adult development and aging. More recently, however, researchers have begun to examine memory performance during all phases of adulthood (see Craik, 1977; Poon, 1985). The results that are emerging are far from simple, but they promise to tell us much about the nature of information processing across the life span.

Factors Involved in Memory Differences

Is memory better in young adults than in elderly individuals? There is no simple yes or no answer to this question. Age-related differences in memory depend on several factors. These factors include (1) the relative involvement of short-term versus long-term memory (see box 6.1), (2) the type of information-processing activities employed during encoding, (3) the nature of the memory test (for example, recall versus recognition), (4) the type of material that must be remembered (for example, familiar or unfamiliar), and (5) the characteristics of the person remembering (including the repertoire of knowledge and skills he or she possesses and can bring to bear on the memory task).

Short-Term versus Long-Term Memory

Adult age-related differences appear more clearly in tasks that depend upon long-term rather than short-term memory (Craik, 1977; Poon, 1985). Consider, for example, the assessment of a person's memory span, a commonly used test of short-term memory. Memory span is defined as the number of digits or letters a person can repeat in order without error. Table 6.1 summarizes the results of a representative study of memory span for letters (Botwinick and Storandt, 1974). Note that the fifty-year-olds performed as well as the twenty-year-olds, and even the sixty- and seventy-year-olds performed almost at that level. Memory span is only approximately one letter shorter among the elderly than among young adults.

In contrast to tests that rely on short-term memory, tests that require long-term memory (typically more than sixty seconds) or the remembrance of events that have left consciousness often show substantial age-related differences. A good measure of long-term memory can be derived from the task of **free recall.** In a free-recall task, a list of items—usually common words—is presented to adults, who then attempt to remember as many items as possible in any order. A classic experiment

---

BOX 6.1

DIFFERENCES BETWEEN SHORT-TERM AND LONG-TERM MEMORY

Many years ago, the famous psychologist William James (1890) distinguished between *primary memory* and *secondary memory.* James identified primary memory with conscious awareness of recently perceived events and secondary memory with the recall of events that have left consciousness. James's distinction was based primarily on his own introspections, but a similar distinction is supported by a great deal of experimental evidence. Today a host of information-processing models incorporate a distinction between primary or **short-term memory,** and secondary or **long-term memory.**

A generalized three-stage model of memory (Murdock, 1967) is presented in box figure 6.1. The model includes a system of sensory stores in addition to short-term and long-term stores. Note that box figure 6.1 indicates processes that transfer information from one store to another: transfer from sensory to short-term memory entails attention, and transfer from short-term to long-term memory requires rehearsal. Finally, the model hypothesizes different laws of forgetting for the three memory stores. Forgetting from sensory stores is thought to result from the process of simple *decay;* information is lost (within less than a second) simply as a function of time. Forgetting from short-term memory generally results from *displacement;* new information bumps out old information. Finally, forgetting from long-term memory results from *interference* that occurs between memory for one piece of information and other information learned previously or subsequently. Indeed, many investigators believe that interference does not destroy information in long-term memory but simply impairs the *retrievability* of information from long-term memory.

Several psychologists are examining the manner by which information is transferred from short- to long-term memory. Today it is recognized that simple rote rehearsal is not the only path, or even a very efficient path, to learning and remembering. Processes of organization, semantic elaboration, and imagery can be highly effective for enhancing long-term memory.

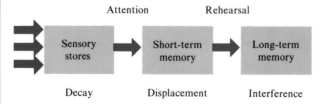

Box figure 6.1 A generalized three-stage model of memory.

Table 6.1

MEMORY SPAN FOR LETTERS PRESENTED AUDITORILY

	Age (Years)					
	20s	**30s**	**40s**	**50s**	**60s**	**70s**
Span	6.7	6.2	6.5	6.5	5.5	5.4

From Jack Botwinick and Martha Storandt, *Memory-Related Functions and Age,* 1974. Courtesy of Charles C Thomas, Publisher, Springfield, Illinois.

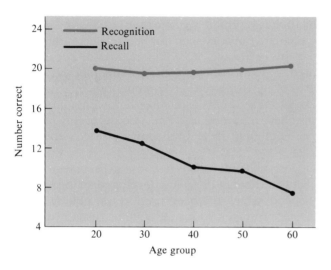

Figure 6.3   Recognition and recall scores as a function of age.

(Schonfield and Robertson, 1966) examined free recall by adults in five age groups. The lower line in figure 6.3 shows the free recall scores for each age group.

As you can see, a clear age-related decline occurs for free recall. This trend differs from the information about the memory span shown in table 6.1. Such comparisons have led some experts on adult cognition, such as Fergus Craik (1977) and Leonard Poon (1985), to conclude that the span or capacity of short-term memory is relatively unimpaired by aging.

Alan Baddeley (1986) suggests that memory-span tasks such as the one employed by Botwinick and Storandt (1974) are overly passive. Baddeley distinguishes between active and passive forms of short-term memory; he uses the term **working memory** to refer to the more dynamic aspect of short-term memory. Perhaps the best way to understand the concept of working memory is to think of a desktop. During the course of a day, new pieces of information (memos, reports, work requests, and so on) constantly accumulate on an individual's desk. At any given time during the work day, the individual has to determine (1) which task is the most important to complete, (2) which pieces of information on the desktop one must attend to in order to complete a task, (3) the best strategy to use to complete a task, and (4) which pieces of information are cluttering up the desktop and should either be discarded or saved. Thus, by analogy, a working-memory task requires an individual to select, coordinate, and process incoming information.

Using Baddeley's concept of working memory as a guide, Dobbs and Rule (1989) presented individuals in five different age groups (in their thirties, forties, fifties, sixties, and over seventy) with a standard memory-span task and a working-memory task. In the latter, participants heard a list of randomly ordered digits at a rate of one digit every 1.8 seconds. After the presentation of each digit, the participants were required to repeat (1) the digit they just heard, (2) the digit prior to the one they just heard, or (3) the digit two prior to the one they just heard. Results showed that performance on the standard memory-span task was related to the participant's education level but *not* to his or her age. More importantly, the age of the participant was significantly related to performance on the working-memory task. Specifically, subjects over sixty years of age displayed very poor performance on this task. Dobbs and Rule concluded that these results "are consistent with a growing literature indicating that aging may have a pronounced effect on the ability to manipulate processing and a lesser or negligible effect on the more passive (storage) aspects of memory." (1989, p. 502)

There is also evidence that suggests that older adults may lose *speed* in searching or scanning short-term memory. Saul Sternberg (1969) has developed an ingenious procedure for measuring search speed, which has been used to test elderly individuals. In this procedure, people are presented with a set of items (usually digits, such as 6, 3, and 9) to hold in memory. Then they are presented another digit (for example, 9). They have to decide as quickly as possible whether the digit matches one of the digits in the memory set. Memory sets of varying lengths are used, and as might be expected, reaction times rise (answers are given more slowly) as the length of the memory set increases. Figure 6.4 shows the results from one study (Anders, Fozard, and Lillyquist, 1972) that compared the speed of short-term memory search for individuals in early, middle, and late adulthood. Note that longer memory sets produced longer reaction times, which is a typical finding. Note also that the slope (that is, the steepness or the angle) of the reaction-time curve is greater for individuals in middle and late adulthood than for those in early adulthood. This difference in slope indicates that the two older adult groups scan through lists of items in short-term memory at a disproportionally slower pace than younger adults. Other studies (for example, Strayer et al., 1987) have shown that when dependent measures other than reaction time are used in memory-search studies (for example, P300 brain wave latency), the speed of memory search does not decline with age.

Scanning is not the only short-term memory process to slow with age. Evidence suggests that *spatial processing* in short-term memory also slows in older people (Cerella, 1985; Cerella, Poon, and Fozard, 1981). Spatial-processing tasks have been used to examine different aspects of mental imagery. The **mental rotation** task (Shepard and Metzler, 1971) is one of the best techniques available for exploring

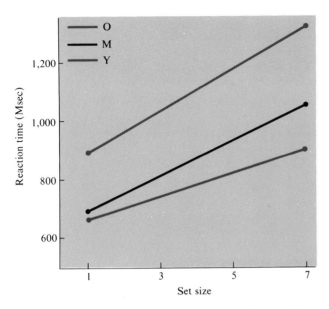

Figure 6.4   Mean reaction times as a function of age and set size.

spatial processes involved in mental imagery. In one version of this task, a capital letter appears on a screen, sometimes normally and sometimes reversed from left to right (reflected). Participants in the task decide, as quickly as possible, whether each letter is normal or reflected. Judgments are made by pressing one of two response keys. The latencies, or how long it takes, to make these responses are then measured. All of this sounds simple enough, except that the letters are usually also presented at a tilt rather than upright. The degree of tilt can range from 0 (upright) to 180 degrees (upside down). The key finding from such studies is that latencies become longer as the tilt increases. This effect of tilt on latency indicates that adults must mentally rotate the tilted letters to upright before making their judgment. (See figure 6.5 for examples of the way the letters are presented.)

Cerella et al. (1981) examined age-related differences in the speed of mental rotation. The results of this study are shown in figure 6.6. Note that the latencies grow longer with greater departures from vertical orientation—this supports the idea of mental rotation. But note also that the slope or steepness of the line relating orientation to latency is greater for older adults. This pattern suggests that mental rotation is slower in older adults than younger adults. A more recent study conducted by Sharps and Gollin (1987) measured the accuracy and speed of mental rotation in young and elderly adults. These researchers found, just as Cerella et al. did, that the speed of mental rotation declined with age. However, they also discovered that elderly participants' judgments were just as accurate as those of young participants.

Original
stimulus

1   2   3

Stimuli 1 and 2 are rotated (tilted)
versions of the original stimulus.

Stimulus 3 is a rotated and reflected version of the
original stimulus.

Figure 6.5   Examples of the stimuli employed in an imagery task examining mental rotation.

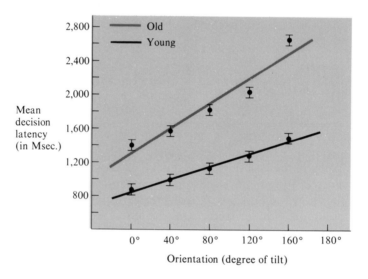

Figure 6.6   Mean decision latency for young and old adults as a function of stimulus orientation.

Research on the speed of scanning and mental rotation in short-term memory raises several interesting questions. One is whether the age-related losses in the speed of short-term memory search reflect the same underlying causes as the age-related losses in mental rotation speed. Cerella (1985) pointed out that the degree of age-related slowing in rotation was quite close to the degree of age-related slowing in memory search. This may be a coincidence. On the other hand, it suggests that a common factor may produce age-related slowing in many different processes (Birren, 1974). A second important question this research raises pertains to the role of life-style and educational factors in producing age-related slowing. To investigate this possibility, Jacewicz and Hartley (1979) compared the performance of young adults with that of elderly adults enrolled in college. No age-related differences in rotation speed were observed in this study. This suggests that education and life-style may be critically important determinants of age-related differences in rotation speed and other processes. A third question is whether practice can eliminate age-related differences in the speed of central cognitive processes. The study by Salthouse and Somberg (1982), discussed earlier, included a Sternberg-type memory-search task. Performance on this task was examined over fifty experimental sessions. After forty sessions, the slope of the function relating reaction time and memory set size was comparable for young and elderly adults. This suggests that extensive practice can increase the speed of central processes.

In summary, the evidence suggests that short-term memory capacity declines only minimally with age. Other aspects of short-term memory (for example, speed of memory search) also show significant age-related declines. The remainder of this section focuses on age-related differences in long-term memory.

Characteristics of the Processing Strategies

Though age-related differences are common in long-term memory, the magnitude of these differences—indeed, their very existence—depends upon the nature of the information-processing strategies individuals use. Three types of encoding processes appear especially important: organization, semantic elaboration, and mental imagery. Research suggests that all three processes—the characteristics of which are summarized in table 6.2—might be less efficient or less likely to occur in old age. This research also suggests that with appropriate techniques, older adults can overcome or at least reduce this deficiency.

Evidence for the influence of **organization** on memory comes in part from George Mandler's (1967) sorting task. In this task, people are asked to sort words into subjectively determined groups or categories. Subsequent recall of words is heavily influenced by the number of categories created; the more categories the person creates (up to about seven), the easier it is to recall the words presented. David Hultsch (1971) compared individuals in early, middle, and late adulthood in sorting and nonsorting conditions. In the latter condition, individuals simply were told to study the words presented. The results appear in figure 6.7. Young adults recalled equally well whether they were told to sort or simply to learn the words. In contrast, the recall of the two older groups improved when they sorted the words. Thus the difference between the younger and older participants decreased when the sorting technique was used. This pattern suggests that older adults may be deficient at organizing material. However, they can reduce this deficiency by a technique—such as the sorting procedure—that ensures that organizational activities take place.

Hilary Ratner and her colleagues (1987) conducted an experiment that examined age-related differences in organizational strategies in three groups of women: (1) young adult female college students, (2) young adult female high school graduates not enrolled in college, and (3) retired elderly females not enrolled in college. All of the women were required to learn different types of stories. Half of the

Table 6.2

CHARACTERISTICS OF THE PROCESSING STRATEGIES

Process	*Time of Occurrence in Memory Task*	*Description of Process*
Organization	Learning the material	The learner actively groups input items together into higher-order units or chunks. For example, in a long list of words, the learner might group together *raisin, apple,* and *pear* and treat them as a single unit (*fruits*).
Semantic elaboration	Learning the material	The learner associates presented items with long-term memory representations that give access to the meaning of the items. Semantic elaboration is usually involved in organization as well as imagery, though it might occur without these processes.
Imagery	Learning the material	The learner generates a "picture in the head," "tape recording in the head," or other mental image.

Note: While there are many different theories of how memory operates, the importance of these and other information-processing activities is widely acknowledged. Thus age-related differences in one or more of these processes would be expected to produce age-related differences in memory. By the same token, improving the utilization of these processes in individuals in middle or late adulthood may markedly improve the memory performance of these older people. Note also that these processes have been explored primarily in the domain of *verbal* memory; much less is known about their nature and importance for nonverbal memory (memory for faces, songs, and so forth).

women in each of the three groups were told simply to learn the stories; the other half were told to memorize the stories *verbatim.* In a memory test on the stories, the college students performed the best. It was discovered that they studied longer than the other groups and were more likely to use a variety of organizational strategies to help them remember the stories. The researchers did not observe the use of complex organizational strategies in either the young nonstudents or the older adults. Without such spontaneously constructed organizational strategies, memory deficits were likely to occur in both of these groups of women. Ratner and her associates concluded that the older women (as well as younger women who do not attend college) generally found themselves in nondemanding social environments. These environments did not require them to develop sophisticated strategies to help them organize information. This suggests that memory deficits in older adults may be attributed to environmental circumstances, not age per se. Results comparable to those obtained by Ratner et al. have also been reported by Zivian and Darjes (1983).

Semantic elaboration of information has also been found to improve older adults' memories. Smith (1977) required adults to study a list of words under three different conditions. Adults in the *no-cue* condition were shown a list of words (for example, *apple*) and instructed to learn them. Those in the *structural-cue* condition saw each word on the list along with its first letter (*apple—A*). In the *semantic-cue* condition, the participants saw each word on the list along with a category the

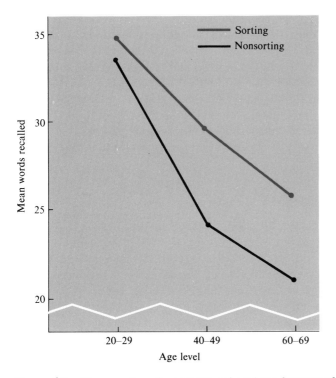

Figure 6.7   Mean number of words remembered as a function of age and sorting condition.

word belonged to (*apple—fruit*). In the first two conditions, age-related differences in free recall appeared. The young group (aged twenty to thirty-nine) had the best recall, the late adulthood group (aged sixty to eighty) showed the poorest recall, and the middle-aged group (aged forty to fifty-nine) was intermediate. However, in the third condition, which involved semantic-category cues, recall was approximately equal in all age groups! These findings suggest that an age-related decline occurs in recall memory, a decline that begins by middle age. But it also appears that this decline can be eliminated by incorporating semantic elaboration of the words to be recalled at the time of study.

Another process relevant to recall is **imagery,** which is known to improve memory in many different situations (Pavio, 1971). One study (Mason and Smith, 1977) focused on the recall of individuals in early, middle, and late adulthood. Those in the imagery condition were instructed to form mental images for each word on a list, but those in the control condition were given no instructions to aid recall. Imagery instructions did not affect recall in the early and late adulthood groups but did improve recall in the middle adulthood groups. Indeed, middle-aged adults in the imagery condition performed as well as young adults, though in the control condition they fell below young adults. Again, these results indicate an age-related deficiency in recall memory that can be eliminated through appropriate learning procedures. In this case, however, the learning procedure effective with middle-aged adults was *not* effective with elderly adults. Indeed, a study by Michael Eysenck (1974) comparing young and elderly adults showed that age-related differences can be greater under imagery instructions than under other types of instruction. And Fergus Craik and Eileen Simon (1980) have described studies in which semantic-categorization tasks (similar to the semantic-categorization task of Smith, 1977) failed to reduce age-related deficits in recall memory. Thus evidence shows that appropriate learning procedures, in many but not all instances, may eliminate age-related deficits in memory.

Characteristics of the Retention Measures

We previously discussed age-related differences in **free recall** observed by Schonfield and Robertson (1966; see figure 6.3). Their experiment also included a **recognition** test. The test included previously studied words along with new words; the participants attempted to recognize the former. Performance on this recognition test is shown by the top line in figure 6.3. As the figure shows, there was no evidence of an age-related deficit in recognition.

Bahrick, Bahrick, and Wittlinger (1975) observed a strikingly similar pattern. These researchers developed a naturalistic memory task—remembering one's high school classmates. The research assessed face recognition, name recognition, and name-face matching. Free recall of names and cued recall of names in response to faces were also evaluated. The participants differed in the number of years that had elapsed since their high school graduation (from three months to forty-seven years since graduation). It is clear from figure 6.8 that recognition and matching performance remained virtually constant (and nearly perfect) up to a retention interval of thirty-four years. This means that adults in their mid-fifties were performing about as well as eighteen-year-olds. In contrast, the recall measures, particularly free recall, showed clear evidence of age-related decline that began shortly after graduation. Note especially the steady drop in free recall from the three-year interval (adults about twenty-one years old) to the forty-seven-year interval (adults about sixty-five years old).

Why are age-related memory deficits attenuated when recognition tests are employed in research? One possibility (Craik, 1977) is that recall tests place a great demand upon effortful search or retrieval from memory. In a recognition test, previously studied items are actually presented to the participant; he or she only has to distinguish these items from distractors that have not been previously studied. This procedure may lessen the need to initiate effortful or controlled search processes. This argument makes sense given the information we have about the dwindling attentional resources available to the elderly.

Although several studies have shown that recognition testing reduces age-related memory differences, it would be wrong to conclude that such testing *always*

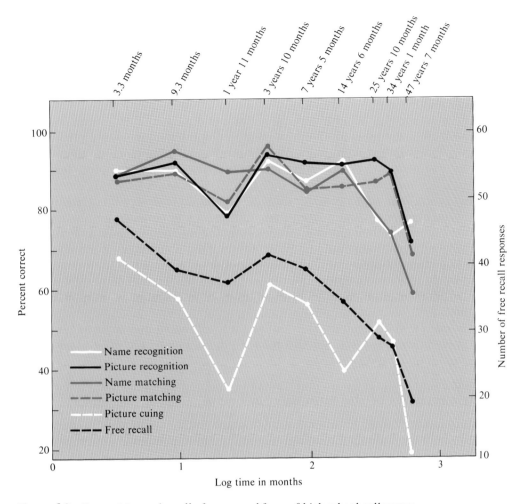

Figure 6.8 Recognition and recall of names and faces of high school colleagues.

removes age-related differences. A safer conclusion is that minimal age-related deficits occur if recognition testing is *combined* with controls over information processing at encoding. One investigation that illustrates this point was conducted by Sharon White (described in Craik, 1977). Elderly and young participants received the same list of words, but the participants in each group were asked different types of questions about the words on their list. In the *capitals condition,* each participant was asked if a word was printed in capital letters or small letters (for example, *goat* versus *GOAT*). In the *rhyming condition,* participants had to determine if each word on the list (for example, *goat*) rhymed with another word (perhaps *boat*). Participants in the *category condition* saw a word (*goat*) and then answered a conceptual question about the word (Is this a type of animal?). In the *learn condition,* participants were simply told to "learn the words." After receiving the list, all participants took both a recall and recognition test for all the words. The results showed age-related differences in recall memory but no age-related differences in recognition memory for words accompanied by questions. Elderly subjects performed more poorly than young adults in remembering the learn-condition words regardless of recall or recognition testing.

Studies such as White's (see also Craik and Simon, 1980; Perlmutter and Mitchell, 1982; Ratner et al., 1987) suggest a complex interplay among the factors of age, processing requirements at input (encoding), and type of test. When adults receive instructions for processing stimulus materials (for example, "learn the words"), age-related deficits often appear, regardless of recall versus recognition testing. In contrast, when elderly adults are instructed to process materials in a semantically elaborate manner, age-related differences in memory are less likely to occur—especially when memory is assessed using recognition tests. As Perlmutter and Mitchell (1982) concluded, "When retrieval support has been provided, and encoding operations directed, age differences seem to vanish." Their conclusion suggests that the encoding abilities of younger and older adults do not differ. What differs is their *spontaneous* use of complex encoding strategies (Perlmutter and Mitchell, 1982).

Besides tests of recall and recognition, tests of retention may include explicit and implicit memory tasks. See box 6.2 for a discussion of age differences on explicit and implicit memory tasks.

Characteristics of the Stimulus Materials

A fourth factor to consider in understanding age-related differences in memory is the nature of the material that adults are required to remember. An excellent demonstration of the power of *familiarity* was provided in a study by Barrett and Wright (1981). These investigators have shown that manipulations of familiarity can eliminate and even reverse memory differences between the young and the elderly. Barrett and Wright examined recall memory for young-familiar words, such as *tweeter, spa, cassette,* and *rip-off;* and, for old-familiar words, such as *poultice, davenport, hollyhock,* and *doily.* The former were more familiar to young adults than to elderly individuals, while the latter were more familiar to older people. The results were clear-cut; young adults outperformed elderly adults on recall of young-familiar words, but elderly adults outperformed young adults on recall of old-familiar words. Clearly, then, any comparison of memory abilities in different age groups must consider the factor of familiarity.

The effects of stimulus familiarity were also addressed in an interesting study conducted by Kathryn Waddell and Barbara Rogoff (1981). Waddell and Rogoff asked middle-aged and elderly women to remember the spatial locations of objects. In one condition, the objects were placed in a naturalistic panorama, while in the other condition, the objects were placed arbitrarily in cubicles. Performance in the two conditions was equivalent among middle-aged women, but elderly women performed more poorly than middle-aged women in the cubicle condition. The authors concluded that elderly people are apparently quite good at remembering the locations of objects as long as the stimulus materials are arranged in a realistic rather than unfamiliar fashion.

It would seem as if the most familiar and meaningful (and therefore the most memorable) experiences, then, are the real events that happen to us in our everyday lives. See box 6.3 for information regarding older adults' memories for earlier life experiences.

Characteristics of the Learner

A fifth factor relevant to age-related declines in memory concerns the learner. Many characteristics of the person apart from age can determine performance in memory tasks. These characteristics include but are not limited to attitudes, interests, health-related factors, and intelligence levels. In one experiment, Craik, Byrd, and Swanson (1987) studied memory ability in three groups of elderly people who ranged from sixty-four to eighty-eight years of age. Group 1 consisted of highly intelligent and relatively affluent individuals. Group 2 was comprised of individuals somewhat lower in intelligence and socioeconomic status who were actively involved in the community. Group 3 contained individuals of even lower intelligence and socioeconomic status who were not involved in community or social affairs. Furthermore, Craik, Byrd, and Swanson studied a group of college students matched on verbal intelligence with the first group of elderly participants. All participants received lists of words to remember. The participants differed, however, in the number of cues (that is, psychological support) they were given at encoding and/or retrieval. Some participants were provided cues when they were initially presented with each word on a list (for example, "a type of bird—LARK") but not during recall. Other participants were given this cue during recall but not during presentation; others were cued during both presentation and recall; and still others were not cued during either presentation or recall. The existence of age-related differences in memory was found to depend on the amount of support offered in the task and the characteristics of the persons performing the task. Among the participants who received the greatest degree of support (cued presentation and cued recall), all of the elderly groups with the exception of group 3 (low IQ, low socioeconomic class) performed just as well as the college students. Among the participants who received an intermediate amount of support (noncued presentation and cued recall), only the first elderly group performed as well as the college students. When participants were not provided with any support (noncued presentation and noncued recall), the college students performed better than all of the elderly groups. Figure 6.9 illustrates the different levels of performance for the participants.

One of the most important characteristics of adult learners is their repertoire of previously acquired knowledge and skills. It now appears that individuals maintain their ability to use well-learned knowledge, strategies, and skills throughout

BOX 6.2

AGE-RELATED DIFFERENCES IN IMPLICIT AND EXPLICIT MEMORY

Age-related differences in long-term memory are more likely to be revealed if memory is measured by a *recall* rather than a *recognition* task. A recall task is quite different from a recognition task but they do share one important characteristic—they both require *conscious* recollection of previous experiences. In both of these tasks, a person is *aware* of the fact that he or she is to remember something experienced in the past. Any memory task in which a person is instructed to consciously recollect (or become aware of) a previous experience is called an **explicit memory task** (Schacter, 1987).

By contrast, an **implicit memory task** is one which does not require an individual to consciously recollect a past event. Implicit memory has been referred to as memory without awareness. A person is not aware of the fact that he or she is remembering something while performing an implicit memory task (Schacter, 1987).

The distinction between implicit and explicit memory was first drawn by studying patients suffering from amnesia. In these experiments (see Squire, 1986, 1987), participants were given an orienting task in which they were required to make judgments about the words on a list. For example, amnesiacs might see the word *sharp* and then be asked a letter-identification question (Is there an *e* in this word?) or a semantic question (Is this word the opposite of *dull?*). Next, they are given an explicit memory task (involving recognition or recall) as well as an implicit memory task. Implicit memory is typically measured by a *word-fragment completion task.* In such a task, an amnesiac is shown a word fragment (that is, they see only some of the letters of a previously encountered word arranged in their correct locations). The participant is then asked to complete the fragment with any letters that pop into his or her mind. If the word *sharp* appeared in the first part of the experiment, for example, the participant might later be asked to complete the fragment *sha ___ ___* . The word-completion task may be given at different time intervals following the initial presentation of the word list (one hour later, one week later, and so on). Results show that profoundly amnesiac patients can remember a substantial number of words on a word-completion (implicit memory) task, yet be incapable of recalling or recognizing any of the words on the original (explicit memory) list. Thus, researchers conclude (Squire 1986, 1987; Schacter, 1987, 1989) that in amnesia explicit memory is impaired, but implicit memory is spared.

Most interestingly, older adults suffering from Alzheimer's disease perform significantly poorer on implicit memory tasks (such as the word-completion task) than either amnesiacs or young adults (Butters, 1987; Shimamura, 1986; Shimamura, Salmon, Squire, and Butters, 1987). As you may remember from chapter 4, AD may reflect an acceleration of normal aging. If this is the case, we would expect that normal elderly adults would exhibit deficits in both implicit and explicit memory in comparison to normal young adults. On the other hand, if AD represents a form of pathological aging distinct from normal aging, we would expect that normal elderly adults would exhibit deficits in explicit memory, but not implicit memory.

In the late 1980s, two teams of researchers, Christine Chiarello and William Hoyer (1988), and Leah Light and Andrea Singh (1987), examined age-related differences in implicit and explicit memory in healthy, community-dwelling adults. As would be expected, these researchers found that older adults performed significantly more poorly than younger adults on tasks of explicit memory (recall and recognition). Furthermore, they reported that older adults scored lower than young adults on tasks of implicit memory (for example, word-fragment completion) than young adults. However, only in the Chiarello and Hoyer (1988) experiment (which seemed to follow a more rigorous methodology than the Light and Singh study) did the differences between the younger and older adults on the implicit memory task achieve statistical significance.

In a review of the most recent literature, Rybash (1990) argues that there seems to be a slight impairment in implicit memory, as measured by word-completion performance, in the normal elderly. This leads Rybash (1990) to conclude that the memory loss displayed by the normal elderly is more similar to that of AD patients than amnesiacs. This means that the neurological changes that accompany normal aging may be more similar to those associated with AD rather than amnesia. Future researchers need to examine the validity and significance of this provocative claim.

BOX 6.3

AGING AND VIVID MEMORIES

When people are asked to remember a real-life experience, they are engaging in an **autobiographical memory task.** For example, can you remember where you were and what you were doing when you first became aware of the explosion of the space shuttle Challenger? This is an autobiographical memory task. On the other hand, being asked to remember the names of the astronauts who died in this crash does not measure autobiographical memory. One of the most important functions of autobiographical memory is to allow each of us to become our own personal historian. At a metaphoric level, we are continually engaged in the process of writing, editing, and updating the story of our own life.

Joseph Fitzgerald has conducted several studies that have examined the relationship between aging and different aspects of autobiographical memory. Fitzgerald and Lawrence (1984), for example, presented a group of older adults with a series of forty common words. Each participant was required to think of a specific autobiographical memory that would trigger each word. The results of this study displayed a typical *retention function*. This means that the participants were most likely to remember events that had just occurred rather than those that had occurred years ago. In fact, most of the autobiographical memories reported by the subjects happened within the last few years prior to the study. In a more recent study, Fitzgerald (1988) asked a group of older adults (approximately seventy years of age) to write a paragraph describing three different *vivid* or *flashbulb memories.* Specifically, the participants were told that a flashbulb memory occurs when an individual's mind takes an exceptionally vivid, detailed, and long-lasting picture of a personally experienced event. The participants were given the freedom to write about vivid memories that occurred at any time over the course of their lives. Finally, Fitzgerald asked the older adults to rate each vivid memory on a number of different dimensions. These dimensions included personal importance, national importance, frequency of rehearsal, and intensity of emotional reaction.

One of the most interesting and unexpected results of this study is displayed in box figure 6.2. Unlike the data collected in the Fitzgerald and Lawrence (1984) study, Fitzgerald's (1988) study shows that vivid memories do *not* exhibit a normal retention function. Participants were very unlikely to recall vivid memories from middle adulthood or old age. Instead, these older adults were most likely to recall vivid memories from their late adolescence and early adulthood. More specifically, the vivid memories reported by the participants were based on personal experiences that occurred, on average, forty years earlier. Also, the data for the study were collected shortly after the Challenger explosion; yet, none of the participants included this event in their list of vivid memories. Some of the older adults' vivid memories possessed a great deal of personal importance and were steeped in emotion (for example, a soldier remembering his friends dying in

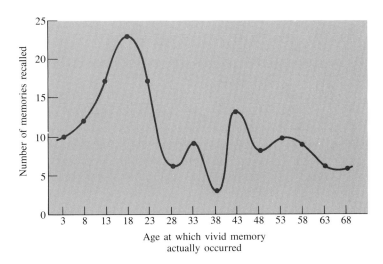

Box figure 6.2 Older adults' retention of vivid memories.

combat, and a mother remembering the birth of her child). However, most of these vivid memories were not of great personal or national importance, nor were they highly emotional (for example, remembering baking a cake or walking to school).

Why doesn't the age distribution of vivid memories show a normal retention function? Why are older adults most likely to recall vivid memories of events that occurred in their youth? Fitzgerald (1988) notes that adolescence and young adulthood may represent that period of the life span when we are in the process of forming unique personal identities. We may use this period as a marker or anchor-point from which to begin the story of our adult lives, of our psychological selves. Thus, because of the special status we attach to youth, we may be likely to have vivid memories from this period of our lives. Fitzgerald (1988) also suggests that because we live in a youth-oriented society, a rich storehouse of vivid memories from youth would allow older adults to maintain contact with a point in the life span when they were young, healthy, and had their lives in front of them.

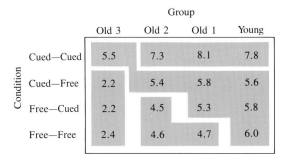

Figure 6.9 Word recall scores grouped into four levels of performance.

middle age and into old age. Tests of common factual knowledge (for example, vocabulary or events of the news) typically show no decline from young adulthood up to old age (Perlmutter, 1980). This seems to be true even when factual knowledge is tested by recall. Janet and Roy Lachman (1980) developed a way to measure recall of previously learned facts while controlling for individual differences in the number of facts known. Using recognition tests to estimate the total amount of knowledge a person possesses, the Lachmans derived a formula for assessing the odds that a given piece of memory knowledge can be retrieved in a recall test. This probability retrieval measure showed no decline between early and middle adulthood, and no decline between middle and late adulthood either.

In reviewing the complex evidence on age-related differences in memory, Marion Perlmutter (1980) suggested that a distinction between *memory processing* and *memory knowledge* may be useful. Aging may be associated with a decline in the speed and efficiency of the processes responsible for establishing new memories. This decline, however, does not affect the amount of knowledge *already stored* within memory, which is available for use in many different tasks. Thus age-related declines may be restricted to tasks in which a person's prior knowledge is not utilized. Tasks that capitalize upon previously learned information may show no age-related declines; indeed, on such tasks older people may even outperform young adults. Perlmutter's distinction between memory processing and knowledge is similar to Horn and Donaldson's distinction between fluid and crystallized components of intelligence (discussed in chapter 5), indicating at least some convergence of psychometric and information-processing ideas.

EXPLANATIONS OF AGE-RELATED MEMORY CHANGE

Why does memory change with age? Leonard Poon (1985) has suggested that changes in adult memory may be considered from three different perspectives: the **biological perspective**, the **processing perspective**, and the **contextual perspective.**

The Biological Perspective

According to the **biological perspective,** age-related differences in memory ability are caused by physical changes in the brain. We know that with increasing age, a number of changes take place within the neurons of the brain (senile plaques, neurofibrillary tangles, and so on, as discussed in chapter 4). These changes, which occur to varying degrees throughout the entire brain but especially within the hippocampus, may produce memory impairments. Also, age-related reductions in the amount of neurotransmitters such as acetylcholine (ACh) affect the consolidation of memories.

Marcel Kinsbourne (1980) has suggested that age-related damage to the cortex may result in attentional deficits which, in turn, cause memory deficits. Older people may have poor memories because they respond more slowly to environmental change and are more distracted by irrelevant task information (Hoyer, Rebok, and Sved, 1979). Albert and Kaplan (1980) have suggested that attentional deficits (and hence memory deficits) in the elderly may be caused by damage to the frontal lobes of the cortex. In fact, Albert and Kaplan (1980) discovered that, when given a number of neuropsychological tests, healthy older adults made the same types of errors as young patients who suffered from frontal lobe damage. Mayes (1986) has also suggested that damage to the frontal lobes leads to memory problems because the ability to plan and execute sophisticated encoding and retrieval processes is located in this part of the brain.

Beyond any doubt, a person's ability to learn and remember is related to the integrity of the brain. Biological models of memory loss are at present most capable of explaining the memory problems that accompany actual physical diseases of the brain (for example, Alzheimer's disease, amnesia, and others). Biological models seem to lose explanatory power when they are applied to healthy, community-dwelling older adults. According to Poon (1985), future researchers need to address two important questions. First, under what conditions are the memory problems of elderly people the result of biological deterioration, and under what conditions are they the result of psychological differences in the way older people process information? Second, under what conditions are biologically-based memory deficits reversible?

The Processing Perspective

The ability to remember information seems to depend on three different psychological processes: *encoding information* (that is, putting information into memory), *storing information* (keeping information in memory), and *retrieving information* (finding information previously placed in memory). The **processing perspective** maintains that older adults are deficient in some (or all) of these necessary memory processes. One idea is that an **encoding deficit** occurs in old age (Eysenck, 1974); elderly persons may simply be less capable of engaging in the organizational, semantic, and imagery processes that are helpful in memory tasks. Encoding deficits might be explained by age-related declines in attentional capacity (Hasher and

Zacks, 1979). That is, elderly people may show processing deficits because they have less of the attentional capacity needed for processing. Alternatively, older adults may not encode information very well because of low motivation, lack of familiarity with the information, and so on. Other psychologists (for example, Schonfield and Robertson, 1966) have called attention to a possible **retrieval deficit** in the elderly. Even if input processing is equivalent in young and elderly adults, the elderly may have difficulty finding previously stored information during the memory test. This theory is consistent with the fact that older adults generally do better on recognition than recall tests.

Poon (1985) has suggested that it is difficult, if not impossible, to trace memory problems to deficits in either encoding or retrieval. These processes are so interrelated and dependent on one another that they cannot be disentangled. For example, the ability to retrieve information depends partly on how well the material is encoded. It seems as if processing deficits experienced by older people may be systemwide.

The Contextual Perspective

The **contextual perspective** suggests that the primary goal of human memory is the reconstruction of previous experience. An individual actively reconstructs (or reinterprets) past experiences from the point of view of the present (just as a historian can only interpret the past from the perspective of the current situation). This viewpoint suggests that the effectiveness of a person's memory depends on the context within which the person is required to learn and remember information.

The degree to which a person's memory functions effectively, therefore, depends on the type of memory task, the type of person performing the task, and the type of materials contained in the task (Craik et al., 1987; Hultsch and Dixon, 1983; Jenkins, 1979). According to Craik et al. (1987):

> . . . it follows that age differences should be most pronounced when little guidance is provided at encoding and retrieval, when the material is not compatible with the subject's knowledge base . . . and when the older subjects themselves are of lower intelligence or what may speculatively be described as *possessing less resources, flexibility of mind, or mental initiative.* (p. 80)

Labouvie-Vief and Schell (1982) argued that older adults may reconstruct the past by developing new processing styles to replace the old ones that have become less effective with aging. For example, when comprehending story information, older adults are more likely to remember the gist of the information, while younger adults are more likely to remember the details. Thus there may be different types of information-processing styles that are more adaptive at certain times in adult development.

The contextual approach highlights the complexity of human memory. It suggests that statements such as, "Older adults have poorer memories than younger adults," and "Memory impairment in the elderly is caused by biological decline and/or processing deficits" are too simplistic and too general.

CONCLUSIONS ABOUT AGE-RELATED DIFFERENCES IN MEMORY

The capacity of short-term memory does not undergo significant changes with age. However, age-related deficits in active short-term memory (working-memory) tasks and in the speed of short-term memory search have been reported. Older adults perform more poorly than young adults on tasks of long-term memory, especially when recall rather than recognition is tested. Long-term memory in the elderly seems more robust, however, when it is measured by implicit rather than explicit memory tasks.

We have shown that older adults, if they are instructed to use efficient encoding strategies, can show a significant improvement in their ability to remember. We have also shown that age-related differences in memory are unlikely to occur when older adults are required to remember familiar information or when they draw upon previous knowledge to help them remember.

To be sure, the biological and processing perspectives have yielded important insights about the causes of age-related memory change. At present, however, the memory abilities of community-dwelling older adults may be best understood by adopting a contextual perspective (Craik et al., 1987; Jenkins, 1979; Poon, 1985). To understand the dynamics of human memory, we need to consider the interrelationship between (1) the characteristics of the person, (2) the characteristics of the material to be remembered, and (3) the situation in which the person is required to remember.

NORMAL VERSUS PATHOLOGICAL MEMORY LOSS

Until now we have focused our discussion on age-related memory differences in normal adults. By "normal" we mean adults who do not suffer from any known biological illness or psychological disturbance. As individuals age, however, they may develop disorders that are characterized by memory loss as one of their primary symptoms. For example, one of the key clinical indicators of Alzheimer's disease is memory loss. Also, one of the most prominent symptoms of depression in elderly adults is memory impairment. It is important for a clinical psychologist, physician, or psychiatrist to differentiate normal memory loss from memory loss due to Alzheimer's disease or depression. Making these types of differential diagnoses is never easy (Zarit, Eiler, and Hassinger, 1985).

Benign Senescent Forgetfulness

The nonpathological loss of memory in the normal elderly has been labeled as **benign senescent forgetfulness** (Kral, 1972). This type of memory impairment is benign because it does not interfere with a person's ability to function in everyday life. Some adults notice a decrease in memory ability as early as fifty to sixty years of age, although it is more common to become aware of memory problems after sixty years of age (Albert, 1984). In many instances, the elderly become very concerned about their self-recognized memory loss. They want to know if their failing memory is normal for their age or a sign of an abnormal disease process.

Many older adults are not very accurate in their self-assessments of memory ability (Hultsch, Hertzog, and Dixon, 1987). They seem to have a distorted picture of their own memory capabilities, often overdramatizing the degree of loss. In fact, Steven Zarit (1980) has argued that relatives, health-care professionals, and the elderly themselves tend to *overestimate* the degree to which healthy older adults suffer from memory problems. Several researchers (Cavanaugh, Grady, and Perlmutter, 1983; Zarit, Cole, and Guider, 1981) have found that older adults not only report more memory failures than younger adults, but they are more likely to become upset and frustrated when they experience a memory failure. It has also been discovered (Hermann and Neisser, 1978; Thompson, 1980; Zarit et al., 1981) that older adults' self-assessments of memory ability do not correlate with their performances on several laboratory tests of memory. Furthermore, it has been shown by Cutler and Grams (1988) that two of the best predictors of self-reported memory problems in older adulthood are the onset of health problems and sensory impairments (problems in seeing and hearing).

Older adults have more negative attitudes about their memories than younger adults, viewing memory loss as proof positive that they are getting old. Older adults are more likely to believe that (1) memory problems cannot be remediated, (2) memory failures are uncontrollable, and (3) memory deficits are caused by age (Berry, Geiger, Visocan, and Siebert, 1987; Person and Wellman, 1987). These beliefs have been found to be predictive of the amount of time older adults spend studying for a memory test and the number of "gloom and doom" verbalizations they make while preparing for the memory test (Berry et al., 1987; Person and Wellman, 1987).

Alzheimer's Disease, Depression, and Normal Memory Loss

How can we tell the difference between memory losses due to Alzheimer's disease, depression, and normal aging? It is extremely important to distinguish between these possible causes. Depression is a treatable or reversible mental disorder, while Alzheimer's disease is not. The result of misdiagnosing Alzheimer's disease as depression, or vice versa, would be disastrous. To make matters more complicated, the diagnosis of benign senescent forgetfulness, Alzheimer's disease, or depression is, in the great majority of cases, based on a behavioral or psychological assessment of the elderly person. Medical tests such as CAT scans, PETT scans, and blood tests are of limited use in conclusively identifying the source of an elderly person's memory problem (Cohen, 1988; Council on Scientific Affairs, 1988).

Donald Read (1987) has developed a useful model from which we can distinguish various memory problems. His model identifies *at what points* memory problems can occur in information processing. First, Read suggested that the ability to recall events from the recent past can be negatively affected by (1) lack of attention to or a difficulty in understanding what has happened (an *encoding deficit*), (2) the brain's failure to record the event (a *storage deficit*), or (3) difficulty recovering events already stored in memory (a *retrieval deficit*). Second, Read argued that the benign memory loss observed in normal elderly adults is caused by a combination of mild deficits in encoding and retrieval, *not* by the brain's inability to store information. Third, he suggested that among elderly adults with depression, poor memory performance stems from both encoding and retrieval deficits that are more severe than those found in the normal elderly. Depressed individuals, for example, may be so wrapped up in their inner worlds that they do not expend the effort needed to encode information in a meaningful way; and even if they encode and store information, they make little effort to retrieve it. Fourth, Read argued that in Alzheimer's disease the major cause of memory loss is the brain's inability to record information (a *storage deficit*). Memory loss in Alzheimer's disease patients should persist, therefore, even if they engage in meaningful encoding processes and are given the utmost support during retrieval. Note that Read does not deny that adults with Alzheimer's disease experience severe deficits in both encoding and retrieval (see Hart, Kwentus, Hamer, and Taylor, 1987). Rather, the thrust of Read's argument is that storage deficits are unique to patients suffering from AD.

Similarly, Grober and Buschke (1987) have made a distinction between apparent memory deficits and genuine memory deficits. **Apparent memory deficits** are memory problems resulting from the use of ineffective encoding and retrieval strategies. Apparent memory deficits can be overcome by inducing individuals to process information in an effective way or by providing individuals with effective retrieval aids. **Genuine memory deficits** are memory problems that persist even after individuals have carried out effective encoding and retrieval activities. Genuine memory deficits, in other words, may be related to the brain's ability to store information and to activate stored information (see also Rissenberg and Glanzer, 1987). Grober and Buschke (1987) suggested that individuals suffering from irreversible forms of dementia such as Alzheimer's disease would be more likely to experience genuine memory deficits than apparent memory deficits. On the other hand, nondemented individuals (both normal elderly and depressives) would be more likely to experience apparent memory deficits than genuine memory deficits.

Grober and Buschke (1987) performed an experiment in which normal older adults and Alzheimer's disease patients engaged in a special set of controlled-learning activities. These activities allowed them to effectively encode and retrieve a list of sixteen common words. Grober and Buschke (1987) hypothesized that the controlled-learning activities should compensate for the apparent memory deficits of the normal elderly adults. The normal elderly, in other words, should display perfect (or near-perfect) memory. The researchers also hypothesized that the controlled-learning activities would not compensate for the genuine memory deficits experienced by the demented patients. The patients, in other words, should have extremely poor memories even when they are given a great deal of help during encoding and retrieval. The results of the experiment were consistent with these hypotheses. See box 6.4 for a more detailed description of the controlled-learning technique developed by Grober and Buschke (1987).

BOX 6.4

MEMORY ABILITIES IN NORMAL
AND DEMENTED ELDERLY

Ellen Grober and Herman Buschke (1987) have developed a methodology that distinguishes between genuine memory deficits and apparent memory deficits. This methodology combines both *controlled learning* and *cued recall.* Controlled-learning procedures insure that an individual encodes information as effectively as possible. Cued recall insures that an individual retrieves information as effectively as possible.

In the controlled-learning component of their experiment, Grober and Buschke presented groups of normal and demented elderly with a list of sixteen common items drawn from different conceptual categories. The items were presented four at a time on four different sheets of paper. Each item was presented as a picture (for example, a picture of a bunch of grapes) with the name of the item boldly printed above the picture (for example, GRAPES). The participants were given the name of a conceptual category (in this case, ''fruit'') and were told to point to and name the picture on the card that corresponded to the category (grapes). After identifying all four items on a sheet of paper, the participants were given an immediate recall task. In this task, the participants had to recall the names of the specific items they had just identified. If a participant could not recall the items, the sheet of paper was represented, the identification procedure was repeated, and the participant was given another chance to recall the item. This entire procedure was repeated again if necessary. Then, the remaining twelve items (four items drawn and labeled on three different sheets of paper) were presented, identified, and recalled in the same manner. All of these controlled-learning procedures insured that the participants attended to all of the items, briefly stored the items, and could immediately recall the items.

Twenty seconds after the controlled-learning phase was over, the participants were given three separate recall trials for the entire sixteen items. Each recall trial consisted of two distinct tasks: a *free recall task* and a *cued recall task.* During the free recall task, participants were allowed two minutes to remember as many of the sixteen items as possible. In the cued recall task, participants were provided with conceptual cues for the items they did not remember in the free recall task. (For example, a researcher might ask, ''What was the type of fruit pictured on the card?'') Two different types of recall scores were obtained for each participant: a *free recall score* and a *total recall score.* The free recall score represented the number of items retrieved without cues on each trial. The total recall score consisted of the total number of items recalled on each trial by both free recall and cued recall.

Grober and Buschke (1987) reasoned that the total recall score should provide a valid estimate of the total number of items stored in memory and potentially available for recall. Thus, a participant's total recall score, rather than free recall score, should be a better predictor of whether he or she belonged to the normal or demented group.

The results of the study were straightforward. First, as can be seen in box figure 6.3, free recall dramatically underrepresents the amount of learning and memory that has taken place in both the normal and demented groups. Box figure 6.3 also shows that the normal group, because they had near-perfect total memory scores, had stored all

BOX 6.4 *Continued*

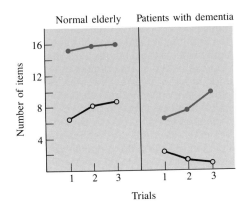

Box figure 6.3 Free recall (open circles) and total recall (closed circles) of sixteen unrelated pictures by normal elderly adults and by elderly patients with dementia. Total recall is obtained by adding items from cued recall to the number remembered from free recall.

Source: Data from E. Grober and H. Buschke, "Genuine Memory Deficits in Dementia" in *Developmental Neuropsychology*, 3:13–36, 1987.

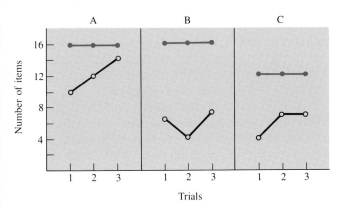

Box figure 6.4 Free recall (open circles) and total recall (closed circles) by (A) a normal 89-year-old man, (B) a normal 87-year-old woman, and (C) an 86-year-old woman with Alzheimer's disease.

Source: Data from E. Grober and H. Buschke, "Genuine Memory Deficits in Dementia" in *Developmental Neuropsychology*, 3:13–36, 1987.

sixteen test items. The demented group, on the other hand, stored only about one-half of the sixteen items.

From the evidence illustrated in box figure 6.3, it appears that knowledge of either a participant's free or total recall score should be equally useful in predicting if he is demented. The data portrayed in box figure 6.4, however, indicates this is not the case—

Box 6.4 *Continued*

total recall is better than free recall at distinguishing normal from demented elderly. More specifically, box figure 6.4 shows the free and total recall scores of three participants. Graph A represents the scores of an eighty-nine-year-old normal participant who had exceptionally good free recall. Graph B represents the scores of an eighty-seven-year-old normal participant who had an average range of free recall scores. Graph C represents the scores of an eighty-six-year-old patient suffering from Alzheimer's disease whose free recall scores are almost identical to those shown in graph B. It should be emphasized, however, that both of the normal participants (A and B) had perfect total recall scores, while person B and the demented person (C) had identical free recall scores but differed in total recall (the normal person (B), but not the demented person (C), had perfect total recall). In other words, total recall proved to be a better indicator of dementia because normal elderly, but not demented patients, displayed near-perfect performance on the total recall score regardless of their free recall scores.

In a related experiment, Hart et al. (1987) reported that depressed elderly patients, but not Alzheimer's disease patients, displayed better memory scores when they were given support in encoding and retrieving information. This finding is consistent with the idea that memory loss in depressives is more apparent than real, and that depressives are more likely to display better memory when they are placed in a supportive context. Even with the extra help, however, depressed patients were found, on the whole, to remember less than the normal elderly.

Another important distinction between normal elderly and the depressed elderly centers around the different response bias displayed by both of these groups (Neiderehe and Burt, 1986). Depressed elderly people have been found to display a conservative response bias on memory-recognition tasks. When they are unsure about a test item, the depressed elderly are likely to respond. "I can't remember," whereas normal elderly individuals are more likely to take chances and guess. In fact, Neiderehe and Burt (1986) have argued that differences in response bias may be the single most important characteristic in differentiating normal from depressed elderly. More information about the differences between dementia and depression is in chapter 12.

Summary

The information-processing approach is one of the most exciting perspectives from which to view age-related changes in cognitive ability. The historical roots of information-processing theory lie in the field of computer science and artificial intelligence. Like a computer, the human mind may be conceptualized as an information-processing device that encodes, stores, and retrieves information.

In this chapter, we have organized information-processing research under the three major headings of perception, attention, and memory. Several aspects of perception appear to show deficits as people age. The evidence for age-related differences in speed of perceptual processing is especially strong. This evidence comes from laboratory experiments that employ masking procedures. It has been shown that age-related perceptual slowing can be attenuated (but not totally eliminated) by extensive practice.

Our discussion of attention began with an examination of the topics of selective attention (the ability to discriminate relevant from irrelevant information), and divided attention (the ability to perform two tasks simultaneously). Overall, the research suggests that divided attention may be more negatively affected by aging than selective attention. On the other hand, several psychologists have argued that age-related differences in divided attention are more apparent than real. They suggest that age-related deficits in divided attention are an artifact of the tendency for older adults to perform more slowly and less accurately on all of the individual components of a divided-attention task.

A growing body of research argues for an age-related decrement in attentional capacity (that is, a decrease in the amount of psychological energy available to perform mental work). Some of this research has compared age-related differences in automatic processing versus effortful processing and suggests that age-related differences in the latter are stronger. Several investigators have found little, if any, age-related changes in attention (or perception) for highly automatic tasks. As a general rule, older adults perform most poorly when confronted with highly unfamiliar tasks that demand a great deal of effortful processing.

The research on memory is extensive. Age-related differences appear to be greater when (1) the memory task taps long- rather than short-term memory, (2) effective processing strategies are not employed during the learning of new material, (3) retention tasks demand a great deal of effortful search or retrieval, (4) the materials are unfamiliar, and (5) the memory task does not draw upon previously acquired knowledge and skills.

It is possible to explain age-related changes in memory from three different perspectives. The biological perspective suggests that the age-related deterioration of the brain causes decrements in memory. The processing perspective suggests that age-related changes in memory are the result of the older person's tendency to employ a number of superficial, shallow, or unsophisticated psychological strategies when called upon to encode or retrieve information. The contextual perspective suggests that memory is a reconstructive process and that the ability to remember any piece of information depends on the relationship between (1) the type of information to be remembered, (2) the characteristics of the individual called upon to remember, and (3) the nature of the situation in which the individual's memory is examined.

With aging, there may be a normal decline in the ability to remember information. This type of benign senescent forgetfulness does not seriously affect an older adult's ability to function in everyday life. Evidence suggests that both young and older adults tend to overestimate the magnitude and the significance of the memory problems experienced by the normal elderly.

Memory impairments may be important signs of physical disease and/or psychological disturbance among the elderly. For example, older individuals suffering from a dementia such as Alzheimer's disease or from a psychological disorder such as depression often display significant problems in remembering. Researchers have discovered, however, that the source of memory loss is different in demented versus depressed elderly.

Review Questions

1. In what ways are the computer and the human mind similar? Give examples of the hardware and software components of both the computer and the human mind.
2. Discuss the research on perceptual change in adulthood. How does practice affect the perceptual abilities of older adults?
3. What is the difference between selective attention and divided attention? Discuss the research that has been conducted in this area.
4. What is meant by the term *attentional capacity?* Do older adults display poorer performance than younger adults on tasks that demand effortful processing or automatic processing?
5. Discuss the nature of short-term and long-term memory and their development during adulthood.
6. How do (a) processing strategies used during learning, (b) the nature of the retention task, (c) the nature of the materials or information, and (d) the characteristics of the learner influence the development of memory during the adult years?
7. Explain the major differences between explicit and implicit memory. What happens to both implicit and explicit memory in amnesiac individuals? How do normal elderly perform on both implicit and explicit memory tasks as compared to older adults suffering from Alzheimer's disease?
8. Discuss the basic differences between the biological, processing, and contextual perspectives on age-related memory impairment. Is one of these perspectives more useful or valid than the others?
9. What is benign senescent forgetfulness?
10. Explain the differences between the memory impairments that occur in the normal elderly versus those that occur in someone who suffers from a dementia such as Alzheimer's disease.

Further Reading

Hoyer, W. J., and Plude, D. J. (1980). Attentional and perceptual processes in the study of cognitive aging. In L. W. Poon (Ed.), *Aging in the 1980s: Psychological issues*. Washington, DC: American Psychological Association.
    A very good summary of some of the basic age-related changes that take place in both attention and perception. Moderately difficult reading.

Poon, L. W. (1985). Differences in human memory with aging: Nature, causes, and clinical implications. In J. E. Birren and K. W. Schaie (Eds.), *Handbook of the psychology of aging*. New York: Van Nostrand Reinhold.
    An excellent overview of the research on human memory and how it ages. Special emphasis is given to an analysis of the clinical aspects of memory decline. Moderately difficult reading.

Salthouse, T. A. (1982). *Adult cognition: An experimental psychology of human aging*. New York: Springer-Verlag.
    This classic text presents an overview of adult cognitive change from an information-processing perspective. Difficult reading.

Siegler, R. S. (1982). Information-processing approaches to development. In P. Mussen (Ed.), *Carmichael's manual of child psychology: History, theories, and methods*. New York: Wiley.
    An authoritative overview of the basic ideas of the information-processing approach and their role in understanding development. Moderately difficult reading.

Squire, L. (1987). *Brain and memory*. New York: Oxford University Press.
    One of the most informative and important books written about the neurological underpinnings of human memory. A special section is devoted to memory and aging. Moderately difficult reading.

CHAPTER 7

APPLICATION OF DEVELOPMENTAL STAGE THEORY TO ADULT COGNITION

IMAGINE

Imagine a Cognitive Ability on Which Older Adults Outperform Younger Adults

The information presented in chapters 5 and 6 indicates that some degree of cognitive decline is an inevitable aspect of the aging process. At best, healthy, well-educated, community-residing elderly adults seem to perform nearly as well as young or middle-aged adults on tasks of mental ability. Developmentalists have been unable to discover any measures of intelligence, attention, or memory on which older adults significantly outperform younger adults. Research stemming from the psychometric and information-processing perspectives seems to reinforce one of the most common images of adult cognitive development—as you age, you become less intelligent, less attentive, and less able to remember.

But another image many of us possess about the older adult's mental abilities is that with advancing age, some older people acquire wisdom. *Wisdom* is a particular mental quality associated with the cognitive abilities of some aged individuals but *not* with younger individuals. With the attainment of wisdom, older people are able to blend personal history and important information from the past for the purpose of resolving a current problem (Clayton and Birren, 1980; Dittmann-Kohli and Baltes, 1988). Those considered to possess wisdom combine reflective abilities such as self-analysis and introspection along with affective components such as "empathy, gentleness, and peacefulness" (Huyck and Hoyer, 1982, p. 184). Wisdom is more than the sum total of an elderly person's cognitive abilities; it is composed of reflection, affect, and knowledge. Certainly traditional psychometric and information-processing approaches have little, if anything, to say about the development of wisdom during older adulthood.

In our society, older individuals occupy many of the leadership roles in politics, religion, art, science, and other fields. Our society, like countless others, could be viewed as a "gerontocracy" (that is, a society where older adults have major input in policy-making decisions and are called upon to assume positions of responsibility). Do gerontocracies evolve because older individuals are more likely to possess wisdom than younger or middle-aged adults?

Which is the more valid image to hold of the cognitive abilities of the older adult? Are the elderly forgetful, inattentive, unintelligent, and foolish, or wise, knowledgeable, and sage? To help you make a meaningful choice between these two contrasting images, this chapter focuses on the application of *stage theory* to adult cognitive development. Stage theories stress the idea that new, more sophisticated ways of thinking emerge during adulthood. These qualitatively unique styles of thinking may lay the basis for what philosophers and laypeople commonly refer to as wisdom.

After reading this chapter, you will be in a position to make a meaningful judgment about which of the contrasting images of adult cognitive development is more credible. You may even decide that both descriptions are valid—cognitive development is typified by losses in some areas along with compensatory gains in others.

INTRODUCTION

This is the last of three chapters that focus on adult cognitive development. Chapters 5 and 6 described the psychometric and information-processing approaches to the study of adult cognition. The research that has been generated by both of these perspectives has painted a somewhat negative picture of adult cognitive development. These approaches suggest that adulthood is characterized by a reduction in basic (or fluid) mental abilities and by decrements in perception, attention, and memory. In this chapter, we'll discuss the application of *stage theory* to adult cognitive development. Stage theorists, in general, portray an optimistic view of adult cognitive functioning. Stage theorists suggest that adulthood is characterized by the growth of sophisticated and powerful ways of thinking about the physical and social worlds in which we live.

We begin this chapter with a description of Piaget's theory of cognitive development, paying special attention to Piaget's description of *formal operations*. This stage was originally thought to be the final, most advanced stage of cognitive development. Next, we'll consider newer research that has sought to identify a stage of cognitive development beyond formal operations. This stage, which only emerges during the adult years, has been referred to as the *postformal* stage of cognitive development. We'll review the basic characteristics of postformal thinking and summarize some of the research studies that have investigated the differences between formal and postformal thinking. A great deal of the research on postformal thinking has focused on *social cognition*. Social cognition refers to the manner in which people understand and resolve the interpersonal problems characteristic of everyday life.

We'll end this chapter with a discussion of the *encapsulation model*. This model, developed by John Rybash, William Hoyer, and Paul Roodin integrates and extends the different theoretical perspectives (the psychometric, information-processing, and developmental stage theories) that bear on the topic of adult cognition. We'll illustrate the basic tenets of the encapsulation model by describing recent research dealing with aging and cognitive expertise and the growth of wisdom during old age.

STAGE THEORIES OF ADULT COGNITIVE DEVELOPMENT

The concept of "stage" is probably one of the most overused and misunderstood terms used by nonpsychologists. It seems as if people often say, "He's in a stage," or "She's going through a stage," in speaking of development. Unlike laypersons, developmental psychologists use a set of very strict criteria to identify a *stage* of development.

Characteristics of Cognitive Stages

Traditionally, psychologists have argued that a true set of cognitive stages must satisfy five different criteria: invariant movement, qualitative change, hierarchical integration, universal progression, and structured wholeness. In this section we'll briefly discuss each of these criteria.

The notion of **invariant movement** suggests that there is a single, unchangeable sequence of stages that individuals must pass through during development. For example, if a stage theorist suggests that cognitive development consists of a four-stage sequence, then individuals must move through the stages in order: stage 1 → stage 2; stage 2 → stage 3; stage 3 → stage 4. It would be impossible to skip stages (for example, to go directly from stage 2 to stage 4 by skipping stage 3). Also, the concept of invariant movement means that it is impossible to regress (or go backwards) through the stages. For example, once an individual is found to be functioning at stage 3, it would be impossible for her to regress to a previous level of functioning (stage 2 or stage 1).

The concept of **qualitative change** suggests that at each different stage an individual actively constructs a completely different set of cognitive structures. Cognitive structures refer to a set of highly abstract, internal, and generalizable rules that are used to represent and understand reality. These thought structures are assumed to be as different from one another as apples are from oranges. Thus, stage theorists assume that mental development involves the growth of *qualitatively* different ways of thinking about the world; this means that cognitive development is not *quantitative* in nature. In other words, mental development is not characterized by the progressive accumulation of more factual information about the world. A stage theorist would argue that a person's intellectual functioning is determined by the *manner* in which the individual understands reality, not by the *amount* of information the individual possesses.

Hierarchical integration implies that each stage in a developmental sequence should be viewed as an incorporation as well as an extension of the stage that preceded it. This means, for example, that stage 3 in a cognitive sequence has its basis in the thought structures laid down in stage 2. It also means that stage 3 extends the structures laid down in stage 2.

The idea of **universal progression** suggests that all individuals in all cultures progress through a set of stages in the same invariant sequence. This means that stage theories do not just apply to certain groups of individuals who live in certain social environments (for example, middle-class, well-educated individuals from an industrialized society). A valid stage theory must apply to all individuals, regardless of social class, race, ethnicity, educational level, or culture.

Finally, the criterion of **structured wholeness,** which may be the most controversial aspect of stage theories, implies that individuals can only understand reality one stage at a time. This means, for example, that if an individual is at stage 2 within a particular cognitive developmental sequence, she will find herself thinking about every issue or problem she might potentially confront from the perspective of that stage. In other words, a person would not be expected to reason about mathematical problems from the perspective of stage 4 and interpersonal problems from the perspective of stage 2—such an inconsistency would violate the concept of structured wholeness.

As you can see, the stage concept is not used loosely by developmentalists. Psychologists demand that the stages within a proposed sequence meet a set of strict and formal criteria.

PIAGET'S STAGE THEORY

Beyond any doubt, Jean Piaget (see Piaget, 1970; Piaget and Inhelder, 1969) has formulated the most important, provocative, and far-reaching stage theory of cognitive development. Piaget suggested that individuals pass through a series of four stages during the course of cognitive growth. Furthermore, he assumed that the stages that comprise this developmental sequence conform to the five criteria that define genuine stages. Although Piaget died in 1980, his theory continues to serve as a basis for a great deal of contemporary research in life-span developmental psychology.

Swiss psychologist Jean Piaget pioneered the stage approach to the study of cognitive development.

Overview of the Piagetian Stages

Piaget identified four stages of intellectual development: the sensorimotor stage, the preoperational stage, the concrete-operational stage, and the formal-operational stage. The **sensorimotor stage** lasts from birth to about two years of age and is thus synonymous with the period most people refer to as infancy. Piaget (1954) argued that infants cannot think about the world by means of internal mental symbols (such as words, visual images, and so on). Instead, infants can only represent objects or events by external body movements. Because infants possess a sensorimotor form of thinking, they cannot solve an object permanence task. This means they cannot successfully search for a hidden object because they cannot form a mental symbol of the hidden object.

During the **preoperational stage,** which begins at about two years of age and last until seven years of age, children can form internal mental symbols. However, at this stage children have a great deal of difficulty in distinguishing between internal mental symbols and their referents. A referent is the object or event a mental symbol stands for. Mental symbols can represent concrete or imaginary events and objects. Thus, preoperational children have a great deal of difficulty distinguishing the real from the imaginary. For example, young children find it difficult to understand that dreams are mental rather than real-life events. They also seem to think that just because they can think of Santa Claus, there must be a real-life Santa Claus. In the preoperational stage, children's thinking may also be *irreversible*. This means that preoperational children do not understand that every action has an opposite action that is the reverse of the original. For example, preoperational thinkers do not understand that addition is the reverse of subtraction. Thus, they do not understand that the best way to solve the following subtraction problem: $? - 7 = 1$ is to transform it into an addition problem: $7 + 1 = ?$.

In the **concrete operational stage,** which lasts from approximately seven to twelve years of age, children and young adolescents become capable of fundamental logical reasoning. That is, they become capable of distinguishing between imaginary mental symbols and real-life events or objects. For example, children this age understand that Santa Claus is not a real person. Also at this stage, individuals can think in a reversible manner. Not only can concrete thinkers understand the complementary relationship between addition and subtraction, they can understand a relationship from different or reversible points of view. For example, when shown two pairs of sticks, the concrete thinker can understand that: (1) if the red stick is taller than the blue stick ($R > B$), and (2) the blue stick is taller than the green stick ($B > G$); then the red stick must be taller than the green stick ($R > G$). Put another way, the concrete thinker is able to reason that, "If the blue stick is shorter than the red stick but taller than the green stick; then the red stick must be taller than the green stick."

Most certainly, concrete operational thinking is a great advance over preoperational thinking. However, there are clear limitations placed on the nature and scope of concrete operational thought. Specifically, concrete thinking is best suited to solve problems that involve concrete stimuli—stimuli that can be seen, heard, touched, smelled, and so on. At the concrete operational stage, individuals cannot reason logically about hypothetical, abstract problems, nor can they reason about contrary-to-fact ideas or propositions. For example, a concrete thinker could easily solve the previously mentioned problem involving the three different-sized sticks, but not the following hypothetical verbal problem: "Imagine there are three girls walking down the street. Of these three girls, Mary is taller than Jane but shorter than Susan. Who is the tallest of the three?" This problem is very similar to the stick problem, but the stimuli in the former problem were concrete (they were actually seen and touched) while the stimuli in the latter task were hypothetical (they had to be imagined).

Piaget maintained that it is only during the fourth and last stage of cognitive development, the stage he termed formal operations, that individuals can reason about hypothetical, abstract relationships.

FORMAL OPERATIONS

The stage of **formal operations,** which according to Piaget emerges somewhere around early- to mid-adolescence, has occupied an important place in the study of adult cognition. The importance of formal operations lies in the fact that since it is the last stage in Piaget's developmental stage theory, it represents Piaget's view of mature adult cognition.

Characteristics of Formal Operations

Piaget and his associates (Inhelder and Piaget, 1958; Piaget and Inhelder, 1969) have discovered three important characteristics of formal thinking. These characteristics are:

1. The creation of a reversal in the relationship between reality and possibility.
2. The ability to think in a hypothetical-deductive manner.
3. The capacity to think about the nature of thinking.

With regard to the first of these characteristics, Piaget and his colleagues suggested that a concrete thinker's understanding of reality consists of a series of generalizations based on specific, real-life experiences. At the level of concrete operations, real experiences are more important than possible (or hypothetical or abstract) experiences. Formal thinkers, however, are capable of creating a reversal in the relative importance they attach to real versus possible experiences. This reversal allows formal thinkers to (1) develop a mode of thinking freed from the constraints of real-life experiences, and (2) think logically about *verbal propositions.* Verbal propositions may be regarded as pure ideas. The truth value of a verbal proposition depends on its logical relationship to other propositions—not on its relationship to concrete, real-life events. Thus, formal thinkers can reason about contrary-to-fact ideas and experiences. For example, think about the following problems:

(1) Would the weather be any different if snow was black, not white? (2) If it was so cold in a freezer that a frozen steak burst into flames, what would happen if this burning steak was placed in a very hot oven? A concrete thinker who can only deal with real-life experiences will respond that both of these problems are silly because in real life, snow is not black and intense cold cannot make things burn. Formal thinkers, on the other hand, can rise above the constraints of reality. They understand that even though snow is not black and cold cannot burn, it is nevertheless logical to conclude that *if* snow was black the weather would change because the temperature would change (if large portions of the earth's surface were covered by a black substance, the earth would become hotter because the dark surface would absorb heat) and, *if* cold could make things burn, then putting the flaming steak into the hot oven should make it freeze.

The concept of *hypothetical-deductive thinking* means that formal thinkers are capable of reasoning like scientists. They are capable of mentally creating abstract hypotheses or theories and then testing the validity of these abstract hypotheses by systematically observing the results of specific, well-controlled experiments. Thus, scientific thinking is deductive in that it proceeds from the general (the abstract hypothesis) to the specific (the construction and observation of the results of a specific experiment designed to test the theory).

The notion of *thinking about thinking* means that formal thinkers can think about the meaning and significance of their mental experiences. For example, an individual at the formal operational stage can think, "I want to be married," and can then generate a number of hypothetical explanations of the meaning and significance of that thought. The ability to think about thinking accounts for the fact that adolescents and adults become very introspective. They often become armchair psychologists who find it intriguing to analyze their own mental activity as well as the thoughts and feelings of others.

To be successful in many of the occupations that exist in contemporary society, individuals are greatly helped by formal thinking. Formal thought is also a necessary prerequisite for success in educational institutions such as high school and college. The successful completion of some adult life-tasks therefore seems to be based on the acquisition of formal operations.

Given the different characteristics of formal thinking, Piaget assumed that formal operations, a mode of thinking first acquired during adolescence, represented the most powerful and adult form of thinking.

Measurement of Formal Operations

There are several different types of tasks that Piaget and his colleagues (Inhelder and Piaget, 1958) invented to determine if an individual has reached the stage of formal operations. In this section we will discuss three of these tasks: the combinatorial-thinking task, the proportional-thinking task, and the isolation-of-variables task.

An individual capable of hypothetical-deductive thinking is capable of reasoning as a scientist does.

The purpose of a *combinatorial-thinking task* is to determine if an individual can generate all of the possible combinations of a number of variables. To generate possibility, a person theoretically must have reached the stage of formal operations. A typical combinatorial-thinking task might be:

> Suppose that you are presented with four different beakers, each of which contains a colorless chemical solution. You are told that if you mix some of the chemicals in the beakers together in a certain way, a chemical reaction will occur and the combined liquids will take on a bright orange appearance. Next, you are given a large number of empty small beakers. You are told that your task is to try mixing different combinations of the chemicals in the four beakers (by pouring some of the contents of the four beakers into the empty small beakers) until you find the combination that produces the orange reaction.

Prior to the formal operational stage, children try to solve this task in a haphazard manner. They simply produce different random combinations of the liquids (for example, $1 + 3$, $3 + 4$, $1 + 2 + 4$, and so on), hoping that one of the combinations will work. Individuals at the formal operational stage, however, solve this problem by using a systematic strategy. In their minds they generate all the different ways in which the chemicals can be combined. Then, they try out each of the combinations in an orderly fashion. For example, all of the different two-way combinations are $1 + 2$, $1 + 3$, $1 + 4$, $2 + 3$, $2 + 4$, and $3 + 4$; the three-way combinations are $1 + 2 + 3$, $1 + 2 + 4$, $1 + 3 + 4$, and $2 + 3 + 4$; and the only possible four-way combination is $1 + 2 + 3 + 4$.

A *proportional-thinking task* involves a type of mathematical problem that can only be solved if an individual thinks about mathematical relationships in an abstract, relational, or proportional manner, rather than a concrete, absolute manner. This type of task helps determine if a person approaches a problem by using simple arithmetic (a concrete operational strategy) or by using algebraic reasoning (a formal operational strategy). For example, imagine being presented with the following problem:

> A large bowl is filled with many white beans; your task is to estimate the number of beans in the bowl. To help you determine a reasonable estimate, a psychologist performs the following experiment. She takes a cup, dips it into the bowl, and pulls out eighty beans. Next, the psychologist takes a red felt-tipped pen and places a large red **X** on each of the eighty beans. The psychologist puts the marked beans back into the bowl and randomly mixes the beans. Then she dips the cup back into the bowl and extracts another sample. She discovers that there are seventy-five beans in the cup and that fifteen of the seventy-five beans have a red **X** on them. What would you estimate the total number of beans in the bowl to be?

A concrete thinker, using simple arithmetic, might answer 140 (adding the 60 unmarked beans in the second sample to the 80 marked beans in the first sample). A formal thinker, using algebraic reasoning, might say 400 (if one-fifth of the beans from the second sample were marked, it is logical to assume that one-fifth of the total number of beans were obtained on the first sample. Therefore, if 80 is one-fifth of the total number of beans, there are 400 beans because $5 \times 80 = 400$).

In the *isolation-of-variables problem,* a person is required to determine which of a large number of variables produces a specific outcome. One of the most widely used problems of this type is the pendulum task. In this task, a participant is asked to determine the factors influencing the speed at which a pendulum swings back and forth. These factors include the length of the pendulum string, the weight of the object placed at the end of the string, the height at which the pendulum is released, and the force with which the pendulum is pushed. To solve this problem, a participant is given a pendulum apparatus that comes with two different strings (a long string and a short string) and two objects of different weights that can be placed on the ends of the strings (a heavy weight and a lighter weight). Given the materials at their disposal, the participants are told to do as many experiments as they need to solve the problem. This task measures formal operational thinking because it requires participants to behave like scientists. The participant must develop a theory about what determines the oscillation of the pendulum and then perform the crucial experiments to test the theory. At the concrete operational stage, children do not act like scientists. Their experiments are not capable of deducing the critical factor because they often vary two or three factors at the same time. Formal thinkers, on the other hand, solve the problem in a much more scientific and systematic manner. They evaluate each of the potential factors one at a time (keeping all of the other factors constant) to determine the frequency of oscillation. Using this approach, they discover that the length of the string, not any of the other factors, determines the speed of oscillation.

Research on Formal Operations

Piaget (1972) assumed that individuals begin to develop formal operational thinking skills at about eleven years of age and that they fully complete the transition from concrete to formal operations at no later than fifteen to twenty years of age. A great deal of research (see Berry and Dasen, 1974; Elkind, 1961; Flavell, 1985; Keating, 1978; Kuhn and Angelev, 1976; Kuhn and Bannock, 1977; Neimark, 1975a, 1975b, 1982; Papalia and Bielby, 1974; Protinsky and Hughston, 1978; Tomlinson-Keasey, 1972) has examined Piaget's assertions about the age at which individuals attain formal reasoning. In these research studies, adolescents and adults were given a number of tasks similar to those described in the preceding section. Surprisingly, the researchers have all reached the same conclusion: a significant percentage of young adults, middle-aged adults, and older adults do *not* attain the stage of formal operations. Thus, contrary to Piaget's original speculations, not all adults display formal-thinking skills! In fact, Diane Papalia (1972) has gathered data that suggests that some older adults may actually regress through the Piagetian stages (that is, they may move backwards from formal operations to concrete operations). It should be noted, however, that serious methodological problems (for example, the confounding of age, cohort, years of education, health status, and so on) cast doubt on the meaning of Papalia's findings.

Overall, the available research seems to indicate that the earliest point in development during which formal operational thinking may appear is early- to mid-adolescence. But this does not mean that all individuals begin thinking in a formal manner at this time; nor does it mean that all individuals will ultimately reach formal operations. These results are both important and somewhat startling. In fact, these findings have forced psychologists to reconsider Piaget's conception of formal operations.

Reconceptualizing Formal Operations

On the whole, previous research with young adults has indicated that Piaget's stage of formal operations violates two basic criteria which define developmental stages: universal progression and structured wholeness. As you may recall from an earlier section of this chapter, universal progression suggests that every individual progresses through each stage within the developmental stage sequence. Clearly, not all individuals attain formal operations. Structured wholeness suggests that if an individual is in a particular stage of cognitive development, he should be able to solve *all* of the different tasks unique to that stage. It has been discovered that being able to solve one type of formal-thinking task does not guarantee that a person will be able to solve another type of formal-thinking task (Bart, 1971; Berzonsky, 1978; Brainerd, 1978). For example, adults who are able to solve an isolation-of-variables task are not necessarily capable of solving a proportional-thinking task, and vice versa.

One of the reasons why not all adults attain formal operations concerns the nature of the tasks used to measure formal thinking. As you may have recognized, the tasks Piaget constructed for assessing formal thought seem to focus on problems from the fields of chemistry, mathematics, and physics. Without the prerequisite educational background and cultural experience, many adolescents and adults are at a distinct disadvantage performing the formal tasks employed by Piaget (Alexander, Roodin, and Gorman, 1980). Thus, we may conclude that Piaget and his associates erred in that they constructed tasks of formal thinking within a very narrow domain. These tasks were probably unfamiliar, uninteresting, and threatening to both adolescents and adults alike.

In an important paper published in 1972, Piaget modified his view on formal operations. Piaget argued that the stage criteria of structured wholeness may not apply to formal operations. He maintained that based on aptitude, educational experience, motivation, professional specialization, and other factors, adults may develop formal thinking in some, but *not* all, areas. For example, an experienced garage mechanic may use formal reasoning to diagnose (and correct) the problem with a faulty automobile engine; but the same mechanic may have a concrete understanding of a critically ill patient's right to refuse medical treatment. On the other hand, a physician may reason at the formal level when thinking about problems involving medical ethics; but the same physician may continue to use concrete thinking to figure out why the family car keeps stalling.

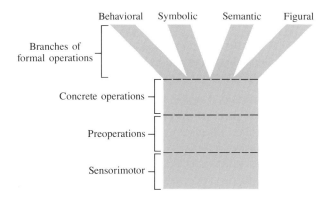

Behavioral   Symbolic   Semantic   Figural

Branches of
formal operations

Concrete operations

Preoperations

Sensorimotor

The behavioral branch involves an understanding of interpersonal and
intrapersonal psychological processes.

The symbolic branch involves the ability to represent and manipulate
arithematic and algebraic symbols.

The semantic branch involves the representation and manipulation of
ideas within a verbal medium.

The figural branch involves the representation and manipulation of
ideas and concrete objects within a visual medium.

Figure 7.1   An illustration of Berzonsky's branching model of formal operations.

One of the more interesting extensions of Piaget's (1972) modified view of
formal operations has been articulated by Michael Berzonsky (1978). Berzonsky
proposed that Piaget's theory can be conceptualized as a tree. The first three stages
of the theory make up the trunk of the tree. The formal operational stage represents
the branches of the tree. These branches, which are based on Guilford's (1967)
ideas about the different dimensions of intelligence, represent the areas within which
an adult could develop formal-thinking skills. Figure 7.1 is an illustration based on
Berzonsky's branching model of formal operations. As you can see, it is possible to
develop formal reasoning in any of a number of different domains (for example,
reasoning about interpersonal relations; reasoning about art, music, and literature;
reasoning about mathematical or scientific issues; and so forth).

Critique of Formal Operations

Formal operational thinking provides a powerful, but somewhat limited, mode of
thought. In this section, we'll discuss some of the limitations of formal thinking as
identified by Rybash, Hoyer, and Roodin (1986).

First, formal operations may *overemphasize the power of pure logic in problem
solving* (Perry, 1968; Labouvie-Vief, 1984). This limitation is expressed in the following passage:

Reason reveals relations within any given context. . . . But there is a limit. In the end,
reason itself remains reflexively relativistic, a property which turns reason back upon

reason's own findings. In even its farthest reaches, then, reason will leave the thinker with several legitimate contexts and no way of choosing among them—no way, at least, that can be justified through reason alone. If he still is to honor reason he must now also transcend it; he must affirm his own position from within himself in full awareness that reason can never completely justify him or assure him. (Perry, 1968, pp. 135–136)

A second limitation of formal operations is it *overemphasizes the importance of the abstract and hypothetical qualities and underemphasizes the pragmatic qualities of real-life cognitive activity.* In late adolescence or early adulthood, individuals become aware of this overemphasis. Labouvie-Vief (1984) reinforced this point when she noted that upon entry into adulthood, "there is a concern with the concrete constraints of real life or the refusal to sever cognition from its affective, social, and pragmatic ties." (p. 159)

Third, formal thinking seems to be *most suited for the solution of problems that call for scientific thinking and logical-mathematical analysis.* Piaget assumed that the goal of the cognitively mature adult was to reason like a scientist or a mathematician. However, Piaget neglected to examine how cognition is applied to real-life social or interpersonal problems. In connection with this point, Flavell (1977) maintained that:

> Real problems with meaningful content are obviously more important in everyday human adaptation (than abstract, wholly logical problems), and it is possible that these are the kinds of problems our cognitive apparatus has evolved to solve. (p. 117)

Fourth, formal operations are *geared for the solution of closed-system problems* (Basseches, 1984a, 1984b; Koplowitz, 1984). A closed-system problem is one in which a person determines how a limited number of controllable and specific variables produce a specific and reliable outcome. For example, in the pendulum task, a series of mini-experiments help to determine how a limited number of controllable and specific variables influence the oscillation of a pendulum. Closed-system problems are also well-defined in that they have a single, correct solution (it *is* the length of the string that controls the oscillation of the pendulum). Real-life problems, in contrast, are open to the extent that they are characterized by an unlimited number of uncontrollable, fuzzy variables. For example, there may be an infinite number of constantly changing variables that a woman must consider when deciding whether to pursue a business career or take time off from business when having a child. Furthermore, open-system problems are ill-defined because they emerge from changeable and uncontrollable variables and do not have a single correct solution (there is no one correct solution, for example, to the woman's problem about whether to pursue her career or take time off when she becomes a mother).

Fifth, the concept of formal operations *does not recognize the relative nature of knowledge and the need to adopt multiple frames of reference.* Several theorists (for example Labouvie-Vief, 1982, 1984; Sinnott, 1981, 1984) have emphasized that formal operations do not allow a thinker to understand the relativistic nature of knowledge and reality. Thinking from a relativistic standpoint has been referred to as "intersystemic thinking" by Gisela Labouvie-Vief (1982). She argued that intersystemic thinking

> . . . reveals the basic duality of logical truth. This realization initiates a movement from logical absolutism to logical relativism. . . . Much as truth now is relativistic, one's actions must be singular and particularized. The erosion of logical certainty throws the self explicitly back on its own resources. (Labouvie-Vief, 1982, p. 182)

Sixth, formal thinking *places a greater emphasis on problem solving than on problem finding* (Arlin 1975, 1984). This means that formal thought is best suited for generating and testing hypotheses that aid in the solution of closed-system, well-defined problems. **Problem finding,** in contrast, represents the ability to generate new questions which arise from ill-defined problems (Mackworth, 1965). It reflects the ability of adults to ask novel questions about themselves, their work, and the events that surround them. Arlin (1984) observed that the essence of problem finding was described by Wertheimer (1945). Wertheimer suggested that "the function of thinking is not just solving an actual problem but discovering, envisaging, and going into deeper questions. Often in great discovery the most important thing is that a certain question is found." (p. 46) Problem finding may be evident in periods of scientific revolution during which insightful adults (such as Darwin, Freud, and Einstein) address old facts from the perspective of new questions and world views (Kuhn, 1970).

POSTFORMAL COGNITIVE DEVELOPMENT

The problems and shortcomings of formal thinking have set the stage for a major conceptual revision of Piagetian theory. It is now assumed that a type of thinking that is qualitatively different from formal operations emerges during the adult years. This type of thinking has been labeled **postformal operations** (Commons, Richards, and Armon, 1984; Commons, Sinnott, Richards, and Armon, 1989). In this section, we will review current theory and research of the growth of postformal thinking during adulthood.

Characteristics of Postformal Thinking

Diedre Kramer (1983) identified three basic features of postformal reasoners. First, postformal thinkers *possess an understanding of the relative, nonabsolute nature of knowledge.* Second, postformal thinkers *accept contradiction as a basic aspect of reality.* For example, a physicist might come to understand light as being both waves and particles, or an individual might realize that his feelings about another person cannot be described in terms of love *or* hate alone, but by the simultaneous existence of these apparently contrasting emotions. Third, postformal thinkers are *capable of dialectic reasoning.* They possess an ability to synthesize contradictory thoughts, emotions, and experiences into more coherent, all-encompassing wholes.

Instead of viewing a contradictory situation as a choice between alternatives, the postformal reasoner views it as a call to integrate alternatives.

Three additional characteristics may be added to Kramer's description of postformal thought. First, Rybash et al. (1986) and Rybash and Roodin (1989) argued that postformal thinkers adopt a *contextual approach* to problem solving. That is, they solve problems by continuously creating new principles based on the changing circumstances of their lives—rather than by applying a set of absolute principles or standards across all contexts and circumstances. This may be especially true when adults reason about the ill-defined problems characteristic of everyday social life. Second, Hoyer, Rybash, and Roodin (1989) and Rybash et al. (1986) have argued that postformal thinking is *domain-specific* in nature. This means that adults develop postformal thinking within some, but not all, areas of knowledge. Third, Patricia Arlin (1975, 1977, 1984, 1989) has suggested that postformal thinking may be more directed toward *problem finding* than problem solving.

The major characteristics of postformal cognitive development are summarized in table 7.1. To gain a more in-depth understanding of postformal thought, read box 7.1. This box describes Michael Basseches's (1984) conception of one of the most important characteristics of postformal cognitive development—dialectic thinking.

Research on Postformal Thinking

In this section, we'll examine research studies focusing on two aspects of postformal thinking: (1) the relativistic nature of knowledge and the limits of pure logic; and (2) the change in emphasis from problem solving to problem finding.

Relativistic Thinking
William Perry (1968) was one of the first researchers to address the topic of postformal thought. He conducted a longitudinal study in which he questioned university students about their educational and personal experiences. Perry found that freshman students approached various intellectual and ethical problems from a dualistic (formal) perspective. These students assumed that any problem or ethical dilemma could have only one correct answer, and that it was the task of authority figures (in their case, perhaps, professors) to teach them the correct answer. In time, the students began to realize the inherent subjectivity of experience. This led the students to conceptualize all knowledge and value systems—even those espoused by authorities—as relative and nonabsolute. At this level, the students felt as if they were adrift in an ocean of uncertainty. They thought that any problem could be approached from a variety of viewpoints, each of which seemed to possess equal merit and validity. Finally, some students reached a developmental level indicating postformal thinking. They still understood the relativity of knowledge, but they were no longer overwhelmed by it. In addition to accepting the contextual and subjective nature of knowledge and values, these students became committed to a self-constructed intellectual and ethical point of view. These students, in other words, were capable of both accepting and transcending relativity.

Table 7.1

MAJOR CHARACTERISTICS OF POSTFORMAL COGNITIVE DEVELOPMENT

1. An understanding of the relative, nonabsolute nature of knowledge
2. The acceptance of contradiction as a basic aspect of social and physical reality
3. The ability to think dialectically (that is, the ability to synthesize contradictory thoughts, emotions, and feelings into more coherent, all-encompassing wholes)
4. The adoption of a contextual approach to problem solving, especially when confronted with ill-defined problems
5. The emergence of sophisticated thinking skills within some (but not all) domains
6. An increased emphasis on problem finding over problem solving

Karen Kitchener and Patricia King (1981) have investigated the relativistic nature of adult thinking in terms of their *reflective judgment model.* This model is similar to Perry's (1968) analysis of the growth of contextual relativism. Kitchener and King's model postulates the existence of a series of seven stages, each characterized by a set of assumptions upon which individuals justify their beliefs about reality and knowledge. Table 7.2 contains a brief description of each of these stages. Several researchers (King, Kitchener, Davison, Parker, and Wood, 1983; Kitchener and Wood, 1987) using interview data have discovered that individuals systematically pass through these different stages from adolescence to middle adulthood. To date, this model has not been extended to research involving the elderly.

Jan Sinnott (1981, 1984, 1989) maintained that relativistic thinking can be directed at several different intellectual domains (for example, the physical sciences or mathematics). But Sinnott also contended that it is easiest to understand the relativistic nature of postformal reasoning within the area of interpersonal reality. Specifically, she applied the term *necessary subjectivity* to describe relativistic thinking within the area of interpersonal relations. Necessary subjectivity means that when adults solve interpersonal problems, they are guided by the premise that subjectivity, or mutually contradictory frames of reference, is a basic characteristic of interpersonal reality. Furthermore, Sinnott assumed that acceptance of subjectivity serves as the basis for personal growth and development. This contrasts with the typical view of physical reality, in which subjectivity is considered to be faulty thinking and eliminated from problem analysis. To examine the relativistic nature of adult cognition, Sinnott (1984) presented a group of adults between twenty-six and eighty-nine years of age with a variety of problems designed to detect the presence of formal thinking and relativistic or postformal thinking. Some of the problems designed to measure formal operations required the use of combinatorial and/or proportional reasoning (for example, putting letters of the alphabet into various combinations). Other problems that measured postformal thinking involved real-life interpersonal issues and conflicts. The results showed that older adults were more likely to use relativistic, postformal thinking styles to deal with real-life rather than abstract problems. Younger participants were more likely to solve all types of problems by adopting a nonrelativistic, formal mode of thinking.

BOX 7.1

BASSECHES'S VIEW OF DIALECTIC THINKING

Michael Basseches (1980, 1984a, 1984b) has developed one of the most provocative models of postformal cognitive development. His conception of postformal thought focuses on the means by which the adult thinker envisions reality as a multitude of relationships or systems that continuously change over time. Furthermore, Basseches proposed that the adult thinker comprehends these constantly changing systems in a constantly changing world through the principle of the *dialectic*. The term *dialectic* refers to an understanding of how transformations occur through *constitutive* and *interactive* relationships.

Relationships are *constitutive* because the elements of a relationship are created by the whole relationship they make up. The whole relationship could not exist, however, without its component parts. Therefore, it is both the relationship which creates the elements and the elements which create the relationship; neither the parts nor the whole of a relationship could exist independently of each other.

Relationships are also *interactive:* they are characterized by mutual (or reciprocal) influence. In other words, the elements of a relationship are changed *by* one another to the same extent that they change one another. Interactive relationships create the changes that transform the system over time.

Let's look at an illustration that contrasts formal thinking with dialectic or postformal thinking. This example, which is drawn from Basseches (1984b, pp. 26–27), deals with the topic of marriage and the problems which could arise between husband and wife.

A formal thinker would probably view the partners of a marriage as two individuals, each of whom possesses a number of fixed and stable traits. The traits that characterize the husband's personality exist independently of those that characterize the wife's personality, and vice versa. Therefore, the marriage of these individuals represents a connection between two elements (husband and wife) that have a separate existence outside of the relationship they are entering. These two sets of fixed traits should give rise to a relationship that remains fixed and stable over time. Finally, the formal thinker would probably give two different explanations for the problems that might develop between a husband and wife. First, marital problems could result from a permanent flaw or shortcoming in either the husband's or wife's personality (for example, one of the marriage

---

Rakfeldt, Rybash, and Roodin (in press) examined the relationship between postformal thinking and the ability to profit from psychotherapy. The participants in this study were adult, first-admission patients in a psychiatric hospital. All of them participated in a series of open-ended interviews. These interviews were designed to assess the manner, formal or postformal, by which the patients conceptualized themselves, their relationships with others, and their psychiatric disorders. The participants also took a large battery of standardized tests that measured their premorbid levels of social adjustment and the degree to which they were benefiting

partners made a bad choice—he or she picked a mate with a totally incompatible personality). Second, it could be that neither of the partners was intrinsically flawed; their marriage developed problems because in some cases the interaction of the personalities of two good people proves to be problematic (they were two nice people who weren't meant for each other).

The dialectic thinker would view a marriage and the problems that might arise within it in a different manner. The dialectic thinker views the elements of a relationship as being in a state of constant flux. Therefore, the traits of the man and the woman who enter the marriage are not regarded as stable and permanent over time. More importantly, it is assumed that the traits of both husband and wife could not exist independently of one another. The traits of the man as a husband are influenced by his relationship with his wife, and vice versa. This means that the marriage is a connection or relationship between two parties that makes the parties of the relationship what (or who) they *are*. In other words, marriage is a constitutive relationship in which the elements of the relationship are totally interdependent on each other. Furthermore, dialectic thinkers view marriage as an interactive relationship—a relationship in which the elements of the relationship (husband and wife) mutually change and are changed by each other. Therefore, a marriage is a relationship between two people, but the nature of the relationship as well as the natures of the people in it are expected to change and evolve over time. Finally, a dialectic thinker would regard marital problems as the results of a relationship that has evolved in an increasingly maladaptive manner. The maladaptivity affects the whole of the relationship—the marriage—to the same extent that it interferes with the growth of the parties of the relationship (the husband and wife who create and are created by the relationship). Viewing a problematic relationship from this perspective allows husband and wife to avoid blaming each other as the cause of the problems. It also allows them to value their relationship as something that was meaningful at some point in its growth and evolution. The crucial question the dialectic thinker asks is, "How does my marriage need to change in response to the changes it has brought about in both of us?"

from psychotherapy. When social adjustment prior to institutionalization was controlled for, it was discovered that patients who displayed relativistic thinking tended to have a more efficacious understanding of themselves, their disorders, and their relationships with others. These patients also seemed to take an active role in their healing. In contrast, patients who adopted an absolute (that is, formal) perspective seemed to make less significant therapeutic gains. Formal thinkers believed it was the duty of authority figures—their psychiatrists—to (1) discover the "true" disorder they suffered from, and (2) treat the disorders while the patients adopted a passive stance. Postformal thinkers, on the other hand, exhibited the opposite set

Table 7.2

STAGES IN KITCHENER AND KING'S REFLECTIVE JUDGMENT MODEL

Stage 1: Characterized by belief in the absolute correspondence between reality and perception. Therefore, beliefs require no justification because to observe reality means to know reality.

Stage 2: Characterized by belief in the existence of an objective reality and absolute knowledge of this reality. It is the role of authority figures (for example, professors) to know and transmit objective knowledge. Therefore, personal beliefs are justified by their correspondence to the beliefs of authorities.

Stage 3: Characterized by the belief that authorities may be temporarily unaware of particular types of absolute knowledge. It is also assumed that while such missing knowledge will ultimately be obtained, it is permissible to believe in what "feels right" to the self.

Stage 4: Characterized by the belief that there is an objective reality which can never be known with certainty. Therefore, all knowledge, even knowledge possessed by authorities, must be conceptualized as relative to the individual's point of view.

Stage 5: Characterized by the belief that not only is knowledge subjective or relative, but that all of reality is subjective or relative as well. Since reality and knowledge of reality can only be understood through subjective interpretation, understanding is contextual and cannot be generalized.

Stage 6: Characterized by the belief that even though all knowledge is subjective, some forms of knowledge may be more valid than others. This claim is based on the premise that there are principles of inquiry which generalize across contexts.

Stage 7: Characterized by the belief that knowledge is the result of critical inquiry. Valid knowledge claims may be made by evaluating the work of many individuals over a long period of time. The process of critical inquiry, however, may give rise to fallible knowledge. Therefore, all knowledge claims must remain open to reevaluation vis-à-vis the formulation of new theoretical paradigms and the accumulation of new data.

From K. S. Kitchener and P. M. King, "Reflective Judgment: Concepts of Justification and Their Relationship to Age and Education" in *Journal of Applied Developmental Psychology,* 2:89–111. Copyright © 1981 Ablex Publishing Corporation, Norwood, NJ.

of attitudes. Rakfeldt et al. (in press) concluded that relativistic thinking allows patients to better understand the complexities and paradoxes of their psychiatric disturbances as well as the choices and options open to them within the therapeutic encounter.

Kramer and Woodruff (1986) investigated the hypothesis that formal operational thinking is a necessary precondition for the development of two distinct forms of postformal reasoning: relativistic thinking (the acceptance and integration of contradiction) and dialectic thinking (the acceptance of contextual relativism). The participants in their study were young, middle-aged, and older adults matched on educational level. They were administered several formal-thinking tasks, along with two dilemmas designed to measure relativistic and dialectic thinking (one dilemma involving the choice of a career and one concerning the resolution of a hostage situation). Results indicated that formal operation was a necessary precondition for the development of dialectic thinking. Contrary to expectation, however, was the finding that an awareness of relativity was a necessary precondition for the development of formal operations! Kramer and Woodruff speculated that dialectic thinking may be more closely allied with postformal thinking than is an acceptance of relativity.

Problem Finding

Patricia Arlin (1975) conducted the first research study that provided evidence for a fifth (postformal) stage in Piagetian theory. She regarded formal thinking as primarily involved in the task of problem solving. Alternatively, she argued that postformal thinking is primarily geared to the task of problem finding, or generating new problems by examining situations from a novel and creative point of view. Arlin presented college freshmen and seniors with measures of both problem-solving and problem-finding skills. The problem-finding task invited participants to raise questions about the arrangement of a number of disparate objects (for example, a C-clamp, a quarter, three candles, a boxtop, and ten thumb tacks). Very generalized and abstract questions were assumed to reflect a problem-finding orientation, while very specific and concrete questions were assumed to reflect a preoccupation with problem solving. Results showed that success on the Piagetian measures of formal operations was a necessary but not sufficient condition to produce high levels of performance on the problem-finding task.

Arlin (1984, 1989) also studied problem finding in a group of young adult artists, all of whom performed equally well on measures of formal thought. These artists were given a problem-finding test similar to that employed by Arlin in her earlier research (Arlin, 1975). Artists who were judged to produce highly creative and original works scored higher on the problem-finding measure than the artists whose work was rated noncreative. Differences between artists who were classified as either formal or postformal in their cognitive orientation were related to their answers to questions such as, "Could any of the elements in your drawing be eliminated or altered without destroying its characteristics?" The formal-thinking artists viewed their works as fixed, unalterable, and finished, while the postformal artists viewed their works as changeable and unfinished. Arlin suggested that the more creative artists were postformal thinkers who (1) did not adopt a single, fixed, and absolute view of their work, (2) accepted the idea that their work could evolve and change over time, and (3) actively tried to find new perspectives from which to view their work.

More recently, Johnson (1987) conducted a study to test Arlin's claims for a fifth stage of adult cognitive development. Based on his results, Johnson argued that problem finding is a cognitive ability which may be characteristic of individuals at *all* stages of cognitive development. He did suggest that adults may be the most likely age group to display problem finding. But they are not the *only* age group to possess this ability.

What, if any, relationship exists between problem finding and creativity? Is problem finding just another label for divergent thinking (see chapter 5)? Or is it a totally different phenomenon? Are the individuals who are most likely to make major contributions to a field problem finders rather than problem solvers? These questions need to be addressed by future researchers.

Conclusions about Postformal Cognitive Development

We have outlined the main features of postformal thinking along with a brief over-view of the research which has investigated the formal/postformal distinction. Clearly, some adults are capable of conceptualizing reality and solving problems in a postformal manner. Furthermore, the postformal cognitive orientation dis-played by these adults is very different from the formal orientation displayed by adolescents. Postformal thinking seems to be a necessity if adults are to truly ap-preciate the complexities of both physical and social reality. It would be a mistake, however, to believe that *all* adults display *all* of the characteristics of postformal development.

Reasoning about social matters clearly occupies a central role in post-Piagetian attempts to identify the levels or stages of postformal cognitive development. Indeed, one characteristic of all of the Piagetian revisionists described in this chapter is the dominant theme that adult cognition involves the interchange of the individual with his or her social world. The reasoning of adults about the social and inter-personal world in which they live is termed **social cognition.**

Our social cognitions are a pervasive aspect of our lives (Flavell, 1985). We may weigh the pitfalls of giving up our independence versus the benefits of rom-ance and marriage; we may make decisions about whether to have children and if so, how many; we may have to decide whether to tell a parent that she suffers from a terminal illness; we may have to determine the best way to deal with the depres-sion experienced by an aging parent. All of these problems and decisions involve social cognition. Quite clearly, considerable cognitive activity is enmeshed in our interpersonal and social lives.

Beyond doubt, the concept of postformal thinking is a most welcomed addi-tion to Piaget's original ideas about cognitive development. However, it seems as if the quality of the research on postformal reasoning has *not* kept pace with the theorizing surrounding this topic (Rybash et al., 1986). This may be because of the inherent difficulty in constructing and scoring measures of postformal thought. The research on postformal reasoning seems to be less rigorous and objective than the research conducted within the psychometric and information-processing traditions. This situation may represent a "paradigm shift" (Kuhn, 1970) in the study of adult cognitive development. When psychologists realized the problems in applying Piagetian theory to adult development, they responded with a rash of new theo-retical ideas before they had time to develop adequate measures of those theoret-ical concepts.

There continues to be a great deal of controversy concerning the stagelike characteristics of postformal reasoning. Some psychologists believe the research indicates that postformal thinking reflects a genuine stage of cognitive develop-ment well beyond formal operations (Commons, Richards, and Armon, 1984b; Commons, Sinnott, Richards, and Armon, 1989; Richards and Commons, 1984). With regard to the stage issue, Lamberson and Fischer (1988) have made a distinction between *optimal level* and *functional level.* Optimal level refers to the best or highest level of stagelike performance a person can achieve under ideal conditions. Functional level refers to a person's stagelike performance under normal, nonoptimal conditions where the individual is offered little environmental support. Lamberson and Fischer argue that it is only possible to observe genuine stages of development if we measure an individual's optimal level, not his or her functional level. They also suggest that we focus our attention on an individual's *developmental range*—the gap between the person's optimal and functional levels. Other psychologists have suggested that developmental changes in thought beyond formal operations, even when measured under optimal conditions, may not meet the criteria which define genuine cognitive stages. Rybash et al. (1986), for example, argued that postformal operations do not represent a genuine stage of cognitive development. They argue that postformal development may be best understood as a set of *styles* of thinking (relativistic thinking, dialectic thinking, problem finding, and so forth) that emerge during adulthood. Also, Rybash et al. (1986) maintained that postformal styles of thinking are domain-specific. For example, some adults may display some of the characteristics of postformal thought when composing music but not when dealing with interpersonal problems. Other adults may display the opposite cognitive profile.

Finally, several developmental psychologists have expressed reservations about the need for the stage concept itself. For example, Brainerd (1978), Gelman (1979), and Gardner (1983) have commented that the cognitive performance of children and adolescents is so inconsistent and variable that it is difficult to embrace the existence of a set of stages which comprise cognitive development. Certainly, adult cognitive performance may reflect even greater individual variability and inconsistency due to the accumulation of different experiences.

THE NEED FOR AN INTEGRATIVE MODEL OF ADULT COGNITION

In the last three chapters of this text, we have reviewed theory and research which bears on the different approaches to the study of adult cognition: the psychometric approach, the information-processing approach, and the stage approach. Each of these different approaches provides valuable information and perspective about the nature of adult cognitive development. However, each of these different theoretical views focuses on a different aspect of cognition, and each has a number of major limitations. To understand the strengths, weaknesses, and focal points of each of these different approaches, refer to table 7.3.

None of the traditional approaches (psychometric, information-processing, and stage) offers a comprehensive and complete account of the nature of adult cognitive change. In this section, we will describe a new perspective on adult cognitive development proposed by John Rybash, William Hoyer, and Paul Roodin (1986). This perspective, referred to as the **encapsulation model,** both integrates and extends the basic features of the traditional approaches to the study of adult cognition.

Table 7.3

A COMPARISON OF THE DIFFERENT APPROACHES TO THE STUDY OF ADULT COGNITION

Approach	Basic Question(s) Asked	Basic Research Findings	Most Important Strengths	Most Important Weaknesses
Stage/Piagetian	Are there qualitative changes in the structural characteristics of thought that are unique to adulthood?	Adulthood is characterized by the emergence of postformal styles of thinking.	Research on postformal thinking seems to capture the unique ways in which adults attempt to understand and deal with social and physical reality. Research on postformal thinking may help us better understand how adults solve ethical problems, develop scientific theories, and produce works of art.	Researchers who have investigated postformal reasoning have (1) neglected to examine age-related changes in the basic building blocks of cognition (for example, memory); (2) relied too much on cross-sectional research designs; (3) not placed enough emphasis on how knowledge affects the quality of an adult's reasoning; and (4) focused their attention on young and middle-aged adults.
Information-processing	Do the speed and capacity of mental operations change over the adult years? How do the fundamental component processes of cognition (memory, attention, perception, and so on) change with aging?	Adulthood is characterized by the tendency to process less information in a progressively slower and less efficient manner. The basic building blocks of cognition (attention, memory, and perception) exhibit age-related decrements. Even with extended practice, older adults cannot outperform young adults.	Researchers who adhere to the information-processing perspective have designed the most well-controlled, scientific studies on the topic of cognitive aging. They are to be praised for the manner in which they have measured age-related differences in the fundamental components of cognition.	Researchers who have examined human information processing have (1) ignored the emergence of postformal styles of thinking unique to adulthood; (2) relied too much on cross-sectional research designs; (3) focused their attention on very young and very old adults to the exclusion of middle-aged adults; and (4) constructed

Psychometric	How do the different components of intelligence (crystallized versus fluid intelligence, the primary mental abilities, and so on) change over the adult years? Are scores of standardized tests of intelligence related to intelligent behavior in real-life situations?	Adulthood is characterized by the growth of some components of intelligence (for example, crystallized intelligence) and the decline of other components of intelligence (for example, fluid intelligence). Performance on the different components of intelligence may be more heavily related to cohort effects, educational level, health status, and factors other than age per se.	Adherents of the psychometric approach have pointed out the multidimensional nature of adult cognitive change (they were the first to point out that intellectual development entails both advances and declines). Also, psychometricians have conducted several large-scale longitudinal and sequential studies which have allowed us to measure intellectual change over the entire range of adulthood and to disentangle the relationship between age, cohort, and time of measurement.	experimental tasks which may be highly unfamiliar and threatening for older adults. Several psychologists have questioned the validity of several psychometric tests of intelligence. Also, psychometricians have (1) made no attempt to examine the unique styles of thinking that emerge in adulthood; and (2) disregarded the important role played by domain-specific knowledge on intellectual functioning.

Source: Data from J. M. Rybash, W. J. Hoyer, and P. A. Roodin, *Adult Cognition and Aging: Developmental Changes in Processing, Knowing, and Thinking.* Copyright © 1986 Pergamon Press, New York, NY.

The Encapsulation Model

The encapsulation model conceptualizes cognition as consisting of three interrelated dimensions: processing, knowing, and thinking. *Processing* refers to the way in which various mental abilities and/or capacities are used to process (encode, store, and retrieve) information. *Knowing* refers to the way in which extant knowledge aids in information processing and problem solving. *Thinking* refers to an individual's understanding or perspective on the knowledge that she has accumulated during her development. Unfortunately, these three facets of cognition have been examined in relative isolation from each other by psychologists interested in the study of adult cognitive development.

Processing has been explored by adherents of the information-processing and psychometric approaches. In general, researchers working within these traditions have viewed adulthood as a period of negative developmental change. They have concluded that adults become less adept at general problem solving because they process reduced amounts of information in a progressively slower and less efficient manner. Research and theory within these traditions, however, are limited in several ways. Advocates of the information-processing and psychometric perspectives have (1) failed to recognize the emergence of qualitatively unique styles of thinking (postformal thinking) during the adult years; (2) displayed too much reliance on the construction of experimental tasks and measuring instruments that are far removed from real-life tasks and circumstances; (3) failed to acknowledge and explain the role played by domain-specific knowledge on the processing of real-life information and the solution of real-life tasks; and (4) focused their research on the subcomponents of the human cognitive system (such as perception, attention, and memory) rather than the whole system itself.

Knowing has been the primary focus of the cognitive-science perspective on cognition. The dominant concern within this tradition has been with the growth and representation of knowledge and with the development of artificial intelligence software systems (see Gardner, 1985; Hillman, 1985; Waldrop, 1984). Cognitive scientists assume that intelligent problem solving has its source in the size and breadth of the individual's knowledge base rather than in the power of the individual's generalized mental abilities (fluid intelligence), mental capacities (attention, memory), or internalized thought structures (postformal thinking). Research conducted within the context of this approach is essentially nondevelopmental. It has been suggested (Charness 1985, 1988; Chi, 1985; Dittmann-Kohli and Baltes, 1988; Hoyer, 1985, 1986), however, that research within the cognitive-science tradition has important implications for the study of adult cognitive development. Adulthood is the portion of the life span during which individuals develop domain-specific cognitive expertise. Furthermore, older adults are likely to display sophisticated cognitive performance in the areas of specialization within which they have developed an expert-like knowledge base. Thus, from the cognitive-science point of view, adulthood may be regarded as a period of positive developmental change. Research and theory within the cognitive-science framework, however, is limited in a number of ways. For example, cognitive scientists

In adulthood, many individuals display sophisticated cognitive abilities in specific areas or domains of expertise.

have (1) failed to recognize the emergence of postformal styles of thinking unique to adulthood; (2) focused on the means by which expert knowledge aids in problem solving but neglected the role it plays in problem finding; and (3) failed to identify the factors that determine the development of cognitive expertise. Read box 7.2 to gain a better understanding of the cognitive-science approach to the study of cognition. As you read, pay close attention to the emphasis placed on expert knowledge in the cognitive-science approach.

Developmental changes in *thinking* have been the focus of theory and research inspired by traditional Piagetian theory. Neo-Piagetian theorists have viewed adulthood as a period of positive developmental change marked by the transition from formal to postformal styles of thinking. Postformal thinking permits adults to

---

BOX 7.2

THE COGNITIVE-SCIENCE APPROACH

Rybash, Hoyer, and Roodin (1986) noted that psychologists studying cognitive development during adulthood are faced with an apparent paradox. Research based on psychometric and information-processing theory indicates a deterioration of generalized cognitive ability with age, while everyday observation of adults within their occupational roles, social interactions, and hobbies indicates that with increasing age comes stability (and sometimes even enhancement) of cognitive performance.

An important line of research that bears on the resolution of this paradox is represented by the *cognitive-science approach* to the study of cognition. This approach suggests that intelligent problem solving lies in the possession and utilization of a great deal of specific *knowledge* about the world. Waldrop (1984), in tracing the influence of the cognitive-science approach on the study of artificial intelligence (AI), comments that:

> The essence of intelligence was no longer seen to be reasoning ability alone. More important was having lots of highly specific knowledge about lots of things—a notion inevitably stated as, "Knowledge is power." (p. 1280)

Thus, in contrast to the earlier approaches (such as the psychometric and information-processing approaches) that represented human problem solving as a generalized mental process, capacity, and/or ability, contemporary cognitive scientists suggest that problem solving in adulthood requires *expert knowledge*.

Expert knowledge has been found to be *domain-specific* and independent of generalized mental abilities. For example, Chase and Simon (1973) and de Groot (1965) carried out a number of ground-breaking studies on chess experts and novices. These researchers found that chess experts (that is, grand masters) could reconstruct the positions of approximately twenty-five chess pieces arranged in a gamelike configuration on a chessboard after having seen the display for only five seconds; novice players, on the other hand, could only remember the positions of about six or seven pieces. When the same twenty-five pieces were arranged in a random configuration on a chessboard, both the experts and the novices remembered the positions of the same number of pieces—approximately seven. Furthermore, experts and novices were not found to differ from each other with regard to generalized measures of memory span and short-term memory. And expert players did not evidence a superiority in general intellectual ability as measured by IQ test performance. It seems safe to conclude that chess experts have exceptionally good memories for gamelike positions on a chessboard because of the vast amount of specific knowledge they possess about gamelike configurations of chess pieces. In fact, it has been estimated that chess experts have stored, in long-term memory, approximately 40,000 different game like configurations!

In a more recent study, Ceci and Liker (1986) investigated the ability of gamblers to handicap horse races. The individuals in the study were avid horse-racing enthusiasts who went to the racetrack nearly every day. Ceci and Liker gave all these participants an early form of a racing sheet. This allowed the gamblers to study the past performances of the horses that would be competing in all ten races the next day at a real racetrack. The researchers asked the men to pick (1) the favorite in each of the ten races, and (2) the top three finishers in each of the ten races in the correct order. The men's selections were compared to the post-time odds for the horses in each race as well as to the actual order of finish for each race. Based on their analysis, Ceci and Liker identified fourteen "experts" and sixteen "nonexperts." The experts selected the horse with the best post-time odds in nine out of the ten races and the top three horses in at least one-half of the races. The nonexperts performed much more poorly. The experts were found to use very complex mental models to make their selections. These models took into account the interaction of about seven different variables: the horse's times during the first and last quarter-miles of a race, the quality of the horses it had competed against in the past, the jockey riding it, and so on. In comparision, the nonexperts used very simplistic models to make their picks.

Most surprisingly, Ceci and Liker found that the experts and nonexperts did *not* differ on a number of variables that would seem to be good predictors of their handicapping skill. For example, these two groups did not differ in IQ score, years of education, occupational status, or number of years of handicapping experience—both groups had been going to the track for about sixteen years! Ceci and Liker concluded that expertise in handicapping is not purely dependent on past experience or general intelligence.

The cognitive-science perspective was not originally developed to explain age-related changes in cognition. Nevertheless, the cognitive-science approach has important implications for the developmental analysis of cognitive change. For example, effective cognitive functioning in adulthood may become less dependent on generalized mental abilities but progressively more dependent on the individual's storehouse of domain-specific knowledge. This may account for the tendency for older adults to perform poorly on laboratory tasks of cognition and psychometric tests of intelligence (because laboratory tasks and psychometric tasks measure generalized mental processes), but competently on everyday occupational and avocational activities (because such tasks draw heavily on domain-specific expert knowledge).

view reality in relativistic and dialectic terms. Such thinking styles provide the necessary basis for the solution of both well- and ill-defined problems and the discovery of new perspectives from which new problems may be identified. The postformal approach certainly has its merits. Postformal theorists may appear, at times, to glorify aging without adequately describing many of the cognitive losses and declines which are a part of the later years of development. More specifically, the postformal approach is limited in that it has (1) ignored the importance played by domain-specific knowledge in adult cognition; (2) failed to take into consideration how such basic cognitive processes as attention and memory change with age; and (3) overemphasized the genuine stagelike characteristics of postformal thinking.

The encapsulation model integrates and extends the three dominant strands of adult cognition: processing, knowing, and thinking. Furthermore, this model accounts for both the cognitive declines and the cognitive competencies of older adults. Specifically, the encapsulation model suggests that basic mental capacities and fluid mental abilities become increasingly dedicated to and encapsulated within specific domains of knowledge during the course of adult development. As general processes and abilities become encapsulated within domains, adults' knowledge becomes more differentiated, accessible, usable, and "expert" in nature.

The encapsulation model also suggests that the acquisition of new knowledge (knowledge *unrelated* to that already encapsulated in specific domains) becomes increasingly less efficient with advances in age. Mastery of new domains is somewhat uncharacteristic of older adults, who are not ideal "learning machines" (see Rozin, 1976). Childhood and adolescence are periods of the life span characterized by the acquisition of new knowledge in a variety of ever-expanding domains. Adulthood may be a time during which individuals refine and develop a perspective on their knowledge.

The reduced capacity to acquire new knowledge during adulthood may be compensated for by the development of expert knowledge within existing domains and by the development of a postformal perspective on that knowledge. Once adults conceptualize their domain-specific knowledge in a relativistic, dialectic, and open-ended manner, they become capable of (1) solving the ill-defined problems characteristic of real life, (2) finding new problems and new perspectives from which these problems may be solved and, (3) producing creative and sophisticated works within defined areas of expertise.

The encapsulation of thinking and knowing within specific domains seems to represent a necessary and adaptive feature of adult cognitive development. Thus, the age-related loss of general intellectual abilities as reported in psychometric and information-processing research may have little functional significance for most adults in most situations. While age-related declines in fluid abilities and mental capacities are indeed documented, these findings seem to result from the practice of assessing mental processes apart from the domains in which they have become encapsulated. Age-related differences in the component processes of cognition (memory, attention, and so forth) cannot be meaningfully assessed apart from the domain in which these processes are encapsulated.

In summary, the encapsulation model suggests that:

1. *Processing, knowing,* and *thinking* are the three dimensions of cognition that must be addressed in any comprehensive theory of adult cognitive development.
2. The processes associated with the acquisition, utilization, and representation of knowledge become *encapsulated* within particular domains as one grows older.
3. Mental capacities appear to decline with age when assessed as general abilities, but show minimal age-related decline when assessed within encapsulated domains.
4. Adult cognitive development is characterized by the growth of expert knowledge and the emergence of postformal styles of thought. Adult styles of thinking and forms of knowing are the result of the process of encapsulation.

We can illustrate the basic claims of the encapsulation model by examining two different lines of research. First, we'll present the results of several studies examining the relationship between aging, information processing, and cognitive expertise. Second, we'll review studies on the growth of wisdom during adulthood.

Aging, Information Processing, and Cognitive Expertise

The encapsulation model suggests that adults continue to accumulate knowledge, which becomes increasingly refined with age and experience. Accumulated domain-specific knowledge can take on a compensatory function for older adults. This means that older adults can continue to function effectively when given tasks that allow them to draw upon their expert knowledge. This occurs in spite of the significant reduction in the generalized information-processing skills and/or fluid intellectual abilities which accompany the aging process. Evidence for this point of view comes from several sources. Neil Charness (1981, 1985, 1988), Timothy Salthouse (1984), and Stephanie Clancy and William Hoyer (1988, 1990) have all shown that expert knowledge can compensate for general losses in processing speed and working memory in older adults.

Charness (1981, 1985) reported that older chess experts were found to be as competent as younger chess experts in choosing the best chess move from four possible alternatives. More specifically, older experts were found to search just as many moves ahead as younger experts. But they were also found to entertain fewer possible moves than their younger counterparts, showing even greater efficiency. Charness concluded that older chess experts compensate for general processing and memory deficits by using an elaborate knowledge base acquired over years of practice. The growth of this vast and highly organized knowledge base allows older experts to search for appropriate moves as quickly as (and even more efficiently than) younger experts.

Salthouse (1984) conducted an experiment with typists who differed in age (young adults versus older adults) and skill level (novices versus experts). As might be expected, Salthouse discovered that the older typists performed more poorly than younger typists on tasks assessing (1) simple reaction time, (2) the fastest speed at which they could tap their fingers, and (3) digit-symbol substitution. (Remember from chapter 5 that the digit-symbol substitution task is a component of the WAIS. In this task, a person is asked to match, as quickly as possible, a series of numbers with a series of abstract geometric patterns.) More importantly, Salthouse also discovered that the participants' typing speed was uncorrelated with age but *was* significantly related to the participants' skill level. The expert typists (both young and old) were significantly quicker than the novice typists (both young and old). Through a set of ingenious experiments, Salthouse was able to determine that older expert typists compensated for age-related declines in speed and reaction time by looking farther ahead at printed text, thereby giving themselves more time to plan what their next keystroke should be. Finally, Salthouse's findings illustrate the domain-specific nature of older adults' compensatory mechanisms. Older expert typists did not employ the same look-ahead strategy on any of the other tasks Salthouse administered (for example, digit-symbol substitution), although the implementation of this strategy would have improved their performance.

Clancy and Hoyer (1988) conducted an experiment with medical laboratory technologists who differed in both age (young adults versus older adults) and skill level (novices versus experts). Keep in mind that a medical laboratory technologist, as an integral part of his or her job, performs a number of complex visual identification tasks such as looking at slides of tissue or blood under a microscope to identify certain diseases. This experiment consisted of two parts. In the first part, the participants had to identify several unfamiliar visual stimuli (for example, abstract geometric figures) that were flashed on a video screen for less than a second. As expected, results showed that younger participants scored better on this domain-general task than older participants. Also, the participants' success on this task was unrelated to their skill level within the field of medical laboratory technology. In the second part of the study, the technologists were briefly shown pictures of complex microscopic slides of actual laboratory specimens. Each slide contained a number of clinically significant and clinically insignificant pieces of information. Clinically significant information was defined as a piece of visual information crucial to the diagnosis of a particular disease. On the other hand, clinically insignificant information was defined as visual information that does not serve as an effective diagnostic aid. The participants were shown a single piece of visual information and asked if it was present in the original complex slide. Results indicated that both the younger and older experts were equally quick and accurate in determining if a clinically significant piece of information was present in a previously seen complex slide. Furthermore, the performance of both expert groups on this task was unaffected by having to perform another task concurrently—pressing a button whenever a tone sounded. In contrast, both younger and older novices performed poorly on this microscopic identification task, especially under dual-task conditions (when they were also required to perform the button-pressing task). This study provides more proof about how older adults can perform competently within their area of expertise yet at the same time function poorly on domain-general measures of cognitive performance.

Finally, note that cognitive expertise is not powerful enough to compensate for the reductions in the mental capacities and physical abilities that underlie performance in all domains. For example, performance in such sports as golf, tennis, basketball, and football declines with age even among individuals who possess a great deal of expert knowledge about these sports. On the other hand, performance within domains that allow more time for planning and reflection, that demand fewer snap decisions and less physical exertion (for example, musical composition or visual art), may actually improve because of the cumulative effects of age and experience. In connection with this point, Charness (1985) has commented that:

> . . . when people can draw upon domain-specific knowledge and when they have developed appropriate compensatory mechanisms, they can treat us to a memorable performance, whether on the keyboard of a typewriter, a piano, or on the podium of an orchestral stage. When the task environment does not afford the same predictability or opportunity to plan ahead, however, as in the case in fast-moving sports environments, degradation in hardware cannot be compensated for by more efficient software. (p. 23)

Wisdom

Wisdom is a mental characteristic or ability that has long been associated with aging within both Eastern and Western cultural traditions (Clayton and Birren, 1980). Wisdom may represent the growth of expert knowledge and postformal thinking within the domain of personal knowledge (Rybash et al., 1986). Personal knowledge refers to an individual's understanding of personal relationships as well as an understanding of how such knowledge can be used to resolve the interpersonal, social, and ethical problems that arise in everyday life. This viewpoint has its roots, in part, in the work of Paul Baltes and his colleagues (Baltes, 1990; Ditmann-Kohli and Baltes, 1988; Smith, Dixon, and Baltes, 1989). They defined *practical wisdom* as the ability to display superior judgment with regard to important but uncertain matters of real life. Dittman-Kohli and Baltes (1988) also distinguished between practical wisdom and *philosophical wisdom*—the understanding of the abstract relationship between one's self and the rest of humanity. Furthermore, they proposed that practical wisdom develops over the adult years and is characterized by:

1. Skill or expertise within the domain of personal knowledge
2. Emphasis on the pragmatic or practical aspects of intelligence and knowledge
3. Emphasis on the context of the problem
4. Recognition of uncertainty as a characteristic of problems and solutions
5. Reflection and relativism in judgments and actions

Notice that the last four characteristics of wisdom are also characteristics of postformal thought. Also, Dittmann-Kohli and Baltes's concept of wisdom may be related to Gardner's (1983) ideas about personal intelligence (see box 5.1).

K. Warner Schaie (1977b) has developed a stage model of adult cognition that bears on the issue of wisdom. Schaie considered the possible existence of four stages of cognitive development: acquisitive, achieving, responsible, and reintegrative. The *acquisitive stage* refers to the periods of childhood and adolescence during which the individual functions in a protected environment and works toward the goal of acquiring knowledge. With the achievement of adult status, the individual is less protected from the consequences of failing at problem solving. At this stage, the goal is no longer the acquisition of knowledge but rather the achievement of potential. Schaie therefore calls this the *achieving stage.* The *responsible stage* corresponds with middle adulthood. At this stage, the individual has attained competence and independence and now has to assume responsibility for others. Schaie believes that this stage requires problem solving that focuses on an individual's family and/or other important people in life. The *reintegrative stage* corresponds to late adulthood. It is during this stage that we may observe the emergence of wisdom. According to Schaie (1977), the older adult's mental resources become focused on aspects of life that are more personally meaningful. Schaie says that the reintegrative stage completes the transition from the what-should-I-know phase through the how-should-I-use-what-I-know phase to the why-should-I-know phase of life.

Speculation about the growth of wisdom abounds. Rebok (1987) has suggested that the next step for developmental psychologists is the construction of a reliable and valid testing instrument to assess practical wisdom. Only if researchers develop such an instrument will they be able to chart the growth of wisdom and differentiate it from other cognitive abilities.

In conclusion, this chapter has described some positive features of adult cognitive development, including postformal styles of thinking and cognitive expertise. These positive features of adult cognition seem to be most apparent when adults grapple with social and/or interpersonal problems characteristic of everyday life. It seems clear, then, that developmental researchers should study cognition in the widest of all contexts. We hope that after having read the last three chapters, you will have concluded that a comprehensive understanding of adult cognition must take into account the theory and research on the psychometric, information-processing, cognitive-science and Piagetian perspectives. The encapsulation model represents a first step in this direction.

Summary

The stage approach to the study of adult cognition offers an important alternative to the psychometric and information-processing perspectives. Genuine cognitive stages must meet a strict set of criteria. These criteria include (1) invariant movement, (2) qualitative restructuring, (3) hierarchical integration, (4) structured wholeness, and (5) universal progression. Jean Piaget developed the most significant stage theory of cognitive development. Originally,

Piaget argued for the existence of four different cognitive stages. The fourth stage, formal operations, which Piaget thought emerged during adolescence, was thought to be representative of mature, adult cognition. Piaget viewed formal operational thought as a form of scientific thinking, described as hypothetico-deductive, logical, and abstract. Formal thought seems best suited for the solution of well-defined, closed-system problems. In the mid- to late-1970s, it became clear that Piaget's stage of formal operations did not capture the essential features of mature adult thought. Thus, psychologists began to search for a fifth, postformal stage of cognitive development. Postformal thought allows adults to solve ill-defined, open-system problems as well as to focus on problem finding, not just problem solving. Several research studies examined two essential features of postformal cognitive development: relativistic thinking and problem finding. We concluded that postformal development may be best understood as a number of unique styles of thinking that emerge during adulthood, not as a genuine stage of cognitive development. We also concluded that postformal accounts of adult cognition place an emphasis on social cognition. Social cognition refers to reasoning about the social, interpersonal, and ethical problems characteristic of everyday living.

Finally, we briefly described the encapsulation model of adult cognition. This model integrates the theory and research stemming from the psychometric, information-processing, cognitive-science, and cognitive-stage perspectives. It suggests that the salient dimensions of cognition are processing, knowing, and thinking. It also suggests that the most important characteristics of adult cognition (the development of domain-specific expert knowledge and postformal thinking) result from the encapsulation of basic cognitive processes and abilities. We illustrated the encapsulation model through a discussion of the relationship between aging, cognitive expertise, and information processing; and by a discussion of the growth of wisdom during the adult years.

Review Questions

1. Describe each of the different criteria that define genuine cognitive stages.
2. Discuss the essential features of formal operations. Describe some of the different problems that may be used to test for the presence of formal thinking.
3. Why did psychologists become disenchanted with Piaget's contention that formal operational thinking was the final stage of cognitive development?
4. Describe the essential features of postformal cognitive development. What aspect of postformal thinking (relativistic thinking, dialectic thinking, or problem finding) do you think has generated the most meaningful and important research? Why?
5. Do you think the research on postformal thinking really captures the essence of postformal development? Explain.
6. What is social cognition? Is the research regarding formal or postformal thinking more focused on the topic of social cognition? Why?
7. Compare and contrast the psychometric, information-processing, and cognitive-stage approaches to the study of adult cognition. Indicate the focal point as well as the strengths and weaknesses of each approach.
8. Explain the basic tenets of the cognitive-science approach to the study of cognition. What are the implications of the cognitive-science approach for psychologists interested in the study of adult cognition?
9. Explain the basic features of the encapsulation model. Explain the differences between processing, knowing, and thinking.

10. Discuss the research studies which suggest that adults continue to function effectively on tasks within which they have developed cognitive expertise.
11. Explain how cognitive psychologists have attempted to examine the concept of wisdom.

For Further Reading

Charness, N. (1988). Expertise in chess, music, and physics: A cognitive perspective. In L. K. Obler and D. A. Fein (Eds.), *The exceptional brain: The neuropsychology of talent and special abilities.* New York: Guilford Press.
This chapter is an excellent overview of the cognitive-science approach to human expertise. Moderately difficult reading.

Commons, M. L., Sinnott, J. D., Richards, F. A., and Armon, C. (Eds.). (1989). *Adult development: Vol. 1, Comparisons and applications of developmental models.* New York: Praeger.
This book contains fifteen different essays which focus on the differences between formal and postformal thinking. It is an important source of information for the postformal movement in developmental psychology. Moderately difficult to difficult reading.

Dittmann-Kohli, F., and Baltes, P. B. (1987). Towards a neo-functionalist conception of adult intellectual development: Wisdom as a prototypical case of intellectual growth. In C. Alexander and E. Langer (Eds.), *Beyond formal operations: Alternative endpoints to human development.* New York: Oxford University Press.
In this important work, Dittmann-Kohli and Baltes articulate their provocative viewpoint on the nature and development of wisdom during adulthood. Moderately difficult reading.

Inhelder, B., and Piaget, J. (1958). *The growth of logical thinking from childhood to adolescence.* New York: Basic Books.
In this classic book, Jean Piaget and his associate Barbel Inhelder first described the essential characteristics of formal operations. Very difficult reading.

Rybash, J. M., Hoyer, W. J., and Roodin, P. A. (1986). *Adult cognition and aging: Developmental changes in processing, knowing, and thinking.* New York: Pergamon Press.
An informative and important overview of all the different theories and research bearing on adult cognition and aging. The authors set forth their own viewpoint of adult cognitive development—the encapsulation model. Moderately difficult reading.

CHAPTER 8

RELATIONSHIPS, MARRIAGE, PARENTING, AND SEXUALITY: DEVELOPMENTAL PERSPECTIVES

IMAGINE

Imagine What It Would Be Like to Have No Friends and to Be Lonely

Imagine what life would be like without close ties to other people—no one to be a companion, no one to share joys and sorrows. Imagine what it would be like not to have anyone who makes you feel secure and give you support when you need it.

Some people lack emotional attachments or a social network, and these conditions are likely to result in feelings of loneliness. Robert Weiss (1973) believes that there are two kinds of loneliness: emotional isolation, which results from the loss or absence of an emotional attachment, and social isolation, which occurs through the loss or absence of social ties. Either type of loneliness is likely to make an individual feel restless and depressed. Weiss also believes that one type of relationship cannot easily substitute for another to diminish the loneliness. Consequently, an adult grieving over the loss of a love relationship is likely to still feel very lonely even in the company of friends.

For many people, divorce or the death of a spouse inevitably produces feelings of loss and loneliness. One divorced woman commented that such a loss gives you the feeling that the whole world has just come to an end and that you are completely alone. From Weiss's perspective, a supportive network of friends and relatives may help a divorced person adapt, but he or she is still likely to experience emotional isolation.

Similarly, people who have close emotional attachments may still feel a great deal of loneliness if they do not also have some social ties. Weiss described one woman who had a happy marriage but whose husband had to take a job in another state where they knew no one. In their new location she listened to her husband describe all the new friends he was developing on his new job while she was home taking care of the kids. She was bored and miserable. Finally the family moved to a suburb where she would have a better opportunity to develop friendships.

Being alone is different from being lonely. Most of us cherish moments when we can be alone for awhile, away from the hectic pace of our lives. Zick Rubin (1979) has commented that for people in high-pressure jobs, aloneness may heal, while loneliness can hurt. In our society we are conditioned to believe that aloneness is to be dreaded, so we develop the expectation that solitude may bring sadness. However, research has revealed that people who choose to live alone are no more lonely than people who live with others (Rubenstein and Shaver, 1981).

Intimacy, love, attachment, and friendship are among the most cherished aspects of adult life. If we do not have an intimate relationship with someone, we may spend endless hours thinking about how to develop such a relationship. And if we don't have any friends, most of us spend time and effort trying to develop friendships. Few of us want to go through the world alone for very long—feelings of loneliness, when they persist for a long time, can be debilitating and lead to symptoms of mental disturbance.

INTRODUCTION

In this chapter we'll explore the personal relationships of adults. We'll begin with an analysis of the building blocks of adult relationships: love, intimacy, and friendship. Then we'll discuss a particularly significant relationship of the adult years—marriage. We'll also highlight the parent and grandparent roles. Finally, we'll discuss the sexual dimension of adult interpersonal relationships from young adulthood to old age.

BUILDING RELATIONSHIPS

Not only are we motivated to seek the company of other people in general, but most of us would like to form close and stable relationships with specific people. Adults usually seek two kinds of relationships with others—one an emotional attachment to one other person (usually a lover or spouse), the other social ties to a number of friends. The two sets of relationships serve different needs: emotional attachments stimulate a sense of comfort and security, whereas social ties create a sense of group identity and integration.

Attachment and Love

Love has been the domain of poets and novelists more than the province of scientific psychology. Though not easily defined and measured, love is, nevertheless, a pervasive aspect of interpersonal relationships in adulthood. Many adults spend hour after hour thinking about love, anticipating a romantic love relationship, watching love relationships on soap operas, reading about love in magazines or books, and listening to music filled with references to love. Psychologist Zick Rubin (1970, 1973) has attempted to measure romantic love. He developed two scales, one for liking and one for loving. Rubin maintains that *liking* refers to the cognitive belief that someone is similar to us and involves our positive evaluation of that person. *Loving,* on the other hand, is the belief that we are close to someone and involves dependency, a more selfless orientation to help the other person, and qualities of exclusiveness and absorption. The qualities of exclusiveness and absorption seem to most strongly differentiate liking from loving. If you like someone, that individual probably does not preoccupy your thoughts and you are not likely to be overly concerned if that person also likes someone else. By contrast, love triggers a preoccupation with another person, including feelings of possessiveness.

Rubin's ideas of loving and liking seem to correspond to more recent theories (Berscheid, 1988; Davis, 1985; Sternberg and Grajeck, 1984). For these researchers, love involves a relationship marked, in part, by three underlying themes: (1) emotionality or passion, (2) a sense of commitment or loyalty, and (3) a degree of sharing, openness, or mutual expression of personal identity. These three themes appear in different proportions in each theory. For example, Robert Sternberg (1986)

Figure 8.1   Davis's conceptualization of the components of love.

George Levinger (1974, 1978), ''mutuality'' supports love relationships over time. Mutuality occurs when partners share knowledge with each other, assume responsibility for each other's satisfaction, and share private information that governs their relationship. In virtually every current theory of love, this theme of mutuality is expressed in one form or another.

Attachment and love are important to our survival and well-being throughout life (see, for example, Bowlby, 1969; Reedy, Birren, and Schaie, 1981; Spitz, 1945). There is increased interest in studying various dimensions of attachment across the life span (for example, Antonucci, 1981; Ingersoll-Dayton and Antonucci, 1988; Hartup and Lempers, 1973; Troll and Smith, 1976; Weinraub, Brooks, and Lewis, 1977). Margaret Reedy, James Birren, and K. Warner Schaie (1981) examined the theoretical and research literature on the developmental nature of attachment in adult love relationships and found two themes. The first indicates that relationships may move toward deeper levels of intimacy over time as the passionate fires of youthful love are somehow transformed into the deeper, more serene and tender love of advanced age. From this perspective, physical attraction, perceived similarity of the loved one, self-disclosure, romance, and passion are important in emerging relationships, whereas security, loyalty, and mutual emotional interest in the relationship sustain love relationships over long periods of time. According to George Levinger (1974, 1978), ''mutuality'' supports love relationships over time. Mutuality occurs when partners share knowledge with each other, assume responsibility for each other's satisfaction, and share private information that governs their relationship. In virtually every current theory of love, this theme of mutuality is expressed in one form or another.

BOX 8.1

ROMANTIC AND AFFECTIONATE LOVE

Love is a very difficult concept to define and study. To help us better understand this elusive concept, Ellen Berscheid (1988) has articulated the distinction between *romantic love* and *affectionate love.*

ROMANTIC LOVE

Berscheid believes that when we say we are "in love" with someone, we are speaking of romantic love. Romantic love is the reason people give for wanting to be married (Kephart, 1987); without love, many feel there is no reason for marriage (Simpson, Campbell, and Berscheid, 1986). Moreover, half of today's men and women believe that no longer being in love is sufficient reason to dissolve a marriage.

Romantic love is especially important to younger adults. In one investigation, unattached college students were asked to identify their closest relationship. More than half named a romantic partner rather than a parent, sibling, or friend (Berscheid and Snyder, in press). About a romantic partner one says, "I am *in love,*" rather than just, "I love." Certainly romantic love has a strong sexual component; this component is an undeniable force in the relationship (Berscheid, 1983, 1988). But romantic love is also established with people we believe can meet our basic emotional, intellectual, and social needs (Berscheid, 1982). Romantic lovers who fail to meet these expectations on a consistent basis can expect to experience strongly negative emotional reactions towards each other. These negative feelings ultimately jeopardize the long-term maintenance of the relationship. In one investigation, romantic lovers were more likely than friends to cause depression (Berscheid and Fei, 1977).

AFFECTIONATE LOVE

Love is far more than simple passion or physiological arousal; it is also affectionate love, which has been called emotional attachment. In affectionate love, we desire to have the other person near us and maintain a deep affection for the other person. While early phases of love center on romantic love and passion (Davis, 1985; Sternberg and Grajek, 1984), affection predominates as love progresses. Phillip Shaver (1986) has described the developmental course of enduring love. Initially, romantic love is fueled by mixtures of sexual attraction and gratification, a reduced sense of loneliness, uncertainty about the security of developing another attachment, and excitement aroused by the novelty of exploring another human being. With time, sexual attraction wanes, attachment anxieties either lessen or produce conflict and withdrawal, novelty is replaced with familiarity, and lovers either find themselves securely attached in a deeply caring relationship or feel distress—in the form of boredom, disappointment, loneliness, or even hostility. In the latter case, one or both partners may eventually seek another close relationship.

A second theme in the literature on the development of love relationships suggests the presence of two basic marital types: institutional and companionship (Hicks and Platt, 1970). The institutional relationship is oriented toward tradition; loyalty and security are primary aspects of the relationship, and normative behavior rules are sex-differentiated along traditional lines. The husband's role is more instrumental, the wife's role more expressive. By contrast, the companionship relationship stresses the importance of affective interaction, including passion, expressions of love, rapport, communication, and respect. Investigators have found that over time tradition may replace companionship as the primary bonding force in love relationships. For example, in a twenty-year longitudinal study, it was found that a decline in marital satisfaction from youth to middle adulthood was associated with a decline in companionship, demonstrations of affection and passion, common interests, and communication (Boland and Follingstad, 1987; Pineo, 1961; Smith, Snyder, Trull, and Monsma, 1988).

To explore the nature of age and sex differences characteristic of satisfying love relationships, Reedy et al. (1981) studied 102 happily married couples in early (average age twenty-eight), middle (average age forty-five), and late adulthood (average age sixty-five). As figure 8.2 shows, the researchers found age-related differences in the nature of satisfying love relationships. Passion and sexual intimacy were more important in early adulthood than late adulthood, while tender feelings of affection and loyalty most predominated in later-life love relationships. Young-adult lovers rated communication as more characteristic of their love relationships than their counterparts in middle and late adulthood did.

Aside from the age-related differences, however, there were some striking similarities in the nature of satisfying love relationships in the Reedy, Birren, and Schaie study. At all ages, emotional security was ranked as the most important factor in love, followed by respect, communication, help and play behaviors, sexual intimacy, and loyalty. Clearly, love is multifaceted and encompasses far more than sex. These findings indicate that a new historical trend in the quality of relationships may be emerging. Earlier there was extensive interest in individual freedom and independence in love relationships, but the data suggest a historical shift toward security, fidelity, trust, and commitment in relationships (Hendrick and Hendrick, 1983). This shift occurs at a time when worldwide concern is focused on acquired immune deficiency syndrome (AIDS), which can be transmitted in several ways, including heterosexual contact with infected carriers (Sande, 1986).

The findings of Reedy et al. (1981) also suggest that the nature of a satisfying love relationship is different for men and women. Women rate emotional security as more important than men do. No gender differences were found for communication and sexual intimacy, but somewhat surprisingly, men more than women rated loyalty as characteristic of their love relationships.

Though this research suggests that intimacy is a more central factor in a satisfying love relationship as marriages age, life-span theorist Erik Erikson believes that early adulthood is the period in which the development of intimacy becomes very important.

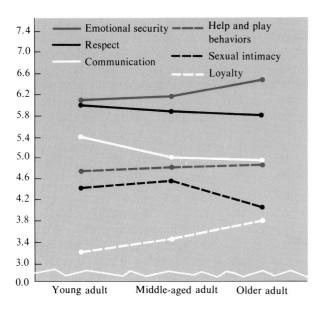

Figure 8.2 Changes in the components of satisfying love relationships across the life span.

Intimacy

Erik Erikson (1968) suggested that intimacy should develop after individuals are well on their way to achieving a stable and successful identity. The development of intimacy, in Erikson's view, is another life crisis—if an individual does not develop intimacy in early adulthood, he or she may be left with what Erikson refers to as isolation.

Erikson (1968) finds intimacy possible in both sexual relationships and adult friendships. He comments:

> As the young individual seeks at least tentative forms of playful intimacy in friendship and competition, in sex play and love, in argument and gossip, he is apt to experience a peculiar strain, as if such tentative engagement might turn into an interpersonal fusion amounting to a loss of identity and requiring, therefore, a tense inner reservation, a caution in commitment. Where a youth does not resolve such a commitment, he may isolate himself and enter, at best, only stereotyped and formalized interpersonal relations; or he may, in repeated hectic attempts and dismal failures, seek intimacy with the most improbable of partners. For where an assured sense of identity is missing, even friendships and affairs become desperate attempts at delineating the fuzzy outlines of identity by mutual narcissistic mirroring; to fall in love means to fall in love with one's mirror image, hurting oneself and damaging the mirror. (p. 167)

An inability to develop meaningful relationships with others during young adulthood can be harmful to an individual's personality. It may lead a person to repudiate, ignore, or attack others. Erikson (1968) asserts that this inability to form a relationship can account for the shallow, almost pathetic attempts of youth to merge themselves with a leader or cult figure. Many youths want to be apprentices or disciples of leaders who will shelter them from the harm of an "outgroup" world. If this fails, and Erikson believes that it must, then sooner or later the individual will recoil into a self-search to discover where he or she went wrong. Such introspection sometimes leads to painful feelings of isolation and depression. It also may contribute to mistrust of others and restrict the individual's willingness to act on his or her own initiative.

Styles of Intimate Interaction

One classification of intimacy suggests five styles of interaction: intimate, preintimate, stereotyped, pseudointimate, and isolated (Orlofsky, Marcia, and Lesser, 1973). The *intimate* individual forms and maintains one or more deep and long-lasting love relationships. The *preintimate* individual has mixed emotions about commitment; this ambivalence is reflected in her strategy of offering love without any obligations or long-lasting bonds. In most instances, the stereotyped individual forms superficial relationships that tend to be dominated by ties with same- rather than opposite-sex friends. The *pseudointimate* individual appears to be maintaining a long-lasting heterosexual attachment, but the relationship has little or no depth or closeness. Finally, the *isolated* individual withdraws from social encounters and has little or no intimate attachment to same- or opposite-sex individuals. Occasionally the isolate shows signs of developing interpersonal relations, but usually such interactions are anxiety provoking. One investigation indicated that intimate and preintimate individuals are more sensitive to their partners' needs, as well as more open in their friendships, than individuals characterized by the other three intimacy statuses (Orlofsky, 1976).

Bernice Neugarten (1980) argues that intimacy is a critical issue not only in early adulthood but also at later stages of life. Next we will explore intimacy as an important concern of individuals in middle and late adulthood.

Intimacy in Middle and Late Adulthood

Intimacy during the adult years must be regarded as a multidimensional concept. Davis (1985), for example, considers intimacy to be composed of six factors: mutuality, openness, commitment, sharing, respect, and enjoyment. As you might expect, intimacy may mean different levels of openness, mutuality, and so on to different people. Furthermore, the levels of these six factors required to create a satisfying love relationship change as couples themselves age and change.

Marjorie Lowenthal and her colleagues suggest that the presence of a confidant is a critical aspect of psychological adaptation to aging as measured by morale, avoidance of psychosomatic symptoms, and the ability to cope with stress (Lowenthal, Thurnher, and Chiriboga, 1975). The presence of a close confidant or mentor helps adult males in their twenties and early thirties to become successful in their

A mentor serves as a coach to younger workers, supervising their work as well as nurturing, supporting, and encouraging them.

careers (Levinson, 1986). The mentor serves as coach to those beginning their careers, providing a supervised internship as well as support, nurturance, and encouragement. By contrast, extreme social isolation is associated with psychiatric illness, poor achievement, failure to thrive, and limited job success (Levinson, 1986; Lowenthal, 1964). Indeed, being embedded in a network of close interpersonal ties is related to general life satisfaction and a sense of belonging, worth, and identity.

Friendships

In our discussion of relationships and intimacy, we have seen that friendships are very important to adults. In this section we'll look further at the nature of friendships in adulthood.

Intimacy and Similarity in Friendships

Friendship involves enjoyment (spending time with our friends); acceptance (valuing our friends as they are without trying to change them); trust (believing that our friends act on our behalf); respect (thinking our friends have the right to make their own judgments); mutual assistance (helping and supporting our friends and allowing them to do so for us); confiding (sharing experiences and confidential matters with our friends); understanding (feeling that our friends know us well and

Friendship is an important part of adult life. It involves enjoyment, acceptance, trust, sharing, and other qualities.

understand what we are like); and spontaneity (doing and saying as we like with a friend) (Davis, 1985; Tesch, Whitbourne, and Nehrke, 1981).

It has been suggested that female friendships are characterized by more intimacy than male friendships (Berndt, 1982). Indeed, in cross-sex dating and marital relationships, females are much more likely to disclose themselves to males than vice versa and are much more prone to share their private inner lives than males (for example, Douvan and Adelson, 1966). Females bring the capacity for intimacy to courtship and then train males to be intimate (for example, Simon and Gagnon, 1969). In other words, women are more oriented toward revealing sensitive, intimate feelings than men are. The importance of friendship among older women in our society continues to emerge in more recent investigations. In one study, both friendships and family supports were found to be equally effective among married and never-married women in combatting loneliness and isolation (Essex and Nam, 1987).

Does intimate friendship have an effect on personality or life satisfaction? Intimacy has been linked to life satisfaction. There is also evidence that having a close and stable best friend is associated with self-esteem (Mannarino, 1979), but we do not know whether the differences are caused by life satisfaction and self-esteem or by intimacy. In other words, it may be that adults with high self-esteem and life satisfaction are more likely to develop close, intimate friendships, or it may be that having a close friend promotes self-esteem and life satisfaction.

Similarity is another important aspect of friendship. Friends are usually similar in terms of age, sex, and race (Baruch, Barrett, and Rivers, 1983; Hallihan, 1979). Friends usually have similar attitudes regarding politics and achievement orientations (Ball, 1981). Friends often like the same kinds of music and clothes and like to engage in the same kinds of leisure activities (Ball, 1981). For the most part, we meet our friends through activities at school or college, at work, in our neighborhoods, or in community activities (Davis, 1985).

Friendships are marked by many of the same characteristics as relationships between spouses or lovers (Davis, 1985). Both share the characteristics of acceptance, trust, respect, confiding, understanding, spontaneity, mutual assistance, and happiness. However, relationships with spouses and lovers, unlike friendships, are marked by strong emotion (passionate love) and strong caring. Interestingly, relationships with friends are perceived to be more stable than relationships among spouses or lovers.

Friendships across the Adult Years

One life-span developmental study of friendships found that newly married young adults have more friends than adolescents, middle-aged adults, or the elderly (Weiss and Lowenthal, 1975). During early adulthood, young married couples report that friendships established in their single days may dissipate. Often friendships among young married adults are based on a four-party relationship (two couples) rather than a two-party relationship (one couple); the two couples may go out to dinner together, play bridge together, and so forth.

By middle adulthood many friends are "old friends." Still, new acquaintances may develop, often through formal organizations, which middle-aged adults participate in at a fairly high rate (Troll, 1975). During middle adulthood, closeness and convenience seem less salient in establishing friendships than in early adulthood. In one investigation of 150 middle-aged adults who had moved within the last five years, a majority of the individuals named someone from their former locale as their best friend (Hess, 1971). One of the most important characteristics of friendships in middle and later adulthood is reciprocity. Friends feel that they give and receive equally in the relationship (Antonucci and Akiyama, 1987; Tesch et al., 1981).

Evidence shows that married middle-aged men often allocate more of their time to friendships than to their families and may rely on the suggestions of friends more than the advice of their spouses. However, throughout the adult years, women seem to maintain their friendships longer than men do (Essex and Nam, 1987; Maas and Kuypers, 1974; Riley, Johnson, and Foner, 1972). Women in old age expect friendships to be as reciprocal as they were in middle adulthood, even though they expect their children to provide more for them than previously (Rook, 1987). Ingersoll-Dayton and Antonucci (1988) reported that older women rarely expected friendships to evolve into nonreciprocity; long-lasting friendships are those in which both parties maintain equal patterns of giving, receiving, and confiding.

In late adulthood, the death of a spouse may narrow the circle of friends for men but expand it for women. Women who have had sustained career commitments often show a more restricted social network in old age because they have not had much time to devote to the nurturance of friendships (Troll, 1971). However, the support derived from friends is comparable among married and single women in old age (Essex and Nam, 1987). Friends and relatives are reported to be equal in their importance as social supports to older women (Ingersoll-Dayton and Antonucci, 1988). Finally, some researchers have suggested that the cohesiveness found in many retirement communities may reflect a loosening of kin relationships (Lowenthal and Robinson, 1976).

DEVELOPMENT OF MARITAL RELATIONSHIPS

For the vast majority of individuals, the most intense and important relationship they enter during adulthood is the marital relationship. In this section, we'll discuss different aspects of marital relationships.

From the time two people marry, an average of two years pass before they have their first child, and the next twenty-five to thirty-five years are devoted to child-rearing and launching. Although this represents a sizable segment of the life span, the typical married couple experiences more than one half of their total years together *after* their last child leaves home. This extended period of shared time is a recent occurrence. Since the turn of the century, as people have married earlier and stayed married longer, an average of ten years has been added to the average length of married life (assuming that divorce has not occurred). In the average family of

1900, the last child left home about two years after the death of one parent. Today, both parents are usually alive when the youngest child departs. The husband will work about fifteen more years, and often both marital partners now live long enough to go from early old age (fifty-five to seventy-four) to late old age (seventy-five plus) in the life cycle (Neugarten, 1975).

Courtship

How do we choose our marriage partners? Initially, physical appearance is often an important factor. Some psychologists believe that the choice of a mate entails a selection process based on mutual qualities and interests (Murstein, 1982). If two individuals discover that they share similar values, attitudes toward life, ideas about the roles of men and women, political and religious beliefs, and attitudes toward sex and marriage, then a closer relationship is likely to develop. Once two people find that they have similar qualities and ideas about many areas of life, the couple may explore the possibility of marriage.

Alternatively, some have argued that complementary needs play an important part in the mate-selection process (Winch, 1974). For example, if one person tends to be introverted, a socially outgoing spouse may complement him or her. Not all marital choices, of course, are made on the basis of such complementary qualities. Most of us choose a mate who shares some characteristics that are similar to our own and some that are not.

The Early Years of Marriage

The first few months of marriage are filled with exploration and evaluation. Gradually, a couple begins to adjust their expectations and fantasies about marriage to correspond with reality. For couples who have lived together before marriage, there may be fewer surprises. Still, as the two explore their new roles, they will negotiate a life-style based on each person's past experiences and present expectations. Surprisingly, couples who live together prior to marriage face exactly the same challenges as other couples in their early years of marriage. In fact, cohabitation and marital satisfaction were reported to be inversely related for couples in first-time marriages (Demaris, 1984). Other research suggests that women who have cohabited have more marital problems than those who have not cohabited with their spouse. Murstein (1982) considers this early process of discovering the core values, attitudes, and beliefs of a spouse a period of value matching. Certainly every couple has had the experience of realizing that their "perfect" mate has faults, defects, and flaws which they previously overlooked. Cohabitation does not eliminate these early phases of marital adjustment.

Since most marriages begin when people are in their twenties, young married couples are not only involved in their marriage roles but also in becoming established in occupations (Levinson, 1978, 1986). As more women become involved in meaningful careers, they must make decisions about when and if they will interrupt their careers to bear children. The process of fitting varied role expectations to each spouse and working through compromises and negotiated settlements is described by Murstein (1982) as role compatibility. It is a process of adjusting strengths and weaknesses, and the likes and dislikes of each mate. More importantly, developing role compatibility is a lengthy process as each marriage partner discards old roles and adopts new ones (such as career roles or parenting).

Early communication patterns set the tone in a marital relationship. Research (for example, Reedy et al., 1981) confirms that good communication is more characteristic of marital relationships in early adulthood than in middle or late adulthood. Early in marriage, each partner needs to relinquish unrealistic fantasies and idealizations because romantic ideas sooner or later clash with reality and produce disillusionment (Rhodes, 1977).

The Childbearing and Childrearing Years

Historically, childbearing and childrearing have been associated with the very beginning of the adult portion of the life span. David Gutmann (1975, 1977), in fact, describes this as a biological period in which adults respond to a "parental imperative" designed to make maximal use of the division of labor between the sexes and to insure the continuity of the social community. In more recent times, couples are delaying childbearing until early middle age, and some are deciding not to have any children. Childlessness has become an acceptable option as more couples choose a personal life-style of freedom and independence or respond to worldwide problems of overpopulation.

Childlessness

Not all married couples want or plan to have children. Generally, these couples are highly educated and strongly career-oriented. Some experts believe that 5 to 10 percent of married couples who remain childless do not make the final decision until their late thirties or early forties (Hoffman, 1982). In one investigation, Veevers (1980) questioned married couples who did not want to have children. Some couples recognized that from as far back as their own childhood or adolescence they knew they did not want to have children. Veevers calls these individuals (usually the wife) *early articulators.* Early articulators clearly conveyed their decisions to their prospective spouses during serious discussions well before marriage. Another group, in contrast, simply continued to delay the decision to have children until it became obvious to the couple that children were not going to be a part of their marriage. These couples, called *postponers,* seemed to let the decision to remain child-free emerge by placing other priorities ahead of childbearing. For these couples, having children might have been acceptable, but since other concerns took precedence in their marriages (for example, their relationships, careers, personal freedom, travel, or other priorities), they accepted the consequences (Richmond-Abbott, 1983; Veevers, 1980). Early articulators have been found to be more expressive of affection toward each other than postponers (Callan, 1984, 1987), and early articulators appear slightly more satisfied with their marriages than postponers (Bram, 1985–1987). Childless couples spend more time together than couples with children as they share plans, discuss activities, and evolve a compatible life-style (Callan, 1984). Overall, being childless has not been found to diminish the quality or satisfaction of marriage (Callan, 1984, 1987; Hoffman, 1982). Perhaps the childless couple invests greater emotional commitment and more time and energy into the marital relationship (Bram, 1985–1987).

Having Children

For the majority of couples who desire children and who are fertile or willing to adopt, a number of potential problems exist. For example, it is during the early years of the child's life that parents report a high degree of dissatisfaction and frustration with marriage (Rollins and Feldman, 1970; Rollins and Gallagher, 1978). Belsky (1981) reports that there are both many stresses as well as immense pleasures in childrearing. With the birth of a child, couples no longer have as much individual freedom, and their own relationship diminishes in importance and satisfaction.

The increasing financial responsibilities of childrearing also play an important role. Most couples feel the child dominates their lives, restricting their outside friendships, hobbies, and community involvement. The financial costs of raising children are considerable. This causes more and more mothers to seek employment. For example, although married women historically have tended to drop out of the labor market, in the 1980s nearly 50 percent of women with preschoolers were employed (U.S. Dept. of Labor, 1987).

Postchildrearing Years: The Empty Nest

A time comes in a couple's life when their children become independent and begin to provide for themselves and form friendships outside the family unit. Instead of maintaining a parent-child relationship at this time, parents and offspring gradually begin interacting with each other as one adult to another. The growing realization of adult children that a parent is an adult like themselves, with strengths and weaknesses, is called **filial maturity.** It enables a mature relationship to unfold between parent and child.

This period is a time of reorganization for parents. Couples who have learned to relate to each other through their children no longer have their children to buffer their relationship. They must now rely more on their relationship with each other (Rhodes, 1977). It is not surprising to find that this is another point in life when the incidence of divorce rises.

When adolescents or young adult offspring leave home, some parents (mothers *and* fathers) experience a deep sense of loss or the **empty nest syndrome.** Researchers have identified a relationship between strict role division and the empty nest syndrome through lengthy interviews with middle-aged women suffering from acute depression after their children left home (Bart, 1973). The greater a mother's involvement with her children, the greater her difficulty in seeing them leave home. Women who defined themselves primarily in terms of the maternal role and whose lives had been focused exclusively on their children felt as though they had nothing to live for when their offspring left the nest. They had dedicated themselves to living selfless, nurturing lives on behalf of their spouses and children and anticipated some reward for this self-denial at the end of their childrearing years. Specifically, they expected to share in their adult children's lives; when children failed to comply with this expectation, the women felt lost and depressed. All of these "super-mothers," when asked what they were most proud of, said, "my children." None mentioned an accomplishment of their own.

Recent research suggests that the empty nest may be welcomed by another group of mothers—those who have maintained a career, hobby, or a work-defined self-concept to which they can return after the nest is empty. For these women, the empty nest means a welcome role loss and the easing of role conflict and stress (Coleman and Antonucci, 1983). The empty nest does not always mean tragic loss; for these women it represents a new beginning and a new opportunity. As evidence that some couples adjust relatively quickly to the empty nest, consider the oft-cited data showing marital satisfaction and the **upswing hypothesis** (see figure 8.3). The upswing hypothesis suggests that marital satisfaction is highest before child-rearing begins, declines during childrearing, and increases when children have left the nest (Anderson, Russell, and Schumm, 1983). Thus, couples whose marriages survive (since many marriages end in divorce long before the children are launched) seem to find renewal in their relationships when the nest is empty. Couples appreciate the increased free time for individual self-enhancement, greater involvement with a spouse, hobbies, and community involvement. Should couples have empty nest parties to celebrate the new opportunities this transition creates?

The Aging Couple

The time from retirement until the death of a spouse signals the final stage of the marriage process. Retirement undoubtedly alters a couple's life-style and requires some adaptation in their relationship. The greatest changes may occur in families in which the husband works and the wife is a homemaker. The husband may not know what to do with himself, and the wife may feel uneasy having him around the house all the time. In such families, both spouses may need to move toward more expressive roles. The husband must adjust from simply being a good provider to helping and supporting his wife around the house, whereas the wife must change from functioning only as a good homemaker to interacting with her husband with love and understanding (Troll, 1971). Such women seem to experience a loss of autonomy following the retirement of their husbands. Marriages in which both husband and wife have worked take on a somewhat different pattern of adjustment to retirement, one marked by a simpler transition. In retirement, these couples displayed more egalitarian and far more cooperative relationships (Tryban, 1985).

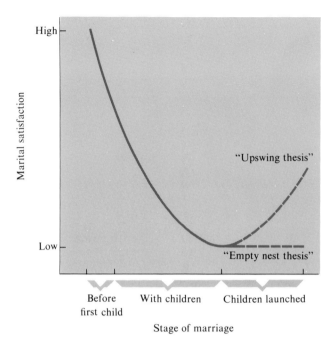

Figure 8.3   The relationship between marital satisfaction and stage of marriage.

Among twenty-one retired working-class couples in one study, the dual-career couples derived increased happiness, satisfaction, and involvement in retirement when compared to single-wage-earner families (Tryban, 1985). Marital happiness in late adulthood may also be influenced by each partner's ability to deal with personal conflicts. For example, older couples are highly vulnerable to a spouse's aging, illness, and eventual death (Gilford, 1984).

Married older adults appear to be happier than those who are single (Lee, 1978). Such satisfaction seems to be greater for women than for men, possibly because women place more emphasis on attaining satisfaction through marriage than men do. However, as more women develop careers, this relationship between satisfaction and marriage may not hold.

Of course, there are many different types of adult life-styles (see chapter 9). Not all individuals in late adulthood are married. At least 8 percent of people who reach the age of sixty-five have never been married. Contrary to the popular stereotypes, those older people seem to have the least difficulty coping with loneliness in old age. Many of them learned long ago to live autonomously, sustain friendships, and maintain self-reliance (Essex and Nam, 1987; Gubrium, 1975).

Eventually, for married couples, one spouse dies and the surviving spouse must adjust to being a widow or widower. As we'll see next, a number of age- and sex-related differences exist among surviving spouses, and individuals vary extensively in their ability to cope with the death of a spouse.

Married older adults tend to report a higher level of satisfaction than their single counterparts.

Widowhood

When a spouse dies, the surviving marital partner goes through a period of grieving. Some researchers call the bereavement process (see chapter 13) of widows or widowers in the year after the death of a spouse **grief work** (Parkes, 1972). The individual's structure or model of the world is disrupted because of the loss of a strong attachment bond (Bowlby, 1980). Grief work may lead to a new identity for the individual, an identity that can be healthy or unhealthy.

Relatively recent data (U.S. Bureau of the Census, 1986) indicate that widows outnumber widowers nearly six to one. Over the course of a year, most individuals come to accept the loss of a spouse and seem to adapt reasonably well. Women seemed to adjust better than men to the death of a spouse, and older people seemed to adjust better than younger people (Carey, 1977). Women are perhaps better able to cope since they are used to managing most of the day-to-day tasks required in the home, have a greater number of intimate friendships to draw upon for support, and seem able to deal constructively with the time alone. At the same time, today's older widow faces difficulties if she cannot drive, manage the complex world of banking, stocks, and insurance, and establish an independent credit rating. Surely such data are, in part, the result of cohort effects. With dual-career marriages, divorce, and separation so common today, we will likely find both men and women now in midlife to be far more independent, self-sufficient, and capable in facing life alone following the death of their spouse. At present, however, most widowers remarry and most widows remain unmarried in old age (U.S. Bureau of the Census, 1986).

The death of a husband may be difficult for a wife who has not developed a separate identity of her own (for example, through a career). When an older woman's identity as a wife is stripped away, she may feel that there is no meaning left in her life. But even for women who have roles and interests outside of their husband's identities, the death of a spouse is a traumatic experience. With no husband to provide for her, the older widow may have to live on public support or find a job. Certainly reduced income and subsistence near poverty level make coping with the death of a husband especially difficult (U.S. Bureau of the Census, 1986). Elderly women reported an average annual income of $5,600 per year, in comparison to $9,800 among comparably aged men. Furthermore, the older a woman is, the poorer she becomes; among women eighty-five years of age or older, one in four was living at or below the level of poverty in the mid-1980s (Bould, Sanborn, and Rief, 1989; Plesser, Siegel, and Jacobs, 1986). Widows may also experience loneliness after years of socializing with other couples or relying heavily for social interaction on their husbands. Yet a widow may be criticized by family and friends for developing a relationship with another man too soon after the death of her husband. Families rarely recognize that widows have attachment or intimacy needs that are often unfulfilled. Widows experience feelings of loneliness as well as a range of emotions including grief, hostility, and ambivalence.

Men are not isolated from the trauma of a spouse's death, either. They have typically relied on their wives for emotional support, intimacy, and sexual satisfaction. The loss of their mates usually triggers a great deal of grief and stress. Support systems, such as a circle of friends, are usually more available to the wife whose husband has died than vice versa, particularly because there are many more older women than older men in our society (Ingersoll-Dayton and Antonucci, 1988). One advantage the widower has over the widow in late adulthood is that if he decides to date and/or remarry the available pool of women is large (Brecher, 1984).

Even though widowed older people report a fairly high degree of loneliness, the marriage rate for those in late adulthood is not very high. The needs for intimacy, sharing emotions, and companionship are among the most frequent reasons older people give for remarriage. However, the older a surviving spouse is at the time of the death of a husband or wife, the less the likelihood of remarriage (Bould, et al., 1989; Ward, 1984). Approximately 20 percent of widowers over sixty-five and less than 5 percent of widows over fifty-five years of age will remarry (George, 1980). Among some older people, remarriage may be viewed as a betrayal of the deceased spouse. Some elderly people are limited by mobility, energy, or budget constraints in their efforts to meet new people, including potential mates. Such limitations suggest why the remarriages that do occur in late adulthood are often between people who have previously known each other (McKain, 1972).

In many marriages, the partners gain a great deal of enjoyment from each other. They treasure their intimate moments, the feeling of love that comes from caring about and sharing oneself with another person, and the satisfaction of having a stable partner in life. Certainly among marriages that survive into old age, the later years are typically marked by marital satisfaction from midlife or the empty nest transition. Yet other marriages without effective communication styles may be rife with conflict, tension, and unhappiness as transitions such as retirement or the divorce of a child demand coping. Next we'll explore the factors that seem to contribute to "good" and "bad" marriages as we evaluate the topic of marital satisfaction and conflict.

Marital Satisfaction and Conflict

Investigators interested in documenting the factors that contribute to marital satisfaction have identified two contrasting views. The first view is represented by the work of Blood and Wolfe (1969), who interviewed 900 Detroit homemakers to find out how the length of marriage and birth of children in the marriage relate to marital satisfaction. In general, they found that marital satisfaction declines in a straight linear fashion from the beginning of a marriage through thirty years of marriage. This decline was reported to occur in a number of different aspects of marital satisfaction: love, compassion, understanding of one's mate, and standard of living. Most interestingly, the researchers also found that it was *not* the addition of children alone that contributed to marital dissatisfaction.

The second view suggests that marital satisfaction peaks in the first five years of marriage and then declines through the period when the children are adolescents. After the children leave home, marital satisfaction increases but never reaches the level of the first five years of marriage (Pineo, 1961). Support for this *upswing thesis* in marital satisfaction has been found in other studies as well (for example, Glenn, 1975; Stinnett, Carter, and Montgomery, 1972; Anderson, Russell, and Schumm, 1983).

David Gutmann (1975, 1977) has offered several reasons for the upswing. He suggests that since the divorce rate has increased, couples who earlier in history were likely to be represented in the married group as dissatisfied are no longer in the middle-aged marital grouping. Also, it may be that fewer parents are feeling the pangs of the empty nest. They may experience an increase in marital satisfaction once their children leave home.

One final note about marital satisfaction. Measuring marital satisfaction is not an easy task (Boland and Follingstad, 1987). Most of our information comes from self-reports by one or both partners. These self-reports may be contaminated by social desirability; that is, each partner may try to place him or herself in a more positive light and characterize the marriage as more satisfactory than it truly is. People also vary in their willingness to disclose information about themselves, particularly on such sensitive issues as how satisfactory their marriage is. There have been almost no observational approaches in the study of marital satisfaction and marital relationships.

Jay Belsky (1981) indicates that another strategy for assessing marital relationships is to focus on marriage as a romance (emphasizing infatuation, passion, and sexuality) and as a friendship (emphasizing efficiency, companionship, and mutuality). Belsky goes on to say that in the transition to parenthood, more stress may occur when the marriage is romance-oriented than when it is partnership-oriented. Support for this viewpoint has been emerging in many investigations. During the transition to parenthood, the least conflict and stress is experienced in marriages in which wives' expectancies regarding division of labor are met and in which husbands (1) share in the early months of child care, (2) hold nontraditional sex roles, and (3) establish equity in home-care tasks (Ruble, Fleming, Hackel, and Stangor, 1988; Tomlinson, 1987).

In this section we have discussed the ties between marital relations and parenting. In the next section we will examine the parenting role in more detail.

PARENTING

Okun and Rappaport (1980) have identified several myths that enshroud parenting, including: (1) the birth of a child will save a failing marriage; (2) because the child is a possession or extension of the parent, the child will think, feel, and behave as the parents did in their childhoods; (3) children will always take care of parents in old age; (4) parents can expect respect and obedience from their children; (5) having a child means that the parents will always have someone who loves them and who will be their best friend; (6) having a child gives the parents a second chance to achieve what they should have achieved; (7) if parents learn the right techniques, they can mold their children to be what they want; (8) it's the parents' fault when children fail; (9) mothers are naturally better parents than fathers; and (10) parenting is an instinct and requires no training.

In earlier times, women considered motherhood a full-time occupation. Currently, couples tend to have fewer children, and as birth control has become common practice, many people choose the time for children and the number of children they will raise. The number of one-child families is increasing. Giving birth to fewer children and reducing the demands of child care free up a significant portion of a woman's life span for other endeavors. Three accompanying changes are (1) women may invest less time in maternal practices than in the past; (2) men are apt to invest a greater amount of time in fathering; and (3) parental care in the home is often supplemented by institutional care (for example, day-care centers). As a result of these changes, questions of how to integrate child care with other roles has become an increasingly important issue (Rossi, 1977). Increasing role conflicts seem to contribute to a high level of dissatisfaction with marriage in the early years (Doherty and Jacobson, 1982). Yet overall, women with multiple roles seem to derive an enhanced sense of self and emotional well-being (Pietromonaco, Manis, and Frohardt-Lane, 1986).

Our culture tends to equate "mothering" with "parenting." In fact, the attachment bond between the mother and the infant is viewed as the basis for the development of a healthy personality later in life. Jerome Kagan (1979) believes this idea is one of the few sacred, transcendental themes in American ideology. Emotions are aroused when discussion of surrogate care outside the home begins. Today more infants and children than ever before in the United States are spending less time with their mothers. More than one of every two mothers with a child under the age of six is employed, and almost 70 percent of the mothers of children aged six to seventeen work outside the home while 50 percent of mothers of preschoolers are employed full-time (U.S. Department of Labor, 1987). While opinion polls indicate that a majority of the public believes that maternal employment harms the family and that day care itself has a negative influence on children (Belsky, 1987a, 1987b, 1987c) much of the research evidence suggests a more positive conclusion (Hoffman, 1979, 1986; Phillips, McCartney, and Scarr, 1987).

The parenting role carries another important distinction. Unlike most adult responsibilities, the parenting role cannot be acceptably changed or discarded. We can quit one job and take another, or we can undergo retraining for an entirely different job. We can also divorce and remarry. However, once children are born, they require a commitment over a period of time—we cannot acceptably revert to nonparent status. Ideally, potential parents must realistically assess whether they are willing to make the extensive investment in time, physical energy, and emotional involvement required to rear competent children.

GRANDPARENTING

Think for a moment about your ideas, images, and memories of grandparents. Although the grandparenting role is prevalent in our society, it still is not well understood nor well researched (Hagestad, 1985; Hess, 1988). We generally think of grandparents as old people, but there are many middle-aged grandparents in their fifties as well (Nahemow, 1984). The average ages for first-time grandmothers and grandfathers are fifty and fifty-two years old respectively (Tinsley and Parke, 1987). With increased life expectancy and modifications in fertility patterns, the duration and experience of grandparenting has significantly changed (Hess, 1988). Hagestad (1985) has identified four shifts resulting from these changing demographics:

1. More people become grandparents than ever before.
2. The entry into grandparent status typically occurs at midlife, and many people spend four or more decades as grandparents.
3. Multigenerational families are common, and many grandparents also become great- and great-great-grandparents.
4. Parenthood and grandparenthood have become distinct from each other, both as individual life experiences and as two kinds of family status.

In earlier generations, most children were fortunate to have one surviving grandparent, let alone four (Uhlenberg, 1980). It appears that the way in which grandparents and grandchildren interact is partially a function of the age of the grandparents. Nahemow (1985) suggests that today's younger grandparents are nontraditional in their interactions with their grandchildren. She believes that our societal definition of the traditional grandparent role is far more likely to be seen among great-grandparents or great-great-grandparents than among grandparents. Wentowski (1985), in fact, reports that great-grandparents engage in a style of distant interaction with their great-grandchildren, a fact not too surprising given the advanced age of great-grandparents. Thomas (1986b) reports that younger grandparents feel far more responsibility for their grandchildren in terms of discipline, caretaking, and childrearing advice than older grandparents. Thomas (1986a) also observes that most grandparents, by age seventy, seek less direct physical intervention and day-to-day care of their grandchildren. "One of the nicest things about being a seventy-two-year-old grandmother," said one woman, "is that you can say goodbye to your grandchildren when they come for a visit." Younger grandparents, however, seem to be far more involved in assisting daughters or sons in the actual care of young grandchildren. They may baby-sit, cook, play, go shopping, and help direct the activities and interests of their grandchildren.

Regardless of age, grandparenting is a role that has few norms in our society. In one investigation (Neugarten and Weinstein, 1984), seventy pairs of grandparents were interviewed about their relationships with their grandchildren. Researchers examined the degree of comfort the grandparents felt in their roles, the significance of their roles, and the styles in which they carried out the roles. At least one-third of the grandparents said they had some difficulties with the grandparent role, in terms of thinking of themselves as grandparents, in how they should act as grandparents, and in terms of conflicts with their own children over how to rear the grandchildren.

Kivnick (1983) has separated grandparenting into three components: (1) the meaning of the grandparenting role—*role meaning;* (2) the behavior a grandparent adopts—*role behavior;* and (3) the enjoyment of being a grandparent—*role satisfaction.* For some individuals, the role meaning in being a grandparent was a source of biological renewal and/or continuity. In such cases, feelings of renewal (youth) or extensions of the self and family into the future (continuity) appeared. For others, being a grandparent meant emotional self-fulfillment, generating feelings of companionship, and finding satisfaction from the development of a relationship between adult and grandchild that was often missing in earlier parent-child relationships (for example, many found meaning in being indulgent with their grandchildren). For still others, the grandparent role was seen as remote, indicating that the role had little importance in their lives (Kivnick, 1983).

In addition to evaluating the meaning of grandparenting, researchers have assessed the behavioral roles exhibited by grandparents in interacting with their grandchildren. In fact, this dimension of grandparent-role behavior is the most frequently studied aspect of grandparenting (Hess, 1988). Kivnick (1983), for example, noted three behavioral roles: formal, fun-seeking, and distant-figure. The *formal role* involved performing what was considered a proper and prescribed role. Although people who assumed this style showed a strong interest in their grandchildren, they left parenting to the parents and were careful not to offer childrearing advice. The *fun-seeking role* was typified by informality and playfulness. Grandchildren were viewed as a source of leisure activity, and mutual satisfaction was emphasized. The *distant-figure role* was characterized by benevolent but infrequent contact between grandparent and grandchild. In the study, a substantial portion of grandparents were distant figures. Grandparents over age sixty-five were more likely to display a formal style of interaction, whereas those under sixty-five were more often fun-seeking. Two new roles adopted by modern grandparents are that of surrogate caretaker (Cherlin and Furstenberg, 1985, 1986) and family watchdog (Troll, 1983).

Grandparents often play a significant role in the lives of their grandchildren. In one investigation (Robertson, 1976), young-adult grandchildren showed highly favorable attitudes toward their grandparents. A full 92 percent indicated that they would miss some important things in life if there had been no grandparents present when they were growing up, and 70 percent said that teenagers do not see grandparents as boring. Such information suggests that the grandparent-grandchild relationship is reciprocal. However, nearly one-third of a sample of grandmothers who found the role of grandparenting uncomfortable and difficult were those who had been asked to assume some of the burden of child care, for instance, while a daughter or daughter-in-law worked (Robertson, 1977). Many factors contribute to

Grandparents and grandchildren often play significant roles in one another's lives.

role satisfaction or the degree to which being a grandparent fulfills individual expectations and leads to feelings of self-worth and personal gratification (Hess, 1988). Some of the factors leading to role satisfaction in grandparenting include perceived control over the timing of entry into the role, proximity to grandchildren, relationships to grandchildren, and the divorce of one's children (Johnson, 1988; Kivnick, 1985).

Despite the tendency of research investigators to view grandparenting as a generic term (Hess, 1988), there are real and significant differences between the roles of grandmother and grandfather. Grandmothers, for example, tend to outlive grandfathers, thus occupying their role for a longer period of time and potentially having a different impact on their grandchildren (Hess, 1988). Grandmothers typically have closer ties to grandchildren of both sexes than grandfathers do (Hagestad, 1982). Grandfathers, however, appear to establish closer ties with their grandsons than with their granddaughters (Bengston, Mangen, and Landry, 1984). Generally maternal grandparents have more contact with grandchildren than paternal grandparents (Kahana and Kahana, 1970). In times of family crisis, the maternal grandparents are more frequently sought for help and more frequently provide assistance (Cherlin and Furstenberg, 1986).

Gender differences in grandparenting lead to different interpretations of this role. In a survey of 177 grandmothers and 102 grandfathers, Thomas (1986a) found that grandmothers derived greater satisfaction from their roles than grandfathers. Interestingly, regardless of gender, the grandparents who had the highest degree of satisfaction with their roles were those who perceived that they were partly responsible for caring and helping with their grandchildren. Grandmothers are more likely than grandfathers to consider grandparenting a second chance at parenting. And grandmothers appear more willing than grandfathers to accept the role of passing along to grandchildren family traditions, history, and customs. Grandfathers appear more as "secretaries of state" (Troll, 1983) or heads of the family, while grandmothers are more "kinkeepers" (Cohler and Grunebaum, 1981), making sure the family stays together and maintains family protocol. Perhaps these factors are responsible for the loss grandparents feel when they witness the divorce of a child and the breakdown of the family in which grandparenthood was practiced (see box 8.2).

In addition to gender, both cultural and ethnic diversity lead to differences in parenting. Black grandmothers, for example, tend to adopt roles that allow them considerable control and authority over their grandchildren. White, Asian, and Hispanic cultures tend to be far more varied in their grandparenting styles (Cherlin and Furstenberg, 1985). In another investigation, Bengston (1985) reported that Mexican-American grandparenting was marked by many more intergenerational relationships (more children, grandchildren, and great-grandchildren) than black or white families. In Mexican-American families, grandparents were extremely satisfied with the frequency and quality of contact with their grandchildren (Bengston, 1985).

The role of great-grandparent has emerged with increasing frequency among the elderly. Families comprised of four living generations represent a fairly new area for study. There is evidence that younger individuals with living grandparents and great-grandparents maintain very positive attitudes toward the elderly as well as great love and affection for these relatives (Bekker, DeMoyne, and Taylor, 1966; Boyd, 1969). Wentowski (1985) interviewed nineteen great-grandmothers about their roles. They identified great-grandparenthood as rather remote and isolated from other family roles. These women saw their great-grandchildren on an intermittent basis, with physical distance a strong factor in predicting the frequency of visits. Great-grandmothers also felt that visits with great-grandchildren had to be brief, in part because they were in their seventies and eighties. Although they considered this role a sign of aging, they derived considerable emotional fulfillment from seeing this fourth generation representing family immortality. In fact, in a study of forty great-grandparents (thirty-five women and five men), 93 percent indicated very favorable attitudes toward and significant emotional significance in their new role (Doka and Mertz, 1988). Most viewed the acquisition of great-grandparenthood as a positive mark of successful aging or longevity. The role of great-grandparent also contributed to a sense of personal and familial renewal and a welcome opportunity for diversion. Two predominant styles of great-grandparenting emerged in the Doka and Mertz's study (1988). For 78 percent of the sample, the role was remote in that they had limited opportunity to see their great-grandchildren or saw them only on special occasions (ritualistic contact) such as holidays or birthdays. For 35 percent of the great-grandparents, however, the new role allowed them an opportunity to be emotionally close to their great-grandchildren. They saw their great-grandchildren at least once each month, spoke nearly once a week with the great-grandchild's parents, often served as baby-sitters, went shopping, and took trips with their great-grandchildren (Doka and Mertz, 1988). Great-grandparents who reported a close relationship with their great-grandchildren all lived within twenty-five miles of them.

Finally, we must emphasize that parenting occurs within a family context, and that the shape and fabric of the American family has changed dramatically over the last several years. See box 8.3 for a description of the strengths and weaknesses associated with different types of family arrangements.

SEXUALITY

One of the most important elements of adult relationships, especially marital relationships, is sexuality. In this section we'll discuss several aspects of adult sexuality. We will focus on various age-related changes in sexual functioning. Finally, we'll pay special attention to menopause and the male climacteric.

Sexual Attitudes and Behavior

Some aspects of our sexuality are probably a consequence of the way we are socialized. Many of us were brought up to believe that premarital sex is acceptable for males but not females. Some parents, fearful of the AIDS virus, caution their adolescents to abstain from sexual relations until marriage. But often males are reared to associate the sexual act with power and masculine worth, and they distance themselves from a caring commitment to the other person. Males also are believed to have more sexual knowledge than females. Men, then, often enter long-term sexual relationships and/or marriage with the belief that they are responsible for the satisfaction of the couple's sexual needs. In a sexual relationship, if either one or both of the partners do not climax, the blame usually rests with the male (Masters and Johnson, 1970). Such a perspective leads the male to think that his most important function is to get the job done rather than to spend time relating to his partner's sensual and emotional needs.

Females who adopt a passive role in sexual relationships and who remain naïve about sexual techniques may contribute to the difficulties many couples experience. In recent decades it has become more culturally acceptable for females to express their sexuality, to be knowledgeable about sexual matters and techniques,

---

BOX 8.2

GRANDPARENTS' VISITATION RIGHTS

During the last ten to fifteen years, most states have passed laws granting grandparents the right to petition a court to legally obtain visitation privileges with their grandchildren. The House of Representatives in 1983 recommended that a uniform, nationwide statute should be developed that ensures grandparents visitation rights. Ross Thompson, Barbara Tinsley, Mario Scalora, and Ross Parke (1989) have noted that this is a significant change from traditional laws that gave grandparents visitation rights only if the child's parents consented to such visitation. Now grandparents may be allowed visitation privileges even if parents object!

What made legislators change their minds about grandparents' visitation rights? One of the most important factors, according to Thompson et al. (1989), is the emerging political influence of older adults. Lawmakers are becoming more likely to pass legislation that will please their growing constituency of older voters. It has also been suggested that grandparent visitation may be one way of preserving intergenerational ties within a family. Moreover, grandparents may provide their grandchildren with a powerful source of psychological support above and beyond that offered by parents.

It seems as if legislators have come to the conclusion that grandparents play an important role in children's development, and that children's development is enhanced by the presence of grandparents.

Thompson et al. (1989) question whether there is sufficient psychological research to substantiate these assumptions. One of the things psychologists know, however, is that the benefits that children derive from interacting with their grandparents are directly related to the quality of the relationship that exists between the grandparents and the child's parents (Johnson, 1988). When this relationship is harmonious, children seem to benefit from interacting with their grandparents. If this relationship is typified by ill-will and hostility, little, if any, benefits may be derived from grandparent visitation. In fact, children may even suffer from extended contact with their grandparents if significant intergenerational conflict exists.

With regard to the issue of intergenerational conflict, Thompson et al. (1989) have commented that:

> Grandparents are likely to turn to the courts only if they cannot come to an agreement with the child's parents about visitation with grandchildren. Children are likely to encounter loyalty conflicts during the judicial proceedings, and if a visitation is granted, loyalty conflicts are likely to be maintained as the child remains the focus of intergenerational conflict. Because a child already experiences distress owing to

the triggering conditions linked to a visitation petition (for example, parental divorce or death), it is hard to see how further legal conflict between the family members can assist the child in coping. (p. 1220)

A similar problem may arise, of course, when a child visits a noncustodial parent after a divorce. But, Thompson et al. (1989) maintain that the relationship a child shares with a noncustodial parent may be more salient than the relationship he or she shares with grandparents. In fact, Thompson (1986a,b) has discovered that children benefit from visiting a noncustodial parent even when there is friction between the custodial and noncustodial parents. At present, we do not know if comparable benefits hold true for children who visit grandparents who squabble with the child's parents.

By granting visitation privileges to grandparents, the courts have broadened the degree of "extraparental" parenting to which the child is exposed. This has eroded the traditional notion that parents have virtual autonomy in childrearing matters. Also, grandparent visitation privileges may inadvertently foster changes in how family disputes are resolved. Bargaining between parents and grandparents over visitation privileges now takes place within the shadow of the law. Thompson et al. (1989) suggest that parents could be at a disadvantage in such circumstances because the conditions that allow grandparents to petition for visitation (for example, divorce or the death of a parent) often render a parent less prepared, both psychologically and financially, for a court battle than the child's grandparents.

Recent changes in the law regarding grandparents' visitation rights were made by well-intentioned legislators. However, Thompson et al. (1989) have pointed out that these new laws may have three potential costs. First, due to court-enforced visitation, a young child may become unnecessarily involved in a stressful intergenerational conflict. Second, the threat of court-enforced visitation may change the way conflicts are resolved in a family. Third, court-ordered grandparental visitation may increase the role played by factors outside the family (for example, the courts) on a child's development.

Should grandparents have visitation privileges over the objections of a parent? Is court-enforced grandparental visitation really in a child's best interests? Thompson et al. (1989) argue that we do not know enough about grandparenthood to answer these questions. Our ideas about grandparenthood are probably too naïve and idealized. We may overestimate the benefits of grandparental visitation and underestimate its costs. Clearly, this is one area where research is needed to help address these basic issues.

BOX 8.3

STRENGTHS AND WEAKNESSES OF DIFFERENT FAMILY FORMS

The American family is changing. With many working parents, a divorce rate of nearly 50 percent, single-parent households, extended families living under one roof, live-in nannies, and alternative life-styles, the idea of a universal family arrangement seems to be on the decline (Lauer and Lauer, 1985; U.S. Bureau of the Census, 1984, 1987). In this box we'll describe the strengths and weaknesses of six different family forms as identified by Sussman (1978).

THE SINGLE-CAREER FAMILY

The single-career family is the intact nuclear family comprised of a husband, wife, and children living in a common household in which one partner, usually the husband, is the breadwinner. It is estimated that no more than 15 percent of all households are of this type.

Among the strengths of this type of family are (1) it is the primary family structure for socializing members throughout the life cycle; (2) it is the main family structure involved in caring for disabled, deviant, and dependent members; and (3) it may be the best-adapted family form for fitting the demands of the corporate economic structure.

The single-career family has weaknesses as well. First, this family form is easily broken. As a result, there is an increase in the intervention of organizations and the amount of money spent to maintain individuals from broken homes and new family forms. Second, the single provider, especially in the working class, is often unable to provide adequately for the maintenance of the family.

THE DUAL-CAREER FAMILY

The dual-career family consists of a husband, wife, and children living in a home in which both adults work. It represents 19 percent of all households.

Two of the strengths of the dual-career family are (1) it is a competent form for providing maximum income and achieving quality-of-life expectations, and (2) it is an adequate family form for attaining gender equality and sharing household and marital responsibilities.

The dual-career family also has weaknesses. Often it is necessary to depend on kin and institutional support systems (such as day care) to function effectively. Furthermore, this type of family often experiences difficulties coordinating career and family responsibilities.

THE SINGLE-PARENT FAMILY

Approximately 16 percent of all households are headed by a single parent. In most cases the parent is single because of divorce, but in some instances the parent never married or lost his or her spouse through death.

Single-parent families may have certain strengths. Often many other adults are around to function as socialization models for children. In some instances, adults other than

---

BOX 8.3 *Continued*

---

parents may be more effective socializers. If appropriate support systems are available, the single parent may be able to attain greater self-expression because his or her accountability is limited to the children, not to a marital partner as well. In some instances marital conflict may have reached a maladaptive point in a nuclear family and been harmful to the children involved. The removal or absence of one parent may lead to a more nurturing, livable family.

Single-parent families have weaknesses, too. They usually need support systems to assist the parent in parenting, economic matters, health maintenance, and social relationships, and sometimes such support systems are not available. Single-parent families often do not have sufficient income, one aspect of the weakness just mentioned but so prevalent it requires special attention. The need to obtain financial support may pressure the parent to remarry, with the possibility that the previous marriage experience may be repeated. For some families in which the single parent is employed, too much of the child's socialization process may be left unsupervised.

THE REMARRIED NUCLEAR FAMILY

The remarried nuclear family consists of a husband, wife, and children; one or both of the adults have been previously married and brought children with them from the previous marriage(s). Sometimes these families are referred to as *blended families*. They represent approximately 11 percent of all households.

Among the strengths of remarried nuclear families: (1) prior marital experiences may lead to an increased stability in subsequent marriage, and (2) parenting that was formerly the sole responsibility of a single adult can now be shared with the new spouse and his or her older children.

Some of the weaknesses in such families include: (1) there may be difficulties blending two formerly independent households into one, and this may lead to stress for one or more family members; and (2) formations of two large families may require considerable economic resources, counseling, and other supports.

THE KIN FAMILY

The kin family is made up of intergenerationally linked members living in the same household. Approximately 6 percent of all households are of this type. Its strengths include the maintenance of family values and transmission of knowledge and skill across generations and the fact that multiple adults are available for socialization and shared household and work tasks.

One of the weaknesses of the kin family is that contemporary demands for geographical mobility are not easily met by such a family. It may be that the resistance to change that characterizes this family form can reduce the motivation of individual members to achieve in society.

BOX 8.3 *Continued*

THE EXPERIMENTAL FAMILY

The experimental family consists of individuals in multiadult households such as communes or households of cohabitating adults. Approximately 4 percent of households are of this type.

In communal settings, large numbers of people are available to form a support network to meet individual needs. For this reason, this family form may be particularly helpful to individuals in transition from one family form to another. Furthermore, people who are not ready or are unwilling to make a commitment to long-term partnerships may be able to experience economic sharing, psychological growth, and expanded interpersonal relationships in an experimental family.

Experimental families have many weaknesses. Few have well-mapped strategies, techniques, or financial bases to maintain their activities or attain their goals. Similarly, in many experimental families, role responsibilities are not clearly defined, with resulting difficulty in implementing parenting, economic, and household functions.

In conclusion, it seems that during the 1990s the family will continue to be an extraordinarily important force in the lives of individuals; but the percentage of people living in family forms other than the single-career family will continue to expand tremendously. Certainly the statistics on divorce alone provide support for this conclusion. And Hetherington et al. (1989) believe that nearly 50 percent of school-age children will spend at least one year in other than a two-parent family before they graduate from high school.

---

and to share responsibility for the success of a sexual relationship. For sexual fulfillment, it is best that both partners be informed and active in exploring their sexuality and in communicating their needs to each other (Sarrell and Sarrell, 1974).

Today, many middle-aged women who spent their early adult years in a more sexually inhibited atmosphere are showing a stronger interest in being active and knowledgeable partners in sexual relationships. Whereas at earlier points in history it was unacceptable for females to achieve orgasm, this is no longer our cultural standard. Achieving orgasm on the part of both male and female is an important part of each individual's sexual satisfaction, but not their sole concern.

Type and Incidence of Sexual Activity

For most American males, the outlet for their sexual drive changes from adolescence to early adulthood. Masturbation is the dominant form of male sexual behavior during adolescence, particularly during the early phases of adolescence; but sexual intercourse is more prevalent in early adulthood (Kinsey, Pomeroy, and Martin, 1948, 1953; Masters and Johnson, 1966).

Premarital Sex

Our cultural standards concerning *premarital sex* have changed substantially during the course of this century. In recent years, our society has suggested that there are times when premarital sex is perfectly acceptable. For example, in a 1969 study of adults, 48 percent of men under age thirty said that premarital sexual relations are not wrong; by 1972, the figure had reached 65 percent. For women, the figures during the same period increased from 27 to 42 percent (Udry, 1974). National surveys indicate that by the time they are twenty-five, 97 percent of males and 81 percent of females have engaged in premarital intercourse (Hunt, 1974).

Although earlier studies (Kinsey et al., 1948) indicated that males were more likely than females to engage in premarital sex, more recent data from a number of studies of college students suggest that women are often as likely as men to have premarital sex (Luria and Rose, 1981). As students progress from the freshman to the senior year of college in the United States, the incidence of premarital sex typically increases. The statistics for men engaging in premarital sex jump from 28 percent at the beginning of college to 82 percent during the senior year; for women, the corresponding figures are 29 and 86 percent, not much different from the statistics for men.

Sexual Intercourse in Marriage

Evidence that sexual intercourse in marriage is a highly satisfying physical experience, particularly for wives, comes from data reported by more than 2,000 middle-class American married women (Bell and Lobsenz, 1979). Married women in their twenties reported that they enjoyed the physical aspects of sexual intercourse more than their counterparts in their thirties, who were more inclined to enjoy its emotional aspects. Most of the women reported that they experienced orgasms, and those who had orgasms more frequently were also more likely to indicate they were happy. Women who had never had an orgasm typically were brought up in restrictive homes and were somewhat religious (Geer, O'Donohue, and Schorman, 1986). Less than 10 percent of women have never had an orgasm (Hunt, 1974), and such women appear clinically to be rather sensitive to criticism and marginally depressive (Derogatis, 1981). Married women in their twenties and thirties said that they practiced oral-genital sex more than older groups of married women. The young women also indicated that their husbands, rather than they, were more likely to initiate love-making sessions. However, because these data were collected in a cross-sectional manner, cohort effects may be involved.

It appears that sexual relations follow a predictable pattern depending on how long a couple has been married. For example, intercourse is practiced frequently in the early months of marriage and then decreases over the length of the marriage.

Figure 8.4   Average monthly frequency of sexual intercourse over thirty years of marriage.
Source: Data from *From Now to Zero: Fertility, Contraception, and Abortion in America.* Copyright © 1968, 1971 Charles F. Westoff and Leslie Aldridge Westoff. Little, Brown and Company, Boston, MA.

Doddridge, Schumm, and Bergen (1987) noted that when married couples reported the preferred frequency of sexual intercourse, the older the couple and the longer the marriage, the lower the preferred frequency. Mirroring these data, figure 8.4 traces the average monthly incidence of intercourse through thirty years of marriage. Research suggests that the frequency of intercourse for married women under age thirty declines by 25 percent after four years of marriage; further declines begin about age thirty for married males and age forty for married females (Katchadourian, 1985, 1987).

The link between frequency of intercourse and marital satisfaction is not the same in every marriage and may not be the same for partners in the same marriage (Doddridge et al., 1987). Nonetheless, there is a substantial association between marital satisfaction and the incidence of intercourse when large numbers of couples are surveyed (Bell and Bell, 1972; Levinger, 1970). The most common reason given for sexual abstinence among married couples is marital conflict. Other reasons include physical illness, loss of interest, and emotional stress (Edwards and Booth, 1976; Gambert, 1987). The greatest obstacle to sexual happiness among couples is the level of tension or anxiety in the marriage. In virtually every case of sexual dysfunction, significant psychological depression, anxiety, and anger are present (Gambert, 1987).

Husbands usually show a stronger interest in sexual activity than wives do (Broderick, 1982). In one novel investigation, participants were asked to select from a list of more than ninety possibilities the five most preferred leisure-time activities (Mancini and Orthner, 1978). The men ranked sexual and affectional activities among their top five choices more often than any of the other activities. The women ranked reading their first choice, with sex and affection tied with sewing for second place.

Extramarital sex, though considered acceptable to some individuals, still is not condoned as morally appropriate conduct by the majority of our society. Pollster Daniel Yankelovich (1981), writing in *New Rules in American Life,* found that 76 percent of adult Americans disapprove of men having extramarital affairs. One estimate reported that nearly 50 percent of married men and 20 to 40 percent of married women have had an extramarital affair (Knox, 1985). Spanier and Margolis (1983) note that reported affairs may often be for only one night.

Men report an interest in extramarital relationships primarily for sex or variety, while women most often seek extramarital relationships for emotional reasons (Glass and Wright, 1985). Women involved in extramarital relationships report more marital dissatisfaction than their male counterparts. After marital dissatisfaction, extramarital affairs appear most often to be based on proximity, availability, and common interests (for example, among coworkers); enhancing self-esteem and excitement are less frequently identified factors (Wiggins and Lederer, 1984).

Sexual Attitudes and Behavior at Midlife

Although there is usually little biological decline in a man or woman's ability to function sexually in middle adulthood, middle-aged adults usually engage in sexual activity less frequently than people in early adulthood. Career interests, family concerns, and energy levels may contribute to a decline in sexual activity. Men peak in sexual activity in the mid-twenties, with females peaking a bit later.

Still, a large percentage of individuals in middle adulthood continue to show moderate or strong sexual interest and continue to engage in sexual activity on a reasonably frequent basis. For example, in one national survey of 502 men and women, approximately 68 percent of the fifty-one to fifty-five-year-old respondents said that they had a moderate or strong interest in sex (Pfeiffer, Verwoerdt, and Davis, 1974). Approximately 52 percent said they had sexual intercourse once a week or more. For men, the influence of psychologically erotic stimuli declines with increasing age. Thus, although physical stimulation remains effective in producing sexual arousal, psychological stimulation loses some of its power. For instance, a spouse's nudity may not arouse as it did in earlier years. Couples often mistakenly view this as evidence that advancing age means waning sexuality (Katchadourian, 1987).

Typically, surveys note sex differences in sexual interest and activity in middle adulthood. Men consistently report greater interest in sex and indicate that they engage in sexual activity more than women. For example, in the survey mentioned in the previous paragraph, 81 percent of the men but only 56 percent of the women between the ages of fifty-one and fifty-five said that they had a moderate or strong interest in sex; 66 percent of the men but only 39 percent of the women said they had sexual intercourse one or more times per week (Pfeiffer et al., 1974). Often postmenopausal women actually show an increase in sexual interest as the fear of pregnancy is removed and family concerns are replaced by healthy self-interests and individual assertiveness. However, if the children depart and a woman's husband is concerned with business, finances, and his own self-esteem, even positive changes in her life may not lead to sexual rediscovery (Katchadourian, 1987).

Menopause

Perhaps the subject of strongest interest to researchers studying sexuality in middle adulthood is the range of changes that accompanies menopause. Let's look at some of the biological and psychological aspects of menopause.

Most of us know something about menopause. But is what we know accurate? Stop for a moment and think about your knowledge of menopause. What is it? When does it occur? Can the symptoms be treated? Here are some comments made by four women who have experienced menopause.

> My first sign of menopause was the night sweat. Even though I knew why I was having the sweats, it was a little frightening to wake up in the middle of the night with my sheets all drenched. It was hard not to feel that something was very wrong with me. And I lost a lot of sleep changing sheets and wondering how long the sweats would go on. Sometimes I felt chilled after sweating and had trouble going back to sleep.
>
> I also had hot flashes several times a week for almost six months. I didn't get as embarrassed as some of my friends who also had hot flashes, but I found the "heat wave" sensation most uncomfortable.
>
> I am constantly amazed and delighted to discover new things about my body, something menstruation did not allow me to do. I have new responses, desires, sensations, freed and apart from the distraction of menses [periods] . . .
>
> I feel better and freer since menopause. I threw that diaphragm away. I love being free of possible pregnancy and birth control. It makes my sex life better. (Boston Women's Health Book Collective, 1976, pp. 327, 328)

These comments suggest both negative and positive reactions to menopause. They help dispel popular stereotypes of the menopausal woman: exhausted, irritable, unsexy, hard to live with, and irrationally depressed.

Biologically, **menopause** is defined as the end of menstruation, a marker that signals the cessation of childbearing capacity. Menopause is accompanied by a reduction of **estrogen,** the primary female sex hormone, to one-tenth of earlier levels. Menopause is considered to have occurred when twelve consecutive months have passed without a menstrual period (Block, Davidson, and Grambs, 1981); the average age at menopause in the United States is fifty. Despite the number of symptoms reported to accompany menopause, only two, hot flashes and the atrophy of the vagina, are believed to be directly related to decreased estrogen levels (Katchadourian, 1987).

The *hot flash,* a feeling of extreme heat that is usually confined to the upper part of the body and often is accompanied by a drenching sweat, is the most commonly experienced symptom of menopause. Hot flashes gradually diminish in frequency and generally disappear completely within a year or two. *Atrophy of the cells of the vaginal walls* means that the vagina becomes drier, the layer of cell walls thinner, and the amount of lubricants secreted during sexual arousal is reduced. These conditions can make sexual intercourse painful for some women. They may require the use of artificial lubrications during intercourse (Gambert, 1987).

Table 8.1

CLINICAL FINDINGS ASSOCIATED WITH MENOPAUSE

Physical Effects

1. Blood pressure disturbance ("hot flashes")
2. Osteoporosis (thinning of the bones, calcium absorption inefficiency)
3. Atrophy of the vaginal walls, vaginal shortening, and reduced lubricity
4. Increase in incidence of cardiovascular disease

Psychological Effects (Wide-ranging Individual Differences)

5. Insomnia
6. Anxiety
7. Depression

Gambert (1987) has identified a large number of physical and psychological effects that may be directly or indirectly associated with menopause. They are outlined in table 8.1. As previously mentioned, hot flashes and atrophy of the vaginal walls are the direct results of menopause. On the other hand, *osteoporosis* (thinning of the bones) is directly caused by a woman's inability to uptake calcium to strengthen her bones; this, in turn, is caused by a reduction in available estrogen. Osteoporosis is a common cause of the postural stoop in older people and a contributor to the brittleness of bones that break easily in old age. None of the psychological effects of menopause identified in table 8.1 are directly related to the physical changes that accompany menopause.

Depression may be associated with menopause, but menopause does not *cause* depression. Menopause comes at a time when some women are losing their full-time jobs as mothers and wives, when some middle-aged men are attracted to younger women, and when other aspects of the aging process (wrinkles, greying hair, and so on) are also appearing. Therefore, it may be these other factors, rather than menopause itself, that cause depression. Indeed, many women handle menopause in very positive ways, as suggested by the quotes from two of the four women at the beginning of this section. Recent estimates indicate that approximately 20 percent of women go through menopause with no intense symptoms at all, whereas 15 percent experience symptoms that are sufficiently severe to warrant treatment (Women's Medical Center, 1977). The majority of women (65 percent) experience mild symptoms and can cope with them without undergoing any medical intervention.

The incidence of insomnia, depression, and anxiety may be traced to the meaning or psychosocial significance individuals attach to menopause (Newman, 1982). Generally those who have the greatest psychological difficulty greatly value their roles as mothers and their capacity to bear children. They also express fears of growing old (Newman, 1982). Holte (1978) compared menopausal adjustment across different cultures. Women who displayed the poorest adjustment to menopause belonged to cultures organized around a patriarchy (social power was primarily in the hands of males). Following menopause, these women had more restricted and less important social roles (Bart, 1971). These cultures interpreted the inability to bear children as a role loss and relegated postmenopausal women to a lowered social status. In other cultures, women actually increased their social standing and prestige following menopause. Bart (1971) reported that in such cultures the role of grandmother, for example, was important and valued. Age, wisdom, and the beneficial effects of experience give older, postmenopausal women a special role and status in some cultures. Our own society seems to make menopause a major negative life stressor (Huyck and Hoyer, 1982). A more balanced view of menopause interprets the experience as a potentially positive transition rather than focusing on role loss.

Many middle-aged and older women undergo hysterectomies, a sort of artificial menopause. In a *simple hysterectomy,* the uterus and cervix are surgically removed, while in a *total hysterectomy* the ovaries and fallopian tubes are removed as well. Hysterectomy is one of the most common operations performed in the United States (Morgan, 1978). In 1987 the figure had reached some 800,000 women per year. A hysterectomy is performed for various reasons. The most common involves the slippage and improper positioning of the uterus, which happens most often in women who have had several children because pregnancy stretches the ligaments that hold the uterus in place. A hysterectomy also may be performed to eliminate fibroid tumors, which as many as 25 percent of all women experience. Such tumors are not cancerous, but they may cause abnormal bleeding. The third most common reason for a hysterectomy is cancer, which, if detected early by a Pap test, is not necessarily life threatening (Block, Davidson, and Grambs, 1981; Gambert, 1987).

One of the most controversial aspects of menopause involves intervention in response to the decrease in natural estrogen levels and the use of estrogen replacement therapy (ERT). *Estrogen replacement therapy* involves replacing the estrogen that a woman's body no longer produces; physicians usually prescribe it only in severe cases, using the lowest dosage for the shortest possible period of time (Gambert, 1987; Katchadourian, 1987).

Marilyn Block, Janice Davidson, and Jean Grambs (1981) state that the use of ERT is highly controversial because of the relationship between estrogen and cancer. Despite some reports that ERT does not cause uterine or breast cancer, the Federal Drug Administration warns that the chances for uterine cancer increase five to seven times with ERT. The linkage is now well documented between ERT and endometrial or uterine cancer (Gambert, 1987). Much of the danger of ERT occurs when the medication is taken for long periods of time. The average amount of time spent on ERT by most women has been nearly ten years.

Do men experience biological changes related to their sexuality as they go through middle adulthood? We'll explore this question next.

The Male Climacteric

The **male climacteric** occurs during the sixties and seventies in most men when they experience a decline in sexual potency or fertility. The male climacteric differs in two important ways from menopause: it comes later and it progresses at a much slower rate. Men experience hormonal changes in their fifties and sixties, but not to the extent that women do. For example, testosterone production declines about 1 percent a year beginning during middle adulthood, but men do not lose their capacity to father children. Consequently, the male climacteric (remember, there can be no male menopause since menopause is the cessation of the menstrual cycle) has less to do with hormonal change than with the psychological adjustments men must make as they are faced with declining physical energy and increased pressures from business, friends, and family. Men in their fifties may have difficulty concentrating, feel fatigued, and become irritable in response to life pressures (Burt and Mecks, 1985; Katchadourian, 1987). The fact that testosterone therapy does not relieve such symptoms suggests that they are not induced by hormonal change.

Certain common characteristics indicate the beginning of a male climacteric in middle adulthood. For example, the older a man gets, the longer it takes him to have an erection but he is able to maintain it longer (Wagenwoord and Bailey, 1978). Although a man's sexual potency may decrease, his sexual desire does not necessarily decline. There also are some changes in secondary sexual characteristics during the climacteric: a man's voice may become higher pitched, his facial hair may grow more slowly, and muscularity may give way to flabbiness (Whitbourne, 1985).

Sexuality in Late Adulthood

Alex Comfort (1980), a noted expert on the elderly, concludes that aging does induce some changes in human sexual performance, more so in males than females. Orgasm becomes less frequent in males, occurring every second or third act of intercourse rather than every time. Men usually need more direct stimulation to produce an erection. In the absence of actual disease and/or the belief that old people are or should be asexual, sexual capacity is lifelong. Many older people believe that in old age one must give up interest in sexual activity to conform to social expectancies (Ludeman, 1981).

With aging comes a moderation of the sexual response for both men and women (Katchadourian, 1985, 1987). Thus, it takes longer for both men and women to become aroused. Erections are softer, not maintained as long as in younger years, and are angled less upright. Climax is less intense, contractions fewer, and the volume of ejaculation diminished in comparison to younger years (Katchadourian, 1985, 1987). Further, increasing time is needed after orgasm to attain another erection (Burt and Meeks, 1985; Katchadourian, 1985). A similar pattern holds for women's arousal and climax. With reduced levels of estrogen, the vaginal walls become

Older adults continue to enjoy and express their closeness through touching, emotional intimacy, and sexual intercourse.

thinner and less elastic and the vagina itself shrinks, becoming shorter. However, even when actual intercourse is impaired by infirmity, physical health, or hospitalization, other sexual needs still persist among the elderly, including closeness, physical touching, emotional intimacy, sensuality, and being valued as a man or a woman. These needs are a vital part of an older person's sexuality.

A direct correlation exists between health and sexual activity. Generally, sexual intercourse is an important part of therapy and treatment following a major illness or surgery and is itself minimally risky to health (Gambert, 1987). Following heart attacks or open-heart surgery, most physicians encourage resuming sexual intercourse within eight to twelve weeks. Patients encounter few physical problems, although they often feel fearful of having a heart attack during intercourse. Sexual intercourse is not terribly taxing, does not lead to an increase in the risk of heart attack, and is roughly comparable to such physical labor as a brisk walk or ascending a flight of stairs (Gambert, 1987).

Fortunately, many elderly people go on having sex without talking about it, free from the destructive social stereotypes of the dirty old man and the asexual, undesirable old woman. Among people between sixty and seventy-one years old, almost 50 percent have intercourse on a regular basis. Fifteen percent of those over seventy-eight years old regularly engage in intercourse (Comfort, 1980). Bear in mind that many individuals who are now in their eighties were reared when there was a Victorian attitude toward sex. In early surveys of sexual attitudes, older people were not asked about their sexuality, possibly because everyone assumed they didn't have sex or thought it would embarrass them to ask them about sex.

Most of the published work in the area of sexuality and aging suggests that there are no known age limits to sexual activity (for example, Kaplan, 1974; Masters and Johnson, 1970). Adults who have always placed a high priority on their sexual lives approach old age with the same values (Pfeiffer, 1983). Healthy older people who want to have sexual activity are likely to be sexually active in late adulthood (Comfort, 1980). Katchadourian (1987) suggests: "If you want to stay sexually alive, you must keep sexually active. Men and women who remain sexually active are more likely to maintain their sexual vigor and interest into their older years—another illustration of the adage, 'Use it or lose it' " (p. 73). The greatest obstacles to continued sexual expression are the lack of an available partner, severe health problems, and the belief that society does not condone this mode of expression in old age. However, societal attitudes are changing. Ludeman (1981), for example, noted the greater acceptance of masturbation by older women without available partners. Nearly 50 percent of older adult females masturbated when faced with the lack of a suitable male partner.

Most certainly, it is incorrect to assume that sexuality disappears in old age. This holds true even when we examine the sexual needs of unique subpopulations of the elderly, those living in nursing homes. See box 8.4 for more information about this topic.

In summarizing his ideas about sexuality in late adulthood, Alex Comfort (1980) made a number of suggestions about how health-care personnel can help the elderly with sexual needs. Sexual responsiveness should be fostered but not preached. The elderly need to be reassured against their own false expectations, the hostility of society—including children and potential heirs—and the interference of some health-care personnel who do not understand such needs. Comfort suggests that when a partner is not available, masturbation should be viewed as an acceptable release of sexual tension. He believes that explicit discussion of masturbation with the elderly may relieve anxiety caused by earlier prohibitions. Group discussion among elderly couples can be a valuable means of ventilating sexual anxieties and needs that may not be sanctioned in conversations with others. Comfort believes that sexual dysfunction is usually produced by culture-based anxiety and that it is never too late to restructure sexual attitudes. Various therapies for elderly people who report sexual difficulties have also been reported to be effective (White and Catania, 1982). For example, in one investigation, sexual education (consisting largely of providing sexual information) led to increased sexual interest, knowledge, and activity in the elderly (White and Catania, 1982).

BOX 8.4

SEXUALITY AND THE INSTITUTIONALIZED ELDERLY

In a provocative investigation of sexual activity and interest, Charles White (1981) evaluated a group of elderly nursing home residents, a population whose sexuality has rarely
been studied. White asked eighty-four males (with a mean age of eighty-one) and 185
females (with a mean age of eighty-three) in fifteen nursing homes about their sexuality.
Attitudes and knowledge about sexuality proved to be significantly related to sexual
activity and habits earlier in adulthood. Seventeen percent of the sexually inactive residents indicated a desire to be sexually active, which conforms with other data collected
from noninstitutionalized individuals in late adulthood and suggests that sexual interest
exceeds sexual activity in this sample (for example, Verwoerdt, Pfeiffer, and Wang, 1969).
Solnick and Corby (1983) found that most nursing homes and elder care institutions
were nominally aware of the sexual needs of their elderly patients. Staff generally felt
that physical health problems were a great obstacle to sexual activity, and they largely
ignored the needs of the elderly who desired expression of their sexuality. One mani-
festation of this attitude toward the elderly is the maintenance of sex-segregated floors
or wings of the institution (Solnick and Corby, 1983). Another example of this attitude
is the tendency of institutional personnel to "infantilize" sexual forms of expression.
Elderly who express an interest in, genuine caring for, and emotional attachment to each
other are often teased, ridiculed, and held up to public scrutiny. For instance, staff might
ask a woman how her "date" behaved at the movie shown in the social hall, or they
might ask a man to explain his interest in his "girlfriend" or account for her wavering
loyalty if she sits next to someone else at mealtime. Adult men and women who display
a healthy life-long interest in their sexuality need *not* be treated as adolescents participating in the "Dating Game" simply because they reside in an institution. They are
entitled to the same privacy and respect that other community-residing elderly receive.

Sexual Dysfunction in Late Adulthood

The older male has to contend with some obstacles to sexual functioning. One of
the most common is the **Widower's syndrome,** which affects men who have not
had sexual intercourse for a lengthy period of time following the loss of a spouse
(Gambert, 1987). A widower with this syndrome may have both the desire and the
opportunity for sexual activity, but his physiological system fails to respond (incomplete penile erection occurs). A comparable condition has been reported among
husbands whose wives had Alzheimer's disease (Litz, Zeiss, and Davies, 1990). A
second factor to consider among older males is the impact of a variety of common
drug treatments and diseases (Gambert, 1987). Drug treatments that may cause impotence include: (1) some of the psychotropic drugs used to treat mental disorders
such as depression; (2) alcohol, if used excessively; (3) many of the drugs used to

Institutionalization of elderly adults does not necessarily mean the demise of their sexual interest (McCartney, Izeman, Rogers, and Cohen, 1987). Even institutionalized elderly with dementia may maintain the competency to initiate sexual relationships although well-intentioned staff may thwart such interests (Lichtenberg and Strzepek, 1990). Following is one example of guidelines written to help staff determine the competencies of institutionalized elderly to engage in intimate relationships:

1. Patient's awareness of the relationship
   a. Is the patient aware of who is initiating sexual contact?
   b. Does the patient believe that the other person is a spouse and thus acquiesce out of a delusional belief, or are they cognizant of the other's identity and intent?
   c. Can the patient state what level of sexual intimacy they would be comfortable with?
2. Patient's ability to avoid exploitation
   a. Is the behavior consistent with formerly held beliefs/values?
   b. Does the patient have the capacity to say no to any uninvited sexual contact?
3. Patient's awareness of potential risks
   a. Does the patient realize that this relationship may be time limited (placement on unit is temporary)?
   b. Can the patient describe how they will react when the relationship ends? (Lichtenberg and Strzepek, 1990 p. 119)

treat high blood pressure (antihypertensive medications); (4) drug treatments that employ steroids; and (5) drugs used to treat diabetes. Diseases that may cause impotence include various illnesses that affect the vascular and endocrine (hormone) systems as well as diabetes, kidney disease, prostate cancer, and neurological lesions in the brain or spinal cord (Gambert, 1987).

In most instances, the older female's sexual problems do not stem wholly from biological causes. For example, many older women do not have sexual intercourse because of the lack of a suitable partner. A spouse may not be physically healthy or may have recently died. Today's older women find it particularly troubling, given their cohort's sexual attitudes, to accept sexual relationships outside of marriage or to engage in masturbation (Ludeman, 1981; Pfeiffer, 1983). However, such restrictive attitudes are less common among their older male counterparts (Pfeiffer, 1983; Pfeiffer et al., 1974).

Summary

Our relationships with others are extraordinarily important to us as adults. Those who do not have emotional attachments or social ties often suffer from loneliness. It may be important to develop not only an emotional attachment but also to have a network of social ties to adequately round out one's life as an adult. Emotional attachments give us comfort and security, and social ties provide us with a sense of group identity and integration. In new relationships, physical attraction, perceived similarity of the loved one, self-disclosure, romance, and passion seem to be important; security, loyalty, and mutual emotional interests are more germane to enduring relationships.

Intimacy is a very important ingredient in such close relationships as spouse, lover, or close friend. Erik Erikson believes that people should develop intimacy after they have developed a stable and successful identity. Intimacy is a part of development in middle and late adulthood as well as early adulthood. Indeed, building a network of close interpersonal ties appears to be closely linked with life satisfaction.

Marriage follows a developmental sequence of courtship, early years of marriage, child-rearing years, postchildrearing years, years as an aging couple, and widowhood. The choice of a mate may be influenced by similarities and complementary needs. Early communication patterns set the tone in a marital relationship. Although not all couples have children, those who do face increased responsibilities and demands. One particularly difficult task is successfully juggling career and family pressures. The time comes later in a couple's life when their children become independent and leave home. Debate focuses on whether the "empty nest" increases or decreases a couple's happiness. The time from retirement until the death of a spouse is the final stage of the marriage process. Considerable adjustment is required at this point in development. Eventually, one spouse dies and the surviving spouse must adjust to being a widow or widower. The initial process usually consists of a period of grieving.

Some marriages are robust and others are not. Why? One view emphasizes the effects of the transition when children leave home; more recently, social scientists have argued that an upswing in mood occurs at this time. There is also some evidence that if individuals assume marital and family roles in a standard age-graded fashion, greater marital satisfaction will result.

Parenting involves a number of interpersonal skills and emotional demands, yet our society provides little formal education for this task. Many parents have mixed emotions and romantic ideas or illusions about having a child. The developmental course of parenting is affected by the parent's gender, age, and emotional commitment. Various meanings have been attributed to the roles, expectations, and emotional fulfillment of grandparenthood. Grandparenting is also affected by gender, age, and personal commitment. Furthermore, researchers have documented different interaction styles among grandparents as well as great-grandparents.

A number of family forms exist today: the single-career family, the dual-career family, the single-parent family, the remarried nuclear family, the kin family, and the experimental family. All of these forms possess both strengths and weaknesses.

Sexuality consists of biological, behavioral, and attitudinal components. Premarital sex is prevalent among young adults, and sexual activity is a source of great pleasure among young married couples. Menopause—the end of menstruation—is surrounded by many myths. The majority of women cope with menopause without having to undergo medical intervention, and for some women, menopause can be a positive event. Although males do not experience comparable rapid hormonal changes during middle age, they do seem to undergo a climacteric, involving a gradual decline in sexual interest, potency or fertility, and sexual functioning. Although little biological decline usually occurs in the ability to function sexually in middle age, many middle-aged adults engage in sexual activity less frequently than in early adulthood. Sexual activity and enjoyment may continue among many individuals in late adulthood. However, many elderly adults who have strong sexual interests do not always have the opportunity to fulfill their needs in this important area of life. Sexuality in middle adulthood reflects mild attenuation in specific areas; sexuality may take many forms in late adulthood.

Review Questions

1. How do adults experience intimate relationships, attachment, and love across the adult years? Why are such relationships important?
2. Describe Erikson's ideas about intimacy. Discuss why he believed we must go through the intimacy stage in early adulthood.
3. Outline the developmental course of marital relations. Suggest some of the major issues involved and adaptations that have to be made at each stage of marriage.
4. What is the *empty nest?* How does this concept relate to the *upswing hypothesis?*
5. Discuss the special problems associated with widowhood.
6. What are the most important characteristics of the grandparenting role? Discuss the meaning of grandparenting to both grandparents and grandchildren from intact families as well as from divorced families.
7. Describe the strengths and weaknesses of each of the six major family forms.
8. Discuss the biological aspects of sexuality in adulthood, placing special emphasis on menopause and the male climacteric.
9. Describe the behavioral and attitudinal components of sexuality through the later adult years.

Further Reading

Katchadourian, H. (1987). *Fifty: Midlife in perspective.* New York: W. H. Freeman.
    A clear and concise summary of the major physical, social, and psychological changes that occur in middle age. Special attention is directed toward sexual intimacy, marriage, relationships, menopause, climacteric, and personality. Moderately easy reading.
Lopata, H. (1988). Widows and their families. In C. S. Chilman, E. W. Nunnaly, and F. M. Cox (Eds.) *Variant family forms.* Newbury, CA: Sage.
    A well-integrated summary of the impact of widowhood and the range of family consequences encountered. Moderately easy reading.
Shuchter, S. R. (1986). *Dimensions of grief: Adjusting to the death of a spouse.* San Francisco, CA: Jossey-Bass.
    A detailed and extended presentation of adjustment among seventy widows who were studied over a five-year period. Their psychosocial reactions and the diverse patterns of needs required to sustain their adjustment are carefully documented. Moderately difficult reading.
Thompson, R. A., Tinsley, B. R., Scalora, M. J., and Parke, R. D. (1989). Grandparents' visitation rights: Legalizing the ties that bind. *American Psychologist 44,* 1217–1222.
    An informative perspective on the legal, social, and psychological impact of divorce on children, parents, and grandparents. The historical background to these problems and current legal and psychological thinking is excellent. Difficult reading.
Troll, L. (Ed.). (1986). *Family issues in current gerontology.* New York: Springer.
    A series of papers concerned with the impact of aging on the family. Readers will derive a sense of the important issues surrounding relationships, intimacy, independence, and widowhood. Moderately difficult reading.

CHAPTER 9

THE SOCIAL CONTEXT OF ADULT DEVELOPMENT

309

IMAGINE

Imagine That You Are a Sixty-Five-Year-Old Homeless Person

You live on the streets of Chicago or another large city. Based on what we know about the homeless, we might assume that you (1) must contend with severe changes in weather and temperature, enduring hot, humid summers and cold, snowy winters; (2) have little certainty about when or where you will have your next meal; (3) have little, if any, chance of receiving medical attention for your health needs, and; (4) have been a solitary, asocial, and somewhat mentally disturbed individual, perhaps a recently deinstitutionalized mental patient. Living under these circumstances would be extremely difficult for an adaptive, creative, healthy young person. How can a homeless elderly person survive? Finally, we, like many Americans, assume that homelessness affects the lives of only a small number of elderly persons. In fact, we are in error. Statistics indicate that homelessness affects a significant number of older individuals. Authors like Jonathon Kozol (1988) have vividly portrayed the plight of America's homeless and their families.

In 1985, the Aging Health Policy Center surveyed shelters in eight large cities in the United States. Their findings revealed that approximately 27 percent of the homeless were over sixty years old! The greatest fear of most elderly persons is that they will be placed in a nursing home. Should the elderly be more concerned with the threat of homelessness?

Recently, Cohen, Teresi, and Holmes (1988) conducted a study of homeless elderly men living in New York's Bowery (Skid Row) section. They described how many of these homeless men successfully obtained basic necessities such as money, food, shelter, and health care. The homeless men established a small but effective informal information and social support network among themselves. They helped newcomers and spread the word on where and how to find food, money, and safe shelters. Thus, these men created a small-scale social system that helped them survive in a harsh world.

In this chapter we will focus our attention on the social forces that influence the aging process. We will see that adults display a diversity of life-styles, few of which are as extreme as that of a homeless older person. We will explore factors (such as economics, health, personality, and sex) that lead to variability in aging across our multilevel social-class system. The homeless elderly, for example, arrive at this point in their lives as a result of many interwoven factors. The homeless are, in fact, a diverse group themselves; they cannot be easily stereotyped as predominately deinstitutionalized mental patients with no place to go, devoid of family and social ties, and without vocational skills. We will also investigate cross-cultural differences in aging. For example, do Eastern cultures such as China and Japan allow their elderly to become homeless? Does homelessness even exist in these cultures? What changes do we need to make in our society to solve the problems of the homeless, especially among the elderly?

INTRODUCTION

In this chapter, we will highlight some of the sociocultural forces that shape adult development. We'll begin with a description of the different life-styles that individuals display within our culture. Specifically, we'll first examine various aspects of being single. Next we'll describe how social class, race, and poverty influence adult life-styles. Then we'll turn our attention to a cross-cultural analysis of aging. In this section we'll compare the aging experience within several different cultures. We'll also explore sex roles as organizers and filters of social interaction across adult development. Finally we'll question the existence of universal age-related changes in sex roles and examine three social theories of aging designed to explain life satisfaction.

THE DIVERSITY OF ADULT LIFE-STYLES

In the previous chapter, we described developmental changes in what many individuals would consider to be the prototypical (most common) life-style adopted by adults in our society: a partner within a marriage. In this next section, we'll turn our attention to adults who are single rather than married. Specifically, we'll discuss the different reasons why adults adopt the single life-style, and we'll point out some of the special problems encountered by single adults.

Single Adults

A greater proportion of the adult population is single now than in the past. In the 1970s, for example, the number of men living by themselves increased 97 percent, while the number of women living alone increased 55 percent. In the 1980s, this growth has slowed somewhat, but it is expected to continue through 1995. In 1985, 20.6 million individuals lived alone in the United States, accounting for 11 percent of adults and 25 percent of all households (U.S. Bureau of the Census, 1986). Some people choose to be single as a preferred life-style. For others, however, singleness occurs by circumstances such as the death of a spouse or divorce, or other situations that hinder a person's selection of a mate. In fact, at any given time, about 30 percent of all adult males and 37 percent of adult females are unmarried (Macklin, 1980). Kasper (1988) reports that nearly one of every three elderly persons lives alone without a spouse, child, sibling, or friends. Table 9.1 shows the distribution of men and women living either with a spouse or alone. Among men sixty-five to seventy-four years of age, 79 percent live with their wives as compared to 67 percent over age seventy-five (Church et al., 1988). Comparable data for women, however, suggest that only 50 percent of those sixty-five to seventy-four years of age and less than 25 percent of those over seventy-five years of age live with a husband. Thus, aging is a different phenomenon depending on one's sex; men more often age with a spouse, while women more often age alone.

Table 9.1

PERCENTAGE OF OLDER PERSONS LIVING WITH A SPOUSE

		Living with a Spouse		*Living without a Spouse*	
		Men	**Women**	**Men**	**Women**
A	65–74	79 percent	50 percent	21 percent	50 percent
G					
E	75 +	67 percent	25 percent	33 percent	75 percent

Source: Data from D. K. Church, M. A. Siegel, and C. D. Foster, *Growing Old in America,* 1988.

Remember that living alone does not necessarily mean being lonely (Kasper, 1988). Elderly people who are able to sustain themselves while living alone typically have good health and few disabilities. They have access to some medical care and experience regular social exchange with neighbors, relatives, or friends either face-to-face or over the telephone. The elderly living alone are predominately widows (Kasper, 1988). Widows who are at greatest risk of being isolated and lonely are those who have no siblings or living children (Church et al., 1988). Among the elderly living alone, however, 23 percent of those with children usually see one child at least once a day, 40 percent receive a visit from a child at least once a week, and 16 percent see a child at least once a month (Advancedata, 1986). Requests for help from elderly people living alone are most often directed at family members. For example, if an older person needs help with personal care, he or she initially asks a spouse to provide assistance, then a daughter, then a son, next a sibling, and then an extended family member such as a niece or grandchild. Elderly people seek women relatives for personal care needs; they ask male relatives to provide home repairs, financial advice, and automobile rides (Church et al., 1988).

In the 1970s the number of never-married people under age thirty living by themselves more than tripled. One circumstance that has caused increasing numbers of women to remain single is called the "marriage squeeze" (Glick and Carter, 1976). In the 1940s and 1950s, the postwar baby boom occurred. Because females often marry males who are older, a shortage of males of desirable age developed in the 1970s and 1980s. In the 1990s there will continue to be a steadily increasing number of women who have difficulty finding a desirable mate.

There are many myths and stereotypes associated with being single (Van Hoose and Worth, 1982). These stereotypes range from the swinging-singles life-style to the desperately lonely, suicidal adult. Most single adults, of course, are somewhere between these somewhat illusory extremes (Libby and Whitehurst, 1977; Kelley, 1982, 1987). Quite commonly, single adults' concerns do center around issues of intimate relationships with other adults, confronting loneliness, and finding a place in a marriage-oriented society. Singles are often challenged by others to get married (Edwards, 1977). Clearly, though, there are advantages to being single. These include time to make decisions about the course of life one wants to follow; time to develop the personal resources to meet goals; freedom to make autonomous decisions and pursue one's own schedule and interests; opportunity to explore new places and try out new things; and availability of privacy (Edwards, 1977).

Today choosing a particular life-style offers flexibility. This freedom partially explains why some adults choose to marry later in life and why the number of single people aged thirty-five and under is rapidly growing. Another factor in this choice is the change in attitude of many women toward careers and personal fulfillment. Many women and men choose to develop their careers before assuming marriage responsibilities. Birth control devices and changing attitudes about premarital sex make it possible for single adults to explore their sexuality outside the bounds of marriage. The era of *safe* sex, however, will have an impact on the sexual behavior of single adults. Some psychologists think that adults will limit the range of their sexual partners (as well as the range of their sexual practices) because they fear contracting AIDS (Lyons, 1983). It remains to be seen if the threat of AIDS has a noticeable impact on the percentage of adults who adopt a single (or married) life-style.

Homosexual Adults

The early recognition that one is homosexual is a challenge that must be confronted throughout the adolescent and early adult years (Remafedi, 1987a, 1987b). Self-acceptance of sexual preferences by gay men and lesbian women is initially difficult as social forces provide painful comparisons that indicate that something is "wrong." In one investigation, males in late adolescence continued to question their sexual orientations despite clear evidence that they were homosexual (Remafedi, 1987a). Young homosexual adults, fearful of the censure of parents, straight peers, and co-workers, continue to feel pressure to protect themselves from disclosure of their sexual preferences. Despite legal mandates, homosexuality carries a threat of discrimination in terms of hiring and career advancement. Gay rights activists have helped many young adults to face their sexual preferences—to come out of the closet willingly, rather than to be dragged out with the threat of lowered self-esteem and anxiety over public disclosure.

Within the homosexual life-style, short-term relationships are the norm in young adulthood, particularly for gay men up to their mid- to late thirties (Corby and Solnick, 1980). It has been estimated that 72 percent of homosexual men had no long-term commitment to a partner, while the percentage of lesbian women who were uncommitted to a partner was less than 55 percent (Bell and Weinberg, 1978; Bell, Weinberg, and Mannersmith, 1981). For those able to establish emotional intimacy and commitment, a long-term relationship or "marriage" may evolve. However, the homosexual couple has no legal rights or obligations recognized by the law at this point in time. Corby and Solnick (1980) suggest that aging homosexual men who remain alone may be at an advantage in having developed coping strategies. These

Gay rights activists encourage homosexual adults to acknowledge their sexual preferences and demand their rights.

strategies help them to deal with loneliness and isolation and to confront identity and sexual preference conflicts in late adolescence and early adulthood.

Our knowledge of long-term homosexual relationships suggests that such couples emerge after an extended period of time as single dating partners. When adult homosexuals no longer feel they are physically attractive enough to compete successfully in playing the field, they are more likely to consider commitment to a long-term relationship (Corby and Solnick, 1980). The period in adulthood in which such commitments are made is often just prior to middle age (in the mid- to late thirties for males). Homosexual couples committed to each other may elect to maintain closed, monogamous relationships or open, nonmonogamous relationships (relationships in which both partners are free to have other partners). A comparison of the satisfaction and life-styles of homosexual male couples in open relationships with those in closed relationships identified closed relationships as characterized by greater levels of social support, interdependency, and positive attitudes toward the relationship, and lower anxiety levels than open relationships (Kurdek and Schmitt, 1985–86).

Concern about the increase in AIDS among the elderly population forces us to focus our attention on aging homosexual and bisexual males. In 1987, these men represented 65.8 percent of all older persons with AIDS (Stall, Catania, and Pollack,

1988). Recent evidence shows that unprotected sexual activity places older homosexual males at risk (Curran et al., 1988; Lifson, 1988). Yet this group is more knowledgeable about safe sex than comparably aged heterosexual males (Catania et al., 1989). Despite the risks, most older homosexual males remain sexually active, although they less frequently engage in one-night encounters (Catania et al, 1989). The question is whether the aging homosexual community will practice what it clearly knows about safe sex.

Formerly Married Adults

William Van Hoose and Maureen Worth (1982) have conducted research investigating the lives of the formerly married. Each year many adults become single through divorce, separation, desertion, or the death of a spouse.

The transition from being married to being single is often marked by grieving focused on the former relationship. This is true even when the marriage ends in divorce. Holidays are difficult times for individuals who are separated from their children or for those who remember previous times when a spouse was present.

Divorced Adults

In many respects divorced and widowed adults experience many of the same emotions. In both instances, the individuals experience the death of a relationship; next to a death of a spouse, a divorce causes the most trauma in the lives of individuals (Pearlin, 1985). Whether an adult initiates the divorce or is divorced by a spouse, the grieving process is the same. However, there are factors that are more likely to lead to emotional problems and poor adjustment, including a sudden divorce, an unexpected separation, or a divorce following a long and emotionally committed marriage (Stroebe, Stroebe, Gergan, and Gergan, 1985).

Until recently, divorce was increasing annually by 10 percent, although the rate of increase slowed as we entered the 1990s. While divorce has increased in all socioeconomic groups, people from lower social classes have the highest divorce rates. Among lower socioeconomic classes, factors associated with divorce include marriage at an early age, low levels of education, and low income (Spanier and Glick, 1981; U.S. Bureau of the Census, 1985). Premarital pregnancy is another critical factor. In one investigation, half of the women who were pregnant before marriage failed to live with their husbands for more than five years (Sauber and Corrigan, 1970). Because the median age for divorce is thirty-eight, many divorced people must rear dependent children (Hetherington, Stanley-Hagan, and Anderson, 1989; Kaslow and Schwartz, 1987).

Divorce is a complex and emotionally charged process. For many it initiates a lifelong process of attempting to gain insights and learning to break prior social scripts and patterns of interaction. Weiss (1975) first suggested that although divorce is a marker event in the relationship between spouses, it often does not signal the end of the relationship. Mavis Hetherington (Hetherington, Cox, and Cox, 1978) reported that of forty-eight divorced couples observed, six of these couples had sexual intercourse during the first two months after separation. Weiss believes that the attachment to each other endures regardless of whether the former couple respects or likes one another or are satisfied with the present relationship. Kelley (1982), however, reported that this attachment bond is more characteristic of one of the partners, not both. One partner is more likely to want a divorce than the other partner.

Further information about the divorce and separation process suggests that former spouses often alternate between feelings of seductiveness and hostility (Hunt and Hunt, 1977). They also may have thoughts of reconciliation. And while at times they may express love toward their former mate, the majority of their feelings are negative and include anger and hate. Certainly, couples find the few months just prior to divorce among the most unpleasant and difficult to endure (Thompson and Spanier, 1983). And the data suggest that the effects of divorce and the experience of stress are heightened among couples over fifty years of age (Chiriboga, 1982a). With late-age divorce, both men and women feel they lack resources and choices when they compare themselves to the younger population playing the dating game or when they search for an available social group.

Sex Differences in Divorce

Divorce may have different effects on a woman than on a man. For example, one investigation found that divorce is more traumatic for women than for men; yet both sexes indicate that the period before the decision to divorce is the most stressful (Hetherington, Stanley-Hagan, and Anderson, 1989). Women who have gained much of their identity through the roles of wife and mother are particularly vulnerable after divorce. Many divorced women must work outside the home and may not be adequately prepared for managing a new job and home responsibilities. Four out of five divorced women have school-aged children (Women's Bureau, U.S. Bureau of the Census, 1979). Women, more often than men, must also cope with less income (Santrock and Warshak, 1979).

The term *displaced homemaker* describes the dilemma of many divorced or widowed women. These women always assumed that their work would be in the home. Although they may have considerable expertise at managing a home, prospective employers do not recognize this as work experience. Donna is typical of this type of woman. She married young, and at eighteen she had her first child. Her work experience consisted of a part-time job as a waitress while in high school. Now Donna is thirty-two and has three children aged fourteen, twelve, and six. Her husband divorced her and married again. The child support payments are enough for food, but little is left for rent, clothing, and other necessities. Without any marketable skills, Donna is working as a sales clerk in a local department store. She cannot afford a housekeeper and worries about the children being unsupervised while she works, particularly on Saturdays and summer vacations. Creating a positive identity as an independent person is essential for divorced women like Donna.

Following divorce, these women need to overcome loneliness, lack of autonomy, and financial hardship (Ahrons and Rodgers, 1987; Kaslow and Schwartz, 1987).

Men, however, do not go through a divorce unscathed. They usually have fewer rights to their children, experience a decline in income, and receive little emotional support. The separation and divorce process also may have negative effects on a man's career (Hetherington et al., 1989).

Family Conflict

Many separations and divorces are highly charged emotional affairs that enmesh the child in conflict (Hetherington et al., 1989; Ahrons and Rodgers, 1987). The child may hear parents yelling and crying. The parents may make statements that place the child in a position of competing loyalties, with one parent trying to persuade the child that the conflict is the other parent's fault. These experiences may make the child depressed and cause the child to "de-idolize" his or her parents (Hetherington et al., 1989).

Conflict is such a critical aspect of family functioning that it appears to outweigh the influence of family structure on the child's behavior. Children in single-parent families function better than those in conflict-ridden nuclear families (Hetherington et al., 1978; Hetherington et al., 1989). Escape from parental conflict may be a positive benefit of divorce for children, but unfortunately, in the year immediately following the divorce, other conflicts do not always decline. In fact, they may increase (Hetherington et al., 1989). At this time, children—particularly boys—in divorced families show more adjustment problems than in homes in which both parents are present (Hetherington et al., 1989; Kaslow and Schwartz, 1987; Kurdek, 1981).

Parenting

The child's relationship with both parents after the divorce influences his or her ability to cope with stress (Hetherington et al., 1989; Kelley 1982, 1987). During the first year after the divorce, the quality of parenting that the child experiences is often very poor; parents seem to be preoccupied with their own needs and adjustment, experiencing anger, depression, confusion, and emotional instability that inhibit their ability to respond sensitively to the child's needs. During this period, parents tend to discipline the child inconsistently, are less affectionate, and are somewhat ineffective in controlling the child. But during the second year after the divorce, parents are more effective at these important childrearing duties (Hetherington et al., 1989; Kaslow and Schwartz, 1987; Kurdek, 1981).

The custodial parent has a strong influence on the child's behavior in divorced families. The psychological well-being and childrearing capabilities of the custodial father or mother are central to the child's ability to cope with the stress of divorce. It appears that divorced mothers have more difficulty with sons than daughters. Hetherington (1979) believes that divorced mothers and their sons often get involved in what she calls a cycle of coercive interaction. But what about boys growing up in homes in which the father has custody—does the same coercive cycle occur? In one investigation, sons showed more competent social behavior when their fathers had custody, whereas girls were better adjusted when their mothers had custody (Santrock and Warshak, 1979).

Support Systems

Most information we have about divorced families emphasizes the absent father or the relationship between the custodial parent and the child, but mental health experts have become increasingly interested in the role of support systems available to the child and the family (Hetherington et al., 1989). Support systems such as the extended family and community-based agencies are particularly important for low-income families following divorce (Colletta, 1978; Kurdek, 1981; Spicer and Hampe, 1975). Competent support systems may be particularly needed by divorced parents with infant and preschool children because the majority of these parents must work full-time to make ends meet. Networks to assist newly divorced women, in particular, provide emotional support, legal counseling, and career advice at a crucial time of crisis. With such networking, women may more easily provide continuity and consistency in parenting (Hetherington et al., 1989).

Marital Separation in Later Life

Although research on divorce has increased tremendously in recent years, little attention has been paid to how this critical life event may influence those who have been married a long time (Chiriboga, 1982b; Kaslow and Schwartz, 1987). One view suggests that since middle-aged adults have more maturity and greater resources, divorce in middle age allows the simplification of life patterns and ends an incompatible relationship (Golan, 1986). However, the emotional commitment to a long-term marriage is not easily cast aside. Many middle-aged individuals perceive the divorce as the failure or repudiation of the best years of their lives. The partner initiating the divorce may view it as an escape from an untenable relationship; the divorced partner, however, usually feels betrayal, sadness over the end of a long-standing relationship, and emotional grief over the loss of trust and commitment (Golan, 1986).

David Chiriboga (1982a) evaluated the psychosocial functioning of 310 recently separated men and women ranging in age from twenty to the mid-seventies. Included in the analyses were measures of morale, psychiatric symptoms, time perspective, self-reported physical health, social disruption, and divorce-induced upset. The older adults showed more distress than younger adults, and the sex differences suggested that men and women may have different vulnerabilities.

People in their fifties stood out as being the most maladapted in the face of divorce, whereas those in their forties functioned more like young adults. Chiriboga's results suggest that older adults have fewer options and a general uncertainty about what to do following divorce. Many older people were unable to project even one year into the future, with men over fifty the most vulnerable in this area, although women may be more open about their vulnerability than men (Uhlenberg, Cooney, and Boyd, 1990).

Remarriage

Remarriage is somewhat less prevalent in our society than was the case nearly two decades ago (Glick and Ling-Lin, 1984). Various authorities have explained this by referring to the greater mobility of our population and the higher rate of cohabitation (Glick, 1980, 1984). Statistics suggest that remarriage is still a popular choice among those couples who have experienced divorce for the first time (Glick and Ling-Lin, 1986). According to the 1986 census report, 80 percent of all divorced people decide to remarry; yet, of these remarriages, 60 percent will end in divorce (versus a 50 percent rate of divorce for first marriages). Divorced people, in other words, seem firmly committed to the institution of marriage.

Men and women seem to look for different people and value different priorities when they enter a second marriage (Furstenberg, 1982). For example, while first marriages are based on idealized images of a spouse and a fantasized blissful relationship, the second marriage often involves a far more reasoned, careful, and analytic approach to choosing a mate and dealing with the realities and effort required to make marriage successful. Second marriages find couples seeking qualities in each other which would lead to stable, long-lasting relationships. The qualities sought in first marriages focus on superficial signs of acceptance: pleasing physical appearance, having a good job, and being hard-working (Furstenberg, 1982). However, divorce does not create a blank slate; one cannot just begin again at the beginning. Wallerstein and Blakeslee (1988) remind us that second marriages are highly complex "second chances," with excess baggage such as "his and her small children, lowered income due to alimony, and the ghost of a failed marriage."

The number of remarriages in which children are involved has been steadily growing. Remarried families are usually referred to as stepfamilies, blended families, or reconstituted families. About 10 to 15 percent of all households in the United States are comprised of stepfamilies which represents more than 500,000 families (Prosen and Farmer, 1982). Projections into the 1990s estimate that approximately 25 to 30 percent of all children will be part of a stepfamily before their eighteenth birthday (Glick, 1980, 1984).

When a remarriage occurs, adjustment may be overwhelming to the new family. The mother who remarries not only has to adjust to having another father for her children but also to being a wife again. There may not be much time for the husband-wife relationship to develop in stepfamilies. The children are a part of this new family from the beginning, a situation that leaves little time for the couple to spend time alone and to grow with each other (Hetherington et al., 1989; Visher and Visher, 1979, 1983; Wallerstein and Blakeslee, 1988). Some experts believe that with the added burdens of children second marriages are very likely to fail (Klags-brun, 1985). Other experts are more optimistic, restricting the problems of children in a remarriage to those of adolescent age (Hetherington et al., 1989).

Remarriages may suffer from some of the same problems that a first marriage encountered, but in many respects second marriages have unique problems of their own since more individuals are involved.

SOCIAL CLASS, POVERTY, AND RACE

In the United States, individuals from different social classes, races, and economic income levels age in a somewhat different manner. In this section, we'll examine how social class, race, and poverty impact on the aging process.

Social Class

You probably already have a general concept of social class. We infer much about people from different social class backgrounds: "He's not making much money and doesn't live in a nice house because he comes from a lower-class background." "She's achievement-oriented because she comes from a middle-class family." The classic methods of defining social class in research include evaluating the amount of income in the family or the social status of the job held by the primary wage earner (Warner and Lunt, 1941). This latter definition may be limiting when both husband and wife are employed.

Social stratification in the United States carries with it certain inequalities. It is generally acknowledged that members of society have (1) occupations that vary in prestige, (2) different levels of power to influence the institutions of a community, (3) different economic resources, and (4) different educational and occupational opportunities. Differences in the ability to control resources and to participate in the rewards of society produce unequal opportunities for individuals as they grow older (Atchley, 1983; Taylor and Chatters, 1988). Specific racial groups, legally de-fined minorities, and the elderly are disproportionately represented within the lower social classes and poverty levels in our society.

Poverty

In 1986, of the nearly 27.6 million citizens in the United States aged sixty-five and over, more than 3.25 million, or 12.4 percent, of the elderly were classified as poor by the federal government (U.S. Bureau of the Census, 1987). The definition of poverty is determined by examining the minimum income needed to sustain fam-ilies of various sizes (Bould, Sanborn, and Reif, 1989). For example, in 1985 the federal poverty level for an elderly person living alone was $5,160; for an elderly couple it was $6,500; while for a three-person family, the level was $8,750. These figures compare dramatically to those elderly defined as affluent whose income is at least five times higher than the poverty level (Duncan, Hill, and Rogers, 1986).

Table 9.2

POVERTY RATES FOR ELDERLY AND NONELDERLY ADULTS: 1959 to 1986

Year	Poverty rate 18 to 64	65 plus	Year	Poverty rate 18 to 64	65 plus
1959	17.4	35.2	1976	9.2	15.0
1966	10.6	28.5	1977	9.0	14.1
1967	10.2	29.5	1978	8.9	14.0
1968	9.1	25.0	1979	9.1	15.2
1969	8.8	25.3	1980	10.3	15.7
1970	9.2	24.5	1981	11.3	15.3
1971	9.4	21.6	1982	12.3	14.6
1972	9.0	18.6	1983	12.1	14.1
1973	8.5	16.3	1984	11.7	12.4
1974	8.5	14.6	1985	11.3	12.6
1975	9.4	15.3	1986	10.8	12.4

Source: Congressional Research Service, with 1985 and 1986 data supplied by U.S. Bureau of the Census.

Affluent elderly couples have incomes of $32,550, while affluent single elderly individuals earn at least $28,500 (Bould et al., 1989). Women currently represent 2.3 million or 71 percent of the elderly poor in our society (Church et al., 1988). As can be seen in table 9.2, the elderly have a higher poverty rate than any other adult age category.

The percentage of elderly poor appearing in table 9.1 would probably be much greater if it included the **hidden poor,** those individuals who could be classified as poor on the basis of their own incomes but who have been taken in by relatives who are not poor. Recent estimates place the number of hidden poor at nearly double the rate determined by official census statistics (Bould et al., 1989). The hidden poor are cared for in the homes of close relatives and listed in census data as part of that relative's household. A significant number (92 percent) of those eighty-five years of age and older are women who live under such arrangements and are not classified as poor. However, for comparably aged women living alone, the poverty rate is nearly 40 percent (Taeuber, 1987).

One of the socioeconomic concerns of individuals in late adulthood is the decrease in income they usually experience. It is rare that people plan sufficiently for their own aging; most fail to assess the impact of inflation and reduced income levels. For example, middle-aged Americans who will be ready to retire in twenty to twenty-five years will need an income equal to 75 percent of their current annual expenditures (adjusted for inflation) to maintain a life-style comparable to their life-style today (Taylor, 1988). Many people expect Social Security to provide the support necessary to live comfortably in retirement, but clearly Social Security is not sufficient by itself. Yet in 1987 the major source of income for those sixty-five years of age and older was Social Security. Social Security accounted for 56 percent of the income of older Americans, with additional income from assets representing 21

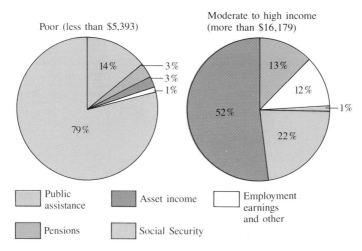

Poor (less than $5,393)

Moderate to high income
(more than $16,179)

Figure 9.1   The relative proportions of income sources for elderly people living alone (1987).

income of older Americans, with additional income from assets representing 21 percent, from pensions representing 13 percent, and from earnings another 7 percent (Commonwealth Fund Commission, 1987). As figure 9.1 illustrates, for those who are poor and living alone, Social Security represents a far more sizable percentage of income than it does for those with moderate or high incomes.

To better appreciate the tenuous line the elderly walk between subsistence and poverty, consider the recent study of the elderly in Massachusetts (Branch, Friedman, Cohen, Smith, and Socholitzky, 1988). The investigation estimated the financial impact of long-term health-care costs among a group of elderly adults. The concept of **spending down** (using up all one's assets to qualify for subsidized care in long-term health-care facilities) was evaluated. Among those seventy-five years of age and older and living alone, spending down assets and current income would cause 46 percent of the sample to reach poverty levels within thirteen weeks of institutionalization in a skilled nursing facility. Spending down for married couples would result in poverty levels for 25 percent of the sample in thirteen weeks and 47 percent of the sample in one year (Branch et al., 1988). Recent data obtained from a national sample of nursing home residents indicate that only 10 percent of older individuals will actually spend down their assets to qualify for subsidized care (Liu et al., 1990).

It is interesting to compare income expenditures between younger and older individuals. Table 9.3 provides comparative data from a single-wage-earner family of four (two parents, two children) and a retired couple over the age of sixty-five (Annual Price Survey—Family Budget Costs, 1986). With retirement and reduced income, elderly couples, when compared to younger couples, spend proportionally more on housing and medical care, but less on food (Community Council of Greater New York, 1986). The percentage of income spent on medical care shows the greatest difference when younger and retired couples are compared.

Table 9.3

ANNUAL BUDGET COSTS FOR INDEX FAMILY OF FOUR PERSONS[1] AND RETIRED COUPLE
[PRICES AS OF OCTOBER 1985, NEW YORK CITY, MODERATE LEVEL]

Item	Four-Person Family		Retired Couple	
	Dollars	Percent Distribution	Dollars	Percent Distribution
Food..	7,074	28.8	3,706	24.0
Housing	7,968	32.5	5,971	38.6
Clothing and upkeep	2,418	9.9	847	5.5
Personal care	843	3.4	546	3.6
Medical care............................	2,413	9.8	2,348	15.2
Transportation	1,535	6.3	1,007	6.5
Other goods and services	2,284	9.3	1,026	6.6
Total	24,535	100.0	15,451	100.0

[1]Index family includes two adults, ages 35–54; one of whom is a wage-earner, and two children, a boy of thirteen and the other a girl of eight.

Source: *Budget Costs,* 22d ed. Copyright © 1986 Community Council of Greater New York.

Table 9.4

MEDIAN INCOME OF PERSONS AGED SIXTY-FIVE AND OLDER BY MARITAL STATUS: 1986

Marital Status	Both Sexes	Male	Female
Married..	$9,041	$12,265	$5,253
Single	8,381	8,867	8,122
Widowed	7,313	9,258	6,993
Divorced..	7,406	7,826	7,000
All persons sixty-five plus	8,154	11,544	6,425

Source: U.S. Bureau of the Census. "Money Income and Poverty Status of Families and Persons in the United States: 1986." *Current Population Reports* Series P-60, No. 157 (July 1987). Unpublished data from the March 1987 Current Population Survey.

Table 9.4 shows that poverty or near poverty is strongly related to sex and marital status. Women who are widowed, in particular, are most likely to experience a severe reduction in income. It also is evident from table 9.4 that a higher rate of poverty exists for elderly women than men. The statistics also show that race is a significant predictor of poverty among the elderly. Black women comprised 31 percent of those living at poverty levels and Hispanic women comprised 22.5 percent, while white males and females together represented only 11 percent of the total population of elderly living at or below poverty levels (Church et al., 1988). The best predictors of poverty in old age continue to be race (black), education (no high school degree), gender (female), marital status (divorced or widowed), and city living environment (Jackson, 1985; Taylor and Chatters, 1988).

It is curious that older Americans appear to have the benefit of having accumulated assets over a lifetime. On the one hand, such accumulation is the result of long, productive years of work, investments, and savings. Many of the assets described in an individual's net worth (assets minus liabilities) seem substantial. An older household in the latest census shows a net worth of $60,300 compared to the average nationwide of only $32,700. On the other hand, this apparent advantage may be illusory since such assets do not represent readily available or liquid assets (Church et al., 1988). It is difficult for elderly people with fixed incomes to sell their homes or assume sizable home equity loans to meet current expenses for medical care, food, clothes, and taxes.

Certainly for one segment of the elderly, the "young-old," lower poverty rates exist than are reported among the "old-old" (Bould et al., 1989). The difference is largely due to the willingness and ability of the young-old to continue to work at either full- or part-time jobs (Schultz, 1985). Among elderly Americans sixty-five to seventy-one years of age, there was only a 4 percent risk of poverty if they had been employed in any capacity for any length of time in the previous twelve months (U.S. Bureau of Census, 1987). For those over seventy-five, poverty rates increase substantially as disability, the physical self-care routine, medical visits, and housekeeping demand increased time and leave minimal chances to work (Bould et al., 1989).

To a real extent, the economic status of an elderly adult is dependent on the outcomes of two different types of "lotteries": the *pension lottery* and the *marriage lottery* (Bould et al., 1989). Box 9.1 describes these lotteries.

Race, Ethnicity, and Life Expectancy

The National Center for Health Statistics (1988) reported that between 1984 and 1986, life expectancy for blacks dropped to 69.4 years, the lowest it has been since 1982 (see figure 9.2). At the same time, corresponding data for whites (males and females combined) increased to 75.4 years. This is the first time that black life expectancy has declined while white life expectancy has risen. Whites generally have shown a pattern of living nearly six years longer than blacks, with both groups increasing in life expectancy at roughly the same rate (one year added every 2.5 years since the turn of the century). A key to understanding the differential life expectancy for black men and women is to recognize that black men are dying far earlier in young and middle adulthood. Black males experience higher rates of murder and intravenous drug use and often face limited access to medical care, poor nutrition, and homelessness or substandard housing. The situation has been concisely summarized by Representative Louis Stokes (D-Ohio): "In a nation where access to health care depends largely upon ability to pay, millions of Americans face barriers to obtaining quality health care. . . . the poor, elderly, and minority Americans experience a higher mortality rate and incidence of chronic illness." There is also evidence that in Hispanic cultures, individuals feel older than their white counterparts of comparable age (Atchley, 1983). Hispanics make few age discrim-

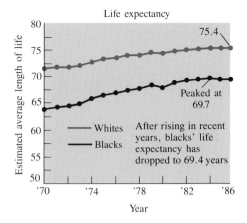

Figure 9.2 Life expectancy and race.
Source: National Center for Health Statistics.

inations among elderly people (Bastida, 1987). Thus, in answer to the question, Do you consider yourself middle-aged, of advanced age, or very old ("anciano")?, elderly Hispanic respondents tended toward the latter descriptor and adopted realistic physical explanations or justifications for their choices (Bastida, 1987).

Housing

Ironically, the bulk of research concerned with the living environments of the elderly has focused on special situations such as nursing homes, public housing, mobile home parks, welfare hotels, or retirement communities. In reality, however, these living conditions account for less than 10 percent of this country's elderly population. The National Center for Health Statistics (1988) indicated that 26.3 million Americans over the age of sixty-five resided in family homes in communities, while less than 10 percent of those over age sixty-five resided in nursing homes or other group care settings. Home ownership represents a sign of achievement among all adults, particularly the elderly (National Center for Health Statistics, 1987).

However, the data concerned with housing quality are less positive. The U.S. Senate Special Committee on Aging estimated that 30 percent of the elderly occupy housing which is deteriorating or substandard and approximately one in five lives in a housing unit which lacks basic plumbing facilities (Carp, 1976).

Suitable living environments directly influence the morale, adjustment, sociability, and intellectual abilities of the elderly (Beland, 1987; Lawton, 1977). The immediate impact of housing is far greater for the elderly since their life-style centers so much more on activities in the home. Among the elderly the overwhelming preference is to maintain ownership of their own homes, assuming they are physically, mentally, and economically able to do so. Beland (1987) reported that 57

BOX 9.1

PLAYING THE LOTTERIES IN OLDER ADULTHOOD

According to Sally Bould, Beverly Sanborn, and Laura Reif (1989), the income of the oldest-old (individuals eighty-five years old and older) is dependent on the outcome of two important lotteries: the **pension lottery** and the **marriage lottery.** The winners of these two lotteries are married persons with adequate pensions. The losers are widows and widowers with minimum Social Security benefits. Unfortunately, the number of losers far outweighs the number of winners. Following is a brief description of these lottery systems.

THE PENSION LOTTERY

The presence or absence of a private pension from a previous employer has a tremendous impact on the financial well-being of an older adult. In several European countries such as Sweden, Germany, France, and the Netherlands, nearly all older persons receive a meaningful pension. In the United States, however, significant pensions are usually provided to a lucky minority of older adults. Typically, the winners of the pension lottery are male, white, and retired from a well-paying position in a private corporation. Bould et al. (1989) recorded a portion of a statement made by a registered professional engineer and a member of the Institute of Electrical and Electronic Engineers, someone who should have been a winner of the pension lottery but wasn't.

> I have pursued a mobile career in engineering, having an average time per employer of approximately five years, not including the self-employment periods or my current employer. Unfortunately, the price my wife and I have paid for my mobility is a forfeiture of opportunities to accrue substantive retirement benefits by remaining with an employer who provided a company-sponsored plan.
>
> In fact, during this period of my employment career, my wife has also had eight different positions in her nursing career, none of whom offered her a pension plan. Even if she had been able to participate, it is unlikely that she would have been able to vest because of my mobility.
>
> In summary, my wife and I have had a collective total of fifteen employers since my engineering career began. We currently have only our IRA investments to depend upon for retirement income (U.S. Senate, Special Committee on Aging, 1985, p. 9; quoted in Bould et al., 1989, p. 134).

Bould et al. (1989) report another case of an elderly woman who was left without a pension because of a practice called "integration."

> After twenty years, I hoped that at least I would get some sort of a retirement pension, but instead, I got a letter which said that I would not get a dime. What it said was that if the Social Security benefits meet the pension plan's retirement income goals, then no benefit is payable from the plan. Since Social Security meets the plan goals, there is no pension payable to me.

I really did not understand what this meant. A friend of mine explained that the plan used Social Security to wipe out the pensions of lower-paid workers like me.

What is so strange about all this is that I received statements from the company each year, telling me that I was fully vested. I guess I was vested in zero.

I should mention that J. C. Penney changed the pension plan after I retired so someone like me would not completely lose out. Under the new plan, someone in my position would get a few dollars a month. But the question is, why should a company be able to take away any of a person's pension by subtracting Social Security?

This is completely unfair. I always thought that the reason a company had a pension plan was to make sure workers can get more than Social Security at retirement. After years of work with the company, they certainly owe us something (U.S. Senate, Special Committee on Aging, 1985, p. 4; quoted in Bould et al., 1989, p. 135).

By the end of the 1980s, federal legislation ended some, but not all, of the problems of the pension lottery. Additional legislation, however, may help future cohorts of older adults more than today's older adults.

THE MARRIAGE LOTTERY

The winners of the marriage lottery are older adults (primarily women) who still have their spouses or who remarry after a spouse's death. The losers are widows who never remarry. There are two reasons why the marriage lottery has a much greater impact on the financial well-being of older women than men. First, today's older women who worked in the past usually had part-time, low-paying jobs. Working under these conditions results in a meager pension, if any pension at all. Second, the vast majority of very old women never worked at all—they receive no direct pension benefits whatsoever. Therefore, the older woman's economic well-being depends on the pension provided to her husband. The death of a husband can spell financial ruin for the elderly woman! At present, widows who are eighty-five years of age or older do not even have the benefit of legislation that provided for a survivor option after a husband's death.

Bould et al. (1989) provide the following hypothetical example of what would happen to Mary Doe upon the death of her husband John:

If John had a pension of $1,000 a month for his lifetime only, plus a Social Security Benefit of $500 a month, and a Social Security dependent's allowance for his wife Mary of $250 a month, then the total monthly income of this married couple would be $1,750. On John's death, however, Mary loses his pension of $1,000 a month and the Social Security dependent's allowance of $250. Without any financial income from stocks or savings, she will now be near poor with only $500 a month, less than one-third of the couple's former income. (p. 136)

percent of an elderly sample preferred to live independently either alone or with a spouse. The remaining elderly who preferred to live with someone else and had already moved into the home of a child, relative, or friend usually had done so because of an emergent problem which prevented their independent living (Beland, 1987). Scheidt (1985), in a study of rural elderly, found that housing quality was a powerful predictor of overall mental health.

One attempt to deal with some of the problems faced by older Americans is to provide subsidized housing. The elderly currently comprise more than 27 percent of people who reside in subsidized housing nationwide. Experts continue to debate issues such as whether housing arrangements for the elderly should be age-segregated or integrated (Cohen, Bearison, and Muller, 1987). Age segregation helps provide a defense against social rejection and social comparison. Age integration provides the opportunity for growth, insight, and understanding of different perspectives. Subsidized housing will continue to be a crucial issue for those examining public policies for the elderly. As we have seen previously, race and ethnicity are factors highly predictive of which elderly adults will experience less than adequate housing.

An example of haphazard matching of life-style and environment is the mode of urban living referred to as SRO (single room occupancy), which is described in box 9.2. Social isolation and lack of socially desirable activity often characterize such settings.

The homeless elderly provide a grim reminder that statistics summarize human lives. While most elderly are able to meet their housing needs in some fashion, there is a segment of our population which is not so fortunate. The Aging Health Policy Center (1985) estimates that at least 27 percent of the homeless are over sixty years of age. Cohen, Teresi, Holmes, and Roth (1988) suggest that this figure is an underestimate since many elderly homeless do not compete for shelter space, fearing beatings, abuse, and the loss of independence in such institutionalized programs (Coalition for the Homeless, 1984). In a recent analysis of elderly homeless men on New York City's Bowery (Skid Row), the use of an informal peer information and social support network helped some homeless elderly men to cope. Poor copers, unable to develop this network, displayed poor physical health, emotional depression, and high levels of stress (Cohen et al., 1988).

Income plays an important role in the living conditions of the elderly. Some elderly choose to insure themselves against long-term costs and escalating inflation, taxes, and home maintenance by enrolling in **Continuity Care Retirement Communities** or **CCRCs** (Branch, 1987; Tell, Cohen, Larson, and Batten, 1987; Cohen, Tell, Batten, and Larson, 1988). They pay a substantial initiation or entrance fee as well as a monthly fee. The fees remain constant regardless of the medical and nursing care a resident may require in the future. The population considering this option is economically advantaged, better educated, and older (but rarely over eighty-five). Tell et al. (1987) expect the number of available CCRCs to increase from 300 to more than 1,500 in the next ten years.

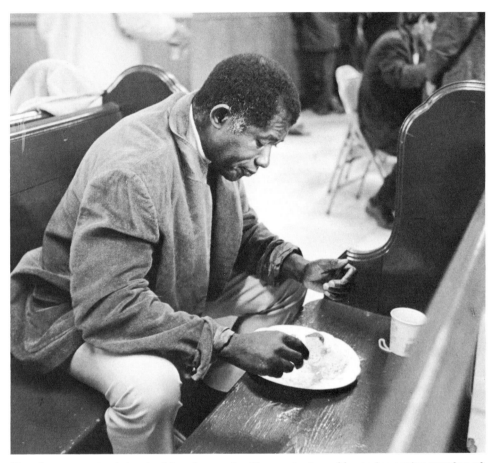

Homelessness and substandard housing are problems experienced by an increasing number of elderly.

Only about 1 percent of aged families and one tenth of 1 percent of unrelated elderly people have incomes of $50,000 or more. For such individuals, housing options are virtually unlimited. At the other extreme homeless individuals with a mean income of $3,250 live in places like the slum hotel described in box 9.2. Currently two of every five older people living at or below the poverty level find that housing represents their primary expense, typically exceeding 45 percent of their limited, fixed income (Church et al., 1988). Of course, most of the elderly fall between these two extremes. Yet for people aged seventy-five and over, housing accounts for almost one half of their budget (Harris, 1978).

Trunzo (1982) has maintained that nursing homes may be the only housing alternative for some of the elderly. About 5 percent (or 1.6 million adults) over sixty-

---

BOX 9.2

LIFE IN THE SLUM HOTEL

An estimated 146,000 poor older persons reside in run-down hotels or rooming houses in the blighted sections of cities (Carp, 1976). Though SROs house a very small percentage of all older persons, residents' life-styles reflect the same staunch desire for privacy, independence, and autonomy that the elderly residing in more desirable homes show.

An ethnography of a slum hotel in a large western city (Stephens, 1976) shows how the elderly who are near the bottom of the economic ladder live. Approximately 30 percent of the occupants of this particular hotel were elderly.

Isolation in one form or another was the hallmark of this social environment. For the most part, the ninety-seven elderly males avoided not only the eleven elderly females but each other as well. These people were virtually required to relinquish their needs for intimacy to survive in the hotel. The two principal reasons for developing or maintaining relationships were common economic interests or shared leisure activities. Relationships among residents seemed to require some justification; simple social interaction never seemed to be enough.

The prime source of income for many older residents involved "hustling"—scavenging, peddling, pushing drugs, or shoplifting. In some cases, two or more residents developed relationships which facilitated hustling schemes. It was also necessary for a "hustler" to let others know of hustling successes since hustling was a key determinant of social status along three dimensions: its profitability, its dependability as a source of income, and the degree of autonomy it provided. Besides socializing over successful hustling feats, residents also related to one another through drinking or betting activities.

Only minimal social activity took place at the hotel, and it served as the focal point for little physical activity other than sleep. Most residents had to go outside the hotel for food and routine health needs. Some took meals at the least expensive places in the neighborhood, where muggings were frequent. The rooms had no cooking or refrigeration facilities, but some residents cooked using a hot iron braced by two bibles as a hot plate. . . . (Williamson, Munley, and Evans, 1980, pp. 259–260).

Locked into this situation by poverty, ill health, and a desire to maintain independence, many older residents of this hotel planned to die there.

---

five are residents of nursing homes, the specific percentages in each age group differ dramatically, as shown in table 9.5 and figure 9.3. Until the mid-1970s, many nursing homes provided poor, slipshod care. Now, the abuses of the past are being corrected. Today's better nursing homes offer a variety of rehabilitation programs to their residents.

Table 9.5

NURSING HOME POPULATION DISTRIBUTED BY AGE

Age	Percentage of entire elderly population who reside in nursing homes
65–74	1.5 percent
75–84	6.0 percent
85 +	23.0 percent

Source: Data from D. K. Church, M. A. Siegel, and C. D. Foster, *Growing Old in America*, 1988.

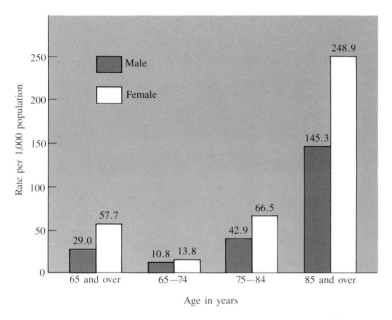

Figure 9.3   The number of nursing home residents per 1,000 of the population of individuals sixty-five years of age and over: by sex and age in the United States.

Source: Use of Nursing Homes by the Elderly: Preliminary Data from the 1985 National Nursing Home Survey. National Center for Health Statistics, May 14, 1987.

CROSS-CULTURAL COMPARISONS OF AGING

The cultural milieu—that is, the physical and social setting in which adults live—has many aspects. It is vital to consider the variety of cultural contexts in which aging occurs. We will examine how the cultural process works by examining societal and cross-cultural views of aging.

The Cultural Process

The term *culture* as used here refers to the existing cluster of behaviors, attitudes, values, and products of a particular group of people. Thus we can refer to the culture of the United States, the culture of China, the culture of the Soviet Union, and so forth. The culture of any nation or group cannot be defined as a single strand. Within each culture are many subcultures with their own sets of behaviors and values.

Think about the community you grew up in. Was it rural or urban? What was the moral climate—conservative or liberal? How strong was the role of religion? How much community organization and interest existed? Was it a young community with few older people, were there lots of older people, or was there a mixture of adult age groups? Were most of the townspeople white- or blue-collar workers? Did most people have two cars and send their children to summer camp? What kind of support systems were available for the elderly? By thinking about questions such as these, you can get a sense of varying community subcultures.

Aging in the United States

One of the biggest problems facing the elderly in the United States may be the stereotypes many people hold about older people. Such misperceptions may be positive (idealizing old age) or negative (viewing the elderly as useless and inadequate). Table 9.6 lists some of these stereotypical beliefs. Evidence suggests that elementary school children already have unrealistic perceptions of the elderly, viewing them in terms of one of two extremes—very kind or very mean. Children also perceive many of the elderly as lonely, bored, and inactive and as having time hanging over their heads (Hickey, Hickey, and Kalish, 1968; Hess, 1988).

Gerald Gruman (1978) has traced the historical background of negative attitudes toward the elderly, concluding that these stereotypes seem to have first appeared as the western frontier was settled in the 1890s. America was striving to become a strong nation, acquiring new territory in the process. Young people were considered a vital resource for this task, whereas the elderly were viewed as weak and inadequate. At this time it was standard practice for industries to make anyone over the age of forty quit working.

The Great Depression of the 1930s eliminated any savings that most elderly people might have had. This period may have been the worst the elderly in America have experienced. Poverty was severe, savings were spent, and younger men needed work. Retirement policies were established, possibly to make room for younger workers who were thought to have more strength and skill and vigorous new ideas. Many of the elderly lived with their children because they had no other option. Society viewed the aged as a problem—what should be done with them? Another study (Covey, 1988) traced historical terms perpetuating the negative stereotyping of elderly people. Since the last part of the nineteenth century older people have

Table 9.6

COMMON MISPERCEPTIONS ABOUT THE ELDERLY THAT ARE BASED ON STEREOTYPES

Examples of Misperceptions Based on Negative Stereotypes

1. Most older persons are poor.
2. Most older persons are unable to keep up with inflation.
3. Most older people are ill-housed.
4. Most older people are frail and in poor health.
5. The aged are impotent as a political force and require advocacy.
6. Most older people are inadequate employees; they are less productive, efficient, motivated, innovative, and creative than younger workers. Most older workers are accident-prone.
7. Older people are mentally slower and more forgetful; they are less able to learn new things.
8. Older persons tend to be intellectually rigid and dogmatic. Most old people are set in their ways and unable to change.
9. A majority of older people are socially isolated and lonely. Most are disengaging or disengaged from society.
10. Most older persons are confined to long-term care institutions.

Examples of Misperceptions Based on Positive Stereotypes

1. The aged are relatively well off; they are not poor, but in good economic shape. Their benefits are generously provided by working members of society.
2. The aged are a potential political force that votes and participates in unity and in great numbers.
3. Older people make friends very easily. They are kind and smiling.
4. Most older persons are mature, experienced, wise, and interesting.
5. Most older persons are very good listeners and are especially patient with children.
6. A majority of older persons are very kind and generous to their children and grandchildren.

Reprinted by permission of the *Journal of Gerontology,* 27:77–81, 1987.

been labelled with increasingly negative and debilitative terms. Covey found terms that clearly separated old men from old women; labels for older men included old-fashioned, feeble, and conservative, and labels for older women included bad-tempered, repulsive, and mystical. Animal terms such as old buzzard or old goat were associated with old men, while old bird and old crow were reserved for women.

As the number of elderly people dramatically increased, our society began to develop programs to meet their needs. In the 1960s and 1970s, greater social concern was directed toward the elderly. Some social scientists, while recognizing that more still must be accomplished, believe that there has been a gradual improvement in the quality of life and status for elderly people since World War II (Tibbits, 1979). In the United States today, the increasing population of older people who are healthy, productive, and intelligent suggests that stereotypes of the elderly as sick, inadequate, and worthless need to be discarded.

Interestingly, David Schonfield (1982) has found that when adults of varying ages are allowed to describe exceptions to their generalizations of the elderly, they engage in less negative stereotyping (see table 9.7). As you can see from the first

Table 9.7

RESPONSES TO TRUTH OF MYTH-STEREOTYPE STATEMENTS AND MEANS OF PERCENT EXCEPTIONS

Statements	Respondents Who Initially Considered Statement True (in %)	Exceptions To Statement Considered: True (M %)	False (M %)
1. As people grow older, they become more alike.	37		
2. If people live long enough, they will become senile.	25	22	25
3. Old age is generally a time of serenity.	52	28	24
4. Older people tend to show little interest in sex.	47	26	22
5. Old people tend to be inflexible.	65	22	27
6. Most older people lack creativity and are unproductive.	20	23	25
7. Older people have great difficulty learning new skills.	46	24	24
8. When people grow old, they generally become cranky.	22	18	24
9. Most older people are lonely and isolated.	66	26	27
10. As people become older, they are likely to become more religious.	77	18	24

Reprinted by permission of *The Gerontologist*, 22:267–272, 1982.

column, 20 to 77 percent of the respondents initially said that one or another generalization was true. But a different picture emerged when participants were asked about exceptions to the generalization. And, as you can see from table 9.8, older respondents were more likely than younger respondents to see exceptions to generalizations about the elderly.

Aging and Ageism

Ageism has become a new word in our vocabulary. Like sexism, it is one of society's uglier words: it refers to prejudice against or negative stereotyping of older adults. Many older adults in the United States face painful discrimination, and they may be too polite or too timid to attack it. Older adults may not be hired for new jobs or may be eased out of old ones because they are perceived as too rigid and feebleminded. They may be shunned socially, possibly because they are expected to be senile or boring. At other times they may be perceived as children, infantilized by descriptions such as "cute" and "adorable." The elderly may be edged out of their families by children who see them as sick, ugly, and parasitic. In sum, the

Table 9.8

AGE DISTRIBUTION OF RESPONDENTS WHO AT LEAST ONCE OPTED FOR 50 PERCENT EXCEPTIONS AFTER SAYING A MYTH-STEREOTYPE STATEMENT WAS TRUE OR FALSE

Age Group (Years)	Total Respondents	Respondents Using "50% Exceptions" (%)
Under 25	46	26
25–44	36	39
45–64	48	38
65–74	33	45
75 +	26	58

Reprinted by permission of *The Gerontologist,* 22:267–272, 1982.

elderly may be perceived as incapable of thinking clearly, learning new things, enjoying sex, contributing to the community, and holding responsible jobs—inhumane (and inaccurate) perceptions to be sure, but often painfully prevalent (Butler, 1987).

Next, let's turn our attention to cultures in which most individuals assume that the elderly are less subject to ageism than in the United States.

Aging in Other Cultures: China and Japan

In China and Japan, the elderly possess a higher status than in the United States. Intergenerational relations are reciprocal rather than linear. *Filial piety* runs high in China—respect and homage to family and community elders is a way of life. For example, one custom permits parents to send weekly or monthly stipends to a married child. This money is not to be spent, even though it is a gift. Rather, the stipend is to be saved and safely invested so that it can be returned to the parents when they reach old age. In Japan, the elderly are more integrated into their families than the elderly in most industrialized countries. More than 75 percent live with their children, and very few single older adults live alone. Respect for the elderly in Japan is evidenced in a variety of everyday encounters: the best seats on public transportation are usually reserved for the elderly, cooking caters to the tastes of the elderly, and people bow respectfully to the elderly. However, such respect appears to be more prevalent among rural than urban Japanese and among middle-aged than young adult Japanese (Palmore, 1975; Palmore and Maeda, 1985).

Recently, critics and governmental agencies in Japan have questioned whether reverence and respect for the old can be expected to continue, given the growing numbers of elderly in the population (Goldsmith, 1984; Lebra, 1979; Nydegger, 1983; Palmore and Maeda, 1985; Sussman, Romeis, and Maeda, 1980). Tobin (1987), for instance, suggested from recent data that Western observers have idealized Japanese old age. The idealization conforms to our own society's ambivalence toward the dependency experienced in old age versus that experienced at other points in the life course. Tobin finds our idealized view of Japanese old age exaggerated, stereotyped, limiting, and one-dimensional. Tobin suggests that there are negative aspects to Japanese aging often overlooked by experts. The observance of Respect for Elders Day and the designation of subway seats as "silver seats" for the elderly and handicapped may mean that such policies are needed to ensure respect and honor toward the elderly. Similarly, although it appears that in Japan more older people live with their children than is true in the United States, the elderly may yet experience loneliness and emotional distance. Living together does not ensure reverence, respect, and belongingness. Finally, Tobin (1987) suggests that the overall percentage of parents living with children in Japan has declined steadily over the past fifty years as modernization, housing space, and population changes have occurred. The language used to refer to Japanese old age has also evolved dramatically. Current usage gives a negative connotation to the traditional term *rojin* or *ecstasy years.* It has been replaced with the more preferable *jitsunen,* translated as *the age of harvest* or *the age of fruition* (Loveridge-Sanbonmatsu, 1989).

It is possible that in earlier times, when so few individuals lived to old age, the elderly were granted high status in many cultures. When few people reached old age, younger members of the society may have believed that these few surviving elders were imbued with special powers and wisdom. However, in most industrialized societies like Japan and the United States, where the aged now constitute a sizable portion of the population, it is no longer a special feat to live to old age.

Jay Sokolovsky (1983), drawing upon the work of Cogwill and Holmes (1972; Cogwill, 1974), has identified seven different factors that seem to be universally associated with high status for the elderly. Specifically, high status should be accorded the elderly in cultures where

1. Older people possess valuable knowledge.
2. Older persons control key family and community resources.
3. Older persons are allowed to perform useful and valued functions as long as possible.
4. There are fewer role shifts and a greater sense of role continuity throughout the life span.
5. Age-related role changes involve gains in responsibility, authority, or advisory capacity.
6. The extended family is an important residential and/or economic unit and the elderly are integrated into it.
7. Less emphasis is placed on individual ego development.

We must not lose sight of our own cultural bias in examining aging, ageism, and stereotyping. Box 9.3 contains information about the cultural-religious ideal for aging in traditional Indian culture. Think about India's cultural norms and the social context in which aging occurs there and compare it to our Western notions.

Are there any areas of agreement? While reading this section, keep in mind the following quotation: ". . . for a happy and long life . . . choose your society . . . carefully (Anonymous, Sokolovsky, 1985, p. 9).

In the next section, we'll turn our attention to changes in sex roles during the adult years. Given the existence of sexist attitudes in almost all cultures, including ours, it would seem as if the aging process is even more burdensome for women than for men.

SEX ROLES

The term **sex role** has been used to describe the different psychological traits or characteristics that individuals display because of their sexes. However, some experts (for example, Spence and Helmreich, 1978) define sex roles as the behaviors *expected* of individuals because they are either male or female. An important aspect of being male or female is sexual or gender identity. We can define this as the extent to which individuals actually take on as part of their personalities the behaviors and attitudes associated with either the male or female role. The development of sex-appropriate sex roles results in "masculine" males and "feminine" females. In past years, researchers assessed the concept of sex roles as a bipolar construct, with masculinity and femininity at opposite poles. More recently, social scientists have developed an alternative view of sex roles. This view is based on the concept of androgyny.

Androgyny

The belief that masculinity and femininity are polar opposites was challenged by psychologists in the mid-1970s. They suggested not only that masculinity and femininity are independent of one another (each involves separate traits) but also that some psychologically healthy males and females possess **androgyny.** Androgyny became a byword in research on sex roles in the late 1970s and early 1980s. What do we specifically mean when we say thirty-five-year-old Bob is androgynous? We mean that his psychological makeup includes both male and female aspects of behavior. Sandra Bem (1974, 1977) and Janet Spence (Spence and Helmreich, 1978; Spence, Helmreich, and Stapp, 1974), pioneers in the study of androgyny, believe every male has some feminine attributes, and every female has some masculine attributes. The androgynous person possesses both male traits (for example, achievement orientation) and female traits (for example, warmth) that are valued by our culture. Androgyny allows individuals to adapt more competently to a wide range of situations.

To measure androgyny, Bem created the Bem Sex-Role Inventory (BSRI) and Spence the Personality Attributes Questionnaire (PAQ). The types of sex-role attributes measured on these two scales include dominance, independence, passivity, competitiveness, loyalty, aggressiveness, and forcefulness, among others. See table 9.9 for a list of some of the items from Bem's inventory.

BOX 9.3

AGING IN INDIA: A CULTURAL-RELIGIOUS IDEAL

Examining other cultural definitions of aging and the treatment of the elderly in diverse cultures gives us important insights into our own values and attitudes toward this topic. There are many acceptable views of aging across many different cultures. Some of these do not fit our own notions of what is "right." However, by increasing our sensitivity and awareness, we can become less ethnocentric, more tolerant and accepting, and perhaps more aware of the limitations of our own culture's approach to aging. Would some cultures find our practice of removing older people from their homes, friends, and family to place them in a hospital or nursing home hard to understand? Do these practices seem cold, cruel, and insensitive? Is illness a legitimate justification for what we do to our elderly?

In Hindu tradition there are four life stages (ashrams). Each stage, while distinct, produces a totality, a balance and harmony between person, nature, life forces, and one's duty (dharma). These stages apply to all but the menial caste and are centered on males. The first stage consists of the *celibate student* in adolescence and early adulthood. This is a time when a teacher (guru) provides both a home and a mentor relationship in transmitting religious knowledge. The second stage of life consists of marriage and the special obligations of a *householder,* which include bringing children into the world and enjoying family life. In traditional Hindu marriages sons bring their wives into the paternal home, creating an extended family from which religious and cultural practices can be preserved by direct transmission to the next generation.

After the stage of householder and the establishment of family, a man is to voluntarily begin to remove himself from his family. The third life stage is that of a "hermit in the forest." This is a time for meditating, studying, and totally absorbing Hindu religious thought and ideas. It involves living a life devoted to asceticism, self-control, and the acquisition of inner spiritual power. A man is ready for this third stage when he sees "his skin wrinkled, his hair white, and the son of his sons." The final stage is complete

Table 9.9

EXAMPLES OF MASCULINE AND FEMININE ITEMS FROM BEM'S SEX-ROLE INVENTORY

Masculine Items	*Feminine Items*
Acts as a leader	Affectionate
Analytical	Compassionate
Competitive	Feminine
Forceful	Gullible
Individualistic	Sensitive to the needs of others
Self-reliant	Sympathetic
Willing to take a stand	Warm

Reproduced by special permission of the publisher, Consulting Psychologists Press, Inc., from the Bem Sex Role Inventory by Sandra Bem, Ph.D., copyright 1978.

separation from all worldly concerns; the elderly man abandons all ties to family, possessions, and home. He wanders unencumbered, free to seek harmony between himself and the universe, free to find the common cord between his existence and the existence of others, both animate and inanimate. The goal of the fourth stage is to become a nonperson, devoid of the need for spirituality, sensuality, psychological bonds, or social dimensions. The individual has no self, no real-world concerns; he waits to die. Death is blissful liberation. It is the deserved attainment of one who has led a perfect life: having committed time to religious study, having married and produced children, and having offered support and help to those in need. Given these accomplishments, his life should be in total harmony.

The Hindu ideal provides a cultural counterpoint to our society. Few in India, even among the highest caste (Brahmins), ever reach the goals outlined for each of the four stages. Yet, these stages provide a model—a path to follow for successful aging. They provide a direction to life, a target for maturity. And obviously, the goals are quite different from those in our society. We encourage and expect the social attachments of older people to serve as anchors and stabilizers in times of crisis, and we look to personal achievements to bring meaning to our existence (Valliant, 1986). But these are obstacles to continued growth in the Hindu cultural-religious system. We emphasize ego integrity, self-awareness, and personal wisdom; these are the very dimensions eschewed in traditional Indian religious culture. The Indian search for connectedness and oneness between self and the cosmos is antithetical to Western notions of personal growth and individual maturity in old age.

The PAQ includes such positively valued "masculine" traits as independence, competitiveness, ability to make decisions easily, unwillingness to give up easily, self-confidence, and a sense of superiority; positive "feminine" characteristics include gentleness, helpfulness, kindness, and awareness of others' feelings. While androgyny had been scored in different ways by researchers, Spence and her colleagues (Spence, Helmreich, and Stapp, 1974) advocate classifying those who score highly on both the feminine and masculine scales as androgynous. Individuals who score low on both the masculine and feminine scales are labeled undifferentiated; and individuals who score high on one scale but low on the other are categorized as masculine or feminine.

Some psychologists are skeptical of the notion of androgyny as developed by Spence and Bem. Box 9.4 provides a critical appraisal of whether androgynous adults are advantaged in their overall adjustment.

Finally, sex-role researchers should pay close attention to the remarks made by Barbara Turner (1982). She maintained that *sex-role research is strongly influenced by the historical-cultural context in which people live.* For example, several pieces of research (Douglas and Arenberg, 1978; Gutmann, 1977; Haan, 1981, Haan, Milsap and Hartka, 1986; Livson, 1976; Valliant, 1977) lead to the conclusion that the young adult male is emotionally inexpressive. This finding is consistent with sex-role expectations for achievement-oriented males. However, there may be some subcultural variations in this developmental theme. For example, young black men in the United States often show more warmth and expressiveness than their white counterparts (Turner and Turner, 1974).

AGE-RELATED CHANGES IN SEX ROLES

Several lines of research suggest that traditional sex-typed traits and behaviors may be more common during young adulthood than during old age. Furthermore, some developmentalists believe that as individuals age they become progressively more androgynous.

Several longitudinal studies have analyzed the personality and sex-role changes that occur in males and females as they age (for example, Chiriboga and Pierce, 1978; Eichorn, Clausen, Haan, Honzick, and Mussen, 1981; Haan et al., 1986; Livson, 1976; Lowenthal, Thurnher, and Chiriboga, 1975; Maas and Kuypers, 1974; Mussen, Honzik, and Eichorn, 1982; Neugarten, 1973). In the Kansas City Longitudinal Study, for instance, Beatrice Neugarten (1973) reported that sex-role differences between the sexes appear with age. Older men were found to be more receptive to their own affiliative and nurturant behavior than younger men; whereas older women were discovered to be more receptive than younger women to their own aggressive and egocentric behavior. Coming to terms with new components of one's personality (for example, nurturance or aggressiveness) may be one of the most important challenges in human development. It is a task, according to developmentalists, that emerges and requires resolution by middle age (Cytrynbaum et al., 1980). With the acceptance and integration of the masculine and feminine components of their personalities, individuals may become more adaptable in facing the additional challenges of old age (Cytrynbaum et al., 1980; Levinson, 1986).

Let's turn our attention to the issue of whether personality change in later life is characterized by a decreasing sense of femininity in women and of masculinity in men. Three specific lines of theory and research bear on this interesting and important issue.

BOX 9.4

BEYOND ANDROGYNY?

Though androgyny has many appealing qualities, some psychologists do not believe that it adequately determines which individuals have the best-adjusted personalities (Locksley and Colten, 1979). Consider the belief that androgynous adults are better adjusted because they are more flexible and are not confined by sex-role stereotypes. In one investigation (Jones, Chernovetz, and Hansson, 1978), Bem's androgyny test was given to evaluate the degree to which adults showed masculine, feminine, or androgynous orientations. The adults were also given a number of other measures: self-esteem, helplessness, sexual maturity, and personal adjustment. The androgynous adults were not better adjusted. Indeed, for both sexes a masculine orientation rather than an androgynous orientation tended to predict better flexibility and adjustment.

Furthermore, serious conceptual criticisms have been leveled at the concept of androgyny. Critics stress that the concept of androgyny is not valid because it implies autonomy from sex-linked social and biological foundations of personality. They point out that such biological and social differences in the sexes are everywhere because sex is a structural feature of contexts and the ongoing organization of life experiences (Locksley and Colten, 1979).

Thus, critics of the androgyny concept believe that sex—being male or female—invariably affects how people see us, what they expect us to be like and to do, as well as what we expect ourselves to be like.

Where do you stand on this controversial issue? Who do you believe are better adjusted—androgynous, traditionally female-oriented, or traditionally male-oriented adults? It may be that for some people better adjustment is determined by the sociocultural-historical context in which they live. Some women who are married, stay home most of the day, take care of their children, and have a traditionally oriented husband may be better adjusted if they have a traditional female orientation. Other individuals who believe in change, who believe that both males and females should have the personality characteristics of both sexes, may be better adjusted if they have an androgynous sex-role orientation. It is likely that none of the three sex-role orientations—masculine, feminine, or androgynous—has exclusive rights to better adjustment as an adult.

David Gutmann's View of Sex-Role Changes during Adulthood

Gutmann's theory (1974, 1975, 1977) suggests that a critical difference in men's and women's **ego mastery styles** is dominant in the early adult years, but that this difference shifts as adults reach middle age. Ego mastery refers to the style adopted in coping with self and others. It is more, however, than just how we respond or behave; ego mastery style is the underlying organization of values and beliefs that govern external behavior. Two ego mastery styles have been associated with age-related personality changes for men and women: active mastery and passive accommodative mastery. **Active mastery** is typified by striving for autonomy, control, and personal competence. One shapes the external environment to fulfill one's own needs and desires. To accomplish active mastery, individuals may employ strategies centered on aggressive themes or intents. **Passive accommodative mastery,** in contrast, is an ego mastery style in which individuals gain control over their environments by accommodating others perceived to be in power. By accommodating the needs and desires of others, the individual gains a sense of ego mastery and control. Passive accommodation to others implies extreme social sensitivity and a mild-mannered, soft-spoken, and gentle demeanor.

These two styles of ego mastery, while present in both men and women, appear to wax and wane at particular periods in the life course. According to Gutmann, active mastery appears to overshadow passive accommodative mastery in younger men. By middle age, however, the two styles have shifted; passive accommodative mastery becomes the dominating male orientation. Interestingly, Gutmann suggests that the situation is exactly the opposite for women. Passive accommodative ego mastery style predominates women in young adulthood, while active mastery predominates by middle age. Gutmann's conclusions, reached after years of research on adults in our society as well as those from other cultures (Mayan Indian, Navajo Indian, and Middle-Eastern Druze), have attracted wide-ranging discussion and debate.

Gutmann offers a biological/genetic explanation for age changes in mastery style among men and women. His explanation rests on the concept of the **parental imperative.** To ensure the biological and social survival of our species, it is imperative that we employ the most effective strategy possible to raise our children. The best childrearing strategy, according to Gutmann, involves a division of labor between males and females. This division of labor, which has evolved over thousands of years, has given rise to the two ego mastery styles. A passive accommodative style, characteristic of young adult women, is uniquely suited to the biological demands of parenting, while the active mastery style of young adult men is suited to providing the necessary economic and material support necessary for family survival. After parenting is over, middle-aged adults begin a process of sex-role reversal. The shift or transition identified by Gutmann is gradual, not abrupt. Men slowly recognize dimensions of their egos which have been unfulfilled and unrecognized. By middle age, men have become more aware of their inner selves, their dependency, social needs, nurturant dispositions, and underlying emotional lives. Corresponding changes in women are also gradually detectable by middle age. For example, women, in becoming more active mastery-oriented, assume far more control of family resources and play a larger role in decision making as they wrest power from husbands.

Critics of Gutmann's theory question whether the observed changes in ego mastery style in middle age are reflective of sex-role reversal or are simply a description of emergent socialization. Linda Cool and Justine McCabe (1983) analyzed research on a number of Mediterranean cultures (for example, rural Lebanon) known for their ideal of female subordination. Their analysis shows that women display a shift in mastery styles consistent with Gutmann's theory. However, they believe that this shift is based not on a biological parenting imperative, but on socialization. They state that

> women's ability to manipulate their own lives and the lives of others around them increases with the passage of years. This emphasis on women as capable, energetic members . . . of society has typically been overlooked. Most studies focus on *de jure* power (or authority, the publicly recognized right to exercise control) which is typically a male domain . . . When anthropologists turn their attention to *de facto* power and control that is exercised in the private rather than the public sphere, the strengths of women begin to appear.
>
> . . . the sources of [women's greater power with increasing age] are: women's socialization to continued changes in their roles and self-concept, their increasing expertise and confidence in their domain (the home), their move from covert use of power (their manipulation of their children's affections) to overt and recognized control in the eyes of the larger community, and the strength and comfort they draw from female solidarity. Such an emphasis seems particularly compelling because the detailed ethnographic examples are drawn from the Mediterranean, an area of the world commonly thought to represent one of the extreme cases of the domination of men and the subordination of women. The message is clear. There is no biological imperative for a submissive (or powerful) female role. Women, like men, are products (and producers) of the particular culture in which they are socialized and live out their lives. (pp. 67, 68)

Other criticism centers on the limited generalizability of Gutmann's theory to our changing modern society. His work may be cohort-specific to the simpler existence of Americans in the 1960s and early 1970s; it cannot easily fit the diversity of life-style and career options selected today by many younger couples with children. Additionally, the changes Gutmann describes as men and women grow older are based on the experience of dealing with children. However, can similar patterns be observed among adults without children? If similarities in dominance-submission patterns are found among both childless couples and those with children, to what may we attribute change in place of the parental imperative? We must wait for more detail before accepting (or rejecting) such a wide-ranging and provocative view of sex differences in adulthood.

Carl Jung's View of Sex-Role Development in Adult Life

Carl Jung broke with traditional Freudian psychoanalytic theory to create his own view of personality. His theory of personality development, with its focus on adulthood, was unique in its time in expanding the study of personality from only childhood to include the adult years (Jung, 1933, 1960). In Jung's view, a healthy personality for adults involves an equilibrium among various components, including the polarities of masculinity and femininity. The period of early adulthood is marked by a decided imbalance between the two, so that one of these components dominates to the exclusion of the other. Masculinity or femininity predominates at this time because of society's coercive influence through sex-role stereotyping or modeling. Ideally, the dominant orientation to masculinity or femininity matches one's biological sex. By middle age, however, masculinity and femininity become more balanced as males become more aware of and able to express their feminine characteristics (for example, nurturance), and females become more aware of and able to express their masculine characteristics (for example, aggression). By old age, Jung suggests, a healthy equilibrium should exist in the personality components of masculinity and femininity. Older males and females see this balance in themselves and recognize their personalities as consisting of *both* masculine and feminine features.

Jeanne Brooks: Sex-Role Behavior and Social Maturity

Jeanne Brooks (1981), in examining data from the longitudinal Berkeley growth study, identified a pattern of sex-role behavior in adulthood analogous to those suggested by Gutmann and Jung. Brooks believes that, beginning in middle age, the distinction between male and female personality characteristics becomes progressively blurred. In fact, social maturity emerges from middle age onward. **Social maturity** consists of three essential components. First is the recognition of how to live easily and comfortably with all people, both men and women. Second is the capacity to adopt unconventional standards, values, or behaviors despite the negative social sanctions which may ensue. Third is the ability to respond humanely, appropriately, and sensitively to those who, like ourselves, experience stressful life circumstances and need help coping. It is Brooks's contention that from middle age onward men and women appear far more alike than different in their articulated sense of social maturity.

Conclusions about Sex-Role Changes in Later Life

Some data suggests that by middle age, males and females become increasingly aware of new or hidden aspects of their personalities and identities. Neugarten (1977), for example, highlights this change as an increase in the incorporation of opposite-sex characteristics. Both Gutmann (1975) and Troll (1985) see the later years as a time of sex-role blending. Men express their nurturance, tenderness, emotion, and dependency, while women increase in independence, assertiveness, and competitiveness (Bengston, Reedy, and Gordon, 1985). Haan and her colleagues (1981, 1986) find a greater expression and acceptance of nurturance among both older men and women. We come to understand and accept traits we share in common with others of the human species. In other words, sex-role differences may be overshadowed by species commonalities in later life.

It seems that the tendency for members of both sexes to become more aware of personality components they have not fully recognized, fostered, or expressed is correlated with aging. Not all investigators, however, believe that this growing consciousness is triggered by changes in age. According to Bengston, Reedy, and Gordon (1985), social forces, rather than one's age, may have a more profound impact on personality in general and sex roles in particular. For example, once children have left home and the day-to-day responsibilities of child care have ended, sex-role distinctions merge (Feldman, Biringen, and Nash, 1981). Yet, among parents with children at home, traditional sex-role differences are at their highest.

Several methodological problems plague the longitudinal research that has been conducted on age-related changes in sex roles. Turner (1982) notes, for example, the select nature of the individuals who serve as participants in many longitudinal studies of personality development. These individuals are usually middle-class, white, and well educated, and they generally have very supportive environments. The data obtained from these samples may not generalize to individuals from other subcultures, and it may not even generalize to individuals with the same demographic characteristics that were (or will be) born into different cohorts. Longitudinal research, even if it is conducted on a representative sample of individuals from all of the different subgroups in a culture, cannot determine whether changes in sex-role orientation are caused by changes in age or by sociohistorical change. This is especially true in a fast-moving society such as ours. What we consider sex-appropriate behavior has changed dramatically over the past few decades. Will it change even more quickly in the future?

SOCIAL THEORIES OF AGING

For some years, two perspectives dominated the thinking of social scientists on the social basis of aging: **disengagement theory** and **activity theory.** Each theory seeks to explain how people can derive the greatest life satisfaction as they age. **Life satisfaction** is a complex construct with various operational definitions. On the one hand, some investigators assume life satisfaction reflects the assessment of "life in general" or "life as a whole" (Schulz, 1985). On the other hand, life satisfaction may be reflective of an individual's morale assessed either in emotional terms or in terms of a cognitive assessment of the quality of life (Schulz, 1985). Regardless of how it is conceptualized, researchers agree that life satisfaction is a feeling or attitude within individuals.

Disengagement Theory

For a number of years, many experts believed that disengagement theory represented the ideal approach to successful aging and would result in great life satisfaction. Developed by Cumming and Henry (1961), disengagement theory argues that as people age, they slowly give up specific roles, interests, and activities and gradually withdraw from society. Disengagement is viewed as a mutual activity; the individual disengages from society at the same rate that society disengages from the individual. According to the theory, an older individual develops increasing self-preoccupation, reduces emotional ties with others, and shows a decreasing interest in the affairs of the world. Such a reduction of social interaction and increased self-preoccupation was considered necessary to maintain life satisfaction in late adulthood.

Disengagement theory has been criticized by a number of prominent theorists and researchers. For example, disengagement theory predicts that low morale is characteristic of older people who maintain high activity. Disengagement theory also predicts that social withdrawal will be inevitable and welcomed by the elderly. An early series of research studies have failed to support these beliefs (see, for example, Maddox, 1964b; Reichard, Livson, and Peterson, 1962). For example, in one investigation (Maddox, 1964b), when age was held constant, the participants showed substantial variation in the indicators of disengagement. Also, when individuals continue to maintain very active lives in late adulthood, they do not necessarily experience a decrease in life satisfaction. Further criticism centers on the idea of mutual withdrawal from activities and roles. Research suggests that this process is rarely mutual, but is instead initiated by forces beyond the control of elderly people (Palmore, 1979). Indeed, when control is lost over life circumstances, morale and life satisfaction decline markedly (Gurin and Brim, 1984; Busse and Maddox, 1985). From forced retirement to the loss of a spouse to the onset of a debilitating handicap, the loss of roles and activities is rarely desired by the elderly.

Activity Theory

In a well-known investigation of engagement and disengagement, Bernice Neugarten and her colleagues (Neugarten, Havighurst, and Tobin, 1968) found that activity and involvement are often associated with life satisfaction. Neugarten et al. (1968) categorized individuals in late adulthood as having four different personality styles: *integrated* (engaged, involved people); *armored-defended* (holding on, particularly to middle-adulthood roles); *passive-dependent* (medium to low activity level, sometimes passive and apathetic); and *unintegrated* (disorganized, deteriorated cognitive processes, weak emotional control). The life satisfaction of the more active personality types, the integrated and armored-defended individuals, was greater than the less involved passive-dependent and unintegrated types.

According to activity theory, then, the more active and involved older people are, the more likely they will feel life satisfaction. Activity theory suggests that it is often healthy for individuals to continue their middle-adulthood roles through late adulthood and that if these roles are taken away (for example, through retirement), it is important to find substitute roles that keep people active and involved in the world. Yet continued activity and involvement alone will not bring about positive adjustment to aging and high life satisfaction in all individuals.

Older adults may adopt different life-styles yet experience similar levels of life satisfaction.

Life Satisfaction in Old Age

A consistent pattern seems to appear in the lives of older people who report they are making good adjustments to aging and deriving high life satisfaction. Those with particular personality styles, for example, may find that disengagement produces the kind of aging that brings them the greatest satisfaction. For instance, disengagement may be desirable for a person who has felt unfulfilled in an occupation and for whom retirement is eagerly anticipated as a chance to be distanced from a career ("I don't have to get up any longer to go to work"). On the other hand, activity may be singularly important for an armored-defended person who clings to an identity in which one's career remains as central in old age as in young adulthood.

Are there other variables beyond personality and life-style that predict positive adjustment to aging and high life satisfaction? Certainly a complex pattern relates to the control and mastery from which life satisfaction and adjustment derive. For example, in one investigation (Baruch, Barnett, and Rivers, 1983) middle-aged women who felt in control and who derived a sense of mastery were most likely to have the highest levels of life satisfaction. Two critical sources of control and mastery for women emerged: careers and close, supportive relationships with children and husbands. The importance of a sense of control over one's life also emerges in the work of Neugarten (1977), Bandura (1989), Gurin and Brim (1984), Lefebvre-Pinard (1984), and Lachman (1986).

Obviously a host of other variables are also predictive of positive life satisfaction and healthy adjustment to aging. Various researchers (Busse and Maddox, 1985; Gurin and Brim, 1984; Kuypers, 1981; Larson, 1978; Palmore, 1979) have reported the relationship of life satisfaction to factors such as income, health, social class, education, spousal communication, interaction style, sexual activity, social support network, peer group and social activities, leisure pursuits, satisfaction with careers, and proximity to friends and relatives. Comparable data based on a measure of subjective well-being identifies the best predictors of life satisfaction to be income, health, degree of social interaction, marital status, independent living arrangements, and availability of transportation (Larson, 1978; Schulz, 1985). Furthermore, Paul Costa and Robert McCrae (Costa, Zonderman, McCrae, Cornon-Huntley, and Barbano, 1987) suggest that basic personality traits and life satisfaction remain stable from a person's early thirties to their seventies and eighties. Clearly, people with personality disorders and difficulty in coping with major life changes are more likely to find the transition to old age difficult, demanding, and problematic. In keeping with Costa and McCrae's theme of continuity and stability, other investigators (George, 1980) have noted that subjectively experienced well-being does not show any appreciable age-related changes across the adult portion of the life span. Those with positive outlooks in middle age remain generally positive, while those with negative views remain so throughout the second half of life.

However, it appears that the source of life satisfaction may change with age (Sears, 1977). Following a group of highly gifted youngsters longitudinally into adulthood, Robert Sears reported that work and marriage were the main sources of life satisfaction in young adulthood and middle age. However, by the time the men were in their sixties, they emphasized family over work as the area which provided them the most personal satisfaction.

Conclusions about the Social Dimensions of Aging

Because of the tremendous variation in cultural and ethnic backgrounds among the aged in the United States, social integration must be considered within the context of cultural value systems. One life-style and set of activities may suit people from one ethnic background better than another. For example, social interaction with family members tends to be more frequent and important for older people of French-American background than their Scandinavian counterparts. The Scandinavian elderly have adapted to an individualized life-style and may seek social integration through organizational participation.

The models of successful aging suggest that individuals in our society may reach their later years with high morale and positive life satisfaction by following a number of different pathways. Some age successfully by becoming disengaged, some by being active, and some by striking a balance between the two. The common predictors of successful aging, however, include a host of demographic variables, social adjustment and personality traits, as well as factors such as personal health and individual control.

Summary

The diversity of family forms includes an increase in the number of single adults. Single adults are often concerned with establishing intimate relationships with other adults, confronting loneliness, and finding a place in a marriage-oriented society. Unique issues face homosexual adults, as well as the large number of formerly married adults affected by divorce. Divorce is a process that all family members find complex and emotionally charged. The most stressful impact seems to occur during the period just after the separation, but over the course of several years the divorced adult seems to adjust to being single. Divorced mothers may be particularly vulnerable to stress because of increased economic and childrearing responsibilities. The effects of divorce on children are mediated by a variety of factors, including postdivorce family functioning and the availability of support systems, particularly for women. Marital separation in later life may be more traumatic than in earlier adulthood because of a greater commitment to the marriage, less resources, and more uncertainty about the future. The number of stepfamilies is increasing; it is estimated that in the 1990s, one-fourth to one-third of all children under age eighteen will have lived in a stepfamily at some point. Difficulties in stepfamilies may arise from financial pressures and from the existence of so many attachments and loyalty bonds.

One important aspect of a culture is social class. One of the major concerns of individuals in late adulthood is the decrease in income they are likely to experience. The elderly have a higher poverty rate than any other age group. Fortunately, more help than ever is available in the form of improving institutions and expanding in-home services.

Unfortunately, aging in our culture still carries with it a number of negative stereotypes. Ageist stereotypes appear early in development; even elementary school children often view the elderly as inactive, lonely, and bored. It appears that negative stereotypes about the elderly in America began in the late 1800s. The Great Depression contributed to the poverty of the elderly, and it wasn't until after World War II that greater social concern was directed toward the elderly, a trend continuing today. Some cultures such as China and Japan appear to possess more positive attitudes toward the elderly than our own. However, recent social, economic, and demographic changes in these cultures have led to more negative attitudes toward the elderly.

The nature of sex roles and how they change is highly complex. Many researchers have focused on the concept of androgyny—the belief that every individual's personality has both masculine and feminine dimensions and that adults who portray positive aspects of both roles may be more flexible and better adjusted. However, the critics of androgyny argue that cultural expectations, socialization, and social learning exert the most influence on sex roles. The degree to which an adult with a masculine, feminine, or androgynous sex-role orientation shows better adjustment may depend, in part, on cultural-historical context. Gutmann's work indicates an increase in sex-typed feminine traits in the personality profiles of older men and a corresponding tendency for older women to display an increase in sex-typed masculine traits.

Two major theories have been developed to explain the social basis of aging: disengagement theory and activity theory. Each theory attempts to explain how some people derive life satisfaction from and make a positive adjustment to aging. An individual's ability to derive life satisfaction may depend not only on relating personality to disengagement and/or activity, but also on demographic, social, and psychologically relevant factors.

Review Questions

1. Discuss the reasons why some adults choose to adopt a single life-style.
2. What is the impact of divorce on both men and women?
3. How does adjustment differ when separation or divorce occurs in later life?
4. Describe the economic hardships that many of today's elderly must endure.
5. Describe the pension lottery and the marriage lottery. What impact do these two lotteries have on the financial well-being of the elderly?
6. Discuss how race affects life expectancy. What factors account for the difference?
7. What is ageism?
8. Trace the historical background of ageist attitudes toward the elderly in the United States.
9. How do attitudes about the aged in countries like China and Japan compare to the attitudes held by Americans?
10. How do sex roles affect adults? What is androgyny?
11. Explain the meaning of the following terms: *active mastery, passive accommodative mastery,* and the *parental imperative.*
12. Describe three different explanations for the sex-role reversal that seems to occur during adulthood.
13. Describe three different theories on the social basis of aging.
14. Is there an optimal way to age? What evidence supports your position?

For Further Reading

Bould, S., Sanborn, B., and Reif, L. (1989). *Eighty-five plus: The oldest old.* Belmont, CA: Wadsworth Publishing.
This excellent book contains an analysis of the social and economic issues facing America's oldest old. Moderately easy reading.

Gutmann, D. L. (1977). The cross-cultural perspective: Notes toward a comparative psychology of aging. In J. E. Birren and K. W. Schaie (eds.), *Handbook of the psychology of aging.* New York: Van Nostrand Reinhold.
This chapter contains an excellent review of the research relating to David Gutmann's theory of sex-role reversals during adulthood. Moderately difficult reading.

Sokolovsky, J. (Ed.). (1983). *Growing old in different societies: Cross-cultural perspectives.* Belmont, CA: Wadsworth Publishing.
In this edited text, Sokolovsky presents a wealth of information about the aging process in different societies across the world. Easy to moderately difficult reading.

CHAPTER 10

WORK, LEISURE, AND RETIREMENT

353

IMAGINE

Imagine That You Have Inherited So Much Money You No Longer Have to Work

Would you stop working? Would you go out and buy a Rolls Royce, a yacht, a mansion? Would you travel around the world? After a year or two of enjoying the money, what would you do?

In one investigation, workers were asked what they would do if they inherited enough money to allow them to stop working (Morse and Weiss, 1968). Only 20 percent said they would quit working. Approximately one-third of the workers believed that joblessness would make them feel lost, useless, and ineffective in deciding how to spend their time. It seems that work is a vital part of our identity as adults and often becomes the organizational center of our lives. Indeed, one of the first things adults ask on meeting one another is, "What do you do for a living?" Occupations often index information about people's intellectual levels, patterns of motivation, life-styles, and community relationships (Bock and Moore, 1986). The world of work becomes a central focus for many people because it represents a primary basis for scheduling time—daily, monthly, yearly, and even over the entire life span.

Most American adults spend at least one of every three waking hours working. In our culture, we are reared to think we can go from rags to riches if we work hard enough. Our society is extraordinarily achievement-oriented. We are taught that imagination, energy, self-denial, and persistence will make us successes in life. A focal point in our culture is the idea of finding pleasure in work. In the 1990s Americans still seem committed to the words of Thomas Carlyle, who in 1843 declared, "Work, and therein have well-being."

How can work promote a sense of satisfaction and well-being in life? Work helps to satisfy our basic needs. It helps us buy food, shelter, and clothing, and it can help us support a family. Work can also contribute to psychological satisfaction since it is the primary setting in which adults develop skills, show competence, apply knowledge, and generally build self-esteem. Other motives that may undergird an adult's strong interest in working include the intrinsic interest of the work, the chance to learn or use new ideas, and the opportunity to socialize and develop relationships with other people.

Because work is such an important aspect of our culture, unemployment can be a tragic experience. Not long ago unemployment reached the highest point since the depression, with about 10 percent of Americans who wanted to work unable to find jobs. Unemployment can be a difficult experience, not just because of loss of income but because of the sense of purpose one may lose as well. Perhaps this explains why only 20 percent of us would choose not to work even if we inherited enough money so that we no longer had to work (Morse and Weiss, 1968).

INTRODUCTION

In this chapter we'll explore one of the most important contexts of adult development—work. Initially, we'll look at the social and historical contexts of work, then we'll outline the changes that take place in work across the adult years. Such changes include occupational choice, finding a place in the world of work, adjusting to work, reaching and maintaining occupational satisfaction, and working in late adulthood. We'll further evaluate the varied meanings of work, looking in detail at the achievement motive, intrinsic motivation, the work ethic, and the impact of unemployment. Then we'll examine perhaps the greatest change in the labor force in the last thirty-five years: the increasing number of women working outside the home. We'll also pay special attention to the career development of men and women in early adulthood.

Not only do people need to learn how to work well, but they also need to develop leisure activities. We'll discuss the nature of leisure activities, leisure at midlife, and leisure in retirement. In the last part of the chapter, we'll explore factors related to retirement, along with describing the phases of retirement and the factors predictive of successful adjustment to retirement.

THE SOCIAL AND HISTORICAL CONTEXTS OF WORK

Robert J. Havighurst (1982) has described the important role of work in all cultures and its evolution in the United States. The society of the United States was *preindustrial* in the nineteenth century. The majority of families farmed land, worked together, and functioned as a unit. Some townspeople also worked as family units, with one or more sons learning from their fathers to be blacksmiths or carpenters, for example. In many parts of the world—much of Africa, Latin America, and Asia—such work conditions still prevail. But by the end of the nineteenth century, the United States was becoming urbanized and industrialized. By 1910, only one-third of the men were farmers or farm laborers.

The year 1910 is often considered the beginning of the industrial revolution in the United States. Factories multiplied, and the labor force changed so dramatically that by 1950 half of all male workers were involved in some form of manufacturing or construction. In an industrial society, machines that operate with mechanical energy substantially increase productivity. Coal, petroleum, and natural gas allowed worker productivity to rise, along with the profits of industrial owners.

At the present time, we are making a transition to a *postindustrial* society. Approximately 65 to 70 percent of all workers are engaged in delivering services. It has been predicted that by the year 2000, only 10 percent of the labor force will be involved in manufacturing and producing goods for the other 90 percent.

The term *services* can refer to many different activities. In earlier times, common services included domestic work, transportation, and the distribution of goods, whereas in the postindustrial society we are witnessing a significant increase in jobs related to human services (such as education and health) and professional and technical services—data processing and communication, for example.

Havighurst (1982) believes that energy costs may control the socioeconomic structure of the twenty-first century. These costs may determine the numbers and age structure of the labor force, the distribution of the population between large and small cities, and the size of housing units. A major increase in the cost of energy is likely to lower the material standard of living. People may respond by working longer hours and/or more years to increase production of goods and services so that they can maintain their standard of living. This would mean that the elderly will be encouraged to stay in the labor force as long as they can remain productive. The average age of voluntary retirement could rise to seventy, seventy-five, or older (Chen, 1987).

Despite these projections, it appears that in the 1980s the percentage of men over the age of sixty-five who continued to work full-time was significantly lower than the percentage at the beginning of this century. Douvan (1983) reports a decline of nearly 70 percent in America's work force over the age of sixty-five since 1900. One important change among the elderly is an increase in part-time employment. The U.S. Bureau of Census reported in 1986 that of the more than three million people in the United States over the age of sixty-five who worked, 54 percent were part-time employees. Table 10.1 shows that the percentage of older part-time workers rose steadily from 1960 to 1986. The 18 percent increase in part-time employment is related to many factors to be examined later in the chapter.

Next let's look at work over the life cycle. We have just seen that earlier in American history, many adolescents engaged in work experiences within their families; but as our society industrialized, schooling began to replace family apprenticeships as training for workers ready to fill newly created jobs. During the twentieth century, vocational choices have broadened considerably.

Table 10.1

PERCENTAGE OF OLDER PERSONS EMPLOYED ON A FULL- OR PART-TIME BASIS: 1960–1986.

Sex and Age	1960		1970		1982		1986	
	Full-time	*Part-time*	*Full-time*	*Part-time*	*Full-time*	*Part-time*	*Full-time*	*Part-time*
Males								
45 to 64	94	6	96	4	93	7	93	7
65 plus	70	30	62	38	52	48	52	48
Females								
45 to 64	78	22	77	23	73	27	75	25
65 plus	57	43	51	49	40	60	39	61

Source: U.S. Department of Labor, Bureau of Labor Statistics. Unpublished data from the *Current Population Survey.*

One change in employment patterns among older adults is the increase in part-time work.

WORK OVER THE LIFE CYCLE

In this section, we'll examine career exploration, planning, and decision making. Then we'll discuss entry into an occupation as individuals attempt to find their places in the world of work. Subsequently, we'll evaluate the flexibility of careers in middle adulthood, occupational satisfaction, and work in late adulthood.

Occupational Choice

At some point toward the end of adolescence or the beginning of early adulthood, most individuals enter an occupation. Most career choice theorists and counselors believe that, before deciding upon a particular career, it is wise to explore a wide number of occupational alternatives. Of all decisions in life, career choices often appear to be the most unplanned; yet, at the same time, they are among the most significant of our adult lives (Super, Kowalski, and Gotkin, 1967). We will briefly examine three theories of occupational choice proposed by Donald Super, Eli Ginzberg, and John Holland. All three theorists believe that exploration of alternative career paths is the most important aspect of career development.

Super's Theory

Donald Super (1969, 1975, 1980) has consistently maintained that occupational choices are influenced mostly by self-concept. People select particular careers or vocations that best express their self-concepts. This theory suggests the presence of five stages in vocational development, with each stage reflecting predictable changes in self-concept as one's vocational choice is seen as more or less successful (Super, 1980). Super suggests that occupational choice is a continuous developmental process from adolescence to old age, with the person making modifications, reassessments, and redirection throughout the life span as self-concept becomes clearer and more distinct.

Super refers to the first stage of career development as *implementation*. At this stage, individuals, usually adolescents, simply try out a number of part- or full-time jobs to explore the world of work. Part of the exploration involves finding the boundaries of acceptable work-role behavior: dress, communication, punctuality, social networks, supervisor expectancies, reward structures, and so forth. In this stage, exploration is healthy and a reflection of adolescent self-concept. In one investigation, Super and his colleagues (Super et al., 1967) studied young adults after they left high school. The investigators found that over half of the position changes made between leaving school and the age of twenty-five involved floundering and unplanned changes. In other words, the young adults were neither systematic nor intentional in their exploration and decision making about careers.

The second stage, the *establishment stage,* involves the transition to a specific career choice. Again, this stage mirrors a young adult's self-concept. Interestingly, Super predicts considerable stability in vocational choice for those at this stage.

There will be little movement away from the specific career selected, although some young adults will try to move up the career ladder by changing positions within a company or moving to a different company. If an adult considers career change, it is usually in midlife that he or she becomes serious about a completely new vocation. Such changes occur after an individual takes stock of the opportunities for self-development within the initially chosen career.

For the majority of people who stay within the career they chose in young adulthood, the *maintenance stage* describes the period from roughly the mid-forties to the mid-fifties. This is a time when most people either achieve the levels of occupational success they hoped to attain or recognize that they will not reach these levels. Super describes this decade of vocational development as early preparation for the disengagement expected with retirement. Individuals remain occupationally involved, committed, and focused, but with reduced intensity on personal achievement and success.

About ten to fifteen years prior to actual retirement, Super believes the individual enters the *declaration stage*. This stage reflects an active readiness for retirement as individuals prepare themselves emotionally, financially, and socially. A distance from one's lifelong career begins to emerge. For workers who have made work a central focus in their lives, this stage represents a significant challenge.

The last stage in Super's model is *retirement*. The individual achieves a physical separation from work and begins to function in life without a career or vocation. Super's theory has been criticized for its narrow focus on self-concept as the prime factor responsible for occupational choice. Super largely ignores the roles of factors such as social class, education, family, and chance. Moreover, his theory implies that most young adults are articulate, mature, and reflective individuals who are able to reason, evaluate, and rationally compare alternative career pathways.

Ginzberg's Theory

Eli Ginzberg has also developed a stage theory of occupational choice (Ginzberg, 1971, 1972). The essential principle underlying the *fantasy, tentative,* and *realistic stages* is the emergence of more and more realistic vocational decisions. Fantasy stages occur as a child imagines and practices various occupations for a few hours, days, or weeks. The tentative stage begins as the early adolescent explores career involvement. Adolescents may closely monitor adults (models) in various careers; they also read about and discuss occupations with family members and friends. The realistic stage begins as the young adult (from high school graduation to the mid-twenties) carefully and rationally analyzes career choices. This stage involves a realistic assessment of the necessary education, apprentice period, and personal qualities (values, attitudes, and aptitudes) required to pursue particular careers. The process of realistic assessment is initiated in young adulthood but continues through the life span. Ginzberg's theory has been criticized for being overly rational in its presentation of occupational choice, with too much emphasis placed on cognitive processes. Also, Ginzberg makes no provision for career change in midlife.

Holland's Theory

John L. Holland (1973, 1985) has developed a theory of career choice that is quite different from the stage views of Super and Ginzberg. Holland believes that career selection is based on the best fit between an individual's personality and the demands of the vocation. A good match between an individual's personality and a specific vocation will lead to job satisfaction and stability, whereas a bad match will lead to job dissatisfaction and the search for a different career. In Holland's view, adults look for careers that are most compatible with their personalities. Psychological tests can help assess an individual's personality profile and match it against the prototypical personality of an individual in a particular career. Holland has identified six basic personality types along with the kinds of careers that best match these personalities (Holland, 1973):

1. *The artistic personality* (creative, emotionally expressive, innovative, original, reflective): This personality might enjoy being an architect, a designer, or working in fashion-related industries.
2. *The conventional personality* (concern for conformity, efficiency, somewhat shy and inhibited): This person might become a bookkeeper, secretary, receptionist, or typist.
3. *The enterprising personality* (high energy and motivation, need to be in control, strong, outgoing, and socially gregarious): This personality thrives in business, management, private companies, and sales work.
4. *The investigative personality* (strong curiosity, intellectual, rational): People of this personality type make good researchers and scientists.
5. *The realistic personality* (concrete, materialistic, mechanical, practical, asocial): This person might be a computer programmer, an engineer, or a mechanic.
6. *The social personality* (cooperative, helpful, social orientation, understanding of human relations): People of this type enjoy being counselors, personnel managers, psychologists, teachers, and social workers.

Some critics of Holland's approach suggest that few adults have the capacity to see themselves, their personalities, and the demands of specific jobs as he suggests. Do adults insightfully, carefully, and slowly compare potential careers to their own unique personal qualities? Moreover, few people are as accurate in their individual self-assessment as Holland suggests. Critics have also found Holland's theory limited in that it ignores the developmental changes in self-knowledge that occur throughout the life span. These changes can lead to career changes (Vondareck, Lerner, and Schulenberg, 1986).

Career Exploration

To insure that students in high school engage in career exploration, educators have adopted a variety of approaches (Osipow, 1987). Some counseling programs are self-oriented (that is, students are left to their own devices to read about, discuss,

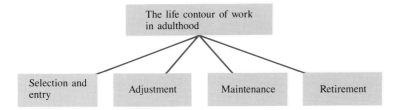

Figure 10.1 The life contour of work in adulthood.

and question particular career options). Others are more directive. They bring students to resource centers with computer-assisted career-information packages that can be examined in stepwise fashion. Still others have mandated that students enroll in specific credit-bearing courses on career exploration (Hamdani, 1974). Studies confirm that self-oriented programs rarely have beneficial effects on students' career exploration and decision making (Corbin, 1974; Hammer, 1974). It is not enough for students to engage in career exploration without any guidance. Most high schools are beginning to recognize the need for directed career guidance and placement in their educational programming and are making positive changes in this direction (Osipow, 1987).

Career exploration, planning, and decision making are important activities for adolescents and young adults. These processes, however, should not be restricted to any single portion of the life span. Indeed, occupational orientation is lifelong and can be conceptualized to consist of four major stages: *selection and entry, adjustment, maintenance,* and *retirement.* Each of these stages is outlined in figure 10.1. These stages are readily identifiable in careers that move in an orderly progression; they become more obscure in disorderly work patterns or work changes that require some form of readjustment.

Entering an Occupation

At some point during the late teens or twenties, one usually *enters an occupation.* For the first several years, an occupation may take an inordinate amount of a person's time, so that other aspects of life such as marriage and family become secondary. Havighurst (1982) believes that getting started in an occupation is more difficult for middle- than lower-class people because success in an occupation is essential to maintaining middle-class status. Many lower-class individuals, however, are socialized to work long and hard at their jobs. Valliant and Valliant (1981), for example, regularly interviewed a group of 465 lower-social-class men about their work as they aged over a thirty-five-year period. The most industrious participants in childhood remained so in adulthood. They also derived the greatest success from their work, had the warmest social relationships, and the best overall adjustment (mental health).

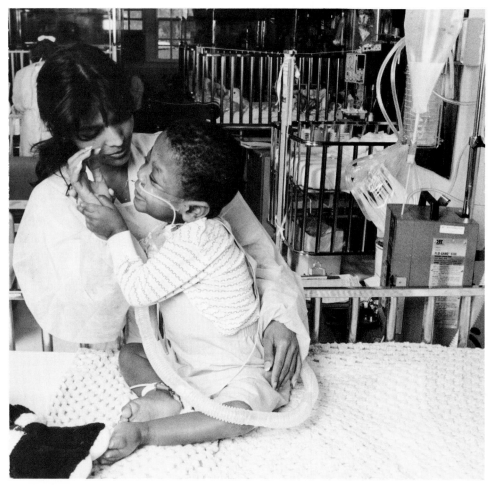

In early adulthood, beginning an occupation takes priority over other life concerns.

Adjustment

Adjustment is the key concept in the second stage of the occupational cycle (figure 10.1). This is the period that Daniel Levinson (1978) calls the *age-thirty transition* in men. According to Levinson, once a man has entered an occupation, he must develop a distinct occupational identity and establish himself in the occupational world. Along the way, he may fail, drop out, or begin a new path. He may stay narrowly on a single track or try several directions before settling firmly on one. This adjustment phase lasts several years. A professional may spend several years in academic study, whereas an executive may spend his early years in lower- or middle-management jobs. Hourly workers typically need several years to explore the work world and move beyond the apprentice status to a permanent occupational role.

The level of attainment a man reaches by his early thirties varies. One executive may be on the bottom rung of the corporate ladder; another may be near the top. An hourly worker may be an unskilled laborer without job security or a highly skilled craftsperson earning more than many executives or professionals.

The occupational cycle for women, even more so than for men, is also marked by a series of adjustments. Women pursuing careers are faced with the same challenges in embarking on a career as men, yet they also may experience an intense need to balance the competing demands of marriage and family (Fitzgerald and Betz, 1983). In our society, men rarely have to decide whether to delay marriage and childrearing in favor of furthering their careers. Those women who marry, bear children, and become committed to full-time mothering ("traditional women") have subordinated the work role to the family role. Osipow (1983) reports that traditional women are strongly motivated by needs of acceptance and love. In the past two decades, increasing numbers of women ("careerists") have developed committed, permanent ties to the workplace that resemble the pattern once reserved for men alone. Osipow (1983) finds careerists strongly achievement-oriented.

Studies show that most women work out of economic need first and foremost, although they may find considerable satisfaction in their careers (Maymi, 1982). Nearly 67 percent of working women in Maymi's study were either single, divorced, separated, widowed, or married to husbands earning less than $10,000 per year. Increasing numbers of women are combining the commitment to both work and family, and recent research shows no sign of this trend changing. Fassinger (1985) found that high-ability women who were juniors and seniors in college showed a strong interest in blending career *and* family in early adulthood. Perhaps no better index of the impact of women in the work force exists than that provided by the increasing number of occupations in which women are now employed. Figure 10.2 shows five professions in which women have made sizable gains in employment over a seven-year period (1979–1986). Given the important jobs that need to be filled in our society, we would think that the sex of a qualified applicant would be irrelevant; indeed, this is the stance our laws take in prohibiting sex discrimination in hiring, salary, and promotion. However, as we shall see, the promises of equal opportunity and equal pay for equal work have not yet produced the intended effects for women in the world of work.

Reaching and Maintaining Occupational Satisfaction and Midlife Career Change

In middle adulthood, most men reach their highest status and income levels in their careers; women, if they have been employed most of their adult lives, do likewise. Those who remain in their careers from early adulthood to retirement generally become increasingly satisfied with their work through their mid-sixties (Rhodes, 1983). Satisfied employees are usually somewhat more productive, while dissatisfied workers show both decreased productivity and increased absenteeism (Iaffaldino and Muchinsky, 1985; Rhodes, 1983). What leads employees to be satisfied or dissatisfied with their work?

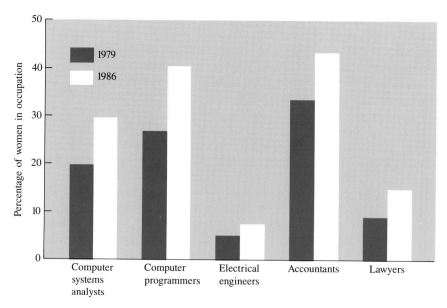

Figure 10.2   Five professions in which women have been historically underrepresented: 1979–1986.

Source: Data from the U.S. Bureau of the Census.

The factors that lead to occupational satisfaction are different for younger and older workers. Younger workers seem concerned with salary, job security, opportunity for advancement, and relationships with both supervisors and coworkers (Nord, 1977). By midlife, established workers focus on different factors: autonomy on the job, the opportunity for individual challenge and mastery, personal achievement, freedom to be creative, and the need to see one's work as contributing to a larger whole (Clausen, 1981). Most older workers are satisfied with their work, have derived recognition for their abilities (enhanced self-esteem), and will not change companies even if offered higher salaries (Havighurst, 1982, Nord, 1977). There are, of course, some interesting exceptions to these general trends (for example, people in middle adulthood who start over and select a new career).

Many men and women who have had relatively routine jobs deliberately seek change to find work that is more interesting and rewarding. Perhaps this helps describe the shift made by traditional women from housework to careers. At present, just over 50 percent of women aged forty to fifty-nine are in the work force, many of them having obtained jobs as they were raising or immediately after raising a family. Approximately 10 percent of men change the nature of their work between the ages of forty and sixty, either for their own reasons or because they lose their jobs (Havighurst, 1982). And some people change jobs because they feel they are not physically fit for the work required of them (for example, professional athletes, police officers, and some armed forces personnel).

Psychological Factors in Midlife Career Change

What are some of the factors that motivate individuals to change their careers at midlife? Daniel Levinson (1978) maintains that one important challenge in midlife involves adjusting idealistic hopes to realistic possibilities in light of how much time is left in an occupation. Middle-aged adults often focus on how much time they have left before retirement and the speed with which they are reaching their occupational goals. If individuals believe they are behind schedule, or if they now view their goals as unrealistic, then some reassessment and readjustment is necessary. Levinson (1978) comments that many middle-aged men feel a sense of sadness over unfulfilled dreams. Levinson and his colleagues also found that many middle-aged men feel constrained by their work, bosses, wives, and children. Such feelings may lead to rebellion, which can take several forms—extramarital affairs, divorce, alcoholism, career change, or even suicide. In one investigation, the incidence of extramarital affairs among thirty-two women and twenty-seven men was reported to be related, in part, to a mismatch between vocation and personality profile (Wiggins and Lederer, 1984). Levinson notes that a person in middle age wants desperately to be affirmed in the roles that he or she values most. At about age forty, Levinson's subjects fixed on some key event in their careers (for example, a promotion or an award) as carrying the ultimate message of affirmation or devaluation by society.

It is important to consider the deeper meanings of career change during the middle years. Midlife career changes are often linked to changes in attitudes, goals, and values (Thomas, 1977). While some people hang onto their jobs despite intense dislike for their work, others change careers even when their jobs are still satisfactory. The decision to remain with a career is in itself no guarantee that an individual has not revised personal attitudes, goals, and values. Even if nothing in the individual's external life changes, the individual does. Middle-aged people begin to see themselves, their life situations, and their careers more introspectively, reflectively, and sensitively. Levinson (1978) notes the importance of these internal psychological changes that give different meanings to life, work, and self (see chapter 11).

One additional stress on careers in midlife is the existence of fiscal events that influence career decisions. For example, in some families midlife is a time of financial strain as children enter college. In other families, a reorientation toward the later years causes concerns to mount about the adequacy of the family's financial resources for retirement (Heald, 1977).

Of particular interest are the factors related to occupational mobility in adulthood. What factors contribute to the likelihood that an individual from a working-class background will take on a middle-class occupation in adulthood? Data from the California Longitudinal Study (Clausen, 1981) allow us to address this question. See box 10.1 for information about the relationship between personality attributes in adolescence and midlife and occupational status at midlife.

BOX 10.1

THE RELATIONSHIP BETWEEN PERSONALITY ATTRIBUTES AND UPWARD OCCUPATIONAL MOBILITY

The California Longitudinal Study compared data collected on the personality attributes of individuals when they were in junior high school with the degree to which the individuals showed upward occupational mobility by the time they reached midlife. Some of the individuals who came from working-class backgrounds ended up with middle-class occupations at midlife. Were there any clues from the personality characteristics of these individuals that were predictive of upward occupational mobility?

John Clausen (1981) found that men who moved from working-class backgrounds into middle-class occupations exceeded their nonmobile peers from comparable backgrounds in dependability, productivity, personal effectiveness, aspiration levels, and intellectual capacities and interests in the junior high school years. The picture that emerged for the working-class mobiles was that of pleasant, dependable, conventional working-class boys who worked productively to get ahead. This contrasted with the more rebellious, self-defensive, less conventional middle-class boys who seemed less pleasant and less dependable. The upwardly mobile working-class boys were also more nurturant and secured more education than their peers who remained in the working class. Further, the upwardly mobile boys continued to increase their intellectual skills and interests as they moved up the occupational ladder. In general, at midlife they more closely resembled men who came from middle-class families than they did their former working-class peers who were employed in blue-collar jobs. Thus a combination of personality characteristics, the socializing influence of higher education, and the requirements of white-collar jobs differentiated these boys from their peers. Furthermore, it was these upwardly mobile men who were the most satisfied with their occupational success.

Work in Late Adulthood

Productivity in old age seems to be the rule rather than the exception. People who have worked hard throughout their lives often continue to do so in old age. Some keep schedules that would exhaust younger workers, and many continue to demonstrate highly creative skills, sometimes outperforming their young and middle adult coworkers. In business and industry, a positive relationship exists between age and productivity that favors the older worker. Younger workers have less commitment to their employers than older workers who have invested a lifetime with a company. Thus, older workers have 20 percent less absenteeism than younger workers. Older workers also have fewer disabling injuries as well as a lower rate of accidents than young adult workers (Sterns, Barrett, and Alexander, 1985). However, fatal injuries or permanently disabling injuries show a U-shaped function across age (Sterns et al., 1985). It appears, then, that the current changes in federal law eliminating nearly all mandatory retirement represent no increased risk to older workers. A rational approach for employers is to encourage older workers to continue in most occupations if they so choose. The limitations of declining health and disease, however, may make it difficult for older workers to maintain occupational roles, even if they would like to continue in their jobs (Sterns et al., 1985). Older workers are at increased risk for certain safety problems and injuries. When comparable accidents occur on the job, younger workers have a greater possibility of recovery and a smaller likelihood of permanent disability. The older worker experiencing severe injury may become disabled, preventing further employment, or may suffer disability, dysfunction, or even death. The consequences of accidents and on-the-job injury are far more serious for older than younger workers (Sterns et al., 1985).

Job Performance and Aging

Research concerning job performance and aging is decidedly unclear (Stagner, 1985). There are equally as many studies suggesting that older people perform as well as or better than younger workers as there are studies reporting an advantage for younger workers. A careful analysis of such conflicting patterns reveals that researchers often employ dramatically different methodologies. Some studies employ objective measures of workers' performance, while others rely on the subjective performance ratings of supervisors. Studies relying on the subjective evaluations of executives and supervisors may contain an inherent negative bias against the older worker. And, perhaps surprisingly, even older workers themselves seem to accept negative stereotypes, frequently believing that they are less effective and productive despite objective evidence to the contrary (Stagner, 1985). Objective assessments reveal a much more positive view of the performance of older workers.

In addition to exploring the developmental course of work in the adult years, it also is important to examine the meaning of work for adults.

THE MEANINGS OF WORK, THE ACHIEVEMENT MOTIVE, AND UNEMPLOYMENT

Virtually all workers view their jobs as a way of earning a living, but as we will see next, work has other meanings as well. In this section we'll examine these meanings, as well as the achievement motive and the implications of unemployment.

The Meanings of Work

Recall from the Imagine section at the beginning of this chapter that a large majority of individuals would continue to work even if they inherited enough money to live without working. Some people view their jobs as a measure of prestige or status,

Table 10.2

THE RELATIONSHIP BETWEEN THE FUNCTIONS AND MEANINGS OF WORK

Work Function	*Work Meanings*
Income	Maintaining a minimum sustenance level
	Achieving some higher level or group standard
Expenditure of time and energy	Something to do
	A way of filling the day or passing time
Identification and status	Source of self-respect
	Way of achieving recognition or respect from others
	Definition of role
Association	Friendship relations
	Peer-group relations
	Subordinate-superordinate relations
Source of meaningful life experience	Gives purpose to life
	Creativity, self-expression
	New experience
	Service to others

From E. Friedmann and R. J. Havighurst, *The Meaning of Work and Retirement.* Copyright © 1954 University of Chicago Press, Chicago, IL.

whereas others may see their jobs as their prime contact with the outside world and a way to develop social relationships beyond the family. The challenge of work varies in each occupation. A salesperson worries about cracking a tough customer; the assembly-line worker complains about the monotony of his job, yet brags that he is the best at his job in the plant; the executive discusses her immense responsibilities in the corporation. But there are some common threads of meaning that run through jobs with diverse functions.

Table 10.2 is a list of some of the meanings individuals assign to their jobs and how these meanings may be linked with more universal functions of work.

In table 10.3, the data from two studies conducted by Robert Havighurst (Friedmann and Havighurst, 1954; Havighurst, McDonald, Perun, and Snow, 1976) reveal that skilled craftpersons and white-collar groups stress the nonfinancial meanings of work to a much greater degree than workers in heavy industry. It may be that the meanings of work described in table 10.3 become more relevant as we move up the occupational and skill ladders.

Next let's look at what many psychologists consider to be an important motive in our culture—achievement—and evaluate its relationship to work.

The Achievement Motive and Work

The **achievement motive** refers to the need to maintain or increase one's competence in activities in which a standard of excellence is involved. If a person is strongly motivated to achieve, he or she will show considerable effort and persistence in succeeding. There is some controversy about how effectively we can measure achievement motivation. The most common strategy has been to use a

Table 10.3

MEANINGS OF WORK[a]

Meanings	Category of Worker (Percent Choosing)						Social Scientists	
	Steelworkers	Miners	PhotoEngravers over 65	Salespersons	Senior Physicians	College Administrators	Male	Female
1. Income for my needs	28	18	11	0	0	4	6	5
2. Routine: Makes time pass	28	19	15	21	15	1	1	1
3a. Self-respect				12	7	14	12	8
3b. Prestige 3a + 3b	16	18	24	11	13	11	14	5
4. Association with peers	15	19	20	20	19	11	10	17
5. Self-expression; new experience; creativity	13	11	30	26	15	27	39	41
6. Service to others; useful	N.D.[b]	16	N.D.	10	32	31	17	22

[a]The interview or questionnaire format varied from one group to another, making strict comparisons questionable. The data are reported in percentages within groups; assuming each respondent to have given his/her favored response.

[b]N.D. = No data

Sources: Friedmann and Havighurst, 1954 (table 26); Havighurst, McDonald, Perun, and Snow, 1976 (table 7.2); and Havighurst, 1982, p. 782.

personality test (for example, the **Thematic Apperception Test** or **TAT**) that requires the individual to tell a story about some pictures likely to elicit achievement themes. However, it seems that the person's story responses about achievement may not correspond closely with actual achievement behavior. Nonetheless, the concept of achievement motivation is thought to be an important part of our orientation toward work.

As a rule, the higher the adult's achievement motivation, the more likely she is to choose work that is characterized by risk and challenge. Starting one's own business would be one example. David McClelland, the architect of much of the early research in the achievement motive (for example, McClelland, Atkinson, Clark, and Lowell, 1953), has suggested the need for achievement-motivation training to improve the performance of small businesses and to increase the employment of minorities (McClelland, Constanian, Regaldo, and Stone, 1978).

What kind of psychological profiles do highly achievement-oriented adults reveal? One effort to investigate this question focused on the interrelationship of work orientation, mastery, and competitiveness (Spence and Helmreich, 1978). The investigators developed self-report procedures to measure separately each of the following motives: (1) *work orientation,* the desire to work hard and do a good job; (2) *mastery,* the preference for difficult and challenging activities; and (3) *competitiveness,* the motivation to beat other people. The highest-achieving adults are consistently high on work and mastery motives but low on the competitive motive. Such a pattern was revealed among college students with the highest grades, business executives with the highest salaries, and scientists who made the most significant contributions (Spence, 1979). Why? It may be that competitiveness can impede achievement, since it is related to **extrinsic motivation** (wanting to outperform one's peers). Some psychologists believe that extrinsic motives can decrease an individual's interest in the activity he is working on and consequently reduce success (Deci, 1975; Lepper and Greene, 1975). By contrast, **intrinsic motivation** (doing something for the pleasure in the activity itself rather than for external rewards such as money or compliments from others) is thought to be an important aspect of work (Deci and Ryan, 1985, 1987).

Currently, Japanese industry is more productive and efficient than American industry in the manufacture of automobiles, steel, appliances, computer chips, and even subway cars (Yankelovich, 1982). Two reasons have been offered for superior Japanese productivity: first, U.S. productivity has declined substantially; and second, the U.S. work ethic has deteriorated badly. In box 10.2 we'll look at the second reason, the work ethic, in greater detail.

Unemployment

Unemployed workers face stress whether the job loss is temporary, cyclical, or permanent. The psychological meaning of job loss may depend on a number of factors, including the individual's personality, social status, and resources. This was the conclusion of an investigation by Terry Buss and F. Stevens Redburn (1983) that focused on how the shutdown of a steel plant in Youngstown, Ohio, affected workers. For example, a fifty-year-old married worker with two adolescent children, a limited education, no transferable job skills, and no pension would not react the same way to the shutdown as a twenty-one-year-old apprentice electrician. Is there any evidence that one type of worker experiences more difficulty with unemployment than others?

In the Buss and Redburn (1983) study, managers and steelworkers were compared in 1978 and 1979. Managers were less affected in 1978, one year after the plant closing. The steelworkers felt more helpless, victimized, and distrustful; they tended to avoid social interaction and were more aggressive. They were also more depressed and showed a greater degree of perceived immobility. Over time, the

---

BOX 10.2

INTRINSIC MOTIVATION, THE WORK ETHIC, AND WORKER PRODUCTIVITY

Sometimes it is argued that people don't work as hard today as they did in the past. But if by the work ethic we mean the sense of intrinsic worth involved in doing the best possible job regardless of financial reward, recent research suggests that the work ethic in the United States is very strong and may be growing even stronger. In a 1980 Gallup poll, though fewer Americans said they enjoy their work now than was true in the past, an overwhelming 88 percent said that it is personally important for them to work hard and do their best on the job (Yankelovich, 1982). Thus, a faulty work ethic may not be responsible for our productivity decline.

Americans seem to believe, however, that people are working less even though the work ethic has not declined. Sixty-nine percent of a national sample of adults feel that workmanship is worse than it was a decade ago, and 63 percent feel that most people do not work as hard as they did ten years ago. Such opinion polls do not prove that we are actually working less effectively than in the past, but it is difficult to ignore such widespread impressions. For example, for a number of years the University of Michigan asked a sample of workers to keep a diary of job activities. Analysis of these diaries suggested that between 1965 and 1975, the amount of time actually spent working declined by more than 10 percent (Yankelovich, 1982).

Why this discrepancy between the work ethic and worker productivity? According to Daniel Yankelovich (1982) the answer is clear. When Gallup's 1980 poll asked workers who would benefit the most from improvement in their productivity, only 9 percent felt that they, the workers, would. A large majority felt that others would benefit most—management, stockholders, or consumers, for example. Thus, in order to increase productivity, we may need to help workers feel that their work is important and that they can derive intrinsic benefits (for example, self-satisfaction) as well as extrinsic rewards (for example, salary) from their work.

The Japanese seem to understand this important point better than Americans. Japanese companies distinguish between the soft factors of production—such as the dedication of the work force—and hard factors—such as technology, capital investment, and development. The managers and executives of Japanese industry believe that the soft factors are just as important as the hard. Yankelovich argues that American business leaders do not have a good understanding of how the soft (intrinsic) and hard (extrinsic) factors are interrelated. Perhaps a better understanding would help increase American productivity.

steelworkers were less trustful and continued to feel immobile, helpless, and stressed. Furthermore, they also reported more health problems and increased their alcohol intake.

In contrast, the managers seemed to cope much better with unemployment. Except for a lack of trust, their psychological profiles either continued to improve or remained the same. However, in the second wave of interviews conducted in 1979, the managers began to report more family problems and a higher tendency to consume over-the-counter drugs. Nevertheless, the steelworkers were still more severely affected by the plant closing, probably because they had fewer job options and less hope for similar employment in the future. Professional managers viewed themselves as likely to become employed in a similar capacity, although not necessarily with the same company. With hope for the future, perhaps more financial resources in the form of savings, and a greater sense of control, managers were less likely to feel helpless, depressed, and distressed. Although unemployment has stressful effects on both laborers and managers, managers seem to handle it better.

Being unemployed in the 1990s may be as bad, or in some cases even worse, than was true in the Great Depression of the 1930s. The unemployed in the 1930s had a strong feeling that their jobs would reopen. Because many of today's workers are replaced by technology, expectations that their jobs will reappear are less realistic. This suggests that many individuals will experience a number of different jobs during their adult years—not a single occupation, as in the past. The tendency for workers to enter and exit several occupations throughout adulthood means that future workers will need to view education as a lifelong process, not something completed during two to four years in young adulthood and marked by the receipt of an associate or baccalaureate degree.

Next let's consider the most dramatic change in the world of work: the increasing participation of women.

WOMEN AND WORK

The most significant change in labor force participation in the past few decades is the huge increase in the employment of women between the ages of twenty and sixty-five, including married women with children. By 1987, 55 percent of females twenty years of age and older were in the labor force, a figure that has increased approximately 14 percent since 1960 (U.S. Department of Labor, 1989).

Although some women are entering previously all-male occupations, the majority of women still have not achieved parity with men in the occupational marketplace. The difference between the average salaries for women and men is still substantial—women earn on average less than 30 percent of the income paid to men (Congressional Caucus for Women's Issues, 1987). While women have entered the work force in greater numbers than ever before, many of the jobs they take are low-paying, low-status positions such as clerical jobs, sales clerk jobs, and part-time positions (Wright, 1982; Jacobs, 1989). In the past few decades, women usually entered the job market while in their forties. They are thus limited in how

One problem women in the work force face is the lack of female mentors.

far they may rise in their occupations, unlike their male counterparts who have a twenty-year head start.

Women who enter careers in middle age are further hampered by the lack of mentors. **Mentors,** readily available to younger adults, are experienced, successful workers about ten to fifteen years older than the fledgling workers they help start on the road to career success. Mentors impart advice, guidance, and perspective through an intense, open, and emotionally close relationship. With males more likely

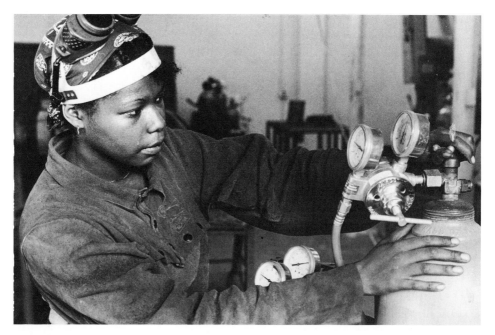

Although women are entering traditionally male occupations in increasing numbers, there are still some fields in which women rarely advance as rapidly as men.

to become managers and executives, many more men than women serve as mentors. As researchers have discovered, when men become mentors to women, the mentoring process is likely to become disrupted by sexual attraction (Roberts and Newton, 1987). Middle-aged women are less likely to have the benefit of a mentor, given their late entry into the work force, and thus are at a distinct disadvantage on the job. Two recent reports document the special problems middle-aged and older women experience in the work force (Herz, 1988; U.S. Department of Labor, 1989). Delaying a full-time career until middle age restricts a woman's options in terms of pensions, Social Security benefits, and retirement. Older women thus may find themselves forced to continue to work well beyond the age they would choose to retire.

Reskin and Roos (1990) provide strong evidence that women are entering many more "traditionally male" occupations. They identified thirty-three occupations where women made significant progress from 1970 to 1980. These occupations included such fields as typesetting, where the rate of increase in women employees was 38.9 percent compared to an overall growth in the nation's work force of 4.6 percent. There are a number of sociocultural factors at work in opening job opportunities for women. According to Reskin and Roos (1990), these factors include the following:

1. Growth in occupations requiring special technical skills (for example, in the computer field) with no readily available pool of trained workers
2. Financial penalties for companies that fail to achieve sex equity in traditionally male-dominated fields (for example, the insurance industry)
3. Technological advances that reduce the importance of physical strength in many jobs (for example, typesetting, which is now largely computer controlled)
4. Training and education of women to increase their employability
5. Legal mandates against sex discrimination that have influenced the attitudes of employers

Despite the appearance of substantial gains in employment for women, we must interpret such progress cautiously. Many of the traditionally male occupations showing dramatic growth in hiring women have been jobs that offer low pay, low status, or less desirable working conditions. Some feminists argue that when traditional male occupations do become open to women, it is usually because these fields are having trouble attracting males to fill the jobs, or because the fields show less earning potential, loss of prestige, and diminished power in society (Reskin and Roos, 1990). The recent surge of women into the field of medicine is a good example. This career is no longer as attractive as it used to be, as evidenced by the more than 50 percent decline in applications to medical school in the past ten years. Doctors cite overregulation, excessive malpractice insurance costs, preset fee schedules, and excessive overhead as factors that restrict the appeal of medicine (Reskin and Roos, 1990). The increase in the percentage of women entering traditionally male occupations must be interpreted cautiously; nearly 50 percent leave such positons within ten years for gender-neutral or traditional female jobs such as teaching or social work (Jacobs, 1989; Reskin and Roos, 1990). There remain many occupations in which males are entrenched, and many fields, such as the corporate world, in which women rarely match men's rate of career advancement.

Work Pathways for Women and Men

Most men begin work in early adulthood and work more or less continuously until they retire, unless they return to school or become unemployed. Unstable patterns of work are much more common among low-income than middle-income workers, although a continuous pattern of work is still the norm among low-income male workers.

Although the majority of college women anticipate having both a career and marriage, many are unrealistic about the difficulties this combination poses (Shields, 1973). The dissatisfaction women feel in combining a family and career seems to result more from role overload than role conflict. Women who cope with time pressures and conflicts by redefining their own and their families' responsibilities are more satisfied than those who attempt to meet all demands alone (Osipow, 1983).

Women who return to higher education or careers after marrying and having children show high levels of commitment. Women who are employed have higher levels of life satisfaction and feelings of adequacy and self-esteem than full-time homemakers (Coleman and Antonucci, 1983). However, the psychological benefits of employment are greater for educated middle-class women and the liabilities greater for lower-class women.

The most common path for both working-class and middle-class women is to work after finishing high school or even college; to marry and cease working when having children; then, when children are a little older, to return to part-time work to supplement the husband's income. As the children begin to leave home, women return to school to update earlier skills or to retrain to better compete for a full-time job. Women in their forties and fifties are relatively free of home and family responsibilities and better able to assume full-time employment.

For professional or career women, the picture is different, since they have committed themselves to maintaining their professional skills. Researchers have identified four career patterns among professional women (Golan, 1986; Paloma, Pendelton, and Garland, 1982). These patterns include: (1) the *regular career pattern,* the woman who pursued her professional training immediately after graduation and who continued to work with no or minimal interruption throughout the years; (2) the *interrupted career pattern,* the woman who began work in the regular pattern but interrupted her career for several years—usually for childrearing—and then went back to work full-time; (3) the *second career pattern,* the woman who started her professional training near or after the time the children left home or after a divorce; and, (4) the *modified second career pattern,* the woman who started her professional training while the children were at home but old enough not to need full-time mothering, then started to work, possibly part-time, until the last child left home, at which time the woman shifted to a full-time career.

We have discussed a number of aspects of work, but as adults, we must not only learn how to work well, we also need to learn how to relax. With the kind of work ethic our country has embraced, it is not surprising to find that many adults view leisure as boring and unnecessary. When elderly people find it necessary to reduce their work loads or retire, they often find themselves with more free time than they know how to handle. Let's look at the nature of leisure in adulthood.

LEISURE

Aristotle recognized the importance of leisure, stressing that we should not only work well but use leisure well. In our society, the idea that leisure is the opposite of work is common. Some see leisure as wasted time and thus antithetical to the basic values of our society: work, motivation, and achievement. John Neulinger (1981), a leading investigator of leisure in the United States, poses this dilemma: Is humanity's ultimate goal a life of leisure? Clearly, most of us would disagree that leisure is what motivates us or is the measure of our life's success. Yet the puzzle remains: What is leisure? How important is it in our lives?

The word **leisure** has usually been used in four different contexts. Burrus-Bammel and Bammel (1985) recognize the *classical* view that leisure is a state of mind. Free time alone is neither a necessary nor sufficient condition for leisure; rather, it is how one chooses to define tasks and situations that is the critical variable (Neulinger, 1981). Thus, some persons define their work as leisure, while others define specific nonwork activities and time away from work as leisure. Generally, the higher one's occupational status and income, the greater the identification with work rather than leisure (Burrus-Bammel and Bammel, 1985; Neulinger, 1981). Viewing work as leisure may also be influenced by the nature of the rewards derived—intrinsic or extrinsic. Intrinsic rewards characterize leisure in that the activity itself is rewarding. Leisure may also depend on *social class.* Historically, only the elite were free to choose and pursue self-selected activities, while those from lower social classes were destined to a life of constant work. Leisure may also lead to particular kinds of *activity* apart from work roles, such as recreation, entertainment, education, or relaxation. Finally, leisure may refer to the availability of *free time* (Burrus-Bammel and Bammel, 1985; Kraus, 1978). For example, our industrial society provides leisure time to retired workers or to employees who choose activities during nonwork hours.

The Nature of Leisure Activities

Ninety years ago the average work week was seventy-one hours. Only in the last several decades has the work week averaged thirty-five to forty hours. We have even created flextime so that workers can complete their week's work without being on the job from 9:00–5:00 P.M. For example, some industries give employees the option of working twelve-hour shifts for three consecutive days with the next four days off. Others let employees set the length of their work days as long as they work a specific minimum number of hours each week. Other companies allow employees to take leaves without pay or to choose part-time employment for significant parts of the year. Workers with such choices have more free time than cohorts in previous generations did. Are we experiencing a growth in leisure activities?

The Role of Television

Within the last twenty-five years have social scientists devoted much time to investigating the activities that adults pursue in their leisure. One emerging trend is the increasing reliance on television over other forms of mass media as a key form of leisure and entertainment (Pepper, 1976). Television viewing has partially displaced other leisure activities and consistently appears as one of the most popular leisure choices (Burrus-Bammel and Bammel, 1985). Table 10.4 is a list of the rankings of preferred leisure-time activities for a representative group of community-dwelling elderly adults (McAvoy, 1979).

It is interesting that a list of preferred leisure activities (see table 10.4) may not reflect how older adults actually spend their leisure time. McAvoy (1979), for

Table 10.4

LEISURE-TIME ACTIVITIES OF ELDERLY COMMUNITY-RESIDING ADULTS

Category	*Rank*
Visiting friends	1
Watching television	2
Reading	3
Gardening	4
Hobbies	5
Driving	6
Walking	7
Indoor games	8
Organization and club meetings	9
Caring for animals	10

From L. McAvoy, "The Leisure Preferences, Problems, and Needs of the Elderly" in *Journal of Leisure Research*, 11:40–47. Copyright © 1979 National Recreation and Park Association, Alexandria, VA.

instance, reported that older adults actually preferred other activities, including travel, hobbies, gardening, and driving for pleasure, to watching television. Yet television watching remains the most common leisure activity for older adults next to visiting friends (Moss and Lawton, 1982). The typical viewing time for older adults is 3.3 hours each day, or over 23 hours per week.

Recent surveys suggest there are few realistic portrayals of aging and older adults on most television programs (Burrus-Bammel and Bammel, 1985). Television presents a highly distorted view of the elderly. Most programs portray older adults living in middle-class settings, without minority representation, free from health concerns, and able to maintain considerable freedom and independence and an active life-style (see box 10.3). Television perpetuates stereotypes of how people age in our society and ignores the problems of loneliness, poverty, health, and dependence. By ignoring the diversity of ways in which people grow old and the special problems of widows or minorities, television may be creating in older people the sense that their own aging is largely negative in comparison to what they see.

The Therapeutic Benefits of Pets

Not all older adults are attracted to television. Many other leisure activities, such as the routine care of pets, become increasingly important as people grow older. For the widowed or single individual, pets can play a therapeutic role, helping them organize each day (Soares, 1985). Routine pet care may also help to increase the number of interactions between the pet owner and other people (Brickel, 1980–1981). Ory and Goldberg (1983) reported that among married older women (sixty-seven to seventy-five years of age), those with strong attachments to pets were happier than those with weaker attachments or with no pets. Kidd and Feldman (1981) also reported that compared to those without pets, older pet owners (sixty-five to eighty-seven years of age) scored higher on measures of happiness, self-confidence, responsibility, and dependability.

Pets may help promote health, emotional well-being, and responsiveness among older adults.

BOX 10.3

PRIME TIME WOMEN

Recently the National Commission on Working Women published an analysis of the image of older women portrayed in television programming (Steenland, 1987). Women over fifty comprise a significant segment of our society, yet on television, the diversity of their experience and living conditions is glossed over in convenient stereotypes. Television portrays older women as having sufficient resources (economic, social, physical mobility, and health) to indulge in leisure pursuits. The image of older women portrayed on television presents a distorted and biased image of females in our society and their individual aging.

Let's examine the stereotypes of aging in our society and try to better understand how television contributes to ageist attitudes. First, consider some basic census data:

1. Among women fifty years of age and older, 13 percent live at or below poverty levels.
2. Among women sixty-five years of age and older, 80 percent currently receive no pension.
3. The normative age for widowhood is fifty-six years—an age which does not qualify a widow for either Social Security or Medicare.
4. Women over age sixty-five represent 71 percent of the elderly living at or below poverty and 80 percent of the elderly living alone.

Now, let's examine the image of the older women (fifty years of age or more) on prime time television. Until the 1970s, the image of the older woman was clear: either she was nonexistent, invisible, or outnumbered significantly by younger characters. The data show that despite the presence of Granny on the Beverly Hillbillies, Maude, and Edith Bunker on All in the Family, 91 percent of all older characters on television were male. In the late 1970s, the Screen Actors Guild reported a study showing a positive correlation between age and increasing unemployment rates for actresses. You may recall the characters of older women on TV who were largely "powerless, befuddled, inflexible, and feeble," as well as devoid of sexuality, romance, substance, and power.

Currently the situation has apparently improved with older women now constituting 20 percent of all the women characters on television. Just as earlier older female images were largely negative, today's older television personalities are portrayed in similarly distorted, although positive, ways. The older female character is "powerful, creative, appealing and affluent" (Steenland, 1987). In the spring of 1986 there were nineteen female characters over the age of fifty on prime time television; their demographic characteristics are presented in box table 10.1 along with comparable figures for older women nationwide.

For older women such as those on Dynasty; Facts of Life; Golden Girls; Hotel; Knots Landing; Murder, She Wrote; Who's the Boss; and other programs "never has life been so good" (Steenland, 1987). The women are predominantly wealthy or middle-class; their power, beauty, money, active life-styles, and need for adventure draw men to them. They remain independent, creative, mobile, and self-sufficient. The ability of viewers to differentiate age among the television characters is particularly hampered since phys-

Box Table 10.1
A Comparison of Prime Time Older Women and Their Real-Life Counterparts

	Prime Time Older Women	*National Statistics on Older Women*
Age (50+)	20 percent of all women characters	38 percent of all women
Marital status	68 percent widowed	32 percent widowed
	16 percent divorced	6 percent divorced
	16 percent married	52 percent married
Economic status	26 percent millionaires	0.2 percent income $75,000+
	68 percent middle class	11 percent income $20,000+
	5 percent working class	76 percent income $5,000–$20,000
	0 percent poor	13 percent poor
Employment	57 percent employed	48 percent employed
	20 percent own corporation	2 percent own corporation
	80 percent managers or professionals	23 percent managers or professionals
Race	89 percent White	89 percent White
	11 percent Black	9 percent Black
	0 percent Asian	1 percent Asian
	0 percent Hispanic	1 percent Hispanic

ical age differences are nonexistent and irrelevant. Steenland notes the physically active, youthful, and vibrant appearance of prime time characters regardless of whether they are fifty or seventy-five. And in the television culture, as many opportunities for older women exist as for women half their age (Steenland, 1987). Only Golden Girls has addressed some of the unique problems of older women, faced the conflicts of widowhood and death, presented some of the economic concerns of women in our society (for example, the four central characters pool their resources to meet the pressures of financial obligations), and made age itself an important variable.

With a few exceptions, television presents a distorted view of aging. The elderly are free from discrimination, free from the ageist attitudes which diminish a woman's inherent worth as she grows older, free from economic hardships, and, through the efforts of screenwriters and make-up specialists, free from the physical changes, losses, and health concerns that are realities for every aging woman! Older women who watch prime time characters on television must surely wonder, "What in the world is wrong with me?"

Brickel (1980–1981, 1985) notes that pets may help to meet the dependency needs and increase the responsiveness of the elderly. Pets also provide a concrete anchor for those whose lives have undergone major change or loss (Brickel, 1985). Pets may even serve as family substitutes, providing comfort and support to those experiencing the negative consequences of aging: death of loved ones, sickness, and feelings of loneliness (Brickel, 1985). Some research suggests that the ability to care humanely for pets gives meaning, purpose, and a sense of control over one's environment for the elderly (Banzinger and Roush, 1983). And caring for pets provides a sense of independence for elderly adults who can take care of something rather than be taken care of by others (Banzinger and Roush, 1983). This view is further echoed by James, James, and Smith (1984) who note the reciprocity involved in pet care leads elderly adults to avoid becoming wholly dependent on others. Pets have also been shown to have positive health benefits in other areas (National Institute of Health, 1988). Friedmann, Kacher, Lynch, and Thomas (1980) indicated that owning a pet was the best predictor of survival one year after leaving a coronary care unit in the hospital. Of fifty-three pet owners, only 6 percent died within one year, while of twenty-eight non-pet owners, 28 percent died within the same period. Pets provided a regularity and predictability in routine care which gave a sense of order to these heart attack patients' lives. Even the presence of minimal-care pets such as goldfish have been reported to help reduce their owners' blood pressure, decrease their sense of anxiety, and increase their leisure satisfaction (Riddick, 1985).

Among the institutionalized elderly, pets can produce similar benefits (National Institute of Health, 1988). For severely depressed residents, pets reduce anxiety, elicit responses (such as care and stroking) when the human environment has been rejected, provide physical reassurance, and help maintain reality, even among those who are terminally ill (Brickel, 1982, 1985; Muschel, 1984). In nursing homes, pet visitations two or three times each week helped break the cycle created by institutionalization: helplessness, hopelessness, dependency, and despair. Some institutions have maintained cats or dogs for a considerable time for this purpose. Others have developed similar programs using tropical fish, or feeders that attract wild birds (Banzinger and Roush, 1983). In these pet therapy programs, investigators have demonstrated that institutionalized older people become less depressed, become more communicative, and evidence higher rates of survival than controls who do not participate in such programs (Langer and Rodin, 1976; National Institute of Health, 1988).

Sports Participation

Sports play an extremely important role in the leisure activities of Americans, either through direct participation or vicariously through attending sports events, watching television, reading newspapers or magazines, discussing sports with friends, and so forth. Active participation in physical sports declines somewhat with increasing age (Ostrow, 1980). Thus, in old age some individuals need to make adjustments in sports activities, reducing the intensity but not necessarily the frequency of their participation (Burrus-Bammel and Bammel, 1985; Schmitz-Secherzer, 1976). For example, rather than jogging five miles each day, older adults may reduce the length of their run, the frequency of their run, or both. Research suggests that the more physically active individuals have been in young adulthood and middle age, the more likely they will continue to be involved in physical activities in old age (Bortz, 1980).

We have seen in earlier chapters, of course, that regular physical activity is one successful way to slow down aging. Physical exercise can improve overall fitness, endurance, muscle tone, flexibility, strength, cardiac output, and respiratory efficiency, no matter what age we begin (Burrus-Bammel and Bammel, 1985). It is difficult for both younger and older people who have remained sedentary to turn over a new leaf. Thus, most older people tend to enjoy leisure activities they have pursued over most of their adult lives and rarely turn to new activities (Schmitz-Scherzer, 1976). One critical feature of successful aging is to make adjustments within physically demanding activities (Burrus-Bammel and Bammel, 1985). Sports activities allow older adults to escape the rigors and pressures of everyday life, even if only for a few hours per week.

Leisure at Midlife

Roger Gould (1978) believes that middle-age is a time of questioning how time should be spent and of reassessing priorities. Midlife seems to be a time when adults want more freedom and the opportunity to express their individuality.

Leisure may be a particularly important aspect of middle adulthood because of the many changes experienced at this point in development: physical changes, changes in relationships with spouse and children, changes in self-knowledge, and career changes. With college expenses ended, mortgages paid off, and women embarking on careers, couples find themselves with more spendable income, more free time, and more opportunity for leisure. For many people, midlife is the first time in their adult lives that they have the opportunity to diversify their leisure interests. Neulinger (1981), in *The Psychology of Leisure,* reminds us that younger adults are more constrained by social and financial pressures and family obligations than middle-aged adults. In midlife adults may select from a number of intrinsically interesting, exciting, and enjoyable leisure activities. Their participation is largely on their terms, at their pace, and at times they select. Younger adults, by contrast, must often carefully program their leisure activities to match social convention and center them around the "right" people for social and/or career success.

Adults at midlife need to start preparing both financially and psychologically for retirement. Constructive and fulfilling leisure activities in middle adulthood are important to this preparation. Leisure activities that can be continued at some level into retirement help ease the transition.

Leisure Activities in Retirement

What do people do with their time when they retire? Studies reveal that they engage in many more activities with the increase in free time (Peppers, 1976). Some of these activities are listed in table 10.5, which summarizes data from five different investigations of leisure activities in retirement (Harris, 1976; McAvoy, 1979; Nystrom, 1974; Roadburg, 1981; Schmitz-Secherzer, 1979). The most common leisure activities chosen by elderly retirees were reading or writing, television, arts and crafts, games, walking, visiting family and friends, physical activity, gardening, travel or camping, organization and club activities, and outings. Of all the data emerging on older people's retirement activities, perhaps the most interesting are those suggesting that, compared to a decade ago, older people today are choosing activities far more like those of people twenty years younger than themselves (Horn and Meer, 1987).

Between the ages of sixty and seventy, many people seem to feel it is time to retire from their occupations. For a person whose job is the central focus of life, retirement can be a difficult and unwelcome experience. Others relish their new freedom and fill their lives with enjoyable leisure activities. One goal for our society is to make the retirement process flexible enough to meet the needs of people with a variety of attitudes toward work (Havighurst, 1982).

RETIREMENT

In the early part of this century, most individuals did not have a choice between work and retirement. The Social Security system in 1935 established benefits to workers who retired at the age of sixty-five; most private pension plans have adopted a comparable age. Social Security, now involving over 90 percent of our nation's work force, was originally designed to *supplement* a worker's personal savings and investments for retirement (Parnes, Crowley, Haurin, Less, Morgan, Mott, and Nestal, 1985). However, for many workers Social Security income has become their only means of support. In 1987, a retired worker with a spouse received $876 per month in benefits from Social Security. Reduced benefits may begin as early as age sixty-two with provision for total disability benefits at any age (Parnes et al., 1985).

The development of a retirement option for older workers is a late-twentieth-century phenomenon. It has emerged for two basic reasons: (1) a strong industrial economy that provides sufficient funds to support the retirement of older workers and, (2) institutionalization of retirement nationwide through public and private pension systems (Palmore, Burchett, Fillenbaum, George, and Wallman, 1985). Today's workers will spend nearly 10 to 15 percent of their total lives in retirement. In 1967, the Age Discrimination Employment Act (ADEA) made it federal policy to prohibit firing, forcibly retiring, or failing to hire workers strictly on the basis of age. In 1978, Congress further extended the mandatory retirement age from sixty-five to seventy in business, industry, and the federal government. In 1986, legislation banned mandatory retirement in all but a few specific occupations (Church et

Table 10.5

A SYNTHESIS OF RESEARCH ON LEISURE PARTICIPATION

Activities	*A*	*B*	*C*	*D*	*E*	*(PERCENTAGES)*
Reading/writing	37	36	55	67	51	
Televison	28	36	89	69	78	
Arts/crafts	26	26	40	46	37	
Cards/games	23	—	56	29	16	
Walking	16	25	—	31	47	
Visiting family/friends	19	47	63	75	56	
Physical activity	10	3	—	—	—	
Gardening	9	39	40	49	27	
Travel/camping	19	—	—	—	29	
Organizations/clubs	2	17	51	29	8	
Outings/driving	9	—	66	32	29	
N	245	2797	65	540	?	

A Roadburg, 1981

B Harris, 1976

C Nystrom, 1974

D McAvoy, 1979

E Schmitz-Secherzer, 1979

Reprinted by permission of *The Gerontologist,* 21, no. 2:142–145, 1981.

al., 1988). These **Bona Fide Occupational Qualifications (BFOQ)** permit mandatory retirement only by demonstrating that *all* workers in a specific job classification, because of age, could not continue to function safely and efficiently (Church et al., 1988). Some of the jobs covered by the Bona Fide Occupational Qualifications include police officers, firefighters, airline pilots, and foreign service officers (the latter having to retire at age sixty because of the hardship and difficulty they meet in "the rigors of overseas duty"). Employers may not fire older workers who have seniority and higher salaries just to save money. The courts, in vigorously defending workers' rights not to suffer age discrimination, have carefully evaluated the justifications made by employers claiming mandatory retirement in BFOQ jobs (see box 10.4). With mandatory retirement in our country and others rapidly disappearing, Belbin (1983) suggests that older individuals will be confronted with the decision of when to retire rather than being forced into retirement.

In the next section, we'll look at factors related to retirement and the different phases that people go through when they retire.

Factors Related to Retirement

A number of factors influence the decision to retire, including financial security, health status, attitude toward work, job satisfaction, and personal interests (Palmore et al., 1985). It is not uncommon for an individual to retire from one job, become restless, and then pursue another job. Elderly women, more than men, are likely

---

BOX 10.4

POLICE OFFICERS AND MANDATORY RETIREMENT: APPLICATION OF THE BONA FIDE OCCUPATIONAL QUALIFICATION

In some jobs, there are compelling reasons for mandatory or forced retirement at specific ages. Such designated jobs are called positions of Bona Fide Occupational Qualification (BFOQ). Employers must show, if challenged in court, that a BFOQ job cannot be handled safely and efficiently by older workers. Church et al. (1988) reviewed some of the challenges which have proven successful in demonstrating age discrimination (for example, when the job was not BFOQ and employers forced retirement to save the company money). Age discrimination is also evidenced by factors such as selective dismissal of or failure to hire qualified older workers. The work of police officers is particularly enlightening in helping us see what the courts accept as a valid BFOQ occupation.

In one case, *Equal Employment Opportunity Commission v. Missouri State Highway Patrol* (748 F.2d 447 1984), an officer challenged the policy mandating forced retirement at age sixty for all officers. The courts ruled in favor of the highway patrol department policy (BFOQ) based on evidence that at age sixty, most individuals would not be physically able to keep up with the demanding routine of a police officer. The safety of the public might be jeopardized by continuing to employ police officers over this age. Nearly 90 percent of older police officers, according to experts, would not have the aerobic capacities needed to handle standard emergency situations typically encountered on the job. Further, older officers would be at a disadvantage in terms of vision, auditory response, reaction time, physical endurance, and physical strength. And any person over the age of sixty would be far more at risk for heart attack. The importance of individual differences in such global descriptions was noted in the record; that is, some sixty-year-olds are physically fit and capable of meeting the demands of the Highway

---

to continue to look for work in old age (Herz, 1988; U.S. Department of Labor, 1989). For example, Frank Baird, a seventy-two-year-old motel manager, found that he could not tolerate the inactivity of retirement:

> "They gave me a gold watch—a beautiful thing—six months pay, a new car, and a fabulous pension," Baird explained. "We spent three months traveling, playing golf, fishing, and getting lazy. At first, I thought it was great. You know, for years you look forward to the freedom, the leisure time, the no hassles. But let me tell you, friend, it gets old. After six months I was bored stiff, and my wife, she was getting fed up too. You know, she had her friends and her activities and didn't need me underfoot. Then I found this job, and it's great. I love it! New people, people from all over, and I am able to make their stay a little more pleasant. Don't ever retire, friend, if you've got a job, stick with it.

Patrol officer. However, the court accepted the difficulty faced by the Highway Patrol in developing, utilizing, and interpreting a battery of tests to measure physical abilities to help them screen which of the sixty-year olds could remain on the job. The policy was justifiable, and the selected age was consistent with expert opinion on the specific behavioral demands and physical requirements of the job of a police officer.

The right of police departments to maintain mandatory retirement policies at similar or even younger ages has been further supported by the courts. A state police officer challenged the right of the Commonwealth of Massachusetts to force his retirement at age fifty [*Massachusetts Board of Retirement* v. Murgia (427 US 307, 1976)]. The Supreme Court accepted the retirement policy of Massachusetts as "rationally" based on the performance demands of the job of a police officer, despite the fact that the officer currently was in excellent health, able to handle the requirements of the job on all dimensions, and faced serious psychological and economic hardships due to forced retirement at such a young age. In a similar case, *Equal Employment Opportunity Commission* v. *Commonwealth of Pennsylvania* (645 F. Supp. 1545, 186), the court accepted that the demanding job of police officer made mandatory retirement throughout the department appropriate and necessary. All officers had to be prepared to respond to crises, even though such crises materialized infrequently, if at all, for most of the police force. However, the demands that routinely emerged and presented obvious difficulties for older officers included "assisting stranded motorists in snowstorms, pushing disabled vehicles off the roadway, chasing suspects on foot, chasing suspects by vehicle at speeds of seventy to eighty miles per hour, subduing suspects, and removing victims of accidents from wrecked vehicles." (cited in Church et al., 1988, p. 102)

Retirement is for the birds. Unless you're a lazy bird." (Van Hoose and Worth, 1982, p. 317)

Still, there are many individuals who look forward to retirement and relish the time when they will no longer have to work long hours. The feelings of Katy Adams, a retired teacher, express this sentiment:

"I don't feel any great loss at all. No, no. I taught math and science for thirty-one years, and if I hadn't taken time out to raise two daughters, I would have made it forty. I loved every minute of it, but now it is time to take a rest. After all that time I have earned it, don't you think? Why would I want to go on teaching? I have my retirement, my insurance, and my health. Now I just want to enjoy it." (Van Hoose and Worth, 1982, p. 317)

This woman's decision to retire may have been influenced by a number of factors such as finances, health status, job satisfaction, and personal interests.

Many older people continue to work. In fact, a growing segment of our nation's work force is comprised of the elderly (Herz, 1988). When given a choice, most people elect to retire as soon as they can afford it (U.S. Department of Labor, 1989). More than 50 percent of those initially filing for Social Security retirement benefits in 1987 were under sixty-five years of age. And nearly 67 percent of federal government employees choose to retire prior to age sixty-two (U.S. Department of Labor, 1989). One of the reasons may be that the U.S. Civil Service Commission has encouraged earlier retirement through rules that allow employees to retire after twenty-five years of service. Some industrial firms and labor organizations have developed programs that allow employees to retire when they are in their mid-fifties. Another reason many people choose to retire is the planning and financial preparation they devote to their retirement. Tax-deferred savings programs, employer pension programs, and personal investments help workers plan to retire. Most people realize the limitations of relying solely on Social Security benefits to meet all their retirement needs. *Thus, today, we note two contrasting trends: an increase in the number of older people in the work force and an increase in the number of people choosing early retirement.* It appears that older women, who comprise an increasing segment of the aging population, are responsible for the increase of elderly people in the labor market. And at the same time, the number of employed males aged sixty-five or older has steadily declined as they elect early retirement (Herz, 1988).

According to Palmore, George, and Fillenbaum (1982), early retirement at ages under sixty-five is influenced strongly by subjective factors such as self-perceptions of health, attitudes toward work and retirement, and perception of the adequacy of one's retirement income. Studies show that those who voluntarily leave their careers early for reasons other than ill health enjoy their retirement as long as they have made adequate preparation for their financial needs (Parnes et al., 1985). Some social scientists believe that many people go through a series of phases before and during retirement. One such perspective has been developed by Robert Atchley (1976, 1983). Atchley (1983) reports that people's attitudes toward retirement are generally positive regardless of sex or age. The only group who seem somewhat less enthusiastic about retirement are those who would like to work but because of other factors (forced retirement, adverse labor market, financial needs, or poor health) cannot maintain their jobs (Atchley, 1983; Parnes et al., 1985).

Phases of Retirement

Atchley (1976) initially suggested that many people go through seven phases of retirement: remote, near, honeymoon, disenchantment, reorientation, stability, and termination. The sequence of these phases is shown in figure 10.3.

Most individuals begin work with the vague belief that they will enjoy the fruits of their labor at some point in the distant future. In this *remote phase* of retirement, most people do virtually nothing to prepare themselves for retirement. As they age toward possible retirement, they often deny that they will eventually quit working.

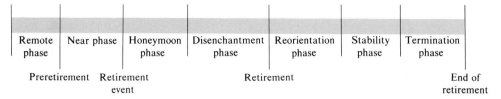

Figure 10.3   Seven phases of retirement.

Only when workers reach the *near phase* do they sometimes participate in preretirement programs. Preretirement planning programs help workers make the transition to retirement and are becoming more common in American businesses. Preretirement programs may help individuals decide when they should retire by familiarizing them with the benefits and pensions they can expect to receive. These programs also discuss more comprehensive issues, such as physical and mental health. Only about 10 percent of the labor force is involved in such preretirement programs, and these programs have a decided emphasis on benefits, pensions, and health insurance. In one investigation (Atchley, 1976), individuals who had participated in a retirement preparation program had higher retirement incomes, engaged in more activities after retirement, and held fewer stereotyped beliefs about retirement than their counterparts who did not participate in a preretirement program.

As indicated in figure 10.3, there are five remaining phases after retirement in this model of the retirement process. Of course, not all people go through all of these phases, nor do they necessarily follow them in the order indicated in the figure. How significant each phase is in the retired person's adjustment depends upon such factors as his or her preretirement expectations and the reality of retirement in terms of money, available options, and the ability to make decisions (Williamson, Munley, and Evans, 1980).

It is not unusual for people to initially feel euphoric during the *honeymoon phase* just after their retirement. They may be able to do many things they never had time for before, and they may derive considerable pleasure from leisure activities. However, people who are forced to retire, or who retire because they are angry about their jobs, are less likely to experience the positive aspects of this phase of retirement. The honeymoon phase eventually gives way to a routine. If the routine is satisfying, adjustment to retirement is usually successful. Those whose life-styles did not entirely revolve around their jobs before retirement are usually able to make the retirement adjustment and develop a satisfying routine more easily than those who did not develop leisure activities during their working years.

Even individuals who initially experience retirement as a honeymoon usually feel some form of letdown or, in some cases, feelings of depression. Preretirement fantasies about the retirement years may be unrealistic. Atchley calls this the *disenchantment phase*. For some, the disenchantment with retirement centers on the experience of loss; loss of power, prestige, status, income, and purpose. Many retired persons also experience the loss of specific work roles (and their own importance) as well as the loss of routine and work-related friendships (Jacobs, 1989).

At some point, most individuals who become disenchanted with retirement begin to reason realistically about how to successfully cope with it. The major purpose of this *reorientation phase* is to explore, evaluate, and make some decisions about the type of life-style that will likely lead to life satisfaction during retirement.

The *stability phase* of retirement is attained when individuals decide upon a set of criteria for evaluating choices in retirement and how they will perform once they have made these choices. For some, this phase may occur after the honeymoon phase, whereas for others the transition is slower and more difficult.

According to Atchley (1983), at some point the retirement role loses its significance and relevance in the eyes of the older person. The autonomy and self-sufficiency developed in the stable phase may begin to give way to dependency on others, both physically and economically. This final phase of retirement is called the *termination phase.*

Because people retire at different ages and for a variety of reasons, there is no immutable timing or sequencing to the seven phases of the retirement process described by Atchley. Some experts question the need for a phase approach. They see retirement, like other life transitions, as a lengthy process of adjustment. Ekerdt, Bosse, and Levkoff (1985), for example, evaluated the adjustment of 293 men to retirement over a three-year period. Examination of life satisfaction and leisure activities at six-month intervals revealed little support for a phase approach to retirement. The men simply took different amounts of time to examine and make choices about this new era in their life. The authors suggest that retirement is best conceptualized as a process of adjustment.

Retirement and Life-Styles

Other experts studying retirement consider the importance of factors such as previous life-style or the importance of work for the individual. Hornstein and Wapner (1985), for instance, questioned whether all individuals experience retirement in the same fashion suggested by phase theorists such as Atchley. Through in-depth interviews of twenty-four individuals obtained one month prior to and six to eight months following retirement, Hornstein and Wapner identified four distinctive retirement styles. The first style they called *transition to old age.* Individuals who typified this style felt that retirement was a time to disengage or wind down rather than undertake new activities. One respondent reported it was too late to create new hobbies or interests: "If you've never been a gardener, you're not going to become one now." The adults in this group believed that retirement marked a transition to old age, much like the rites of passage marked transitions at other periods of development. For them, retirement was the shedding of pressure-filled work roles and the adoption of a restful and enjoyable life-style as they moved into old age.

A second style, the *new beginning,* viewed retirement as a welcome opportunity; a chance to live life on one's own terms and to have the freedom to devote time and energy to oneself. For individuals in this group, retirement was marked by feelings of renewal, revitalization, enthusiasm, and increased vigor. These individuals responded to retirement enthusiastically: "It's a whole new life. There's so much I want to do that I almost don't know where to start." People with this style view the future positively as a time to gain control over long-overdue goals and pleasures (hobbies, interests, volunteerism, and so on) and to become the person they always wanted to be. Retirement for these individuals is a new beginning and wholly unconnected to becoming old.

A third style was that of *continuation.* For individuals who adopted this style, retirement carried no major personal impact. These adults were able to continue working, despite having retired. They either changed positions, shifted careers, or devoted greater time to a special skill, hobby, or interest. Thus, work remained a central organizer in their life structure because they voluntarily chose this activity. These individuals differentiated preretirement and retirement not by activity, but by the lessened pace and intensity of the work role. Retirement for people with this style was essentially a nonevent that signified neither an end nor a beginning.

The last retirement style, *imposed disruption,* represented a significant role loss. The people with this style saw retirement in largely negative terms (loss of work, the inability to continue achievement). For the individuals representing this style, work was a role in which they had invested significant parts of their self-identity; without work, a crucial part of their identity was terminated. Although in time retirement becomes a period in which substitute activities evolve, an underlying sense of frustration and loss remains. Nothing seems to replace work for these individuals and retirement is never truly accepted well. Table 10.6 summarizes these four unique styles of adapting to retirement. Hornstein and Wapner (1985) help us see that the transition to retirement depends on a person's previous orientations to work, to life, and to self.

Braithwaite, Gibson, and Bosly-Craft (1986) have also examined the differential styles of adjusting to retirement. Their research focused on the elderly who really never come to terms with their retirement and continue to have problems coping. Those poorly adjusted to retirement generally showed (1) poor health, (2) negative attitudes toward retirement, (3) difficulty making transitions and adjustments throughout the life span, and/or (4) inability to confront job loss. The first two traits predicted retirements characterized by low levels of activity and involvement, physical and mental health problems, insufficient income, and low levels of life satisfaction. The latter two traits were problems for the short-term only; these individuals usually made more adaptive responses to retirement over time.

Adjustment to Retirement: Activities and Life-Styles

There is evidence that no single life-style will bring about a successful adjustment to retirement. However, it is important that retirees feel that they have choice and control in the way they experience retirement. The less choices a person perceives, the greater the dissatisfaction with retirement. If social contacts are sought and maintained, individuals in retirement will be happy. On the other hand, some retirees derive considerable pleasure from having the freedom to spend time alone. Larson, Zuzanek, and Mannel (1985) reported that among retired persons 50 percent of the waking day was spent alone. Even among married couples in retirement, 40 percent of the waking day was spent in solitude. The investigators hypothesize that the social needs of some older individuals are less intense than those of younger people, since time spent alone was not viewed negatively by the retirees themselves.

In contrast, a study by Hooker and Ventis (1984) reported that satisfaction with retirement among thirty-four men and forty-two women, all between the ages of fifty-three and eighty-eight, was directly proportional to the total number of activities in which they were involved. Moreover, when such activities were perceived by retirees to be "useful," satisfaction in retirement was enhanced. Hooker and Ventis provide support for the **busy ethic,** a theory of successful retirement developed by Ekerdt (1986). Ekerdt believes that in retirement individuals must transfer or channel the work ethic into productive, useful activities. By keeping busy, retirees remain productive within the freedom provided by retirement. Among the most common busy activities are community service, skill development and enhancement, profitable hobbies, and education. The retiree retains the feeling of being useful and a contributing part of society. In addition, these activities provide justification for taking time out for oneself (for example, scheduling vacations between volunteer activities or resting after a morning of running errands for a friend). The busy ethic also provides a way to distance oneself from the effects of aging. And, Ekerdt suggests, through the busy ethic, retirees are viewed as still a valuable and contributing part of society. Of course, not all retirees adhere to this ethic (see, for example, Hornstein and Wapner, 1985), nor should they.

Adjustment to Retirement: Predictive Factors

Who adjusts best to retirement? Overall, older adults who adjust best to retirement are healthy, have adequate incomes, are active, are well educated, have extended social networks including both family and friends, and usually were more satisfied with their lives before they retired (Palmore et al., 1985). Older adults with inadequate incomes, poor health, and other stresses that occur at the same time as retirement, such as the death of a spouse, have the most difficult time adjusting to retirement (Stull and Hatch, 1984). Only about 15 percent of older people have major difficulties adjusting to retirement.

Research by Toni Calasanti (1988) focused on the importance of the type of job held by workers in determining their adjustment to retirement. In the past, most investigators were concerned with assessing the degree to which blue-collar versus white-collar workers adjusted to retirement. Today, however, there seems to be a

Table 10.6

DIMENSIONS OF THE FOUR MODES OF ADAPTATION TO RETIREMENT

Dimension	Group 1—Transition to Old Age	Group 2—New Beginning	Group 3—Continuation	Group 4—Imposed Disruption
Significance or central meaning of retirement	End of working life; time to slow down; beginning of transition to last phase of life (old age)	Beginning of new phase of life; time to live in accordance with *own* needs, not those of others	No major significance except as time to continue preretirement activities in more self-chosen way	Loss of most highly valued activity; period of frustration, lack of focus
Style of making the transition itself	Gradual disengagement from work; transition taken as very meaningful	Rapid disengagement from work; desire to plunge ahead into retirement itself	Minimal sense of transition	Abrupt break with work; "in shock," at a loss for how to proceed
Dominant emotions during the transition period	Reflectiveness; introspection	Excitement; enthusiasm; revitalization; sense of freedom	Quiet satisfaction	Depression; anger; powerlessness
Attitude toward work	Enjoyable but pressured; often frustrating in recent years	In many cases, unsatisfying; in others, satisfying but pressured and draining	Either highly valued and satisfying or not very meaningful, no real investment	Main source of self-definition and identity; allowed time to actualize valued parts of self
Relation of retirement to sense of self	No change—continuity of self before and after	Retirement allows for birth of new part of self	No change—continuity of self before and after	Retirement represents loss of valued part of self
Orientation toward time	Past is satisfying but over; future is constricted; focus is on present	Relief that past is over; future is expanding, filled with opportunity; focus is on actualization of future in present	Future is expanding but based on past; focus is on continuing past in present and future	Past is highly valued; future is constricted; present is "a void," focus is on maintaining past in the present
Extent of change in overall life focus	Preretirement focus abandoned	Preretirement focus replaced with new focus	Preretirement focus maintained in slightly changed form	Attempt to maintain preretirement focus despite changed circumstances
General level of activity (postretirement)	Tired, less energy than before; generally passive	Highly active, energetic	Moderately active; no real change	Largely immobilized (in a psychological sense); passive, low activity

Nature of retirement goals and activities	No clear sense of direction; too late to start major new projects; mainly continuation on diminished level of earlier activities and hobbies in satisfying way	Either clearly articulated specific goals for new projects and activities or movement toward articulation of such goals	Clearly articulated goals but no new activities; previously valued activities continued in generally same form	Some goals, but not experienced as satisfying; frustrated attempt to find activities to substitute for work; mainly involved with daily activities, hobbies in nonsatisfying way
Attitude toward old age	Inevitable next stage of life; no choice but to accept it	Denial of connection between retirement and old age; no sense of identification with "old people," "retirees"; feel younger, not older	No particular feelings about it; no clear sense of connection between retirement and old age	Feel as if others see them as old; feel they are not old and should be working; apprehension about idea that retirement is connected to old age

From G. A. Hornstein and S. Wapner. "Modes of Experiencing and Adapting to Retirement" in *International Journal of Aging and Human Development*, 21 (4):302–303, 1985.

greater variation in salary *within* blue- and white-collar groups of workers than *between* these groups. Also, the distinction between white- and blue-collar jobs has become blurred. White-collar workers, for example, possess less authority and perform more routinized jobs than they did in the past; while the opposite trends have been observed for blue-collar workers.

Calasanti (1988) suggests that to best understand retirement, researchers should begin with the *dual economic model.* This model proposes the existence of two types of firms: *core firms* and *peripheral firms.* Core firms are large and monopolistic. They produce many and varied products so that their income is never totally dependent on one product. Core firms wish to maintain a stable work force because they make use of complex technology and employee training is costly. Thus, employees of such firms receive high wages, command great amounts of power and prestige, and possess the ability to unionize. Peripheral firms make up the competitive sector of our economy. They are usually small, produce one product, and are affected by short-term swings in the national economy. Workers in peripheral companies earn lower salaries and possess less prestige and power than their counterparts in core firms. Both women and blacks are overrepresented in peripheral firms. See table 10.7 for a list of the types of manufactured nondurable goods that are produced by companies within core and peripheral firms in our economy.

Calasanti (1988) compared the responses of retirees from core and peripheral firms on several measures of life satisfaction, happiness, and estrangement. Results showed that the amount of satisfaction and happiness displayed by retirees from core firms was most highly related to their health and physical condition. Retirees from peripheral firms, however, based their satisfaction and happiness primarily on their financial well-being rather than their health. Surprisingly, the educational levels of the retirees from both core and peripheral firms was found to be unrelated to the amounts of satisfaction and happiness they experienced during retirement. Calasanti's work suggests that adjustment to retirement is (1) critically dependent on which portion of the economic sector (core or peripheral) one belongs to during adulthood, and (2) somewhat independent of the demographic factors (for example, educational level) that in the past have been found to be successful predictors of retirement satisfaction.

Theories of Retirement

There are three types of theories about the effects of retirement on the retiree (Palmore, 1984; Palmore et al, 1985). Some, such as Atchley's, consider retirement to have particular influences in phaselike fashion. Other theories consider retirement a "crisis" with retirees experiencing generally negative transitions due to loss (for example, the loss of occupational role identity). A third class of theories views retirement from the standpoint of continuity or positive adaptation. In continuity theories, one's occupational identity, while important, is not the sole basis for one's self-concept or feelings of worth. In fact, for many older Americans, retirement is a challenge for positive adaptation. New leisure roles, the furthering of long-standing

Table 10.7

TYPES OF PRODUCTS PRODUCED BY CORE AND PERIPHERAL INDUSTRIES INVOLVED IN THE MANUFACTURE OF NONDURABLE GOODS

Products of Core Industries	*Products of Peripheral Industries*
Food	Textiles—knitting mills
Tobacco	Textiles—floor coverings
Paper	Apparel
Printing, publishing	Tanned and finished leather
Chemicals and petroleum	Miscellaneous plastic products

friendships and the development of new ones, time for self-indulgence, hobbies, family, and travel are positive aspects of retirement. Retirement, in this view, is not a decision or a single event but a long-term process that presents continual opportunities and challenges as retirees structure, define, and construct adaptive responses.

Summary

Work has been an important part of all cultures throughout history. In the last hundred years, substantial changes in the nature of work have taken place. In our postindustrial society we have witnessed a significant increase in jobs related to human services, jobs that usually require extensive training and education. In the future, changes in the nature of work are likely to be influenced by energy costs.

Virtually all vocational theories stress the importance of the exploration of a wide array of career alternatives. At some point in the late teens or twenties, individuals usually enter an occupation. Doing so signals the beginning of new roles and responsibilities. Career expectations are high and the demands are real; older workers may serve as mentors in socializing young workers to occupational success. In middle adulthood, most men attain the highest status and income in their careers; women do likewise if they have been employed most of their adult years. But there are some interesting exceptions in middle adulthood of people who start over and select a new career for various reasons. One aspect of midlife career change involves adjusting idealistic hopes to realistic possibilities in light of how much time is left in an occupation. Of particular interest are the factors related to occupational mobility in adulthood. Many individuals continue their work into late adulthood, and productivity in old age is often the rule rather than the exception.

Almost all workers see their jobs as a way of earning a living. But work also has other meanings for most workers—prestige, contact with the outside world, and social relationships. The achievement motive is one of the most important human motives involved in work. As a rule, the higher the adult's achievement motivation, the more likely he or she will choose work characterized by risk and challenge. Our work ethic—the intrinsic worth involved in doing the best possible job regardless of financial reward—seems currently to be very strong. Nonetheless, worker productivity is either stagnant or decreasing. One explanation for this suggests that workers believe they are the least likely to benefit from increased productivity.

No change in the labor force has been as great as the increased participation of women. Though discrimination has been reduced, it has not been eliminated. Early adulthood is a critical time in a woman's decision making about work. The timing of decisions about marriage, childrearing, education, and the commitment to work have long-term implications for the lives and careers of women.

We not only need to learn how to work well, we also need to learn how to relax. Although television viewing dominates the leisure time of older adults, many actually prefer a variety of other activities if given a choice. Sports, experienced either directly or vicariously, also play an important role in the leisure activities of many adults. Constructive leisure activities in midlife may be helpful in making the transition from work to retirement. Pets are one leisure interest that assist both community-residing adults in retirement and older adults in institutions.

By sixty-two years of age, many workers choose to retire—men far more so than women. In a recent analysis of predictors of early retirement, subjective factors such as health, attitudes toward work and retirement, and adequacy of current finances were all significant predictors. With the virtual elimination of mandatory retirement, the roles of health, finances, personality, life-style, commitment to work, and the nature of the job become critical predictors of when people choose to retire. Some social scientists believe that we go through a series of phases before and after retirement—the remote, near, honeymoon, disenchantment, reorientation, stability, and termination phases. Others see retirement as a continuous process of adjustment with distinctive styles of adaptation rather than a single event with a phaselike mode of adaptation.

Review Questions

1. Describe the social and historical contexts of work.
2. What are the main theories of occupational choice? Describe the roles of exploration, planning, and decision making in occupational choice.
3. Discuss the developmental course of work once one enters an occupation.
4. What are some of the different meanings of work for men and women?
5. Discuss the achievement motive and work.
6. What factors influence the psychological meaning of job loss? How do they operate?
7. Describe the changing role of women in the labor force. Discuss the achievement orientation and career development of females in early adulthood.
8. Describe the importance of leisure in adult life, in particular during the middle adult years. Outline the kinds of leisure activities adults engage in after they retire.
9. If you could revise social policy about work and retirement, what changes would you recommend? Explain.
10. Describe the factors promoting successful retirement. What factors help determine successful adjustment to retirement?

For Further Reading

Gerson, K. (1986). *Hard choices: How women decide about work, career, and motherhood.* Berkeley, CA: University of California Press.
This book addresses the potential conflicts between career and family faced by women. Includes many case studies of the lives and career paths of women. Easy to read.

Neulinger, J. (1981). *The psychology of leisure.* New York: Thomas.
This book summarizes and integrates the available information on leisure in an interesting manner. Easy to moderately difficult reading.

Okun, B. F. (1984). *Working with adults: Individual, family, and career development.* Monterey, CA: Brooks/Cole.
This book includes valuable information on counseling individuals about career decisions at midlife.

Palmore, E. B., Burchett, B. M., Fillenbaum, G. G., George, L. K., and Wallman, L. M. (1985). *Retirement: Causes and consequences.* New York: Springer.
This book addresses such questions as Why do we retire? and What happens to us after we retire? Easy to moderately difficult reading.

Smelser, N. J., and Erikson, E. H. (1980). *Themes of work and love in adulthood.* Cambridge, MA: Harvard University Press.
An edited volume of essays on the themes of work and love in adulthood, written by experts such as Erik Erikson, Neal Smelser, Robert LeVine, Melvin Kohn, Marjorie Fiske, Roger Gould, and Daniel Levinson. Easy to read.

CHAPTER 11

PERSONALITY AND MORAL
DEVELOPMENT DURING ADULTHOOD

IMAGINE

Imagine What Your Personality Would Be Like If You Were a Sixty-Five-Year-Old Man Living in the United States in 1980

Suppose that you had immigrated to the United States with your parents from Eastern Europe in 1917, when you were two years old. While living in Europe, your parents had little formal education—the equivalent of two or three years of elementary school—and were very poor. Once you reached the shores of America, your family settled in a large, industrialized city and your father took a job as a laborer in a steel mill. Unfortunately, you only received an elementary school education. At an early age, you were encouraged to work to provide extra income for your family—you never were given the chance to enroll in high school. Then the Great Depression came. Times were very difficult for you; you had no money, no job, and your parents were in failing health. You joined the Army when World War II broke out. After the end of the war you came home, married a woman who lived in your old neighborhood, and had two children. Despite your lack of education, you have always encouraged your children to attend school so they can have a more affluent life. Your family and friends all characterize you as well-adjusted, hard-working, cautious, and somewhat introverted. Furthermore, you consider yourself to be less hot-headed and selfish than you were during your younger years; you also seem to be a bit more rigid and politically conservative than you were in the past. Finally, several of your lifelong friends and family members seem to have the same impressions concerning your past and present personality. There are four types of questions a developmental psychologist might have about the personality characteristics you exhibit at this time of your life. First, and perhaps foremost is, *What does your age have to do with your personality?* Is there a preprogrammed set of age-related stages or transitions that all individuals pass through in adult personality development? Do these transitions result in particular personality changes (introversion, rigidity, conservatism, and so on) at predictable ages? If this is true, would the vast majority of sixty-five-year-olds possess personalities similar to yours? Alternatively, it has been suggested by some psychologists that an adult's personality depends on the year in which he was born (his birth cohort or generation). Age, by itself, may have little bearing on personality. Just imagine the dramatically different experiences you would have had if you were sixty-five-years-old in 1900 compared to being sixty-five-years-old in the year 2000 ! Surely, the sociohistorical context you develop in must have a profound influence on your personality. For example, cautiousness, rigidity, and conservatism could be viewed as adaptive traits for an individual who had to live through the Depression and World War II.

A second question a developmental psychologist might ask is, *How has the resolution of prior life tasks affected the structure of your personality?* For example, is your present personality influenced by the type of identity you formed in adolescence? Or is your current personality a reflection of the manner by which you handled a midlife crisis? If you became sixty-five-years-old in 1920, the answer to both of these questions would most certainly be "no." This is because the notions of *identity formation* and *midlife crisis* as we know them today did not exist for individuals of your family background and social class during the time period in which you would have entered adolescence (about 1870) or midlife (about 1895). But if you become sixty-five-years-old in the year 2000, the answer to both of these questions might be an unqualified "yes," (because you would have reached adolescence (about 1950) and midlife (1975) when it was expected, if not fashionable, to experience adolescent and midlife crises.

A third question about your personality might be, *How stable has your personality been over your adult life?* You consider yourself to be more rigid, conservative, and introverted than in the past. Is this because these traits normally change with age? Or because your life over the last several decades has become more predictable, stable, and easier to cope with? Or is it because you are comparing your personality to today's younger adults (people from other cohorts) rather than to the personality you had in your youth? Is it possible for a person to remain introverted from adolescence to older adulthood, while at the same time experiencing a number of life crises?

One final question a psychologist might have is, *How much potential for change exists for your personality?* Are you at an age where your personality is set in concrete? Or could your personality be radically altered if you experienced the right mix of life events?

You probably have some ideas about the nature of adult personality development. Do you feel that personality develops in an abrupt, stagelike manner; or do you believe that adult personalities emerge smoothly? Do you feel that biological maturation plays a crucial role in one's personality development as an adult, or is personality mainly influenced by social experiences? What types of research designs do you think psychologists should use to investigate these issues? As you will soon see, these are some of the concerns of psychologists who attempt to describe and explain adult personality development.

INTRODUCTION

In this chapter we will attempt to define personality and survey a number of theoretical perspectives used in studying adult personality development. We'll begin our discussion with theories that emphasize different stages of personality development, including Erik Erikson's view of personality stages and both Roger Gould's and Daniel Levinson's stage theories of adult personality development. Next, we'll describe the life-events views of Bernice Neugarten and discuss the importance of individual variation in adult personality. Then we'll turn our attention to a number of longitudinal studies that have examined the stability of a variety of personality traits over the adult years. We'll end this chapter with a discussion of another important aspect of adult personality: the development of morality. We'll devote special attention to the relationship between moral development and an adult's ability to cope with significant life events.

WHAT IS PERSONALITY?

First of all, what is personality? It is hard to find agreement on an answer to this question because the answer often hinges on the theoretical view one adopts. Personality is sometimes thought of as a person's most revealing or dominant characteristic. Thus we might describe one person as having a "shy personality" and another person as being an "extrovert." Following are three more formal definitions of personality:

> [Personality is] the dynamic organization within the individual of those psychophysical systems that determine his characteristic behavior and thought. (Allport, 1961, p. 28)

[Personality is] a person's unique pattern of traits. (Guilford, 1959, p. 5)

[Personality is] the most adequate conceptualization of a person's behavior in all its detail. (McClelland, 1951, p. 69)

As Walter Mischel (1981) concludes, there is a common theme running through these and other definitions of personality, namely that **personality** refers to distinctive patterns of behavior, thought, and emotion that characterize each person's typical adaptation to situations in his or her life.

Personality psychologists often differ substantially in their views of human behavior. Sigmund Freud emphasized the importance of unconscious motives outside the adult's awareness, the sources of which lie deeply buried in the past. John Watson and B. F. Skinner, in contrast, stressed the importance of learned behavior in understanding personality. They suggested that the things a person does—his or her overt behaviors, not his or her unobservable, unconscious wishes—are the primary sources of personality. Clearly, great variability exists in the way theorists view personality.

Disagreement also exists about how effectively we can measure personality. To assess the validity of various personality theories, we need to state the theories in scientifically testable terms. Behavioral theories are stated in perhaps the most testable terms, whereas psychoanalytic theories are stated in the least testable terms. For behaviorists, personality is observable behavior. Many theorists, however, believe that the behavioral view leaves out much of the richness and complexity of personality. Psychoanalytic theorists believe that the internal dynamics of a person's mind, not observable behavior, constitute the core of personality. But it is not easy to measure the internal dynamics of personality.

How do we measure something so global and yet so rich in diversity as an adult's personality? Many psychologists suggest a simple procedure: ask the person about his or her personality. However, people do not always perceive themselves in objective terms. Some personality psychologists believe that we must study people under carefully controlled experimental conditions; others argue that we can only understand individuals by studying them under naturalistic, lifelike conditions. One astute observer of personality in adulthood, George Valliant (1977), stressed that lives are "too human for science, too beautiful for numbers, too sad for diagnosis, and too immortal for bound journals" (p. 11).

THE STAGE APPROACH TO ADULT PERSONALITY DEVELOPMENT

Recall that one of the major issues in our study of adult lives is the extent to which a person develops in a stage or nonstage manner. A number of personality theories have emphasized stages of child development while virtually ignoring possible stages of adult development. The assumption in such theories—the most prominent being Freud's psychoanalytic theory—is that the major changes in personality development occur during childhood, *not* adulthood. Freud, for example, asserted that an individual enters the final stage of personality development during adolescence.

Other stage theories, however, are not so narrow in focus. Life-span developmental theories emphasize the series of stages that unfold throughout the life cycle. The most prominent of these views is the psychosocial theory of Erik Erikson, who has described life-span personality development in terms of eight stages.

Erik Erikson's Life-Span Developmental View of Personality

One serious problem with traditional psychoanalytic thinking arises from the fact that Freud neglected the importance of culture. He failed to see that each society socializes children and adults in very different ways. The strong influence that culture exerts on the timing and dynamics of each stage is a theme reflected in the work of Erik Erikson.

Erikson's theory (1963, 1968, 1982) is particularly important because it traces the development of rational or ego processes and because it casts a life-span frame of reference on development. Erikson accepted the basic outline of Freud's theory. He thought that psychologists should study the **psychosexual development** of the child. That is, we should be interested in how developing individuals deal with pleasurable body sensations. At the same time, however, Erikson saw the need to pay closer attention to the individual's **psychosocial development** across the entire life span. That is, Erikson believed that we should place our strongest emphasis on the lifelong relationship between the developing individual and the social system of which she is a part. Borrowing from the terminology used in chapter 7, it seems reasonable to suggest that Erikson envisioned a dialectic relationship between the individual and society. Both the society and the individual *change* each other and *are changed by* each other.

However, Erikson did not view individuals or societies as changing in a random or chaotic manner. Instead, Erikson's theory is based on the premise that development throughout life is influenced by an underlying genetic plan common to all members of our species. The guiding impetus for growth according to this genetic plan is what Erikson called the **epigenetic principle.** Epigenesis operates in a social and cultural context, not in a vacuum. Furthermore, Erikson believed that human cultures are structured to help the individual along the epigenetic path. His theory places considerable emphasis on the interaction between epigenesis (genetics) and culture (environment) in understanding human development. Erikson's views on this matter are beautifully summarized in the following passage:

> The human personality develops in stages predetermined in the growing person's readiness to be driven toward, to be aware of, and to interact with a widening social radius;

and society, in principle, tends to be constituted so as to meet and invite this succession of potentialities for interaction and attempts to safeguard and encourage the proper rate and the proper sequence of their unfolding. (Erikson 1963, p. 270)

Erikson postulated eight stages of development—sometimes called the *eight ages of man.* Each stage centers around a salient and distinct emotional concern stemming from biological pressures within the person (epigenetic principle) and sociocultural expectations outside the person (environment). The concerns or conflicts at each stage may be resolved in a positive and healthy manner or in a pessimistic and unhealthy way. Each conflict offers a polarity and overshadows all the others for a unique time period. Earlier stage conflict must be resolved satisfactorily for the successful resolution of conflicts appearing at later stages of development.

Erikson did not believe that successful resolution of a stage crisis is always completely positive in nature. Some exposure and/or commitment to the negative end of a conflict is often inevitable. However, in a healthy solution to a stage crisis, the positive resolution of the conflict is dominant.

Erikson's stages of psychosocial development are listed in table 11.1. The table also indicates (1) the different social spheres within which each conflict occurs, (2) the different self-definitions which arise during the course of each conflict, and (3) the virtues (psychological strengths) that may evolve if an individual resolves each conflict positively. Each of these virtues influences the person's thoughts, feelings, and behaviors for the rest of his or her life.

The first stage, *trust versus mistrust,* corresponds to the oral stage in Freudian theory. An infant is almost entirely dependent upon parents for food, sustenance, and comfort. The caretaker is the primary representative of society to the child. When responsible caretakers meet the infant's needs with warmth, regularity, and affection, the infant will develop a feeling of trust toward the world. The infant's trust consists of that comfortable feeling that someone will always be around to care for his or her needs, even though the mother occasionally disappears. Alternatively, a sense of mistrust or fearful uncertainty can develop if the mother fails to provide for these needs in the caretaking setting.

Autonomy versus shame and doubt is the second stage and corresponds to the anal stage in Freudian theory. The infant begins to gain control over bowels and bladder. Parents begin imposing demands on the child to conform to socially acceptable methods for eliminating wastes. The child may develop the healthy attitude of being capable of independent or autonomous control over his or her own actions (not just bowel and bladder) or may develop the unhealthy attitude of shame and doubt because he or she is incapable of control.

Initiative versus guilt corresponds to the phallic period in Freudian theory. The child is caught in the midst of the Oedipal or Electra conflict, with its alternating love-hate feelings for the parent of the opposite sex and with fear of fulfilling the sexual fantasies that abound. The child may discover ways to overcome feelings of powerlessness by engaging in various activities. If so, a healthy attitude of being the initiator of action results. Alternatively, the child may fail to discover such outlets and feel guilt at being dominated by his or her primitive urges.

Table 11.1

AN OVERVIEW OF ERIKSON'S THEORY OF PSYCHOSOCIAL DEVELOPMENT

Epoch of the Life Span	Specific Stage or Psychosocial Crisis	Specific Sphere of Social Interaction	Self-Definition	Virtue
Early infancy	Trust vs. mistrust	Mother	"I am what I am given."	*Hope*—the enduring belief in the attainability of primal wishes in spite of the urges and rages of dependency.
Late infancy/Early childhood	Autonomy vs. shame	Parents	"I am what I will to be."	*Will*—the unbroken determination to exercise free choice as well as self-restraint in spite of the unavoidable experiences of shame, doubt, and a certain rage over being controlled by others.
Early childhood	Initiative vs. guilt	Family	"I am what I can imagine."	*Purpose*—the courage to pursue valued goals while guided by conscience and not paralyzed by guilt.
Middle childhood	Industry vs. inferiority	Community, school	"I am what I learn."	*Competence*—the free exercise of dexterity and intelligence in the completion of a serious task.
Adolescence	Identity vs. confusion	Nation	"I am who I define myself to be."	*Fidelity*—the ability to sustain loyalties freely pledged in spite of the inevitable contradictions of value systems.
Early adulthood	Intimacy vs. isolation	Community, nation	"We are what we love."	*Love*—the mutuality of devotion greater than the antagonisms inherent in divided function.
Middle adulthood	Generativity vs. stagnation	World, nation, community	"I am what I create."	*Care*—the broadening concern for what has been generated by love, necessity, or accident.
Late adulthood	Integrity vs. despair	Universe, nation, community	"I am what survives me."	*Wisdom*—a detached yet active concern for life bounded by death.

Industry versus inferiority coincides with the Freudian period of latency. This stage represents the years of middle childhood when the child is involved in the absorption of knowledge and the development of physical skills as the child is drawn into the social culture of peers. If children view themselves as basically competent in these activities, feelings of productivity and industry will result. On the other hand, if children view themselves as incompetent, particularly in comparison with peers, then they will feel unproductive and inferior.

Identity versus identity confusion is roughly associated with Freud's genital stage. The major focus during this stage is the formation of a stable personal identity. For Freud, the important part of identity formation resided in the adolescent's resolution of sexual conflicts; for Erikson, the central ingredient is the establishment of a sense of mutual recognition between the adolescent and the society of which he is a part. The adolescent needs to view his society as decent, moral, and just. And the adolescent must come to believe that his existence is valued by society-at-large. Mutual recognition of this sort leads to feelings of personal identity, confidence, and purposefulness. Without mutual recognition, the adolescent may feel confused and troubled.

More information about Erikson's view of identity formation is contained in box 11.1. This box contains excerpts from Erikson's analysis of the identity crises faced by Adolf Hitler, Martin Luther, and Mahatma Gandhi. Try to draw a connection between the identity struggles of these individuals and their adult personalities.

Most of Erikson's work on identity formation has focused on young men. Ann Constantinople (1976) was one of the first psychologists to study identity formation in women. She discovered that both males and females showed positive identity growth throughout the college years. She also found that women possessed a better sense of personal identity than men when they entered college. But at the end of the college years, men, rather than women, displayed a more positive identity! Differences in the manner in which males and females were socialized in the 1960s may explain these results. Men were usually expected to become independent during adulthood, to "become their own person." Conversely, women were socialized to find husbands and develop an identity as a wife. Because of important sociohistorical change (the growth of the women's movement during the 1970s and 1980s), few women rely on a male figure as a basis for their own identity (Skolnick, 1986). In fact, more recent research (Waterman, 1982) has revealed that sex differences in identity formation are gradually dissipating. However, some women may still find identity formation more difficult than men do. Consider the following statement made by an adult female college student: "I have always been somebody else's something: my father's daughter, my husband's wife, my children's mom. Now I can begin to be me."

Erikson described three stages of adult personality development. These stages, unlike the earlier ones, do not have parallels in Freudian theory. The first of these adult stages occurs during early adulthood and is termed *intimacy versus isolation*. Young adulthood usually brings a job and the opportunity to form an intimate relationship with a member of the opposite sex. If the young adult forms friendships with others and has a significant, intimate relationship with one individual in particular, a basic feeling of closeness with others will result. A feeling of isolation may result from the inability to form friendships and an intimate relationship.

An inability to develop meaningful realtionships with others in early adulthood can be harmful to a person's personality. Such circumstances may account for the shallow and short-sighted attempts of adolescents and young adults to merge themselves with a leader or cult figure. Many youths want to be disciples of leaders who will shelter them from the harm of the outgroup world. If this strategy fails, and Erikson believes that it must, sooner or later the individual will recoil into a self-search to discover where he or she went wrong. This introspection sometimes leads to painful depression and isolation. It may also contribute to a mistrust of others and restrict the willingness to act on one's own initiative.

As we have indicated, the early adult years are a time when individuals usually develop an intimate relationship. At the same time, however, young adults maintain a strong need for independence and freedom. Development during early adulthood, then, often involves an intricate balance of intimacy and commitment on the one hand and independence and freedom on the other. Keep in mind, however, that intimacy and independence are not just concerns in early adulthood; they remain important themes that must be worked and reworked throughout the adult years.

The chief concern of middle-aged adults is to resolve the conflict of *generativity versus stagnation.* The concept of generativity refers to the concern adults have for members of their own generation as well as future generations. Generativity may manifest itself as the desire to help children and adolescents unlock their human potential. Or it may be expressed as the need to become a caring and productive member of one's own generation. Thus, generative adults may conceptualize themselves as caring, giving, and productive. It is during this stage that adults may experience a midlife crisis. For example, some adults may feel a sense of stagnation because they are without children or because they have jobs that have no meaning either for themselves or society. Certain occupations seem to engender generativity such as teaching, nursing, and social work; however, it is the reflective view of the adult which is the final determinant of generativity or stagnation at this stage.

Recently, Erikson made the following commentary concerning the manner by which members of our society are dealing with the crisis of generativity versus stagnation:

> The only thing that can save us as a species is seeing how we're not thinking of future generations in the way we live . . . What's lacking is generativity, a generativity that will promote positive values in the lives of the next generation. Unfortunately, we set the example of greed, wanting a bigger and better everything, with no thought of what will make it a better world for our great-grandchildren. That's why we go on depleting the earth: we're not thinking of the next generations. (Goleman, 1988).

BOX 11.1

THE IDENTITY DEVELOPMENT OF ADOLF HITLER, MARTIN LUTHER, AND MAHATMA GANDHI

Erik Erikson is a master at using the psychoanalytic method to uncover historical clues about identity formation. Erikson has used the psychoanalytic method both with the youth he treats in psychotherapy sessions and in the analysis of the lives of famous individuals. Erikson (1963) believes that the psychoanalytic technique sheds light on human psychological evolution. He also believes that the history of the world is a composite of individual life cycles.

In the following excerpts from Erikson's writings, Erikson uses the psychoanalytic method to analyze the youths of Adolf Hitler, Martin Luther, and Mahatma Gandhi.

In one passage, Erikson (1962) describes the youth of Adolf Hitler:

I will not go into the symbolism of Hitler's urge to build except to say that his shiftless and brutal father had consistently denied the mother a steady residence; one must read how Adolf took care of his mother when she wasted away from breast cancer to get an inkling of this young man's desperate urge to cure. But it would take a very extensive analysis, indeed, to indicate in what way a single boy can daydream his way into history and emerge a sinister genius, and how a whole nation becomes ready to accept the emotive power of that genius as a hope of fulfillment for its national aspirations and as a warrant for national criminality. . . .

The memoirs of young Hitler's friend indicate an almost pitiful fear on the part of the future dictator that he might be nothing. He had to challenge this possibility by being deliberately and totally anonymous; and only out of this self-chosen nothingness could he become everything. (Erikson, 1962, pp. 108–109)

The identity crisis of Adolf Hitler led him to turn toward politics in a pathological effort to create a world order. The crisis experienced by Martin Luther in a different era, however, led him to turn toward theology in an attempt to deal systematically with human nothingness or lack of identity:

In confession, for example, he was so meticulous in the attempt to be truthful that he spelled out every intention as well as every deed; he splintered relatively acceptable purities into smaller and smaller impurities; he reported temptations in historical sequence, starting back in childhood; and after having confessed for hours, would ask for special appointments in order to correct previous statements. In doing this he was obviously both exceedingly compulsive and, at least unconsciously, rebellious. . . .

At this point we must note a characteristic of great young rebels: their inner split between the temptation to surrender and the need to dominate. A great young rebel is torn between, on the one hand, tendencies to give in and fantasies of defeat (Luther used to resign himself to an early death at times of impending success), and the absolute need, on the other hand, to take the lead, not only over himself but over all the forces and people who impinge on him. (Erikson, 1968, pp. 155–157)

In his Pulitzer Prize-winning book on Mahatma Gandhi's life, Erikson (1969) describes the personality formation of Gandhi during his youth:

Straight and yet not stiff; shy and yet not withdrawn; intelligent and yet not bookish; willful and yet not stubborn; sensual and yet not soft. . . . We must try to reflect on the relation of such a youth to his father, because the Mahatma places service to the father and the crushing guilt of failing in such service in the center of his adolescent turbulence. Some historians and political scientists seem to find it easy to interpret this account in psychoanalytic terms; I do not. For the question is not how a particular version of the Oedipal Complex ''causes'' a man to be both great and neurotic in a particular way, but rather how such a young person . . . manages the complexes which constrict other men. (Erikson, 1969, p. 113)

In these passages, the workings of an insightful, sensitive mind is shown looking for a historical perspective on psychological development. Through analysis of the lives of famous individuals such as Hitler, Luther, and Gandhi, and through the thousands of youth he has talked with in person, Erikson has pieced together a descriptive picture of identity development.

The process of constructing a personal identity is a lifelong task.

In the later years, adults enter the stage of *ego integrity versus despair.* This is a time when individuals face their own deaths by looking back at what they have done with their lives. The older person may develop a positive outlook on each of the preceding periods of emotional conflict and resolution. If so, his retrospective glances will reveal a picture of a life well spent, a significant and meaningful life, and the person will be satisfied (ego integrity). However, the older person may have resolved one or more crises in a negative way or been unable to exercise control over life decisions. If so, retrospective glances will yield doubt, gloom, and despair over the worth of one's life. Erikson's own words best capture the richness of his thoughts about the crisis of ego integrity versus despair:

> A meaningful old age, then . . . serves the need for that integrated heritage which gives indispensible perspective on the life cycle. Strength here takes the form of that detached yet active concern with life bounded with death, which we call *wisdom* . . .
>
> To whatever abyss ultimate concerns may lead individual men, man as a psychosocial creature will face, toward the end of his life, a new edition of the identity crisis which we may state in the words, "I am what survives me." (1968, pp. 140–141)

Robert Butler (1963) has given a special name to the older adult's tendency to look back in time and analyze the meaning of his or her life: the **life review.** To learn more about this phenomenon, read box 11.2. Note that other psychologists have used the term **reminiscence** to refer to the same process (Romaniuk, 1981).

It seems obvious that Erikson conceptualized the crises that make up the human life span in a linear manner. Moving through the Eriksonian crises seems akin to climbing a ladder. The bottom rung consists of the crisis of trust versus mistrust, while the top rung is represented by the crisis of ego integrity versus despair. This is *not* the picture of the life span, however, that Erikson tried to paint. Erikson envisioned the life span in a cyclical or circular manner. He thought the individuals who are just beginning life (infants and very young children) may be profoundly influenced by individuals who are about to leave life behind (the elderly). Erikson has stated his thoughts on this matter in the following way:

> And it seems possible to paraphrase the relation of adult integrity and infantile trust by saying that healthy children will not fear life if their elders have integrity enough not to fear death. (1963, p. 268)

A Critique of Erikson's Theory

Erikson's theory has a strong intuitive appeal. But like all psychoanalytically based theories, it is difficult to verify through empirical research (Langer, 1969; Miller, 1983). How does one find out whether an individual has experienced Erikson's stages of development? You might follow Erikson's pattern of probing the depths of an individual's personality by conducting a series of open-ended interviews. Or you might decide to develop a questionnaire or survey that asks adults how they

BOX 11.2

THE LIFE REVIEW: AN INTERPRETATION
OF REMINISCENCE IN THE AGED

The *life review* is a looking-back process set in motion by looking forward to death. This process has the potential to result in personality reorganization. Thus, the life review, while including reminiscence, is not synonymous with it, it is not simply the unbidden return of memories or the purposeful seeking of them, although both may occur.

The life review sometimes proceeds silently, without obvious manifestations. Many elderly persons may be only vaguely aware of the experience. But alterations in the defensive operations of the personality do occur. Speaking broadly, the more intense the unresolved life conflicts, the more work must be accomplished toward reintegration. Although the process is active, not static, the content of one's life usually unfolds slowly; the process may not be completed prior to death. In its mild form, the life review is reflected in increased reminiscence, mild nostalgia, mild regret; in severe form, anxiety, guilt, despair, and depression may set in. In the extreme, the life review may involve the obsessive preoccupation of the older person with her past and may proceed to a state approximating terror and resulting in suicide. Thus, although considered a universal and normative process, it may manifest itself as a psychopathological state.

The life review may first be observed in stray and seemingly insignificant thoughts about oneself and one's life history. These thoughts either continue to emerge in brief, intermittent spurts or become almost continuous. They may undergo constant reintegration and reorganization at various levels of awareness. As a seventy-six-year-old man said:

"My life is in the background of my mind much of the time; it cannot be any other way. Thoughts of the past play upon me; sometimes I play with them, encourage and savor them; at other times I dismiss them."

ADAPTIVE AND CONSTRUCTIVE MANIFESTATIONS
As the past marches in review, the ego surveys it, observes it, and reflects upon it. The individual reconsiders previous experiences and their meanings, often revising or ex-

feel about themselves. But neither of these methods is really adequate for fully and accurately evaluating the adult's ability to resolve the eight crises. The problem becomes particularly acute when one is faced with having to investigate life crises in large numbers of adults. While experts in adult development recognize the importance of Erikson's theory as an integrative framework, they point out that aside from clinical studies and psychobiographies, there is very little empirical information to help evaluate the theory. There is even some debate about whether the stages and concepts are spelled out in adequate detail to allow empirical studies to be derived from Erikson's theory. At present, the number of such attempts is

panding their understanding of past events. This reorganization of past experience may provide a more valid picture, giving new and significant meaning to one's life; it may also mitigate fears and prepare one for death.

Many times, then, the life review serves a creative and constructive purpose. For example, a seventy-eight-year-old man, optimistic, reflective, and resourceful, who had had significantly impairing egocentric tendencies, became increasingly responsive in his relationships to his wife, children, and grandchildren. These changes corresponded with his purchase of a tape recorder. In reference to the tapes he made, he wrote: "There is the first reel of tape on which I recorded my memory of my life story. To give this some additional interest I am expecting that my children and grandchildren and great-grandchildren will listen to it after I am gone. I pretended that I was telling the story directly to them."

Ingmar Bergman's remarkable Swedish motion picture, *Wild Strawberries,* provides a beautiful example of the constructive aspects of the life review. Envisioning and dreaming of his past and his death, the protagonist-physician realizes the nonaffectionate and withholding qualities of his life; as the feeling of love reenters his life, even as death hovers over him, the doctor changes.

In the course of the life review, the older person may reveal to his wife, children, and other intimates unknown qualities of his character and unexplained actions of his past; in return, they may reveal previously undisclosed or unknown truths. Hidden themes of great vintage may emerge, changing the quality of a lifelong relationship. Revelations of the past may forge a new intimacy, render a deceit honest; they may sever peculiar bonds and free tongues; or they may sculpture terrifying hatreds out of fluid, fitful antagonisms. (1975, pp. 331, 332, 338, Copyright 1975 by Robert N. Butler, M.D. By permission of Harper & Row, Publishers, Inc.)

small, and the theory has not been adequately examined in a longitudinal fashion. Other criticisms have questioned whether Erikson's rich, descriptive language and loosely connected descriptions qualify as a researchable theory (Miller, 1983).

Roger Gould's *Transformations*

A well-known perspective that links stage and crisis with adult development has been proposed by UCLA psychiatrist Roger Gould (1975, 1978, 1980b). Gould emphasizes that midlife is every bit as turbulent as adolescence, except that during middle adulthood, striving to handle crisis is likely to lead to a healthier, happier life. Gould first explained his views in the book *Transformations* (1978).

Gould's research led him to propose seven developmental stages of adult life, which are listed in table 11.2. At each stage, persons are seeking to leave behind the **false emotional assumptions** of childhood. Adult transformations require the person both to recognize these false assumptions and to create new techniques for coping with new insights. For example, four of the false emotional assumptions identified by Gould (1980a) are, "I'll always belong to the world of my parents," "With enough will power and perseverance I'll always succeed," "When I'm frustrated and confused someone will step in and show me the way," and "Life is simple, not complicated." Overcoming these false emotional assumptions is difficult and painful. Each assumption provided, in the past, an illusory sense of security. These assumptions must be discarded as an individual successfully masters the challenges of adult life.

Gould believes that our forties may be an especially turbulent time period. We begin to feel a sense of urgency when we realize that our lives are speeding by as parents and elderly relatives begin to die. It is only when we realize that this midlife crisis is a natural step in our development, Gould believes, that we will be on the path to adult maturity.

One of the shortcomings of Gould's theory is that it is based only on clinical observations and questionnaire data. Gould used two different techniques to obtain information about adult development. First, eight medical students listened to tape recordings of patient therapy sessions. The medical students were asked to note the personal feelings of the patients that stood out. Second, a questionnaire was developed and given to a "normal, nonclinical" sample of 524 white, middle-class adults. The clinical ratings by medical students is a questionable strategy. For instance, the likely middle-class bias of both the clinical and the nonclinical sample leads to problems generalizing to a lower-class sample, and in neither the clinical observations nor the questionnaire was there any attempt to measure the reliability of the information obtained. Finally, no statistical analysis was conducted in Gould's work.

Daniel Levinson's *The Seasons of a Man's Life*

Daniel Levinson's vision of adult development was first set out in his well-known book, *The Seasons of a Man's Life* (1978). This book grew out of his research on the personality development of forty middle-aged men. Levinson used biographical case material to illustrate the stages of personality development in adulthood. His interviews were conducted with hourly workers, business executives, academic biologists, and novelists. Though Levinson's major interest was midlife transition, he described a number of phases, stages, and transitions in the life cycle, as indicated in figure 11.1. Levinson has expanded upon his original work (Levinson, 1980, 1986, 1987) and has argued that his theoretical viewpoint holds true for women as well as men from different cultures, classes, and historical epochs. In a review of recent research, Roberts and Newton (1987) found that Levinson's model applies to female

Table 11.2

GOULD'S DEVELOPMENTAL STAGES OF ADULT LIFE

Stage	Approximate Age	Development
1	16–18	Desire to escape parental control
2	18–22	Leaving the family: peer group orientation
3	22–28	Developing independence: commitment to a career and to children
4	29–34	Questioning self: role confusion; marriage and career vulnerable to dissatisfaction
5	35–43	Urgency to attain life's goals: awareness of time limitation; realignment of life's goals
6	43–53	Settling down: acceptance of one's life
7	53–60	More tolerance: acceptance of past; less negativism; general mellowing

adult development. However, the path of adult development seems more complex for women than men.

The most important concept articulated by Levinson is the individual's **life structure.** The term *life structure* refers to the "underlying pattern or design of a person's life at any given time" (Levinson, 1986, p. 41). A person's life structure is revealed by the choices he makes and by the relationships he enters into. For example, a person may choose to devote a significant amount of time and energy to his occupation and foresake his relationships with his wife, children, and fellow coworkers. Another individual may choose to use her time and energy to help others acquire new competencies and job skills and to become closer to her family. Levinson reminds us that the choices we make concerning marriage and family and occupation are the two most important facets of our life structure. The relationships we have with others, as well as with our work, " . . . are the stuff our lives are made of. They give shape and substance to the life course. They are the vehicle through which we live out—and bury—various aspects of ourselves and by which we participate, for better or worse, in the world around us." (Levinson, 1986, p. 6) Finally, Levinson argues that the life structure changes and evolves over the different periods of the adult life span.

According to Levinson, the human life cycle consists of four different **eras,** each of which has a distinctive character. Like Robert Havighurst (1972), Levinson emphasizes that developmental tasks must be mastered during each of these eras. The eras partially overlap one another—a new era begins as an old era comes to an end. These periods of overlap are referred to as **transitions** and last for approximately five years. As Levinson notes, "The eras and cross-era transitional periods form the macrostructure of the life cycle, providing an underlying order in the flow of all human lives yet permitting exquisite variations in the individual life course." (1986, p. 5)

The first era, *preadulthood,* lasts from conception to about seventeen years of age. During this time, the individual grows from a highly dependent infant to be-

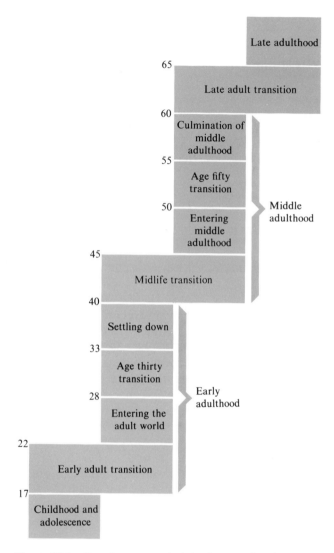

Figure 11.1   Development periods in the eras of early and middle adulthood.

ginning to be an independent, responsible adult. The years from seventeen to twenty-two comprise the *early adult transition.* It is at this time that the developing person first starts to modify her relationships with family and friends to help build a place in the adult world.

The next era, *early adulthood,* spans the approximate ages of twenty-two to forty. This is an era that is characterized by the greatest energy, contradiction, and stress. The major tasks to be mastered are forming and pursuing youthful aspirations (fulfilling a dream), raising a family, and establishing a senior position in the adult world. This period can be immensely rewarding in terms of love, occupational advancement, and the realization of one's major life goals. But, due to the demands of parenthood, marriage, and occupation, this era can also be marked by major stressors. We may be terrorized by our own ambitions as well as by the demands of family, community, and society.

The *midlife transition* lasts from about forty to forty-five years of age. By the time many individuals enter this transitional period, they realize they have not accomplished what they set out to do during the early adulthood era. This realization leads to feelings of disappointment and forces the individual to recast earlier life goals. Alternatively, some individuals meet or even exceed their initial dreams. These individuals may soon realize, however, that their outstanding accomplishments did not insulate them from feelings of anxiety and crisis. These negative emotions emerge from several different sources. For example, individuals start to experience themselves as old and physically vulnerable. They become aware of their own aging, as well as the aging (and deaths) of their parents. They begin to view themselves as next in line for death. And they view themselves as the oldest surviving members of their families. Individuals still want to accomplish much, but they feel they have little time left. This leads them to refine their goals and prove themselves while separating themselves from mentors and parents—a process that Levinson calls BOOM (Becoming One's Own Man).

In the final analysis, Levinson suggests that the midlife transition provides us with the opportunity to either become more caring, reflective, and loving or more stagnated, depending on how we accept and integrate the following polarities of adult existence: (1) being young versus old, (2) being masculine versus feminine, (3) being destructive versus constructive, and (4) being attached versus separated from others.

The third era, *middle adulthood,* lasts from about forty-five to sixty years of age. This is the time period during which most individuals have the potential to have the most profound and positive impact on their families, their professions, and the world they live in. Individuals no longer concern themselves with their own ambitions. They develop new long-range goals which help them to facilitate the growth of others. This is the time during which adults have the capacity to become mentors to younger individuals. They take pride in the competence and productivity of younger individuals rather than being threatened by them. Furthermore, as individuals enter middle adulthood, they are more able to reap the benefits of family life. In essence, Levinson's ideas about middle adulthood correspond to Erikson's notion of generativity.

The *late adult transition* occurs from ages sixty to sixty-five. It is during this time that older adults experience anxiety because of the physical decline they see in themselves and their agemates, and because they are now "old" in the eyes of their culture. In the *late adulthood era* (sixty-five years of age to death), the individual must develop a way of living that allows him to accept the realities of the past, present, and future. During this era, the individual must come to grips with a crisis that is similar to the Eriksonian idea of ego integrity versus despair.

Levinson's publications, like Gould's, are not research reports in any conventional sense. They include no statistics to speak of and no quantified results. However, the data reported by Levinson are consistent with the clinical tradition, and the quality and quantity of the rich biographical reporting are certainly intriguing.

Conclusions about Adult Stage Theories

There seems to be reasonable agreement among Erikson, Gould, and Levinson about the nature of stages in adulthood. All would concur with a general outline of adult development that begins with a shift from identity to intimacy, followed by a change from career considerations to generativity, and finally marked by the shift from searching for meaning in life (in the face of death) to some final integration. Thus, although each theorist labels the stages differently and views the processes responsible for developmental change uniquely, the underlying themes of adult development are remarkably similar. See figure 11.2 for a comparison of these three viewpoints.

The perspectives advocated by Erikson, Gould, and Levinson emphasize the importance of phases or stages in adult personality development. Though the idea of stages in the life cycle can be helpful in pointing out dominant themes that characterize many people at particular points in adult development, there are several ideas to keep in mind when considering these theoretical perspectives as viable models of adult development. First, the research on which they are based often is not empirically sound. Second, there is a tendency for these theorists to focus too extensively on stages as crises in development, particularly in the case of the midlife crisis. Third, there is an increasing tendency for theory and research on adult development to emphasize the importance of life events rather than using stages or phases to organize development. Fourth, there may be a great deal of individual and societal variation in the manner in which the themes, stages, and phases of adult life emerge. Refer to box 11.3 for an in-depth critique of stage theories of personality development. This box shows how individuals from different cohorts may experience different degrees of crisis and transition as they move through adulthood.

THE LIFE-EVENTS FRAMEWORK

An alternative to the stage approach to adult personality development is the **life-events framework.** In the earlier versions of the life-events framework (for example, Holmes and Rahe, 1967), it was suggested that major life events produce taxing circumstances for individuals, forcing them to change their personalities. Events such as the death of a spouse, marriage, and divorce were thought to produce increasing degrees of stress and therefore were likely to have an influence on the individual's personality.

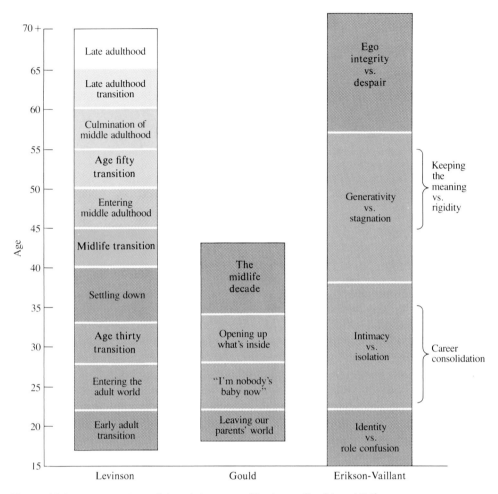

Figure 11.2   A comparison of the adult stages of Levinson, Gould, and Erikson.

More sophisticated versions of the life-events framework (Brim and Ryff, 1980; Dohrenwend, Krasnoff, Askensay, and Dohrenwend, 1978; Hultsch and Plemons, 1979), emphasize the factors that mediate the influence of life events on adult development—physical health, intelligence, personality, family supports, income, and so forth. Some individuals may perceive a life event as highly stressful, while others perceive the same event as a challenge. We also need to consider the sociocultural circumstances within which life events occur. For example, divorce may be more stressful after many years of marriage, when individuals are in their fifties, than when they have only been married a few years and are in their twenties (Chiriboga, 1982b). Also, individuals may be able to cope more effectively with divorce in 1990 than in 1950 because divorce is more commonplace in today's society.

BOX 11.3

COHORT AND CRISIS

Daniel Levinson, Roger Gould, and a number of other personality theorists believe that the middle-aged adult is suspended between the past and the future, trying to cope with a gap that threatens life's continuity. In agreement with Levinson and Gould, George Valliant (1977) concluded that midlife is a time for reassessing the "truth" about the adolescent and adult years. Valliant's claims about adult personality development were based on data collected during a thirty-year longitudinal research project called the Grant Study. The subjects in this study were initially interviewed when they were students at Harvard University. Valliant described the unique character of midlife as follows:

> Adolescence is a period for acknowledging parental flaws and discovering the truth about childhood, so the forties are a time for reassessing and reordering the truth about adolescence and young adulthood.
> At age forty—give or take a decade—men leave the compulsive, unreflective busy-work of their occupational apprenticeships, and once more become explorers of the world within. (1977, p. 220)

However, while Levinson and Gould see midlife as a crisis, Valliant believes that only a minority of adults experience such a crisis:

> Just as pop psychologists have reveled in the not-so-common high drama of adolescent turmoil, the popular press, sensing good copy, has made all too much of the midlife. The term *midlife crisis* brings to mind some variation of the renegade minister who leaves behind four children and the congregation that loved him in order to drive off in a magenta Porsche with a twenty-five-year-old striptease artist. Like all tabloid fables, there is much to be learned from such stories, but such aberrations are rare, albeit memorable, caricatures of more mundane issues of development. As with adolescent turmoil, midlife crises are much rarer in community samples than in clinical samples. (1977, pp. 222–223)

Bernice Neugarten and Nancy Datan (1973) were among the first psychologists to suggest that understanding the nature of adult personality development depends on an analysis of the sociohistorical and personal circumstances within which adult life occurs. They suggested that chronological age has little, if any, bearing on adult personality. For example, Neugarten (1980, 1989) proposed that the admonition "Act your age" has become progressively less meaningful since the middle part of this century. We are constantly aware of adults who occupy roles that seem out of step with their biological ages (for example, the twenty-eight-year-old mayor, the sixty-year-old father of a preschooler, and the seventy-year-old college student). Neugarten also has deep-seated doubts about an increasing number of popular books

It may be that the notion of midlife crisis is a psychological phenomenon unique to individuals living in our current (or not-so-distant) culture. Bernice Neugarten (1964) has emphasized the power exerted by the generation (or cohort) within which individuals develop. She argues that our values, attitudes, expectations, and behaviors are influenced by the period within which we live. For example, individuals born during the Great Depression may have a different outlook on life than those born during the optimistic 1950s, says Neugarten.

Neugarten (1968) believes that the social environment of a particular age group can alter its **social clock**—the timetable according to which individuals are expected to accomplish life's tasks, such as marrying, establishing a career, and even *experiencing a monumental crisis at midlife*. Social clocks provide guides for our lives. And events and trends unique to specific cohorts "set" the social clock for that cohort.

Alice Rossi (1984) also observes that trying to tease out universal patterns in adult development is fantastically complicated because the findings obtained from one cohort may not apply to another. Most of the individuals studied by Levinson and Gould were born right around the time of the depression. What was true for these individuals when they reached age forty may not be true for the members of more recent cohorts when they reach forty. Rossi suggests that the men studied by Levinson and Gould may have been burned out at a premature age (because of the pressures put upon them by their generation) rather than moving through a normal developmental pattern that all adults go through upon entry into midlife.

What events or societal changes do you think have occurred during the latter part of this century that may have led to the birth of the midlife crisis? Do you think that changes in society will heighten or diminish the tendency for members of future cohorts to experience a crisis at midlife?

such as Gail Sheehy's widely read *Passages* (1976) or *Pathfinders* (1981) that emphasize predictable, age-related life crises. People who read such books worry about their midlife crises, apologize if they don't seem to be coping with them properly, and appear dismayed if they aren't having them. These crisis theories, Neugarten maintains, do not really define the typical pattern of adult development. It may be that adults change far more, and far less predictably, than many oversimplified stage theories or crisis theories suggest. As Neugarten (1980b) has asserted:

> My students and I have studied what happens to people over the life cycle . . . We have found great trouble clustering people into age brackets that are characterized by particular conflicts; the conflicts won't stay put, and neither will the people. Choices and dilemmas do not sprout forth at ten-year intervals, and decisions are not made and then left behind as if they were merely beads on a chain. (p. 289)

In earlier periods in our society, it may have been reasonable to describe life as a series set of discrete, predictable stages or crises. More people seemed to experience the same life events at the same ages. People knew the "right age" for marriage, the first child, the last child, career achievement, retirement, and even death. In the last few decades, however, chronological age has become nearly irrelevant as an index of such significant events within adult development (Neugarten, 1989).

During the latter part of this century, our social time clocks have changed dramatically. New trends in work, family size, health, and education have produced phenomena that are unprecedented in our history. We see, for example, a significantly longer empty nest period after the children leave home that may require major readjustments in the parents' relationship. Also, we see an increase in the numbers of great-grandparents as well as those who start new families, new jobs, and new avocations when they are forty, fifty, or sixty years old (Neugarten, 1980, 1989).

The life tasks that we used to associate with one particular stage of adult development seem to reoccur over the entire course of the adult life span. Neugarten has articulated this point in a most eloquent manner:

> Most of the themes of adulthood appear and reappear in new forms over long periods of time. Issues of intimacy and freedom, for example, which are supposed to concern young adults just starting out in marriage and careers, are never settled once and for all. They haunt many couples continuously; compromises are found for a while, then renegotiated. Similarly, feeling the pressure of time, reformulating goals, coming to grips with success (and failure)—these are not the exclusive property of the forty-eight to fifty-two-year-olds, by any means. (Neugarten, 1980, pp. 289–290)

Applying a Life-Course Perspective to Life Events

It is important to make connections between age or life stage, the probability of certain events taking place, and the power of the event as a stressor (Brim and Ryff, 1980). Some events, such as a serious automobile accident, are not necessarily age-linked and have a low probability of occurring. Therefore, we are seldom prepared for such events psychologically. However, other events, such as menopause, retirement, or the death of a parent have stronger ties with age. This allows us to anticipate the events and to develop coping strategies that may help alleviate some of the stress these events engender (Neugarten, 1989; Pearlin and Lieberman, 1977). Figure 11.3 shows how a life-course perspective can be applied to life events (Hultsch and Plemons, 1979). This figure considers variations in the probability of certain events, their timing and sequencing, the motivational factors stimulated by the events, the coping resources available for dealing with them, and adaptational outcomes.

The life-events framework described in figure 11.3 has four main components: antecedent life-event stressors, mediating factors, a social/psychological adaptation process, and consequent adaptive or maladaptive outcomes. From this perspective,

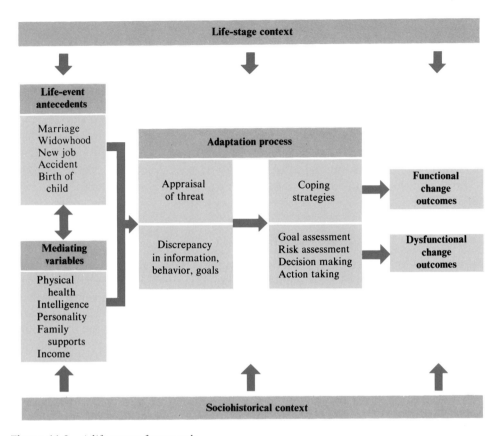

Figure 11.3   A life-events framework.

all life events, regardless of whether they are positive (marriage, being promoted at work) or negative (divorce, the death of a spouse), are viewed as potentially stressful. Factors that may mediate the effects of life events on the individual can be categorized as internal (physical health or intelligence) or external (salary, social support network). Social-psychological adaptation refers to the individual's coping strategies, which may produce either a positive or negative outcome.

As indicated in figure 11.3, it is also important to consider both the life stage and the sociohistorical context in which a life event occurs. Two time lines that are important in our lives, then, are **individual time** and **historical time.** An event (such as the death of a spouse) that occurs at age thirty may have a different impact on the individual than at age seventy-three. Similarly, an event (such as a woman being promoted over a man at work) would have a different impact if it occurred in 1990 rather than 1950.

The life-events framework provides valuable insights into adult development. Like all the other theories described in this chapter, however, it is not without flaws

(Dohrenwend and Dohrenwend, 1978; Lazarus and DeLongis, 1983; Maddi, 1986). One of the most significant drawbacks of the life-events framework is that it may place too much emphasis on change. It does not recognize the stability that, at least to some degree, characterizes adult development. Another potential drawback is that this perspective may place too much emphasis on major life events as the primary sources of personality change. Enduring a boring and tense job, a dull marriage, or living in poverty do not qualify as major life events. Yet the everyday pounding we take from these types of conditions can add up to a highly stressful life. Some psychologists (for example, Lazarus and Folkman, 1984) believe that we can gain greater insight into the source of life's stresses by focusing on daily hassles and uplifts rather than focusing so much on the catastrophic experience of major life stressors.

Recognizing Individual Variation

Broadly speaking, there are two theoretical approaches to the study of personality development—one focuses on similarities, the other on differences. The stage theories of Erikson, Gould, and Levinson all attempt to describe universal forms of intraindividual change that take place during adult development. The life-events framework, as championed by Neugarten, focuses on the interindividual variability that is characteristic of adult personality change.

In an extensive investigation of a random sample of 500 men at midlife, Michael Farrell and Stanley Rosenberg (1981) discovered a wide range of individual differences in adult personality. They concluded:

> While some studies have found middle age to be the apex of satisfaction and effectiveness, others found it to be a period of identity crisis and discontent. . . . Both our research design and our findings suggest a more complex model [than the universal stage model], one anchored in the idea that the individual is an active agent in interpreting, shaping, and altering his own reality. He not only experiences internal and external changes, he gives meaning to them. The meaning given shows a wide range of variation. (1981, p. 2)

Think about yourself and other people you know. There are certain things you have in common with others, yet many ways in which you differ. Individual variation must be an important aspect of any viable model of adult development.

STABILITY AND CHANGE: TRAIT VIEWS OF ADULT PERSONALITY

In the previous section of this chapter, we showed that there are wide individual differences in adult personality. In this section, we'll discuss the issue of how changeable or stable such individual differences are across the adult life span.

The degree to which personality is stable or changes is a major issue in adult development. This issue can be approached in many different ways. We may evaluate the extent to which childhood personality characteristics predict adult personality characteristics. For example, is an introverted child also an introverted adult? Is a neurotic adolescent also a neurotic adult at midlife? We can ask whether an achievement-oriented woman in early adulthood is still striving hard to be successful at the age of fifty. Or to what extent a depressed thirty-year-old is still depressed at the age of seventy? Further, rather than looking only at the stability of a single personality characteristic, such as introversion, we may evaluate how one or several characteristics present at specific points in the life cycle predict other characteristics at a later point in life. We might also be interested in how social experiences, family experiences, and work experiences predict personality characteristics later in life.

To the extent that there is consistency or continuity from one period of time to another in some attribute of personality, we usually describe personality as being *stable*. In contrast, to the extent that there is little consistency from one period of time to another, we refer to *change* or *discontinuity* in personality.

Personality theorists are often categorized by whether they stress stability in personality across time as well as across situations. Personality theorists called **personologists** or **traditional trait theorists** argue for consistency and stability, whereas, contextual, life-events, or stage theorists are likely to maintain that personality changes over time.

What is a trait? What are the major assumptions that underlie the trait approach to personality? To help answer these questions, it may be useful to consider the ideas of Paul Costa and Robert McCrae (1980). These psychologists, two of the most influential researchers studying adult personality, have listed a set of principles underlying the trait approach:

1. Traits may be regarded as generalized dispositions to thoughts, feelings, and behaviors that endure over substantial periods of time.
2. Traits have relatively little to do with the determination of single, specific behaviors. Specific behaviors are usually controlled by situational influences. Traits do, however, show an appreciable influence over behaviors that are averaged over long periods of time and over a range of diverse situations.
3. Traits, by their inherent nature, are highly interactive (for example, trait anxiety is the tendency to experience fear when threatened, sociability involves the tendency to act friendly when in the presence of other people, and so forth). Thus, trait theory recognizes the importance of the *Person* × *Situation* interaction.
4. Traits are not merely reactive. Traits possess dynamic, motivating tendencies that seek out or produce situations which allow for the expression of certain behaviors. For example, a person who is open to experience may react with interest when presented with a new idea and may actively seek out new

situations (by attending lectures, reading books, changing an occupation, and so on) that lead to new experiences.

5. The enduring quality of generalized traits may manifest itself by the emergence of seemingly different types of behaviors that occur at different times in the adult life span. For example, an anxious person may be afraid of rejection in high school, economic recession in adulthood, and illness and death in old age.

6. Traits need not be purely inherited or biologically based. The origin of personality traits can (and should) remain an open question.

7. Traits are most useful in describing and predicting psychologically important global characteristics in individuals. Since traits are sensitive to the generalities in behavior, trait theory is especially useful in giving a holistic picture of the person. It is this feature of trait theory that makes it the ideal basis for the study of personality and aging. If one adopted a radical interactionist or contextual model of personality, one would never attempt to address such global matters as how personality changes with age.

8. The aims of trait theory are compatible with the aims of longitudinal and sequential research. If traits are assumed to endure over time, they must be measured over time. And the influence of cohort and time of measurement on the assessment of traits must be differentiated from age and true developmental relationships.

Now that we have a general understanding of the trait approach, let's look at some of the major studies of personality development that shed light on the stability-change issue as it relates to personality in the adult years.

The Kansas City Study

One of the earliest longitudinal studies of personality in adulthood was conducted by Bernice Neugarten on a large sample of people aged forty to eighty (Neugarten, 1964, 1973, 1977, Neugarten and Gutmann, 1977). This study took place over a ten-year period in Kansas City, Missouri. The Kansas City Study was not completely grounded in the trait approach, but the results derived from this research have important implications for trait theory. Dependent measures included a number of projective tests, questionnaires, and several types of interviews designed to gain information about the participants. Neugarten concluded that personality is continuous or stable in a number of respects but that some age-related changes occur as well. The most stable characteristics of personality were socioadaptive characteristics, such as coping styles, methods of attaining life satisfaction, and the strength of goal-directed behaviors. Some consistent age-related differences occurred in various intrapsychic personality dimensions that reflect different feelings about the extent to which one can control one's environment. For example, forty-year-olds felt that they had considerable direct or active control over their environments and risk taking was not a primary concern. However, sixty-year-olds were more likely to perceive the environment as threatening and sometimes dangerous. They also

Research indicates that personality is largely stable, although some age-related changes may occur.

had a more passive view of the self. This personality change in adulthood was described by Neugarten as moving from *active to passive mastery.*

Movement from active mastery in midlife to a more passive orientation in late adulthood seems to be a salient characteristic of adult development in a number of diverse cultures. Groups of individuals such as Navajo Indians, isolated groups in Israel, and the Mayans of Mexico also seem to move from an active, controlling view of their interactions with the world to a more passive, receptive, less controlling orientation as they age (Gutmann, 1977).

According to Neugarten, older adults also seem more concerned about inner life than middle-aged adults. Older adults in her study were found to be more introspective and self-reflective than younger adults. Neugarten refers to this change in the personality of older adults as **interiority** (Rosen and Neugarten, 1964).

In addition to the growth of passive mastery and interiority, a shift in sex-role expressiveness seemed to occur in late adulthood in the participants of the Kansas City Study. More specifically, it was found that significant sex-role reversals began to take place as people grew older—men became more tolerant and expressive of their nurturant impulses, and women became more tolerant and expressive of their aggressive tendencies (Neugarten, 1973).

With regard to trait theory, the Kansas City data seem to suggest age-related changes on two important personality dimensions: introversion-extroversion, and masculinity-femininity. With age, adults become more introverted, men become more feminine, and women become more masculine. These conclusions seem consistent with David Gutmann's (1977) ideas of adult personality development (see chapter 8).

The Normative Aging Study and the Baltimore Aging Study

As already mentioned, two of the strongest advocates of the trait approach to personality are Paul Costa and Robert McCrae. The majority of their research comes from two massive longitudinal studies derived from the Normative Aging Study, which is associated with the Veterans Administration Outpatient Clinic in Boston, and the Baltimore Longitudinal Study of Aging, which is being conducted by the National Institute on Aging. The participants in both of these studies were thousands of relatively well-educated, primarily white, mostly healthy men. They ranged from twenty to eighty years of age. Data collection began in the late 1950s to mid-1960s and is still going. Most importantly, the way the data were collected allowed for cross-sectional, longitudinal, and sequential analyses. Thus, the effects of age, cohort, and time of measurement could be determined. Finally, participants in both of these studies were administered an extensive battery of standardized psychometric personality tests. These personality tests, called **self-report inventories,** are designed in such a way that a participant is required to report his or her opinions, feelings, and activities on a wide range of topics.

Costa and McCrae's research (Costa, 1986, Costa and McCrae, 1977, 1978, 1980, 1982, 1985, 1986; McCrae and Costa, 1984, 1987) has yielded two important findings. First, they discovered that personality can best be conceptualized as consisting

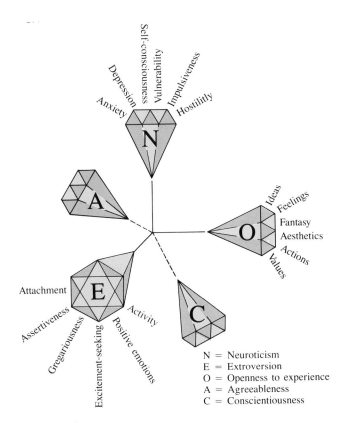

Figure 11.4   An illustration of Costa and McCrae's five-factor model of personality.

of five independent dimensions or factors: neuroticism, extroversion, openness to experience, agreeableness, and conscientiousness. These five dimensions make up what Costa and McCrae call the **five-factor model** of personality (see figure 11.4). The vast majority of the research on this model involves an analysis of the dimensions of neuroticism, extroversion, and openness to experience. Each of these dimensions of personality contains six different facets. **Neuroticism** encompasses how anxious, stable, depressed, self-conscious, impulsive, and vulnerable the individual is; **extroversion** measures the individual's attachment, gregariousness, assertiveness, activity, excitement-seeking, and positive emotions; and **openness to experience** pertains to the individual's openness with respect to fantasy, aesthetics, feelings, actions, ideas, and values.

The second major finding of this research is that these three dimensions of personality remain remarkably stable over the adult years. This is especially true when the data from these studies are analyzed in a longitudinal or sequential manner rather than a cross-sectional manner. This is not to say that the men did not change in a number of ways. In fact, some of the men and their lives changed a great deal. For example, men who were found to be open to experience were likely to change occupations, live eventful lives, and experience good as well as bad in very forceful ways. Individuals who were rated high in neuroticism found new things about which to complain, worry, and become dissatisfied. What endured over time, of course, were the general orientations or dispositions (that is, the traits) that the men used to structure their lives.

Perhaps the results of these studies can be best summed up by examining the following excerpts from a recent interview with Paul Costa:

> I see no evidence for specific changes in personality due to age. What changes as you go through life are your roles and the issues that matter most to you. People may think that their personality has changed as they age, but it is their habits that change, their vigor, their health, their responsibilities and circumstances—not their basic personality.
>
> There is no evidence for any universal age-related crises; those people who have a crisis at one point or another in life tend to be those who are more emotional. Such people experience some degree of distress through most of life; only the form of the trouble seems to change.
>
> After twenty-five, as William James said, character is set in plaster. (*New York Times,* June 1987)

Other psychologists who have analyzed various aspects of the data collected in the Baltimore Longitudinal Study have reported the same findings as Costa and McCrae. Douglas and Arenberg (1978) found that when this data was analyzed in a cross-sectional manner, there were several traits on which young and older adults differed. For example, older adults were found to be submissive, restrained, or serious-minded—this appears to be an increase in introversion. But more sophisticated statistical analyses revealed that these differences were really due to cohort differences between the participants. In fact, the only differences in personality that were found to be due to age (rather than cohort and/or time of measurement) were that the men (1) became less masculine as they aged, and (2) displayed a lower activity level (preferred a slow pace in their lives).

The Seattle Longitudinal Study

K. Warner Schaie and his associates have been involved in a large-scale longitudinal study in the Pacific Northwest, with a great many participants from the city of Seattle, Washington. As we mentioned in chapter 5, this research project has yielded a number of important findings about intellectual development during adulthood. As we will now see, this study has also yielded a number of important findings about personality development as well.

Schaie and Parham (1976) used a variety of methods to analyze the data collected during 1963 and 1970 on a large number of men and women who ranged from twenty-one to eighty-four years of age. All of these participants completed a self-report inventory that measured sixteen different personality traits. When the data were analyzed cross-sectionally, many traits (most notably introversion) seemed to change with age. Older adults were found to be more reserved, less outgoing, and so forth. Upon closer scrutiny, however, these age-related differences were found to be due to cohort effects—adults born in earlier generations were more introverted than those born in later generations. In fact, the only dimension of personality that was found to change with age was excitability. This means that older adults were more likely than young adults to become frazzled, annoyed, and frustrated by many of the events of everyday life.

Conclusions about the Stability of Adult Personality

We believe that Schaie and Willis (1986) have offered an excellent summary of the research examining adult personality development. First, they observed that once the adult personality is formed, it appears remarkably stable. Adult personality is characterized largely by stability and continuity rather than extensive change and reorganization. The adult personality seems to be an organized system of traits that resists major alteration. Can you imagine how difficult it would be to adapt to the changing demands of our lives if our core personalities (as well as the personalities of our friends and family members) underwent frequent change? It seems that adults may exaggerate the age-related changes they think occur in their personality (just as they seem to overestimate the degree to which their memory changes with age). In fact, it has been shown that as individuals age, they tend to perceive their personalities as changing to a considerable degree when in reality their personality remains very stable (Woodruff, 1983; Woodruff and Birren, 1972).

Second, Schaie and Willis (1986) maintained that many of the apparent personality differences between young, middle-aged, and older adults are really caused by generational (cohort) differences rather than age-related differences. Thus, one of the most salient predictors of an adult's personality may be her year of birth rather than mere chronological age. The only personality differences that seem to be due primarily to age are that (1) men seem to become a little more feminine as they age, while women become a little more masculine, (2) many older adults decrease their activity levels or their pace of life, and (3) some older adults become more excited or perplexed about the occurrences of everyday life.

Third, Schaie and Willis (1986) argue that despite the inherent stability of adult personality, the potential for change still exists. For example, even when psychologists find correlations as high as + .70 between personality inventory scores administered over long periods of time, about 50 percent of the variability in the participants' test scores remains unexplained. Obviously, a portion of this variability is caused by imperfections in the test and the conditions under which it was administered. But another source of variability is probably the real shifts that occur in the personality trait in question. According to Schaie and Willis:

> The *average* score for a given trait is likely to remain the same, which means that the people whose scores on the trait increase are balanced by people whose scores decrease. As they grow older, people experience a variety of nonnormative events, changing

them in different ways. There is very little *general* change, but there is quite a bit of *individual* change. (1986, p. 157)

Furthermore, the trait approach to adult personality is not totally antagonistic to the stage perspective. For example, it is possible that a specific individual may go through adulthood with a constellation of stable, enduring personality traits; yet this adult may use these stable traits to tackle the different tasks and psychosocial crises that writers like Erikson and Levinson have identified. A person may deal with an identity crisis in adolescence, a midlife crisis at age forty, and a life review at age seventy-five with the same stable degrees of openness to experience, introversion-extroversion, and neuroticism.

In conclusion, developmentalists should concentrate their energies on both change and stability as well as on the interdependence between the individual and the events of his or her life.

MORAL DEVELOPMENT

In this section, we will look at another important aspect of personality in adulthood—moral development. It has long been recognized that morality represents a central feature of personality. Freud, for example, regarded the superego (one's sense of morality) as one of the primary structures of personality.

Moral development is a multidimensional construct. Most psychologists, in fact, conceptualize morality as possessing three interrelated aspects. The first component is *moral thought:* how do people reason or think about rules of ethical conduct? For example, an individual may hear a story in which the central character is faced with the dilemma of whether to steal to save the life of another person. Then the individual may be asked how the character should resolve the moral conflict. In this procedure, primary emphasis is placed on the individual's rationale, or the type of reasoning he or she uses to justify the character's moral decision.

A second issue in moral development involves the *moral behavior* of individuals in real-life situations. Here the primary concern is whether an individual would, for example, actually steal to help another. In this case, psychologists are concerned with factors which lead to rule transgression or behavioral control.

A third domain of interest is *moral emotion:* how do individuals feel after making a moral decision and engaging in a particular behavior? Psychologists often are particularly interested in emotions that follow either altruistic behavior (helping others, donating to charity) or rule violations (stealing, cheating, lying).

In the next section, we'll describe Lawrence Kohlberg's theory of moral development. Kohlberg's theory, which is one of the most important and influential theories of morality, focuses primarily on the first of the above-mentioned aspects of morality—moral reasoning. But as we shall see, Kohlberg's theory has important implications for how adults adjust to emotionally charged life events and how adults behave in moral contexts.

Kohlberg's Theory

Kohlberg (1958, 1964, 1969, 1976, 1984, 1987) argued that morality is not formed all at once, early in life. Instead, moral development unfolds in a series of discrete stages. Kohlberg's stages of moral development have much in common with Piaget's stages of cognitive development (see chapter 7). For example, the stages develop in an invariant or unchangeable sequence, and they develop in the same way for all individuals (that is, the stages are universal). Furthermore, Kohlberg claims that the stages that comprise moral development are qualitatively different from one another. Finally, Kohlberg maintains that each stage represents the integration and elaboration of the previous stage in the sequence.

Levels and Stages of Moral Development

Kohlberg (1987) proposed that moral development involves three different *levels* (preconventional, conventional, and postconventional) with two different *stages* within each level. An individual's level and stage of moral development are measured by evaluating that individual's response to a number of hypothetical moral dilemmas. One of Kohlberg's well known dilemmas, "Heinz and the Drug," is presented as follows:

> In Europe a woman was near death from cancer. One drug might save her, a form of radium that a druggist in the same town had recently discovered. The druggist was charging $2,000, ten times what the drug cost him to make. The sick woman's husband, Heinz, went to everyone he knew to borrow the money, but he could only get together about half of what the drug cost. He told the druggist his wife was dying and asked him to sell it cheaper or let him pay later. But the druggist said no. The husband got desperate and broke into the man's store to steal the drug for his wife. Should the husband have done that? Why? (Kohlberg, 1969, p. 379)

A person's stage of moral development is determined by his or her answer to the question "Why?", not to the question about what Heinz should have done. In other words, it is the *type* of reasoning a person uses to justify his or her judgment that counts; whether the person thinks Heinz should or shouldn't have stolen the drug is unimportant. Put somewhat differently, Kohlberg's theory places primary emphasis on the *structure* of moral judgment, not the *content* of moral judgment. The former refers to the underlying rule-system that gives rise to a specific moral decision; the latter refers to the decision itself.

The first two stages comprise the **preconventional level** because the individual interprets moral problems from the point of view of physical or material concerns (punishment and reward, the maintenance of power and wealth, and so on) or his own hedonistic wishes. At the preconventional level, then, rules and social expectations are viewed as something external to the self.

The third and fourth stages make up the **conventional level.** At this level, the individual's understanding of morality is dependent on her (or his) internalization of the expectations that other individuals such as friends, family, or society have of her. Maintaining these expectations leads to interpersonal trust and loyalty as well as the preservation of the social system of which the individual is a part. At the conventional level, therefore, the person has identified with or internalized the rules and expectations of other individuals or of a more generalized social system.

The **postconventional level** consists of the fifth and sixth stages in Kohlberg's sequence. At this level, the individual becomes capable of distinguishing between basic human rights and obligations, which remain constant over different cultures and historical epochs, versus societal and legal rules, which can change over sociohistorical contexts. In other words, the postconventional reasoner can construct a set of universal moral principles by differentiating his or her moral point of view from the rules and expectations of significant others and society.

Table 11.3 provides a more complete description of the different stages and levels that make up Kohlberg's theory. Also, table 11.4 provides examples of the type of moral reasoning generated by an individual at each of Kohlberg's stages.

Age-Related Changes in Moral Reasoning

Kohlberg's initial research (Kohlberg, 1958) led to the conclusion that individuals completed the moral stage sequence by the end of adolescence. However, longitudinal data collected by Kohlberg and Kramer (1969) showed that the adolescents who had attained postconventional morality during high school regressed to a preconventional level in their college years. Such a clear violation of the stage criterion of invariant progression forced Kohlberg and his associates to undertake major changes in the theory and measurement of moral development.

Using a revised and more stringent scoring system, Colby, Kohlberg, Gibbs, and Lieberman (1983) reanalyzed Kohlberg and Kramer's longitudinal data and found no evidence of regressive stage movement—the principle of invariant progression had been reconfirmed. Furthermore, Colby et al. (1983) analyzed the data from a twenty-year longitudinal study of moral development which began in the late 1950s. The results of this study are illustrated in figure 11.5. This figure shows the mean percent of moral reasoning displayed by the participants at each of the first five stages in Kohlberg's theory across the entire twenty years of the study. As you can see, there is a clear relationship between age and moral reasoning. Over the twenty-year period, reasoning at stages 1 and 2 decreased. Stage 3 peaked in late adolescence or early adulthood and declined thereafter. Reasoning at stage 4 did not appear at all among the ten-year-olds in the study; yet it was reflected in 62 percent of the judgments of the thirty-six-year-olds. Stage 5 moral reasoning did not appear until the age of twenty to twenty-two. Furthermore, it never rose above 10 percent of the total number of the participants' judgments.

In analyzing these results, Kohlberg (1987) and his associates suggested that children and young adolescents reason at the preconventional level; most older adolescents and adults reason at the conventional level; and a small percentage of adults (mostly middle-aged and older) reason at the postconventional level. Therefore, it seems as if adulthood (not adolescence, as originally suggested) is marked by the ability to construct a universal set of moral principles. Earlier studies (for example, Bielby and Papalia, 1975) have found that moral reasoning declines from middle to late adulthood. These results, however, are based on cross-sectional data and are probably colored by cohort effects.

Stage theories based on data collected only from children and adolescents have limited value for psychologists interested in adult and/or life-span development. Thus, Kohlberg's discovery that moral development occurs during all epochs of the life span—childhood, adolescence, and adulthood—as well as his claim regarding the existence of distinct adult moral stages have been viewed positively by developmentalists.

Determinants of Moral Development

What causes a person to move from one moral stage to the next? There is no reason to believe that chronological age, by itself, is a prime determinant of moral change. Since moral development involves reasoning, Kohlberg (1973) believes that the individual's moral stage is closely related to advances in logical thinking as outlined in Piaget's theory of intellectual development. More specifically, several researchers (Tomlinson-Keasey and Keasey, 1974; Kuhn, Langer, Kohlberg, and Haan, 1977) have maintained that cognitive development is a necessary but not sufficient cause for moral development. They showed that to attain postconventional moral thinking it is necessary for individuals to possess formal operations; however, formal operational thought in itself is not sufficient to automatically produce postconventional morality.

In addition to logical thinking (formal operations), psychologists have examined a number of other factors responsible for the transitions in moral development. After all, if moral development is nothing more than logical thinking applied to moral problems there should be no need to have a theory of moral development separate from cognitive/intellectual theories of development. Kohlberg (1976) suggested that moral development is also heavily dependent on the *sociomoral perspective* a person brings to a moral problem (refer to table 11.3 for a description of the sociomoral perspective that accompanies each stage of moral reasoning). These stages of sociomoral perspective are actively constructed through the reciprocal interactions which take place between an individual and his or her social environment. Moral development should thus be promoted by social environments that (1) give the individual a broad range of role-taking experiences, so that the person becomes aware of the thoughts, feelings, and attitudes of other people and/or adopts the perspectives of various social institutions; and (2) place the individual in real-life positions of moral responsibility (for example, a physician who is forced to make important health-care decisions).

Roodin, Rybash, and Hoyer (1984, 1985) have suggested that advanced moral reasoning during adulthood is dependent on the growth of postformal styles of thinking within the domain of personal knowledge. In fact, it seems that postconventional morality has much in common with Dittmann-Kohli and Baltes's (1988) concept of wisdom (see chapter 7).

TABLE 11.3

AN OVERVIEW OF THE LEVELS AND STAGES THAT COMPRISE KOHLBERG'S THEORY OF MORAL DEVELOPMENT

Level and Stage	What Is Right	Reasons for Doing Right	Sociomoral Perspective
LEVEL I—PRECONVENTIONAL Stage 1—Heteronomous morality	To avoid breaking rules backed by punishment, obedience for its own sake, and avoiding physical damage to persons and property.	Avoidance of punishment, and the superior power of authorities.	*Egocentric point of view.* Doesn't consider the interests of others or recognize that they differ from the actor's; doesn't relate two points of view. Actions are considered physically rather than in terms of psychological interests of others. Confusion of authority's perspective with one's own.
Stage 2—Individualism, instrumental purpose, and exchange	Following rules only when it is to someone's immediate interest; acting to meet one's own interests and needs and letting others do the same. Right is also what's fair, what's an equal exchange, a deal, an agreement.	To serve one's own needs or interests in a world where you have to recognize that other people have their interests, too.	*Concrete individualistic perspective.* Aware that everybody has his own interest to pursue and these conflict, so that right is relative (in the concrete individualistic sense).
LEVEL II—CONVENTIONAL Stage 3—Mutual interpersonal expectations, relationships, and interpersonal conformity	Living up to what is expected by people close to you or what people generally expect of people in your role as son, brother, friend, and so on. "Being good" is important and means having good motives, showing concern about others. It also means keeping mutual relationships, such as trust, loyalty, respect and gratitude.	The need to be a good person in your own eyes and those of others. Your caring for others. Belief in the Golden Rule. Desire to maintain rules and authority which support stereotypical good behavior.	*Perspective of the individual in relationships with other individuals.* Aware of shared feelings, agreements, and expectations which take primacy over individual interests. Relates points of view through the concrete Golden Rule, putting yourself in the other guy's shoes. Does not yet consider generalized system perspective.

438

| Stage 4—Social system and conscience | Fulfilling the actual duties to which you have agreed. Laws are to be upheld except in extreme cases where they conflict with other fixed social duties. Right is also contributing to society, the group, or institution. | To keep the institution going as a whole, to avoid the breakdown in the system "if everyone did it," or the imperative of conscience to meet one's defined obligations. | *Differentiates societal point of view from interpersonal agreement or motives.* Takes the point of view of the system that defines roles and rules. Considers individual relations in terms of place in the system. |

LEVEL III—POSTCONVENTIONAL, OR PRINCIPLED

| Stage 5—Social contract or utility and individual rights | Being aware that people hold a variety of values and opinions, that most values and rules are relative to your group. These relative rules should usually be upheld, however, in the interest of impartiality and because they are the social contract. Some nonrelative values and rights like *life* and *liberty*, however, must be upheld in any society regardless of majority opinion. | A sense of obligation to law because of one's social contract to make and abide by laws for the welfare of all and for the protection of all people's rights. A feeling of contractual commitment, freely entered upon, to family, friendship, trust, and work obligations. Concern that laws and duties be based on rational calculation of overall utility, "the greatest good for the greatest number." | *Prior-to-society perspective.* Perspective of a rational individual aware of values and rights prior to social attachments and contracts. Integrates perspectives by formal mechanisms of agreement, contract, objective impartiality, and due process. Considers moral and legal points of view; recognizes that they sometimes conflict and finds it difficult to integrate them. |
| Stage 6—Universal ethical principles | Following self-chosen ethical principles. Particular laws or social agreements are usually valid because they rest on such principles. When laws violate these principles, one acts in accordance with the principle. Principles are universal principles of justice: the equality of human rights and respect for the dignity of human beings as individual persons. | The belief as a rational person in the validity of universal moral principles, and a sense of personal commitment to them. | *Perspective of a moral point of view* from which social arrangements derive. Perspective is that of any rational individual recognizing the nature of morality or the fact that persons are ends in themselves and must be treated as such. |

From "Moral Stages and Moralization" by Lawrence Kohlberg in *Moral Development and Behavior*, edited by Thomas Lickona. Copyright © 1976 by Holt, Rinehart and Winston.

Table 11.4

RESPONSES AT EACH STAGE LEVEL TO THE "HEINZ AND THE DRUG" DILEMMA

Stage 1

Pro	Con
It's not really bad to steal the drug. It's not like he did not ask to pay for it first. The drug really isn't worth $2,000; at most it costs about $200. Also, letting your wife die would be the same as killing her—and God's commandments say that killing another person is wrong.	Heinz shouldn't steal; he should buy the drug instead. Also, if he steals the drug he'd be committing a big crime and the police would put him in jail for a long time. Finally, God's commandments say that stealing is wrong.

Stage 2

Pro	Con
Heinz should steal the drug because he'd be lonely and sad if his wife dies. He wants her to live more than anything else. Anyway, if he gets sent to jail (that would make him sad), but he'd still have his wife (and that would make him really happy).	Heinz should not steal the drug if he doesn't like his wife a lot. Also, the druggist isn't really a bad person; he just wants to make a profit from all his hard work. That is what you are in business for, to make money.

Stage 3

Pro	Con
If I were Heinz, I'd steal the drug for my wife. Heinz could not be so heartless as to let his wife die. The two partners in a marriage should naturally expect that they will come to each other's aid. Also, you can't put a price on life; and, any decent person should value life above anything else.	Heinz shouldn't steal. If his wife dies, he cannot be blamed. After all, everybody knows that Heinz is not cruel and heartless, he tried to buy the drug legally. The druggist is the selfish one. He deserves to be stolen from.

Stage 4

Pro	Con
When you get married, you take a vow to love and cherish your wife. Marriage is not only love, it's an obligation as well. Marriage is like a legal contract that must be obeyed. Also, by stealing the drug and going to court, Heinz will be able to show the members of his society how dumb the laws about stealing are. This might lead to positive changes in the judicial system.	It's a natural thing for Heinz to want to save his wife, but it is still always wrong to steal. If everybody took the law into their own hands—like Heinz wants to do—his society would be in total chaos. In the long run, nobody in Heinz's society will benefit from this; not even Heinz and his wife!

Table 11.4 *Continued*

Stage 5

Pro	Con
The law is not set up to deal with the unique circumstances of the Heinz case. Taking the drug in this situation is not correct from a "legal" point of view. But, there may be a set of basic human rights (such as the right to life) that must be preserved regardless of what the law may happen to say. The law of the land should protect peoples' basic rights. It certainly isn't in this case. Therefore, Heinz should steal the drug.	You cannot completely blame Heinz for stealing; but extreme circumstances do not really justify violating the law. This is because the law represents a commitment that Heinz and the other members of his society have made to one another.

Stage 6

Pro	Con
Heinz has to act in terms of the principle of preserving and respecting life. It would be both irrational and immoral to preserve the druggist's property right to the drug at the expense of his wife's right to life. After all, people invented the concept of personal property; it is a culturally relative concept. Alternatively, the right of a person to claim their right to life should be absolute.	Heinz is faced with the decision of whether to consider the other people who need the drug just as much as his wife. Heinz ought to act not according to his own feelings toward his wife but on his consideration of all of the lives involved.

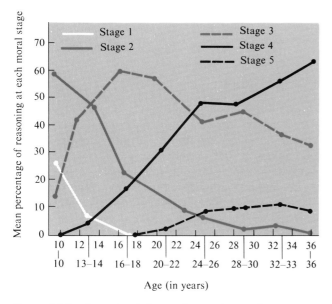

Figure 11.5 Age-related changes in moral reasoning.

How can Kohlberg's theory of moral development help explain the different reasons that adults become involved in issues such as abortion?

The Importance of Moral Development

Why do psychologists attach so much importance to Kohlberg's theory? What is the practical significance of being a postconventional rather than a conventional moral reasoner? Should one try to promote moral development in adults, and if so, how? These important questions can be answered in a variety of ways.

First, as individuals progress through the different moral stages, they should be able to make better or more effective decisions about the moral dilemmas that occur within their own lives. This does not mean that advanced (postconventional) moral reasoners are better people than lower-level moral reasoners. Instead, it means that postconventional reasoners bring a broader, more all-encompassing, and balanced point of view to a moral problem. A postconventional point of view does not have its primary roots in self-centered interests or social/interpersonal expectations. Thus, it allows individuals to more fully consider the conflicting claims that surround a moral dilemma.

Second, it has been shown that a person's level of moral reasoning is related to a person's *moral behavior.* In a review of the literature, Kohlberg and Candee (1984) have shown that as individuals progress through the moral stages, they engage in more consistent instances of moral action: honesty, altruism, political and civil rights activism. Furthermore, they are less likely to comply with immoral orders given by authority figures.

Third, it has recently been reported that moral reasoning is related to the manner in which adults cope with negative life events. Box 11.4 contains more detailed information about the relationship between coping and moral reasoning.

Alternatives and Criticisms to Kohlberg's Theory

A number of studies have validated Kohlberg's claims about the invariance and universality of his moral stage theory (see Colby and Kohlberg, 1984; Harkness, Edwards, and Super, 1981; Nisan and Kohlberg, 1982; Tietjen and Walker, 1985; Walker, deVries, and Bichard, 1984). However, no theory escapes criticism.

Carol Gilligan (1982) believes that Kohlberg's view is not as applicable to females as to males. She points out that adult males, on average, score higher (stage 4) than adult females (stage 3) on Kohlberg's measure of moral reasoning. This is not, in her opinion, due to the fact that men are more moral than women. Instead, Gilligan argues, this sex difference in moral reasoning has its basis in the different *orientations* that men and women bring to moral problems. A man's orientation toward morality is based in abstract principles of justice, while a woman's orientation toward morality is grounded in her relationships with others. These differences have their basis, according to Gilligan (1985), in the socialization of the sexes during childhood. Thus, Gilligan maintains that women score lower on Kohlberg's assessment of moral stage reasoning because Kohlberg's measure is biased in favor of males (in other words, Kohlberg's test measures a person's understanding of abstract principles of justice, rather than the sense of connectedness that binds individuals together). Research inspired by Gilligan's theory (Gilligan, 1977, 1982; Gilligan and Belenky, 1980; Lyons, 1983) has found that women make moral judgments by focusing on their responsibilities to people: their families, their friends, and themselves. However, several psychologists have not observed the sex differences in moral reasoning reported by Gilligan (Gibbs, Arnold, and Burkhart, 1984; Walker, 1986; Walker, deVries, and Trevethan, 1987). Therefore, Gilligan's viewpoint has not achieved unequivocal support.

Another criticism of Kohlberg's theory that bears on adult development has been raised by Rybash, Roodin, and Hoyer (1983). These researchers argued that the problems encountered by adults in real-life contexts, especially older adults, may have little in common with the hypothetical dilemmas that Kohlberg uses to measure moral development. Thus, older adults may be at a disadvantage when using Kohlberg's assessments of moral reasoning. In support of Rybash et al. (1983), Pratt, Golding, and Kerig (1987) found that older adults experienced quite different

---

BOX 11.4

MORAL REASONING AND COPING

A sophisticated series of studies about the relationship between life experiences and adult moral development was conducted by Edward Lonky, Cheryl Kaus, and Paul Roodin (1984). Their research had its basis in John Gibbs's reformulation of Kohlberg's theory of moral reasoning.

Gibbs (1977, 1979) proposed the existence of two distinct phases of moral development: the **standard phase,** and the **existential phase.** The standard phase consists of the four stages that comprise the first two levels (preconventional and conventional) of Kohlberg's theory. Gibbs used the term *standard* to mean normal or expected. That is, it is the norm for the majority of adults to progress through the first four stages in Kohlberg's theory. This is because these stages are directly tied to changes in logical thinking and perspective-taking that occur in the vast majority of adults. The existential phase incorporates the stages that make up the last (postconventional) level in Kohlberg's theory. Gibbs argued that these two stages (5 and 6) do not meet the criteria which define true developmental stages. Gibbs maintained that (1) postconventional morality is displayed in only a very small percentage of adults in our Western culture and is absent in a variety of non-Western (or traditional) societies; and (2) unlike the first four stages, stages 5 and 6 of Kohlberg's theory are subject to reversals and regressions.

More specifically, Gibbs argued that existential or postconventional morality only develops when an adult comes to grips with the core needs that underlie human existence. These core needs, initially identified by Eric Fromm (1955), are: *relatedness* (the need to overcome feelings of aloneness), *transcendence* (the need to surpass passivity and demonstrate competence), *rootedness* (the need for warmth, protection, and security), *identity* (the need to control one's own destiny and be aware of oneself as a separate entity), and *meaning* (the need for a guiding set of principles and beliefs).

Gibbs (1979) argued that these core needs are experienced within the context of salient life events and experiences. He also noted that once an individual experiences

---

real-life moral problems from those presented in Kohlberg's dilemmas. Furthermore, older adults were found to be more reflective when they reasoned about real-life problems than about the hypothetical moral problems used in Kohlberg's assessment procedure. Pratt et al. (1987) also found a great deal of consistency between the stage of moral reasoning used by young and middle-aged adults when they reasoned about real-life versus hypothetical dilemmas, but *no* consistency in stagelike reasoning when older adults reasoned about different types of dilemmas. Somewhat similar results have been obtained by Walker et al. (1987).

a need, she seeks a mode of coping with it. Coping may be characterized as either **affirmative** (essentially positive) or **abortive** (essentially negative and nonproductive). An affirmative mode of coping lays the basis for mutual love, productive creativity, egalitarian community, responsive individuality, and a system of reason and devotion. An abortive mode of coping generates an obsession with power or submission, wanton destructiveness, in-group chauvinism, herd conformity, and rationalizing ideology.

These speculations led Lonky et al. (1984) to wonder if an abortive coping style would be related to a fixation at the standard phase of moral development, while an affirmative mode of coping would be associated with the existential phase of moral development. They studied a group of adult women who had experienced a major loss or separation (the death of a loved one, divorce, and so on) during the past twelve months. These women participated in a semistructured interview that assessed the manner in which they coped with their negative life experiences. The researchers also measured the women's level of moral reasoning. Results indicated that women in the standard phase of moral development (conventional reasoners) tended to deal abortively with the needs they experienced within the context of these life events; while women in the existential phase (postconventional reasoners) dealt with the same needs in an affirmative manner. Lonky et al. also showed that affirmative coping is related to the personality trait of openness to experience as identified by Costa and McCrae (1980) and a problem-solving, action-oriented coping style labeled *problem-focused coping* by Lazarus and Folkman (1984).

Lonky et al. (1984) recognize that it is not possible, based on the design of their research studies, to determine if coping determines moral reasoning or vice versa. But these researchers have established an important link between these two psychological phenomena.

Summary

There are several definitions of personality and wide-ranging theoretical views of how personality should be conceptualized and measured.

Some personality theorists adopt a stage perspective. Among the stage theorists, Freud believed that there is little or no personality change during the adult years, whereas Erikson stressed personality changes throughout the life cycle. Four of Erikson's eight stages are particularly important in terms of personality development in adulthood—identity versus role confusion, intimacy versus isolation, generativity versus stagnation, and ego integrity versus despair. Erikson's theory has stimulated a great deal of interest in themes of personality at different points in adulthood, but it has been hard to develop the empirical data to support his theory.

Several other views emphasize stages of adult personality development. Roger Gould argues that in our twenties we assume new roles, in our thirties we begin to feel stuck with our responsibilities, and in our forties we begin to sense an urgency when we see our lives speeding by. When we realize that these steps are natural, we are on the path to adult maturity. Daniel Levinson's stage theory focuses on personality change during adulthood and midlife transition. He proposed that the middle-aged adult faces four conflicts: being young versus old, being masculine versus feminine, being destructive versus constructive, and being attached to others versus separated from them. The success of the midlife transition depends on how effectively individuals are able to reduce these polarities. Despite the richness and intrinsic appeal of these theories, there are a number of methodological shortcomings in Gould's and Levinson's work. Furthermore, these theorists may have underestimated the role played by generational factors in adult personality development.

Life-events theorists believe that personality itself often changes because of the unique life events that individuals experience during adulthood. Bernice Neugarten, one of the major pioneers of the life-events framework, has argued that we need to consider the sociohistorical circumstances in which life events occur. She leaves the impression that sociohistorical influences are more important in the personality equation than chronological age. Life-events theorists believe that too much emphasis has been placed on stages of adult development and the concept of predictable life crises at the same points in adult life. In particular, they attack the midlife crisis theorists, arguing that events at midlife only take on crisis proportions when powerful, nonnormative life events occur.

Many theorists also recognize the importance of individual differences in adult personality. Not all people go through stages, crises, or life events in the same way, so there is a great deal of individual variation in adult personality development.

Some developmentalists measure the stability of individual differences in personality by adopting a trait approach. Traits may be best conceptualized as enduring characteristics or dispositions which help to organize a person's thoughts, feelings, and behaviors. Two of the most well-known trait theorists are Paul Costa and Robert McCrae. There are many complex aspects to the question of how stable personality is in adulthood. Some overall themes do appear, however, in the longitudinal studies of personality development: the Kansas City Study, the Normative Aging Study, the Baltimore Study, and the Seattle Study. These studies show that adult personality traits such as neuroticism, extroversion, and openness to experience remain remarkably stable over the adult life span. They also revealed that major changes, transitions, and upheavals in adult personality are more apparent than real. Moreover, these studies have also shown that generational or cohort differences can have a significant impact on the structure of adult personality. Finally, the proponents of the trait approach acknowledge that there is always the potential for personality change during the adult years.

A person's sense of morality is an important component of his or her personality. Psychologists have studied three aspects of moral development—moral reasoning, behavior, and feeling. At the core of Lawrence Kohlberg's major theory of moral development is an analysis of how people reason about and understand complex moral dilemmas. Kohlberg believes that moral development occurs in a stagelike sequence. Specifically, his theory proposes the existence of three moral levels (preconventional, conventional, and postconventional), with two stages within each level. Kohlberg also argues that moral development continues during childhood, adolescence, and adulthood. Most adults reason at the conventional moral level, although a small percentage of adults attain postconventional morality. Development through the different stages in Kohlberg's theory is dependent on (1) a person's thinking ability and sociomoral perspective-taking skills, and (2) the degree to which an individual is afforded the responsibility to make critical ethical decisions.

Adults who reason at the postconventional level seem to cope with negative life events in a much more affirmative manner than conventional reasoners. Moreover, it appears that adults at the postconventional level are more likely to engage in moral action than individuals at lower levels.

Kohlberg is not without his critics. Carol Gilligan has argued that Kohlberg's theory is biased in favor of men. Other psychologists argue that the dilemmas Kohlberg uses to assess moral reasoning are very different from the ones that adults experience in their everyday lives.

Review Questions

1. Describe the differences between the views of personologists, or traditional trait theorists, and those of stage and life-events theorists.
2. Compare and contrast the stage theories of Erikson, Gould, and Levinson. What seem to be the strongest and weakest points of these theories?
3. How do the proponents of the life-events framework explain the notion of midlife crisis? Why do life-events theorists attach more importance to sociohistorical influences than stage theorists do?
4. What are personality traits? Briefly describe the three different personality traits that make up Costa and McCrae's five-factor model of personality.
5. What are the findings of the major longitudinal studies of adult personality development?
6. What is the advantage of having a personality structure that remains stable over time?
7. Given all of the information presented in this chapter, do you think that a person's age or year of birth is a more important determinant of his or her personality?
8. Describe the levels and stages which make up Kohlberg's theory of moral development. What level of moral development is unique to adulthood?
9. From the perspective of Kohlberg's theory, what are the factors responsible for moral development?
10. Briefly describe John Gibbs's reformulation of Kohlberg's theory of moral development. Explain how Gibbs's viewpoint may relate both to moral reasoning and coping style.
11. Briefly describe Carol Gilligan's major criticism of Kohlberg's theory.

For Further Reading

Brim, O. G., Jr., & Kagan, J. (Eds.). (1980). *Constancy and change in human development*. Cambridge, MA: Harvard University Press.

Includes detailed information about physical, cognitive, and personality development. Provides insight into some of the difficulties in measuring constancy and change over long time periods. Moderately difficult reading level.

Erikson, E. (1963). *Childhood and society*. (2d Ed.). New York: Norton.

In this famous book, Erik Erikson first proposed his life-span view of personality development. This book is a classic in developmental psychology. Moderately difficult reading level.

Gilligan, C. (1982). *In a different voice: Psychological theory and women's development.* Cambridge, MA: Harvard University Press.

In this well-written book, Gilligan outlines Kohlberg's theory of moral development and her objections to it. She articulates an important and a thought-provoking theory of female moral development. Moderately easy reading level.

Levinson, D. J. (1978). *The seasons of a man's life.* New York: Knopf.

In this major work, Levinson outlines his theory of male adult personality development. The book is extremely well-written and contains a number of clinical, interviewed-based insights into development. It would be very informative to read this book before reading the next suggested reading by McCrae and Costa. Moderately easy reading level.

McCrae, R. R., and Costa, P. T., Jr. (1984). *Emerging lives, enduring dispositions: Personality in adulthood.* Boston, MA: Little Brown.

This book provides an interesting and informative account of Costa and McCrae's longitudinal research on personality development. Strong evidence is provided in support of the view that personality remains stable over time. Moderately difficult reading level.

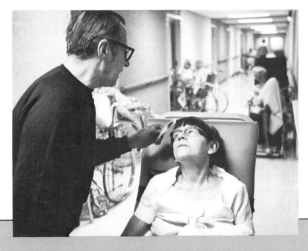

CHAPTER 12

COPING, ADAPTATION, AND MENTAL HEALTH

449

IMAGINE

Imagine That within the Last Six Months You Have Been Fired from Your Job, Separated from Your Spouse, and Experienced the Death of Your Last Remaining Parent

Some psychologists believe that life events can be ranked in terms of the magnitude of stress they produce. These psychologists maintain that the greater the stress produced by specific life events, the greater the likelihood a person will experience physical health problems, diseases, and psychological problems. Holmes and Rahe's Social Readjustment Rating Scale (table 12.1) has often been used as an index of the stress that specific life events produce.

How do researchers arrive at the stress values of various life events? An event such as marriage is used as an anchor point and assigned a value. In the case of the Social Readjustment Rating Scale, marriage was assigned the value of 50. A sample of adults was then asked how much readjustment would be required if each of the events listed in the table occurred in their lives. This question was asked in relation to marriage: for example, would being fired at work require more or less readjustment than marriage? How about sex difficulties, divorce, or the death of a close friend? The average score for an event was then divided by ten to arrive at the number you see beside each life event in the table. Look at the life events and their readjustment scores and rankings. Do you agree with their order?

Generally, a significant but modest relationship has been found between degree of stress and physical illness; there also seems to be an increase in the symptoms of physical illness with increasing age (Aldwin, Spiro, Levinson, and Bosse, 1989). Many individuals—but not all—who have experienced stressful life events seem to show more physical and health-related problems (Rabkin and Struening, 1976; Taylor, 1990). Some people handle stress better than others, resisting illness even in the face of highly stressful life events. For example, when business executives have vigorous attitudes toward challenging situations, they experience fewer physical problems and less illness than their counterparts with opposite attitudes (Kobasa, 1979). People who face stress but retain their health probably perceive change as a challenging opportunity, not a threat.

We can ask several questions about the relationship between aging and stress. For example, do we experience an ever-increasing number of stressors as we age? Do we develop more effective strategies for coping with stress as we grow older? Or do older adults, faced with a barrage of stressful experiences, find their adaptive abilities simply overwhelmed?

INTRODUCTION

In this chapter, we'll deal with issues concerning the adaptation, coping, and mental health of older adults. We'll begin with a discussion of the methods adults use to adapt to stress and examine how coping strategies may evidence age-related changes. Next, we'll turn our attention to the most common mental disorders in older populations—dementia and depression. We'll describe different types of dementia, and we'll discuss the difficulty involved in distinguishing dementia from depression in older adults. After a discussion of some of the more salient mental health concerns of older adults (suicide, fear of crime, and elder abuse), we'll focus on special problems encountered by the institutionalized elderly and the role of rehabilitation programs.

STRESS, COPING, AND ADAPTATION

Psychologists have long been interested in stress and helping people develop more adaptive ways of coping with it. Experts have different theories of stress, different assessment procedures, and different views of the degree to which stress is experienced at critical points in adult life. Too often, simple notions about stress in adult life can lead to erroneous conclusions. Richard Lazarus and his coworkers Anita DeLongis (1983) and Susan Folkman (1984) believe that to better understand psychological stress and coping in aging, we should distinguish between two models of stress: the **life-events model** and the **cognitive model.** They further believe that to delineate more effective ways to cope with stress, we should study how adults cognitively appraise, personally interpret, and individually define the stressors of life.

Models of Coping and Adaptation: The Life-Events View

The earliest life-events model of stress and coping was developed by Holmes and Rahe (1967). These researchers believed that the degree of changes brought about by various life events influenced the levels of stress experienced by individuals. Thus, key life events mandate change and adaptation (Whitbourne, 1985a). This model is briefly summarized in figure 12.1.

One of the predictions from the life-events model is that increased stress leads to physical and emotional problems. Recall the Imagine section and the Social Readjustment Rating Scale, which ranked the levels of stress produced by specific life events. Some believe that this model predicts that the more changes a person has to make, the greater the stress.

However, other psychologists believe the life-events model places too much emphasis on change and largely ignores mediating processes such as the personal significance and subjective interpretation of the events themselves (Rybash et al., 1986; Whitbourne, 1985a). For example, the death of a parent, while stressful, may be interpreted quite differently by a child sixteen years of age and a "child" forty-five years of age. Thus, the same traumatic event may produce different levels of stress for each person. Furthermore, even when faced with comparable stressful events, people do not choose the same coping strategies and solutions. Most people examine their coping resources and strategies in deciding how to face a stressful experience (Lazarus and DeLongis, 1983; Lazarus and Folkman, 1984; Sarason and Spielberger, 1980; Whitbourne, 1985a).

Table 12.1

THE SOCIAL READJUSTMENT RATING SCALE

Rank	Life Event	Mean Value	Rank	Life Event	Mean Value
1	Death of spouse	100	23	Son or daughter leaving home	29
2	Divorce	73	24	Trouble with in-laws	29
3	Marital separation	65	25	Outstanding personal achievement	28
4	Jail term	63	26	Wife begin or stop work	26
5	Death of close family member	63	27	Begin or end school	26
6	Personal injury or illness	53	28	Change in living condition	25
7	Marriage	50	29	Revision of personal habits	24
8	Fired at work	47	30	Trouble with boss	23
9	Marital reconciliation	45	31	Change in work hours or conditions	20
10	Retirement	45	32	Change in residence	20
11	Change in health of family member	44	33	Change in schools	20
12	Pregnancy	40	34	Change in recreation	19
13	Sex difficulties	39	35	Change in church activities	19
14	Gain of new family member	39	36	Change in social activities	18
15	Business readjustment	39	37	Mortgage or loan less than $10,000	17
16	Change in financial state	38	38	Change in sleeping habits	16
17	Death of close friend	37	39	Change in number of family get-togethers	15
18	Change to different line of work	36	40	Change in eating habits	15
19	Change in number of arguments with spouse	35	41	Vacation	13
20	Mortgage over $10,000	31	42	Christmas	12
21	Foreclosure of mortgage or loan	30	43	Minor violations of the law	11
22	Change in responsibilities at work	29			

From *Journal of Psychosomatic Research,* Vol. 11:213–218, T. H. Holmes and R. H. Rahe, "The Social Readjustment Rating Scale." Copyright 1967, Pergamon Press, Ltd.

Models of Coping and Adaptation: The Cognitive View

A second model of coping and adaptation to stress (see figure 12.2) emphasizes the importance of a person's subjective perception of potentially stressful life events. Thus, not all people see highly ranked stressful life experiences (table 12.1) as traumatic and serious problems in their lives. The process of determining if an event is stressful is called **primary appraisal.** The subjective determination of an event as stressful produces emotional reactions of tension, anxiety, and dread, while events considered nonstressful provide challenge and growth, typically producing emotions of hope, excitement, and joy (Lazarus and Folkman, 1984). Once primary appraisal has occurred, a person can decide how to adapt by choosing resources and

Figure 12.1   The life-events model of coping and adaptation.

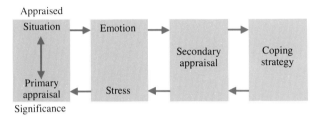

Figure 12.2   Lazarus's cognitive model of coping and adaptation.

determining the costs of using such resources—a process called **secondary appraisal.**

In research on stress in the adult years, Richard Lazarus and his colleagues (DeLongis, Coyne, Dakof, Folkman, and Lazarus, 1982; Lazarus and Folkman, 1984) found an inverse relationship between stressful life events and age for people aged forty-five to sixty-four. Does this mean that people experience fewer stressful life events as they age? We cannot conclude that just because the frequency of stressful life events decreases with age, older people experience less stress. We must also take into account the meaning or subjective interpretation of stress (primary appraisal). A simple frequency analysis on the number of stressful life events ignores the different coping demands of younger and older people. Older individuals, for example, may find that a single minimally stressful life event, such as leaving home for a vacation, may overwhelm them if they also have to deal with a chronic infirmity such as arthritis and nonsupportive relatives who question the wisdom of their decision to travel.

Daily Hassles and Uplifts: The Broken Shoelace Syndrome

Daily hassles are the little, irritating annoyances that punctuate our day-to-day existence (DeLongis et al., 1982; Lazarus and Folkman, 1984). Some hassles are transient, such as having a rude and uncaring waiter, while others may be chronic, such as having to wait hours in traffic each day as we travel to and from work. Lazarus and his colleagues (Folkman, Lazarus, Pimley, and Novacek, 1987; Monat and

Small daily hassles cause stress in the lives of most adults.

Lazarus, 1985) have developed a hassles scale that evaluates the frequency and intensity of everyday stresses such as misplacing belongings, not having enough time for family, filling out forms, or breaking a shoelace. Counterbalancing such hassles are corresponding **uplifts,** or positive experiences, which we also may encounter each day (Lazarus and Folkman, 1984).

In their research, Lazarus and his colleagues have found little difference between men and women in the type and frequency of hassles encountered (Folkman, Lazarus, Dunkel-Schetter, DeLongis, and Gruen, 1986; Folkman, Lazarus, Gruen, and DeLongis, 1986). Interestingly, the measurement of daily hassles is a strong predictor of a person's overall adaptation. The individual's ability to cope with hassles, in fact, is a far better predictor of morale and life satisfaction, psychological symptoms, and somatic illness than the number of major life stresses the person has endured (DeLongis et al., 1982; Kanner, Coyne, Schaefer, and Lazarus, 1981;

Lazarus and Folkman, 1984). Why might this be so? Daily hassles seem to have a stronger link with health outcomes because they evaluate proximal aspects of stress, whereas life-event rankings measure distal aspects. *Proximal* aspects are the adult's immediate perceptions of the environment, whereas *distal* aspects are more removed perceptions that may not have common meanings for all people.

In studying the daily hassles of college students, young adults, and middle-aged adults, Lazarus and his colleagues (Folkman et al., 1987; Lazarus and Folkman, 1984) found that younger adults often reported more hassles than older adults in two areas: economics or finances and work (although personal-social concerns were also problematic). Younger college students had to cope with academic and social problems—wasting time, meeting high standards, being lonely. Older adults experienced hassles most often in the areas of environmental and social problems, home upkeep, and health. Lazarus's sample was essentially white, healthy, middle class, and well-educated. The daily hassles of other adults probably vary from this pattern.

Coping and Adaptation: The Timing of Significant Experiences

The extent to which individuals cope and adapt to stressful experiences has also been related to the timing of such events. Neugarten and Neugarten (1987) have suggested that negative events may produce minimal levels of stress when experienced at predictable points in the life course. Neugarten (1968) has provided evidence that adults construct a kind of social timetable from which they evaluate their developmental progress: they judge the "right" age for marriage, the "right" time to have children, and the predictable time to experience losses, such as the death of a parent (most often between forty and fifty years of age). Events that occur "on time" usually cause minimal stress, while those that are unexpected produce considerable stress. For example, pregnancy can be a wonderful and exciting time for a married women in her twenties or thirties; the same event can bring considerable stress to an unmarried adolescent girl or a forty-five-year-old woman with a demanding career. Similarly, the death of a parent is a very different experience for a fifty-five-year-old as opposed to a fifteen-year-old.

The significance of an illness may also vary according to the time it occurs in a person's life. For example, in one study (Mages and Mendelsohn, 1979), older people who discovered they had cancer often accelerated processes associated with the ending of life such as disengagement from external commitments, increased dependency, and the life-review process. Older adults were also more likely to confront cancer with less anger than younger adults, who feel they should have much of their lives ahead. Such findings illustrate the importance of considering the personal meanings of stressful events at different points in adult development (Hultsch and Plemons, 1979; Lazarus and DeLongis, 1983).

Coping and Adaptation: Life-Threatening Illness

Shelley Taylor (1983) and her colleagues (Wood, Taylor, and Lichtman, 1985) investigated how women cope with the diagnosis of breast cancer. Taylor reported that women interpreted this life-threatening illness through a series of active distortions of reality. Of seventy-eight women interviewed, 95 percent tried to derive a new sense of personal meaning from their illness (for example, "I was very happy to find out that I am a very strong person"). A second theme in their coping with this life-threatening disease was an earnest attempt to gain "magical mastery" or control over their cancer. For example, many believed dietary changes, life-style changes, or maintaining a positive attitude would help them win their battle against the disease. A third theme was the attempt to regain feelings of self-esteem. The women selected a reference group to compare themselves to, deriving a more favorable view of themselves and their disease. Thus, older women felt better off than younger women, married women felt sorry for unmarried women, and those with a poor prognosis consoled themselves that at least they were still alive. The women who coped most successfully with cancer tried to master their dilemma and take charge of their lives regardless of the probabilities and realities of their situations.

Coping and Adaptation: The Use of Resources and Defenses

Adults use coping strategies to adapt to, respond to, reduce, or avoid stress. We rarely respond passively to stress. We attempt to change circumstances when possible; when we can't, we often invoke cognitive strategies to alter the meaning of stressful circumstances, as the women with breast cancer did (Taylor, 1983; Wood et al., 1985). Individuals employ many common defense mechanisms and unconscious strategies to protect the ego from threat and anxiety. It is not an easy task to measure coping resources and strategies (Carver, Scheier, and Weintraub, 1989). Too often, coping has been assessed as a trait or style using a single measure at one point in time. Such simple measurements do not predict how adults will react across time and in various situations. Lazarus and his associates (for example, Folkman and Lazarus, 1980) have constructed a checklist of coping strategies. This checklist focuses on what adults thought, felt, and did in a number of specific stressful circumstances. Using this measure, the researchers identified two basic coping strategies used by adults: **problem-focused coping** and **emotion-focused coping.** When people use problem-focused coping strategies, they attempt to obtain additional information to be more effective in problem solving or to actively change the stressful situation or event. When adults use emotion-focused coping strategies, they employ behavioral and cognitive techniques to help manage the emotional tension produced by the stressful life situation. This strategy does not necessarily remove the perceived stress, but rather helps in managing or reducing the accompanying emotional distress.

Most people use both problem-focused and emotion-focused strategies rather than relying solely on one or the other. When coping patterns are charted according to age, some interesting trends emerge. Folkman et al. reported that

> . . . younger respondents used proportionately more active, interpersonal, problem-focused forms of coping (for example, confrontive coping, seeking social support, planful problem solving) than did the older people, and the older people used proportionately more passive, intrapersonal emotion-focused forms of coping (for example, distancing, acceptance of responsibility, and positive reappraisal) than did the younger people. (Folkman et al., 1987, p. 182)

Carver, Scheier, and Weintraub (1989) further suggest that the emotion-focused and problem-focused distinction made by Lazarus may be far too simple and that additional dimensions may need to be considered in examining age-related differences in coping. Interestingly, older adults perceive the sources of stress as potentially less controllable than younger persons (Blanchard-Fields and Robinson, 1987). And it appears that older adults are far more likely to cope successfully than younger adults and adolescents (Blanchard-Fields and Irion, 1988; Blanchard-Fields and Robinson, 1987).

George Valliant (1977), who conducted a longitudinal study of personality and coping, considers active distortion a primitive form of coping as compared to other ego defense mechanisms. The denial and distortion of reality appears to be at the lowest level of adult coping mechanisms (Valliant, 1977). The most mature coping strategies were characterized by altruism; humor (that is, a method of expressing emotions that is free from consequences); suppression (being optimistic in the face of problems, waiting for a desired outcome, looking for a silver lining); anticipation (planning and preparation for realistic outcomes such as death of a loved one); and sublimation (channeling unacceptable impulses and emotions into socially valued and personally rewarding activities).

It is interesting to contrast Valliant's view that denial and distortion of reality represent immature coping with the views that consider denial to be an acceptable and healthy mode of adjustment under certain conditions (Kemp, 1985; Monat and Lazarus, 1985). On a short-term basis, denial may allow an individual to gain the emotional resources to face reality. Thus, a victim of a severe spinal cord injury may be helped by denying the extent of the injury and being optimistic that some recovery of function may be gained (Kemp, 1985, Monat and Lazarus, 1985). However, in time, denial must be abandoned in favor of more realistic approaches. Some denial and distortions of reality, then, may be helpful in coping, depending on the context and the length of time such strategies are maintained.

Coping in Action: Caring for an Older Relative

There are, of course, many predictable stressors across the life course. One such stressor involves caring for an ill parent or other relative. Providing such care often produces strong feelings of obligation, guilt, and resentment over the time taken from spouse and children. Through interviews conducted over a number of months, researchers identified three styles of coping with an ailing parent: *confrontational* (focusing on dealing with anger, guilt, and sadness, and attempting to bring stressful encounters with the parent to an end); *denial* (suppression and eventual repression of negative feelings); and *avoidant* (consistent suppression rather than denial or repression of negative emotions). The stressful nature of caring for a spouse with dementia or stroke has also been documented (Anthony-Bergstone, Zarit, and Gatz, 1988; George and Gwyther, 1986; Gilhooly, 1984; and Moritz, Kasl, and Berkman, 1989). It appears that such caregiving contributes to increased levels of depression and hostility. Younger and older women (sixty and over) reported increased levels of anxiety when they acted as caregivers (Anthony-Bergstone, Zarit, and Gatz, 1988). Stephens, Norris, Kinney, Ritchie, and Grotz (1988) found both avoidance coping strategies and depression among caregivers sixty years of age and over who were responsible for the care of an older spouse or relative recently discharged from a rehabilitation hospital. Avoidance strategies may help people cope with the immediate impact of stress or a short-term problem (Roth and Cohen, 1986). However, if employed consistently as a strategy to deal with problems of extended duration (more than six to nine months), avoidance generally produces negative outcomes (Roth and Cohen, 1986).

The Search for Meaning

The attempt to make sense out of what is happening to us shapes our cognitive appraisal of stressful encounters and our choice of coping strategies. It is part of our continuous search for mastery and control over difficult situations (Bandura, 1982, 1989; Lachman, 1986; Lefebvre-Pinard, 1984; Rodin, 1986; Rybash et al., 1986). The cognitive-affective struggle we call coping has important implications for our health, psychological functioning, competence both at work and at home, and the success we find in interpersonal relationships. According to Lazarus and DeLongis:

> . . . the significance of such a process-oriented perspective may be even greater in the study of aging than in midlife because of the presence of widespread losses of roles and relationships. But whether viewed in the context of the entire life course or more narrowly in aging, we must see people as engaged in a life drama with a continuous story line that is best grasped not as a still photo but as a moving picture with a beginning, middle, and end. (1983, p. 24)

As we have seen, adaptation and coping are important ingredients in understanding the adult's experience of stressful events. Next, we'll see that the personality profiles of adults who seem to cope well with stress include both resources and deficits.

Personality Profiles of Adults Who Cope Effectively with Stress

Marjorie Fiske (1980) indicates that virtually every individual harbors both deficits and resources within her or his psychological makeup. Fiske believes that we must

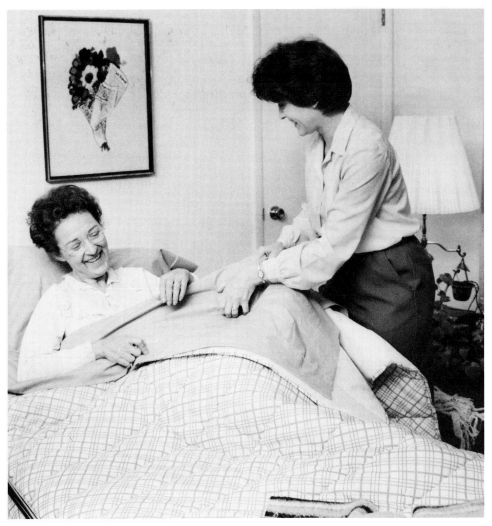

One common stressor in adult life is the need to care for an older relative.

learn more about the adaptive coexistence of both deficits and resources because one strong resource may offset or counterbalance several deficits. In an ongoing longitudinal study, Fiske is attempting to assess the balance between inner resources and deficits among men and women at different stages of the life course, the relationship between these dimensions, and the individual's sense of well-being. Looked at separately, the two dimensions are related to life satisfaction in an entirely rational fashion. People with the most resources (such as the capacity for mutuality, growth, competence, hope, and insight) tend to be satisfied with themselves and their lives; those with deficits (psychological symptoms, including anxiety, hostility, and self-hatred) are the least satisfied. But these expected results were found among fewer than one-third of the people studied. Among the other two-thirds, a combination of many positive and negative attributes seemed to increase the individual's sense of well-being.

Such findings suggest that it may be misleading to look only at the degree of impairment in a particular individual, because when we look closely at people who are the most satisfied with their lives, they harbor an array of both positive and negative attributes, are deeply involved in their worlds, and cope well with the diversity of stresses that in-depth encounters with work and with people involve (Chiriboga and Cutler, 1980; Chiriboga and Thurnher, 1975; Lowenthal, Thurnher, and Chiriboga, 1975). See box 12.1 for a specific example of the confluence of positive and negative attributes in adult life.

MENTAL HEALTH IN LATE ADULTHOOD

We all experience stressors that demand coping and adaptation. Unfortunately, some older individuals lose the ability to cope with the demands and complexities of everyday life. A breakdown in coping strategies and the loss of the ability to function psychologically are two of the hallmarks of mental illness. The importance of understanding and treating mental disorders in older adults is captured in Seymour Kety's foreword to the *Handbook of Mental Health and Aging* (1980). Specifically, Kety commented that:

> "A national health problem that is most severe in terms of its prevalence and cost is a group of mental disorders and dysfunctions which are associated with aging. . . . As the result of progress in medical science, a substantial segment of the population can now look forward to a longer life, but one which may unfortunately be hampered by mental disability. This is a prospect that is both troubling to the individual and costly to society. Since mental handicap makes an individual increasingly dependent on the help and care of others, the cost of these services and prerequisites to other members of the family and to the whole of society as well represents a burden which has been estimated at 36.78 billions of dollars per year in the United States. More important, perhaps, is a cost that cannot be measured or tabulated: the loss of human potential and of the affected person's capacity for adaptation and ability to contribute to human welfare. (p. xi)

Defining *mental health* is not an easy task, although the term has become commonplace in our society. It presumably not only embraces the absence of mental illness, but also reflects one's ability to deal with the issues of life in an effective if not pleasurable or satisfying manner. Because older adults are more likely than younger adults to have some type of physical illness, the interweaving of physical and mental problems is more likely to occur in later adulthood than in younger adulthood (Birren and Sloane, 1980; Gambert, 1987).

BOX 12.1

MANIC-DEPRESSIVE DISORDERS AND CREATIVITY

Experts examining psychological adjustment and coping processes have noted that frequently (but *not* always), those who make unique and outstanding contributions to the creative arts demonstrate cycles of manic-depressive behavior during their lives. It is curious that many of the musical genuises of the past two centuries suffered from bouts of manic-depression, or bipolar affective disorder. DeAngelis (1989) recently examined the suffering and personal anguish this mood disorder brought to the lives of talented composers such as George Frederic Handel, Hugo Wolf, Robert Schumann, Hector Berlioz, and Gustav Mahler. The cyclic effects of intense periods of activity or mania obviously contributed to the immense musical productivity of this group of outstanding and creative composers. Yet their corresponding bouts of debilitating depression, leading at times to suicidal thoughts or behaviors, also affected these composers.

The following diary excerpts and letters reveal how difficult it was for these composers to cope with their manic-depressive episodes. Berlioz, for instance, described his two moods as "the two kinds of spleen; one mocking, active, passionate, malignant; the other morose and wholly passive." Schumann likened his mood swings to two imaginary people, the first "impulsive, widely energetic, impassioned, decisive, masculine, high-spirited, and iconoclastic; the other gentle, melancholic, pious, introspective, and inwardly-gazing." According to musicologist Robert Winter, Gustav Mahler recognized the emergence of the condition as early as age nineteen, writing, "I have become a different person. I don't know whether this new person is better; he certainly is not happier. The fires of a supreme zest for living and the most gnawing desire for death alternate in my heart, sometimes in the course of a single hour."

Is manic-depression a prerequisite to creative expression in the arts? Are all creative people likely to experience manic-depression? While many creative people in music, writing, and the visual arts have experienced manic-depression, the percentages rarely exceed 66 percent in any of the samples selected for study. However, even more modest estimates that 25 to 50 percent of a sample of creative persons experience and/or have been treated for manic-depressive disorders represents a "disproportionate rate of affective illness in the highly creative," according to Kay Jamison of Johns Hopkins University of Medicine. However, not all persons who are creative, talented, and gifted in the arts experience manic-depressive disorders. Nor are all those with manic-depression necessarily creative.

Current research and theory suggests that manic-depression stems from biological factors which are expressed psychologically. The condition is apparently triggered when an environmental stressor primes the pump and the affective disorder begins its inevitable progression. The most effective treatments are based on a combination of psychotherapy and the use of lithium, a drug used to level extreme moods. But researchers estimate that fewer than two-thirds of the more than two million adults with manic-depression are diagnosed or treated. Thus, even in the 1990s, many people continue to experience the sufferings described by the composers a century or more ago. Many of these untreated adults are elderly.

Beyond any doubt, there is a need to address the mental health needs of the ever-growing population of older adults. However, it should not necessarily be assumed that growing old increases the risk of mental illness. In one study that used a sequential research design and involved over 2,000 participants ranging from mid-life to old age, Aldwin et al. (1989) found no support for the hypothesis that the symptoms of mental illness increase with age. Most interestingly, Aldwin et al. (1989) discovered that with increasing age came greater variability in the extent to which individuals experienced emotional distress. This increased interindividual variability in mental health among the elderly may be due to varying life circumstances. For example, Aldwin et al. (1989) suggested that for some individuals, mental distress may increase with age because of the death of friends and loved ones and the onset of chronic illness; other older adults may show improvements in mental health as the strains caused by an unbearable job or caring for ill parents come to an end. Aldwin et al. concluded that

> . . . rather than asking whether mental health changes with age, perhaps we should ask what patterns of change are characteristic of different groups of adults, and what are the antecedents and consequences of long-term change or stability in mental health? In this manner we can begin to understand the process of "successful" aging . . . (1989, p. 305)

Next, let's look at some of the categories of mental disorders that afflict the elderly. These disorders, along with several others not mentioned in this text, are more fully described in the *DSM-III-R (Diagnostic and Statistical Manual of Mental Disorders, Third Edition, Revised)* published by the American Psychiatric Association (1987).

Categorizing the Mental Health Problems of the Elderly

In categorizing mental health problems, a distinction is usually made between organic and functional disorders. **Organic disorders** are associated with some physical cause, such as brain damage. Authorities estimate that about 10 to 20 percent of organic disorders are reversible or partially reversible and that the number of preventable cases is nearly 25 percent (Gambert, 1987; LaRue, Dessonville, and Jarvik, 1985). By contrast, **functional disorders** are unrelated to physiological problems and are caused by psychological or socioenvironmental factors. Two forms of organic disorders researchers have studied are **acute brain syndromes,** which are reversible, and **chronic brain syndromes,** which are not reversible. An acute brain syndrome is a kind of medical emergency requiring rapid diagnosis and treatment to prevent losses and reverse damage. Like other medical emergencies, acute brain syndrome may come on suddenly, without warning. Table 12.2 contains a list of some of the most common causes of acute brain syndromes.

Table 12.2

ACUTE BRAIN SYNDROMES: PREVENTABLE AND REVERSIBLE CAUSES

Drug toxicity (medications and alcohol, heavy metals, carbon monoxide)
Metabolic disorders (salt and water imbalance)
Endocrine abnormalities (hyper- and hypoglycemia, thyroidism)
Nutritional problems (general malnutrition, vitamin B12 deficiency)
Heart and lung disease
Kidney disease
Head injury (tumor and trauma)
Infections (central nervous system)
Emotional problems (depression)
Communication deficit (vision, hearing, aphasis)

A special type of acute brain syndrome is **delirium.** Delirium is marked by minimal awareness of self and environment, disorientation, hallucinations, delusions (often paranoid), attentional disorders, and sleep disorders (Lipowski, 1980; Zarit and Zarit, 1983). Its incidence seems correlated with factors related to cerebral metabolism. Delirium often occurs following surgery, accompanying severe malnutrition, or as the result of toxic levels of drugs, drug-drug interactions, electrolyte imbalances, or potassium deficits (Zarit and Zarit, 1983). Acute brain syndrome or delirium may be misdiagnosed as dementia; medical personnel must rule out such problems as those listed in table 12.2 *before* they diagnose an irreversible dementia or organic brain syndrome (Gambert, 1987; Zarit, Eiler, and Hassinger, 1985).

Chronic brain syndromes usually involve permanent brain damage. They may produce a variety of symptoms, such as confusion, suspiciousness, lack of concern for amenities, and loss of control over bodily functions. Since brain tissue appears unrecoverable once destroyed, it is critical to understand the possible causes of such problems and to undertake rapid intervention, if possible.

David Kay and Klaus Bergmann (1980) concluded that chronic brain syndrome is the most prevalent mental disorder among people aged sixty-five and over. Of these individuals, 1 to 2 percent are severely impaired and 3 to 4 percent are moderately impaired. The majority live at home rather than in institutions and are cared for by relatives and neighbors.

Dementia

Perhaps the most controversial, confounding, and debilitating set of mental disturbances afflicts individuals who have been classified as having some type of dementia. **Senescence** describes normal aging; unless we die early, all of us will experience it. Senescence is the point at which degenerative processes overwhelm the biological capacity of the individual to recover from such losses (Rockstein and Sussman, 1979). On the other hand, **dementia** is an abnormal clinical condition, a mental disorder which is not part of the universal process of aging. **Senility** is a term used by the general public to describe the severe mental deterioration displayed by some older adults. In reality, the common term *senility* is nearly identical in meaning to the medical term *dementia*. Unfortunately, many members of the general public equate *senility* with *senescence*. They mistakenly believe (and perpetuate the unfounded myth) that normal aging is always accompanied by severe mental disorganization.

Dementia is estimated to affect 5 percent of those over the age of sixty-five, but more than 20 percent of those over the age of eighty (Gurland and Cross, 1982; LaRue et al., 1985). Dementia is characterized by a gradual deterioration of intelligence and cognitive ability, often with associated behavioral changes in areas such as self-care. In an overview of the causes and treatments of dementia, Gary Small and Lissy Jarvik (1982) concluded that dementia is best understood as a clinical syndrome—a cluster of symptoms and signs that should lead to a search for the cause of the disorder. Dementia is present in the elderly whenever the following diagnostic symptoms appear (LaRue et al., 1985, p. 676):

1. Loss of intellectual ability severe enough to interfere with social or occupational functioning
2. Memory impairment
3. Impairment in abstract thinking, judgment, or higher cortical functions, or personality change
4. Clear state of consciousness (no delirium or intoxication)
5. Documented or presumed evidence of an organic cause

Note that it is almost impossible to differentiate a reversible (acute brain syndrome) from an irreversible (chronic brain syndrome) dementia using the five criteria suggested above (National Institute of Aging Task Force, 1980; Zarit and Zarit, 1983). A discussion of the several forms of dementia follows. These variants of dementia include Alzheimer's disease, multi-infarct dementia, mixed type, Creutzfeldt-Jakob disease, and AIDS dementia complex.

Alzheimer's Disease

Alzheimer's disease is one form of dementia. (It was described extensively in chapter 3.) It accounts for the largest proportion (60 percent) of dementias among people over sixty-five years old (Zarit and Zarit, 1983a) and is diagnosed by the presence of progressive cognitive and memory impairments. Researchers have identified an abnormal gene on chromosome 21 in families in which Alzheimer's disease appears in generation after generation with cyclic regularity (Goldgaber, Lerman, McBride, Saffiotti, and Gajdusek, 1987; St. George-Hyslop et al., 1987). However, the majority of cases of Alzheimer's disease do not seem to be genetic or familial in origin and are unrelated to specific chromosome defects. Currently, scientists do not understand the cause of Alzheimer's disease, nor have they discovered a successful treatment (Cohen, 1988). Clinical tests of the powerful drug-THA (tetra-hydroaminoacridine) appeared to reduce memory problems in Alzheimer's patients, but side-effects, including severe liver damage, led to the suspension of its use. Alzheimer's disease may be a generic label for a heterogeneous group of disorders involving any of several causes, including hereditary factors (Mohs, Brietner, Silverman, and Davis, 1987). The unmistakable pattern of slow onset, gradual irreversible losses, and associated changes in brain structure and processes such as neurofibrillary tangles, senile plaques, and neurotransmitter defects (for example, underproduction of acetylcholine) are among its defining characteristics (Cohen, 1988).

Multi-Infarct Dementia

Multi-infarct dementia has been estimated to account for 20 to 25 percent of cases of dementia (Gambert, 1987; Zarit and Zarit, 1983a). Multi-infarct dementia arises from a series of ministrokes in the cerebral arteries. The condition is more common among men with a history of hypertension (high blood pressure) and arises when the arteries to the brain are blocked (for example, by small pieces of atherosclerotic plaque dislodging from the artery walls in other parts of the body and traveling to the brain). The clinical picture for multi-infarct dementia is different from that of Alzheimer's disease, since the individual typically shows clear and predictable recovery from the former versus the gradual deterioration of the latter. Symptoms may include bouts of confusion, slurring of speech, difficulty in writing, or weakness on the left or right side of the body, hand, or leg. However, after each such occurrence, rapid and steady improvement usually occurs. Each succeeding occasion leaves a bit more of a residual problem, making recovery from each new episode increasingly difficult.

A relatively minor stroke or infarct is usually termed a **transient ischemic attack** or **TIA.** See figure 12.3 for more information about this disorder.

Mixed Dementia

In some cases two forms of dementia coexist (for example, Alzheimer's disease and multi-infarct dementia) and it is impossible to determine with accuracy the cause of the observed symptoms. Such cases are reasonably common and not the "medical zebras" clinicians report to their colleagues to highlight their diagnostic skills. Obviously, treatment and intervention for a person with mixed dementia presents an especially difficult challenge.

Creutzfeldt-Jakob Disease

This form of dementia is infrequently encountered in clinical diagnosis. It has aroused great interest in those seeking to understand the etiology of Alzheimer's disease because Creutzfeldt-Jakob disease is caused by a *slow-acting virus.* In experimental studies, an analogous slow-acting virus has been found to be transmitted from lower animals to other primates. The analog virus in sheep produces a disease called *scrapie* whose symptoms and destruction of brain tissue are similar to the

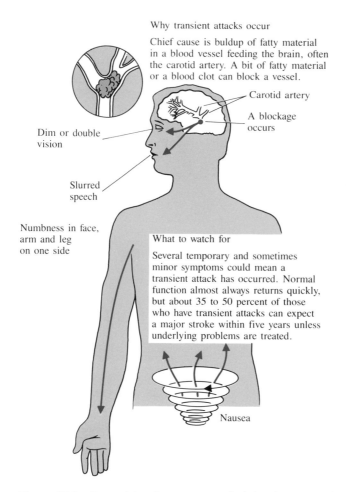

Why transient attacks occur

Chief cause is buildup of fatty material in a blood vessel feeding the brain, often the carotid artery. A bit of fatty material or a blood clot can block a vessel.

Carotid artery

A blockage occurs

Dim or double vision

Slurred speech

Numbness in face, arm and leg on one side

What to watch for

Several temporary and sometimes minor symptoms could mean a transient attack has occurred. Normal function almost always returns quickly, but about 35 to 50 percent of those who have transient attacks can expect a major stroke within five years unless underlying problems are treated.

Nausea

Figure 12.3   Recognizing the symptoms of ministrokes or transient ischemic attacks.

symptoms of Cruetzfeldt-Jakob disease. Scrapie can be transmitted directly to chimpanzees and monkeys in laboratory investigations (Cohen, 1988). This leads to the question of whether the more common dementias such as Alzheimer's may also be the product of a virus—transmitted either from animal to human or from human to human. There is also evidence from work in New Guinea that another rare neurologic brain disorder, *Kuru,* can be virally transmitted (Zarit and Zarit, 1983b). The pattern of symptoms in Creutzfeldt-Jakob disease is highly variable. The emergence of specific symptoms and the rate of progressive deterioration in cognitive functioning, judgment, memory, and personal and social competence depends on the overall rate and extent of neuron loss in the brain, the initial level of intellectual ability, and the availability of a socially supportive and simplified environment in which to live.

AIDS Dementia Complex

This neurological disorder is characterized by progressive cognitive, motor, and behavioral loss. It arises in concert with the **acquired immunodeficiency-syndrome (AIDS)** and is a predictable part of the infection (Price, Sidtis, and Rosenblum, 1988). **AIDS dementia complex (ADC)** is the result of direct brain infection by the human immunodeficiency virus (HIV). An HIV by-product, a protein called gp 120, is responsible for the death of neuron cells, which ultimately produces dementia. Early symptoms include inability to concentrate, difficulty performing complex sequential mental tasks, and memory loss in tasks requiring concentrated attention (reading, meeting the demands of independent living and working). Motor symptoms include clumsiness and weakness in the limbs, while behavioral changes include apathy, loss of spontaneity, social withdrawal, and personality alterations. As the ADC progresses, mental performance becomes noticeably worse and motor behaviors become impaired. Fine motor responses weaken, walking without assistance becomes difficult, and bowel and bladder control are lost. The terminal phase is marked by confinement to bed, vacant staring, and minimal social and cognitive interaction (Price et al., 1988). By learning how the virus invades the brain, scientists hope to learn more about how AIDS itself is transmitted within the body so that they can develop biochemical barriers that prevent the disease from spreading.

Focal Brain Damage

Zarit and Zarit (1983a) have suggested that the sudden emergence of selective (rather than global) impairment of specific cognitive abilities is typical of focal brain damage. Focal brain damage is not considered a dementia and is not marked by progressive deterioration. The likelihood of localized brain damage due to head trauma, stroke, or tumor is a common occurrence among young adult patients, but is frequently overlooked among the elderly (Zarit and Zarit, 1983a). The defining characteristic of focal brain damage is the rapid and sudden onset of limited, specific cognitive impairments. Once identified, further losses in intellectual function can be prevented with timely and appropriate intervention.

Dementia Caused by Psychiatric Disorders

The clinical picture of depression in the elderly often mimics dementia—some clinicians have even labeled depression as **depressive pseudodementia** (Kiloh, 1961; LaRue et al., 1985; Zarit and Zarit, 1983). Table 12.3 presents the difference in symptoms between true dementia and depressive pseudodementia. At least 30 percent of the elderly diagnosed with dementia have been misdiagnosed and in fact have treatable depressive pseudodementia (National Institute on Aging Task Force, 1980; LaRue et al., 1985). Symptoms such as apathy, psychomotor retardation, impaired concentration, delusions, and confusion in a depressed elderly person may easily be mistaken for dementia, particularly when they are accompanied by complaints of memory loss. Interestingly, clinicians observe that persons with depressive pseudodementia may complain far more about memory loss than those with true

Table 12.3

**DEPRESSIVE PSEUDODEMENTIA VERSUS TRUE DEMENTIA:
DIFFERENTIAL SYMPTOMS**

	Depression	*Dementia*
Onset	Rapid; exact onset can often be dated	Insidious and ill-defined
Behavior	Stable; depression, apathy, and withdrawal common	Labile; fluctuates between normal and withdrawn and apathetic
Mental competence	Usually unaffected; however, may appear demented at times; complains of memory problems	Consistently impaired, tries to hide cognitive impairment
Somatic signs	Anxiety, insomnia, eating disturbances	Occasional sleep disturbances
Self-image	Poor	Normal
Prognosis	Reversible with therapy	Chronic; slow progressive decline

dementia. At present, the only way of definitively identifying depressive pseudo-dementia from true dementia is by retrospective means. Thus, if any of the treatments effective in helping depressives produce dramatic improvements in a person's cognitive deficits and other symptoms, then the diagnosis of depressive pseudo-dementia must be correct (LaRue et al., 1985). Clinicians are thus advised to treat such symptoms not as dementia but as depressive pseudodementia. Given the difficulty of diagnosing either problem prior to treatment, the scientific utility of the concept of depressive pseudodementia has been questioned (LaRue et al., 1985).

Other reversible dementias may be caused by drugs, toxins, and physical illness. The sedative effects of some drugs (including alcohol) on older persons and drug-drug interactions may also contribute to memory impairment, delirium, or acute brain syndrome/reversible dementia (Cohen, 1988; Schuckitt, Morrissey, and O'Leary, 1979; Zarit and Zarit, 1983b). Disorders of thyroid metabolism (such as hyperthyroidism) may impair cognitive ability and represent still another reversible cause of the dementia syndrome. And almost any intracranial lesion or tumor may produce memory loss or dementia (Gambert, 1987; Zarit, Eiler, and Hassinger, 1985).

Seeking the particular cause of dementia is important because treatment can be somewhat successful in at least 10 to 30 percent of the cases (Smith and Kiloh, 1981; LaRue et al., 1985). Some experts would like to discard labels such as dementia because of the problems in defining and diagnosing it.

Depression

Depression seems to be the most common psychiatric complaint among older adults. The actual incidence of depression varies widely since different methodologies, samples, nationalities, and criteria have been employed in research studies (LaRue

Table 12.4

SYMPTOMS OF DEPRESSION: DIAGNOSTIC CRITERIA FOR MAJOR DEPRESSIVE EPISODES

A Major Depressive Syndrome is defined as criterion A.

  A. At least five of the following symptoms have been present during the same two-week period and represent a change from previous functioning; at least one of the symptoms is either (1) depressed mood, or (2) loss of interest or pleasure. (Do not include symptoms that are clearly due to a physical condition, mood-incongruent delusions or hallucinations, incoherence, or marked loosening of associations.)

 1. Depressed mood (or can be irritable mood in children and adolescents) most of the day, nearly every day, as indicated either by subjective account or observation by others
 2. Markedly diminished interest or pleasure in all, or almost all, activities most of the day, nearly every day (as indicated either by subjective account or observation by others of apathy most of the time)
 3. Significant weight loss or weight gain when not dieting (e.g., more than 5 percent of body weight in a month), or decrease or increase in appetite nearly every day (in children, consider failure to make expected weight gains)
 4. Insomnia or hypersomnia nearly every day
 5. Psychomotor agitation or retardation nearly every day (observable by others, not merely subjective feelings of restlessness or being slowed down)
 6. Fatigue or loss of energy nearly every day
 7. Feelings of worthlessness or excessive or inappropriate guilt (which may be delusional) nearly every day (not merely self-reproach or guilt about being sick)
 8. Diminished ability to think or concentrate, or indecisiveness, nearly every day (either by subjective account or as observed by others)
 9. Recurrent thoughts of death (not just fear of dying), recurrent suicidal ideation without a specific plan, or a suicide attempt or a specific plan for committing suicide

Reprinted with permission from the *Diagnostic and Statistical Manual of Mental Disorders,* Third Edition, Revised. Copyright 1987 American Psychiatric Association.

et al., 1985). There is some agreement that about 4 to 7 percent of the elderly experience depression serious enough to require intervention (Gallagher and Thompson, 1983; Gurland and Cross, 1982). Gurland (1976, 1980) initially noted that the highest rates of depressive symptoms appear among those older than sixty-five; yet the frequency of depression as a psychiatric diagnosis is highest among those twenty-five to sixty-five years of age.

It appears that depression among older adults is identical to that experienced by younger adults; however, far fewer older adults recognize the problem or are treated for this mental condition (LaRue et al., 1985). An estimated 80 percent of older adults with depressive symptoms receive no treatment at all (Gallagher and Thompson, 1983). The oft-held assumption among the elderly and their families is that depressive symptoms are a natural consequence of growing older, reflecting the many losses (spouse, job, friends, family, housing) and the increasing physical health problems experienced by the elderly. While these events are part of the culture of growing old, experiencing clinical depression for months or years demands intervention. Older people can expect to find that depressive symptoms improve or even disappear with intensive, brief psychotherapy just as they do in younger adults (Gallagher, Thompson, and Breckenridge, 1986).

The actual symptoms of depression as identified in *DSM-III-R* are listed in table 12.4.

Gatz, Smyer, and Lawton (1980) have described some of the problems associated with the treatment of depression in the elderly:

> Two aspects of depression in older adults make it particularly troublesome to treat. The first is that there are often real reasons for feeling depressed, for instance, personal losses that may trigger existential questions. . . . The second difficult aspect of depression is that family and friends do not enjoy being around depressed people. The depressed person tends to be dependent and demanding, thereby discouraging the very people who might be supportive. Thus, the families and caretakers need assistance, and the depressed older adults need interventions that will mobilize their resources while recognizing their concerns as valid. (pp. 11–12)

See box 12.2 for a case history that gives a concrete illustration of the difficulties involved in diagnosing depression.

Suicide

The major consequence of undiagnosed and untreated depression is the increased incidence of suicide among people of all ages. Among the elderly, as we have seen, depression is frequently ignored or accepted as the natural consequence of aging. In fact, older people with depression are at a high risk for carrying out suicidal wishes. Estimates suggest that one of every six elderly with severe depression actually brings about their own death (Kivela, 1985; Thomas and Gallagher, 1985). Statistics also reveal that nearly 25 percent of those who commit suicide are older than sixty-five, with rates of 18 per 100,000 for those sixty-five to seventy-four, 22 per 100,000 for those seventy-four to eighty-five, and 19 per 100,000 for those eighty-five and older (Church et al., 1988). Figure 12.4 presents the incidence of suicide as a corollary of age. These analyses also suggest that the four greatest risk factors related to suicide among the elderly include (1) living alone, (2) being male, (3) experiencing the loss of a spouse, and (4) failing health. There is *no* evidence that the rate of suicide increases following retirement (Atchley, 1983).

Among older adults, the male suicide rate is nearly seven times that of the female rate (Atchley, 1983; Porcino, 1985). However, the incidence of depression is more prevalent among females than males! Suicides among the elderly are sometimes preceded by clear signals which, unfortunately, are largely ignored (Achete and Karha, 1986). Since older people are usually successful in committing suicide, intervention must be directed at preventing the attempt itself (Achete and Karha, 1986; Atchley, 1983; Blazer, Bacher, and Manton, 1986). Mental health professionals must look for signs of extreme despair, overwhelming helplessness, and hopelessness in the elderly. The signs appearing among at-risk individuals, regardless of age, include:

1. Extreme mood or personality changes
2. Discussion of suicide and death
3. Preoccupation with the futility of continuing the struggle of daily living
4. Giving cherished personal possessions to friends and relatives

---

BOX 12.2

THE MISDIAGNOSIS OF DEPRESSION: A CASE STUDY

Dolores Gallagher and Larry W. Thompson (1983) have recorded an excellent example of the difficulty involved in making a correct diagnosis of depression in an elderly adult. Following is the case history of Mr. M. and the diagnoses arrived at by two different clinicians.

Mr. M. is an eighty-seven-year-old male who had lived alone for twenty years after the death of his wife. He had recently been forced to give up housekeeping and move into a nursing home. This occurred because of a gradual weakening of his visual and auditory abilities along with an increased muscular weakness. His memory and other aspects of his cognitive functioning seemed intact. He appeared quite apathetic and withdrawn and did not communicate very much with the nursing home staff. Therefore, he was referred for evaluation and for treatment of possible depression. Initially, he was interviewed by an inexperienced staff member who decided that Mr. M. was not suffering from any diagnosable psychological disorder. Another evaluation by a more experienced clinician revealed that Mr. M. was experiencing a major depressive episode that was characterized by intense feelings of self-reproach and death fantasies.

Why were these two different diagnoses made? The first interviewer indicated that she thought Mr. M.'s symptoms were caused by generalized "frailty" and were primarily due to normal aging. Also, she attributed his lack of communication to having lived alone for twenty years, assuming that few interpersonal demands were placed on him during that time. The second interviewer, in contrast, found that Mr. M.'s hearing loss might be a significant factor in the interview process. She asked questions in a loud voice and occasionally wrote them out. Mr. M. indicated that he could not hear the questions posed by the first interviewer and felt "too bad" to make an issue out of it. He felt frustrated and dissatisfied by the first interview and he appreciated having a second chance to express his true feelings.

On the other hand, there are pitfalls to correct diagnosis when a patient *does* report emotional distress during an interview. For example, complaints that typically accompany the aging process may be erroneously interpreted as depressive symptoms, particularly if the interviewer does not carefully question to determine whether there are alternative explanations. This could lead to a number of false positive diagnoses (misdiagnosing a healthy person as depressed). An examination of *DSM-III-R* criteria indicates that many of the signs used to classify patients as depressed routinely occur with advancing age. For example, older adults frequently report that they are slowed down, lack energy, and experience fatigue. Healthy, normal adults also complain of sleep and memory problems. Finally, age-related changes in the senses of taste and smell may cause a reduction of appetite in older adults. These similarities between the symptoms of depression and the changes that accompany normal aging emphasize the need to recognize the role of age-related changes when formulating a diagnosis of depression.

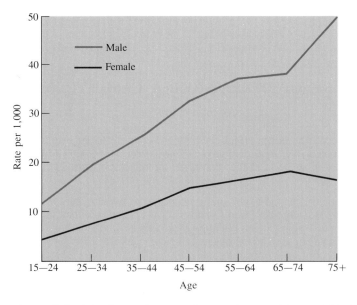

Figure 12.4   Suicide rates by age and sex in the United States:1950–80.

Source: Robert Atchley, "Aging and Suicide" in U.S Department of Health and Human Services, *Epidemiology of Aging,* NIH Publication No. 80–969:146, 1980.

5. Disturbances in sleeping and/or eating
6. Severe threat to identity and self-esteem
7. Death of loved ones and/or long-term friends

Without a social support network to monitor depressive or presuicidal feelings on a daily basis, it is understandable that suicidal thoughts among the elderly easily become actions (Achete and Karha, 1986). Suicide techniques employed by older people are somewhat more passive than those used by younger groups. They include starvation, single-car automobile accidents, failure to take needed medications, mixing medications, combining medications with dangerous drugs such as alcohol, or overdosing on prescription medications (Church et al., 1988).

Ernest Hemingway, the famous author, suffered from major depression including suicidal tendencies. To learn more about Hemingway's depression and his subsequent suicide, refer to box 12.3.

Schizophrenia

Schizophrenia is a label for a group of disorders marked by the presence of hallucinations, delusions, inappropriate affect, disturbances in speech, and alterations in logical thought processes. In short, the schizophrenic patient has broken from reality. Although there are a number of older schizophrenics, schizophrenia is *not* a disorder of old age. Schizophrenia is a chronic condition that usually begins in

---

BOX 12.3

HEMINGWAY

Suicide was a recurrent theme in Ernest Hemingway's (1899–1961) life. Even before his father's suicide, Hemingway seemed obsessed by the theme of self-destruction. As a young boy, he enjoyed reading Stevenson's "The Suicide Club." At one point in his adult life, Hemingway said that he would rather go out in a blaze of light than have his body worn out and old and his illusions shattered.

Hemingway's suicidal thoughts sometimes coincided with his marital crises. Just before marrying his wife Hadley, Hemingway became apprehensive about his new responsibilities and alarmed her by the mention of suicide. Five years later, during a crisis with wife Pauline, he calmly told her that he would have committed suicide if their love affair had not been happily resolved. Hemingway was strangely comforted by morbid thoughts of death. When feeling low, he would think about death and ways of dying; the best way, he thought, unless he could arrange to die in his sleep, would be to jump off an ocean liner at night.

Hemingway committed suicide during his sixties. His suicide raised the question of why a man with good looks, sporting skills, friends, women, wealth, fame, genius, and a Nobel Prize would kill himself. Hemingway developed a combination of physical and mental disturbances. He had neglected his health for many years, suffering from weight loss, skin disease, alcoholism, diabetes, hypertension, and impotence. His body was in a shambles, he dreaded becoming an invalid, and he feared the slow death he felt was coming. At this point, the severely depressed Hemingway was losing his memory and could no longer write. One month before his death, Hemingway wrote, "Staying healthy. Working good. Eating and drinking with friends. Enjoying myself in bed. I haven't any of them." (Meyers, 1985, p. 559)

---

late adolescence or early adulthood and persists, if untreated, throughout adult life. It is very much out of the ordinary for schizophrenic symptoms to first manifest themselves in old age. In fact, it seems as if the symptoms of schizophrenia may burn out or lessen with age (Cohen, 1988).

Schizophrenia seems to have a genetic and/or biological basis. For example, schizophrenic symptoms have been traced to the overproduction of (or hypersensitivity to) the neurotransmitter **dopamine.** Treatment for schizophrenia usually involves the administration of drugs that block the effects of dopamine. During the course of normal aging, the amount of neurotransmitters (including dopamine) manufactured by the brain decreases. This natural reduction in the amount of dopamine would explain why the onset of schizophrenia is inversely related to age (Cohen, 1988).

Parkinson's Disease

Tremors of the voluntary small muscle groups are the most noticeable symptoms of **Parkinson's disease.** They occur between three and seven times per second and appear as jerky motions. The risk of falling increases among the aged with Parkinson's disease (Ochs et al., 1985). As you recall from chapter 4, reduced amounts of dopamine seem to be the primary cause of Parkinson's disease (Cohen, 1988). This neurological disorder produces not only disturbances in psychomotor functioning but in some cases is characterized by dementia. Symptoms include unnatural immobility of the facial muscles, staring appearance of the eyes, and the characteristic tremors or shaking. In the initial phases of the disease, tremors appear in an upper limb and then alternate to the lower limb on the same side.

The standard treatment for Parkinson's disease is the administration of a drug called L-dopa. L-dopa is converted by the brain into dopamine. It is sometimes difficult to determine the correct dosage of L-dopa. For example, if a Parkinson's patient is given too much of this chemical, he or she may display what appear to be schizophrenic symptoms. Conversely, if a young schizophrenic patient is given too much of a drug that blocks the effects of dopamine, he or she may develop what appear to be the symptoms of Parkinson's disease.

Another treatment for Parkinson's disease involves transplanting cells into the brain which help stimulate the production of dopamine. This form of treatment, although promising, is still in the initial, experimental stages (see chapter 4).

MEETING THE MENTAL HEALTH NEEDS OF THE ELDERLY

How can we meet the mental health needs of the elderly? First, psychologists must be encouraged to work with the elderly, and the elderly must see that they can and do benefit from therapy (Gallagher et al., 1986). Second, we must make mental health care affordable. (Medicare currently pays lower percentages for mental health care than for physical care.) Third, we need to increase the number of geropsychologists (Reveron, 1982). Perhaps this could be accomplished by mandating that courses on aging be built into undergraduate and graduate programs of psychology, human services, nursing, and related areas such as sociology. If students are required to study the field of aging and gerontology, they may become interested in working with the elderly.

Autonomy and Control

Mental health experts have recognized the importance of providing the elderly with a sense of control and autonomy. Without individual control, human beings experience emotional distress, depression, lowered motivation, reduced feelings of well-being and life satisfaction, and deficits in cognitive and motor performance (Gallagher and Thompson, 1983; Rodin, 1986; Shupe, 1985).

Older people encounter many circumstances that limit their sense of autonomy and control. These include physical impairments, reduced economic resources, and changes in residence (Rowe and Kahn, 1987). In some studies, researchers have observed that genuine concern and love may lead a caregiver or human service professional to do too much for an older person. These behaviors may unintentionally produce dependency, helplessness, and hopelessness among the elderly (Rowe and Kahn, 1987). When control and autonomy are given to residents of nursing homes and other institutions, beneficial outcomes are routinely found. Interventions include providing choice over the *timing* of a move in living arrangements; providing *options* for residents to select in their nursing home environment; giving residents *control* over the length and timing of student volunteer visits; and having residents *care* for pets and plants (Langer and Rodin, 1976; Rodin, 1986). These interventions have been reported to improve health, emotions, subjective well-being and satisfaction, activity levels, eating, and sleeping. Encouraging control and autonomy also means discouraging well-intentioned caregivers from infantilizing the elderly—treating them as cute children rather than dignified adults. Overprotecting and infantilizing robs the elderly of their dignity, self-worth, mastery, and sense of achievement.

Fear of Crime

The biological decrements, physical limitations, and functional impairments of older persons may contribute to a sense of growing vulnerability and increased fear. One of the most striking manifestations of the older person's sense of vulnerability is the fear of being the victim of a crime. The fear of crime may become a deterrent to travel, social contacts, and the pursuit of an active life-style among some elderly persons. In one analysis, nearly one-quarter of all those sixty-five years of age and older expressed a basic fear of being the victim of a crime (National Institute on Aging, 1982). This contrasts with actual data that reveal that becoming a victim of crime was less likely among those sixty-five years of age and older than among younger adults (see table 12.5).

Violent crime represents a small percentage (6 percent) of offenses against the elderly (Bureau of Justice Department Statistics, 1987). More common are nonviolent crimes such as fraud, vandalism, purse snatching, pickpocketing, and harrassment. The estimate of the incidence of such nonviolent crime is likely low due to underreporting. Older people may fear retribution, believe the criminal justice system cannot help them, or not want publicity that causes personal shame and embarrassment. More crimes against the elderly occur in or near their homes as compared to younger victims (Church et al., 1988).

The factors that predict victimization include age (over sixty-five), race (black), sex (male), and residential status (inner city). Thus, for the older black American male living in the inner city, the fear of crime is based on reality (Jackson, 1988).

Table 12.5

AGE DISTRIBUTION OF VICTIM AND TYPE OF CRIME: 1980–1985

	Age of victim			
	12–24	*25–49*	*50–64*	*65 and older*
Victimization rate				
Crimes of violence	67.5	34.0	11.3	6.0
Rape	2.0	.8	.1[a]	.1[a]
Robbery	11.4	6.0	3.4	2.7
Assault	54.2	27.1	7.8	3.2
Aggravated	18.4	9.1	2.7	1.0
Simple	35.8	18.0	5.1	2.3
Crimes of theft	126.5	82.4	46.1	22.3
Personal larceny with contact	3.5	2.8	2.8	3.1
Personal larceny without contact	123.0	79.6	43.4	19.2
Household crimes	371.4	242.6	164.4	102.7
Burglary	144.3	86.9	59.4	44.0
Household larceny	196.8	136.5	92.3	53.7
Motor vehicle theft	30.3	19.3	12.7	5.1
Number of victimizations				
Crimes of violence	3,429,700	2,703,500	375,300	154,200
Rape	99,000	65,600	4,600[a]	1,900[a]
Robbery	579,300	480,300	113,800	69,000
Assault	2,751,400	2,157,500	256,900	83,400
Aggravated	934,100	727,200	89,300	24,600
Simple	1,817,300	1,430,400	167,600	58,800
Crimes of theft	6,423,800	6,553,900	1,527,200	576,400
Personal larceny with contact	176,700	225,500	92,500	79,600
Personal larceny without contact	6,247,100	6,328,400	1,434,700	496,900
Household crimes	2,708,700	10,195,400	3,151,300	1,809,500
Burglary	1,052,300	3,651,300	1,138,300	775,100
Household larceny	1,435,600	5,733,900	1,768,800	945,300
Motor vehicle theft	220,700	810,200	244,200	89,100
Number of persons in age group[b]	50,792,400	79,549,900	33,091,500	25,811,700
Number of households in age group[b]	7,293,100	42,018,500	19,172,300	17,614,400

Note: The victimization rate is the annual average of the number of victimizations for 1980–1985 per 1,000 persons or households in that age group. Detail may not add to total because of rounding.
[a]Average annual estimate is based on ten or fewer sample cases. [b]Annual average for 1980–1985.
Source: *Elderly Victims*. Bureau of Justice Statistics (WDC, November, 1987).

One striking effect of increased vulnerability among the elderly is the fear of crime.

More than 60 percent of our nation's population of elderly reside within the boundaries of a metropolitan city and are likely targets for criminals as they walk the streets, ride public transportation, or enter large apartment buildings (Church et al., 1988). Given their physical limitations and reduced functional reserve, most elderly residents will not resist or protest when a crime is perpetrated. In fact, when older people protest, they are more likely to need medical treatment than younger people who experience identical violent crimes. Tragically, older persons who experience a violent crime believe strongly that they will be victimized again. They become worrisome, fearful, and obsessed with protecting themselves from another incident.

Elder Abuse

The phenomenon of elder abuse has become an increasingly visible part of American life. Pillemer and Wolf (1986) believe elder abuse, like other forms of family violence such as child abuse and spouse abuse, is a reflection of our violent society. Because of varying definitions and state reporting standards, the incidence of elder abuse nationwide is estimated to be in the range of 1 to 10 percent (Pillemer and Wolf, 1986). In a recent study in a large metropolitan city, a random sampling of incidents of physical violence, verbal aggression, and neglect revealed rates of 32 per 1,000 among older adults (Pillemer and Finkelhor, 1988). Estimates put the incidence of elder abuse at between 700,000 to 1.1 million cases per year nationwide (Pillemer and Finkelhor, 1986). A comprehensive definition of elder abuse includes physical, psychological, and financial dimensions, as illustrated in table 12.6.

Passive forms of neglect are more prevalent than active forms of physical violence. The House Select Committee on Aging estimates that four of every five cases of elder abuse goes unreported and uninvestigated (Church et al., 1988). Furthermore, elder abuse is a repetitive pattern of behavior, not an isolated or single occurrence.

The elderly are most often abused by their own spouses (Pillemer and Finkelhor, 1988). Previous research (Yin, 1985) suggested that women were more likely to be abused than men; however, more recent evidence has revealed nearly equal rates of abuse among older men and women (Pillemer and Finkelhor, 1988). It is clear that abusers of the elderly are typically relatives who act as caregivers (Pillemer and Wolf, 1986). And it appears that abuse is far more likely among the elderly who live with a spouse, child, or another relative than among the elderly who live alone (Quinn and Tomita, 1986).

The causes of elder abuse are varied. Investigators have focused their attention on a *recurrent stress pattern* found among both abused and abuser (Pillemer and Wolf, 1986). The constant responsibility for the care of an older, frail adult often falls on those who neither choose this relationship nor are able to cope with the financial, interpersonal, and time demands placed upon them (Lau and Kosberg, 1979). Abusers are frequently those who have experienced marital problems, financial hardships, drug abuse, alcoholism, and child abuse (Church et al., 1988). Pillemer (1986) notes another common factor in the background of the abused elderly: *dependency.* Initially, researchers focused on the abused's dependency on the perpetrator of abuse (Quinn and Tomita, 1986). However, other data (Pillemer, 1986) suggest that caretakers who abuse the elderly are dependent on those whom they target for abuse. The abuser may be dependent on the elderly victim for housing, for assistance with routine household tasks, or for financial support.

Research also supports the notion that through abuse, the caretaker is able to continue a cycle of abuse which characterized the relationship at earlier periods of development (Steinmetz, 1978, 1981). Resentment over the lack of freedom and free time are also implicated in the development of abusive patterns by those who care for the elderly. The commitment caregivers must make to the elderly person

Table 12.6

DIFFERENT FORMS OF ELDER ABUSE

Physical abuse: Lack of personal care, lack of supervision, visible bruises and welts, repeated beatings, and lack of food
Psychological abuse: Verbal assaults, isolation, fear and threats
Financial or material abuse: Misuse or theft of money or property
Extremely unsatisfactory individual environment: Dirty and unclean home, urine odor in the home, hazardous living environment
Violation of Constitutional rights: Reduction of personal freedom, autonomy, involuntary commitment, guardianship, protection, psychiatric "incompetence," false imprisonment

for whom they care is often not recognized by anyone—neither the elderly person nor others in the immediate family. The individual sacrifice and effort required of caretakers is not sufficiently rewarded socially or economically, and the absence of reward and recognition leads to further cycles of abuse (Myers and Shelton, 1987). In providing care for an elderly parent, for example, adult children in their late thirties and forties are forced to make difficult choices: (1) limiting their career to provide routine elder care; (2) postponing vacations or forgoing evenings out with spouse or friends; (3) providing financial assistance (nursing care or a special diet) at a time when most families face the burgeoning costs of their growing children; and (4) giving retirement planning and financial savings secondary concern (Church et al., 1988). Finally, it should be noted that elderly victims of neglect are generally old, frail, and cognitively and/or physically impaired; they view themselves as helpless and dependent (Myers and Shelton, 1987; Pillemer and Wolf, 1986).

Alcoholism

Among today's cohort of elderly Americans, the excessive use of alcohol is the most common drug abuse problem. Statistics reveal the paradoxical finding that with increasing age, beginning at age fifty, the number of people classified as alcoholics decreases (Simon, 1980). However, among those who continue to use alcohol, the rate of alcoholism holds between 4 and 10 percent (Department of Health and Human Services, 1990). Those who develop alcoholic behaviors in early adulthood **(early-onset alcoholism)** often do not survive to reach middle or old age or develop multiple health problems which force them to either abstain or prepare for imminent death (Atkinson and Schuckit, 1981). Alcoholics who do reach old age are beset with a variety of physical health problems including liver damage, drug-alcohol interactions, and alcohol-based organic brain syndrome. The latter condition, called **Korsakoff's syndrome,** is marked by behavioral disorientation, confusion, delusions, and irreversible memory disorder. Alcohol-based organic brain syndrome is related to the destruction of brain cells and the correlated incidence of malnourishment, vitamin deficiency, and inadequate protein. Alcoholics typically forgo basic nutritional needs in favor of gratifying their substance dependency.

With increasing age, the body becomes less able to tolerate the effects of alcohol. Nearly 10 percent of alcoholics receiving treatment for their condition are over age sixty. Reasonably high rates of success are reported with treatment in this older population, in contrast to that reported among young adult alcoholics (Atkinson and Schuckit, 1981).

Late-onset alcoholism emerges in middle-to-late life, usually in response to multiple stressors (for example, loss of spouse). This form of alcoholism is, at present, underdiagnosed (Beresford, Blow, Brower, Adams, and Hall, 1988; Department of Health and Human Services, 1990).

Independent Living and the Need for Assistance

As people grow older, their ability to lead an independent life is challenged. Older people may require increasing help from concerned relatives, friends, or neighbors. The assistance provided may include transportation to church, the doctor's office, or the market; it may also include assistance in cleaning a home or apartment, preparing meals, and balancing the checkbook. Table 12.7 describes the types of assistance older persons increasingly need. Many require regular assistance with routine personal needs: bathing, dressing, eating, or toileting. The burden of providing these services to older males usually falls to a spouse, while for elderly females, who usually outlive their husbands, adult children are most likely to provide such services (Cicirelli, 1981).

As parents age, we find a kernel of truth to the notion that adult children become parents to their own parents. The need for daily care reminds us that a parent is mortal and moving closer to the end of life. Blenkner (1965) has used the term **filial maturity** to reflect the growing understanding of our parents. In our culture, the adoption of filial responsibility roles brings about basic tensions, although few adult children ever totally reject their parents at this point in life. Tobin (1978) suggests that routine day-to-day care is usually provided by daughters for their mothers, while sons usually assist by hiring housekeepers or home health aides. It is the emotional support, the daily worries, and the physical closeness of daughters living near their mothers that often leads to tension and resentment between siblings over caretaking responsibilities. The data in table 12.7 reveal that an older person's needs for assistance may escalate with age until the person requires full-time nursing care.

Living with an Older Parent

Many families, prior to placing an elderly parent in a group or institutionalized living arrangement, elect to have the parent live with them. Few adult children appreciate the physical and emotional demands of this decision. Unmarried adult children are more likely to move into the residence of an elderly parent, while the reverse holds for married adult children (Bernard, 1975; Tobin, 1978). Usually widows move in with their married daughters rather than their married sons (Bernard, 1975; Sussman,

Table 12.7

PERCENTAGE OF PERSONS OVER SIXTY-FIVE YEARS OF AGE REPORTING DIFFICULTY WITH SELECTED PERSONAL HEALTH CARE ACTIVITIES (1984)

Age	Personal care activity						
	Bathing	Dressing	Eating	Transferring	Walking	Getting outside	Using toilet
65 years and over	9.8	6.2	1.8	8.0	18.7	9.6	4.3
65–74 years	6.4	4.3	1.2	6.1	14.2	5.6	2.6
65–69 years	5.2	3.9	1.2	5.3	12.2	4.9	2.2
70–74 years	7.9	4.8	1.1	7.1	16.6	6.6	3.0
75–84 years	12.3	7.6	2.5	9.2	22.9	12.3	5.4
76–79 years	9.8	6.4	2.1	7.5	19.5	9.9	4.1
80–84 years	16.8	9.7	3.2	12.4	29.0	16.8	7.8
85 years and over	27.9	16.6	4.4	19.3	39.9	31.3	14.1

Source: *National Health Interview Survey,* 1984. National Center for Health Statistics.

1985). The stresses in the family are great as both adult children and their parents forgo freedom, independence, and personal autonomy in favor of maintaining an interdependent relationship. With these added stresses, it is difficult to maintain such living arrangements for more than a few years; yet families often feel guilty when they can no longer continue to care for parents at home (Tobin and Lieberman, 1976). Escalating caretaking demands that few adult children are trained to deliver include personal hygiene, health care, and medical or nursing care. In fact, Roodin, Rybash, and Hoyer (1985) have suggested that it is the increase in these demanding caretaking responsibilities over the years that provides a caregiver a rationale for placing a parent in a nursing home or residential institution.

THE INSTITUTIONALIZED ELDERLY

The decision to institutionalize an elderly parent or relative presents many conflicts. It often follows a number of years of trying to handle the increasing physical and emotional demands of caretaking. Institutional placement brings emotional turmoil to the extended family and the elderly person (Beland, 1984). But as families discover, once the decision is made, it is usually viewed as a wise choice, if not the most emotionally satisfying to all family members.

Some older adults decide to give up their homes voluntarily. In one investigation (Beland, 1984), the decision to consider a change in residence was related to age, widowhood, social class, and physical problems requiring medical supervision. Other studies have revealed the importance of perceived health status, traveling distance and time to the nearest relative, familiarity with the neighborhood, and number of years in residence in predicting residence choices (Lawton, 1980). Interestingly, neither the degree of assistance required nor the extent of physical disabilities alone predict either when an older person will decide to leave their residence or the type of residence they will choose (supervised residence, nursing home, and so on).

The steps prior to and just following institutionalization have been studied for some time (Tobin and Lieberman, 1976; Stein, Linn, and Stein, 1985). The initial period of anticipation of a move to a nursing home is marked by a variety of concerns among the elderly, including (1) orientation and adjustment to the new facility, (2) family and dependency concerns, (3) quality and availability of medical care, (4) provision of tender loving care, and (5) availability of sufficient space (Stein et al., 1985). The actual move may lead to a period of confusion, disorientation, and withdrawal which lasts about two months (Borup, 1983; Tobin and Lieberman, 1976). The somewhat difficult and uncooperative nursing home residents who nonetheless perceive quality care and a concerned staff during this initial phase show better adjustment and longer survival rates than their docile, cooperative counterparts (Lieberman and Tobin, 1983; Simms, Jones, and Yoder, 1982). In a more recent study, levels of stress were higher among elderly planning a move to a lower-quality nursing home than among those planning a move to a better facility (Stein, Linn, and Stein, 1986). And in a three-month follow-up, these anticipated differences were

Table 12.8

ANTICIPATED POPULATION GROWTH OF AMERICANS AGED SIXTY-FIVE AND OLDER (2000–2080)

Year	Total U.S. population	Percent older than sixty-five
2000	267,915,000	13 percent
2030	304,807,000	21 percent
2050	309,488,000	22 percent
2080	310,762,000	24 percent

Source: U.S. Bureau of the Census, *Current Population Reports,* Series P-25, no. 962, May 1984:7.

predictive of the residents' adjustments. Higher-quality nursing programs provided residents more of the "tender loving care" they hoped to receive, while lesser programs, as residents predicted, did not meet their anticipated needs (Stein et al., 1986). Certainly with the public interest in nursing homes and the deficiencies often discovered by state monitoring and the media, the nursing home industry will continue to be regulated. The projected population growth among the elderly makes high-quality care a continued goal for nursing homes (see table 12.8).

Nursing Home Living

Statistics reveal that only about 5 percent of the elderly reside in nursing homes at any time in our society. Yet this relatively small percentage represents an increasingly large number of people. For example, given the projections listed in table 12.8, we can estimate that by the year 2000 about 1,800,000 individuals sixty-five years of age and older will reside in nursing homes (Haber, 1987)! However, only a small percentage of nursing home residents remain there permanently; the majority are temporary. There are three times as many residents discharged from nursing homes as die in such facilities (Haber, 1987). As figure 12.5 shows, the chances that an older person will spend some time in a nursing home are directly related to increased age. One estimate is that 20 percent of the elderly population will spend some time in a nursing home (American Health Care Association, 1984). The average cost of nursing home care nationwide is about $25,000 per year, with higher rates between $3,000 and $4,000 per month at private facilities. For a typical older person living alone with an annual income between $9,700 and $15,000, a seventeen-week stay in a nursing home would result in financial destitution (Church et al., 1988).

Nursing homes may be divided into three classifications (Bould, Sanborn, and Reif, 1989; Haber, 1987): (1) proprietary homes, (2) voluntary nonprofit nursing homes, and (3) government facilities. **Proprietary homes** represent a business arrangement in which the overall goal is to secure a profit for those providing the building, maintenance, and day-to-day costs of this service. Rates are competitive to attract prospective clients as well as to ensure a profit. Proprietary homes operate in the free-market economy—elderly individuals and their families may select a

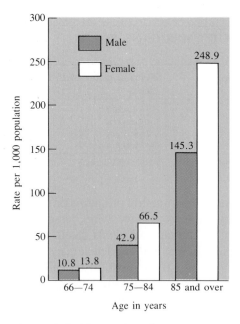

Figure 12.5 The number of nursing home residents per 1,000 of the population of individuals among people sixty-five years of age and over.

Source: *Use of Nursing Homes by the Elderly: Preliminary Data from the 1985 National Nursing Home Survey.* National Center for Health Statistics, May 1987.

facility which provides the environment, services, and care they are seeking. *Voluntary nonprofit nursing homes* are usually designed for those with a specific religion, fraternal, or union affiliation. The voluntary nonprofit home must by law establish rates that generate no excess capital. The most common type of voluntary nonprofit nursing home is the religiously affiliated, although all faiths and beliefs are accepted into the facility. Residents are provided a specific social and moral climate as well as traditional nursing services, meals, and other services comparable to those found in the proprietary homes. *Government nursing homes* are run by the federal government, individual states, or local counties. This third category has the fewest number of nursing homes (Haber, 1987).

There are three kinds of services or levels of nursing care provided by any nursing home (Haber, 1987). The most highly intensive nursing care is found in a *skilled nursing facility.* This category of care requires careful adherence to standards established by the federal government and enforced by each state. The next level of care is *intermediate* or *ordinary nursing care,* which is less intensive than that provided in a skilled nursing program. A *residential care facility,* which meets the least restrictive set of standards, offers a minimal level of nursing care. Residential care is largely routine maintenance and personal assistance in meeting day-to-day needs. Residential care may include provision for some rehabilitation, if needed, and other simple intervention services.

Nursing homes vary in the kinds and quality of services they offer.

Table 12.9

AVERAGE COSTS PER DAY FOR NON-MEDICAID PATIENTS IN NURSING HOMES IN DIFFERENT REGIONS OF THE UNITED STATES

	Level of care		
Ownership and region	*Skilled*	*Intermediate*	*Residential*
Ownership			
Proprietary	$58.67	$47.28	$28.00
Voluntary nonprofit	66.37	50.57	35.82
Government	68.27	48.25	41.81
Census region			
Northeast	79.85	63.33	29.73
North Central	57.06	46.01	35.84
South	53.19	43.83	29.63
West	58.22	47.44	28.52

Source: Data from *Nursing Home Characteristics: Preliminary Data from the 1985 National Nursing Home Survey.* National Center for Health Statistics, Advancedata, March 27, 1987.

The costs of residential care are lower than those in the other two categories (Bould, Sanborn, and Reif, 1989). Recent data (see table 12.9) reveal the costs of skilled, intermediate, and residential private (nonsubsidized by Medicaid) nursing homes (National Nursing Home Survey, 1985). Nursing costs in the Northeast United States are substantially higher for skilled care, moderately higher for intermediate care, and roughly comparable to other regions for residential care. These costs reflect the availability of nursing homes; they are most available in the North Central region, and least available in the Northeast (Haber, 1987). More than 75 percent of the nursing homes in our country are proprietary, 18 percent are voluntary nonprofit, and the remaining 7 percent are government run. In 1979, there were only 3,600 nursing homes designated as skilled nursing facilities, with only 2,100 accredited by Medicare and Medicaid (Haber, 1987). Those who must often obtain nursing home placement are elderly persons who are unmarried, widowed, and who have no close family or relatives (National Center for Health Statistics, 1987).

Economic Considerations

When major health problems strike older people, they often require medical or nursing care. Nursing home care and reimbursement policies are linked to current health-care policies, which are designed to contain hospital and medical costs. National health-care policy requires that each patient with a specific medical condition or **Diagnostic Related Group (DRG)** should conform to the average cost and length of treatment in a hospital comparable to other patients with this condition (Church et al., 1988). Hospitals receive federal support for each patient in a specific DRG based on this average. If some patients require longer stays or more complex treatment, the hospital must absorb the differential in cost between the patient care provided and that reimbursed by federal programs such as Medicare (Church et al., 1988).

Treating patients within the norms of the DRGs for comparable conditions is difficult. Hospital stays and medical costs above these DRG averages must be provided by the hospital, corporation, and physician; those under the averages still receive the same reimbursement. The result is that patients are now discharged as soon as practically possible and sent home or to a nursing home facility. The most commonly treated medical conditions among nursing home residents (Gambert, 1987; Haber, 1987) include circulatory diseases (40 percent), mental disorders and various forms of dementia (20 percent), endocrine, nutritional, and metabolic diseases (6 percent), and neoplasms including cancer (2.5 percent). Additional surveys reveal that nearly half of the residents in nursing homes suffer severe forms of mental disorder, often in conjunction with other medical problems; and almost one-third have lost bladder control (American Association of Retired Persons, 1986). Nursing home placement may become necessary when older people live alone or far away from friends or relatives. This explains, in part, why women occupy more than 75 percent of the available beds in nursing homes (U.S. Bureau of the Census, 1983).

Nursing home costs continue to escalate year after year. The typical nursing home stay is about seventy-five days. Who pays for such services? Medicare and Medicaid are federally subsidized programs that provide the basic coverage older people need, but they rarely cover the complete costs of such services. **Medicaid** is restricted to lower-income people over the age of sixty-five and typically covers about two-thirds of the cost of health services (Rivlin and Wiener, 1988). **Medicare** is part of the Social Security system and provides some support, but not complete coverage, for medical services for any individual over age sixty-five. Medicare specifically does not apply to an older person's long-term health-care needs (Haber, 1987; Rivlin and Wiener, 1988).

Most older persons need supplemental nursing home insurance coverage, yet few obtain this protection. They believe that Medicare or Medicaid will meet their hospital and nursing home needs (AARP, 1986). Those who do seek private insurance for nursing home care find the costs very high. Insurance policy charges range from $318–$684 per year for those aged sixty-five; yet the same policy costs $728–$1,496 for those seventy-nine years old. Insurance companies do not accept those most likely to use nursing home services—older people with prior illnesses, prior nursing home utilization, and chronic disabilities. Many policies may specifically exclude disorders such as Alzheimer's disease. Finally, most policies provide a *fixed* daily rate of reimbursement (indemnity) rather than meeting the costs of services required. The reimbursement rate varies from $10 to $120 per day. These rates do not increase year by year to take inflation and the generally escalating costs of nursing home stays into account. When they purchase policies ten to fifteen years in advance of their use, policyholders often discover that their own projections of nursing home costs are far out of line with current charges (Rivlin and Wiener, 1988).

Investigative reports of nursing homes have reinforced the need for vigilance and careful monitoring. More than one-third of nursing homes investigated were reported to be seriously deficient in at least one major area. Medicare and Medicaid programs will not provide reimbursement to unaccredited nursing homes (that is, to homes that fail federally mandated inspections). Haber (1987) notes that nearly one-third of the available skilled nursing facilities are not eligible for this reimbursement. Many simply cannot meet the minimum requirements for availability of physicians, pharmacists, and various rehabilitation professionals (such as occupational and physical therapists). Further concern has been directed at ensuring patients' rights, which include the right to privacy, access to information (open access to medical files), a life-style in keeping with the resident's mental and physical capacities, safety, and maintenance of personal items (Haber, 1987).

AGING IN SPECIAL POPULATIONS: THE IMPORTANCE OF REHABILITATION

Rehabilitation is a growing field devoted to appraising, intervening, and ameliorating the effects of disabilities. Most of the disabilities experienced by older adults are chronic and have little chance of being cured. They include conditions such as stroke, Parkinson's disease, osteoarthritis, rheumatoid arthritis, multiple sclerosis, diabetes, coronary artery disease, and cancer, as well as conditions occurring early in development such as mental retardation or cerebral palsy (Kemp, 1985). A disability (1) is caused by a physical injury or exists as the result of a physical or mental illness, (2) produces long-term interference in day-to-day function, and (3) produces a clear disruption in a person's typical style of social or physical response to the environment (Kemp, 1985).

The underlying theme of rehabilitation is the concept of normalization, meaning that as much as possible every citizen, regardless of age and disability, is entitled to participate fully in every aspect of life. Thus, intervention is designed to maximize individual functioning and promote independence, personal autonomy, self-worth, and positive self-concept. In implementing this approach, rehabilitation programs for the elderly face a variety of challenges. Older adults often have multiple chronic illnesses as well as mental disorders such as depression. Health professionals and the elderly themselves maintain negative attitudes toward older people (ageism), perhaps because of their slower rate of progress as compared to younger persons in rehabilitative programs (Kemp, 1985). While the goals of rehabilitation for younger people include improving functioning to enable a person to lead an independent, community-based life-style with social supports from friends and family, the goals are somewhat different for the elderly. With severe arthritis, heart disease, or stroke, an older person may not be able to resume independent living. A rehabilitation program for an elderly person may be more concerned with preserving some degree of independence in a supervised residence (Kemp, 1985).

Failing health and increased disabilities, you may recall, are among the predictors of suicide among the elderly (Blazer, 1982). In old age, disabilities often emerge without any warning and without any opportunity to develop coping resources to deal with them (Kemp, 1985). Some experts believe a series of adjustments or phases are required when a disabling condition suddenly strikes (Athelstan,

The goal of rehabilitation is to promote independence and self-worth no matter what a person's age or disability.

1981; Steger, 1976). The initial phase is one of *shock,* when the total impact of the disability is not yet fully understood. Next a phase of *defensive retreat* emerges, in which the individual realizes what has occurred. The individual is terrified and in crisis as he or she seeks to cope. Often, primitive defense mechanisms are adopted in this stage; the person may deny and regress to protect him or herself against the fear, anxiety, and depression that arise from the reality of the disability. As we have seen earlier in this chapter, individuals under stress frequently distort reality; older adults, for instance, may believe a disability was not correctly diagnosed or will not be permanent. Such beliefs may continue for many months or even years. Final recognition of the reality of the disability and its permanence occurs during the *acknowledgment* phase. The final phase, *adaptation,* reflects the attempt to face the difficult challenges the disability presents—becoming as well-integrated as possible into the mainstream of social action (Kemp, 1985).

For some elderly adults, the emergence of late-onset disability may not neatly follow the progressive pattern just outlined; rather, the disability may represent just one more loss in a lengthy string of other loss experiences (Kemp, 1985). While the presence of high-functioning role models (for example, athletes with diabetes) helps the younger adult to look ahead, older individuals have few such role models. Older adults may compare their current functioning with a disability to their previous functioning without the disability. Such comparisons frequently produce negativism and depressive reactions (Kemp, 1985). Rehabilitation goals for older persons center on both normalizing and preserving functional integrity within the limits of the disability. Rehabilitation requires a variety of contextual assessments, including the current family situation, other social supports, type of home environment, perception of the disability by the person, relatives, and friends, and a variety of other personality, cognitive, and emotional evaluations. It is important to examine the person's view of the rehabilitation goals as well as their motivation for improvement. With this background, intervention in the forms of therapy and family involvement can help improve the ability of the disabled older adult to function (Kemp, 1985).

Summary

The ability to cope and adapt to life is an important feature of adult development. One view of stress focuses on the impact of life events, attempting to determine the relative severity of the stresses. However, most experts agree that simply rating stressors does not accurately predict adaptation and adjustment. Lazarus and his colleagues believe that *how* the individual cognitively perceives and understands events is far more significant than a rating of the severity of the stress caused by a life event. Additional support for the cognitive view is found in the concept of daily hassles and uplifts.

Some experts believe that adaptation is best predicted by examining the timing of significant life experiences. Neugarten and her colleagues, for example, report that off-time events are more likely to be experienced as stressful than events that are predictable or on-time. In one study the strategies used by women with a life-threatening illness, active distortion and denial seemed to be essential features for successful coping. The use of active distortion, basic denial, and control or mastery has been downplayed, however, in other views of adaptation. The care of an older relative demands effective coping as caregivers struggle to provide increasingly complex health care, personal help, and nursing care over a period of years. The resulting conflict over providing assistance to an elderly relative versus meeting personal needs and the needs of one's family causes great stress in such situations.

Although we need to address the mental health needs of the elderly, we need not assume that the incidence of mental disorders increases with age.

A basic distinction may be made between acute brain syndromes, which are reversible, and chronic brain syndromes, which are not. Chronic brain syndromes include Alzheimer's disease, multi-infarct dementia, mixed dementia, Creutzfeldt-Jakob disease, and the AIDS dementia complex. Dementia and senescence are not interchangeable terms. The former refers to an abnormal condition of aging, the latter to the universal processes of aging. There are many conditions which mimic chronic brain syndromes but are in reality reversible features of acute brain syndromes. One of the more common of these conditions is focal brain damage, in which a temporary slowing or obstruction of blood flow to the brain (for example, a transient ischemic attack) produces the symptoms of chronic brain syndrome. Pseudodementia is another condition which mimics dementia. Pseudodementia is typically caused by undiagnosed and untreated depression. Depression remains one of the most overlooked and yet common mental health problems of the elderly. If untreated, depression in older adults may lead to suicide; the suicide statistics are particularly grim for older men. Both schizophrenia and Parkinson's disease also have implications for those studying the processes of aging.

To help promote the mental health of the elderly, we must focus on maintaining and preserving a sense of autonomy and personal control in their lives. It is important to recognize the elderly individual's perception of vulnerability. Fear of crime, rather than the actual incidence of crime, can itself limit older people's freedom and autonomy. Such fears become more prevalent among the elderly, especially for those who have been victimized by crime. Their life-styles are sometimes dominated by the threat of the crime occurring a second time. Elder abuse also has become increasingly common. Investigators have found it to be cyclical and to be related to dependency, to inadequate recognition of the sacrifices made by the caretaker, and to a lack of reward or appreciation from the older adult who receives the care. Alcoholism among elderly individuals is less of a mental health problem than it is for younger adults. However, alcoholic behavior, whether of early or late onset, leads to increasingly complex medical problems.

Caring for an elderly parent is emotionally demanding and requires an immense commitment of personal energy and resources. Home care is often a prelude to nursing home care. Custodial, residential, and skilled nursing homes involve different levels of nursing care and intervention. Psychological, physical, and economic factors must be evaluated in a nursing home placement. Only 5 percent of our elderly reside in nursing homes at any time; for every person who dies in a nursing home, three are able to return to and live in the community. Rehabilitation must be a goal for special older populations. Rehabilitation is a critical strategy for those with chronic arthritis, diabetes, stroke, and other disabilities. Through rehabilitation, elderly individuals may spend their later years in as normal a way as possible within the limits of their disabilities. Rehabilitation has become a vital intervention strategy for the elderly.

Review Questions

1. Discuss two major views of stress.
2. Outline Lazarus's ideas about stress and coping.
3. What are the differences between dementia, senility, and senescence? Describe how some forms of mental illness have been misdiagnosed in terms of irreversible or chronic dementia.
4. List two aspects of depression in elderly adults that make it difficult to treat.
5. What are some of the predictors of elder abuse?
6. What is the relationship between depression and suicide in the later years? Why does this particular pattern exist?
7. Describe the typical transfer of an elderly individual into a nursing home. What factors are most likely to be worrisome to the older person making such a move? What can be done to reduce these fears?
8. What impact does the personal search for meaning have on the process of coping and adaptation in the adult years?
9. Describe an off-time event and an on-time event and indicate how timing influences the perception of stress.
10. Describe some of the coping strategies used by women facing a diagnosis of breast cancer.

For Further Reading

Gatz, M., Popkin, S. J., Pino, C. D., and VandenBos, G. R. (1985). Psychological intervention with older adults. In J. E. Birren and K. W. Schaie (Eds.), *The handbook of the psychology of aging.* (2d ed.). New York: Van Nostrand Reinhold.
An important overview of the type of psychological interventions that address the mental health needs of the elderly. Moderate reading level.

Lazarus, R. S., and Folkman, S. (1984). *Stress, appraisal, and coping.* New York: Springer.
A complete presentation of the cognitive view of stress and coping, which has stimulated considerable research and debate in psychology, psychiatry, and the health-care professions. Moderate reading level.

Lewinsohn, P. M., and Teri, L. (Eds.) (1983). *Clinical geropsychology: New directions in assessment and treatment.* New York: Pergamon Press.
An excellent edited volume that contains a number of important chapters about different aspects of the mental health needs of older adults. Moderate reading level.

Pillemer, K. A., and Wolf, R. S. (1986). *Elder abuse.* Dover: Auburn House.
A synthesis of the current theories, data, and demographics of this recently documented form of family violence. Moderate reading level.

CHAPTER 13

DEATH AND THE DYING PROCESS

IMAGINE

Imagine That You Just Found Out Your Best Friend Has Cancer and Does Not Have Long to Live

It is important to remember that your friend, though dying, is still alive now. Your friend has value as a human being and continues to experience emotional and physical needs. A dying person experiences many feelings while trying to make sense out of what has happened and is trying to find a way to face death. Typical emotions include anger, hope, fear, curiosity, envy, apathy, relief, even anticipation; these emotions may come and go as moods change rapidly (Kalish, 1985).

Some people facing a terminal illness are unable to rely on external signs of achievement. In such instances, it may be important to focus your conversations on internal and personal issues; perhaps even looking back at happy moments you have shared. Dying and death are frightening, so don't be afraid to admit that you, like every human being, are afraid of death. However, therapists suggest that it is also important for the dying person to maintain hope. Assure the person that the physicians are doing everything they can to help him. Assure the person that you will be there as long as he needs you. Holding and touching, mourning and weeping, and recognizing how hard it must be to die are all ways to express love and support to a dying person. This is not a time to be stoic.

Ask if there is anything you can do to make your friend feel more secure or comfortable. Let the person make as many choices or decisions as he wants. You might offer to help him put his affairs in order, write messages, and carry out specific directions. If you are willing and able, offer to help the survivors cope with their emotions after the person has died. You can listen while your friend reminisces about happy times.

Therapists suggest that many dying people need to express grief and rage without fear of criticism. If your friend is severely depressed, it may not be in his best interest to try to act cheerful around him. Above all else, try not to make him feel guilty for his feelings. Be willing to share your feelings with him as openly and honestly as you can.

Avery Weisman (1972) reminded those of us who are close to someone who is dying to avoid stereotypes about dying or aging people, which distance us from the individual herself. Often we try to distance ourselves emotionally from family members or others we know who are near death; **distancing strategies** protect us from our own fear of death. One such strategy is to use the third person rather than a first name ("How is she today?") Another is to ask how the person is—as if *better* were a possibility to consider . . . as if *cured* might be today's prognosis. Distancing strategies also includes labeling or placing those who are dying into stereotypical categories. Whenever we categorize people, they become less than they are or could be. How much better to treat every dying person as the unique individual he or she has been throughout life. Since each person is unique and lives life differently, each will also choose to deal with death on their own terms. As James Peterson (1980), commenting on the mental health of dying people, suggests:

One must have looked into the greyness of the night that every man passes through and not flinch in order to hold the hands of those who are making the great transition. All of the defenses and denials we ascribe to others may in reality be projections of our own extinction. When one has achieved some composure about his own death, he may finally be able to listen creatively with responses and silences that help others have an appropriate death. (p. 941)

Later in the chapter, we will comment further on counseling and communication with a dying person, including a discussion on the extent to which the person needs to know that she is going to die.

INTRODUCTION

The process of dying and the event of death is as much an integral part of the human life cycle as the process of birth. In this chapter, we will evaluate different ways in which death is defined, survey the sociohistorical contexts of death, and comment on the practice of euthanasia. We'll describe attitudes toward death at different points in the life cycle, noting in particular attitudes toward death and the dying process in the adult years. In our discussion of facing death, we'll critically evaluate Elisabeth Kubler-Ross's theory on the stages of dying, and then outline the phases of dying suggested by E. Mansell Pattison. We'll focus on the need for open communication and the process of denial. Next, we'll turn to the contexts in which people die—hospitals, hospices, and at home—and evaluate how we cope with the deaths of those we love. We'll detail various forms of mourning and take a critical look at our society's funeral rituals. Finally, we'll focus on grief, including stages of grief, impediments to successful grieving, and coping with being a widow or widower.

DEATH: AN ETHICAL, MEDICAL, AND LEGAL DILEMMA

Definitions of Death

In previous decades, death was a simple matter. The cessation of biological functioning—the termination of the heartbeat, the cessation of breathing, the absence of blood pressure, rigidity of the body (*rigor mortis*)—was a clear and specific sign of death. With advances in medical terminology, it has become increasingly difficult for a physician to make the medical pronouncement that a patient is dead. We understand that death has fundamental properties, including the cessation of essential biological functions such as circulation and respiration (Kalish, 1985). We also know that death is irreversible. But if a patient is dependent on some sort of specialized medical treatment, how can we determine exactly *when* he or she is no longer really living?

Physicians today accept brain death indicators as binding, legal criteria for death. At least thirty-seven states and Puerto Rico have enacted laws defining brain death as equivalent to cardiopulmonary death (Kaufman and Lynn, 1986). Harvard Medical School (1968) developed four neurological criteria to define brain death. These criteria are outlined in table 13.1. **Brain death** means that all electrical activity in the brain has ceased for a specified period of time as determined by an electro-

Table 13.1

HARVARD CRITERIA FOR BRAIN DEATH (MODIFIED)

1. *Unreceptivity and unresponsivity*
   Even the most intensely painful stimuli do not evoke a vocal or other response.
2. *No movements or breathing*
   Observation covering a period of at least one hour by a physician is adequate to satisfy the criterion of no spontaneous muscular movements or spontaneous respiration or response to stimuli. The total absence of spontaneous breathing may be determined by turning off a respirator for three minutes and observing whether there is any effort on the part of the individual to breathe.
3. *No reflexes*
   The pupil will be fixed and dilated. It will not respond to a direct source of bright light. Eye movement and blinking are absent. Swallowing, yawning, coughing and vocalizing are absent. As a rule, the stretch or tendon reflexes cannot be elicited.
4. *Flat electroencephalogram*
   Of great confirmatory value is the presence of a flat or isoelectric electroencephalogram. There should be an absence of EEG activity in response to pinch or noise stimuli. Furthermore, a minimum of ten minutes recording time should be observed. All of the above tests should be repeated at least twenty-four hours later with no change in results. Also, the presence of hypothermia (body temperature below 32.2° C/90° F) and central nervous system depressants such as barbiturates must be ruled out.

From the *Journal of the American Medical Association,* Vol. 205:307–340. Copyright 1968, American Medical Association.

encephalogram (EEG). The absence of blood flow to the brain, determined by cerebral angiography—monitoring the passage of injectable dye through the arteries—confirms this fact. If an individual's heartbeat has stopped but is restored through cardiopulmonary resuscitation (CPR), then a person who has technically died can be revived. This is because lower brain stem centers (such as the medulla) that monitor heartbeat and respiration may die somewhat later than higher brain centers. However, when the higher brain centers have been deprived of oxygen for more than five to ten minutes, the individual will either never recover mental and motor abilities or will recover them only with severe impairment (Weir, 1986).

The major criticism of the Harvard criteria has been that they are too stringent to be of much use in actual practice (Collaborative Study, 1977). In one investigation of more than 503 neurological patients who were likely brain dead, only 19 actually met the criteria completely (Black, 1983a, 1983b). The Medical Consultants of the President's Commission on Ethics in Biomedical and Behavioral Research has formulated new guidelines for determining brain death (1981); they are presented in box 13.1. The modifications suggest that the Harvard criteria may not be applied routinely to infants and young children under five; that all tests need not be repeated at least twenty-four hours later, but *may* be repeated in accord with accepted clinical-medical judgment; and that the presence of fixed pupils (non-responsive to bright light) may be differentiated from widely dilated pupils, which

---

BOX 13.1

CURRENT BRAIN DEATH CRITERIA

Guidelines for Brain Death Proposed by Medical Consultants on the Diagnosis of Death to the President's Commission for the Study of Ethical Problems in Medicine and Biomedical and Behavioral Research

Statement: An individual with irreversible cessation of all functions of the entire brain including the brain stem is *dead*. The determination of death must follow accepted medical standards.

1. *Cessation* is determined by evaluation of a *and* b:
   a. *Cerebral functions are absent*—Deep coma with unreceptivity and unresponsivity; confirmation by flat EEG (no electrical activity) or blood flow analysis/angiography showing no circulating blood to brain for at least ten minutes may be done to confirm evaluation.
   b. *Brainstem functions are absent*—No pupillary reflex to bright light in either eye; no extraocular movements (no eye movements when head turned from side to side or when ear canals are irrigated with ice water); no corneal reflex when the cornea is lightly touched; no gag reflex when a tongue depressor is touched against the back of the pharynx; no cough reflex; no respiratory (apnea) reflexes. Note that some primitive spinal cord reflexes may persist after brain death.
2. *Irreversibility* of death is determined when evaluation discloses a *and* b *and* c:
   a. The cause of coma is determined and is sufficient to account for the loss of brain functions.
   b. The possibility of recovery of any brain function is excluded.
   c. The cessation of all brain functions persists during a reasonable period of observation and/or trial of therapy; and confirmation of this clinical judgment, when appropriate, is made with EEG or blood flow data (cessation of blood flow for at least ten minutes).

Conditions Limiting the Reliable Application of the Above-Mentioned Criteria:

   a. *Drug and metabolic conditions*—If any sedative is suspected to be present, there must be toxicology screening to identify the drug.
   b. *Hypothermia*—Temperature below 32.2 degrees C/90 degrees F.
   c. *Developmental immaturity*—Infants and young children under the age of five have increased resistance to damage and greater potential for recovery despite showing neurologic unresponsiveness for longer periods of time than adults.
   d. *Shock*—Produces significant reduction in cerebral blood flow.

From the *Journal of the American Medical Association*, November 13, 1981:2184–2186. Copyright 1981, American Medical Association.

may or may not indicate brain death (Hospital Law Manual, 1982). In addition, several specific conditions make the application of brain death criteria invalid: drug or metabolic intoxication, hypothermia, developmental immaturity, or shock.

Others have suggested that more qualitative criteria should be recognized. For example, minimal electrical brain stem activity sufficient to control respiratory reflexes or heartbeat may *not* be sufficient to meet the *psychological* definition of living (Veatch, 1981). Can primitive reflexes at the level of the medulla be sufficient to engage a person in the experience of life—the conscious, reflective, and personally involving experience of living, self-care, and social interaction? Questions of ethics, medical responsibility, law, and personal values make the issue of defining death a central concern to society. Despite having the legal right to pronounce a person brain dead, no more than 13 percent of a sample of nearly 650 neurosurgeons and no more than 2 percent of 1,410 internists would simply turn off a respirator without also obtaining consent from either family members or colleagues (Pinkus, 1984).

The Need for a Definition of Death

The need for a precise definition of death assumes greater importance because of recent advances in medical science that have the potential to sustain essential biological functions for a prolonged time period. Physicians and hospital staff have the ability to "pull the plug" and terminate life-sustaining technological interventions. But family members rarely discuss the conditions under which they would like their lives to be continued using so-called heroic life-support measures. Ideally, each person should have a chance to communicate with a physician regarding their status, their chance of survival, and the possibility of recovery. Since this is impossible for those who unexpectedly become brain dead through accidents or sudden illnesses such as cerebral hemorrhage, we are sometimes forced to judge how a person would feel or react to the use of life-sustaining interventions. Physicians may hear a family member say, "Dad was always an active person. For him to simply remain flat in bed, unconscious, hooked to a respirator, is totally contrary to his view of life and living. Please unhook this machine and let him die." Should a physician act in accordance with such statements from the family? What if not all family members agree?

The **living will** was created to insure the right of all individuals to choose whether heroic measures will be used to sustain their lives. Accepted in thirty-eight states, this document, presented in figure 13.1, allows individuals the choice of how, when, and under what circumstances life-sustaining treatments will be provided or withheld. It establishes a contract between the person, the medical community, and close relatives. However, in states without a living will statute, the individual's choice of receiving, denying, or terminating treatment may not be respected.

A living will should, in principle, make life-sustaining treatment a less complex decision for physicians and family members. In actual practice, many difficulties may arise. For example, if one relative objects to the wishes outlined in a living will

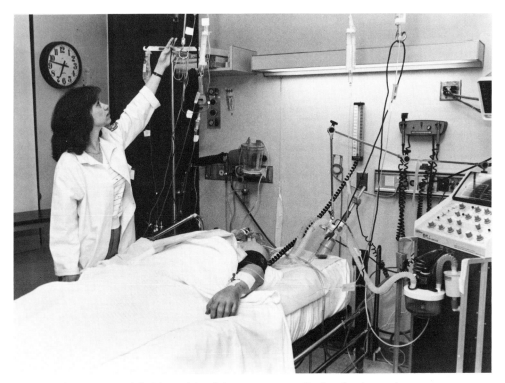

The need for a precise definition of death increases as medical technology advances.

at the time of a medical crisis, the will may not be enforced (Society for the Right to Die, 1987). Another possible complication is that physicians, relatives, and the patient may be at odds regarding treatment outcomes. Additionally, in many gray areas, the person's wishes and acceptable medical treatment standards may conflict. For instance, a patient may not want to accept tubal feeding to sustain life, yet a physician may be unwilling to withhold nutrients and water knowing the consequences will be death. The **medical directive** (see figure 13.2) has been proposed to deal with such problems. It anticipates conditions not specified in the living will.

The State of New York in 1988 passed a **Do Not Resuscitate Act** that is likely to become a model for other states seeking guidance in this complex health-care area. Do Not Resuscitate (DNR) orders in the charts of hospitalized patients specifically direct that physicians and hospital staff *not* initiate resuscitation measures (such as CPR, electric shock, medication injected into the heart, open chest massage, or tracheotomy) when breathing or heartbeat has stopped. Similar DNR orders apply to nursing home residents for whom transfer to a hospital for these procedures will not be permitted. Hospital and nursing home residents themselves can request and consent to a DNR order *orally* provided two witnesses are present, one of whom is a physician. DNR orders can also be made in writing prior to or during

Society for the Right to Die

250 West 57th Street/New York, NY 10107

Living Will Declaration

INSTRUCTIONS
Consult this column for help and guidance.

To My Family, Doctors, and All Those Concerned with My Care

I, _____, being of sound mind, make this statement as a directive to be followed if I become unable to participate in decisions regarding my medical care.

This declaration sets forth your directions regarding medical treatment.

If I should be in an incurable or irreversible mental or physical condition with no reasonable expectation of recovery, I direct my attending physician to withhold or withdraw treatment that merely prolongs my dying. I further direct that treatment be limited to measures to keep me comfortable and to relieve pain.

You have the right to refuse treatment you do not want, and you may request the care you do want.

These directions express my legal right to refuse treatment. Therefore I expect my family, doctors, and everyone concerned with my care to regard themselves as legally and morally bound to act in accord with my wishes, and in so doing to be free of any legal liability for having followed my directions.

You may list specific treatment you do not want. For example:
Cardiac resuscitation
Mechanical respiration
Artificial feeding/fluids by tube
Otherwise, your general statement, top right, will stand for your wishes.

I especially do not want: _____
_____
_____
_____
_____
_____

You may want to add instructions for care you do want—for example, pain medication; or that you prefer to die at home if possible.

Other instructions/comments: _____
_____
_____
_____

If you want, you can name someone to see that your wishes are carried out, but you do not have to do this.

Proxy Designation Clause: Should I become unable to communicate my instructions as stated above, I designate the following person to act in my behalf:

Name _____

Address _____

If the person I have named above is unable to act on my behalf, I authorize the following person to do so:

Name _____

Address _____

Sign and date here in the presence of two adult witnesses, who should also sign.

Signed: _____ Date: _____

Witness: _____   Witness: _____

Address: _____   Address: _____

_____   _____

Keep the signed original with your personal papers at home. Give signed copies to doctors, family, and proxy. Review your Declaration from time to time; initial and date it to show it still expresses your intent.

Figure 13.1   The *Living Will.*

The Medical Directive: An Introduction

As part of a person's right to self-determination, every adult has the freedom to accept or refuse any recommended medical treatment. This is relatively easy when people are well and can communicate. Unfortunately, during severe illness, people are often unable to communicate their wishes at the very time that many critical decisions about medical interventions need to be made.

The Medical Directive states a person's wishes for or against types of medical interventions in several key situations, so that the person's wishes can be respected even when he or she cannot communicate.

A Medical Directive only comes into effect if a person becomes incompetent, or unable to make decisions or to express his or her wishes. It can be changed at any time up until then. Decisions not involving incompetence should be discussed directly with the physician.

The Medical Directive also allows for appointing someone to make medical decisions for a person should he or she become unable to make his or her own; this is a proxy or durable power of attorney. The Medical Directive also allows for a statement of wishes concerning organ donation.

A copy of the completed Medical Directive should be given to a person's regular physician and to his or her family or friend to ensure that it is available when necessary.

Medical Directives should be seen not only as legal protection for personal rights but also as a guide to a person's physician. Discussion of Medical Directives with the physician can help in making plans for health care that suit a person's values.

* * *

A person's wishes usually reflect personal, philosophical, and religious views, so an individual may wish to discuss the issues with his or her family, friends, and religious mentor as well.

Before recording a personal statement in the Medical Directive, it may be helpful to consider the following question: What kind of medical condition, if any, would make life hard enough that attempts to prolong life would be undesirable? Some may say none. For others the answer may be intractable pain. For other people the limit may be permanent dependence on others, or irreversible mental damage, or inability to exchange affection.

Under such circumstances as these, the goal of medical treatment may be to secure comfort only, or it may be to use ordinary treatments while avoiding heroic ones, or to use treatments that offer improved function (palliation), or to use all appropriate interventions to prolong life independent of quality. These points may help to clarify a person's thoughts and wishes.

Durable Power of Attorney

I understand that my wishes expressed in these four cases may not cover all possible aspects of my care if I become incompetent. I also may be undecided about whether I want a particular treatment or not. Consequently there may be a need for someone to accept or refuse medical interventions for me in consultation with my physicians. I authorize:

_____

_____

as my proxy(s) to make the decision for me whenever my wishes expressed in this document are insufficient or undecided.

Should there be any disagreement between the wishes I have indicated in this document and the decisions favored by my above-named proxy(s), I wish my proxy(s) to have authority over my Medical Directive/I wish my Medical Directive to have authority over my proxy(s). (Please delete as necessary.)

Should there be any disagreement between the wishes of my proxies,

_____

shall have final authority.

Organ Donation

I hereby make this anatomical gift to take effect upon my death.

I give: _____ my body; _____ any needed organs or parts; _____ the following organs or parts _____ to the following person or institution: _____ the physician in attendance at my death; _____ the hospital in which I die; _____ the following named physician, hospital, storage bank, or other medical institution _____ ; for the following purposes: _____ any purpose authorized by law; _____ transplantation; _____ therapy; _____ research; _____ medical education.

My Personal Statement (use another page if necessary.)

_____

_____

_____

Signed _____ Date _____

Witness _____ Date _____

Witness _____ Date _____

Figure 13.2 The *Medical Directive.*

My Medical Directive	Situation A	Situation B
This Medical Directive expresses, and shall stand for, my wishes regarding medical treatments in the event that illness should make me unable to communicate them directly. I make this Directive, being eighteen years or more of age, of sound mind, and appreciating the consequences of my decisions.	If I am in a coma or in a persistent vegetative state, and in the opinion of my physician and several consultants have no known hope of regaining awareness and higher mental functions no matter what is done, then my wishes regarding use of the following, if considered medically reasonable, would be:	If I am in a coma, and I have a small likelihood of recovering fully, a slightly larger likelihood of surviving with permanent brain damage, and a much larger likelihood of dying, then my wishes regarding the use of the following, if considered medically reasonable, would be:

	Situation A				Situation B			
	I want	I do not want	I am undecided	I want a trial: if no clear improvement stop treatment	I want	I do not want	I am undecided	I want a trial: if no clear improvement stop treatment
1) Cardiopulmonary resuscitation—if on the point of dying the use of drugs and electric shock to start the heart beating, and artificial breathing				■				■
2) Mechanical breathing—breathing by a machine								
3) Artificial nutrition and hydration—nutrition and fluid given through a tube in the veins, nose, or stomach								
4) Major surgery—such as removing the gall bladder or part of the intestines				■				■
5) Kidney dialysis—cleaning the blood by machine or by fluid passed through the belly								
6) Chemotherapy—drugs to fight cancer								
7) Minor surgery—such as removing some tissue from an infected toe				■				■
8) Invasive diagnostic tests—such as using a flexible tube to look into the stomach								
9) Blood or blood products—								
10) Antibiotics—drugs to fight infection								
11) Simple diagnostic tests—such as blood tests or X rays				■				■
12) Pain medications, even if they dull consciousness and indirectly shorten my life				■				

Figure 13.2   *Continued*

	Situation C				Situation D			
	If I have brain damage or some brain disease which cannot be reversed and which makes me unable to recognize people, or to speak understandably, *and I also have a terminal illness,* such as incurable cancer which will likely be the cause of my death, then my wishes regarding use of the following, if considered medically reasonable, would be:				If I have brain damage or some brain disease which cannot be reversed and which makes me unable to recognize people, or to speak understandably, *but I have no terminal illness,* and I can live in this condition for a long time, then my wishes regarding use of the following, if considered medically reasonable, would be:			
	I want	I do not want	I am un-decided	I want a trial: if no clear improvement stop treatment	I want	I do not want	I am un-decided	I want a trial: if no clear improvement stop treatment
1) Cardiopulmonary resuscitation—if on the point of dying the use of drugs and electric shock to start the heart beating, and artificial breathing				■				■
2) Mechanical breathing—breathing by a machine								
3) Artificial nutrition and hydration—nutrition and fluid given through a tube in the veins, nose, or stomach								
4) Major surgery—such as removing the gall bladder or part of the intestines				■				
5) Kidney dialysis—cleaning the blood by machine or by fluid passed through the belly								
6) Chemotherapy—drugs to fight cancer								
7) Minor surgery—such as removing some tissue from an infected toe				■				■
8) Invasive diagnostic tests—such as using a flexible tube to look into the stomach				■				
9) Blood or blood products—								
10) Antibiotics—drugs to fight infection								
11) Simple diagnostic tests—such as blood tests or X rays				■				■
12) Pain in medications, even if they dull consciousness and indirectly shorten my life								

Figure 13.2 *Continued*

hospitalization as long as two adults are present to sign as witnesses (just as a living will provides). Limits on DNR orders can also be established in advance (for example, do not resuscitate if a terminal illness or irreversible coma exists).

The obligations and choices physicians have in following DNR orders are also specified. A physician given a DNR order has three choices: (1) enter the order as given in the chart and follow the specifications; (2) transfer a patient requesting DNR orders to another physician; or (3) bring the DNR order to the attention of a mediation panel in the hospital or nursing home (mediation panels cannot over-rule a patient's request for DNR). For individuals who are incapacitated or mentally unable to elect a DNR decision, a list of those who may make this decision on the patient's behalf has been established. These proxy decision-makers may include (1) a person previously designated to make a DNR decision; (2) a court-appointed guardian; (3) the closest relative; or (4) a close friend. The proxy decision must represent the patient's own wishes, religious and moral beliefs, or best interests. Any family disagreements regarding DNR decisions must be mediated. For those with no one to serve as proxy, a DNR decision may be made if two physicians agree that resuscitation would be medically futile. DNR orders may be changed by informing the relevant health-care staff of the changes using appropriate notification procedures (New York State Department of Health, 1988).

Euthanasia

Euthanasia, or mercy killing, is the act of putting to death an individual with a terminal illness, a massive disability, or an intensely painful disease. **Active euthanasia**—death induced by positive action such as the injection of a deadly drug or the administration of a drug overdose—may be contrasted with **passive euthanasia**—death induced by the failure to act or the withdrawal of a life-sustaining medication or machine. Physicians, in taking the Hippocratic Oath, have vowed to act "to benefit the sick" by choosing treatments believed "most helpful to patients." Any form of euthanasia is antithetical to these principles. Similarly, it is illegal for laypersons to engage in euthanasia in every country worldwide, although the Netherlands exempts a few specific conditions (Levinson, 1987). Leading ethicists have raised questions about euthanasia: As our medical technology becomes more and more sophisticated, are we adding to life or merely prolonging death? Could families be spared agonizing decisions, painful memories and guilt, and considerable financial expense if euthanasia were legal? Should hospitals and the health-care system use increasingly scarce resources and expensive nursing and medical care for patients with little or no hope of recovery? These decisions are becoming a matter of joint responsibility among all concerned: patient, physician, and family members. Box 13.2 presents one illustration of the ethical difficulties in prolonging life.

BOX 13.2

THE ETHICS OF PROLONGING LIFE

Many clinical, ethical, and legal issues arise when we ask whether it is justifiable to withhold or discontinue aggressive life support to allow severely ill or injured persons to die. In our pluralistic society, the attempt to resolve these issues generates new conflicts within medical ethics, the law, and the general perceptions of the public.

The Refusal to Prolong Life: A Case Study

A forty-seven-year-old woman suffers from a progressive spinal muscular atrophy called *Kugelberg-Welander's disease*. She has deteriorated to the point where she cannot move or eat by herself. She is intelligent and utterly lucid, knows she has an untreatable fatal disease, realizes she must remain on a respirator with a tracheotomy for the rest of her life, and recognizes that she could live for quite a while. Should a doctor respect this woman's lucid, repeated, and unvacillating demand to disconnect the respirator?

Many would hold to the principle that the will of the patient, not the health of the patient, should be the supreme law. The Vatican Declaration on Euthanasia gives additional support to self-determination. It proposes that

> One cannot impose on anyone the obligation to have recourse to a technique which is already in use but which carries a risk or is burdensome. Such a refusal is not the equivalent of suicide; on the contrary it should be considered as an acceptance of the human condition, or a wish to avoid the application of a medical procedure disproportionate to the results that can be expected, or a desire not to impose excessive expense on the family or community. (Vatican Congregation for the Doctrine of the Faith, 1980).

These clear and reasonable principles may conflict sharply with strongly held clinical perceptions and certain dominant values in our culture. For example, a doctor may be repulsed by the thought of disconnecting a respirator from the intelligent, conscious, and lucid patient described above; particularly when her prognosis is for continued life over an extensive period of time. This reluctance may stem from bonds to this woman forged during preceding fights for life. Distressed family members may also offer sharp dissent when a patient refuses or wants to discontinue life support.

Clinical ethics involve more than the deductive application of principles to cases of this sort. Physicians may experience the "executioner syndrome" when a lucid patient asks to discontinue life support; the physician must weigh the patient's desires against the personal perception that to do so would be to become a killer.

Source: D. J. Roy, D. Verret, and C. Roberge, "Death, Dying, and the Brain: Ethical Moments in Critical Care Medicine" in *Critical Care Clinics, 2*, 1, 168–169.

SOCIOHISTORICAL VIEWS OF DEATH

Historically, the relationship between death and age has changed considerably (Kalish, 1985). In earlier times, death occurred with equal probability among young infants and young children, adolescents, young adults, and older individuals. As we have advanced in the treatment of disease and improved the likelihood that infants will reach adulthood and old age, growing old has acquired a parallel meaning: aging means drawing close to death (Kalish, 1985). Life expectancy has increased from forty-seven years for a person born in 1900 to more than seventy-five years for a person born today. Over the years, death has become more closely associated with old age.

This recent change has also led to a variety of different meanings for death in our society. Kalish (1985) notes that death has become an important *organizer* of time. Older individuals are more likely than younger people to use their current age to mark their probable longevity (Reynolds and Kalish, 1974; Keith, 1981–1982). Numerous authors have noted how aging makes one appreciate the importance of time and the fleeting or transitory nature of life itself. Death also is important as a passage or *transition* (Kalish, 1985). Nearly 75 percent of an American sample of older adults reported they believed in and hoped for some form of life after death (Argyle and Beit-Hallahmi, 1975; Kalish and Reynolds, 1976, 1981). Finally, death is a significant *loss* experience: loss of immediate experience, of memories of past events, people, and places; loss of being able to achieve, produce, or create; loss of body, mind, personal identity, and physical existence (Kalish, 1985).

Just as each person must come to terms with death, each society in history has had to confront death. The ancient Greeks faced death as they faced life—openly and directly. To live a full life and die with glory was the prevailing attitude among the Greeks. Currently, our society largely avoids or denies death. Such a denial can take many forms:

1. The tendency of the funeral industry to gloss over death and to fashion lifelike qualities in the physical appearance of the dead.
2. The adoption of euphemistic language for death, such as *passing on, passing away,* and *no longer with us.*
3. The persistent search for the fountain of youth in cosmetics, plastic surgery, vitamins, and exercise.
4. The rejection and isolation of the aged, who remind us of the inevitability of death.
5. The appealing concept of a pleasant and rewarding afterlife, suggesting we are immortal.
6. Emphasis by the medical community on prolonging biological life even among patients whose chances of recovery or quality life-style is nil.
7. The failure to discuss emotional reactions to death with our children.
8. The attempt to cover up emotions at funerals and afterwards as mourners adopt a "stiff upper lip" or are encouraged to "get over it quickly and get on with life."

While Americans are conditioned from early life to live as though they were immortal, this idea cannot easily be maintained elsewhere in the world. People are more conscious of death in times of natural disaster, plague, and war. Death crowds the streets of Calcutta and the scrubby villages of Africa's Sahel. Children live with malnutrition and disease, mothers lose as many babies as they see survive into adulthood, and it is the rare family that remains intact, insulated from death. Even in peasant areas where life is better and health and maturity may be reasonable expectations, the presence of dying people in the house, the large attendance at funerals, and the daily contact with those who are dying help prepare the young for the fact of death and provide them with guidelines about how to die. By contrast, in the United States, it is not uncommon to reach maturity without ever having seen someone die (Foster and Anderson, 1978).

Most societies throughout history have had philosophical or religious beliefs about death, and most societies have some form of ritual that surrounds death. For example, elderly Eskimos in Greenland who can no longer contribute to their society may walk off alone never to be seen again or may be given a departure ceremony at which they are honored, then ritually killed. Freuchen (1961) describes such a departure ceremony among one Eskimo tribe:

> In some tribes, an old man wants his oldest son or favorite daughter to be the one to put the string around his neck and hoist him to his death. This was always done at the height of the party where good things were being eaten, where everyone—including the one who was about to die—felt happy and gay, and which would end with the angakok conjuring and dancing to chase out the evil spirits. At the end of his performance, he would give a special rope made of seal and walrus skin to the "executioner" who then placed it over the beam of the roof of the house and fastened it to the neck of the old man. Then the two rubbed noses, and the young man pulled the rope. Everybody in the house either helped or sat on the rope so as to have the honor of bringing the suffering one to the Happy Hunting Grounds where there would always be light and plenty of game of all kinds. (pp. 194–195)

In most societies, death is not viewed as the end of existence; although the body has died, the spirit is believed to live on. This is true in most religions: ardent Irish Catholics celebrate a wake as the arrival of the dead person's soul in God's heavenly home; the Hindu believes in the continued existence of the person's life through reincarnation; Hungarian gypsies gather at the bedside of a dying loved one to ensure support and an open window so that the spirit can leave and find the way to heaven. Perceptions of why people die are many and varied. Death may be punishment for one's sins, an act of atonement, or the action of a higher being or deity (Kalish, 1985).

Attitudes toward Death

In general, we adopt attitudes toward death consistent with our culture, our family values, and our cognitive and emotional maturity (Kastenbaum, 1985). Clearly, attitudes toward death change as we ourselves age. The awareness of death increases with age, yet older persons also show a greater acceptance and less fear of death than younger or middle-aged individuals (Kalish, 1985; Kalish and Reynolds, 1976). Kalish (1985) notes that the elderly show (1) greater knowledge of the limits of their life and a more realistic assessment of their longevity; (2) an awareness that many significant life roles are no longer available; (3) a sense of achievement in being able to live beyond normal life expectancy, or alternatively, a sense of loss if unable to reach expected years of survival; and (4) a sense of sadness, loss, and emptiness as loved ones and close friends die—but also relief *and guilt* as they continue to escape death.

A Developmental View of Death

Children two or three years old are rarely upset by the sight of a dead animal or by hearing that a person has died. Children at this age really do not understand death cognitively or emotionally. They may even blame themselves for the deaths of those closest to them, illogically believing that they caused the death by disobeying the person who died. For young children, death is equated with sleep. They expect that someone who has died will wake up, return to be with them, and come back to life. Five-year-olds, for example, do not believe that death is final and expect those who have died to come back to life (Speece and Brent, 1984). Given the Piagetian cognitive characteristics of preoperational thinking, children up to seven or eight years of age may not understand that death is universal, inevitable, and irrevocable. Most preoperational children (those of preschool age) assume that dead people continue to experience the same life processes as they did when they were alive. The dead simply have "moved away" and continue to live in Heaven, working, eating, bathing, shopping, and playing. Preschoolers believe that those who die continue to have concrete needs, feelings, and experiences as they did when they were alive (Blueband-Langner, 1977). Even children older than seven or eight years of age view death as an event that will occur for some people, but not all. Usually by age nine or so, children recognize both the finality and universality of death (Nagy, 1948). Adolescents typically deny death, especially the possibility of their own death. The topic is avoided, glossed over, kidded about, neutralized, and controlled as adolescents distance themselves from death. Adolescents do, nonetheless, experience a good deal of anxiety about death.

Despite the appearance of an age-related decline in death anxiety, some researchers suggest that age itself is *not* the best predictor of death anxiety but rather past experiences and confrontations with death (Oleshansky, Gamsky, and Ramsmeyer, in press). Numerous therapeutic programs have recognized the need to provide an opportunity for children and adolescents to discuss their responses to the deaths of people close to them (McDonald, 1981). In such death education programs, professional counselors emphasize honest and open exchange as the best strategy to help younger people cope with death. Yet most of us have grown up in a society in which death is rarely discussed. In one investigation that surveyed the attitudes of 30,000 young adults, more than 30 percent said they could not recall any discussion of death during their childhoods; and an equal number said that while death was discussed, the discussion took place in an uncomfortable atmosphere (Shneidman, 1973). It was also found that the majority of young people initially became aware of death sometime between the ages of five and ten. Almost one of every two respondents said that the death of a grandparent represented their first personal confrontation with death. Generally, the more freedom to discuss death, the more mature (emotionally and cognitively) the attitude toward death. It seems that even religious orientation plays a role. The data suggest a curvilinear pattern, with strong or weak religious *beliefs* leading to less fear of death but moderate beliefs associated with higher levels of death anxiety (Feifel and Nagy, 1981; Kalish, 1985; Nelson and Nelson, 1973).

Middle adulthood, you may recall, is a time when men and women begin to think more intensely about how much time is left in their lives. Middle age may be a time for talking with other family members about death as life insurance needs grow, as wills are written or revised, as one's children reach early adulthood, and as one's parents age and die. Certainly the elderly have direct experience with death as friends and relatives become ill and die. Kastenbaum (1981) suggests that the elderly may experience **bereavement overload** from the cumulative effects of having to cope with the deaths of friends, neighbors, and relatives in a short time span. The elderly are forced to examine the meanings of life and death much more often than those in middle age or young adulthood. There are also, of course, considerable individual differences. Some elderly are able to see their lives draw to a close and recognize that there is not much else to live for, while others cling passionately to life, savoring each activity, personal relationship, and achievement (Kastenbaum, 1969; Kalish, 1987).

FACING ONE'S OWN DEATH

In his book, *The Sane Society,* Erich Fromm (1955) comments, "Man is the only animal that finds his own existence a problem which he has to solve and from which he cannot escape. In the same sense, man is the only animal who knows he must die." (p. 23) It is this knowledge that we will someday die that gives meaning to life, that causes us to establish priorities, and that demands that we use our time wisely. Over the centuries philosophers, theologians, poets, and psychologists have attempted to explain the phenomenon of death and theorized about why all people must die and whether there is some form of existence beyond life on earth.

Most dying individuals want the opportunity to make some decisions regarding death. Some individuals want to complete **unfinished business.** For example, resolving problems and mending fences in personal relationships. When asked how they would spend their last six months of life, younger adults described activities such as traveling and accomplishing things they previously had not done; older adults, in contrast, described more inner-focused activities such as contemplation and meditation (Kalish and Reynolds, 1976, 1981). Box 13.3 describes such a shift in focus among classical musical composers nearing the end of life.

BOX 13.3

SWAN SONGS: CHARACTERISTICS OF LAST COMPOSITIONS

In an article in the journal of *Psychology and Aging,* Dr. D. K. Simonton from the University of California at Davis reported the results of his analysis of the final musical works of 172 classical composers. He wondered whether there would be any unique characteristics in the very last musical work or "swan song" of each of these composers.

In a series of complex computer analyses performed on these varied pieces, Dr. Simonton surprisingly discovered some commonalities in these final musical compositions. Seven basic variables were used to compare earlier works with the last work of the composer: melodic originality and variation, repertoire popularity, aesthetic significance, listener accessibility, performance duration, and thematic size. Unlike earlier investigators' attempts to examine swan songs, Dr. Simonton was able to rule out statistically contaminating factors such as the average age at which the last composition was written and individual differences in terms of fame, reputation, and success. In examining each individual composer's last musical work, or swan song, and comparing it to earlier compositions, Simonton found that the last work was somewhat shorter in length. Swan songs were also typically far more simple in their organization or structure. Also, the swan songs have become some of the most enduring, well-recognized, and cherished, pieces in the field of classical music. These musical finales are characterized by a degree of aesthetic significance that earlier works do not have. Examples of legendary swan songs include Mozart's *Requiem,* Tchaikovsky's *Sixth Symphony,* and Schubert's *Unfinished Symphony.* As composers near the end of their lives, their musical works seemed to reveal personal contentment, inner harmony, and acceptance rather than depression, sorrow, or tragedy.

The ability of composers to construct such enduring works at the end of their lives remains puzzling. The swan song structure found by Simonton is understated in its aesthetic beauty and simplicity. Yet the simplicity is not that of a country melody or peasant folk tune. What emerges is the elegance of a musical composition that is not too complex, not too simple; music that is "just right." The swan song demonstrates that the composer knew how to produce a work that presented the pure essence of a feeling, mood, or theme in the clearest and most direct fashion. It might be argued that this happened because the composers knew that their lives were nearly over. However, most of the composers did not know they were near death; they did not consciously attempt to produce a final composition. The swan song phenomenon is even more striking when juxtaposed against possible "false alarms"; many of the composers produced musical works against the backdrop of serious disease that brought them to the brink of death. Yet during these near brushes with death, the musical compositions created are similar to those produced at other times throughout their careers. It is only the swan song that contains the unique qualities that separate it from a composer's earlier musical compositions.

In the next section, we'll examine the often-cited psychological stages of dying developed by Elisabeth Kubler-Ross and then explore the dying phases or dying trajectories. We'll also consider the concept of appropriate death, as well as the variety of coping strategies individuals develop to deal with the stress of knowing they are dying.

PSYCHOLOGICAL STAGES OF DYING?

The most widely cited view of how people cope with death was developed by Elisabeth Kubler-Ross (1969, 1981). This view, however, has received little empirical support and has been the subject of much theoretical criticism (Shneidman, 1980; Kastenbaum, 1981). Kubler-Ross's theory, which suggests the existence of stages in dealing with the dying process, helped focus professional concern on death education and counseling—topics that had been largely ignored. In her psychiatric work with hospitalized patients dying from cancer, Kubler-Ross reported the existence of five stages: denial/isolation, anger, bargaining, depression, and acceptance. In the first stage, a common initial reaction to terminal illness is **denial/ isolation.** The individual denies that death is really going to occur, saying, "No, it can't happen to me," "It's not possible," or "There must be a mistake, an error in the laboratory or in the diagnosis." Denial is considered a transitory defense and is eventually replaced with increasing acceptance when the individual confronts such matters as finances, unfinished business, and arrangements for surviving family members.

In the second stage, **anger,** the dying individual recognizes that denial can no longer be maintained; anger, resentment, rage, and envy are expressed directly. Now the issue becomes, "Why me?" At this point, the individual becomes increasingly difficult to care for as anger is displaced and projected onto physicians, nurses, hospital staff, family members, and even God. The realization of loss is great, and those who symbolize life, energy, and competent functioning are the targets of the dying individual's resentment and jealousy.

In the third stage, **bargaining,** the individual develops hope that death can somehow be postponed or delayed. Some individuals enter into a brief period of bargaining or negotiation—often with God—as they try to delay their deaths. Psychologically, these people are trying to buy a few more weeks, months, or years in exchange for leading a reformed life or for choosing a life dedicated to God or the service of others.

In the fourth stage, **depression,** the dying individual begins to accept the certainty of his or her death; as she recognizes the growing severity of specific symptoms, a period of depression or preparatory grief may appear. The dying individual is often silent, refuses visitors, and spends much of the time crying or grieving. These behaviors represent an attempt to disconnect the self from all love objects. Attempts to cheer up dying individuals at this stage should be avoided, says Kubler-Ross, because of the dying person's need to contemplate and grieve over impending death.

In the fifth stage, **acceptance,** the individual develops a sense of peace, a unique acceptance of fate, and in many cases, a desire to be left alone. This stage may be devoid of feeling; physical pain and discomfort are often absent. Kubler-Ross describes this stage as the last one before undertaking a long journey and reaching the end of the struggle.

No one has yet been able to provide independent confirmation that people actually go through all five stages in the order described by Kubler-Ross (Kastenbaum 1981; Schulz and Alderman, 1974; Shneidman, 1973, 1980). Theoretically and empirically, the stages have raised many questions, although Kubler-Ross feels that she has often been misread and misinterpreted. For instance, she maintains that she never intended the stages to be an invariant sequence of developmental steps toward death. And she has consistently recognized the importance of individual variation in how we face death (Kubler-Ross, 1974). Nevertheless, Kubler-Ross still believes that the optimal way to face death lies in the sequence she has proposed. Other investigators have not found the same five stages (Metzger, 1979); many report that a single stage (for example, depression or denial) dominates the entire dying experience, while still others identify dying patients as being in two or three stages simultaneously (Kalish, 1985; Shneidman, 1973, 1980). The fact that Kubler-Ross used primarily interview data without sophisticated statistical evaluations provides yet another criticism of her work. Even in her earliest work, it is clear that many patients remain at one of the first stages (denial or anger) and never pass through all five stages of the sequence. Moreover, some patients move backward or regress into stages already completed (Shneidman, 1973). We are left with a provocative and historically important theory of dying, but one which has few developmental or stage properties.

An Appropriate Death

In many ways, the ways in which people face death are a reflection of how they face life. The concept of an **appropriate death** (Weisman, 1972) suggests that individuals should be granted the freedom to face dying as they choose; a death which fits one's expectations and style of coping. An appropriate death permits people to die with dignity on their own terms (Kalish, 1985). There is no mandate to move through a set of stages, no requirement to push to acceptance, no social pressure to face death in a prescriptive way. By permitting individuals an appropriate death, we allow them to maintain a sense of hopefulness. Hopefulness refers to the positive anticipation of the future: birthdays, wedding anniversaries, visits from friends or relatives, seeing the new year arrive. As studies suggest, hopefulness provides one means of control or mastery over terminal illness and allows the process of living to coexist with the process of dying (Kastenbaum, 1981). Some dying persons continue to participate in living each day, *resisting* rather than denying death. Their spirit and hope should not be confused with outright denial; resisting death implies a choice and involves an active decision. With an appropriate death, individuals can maintain their dignity, their self-esteem, their identity, and their individuality. Kalish (1981) notes that "different people die in different ways and

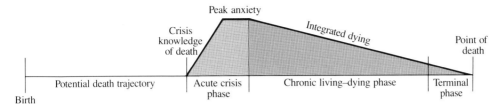

Figure 13.3   **Acute, chronic, and terminal phases of the dying process.**
From the book, The Experience of Dying, by E. Mansell Pattison. © 1977 by Prentice-Hall, Inc. Published by
Prentice-Hall, Inc., Englewood Cliffs, NJ.

experience a variety of feelings and emotions during the process . . ." (p. 186).
Kalish (1985) also identified three factors necessary to permit an appropriate death:
(1) a warm, intimate personal relationship with family, friends, or health professionals; (2) an open environment in which emotions, information, and the terminal
condition can be discussed by all involved; and (3) a sense of meaning derived
from this experience, from one's life, or from religion.

Pattison's Phases of the Living-Dying Interval

The **trajectory of life** has been defined by E. Mansell Pattison (1977) as our anticipated life span and the plan we make for the way we will live out our life. When
an illness or serious injury occurs and leads to a revision of our anticipated life span,
the life trajectory must be revised because we perceive that we are likely to die
much sooner than we had anticipated. Pattison calls the time interval between our
discovery that we will die sooner than we had thought and the time when we actually die the **living-dying interval.** The living-dying interval is characterized by
three phases: acute, chronic, and terminal. The goal of those who treat individuals
in the living-dying interval is to assist them in coping with the first or acute phase,
to help them to live as reasonably as possible through the second, or chronic phase,
and to move them into the third or terminal phase (see figure 13.3). Pattison sees
a pattern to the phases. Depending on the nature of the illness, different people
may spend vastly different periods of time in each phase. For example, some illnesses allow a pattern of chronic living-dying for only a few weeks, while others
allow a more protracted period of months or even years.

Pattison describes each phase in terms of the individual's reactions and coping
needs. In the *acute phase,* individuals face what is probably the most severe crisis
in their lives—the realization that they will die sooner than they thought and will
not get to accomplish and experience all they had hoped. People in this stage feel
immobilized, experience high levels of anxiety, and call into play a number of defense mechanisms to deal with the extreme fear and stress they are confronting. In
this phase, people need a great deal of emotional support from others and need
help to deal rationally with the fact that they are going to die.

In the *chronic phase,* Pattison believes that individuals begin to confront directly their fear of dying. Fears about loneliness, suffering, separation from loved ones, and the unknown often surface. Health professionals can assist dying people by helping them put life into perspective, working through some of the defense mechanisms, and allowing open discussion of death and basic fears.

In the *terminal phase,* individuals begin to withdraw as their hope of getting better gives way to the realization that they are probably going to get worse. At the end of this phase, individuals turn inward, distancing themselves from people and everyday experience.

Just as Kubler-Ross's stages are neither fixed nor invariant for all people, Pattison's dying phases do not represent the trajectory every individual goes through.

COMMUNICATING WITH THE DYING PERSON AND THE CONTEXTS IN WHICH PEOPLE DIE

To help the dying person and the family cope more effectively with death, health-care professionals are placing increasing emphasis on effective communication, understanding, and the context in which the person will die. We'll discuss each of these issues in this section.

Communicating with the Dying Person

It is generally agreed that the situation is optimal when the dying person knows she is dying and significant others also recognize this fact. Research has consistently revealed that people believe dying persons have the right to know their condition and prognosis (Kalish, 1985). This is in contrast to **mutual pretense,** when the dying person, friends, relatives, and staff pretend that the person will recover (Glaser and Strauss, 1965). With mutual pretense, people are isolated from each other at a time when they should be close and able to freely express their thoughts and feelings (Kalish, 1985). Richard Kalish (1981) describes the advantages of an open-awareness context for dying persons:

1. Dying individuals can close life in accord with their own ideas about proper dying.
2. They can complete some plans and projects, make arrangements for survivors, and participate in decisions about a funeral and burial.
3. They have the opportunity to reminisce, to converse with others who have been important in their lives, and to be near to death conscious of what life has been like.
4. They have more understanding of what is happening within their bodies and of what the medical staff is doing.

BOX 13.4

OPEN COMMUNICATION WITH THE DYING PERSON

My eighty-one-year-old aunt was extremely ill and had been for two years; the indications were that she would probably not live for many more weeks. My home was 800 miles away, but I was able to get to visit her and my uncle for a couple of days. It bothered me to see her hooked into a machine that held her life; the ugly wig she had worn during the past couple of years had been discarded, and there were only a few wisps of hair left, but at least they were hers. Her teeth had been placed in the drawer by her bed since she couldn't take solid food and at this point she was not concerned about how she looked.

My uncle and I were in her room talking with her as she moved in and out of awareness. He was standing at the foot of the bed and I was sitting next to her, holding her hand. He began to talk to her about coming to visit me as soon as she could get up and around again, probably next summer. I noticed that she tuned his comments out. Then I found a pretext to get him out of the room.

When we were alone, I stood up and kissed her, I'd like to say that it was easy, but it really wasn't. I told her that I loved her, and I realized that I had never said that to her before, hadn't even thought about it, hadn't even consciously thought that I loved her. I just . . . loved her.

Then I said, "Bea I have to leave now. I may never see you again, and I want you to know how much I love you." Her eyes were closed and she was breathing strangely, but she winced at my words, and I became frightened that I'd said too much, so I hesitated. "Well, I hope that I'll see you again, but I might not." And I left.

She died before I could visit again, and I always wondered whether I should have said what I did, but it seemed important to say it. Even if it pained her to hear me, she knew it was true, and she had not shrunk from painful situations before. It had been easy for me over many years to talk and write about death and dying, but it was very difficult for me to be in the situation where someone I loved was dying. I did what I have told other people to do, and it wasn't at all natural—I had to force myself. But when I heard, three weeks later, that she had died, I considered myself fortunate to have had the chance to be with her before she died and to have been both caring and honest. (p. 172)

From *Death, Grief, and Caring Relationships,* by R. A. Kalish. Copyright © 1981 Wadsworth, Inc. Reprinted by permission of the publisher, Brooks/Cole Publishing Company, Pacific Grove, CA.

It may be easier to die when people we love can converse freely with us about what is happening, even if it entails considerable sadness. Box 13.4 describes a circumstance in which open communication with a dying person occurs and proves beneficial.

For the dying person, external accomplishments and continued achievements become less possible. The focus of communication thus needs to be directed more at internal processes, past experiences, endearing memories, and personal successes. A caring relationship is a very important aspect of the dying person's life. But such caring does not have to come from a mental health professional; a concerned nurse, an attentive physician, an interested chaplain, a sensitive spouse or a friend all provide important communication resources for the dying person. Rather than focusing on the mental health needs of the dying or helping them prepare for death, we should try to emphasize the person's strengths and preparation for the remainder of life (LeShan, 1969).

Denial of Death

Not all people close to death are able to communicate openly. Denial is characteristic of some individuals' approach to death. In fact, it is not unusual for some dying individuals to continue to deny death right to the end. Life without hope is unbearable, and denial serves to protect them from the tortuous reality that they are going to die. Box 13.5 describes denial in coping with impending death.

Some psychologists believe that the more denial, the more difficulty an individual will have facing death and dying in a peaceful and dignified way. Others feel that not confronting death until the very end may be highly adaptive (Kalish, 1981, 1987; Lifton, 1977; Shneidman, 1973).

Denial of death takes many forms (Weisman, 1972). For example, a man scheduled for an operation for cancer of the colon denies the facts and believes that the operation is only for benign polyps. Refusing to acknowledge the implications of a disease or a life-threatening situation is another form of denial. For example, a woman may accept the fact that she has a severe kidney disease but deny its life-threatening consequences. Finally, we may deny our own mortality; that is, even if we accept biological death, we maintain faith in our spiritual immortality.

Denial can be used adaptively to delay dealing with one's death and thus delay the shock. Denial can insulate an individual from having to cope with intense feelings of anger and hurt. Yet, denial does have maladaptive features. For example, it may keep us from seeking medical diagnosis and treatment when life-threatening symptoms appear, or it may block communication and other forms of adjustment to dying. The use of denial must be evaluated in terms of its adaptive qualities for the individual (Kalish, 1981).

The Contexts in Which We Die: Hospital, Home, and Hospice

Most people in the United States, Canada, and England die in some type of health-care institution, typically a general hospital (Cartwright, Hockey, and Anderson, 1973; Kalish, 1985; Lerner, 1970; Marshall, 1980). The majority of individuals, when asked

BOX 13.5

THE DENIAL OF DYING

Denial can be a protective mechanism that enables people to cope with the torturous feelings that accompany the realization that they are going to die. People who are dying can either deny the existence of information about their impending death or they can reinterpret the meaning of the information to avoid its negative implications. There may be three forms of denial (Weisman, 1972). The first involves the denial of facts. For example, a woman who has been told by her physician that a scheduled operation is for cancer believes that the operation is for a benign tumor. The second form of denial involves implications. A man accepts the fact that he has a disease but denies that it will end in death. A third form of denial involves extinction, which is limited to people who accept a diagnosis and its implications but still act as if they were going to live through the ordeal. This last form of denial does not apply to people whose deep religious convictions include some form of belief in mortality.

Another classification includes the categories of *brittle* and *adaptive denial*. Brittle denial involves anxiety and agitation. The individual often rejects attempts to improve his or her psychological adaptation to impending death. However, adaptive denial occurs when the individual decides not to dwell on this aspect of his or her life but to emphasize strengths and opportunities during what remains of life. Adaptive deniers want help and support. Such adaptive denial fits well with the ideas of perceived control and the elimination of learned helplessness.

In discussing the role of denial, Richard Kalish (1981) concluded that denial can be adaptive, maladaptive, or even both at the same time. One can call on denial to avoid the destructive impact of shock by delaying the necessity of dealing with one's death. Further, denial can insulate a person from coping with feelings of anger and hurt, emotions that may intrude on other behaviors and feelings because they are so intense. Denial is neither good nor bad in itself. An evaluation of its adaptive qualities must be made on an individual basis.

where they would want to die, indicate a preference to be at home (Kalish and Reynolds, 1981). However, dying people do feel they may be a burden at home, recognize the problem of limited space, and know they may place undue stress on family members. Those who are dying also worry about the competency and availability of emergency medical treatment if they remain at home. Hospitals offer a number of advantages to the dying person and the family: professional staff members are available and advanced medical equipment is accessible. Yet a hospital may not be the best location for the dying person to engage in meaningful, intimate relationships or retain autonomy. Dying at home is a choice many elderly individuals cannot elect since they typically require extensive medical care, are often in failing condition, and require sophisticated nursing skills (Kalish, 1985).

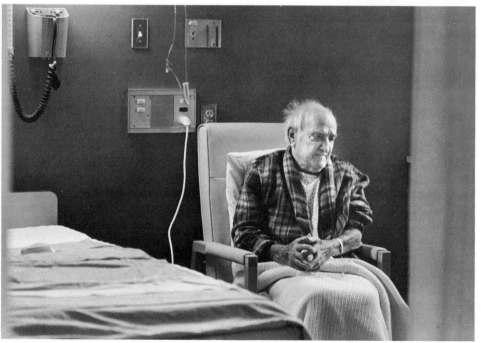

Hospices offer medical care within a personalized, supportive setting (top). Hospitals primarily offer medical care (bottom).

The **hospice** provides an alternative to dying at home or in a hospital. The hospice is designed to blend institutional care and home care as well as provide some significant innovations. Many experts on the care of the dying view the hospice as a unique and humanistic program for the care of the terminally ill, particularly the elderly (Kastenbaum, 1985). The hospice movement has attracted interest among health-care providers in the United States; by 1987 there were nearly 200 hospices nationwide (Kitch, 1987). The hospice program emanates from the pioneering work in London, England of Dr. Cicely Saunders, medical director of St. Christopher's Hospice (Saunders, 1977). When medical treatments are no longer effective and when hospitalization is inappropriate, the hospice may be chosen (Kalish, 1985). The hospice program advocates two goals: (1) the control of pain for dying individuals, and (2) the creation of an open, intimate, and supportive environment to share the ending of life with loved ones. The hospice maintains the humanity, dignity, and personal identity of each dying individual. Pain control is under the direction of the patient and medications that preserve alertness are employed. Thus, patients do not need to wait until they are overwhelmed with pain to ask for assistance. In the hospice, the dying patient remains an integral part of his or her family. The family is welcomed at any time and the entire staff is skilled in death education and counseling. Staff not only help the patient, but also help the family in discussing their feelings over the impending death, the meaning of the loss, and the significance of the dying person in their own life. Hospice programs even provide counseling and support to staff members, who themselves need a regular opportunity to share their feelings (Stephenson, 1985). Such support continues even after the death. The hospice program encompasses a philosophy of care for the terminally ill and ultimately will help to humanize the care of dying patients in all contexts (Hayslip and Leon 1988; Kastenbaum, 1985; Koff, 1981).

To date, only a few research studies have been conducted on the effects of hospice care (Kalish, 1985; Mor, 1982; Morris, 1982). Most hospice patients have been terminally ill with cancer. Hinton (1972, 1979) reported that with hospice care, patients showed less anxiety, less depression, less hostility, and more acceptance of the efforts of the staff than patients in traditional hospitals. Patients appreciated the chance to talk about death, which may have also reduced the guilt of family members and led to more satisfaction with the treatment provided (Lack and Buckingham, 1978). Current concern over the high cost of health care makes the hospice program a cost-effective option for insurance providers. Hospice care receives the strong endorsement of those at the local, state, and national levels who establish health-care priorities (Mor, 1982). Hospice treatment is now provided under Medicare coverage. More than 1,500 community groups nationwide are involved in establishing hospice programs (Stephenson, 1985).

COPING WITH THE DEATH OF A LOVED ONE

Loss comes in many forms in our lives—divorce, a pet's death, loss of a job. No loss, however, is greater than the loss that comes from the death of someone we love and care for—a parent, a sibling, a spouse, a relative, or a friend. In rating life stresses, the death of a spouse is consistently identified as the most stressful life experience (Holmes and Rahe, 1967).

Significant loss can lead to bereavement, grief, and mourning (Kalish, 1985). The term **bereaved** describes the status of a person who survives the death of a loved one. **Grief** refers to the feelings associated with loss and usually encompasses the deep sorrow, anger, guilt, and confusion that often accompany a loss. The process of grieving is considered essential to full recovery from the loss of a significant person in our life. Grief is one of the most powerful of human feelings and produces intense emotional pain and suffering. **Mourning** is the overt expression of grief by the bereaved as defined by cultural, social, and religious custom. Mourning is expressed in various rituals—how we dress, what burial customs we follow, whether we say prayers, and so forth.

Forms of Mourning and the Funeral

There are many cultural differences in mourning. For example, **sati** is the ancient and infrequently practiced Hindu ritual of burning a dead man's widow to increase his family's prestige, enhance the importance of the village, and create an image of the widow as a goddess in whose memory prayers will be offered at the site of the funeral pyre (*India Today,* 1987). Other cultures hold a ceremonial meal for the mourners; in still others, mourners wear black armbands for one year following a death. In the United States, the funeral offers a variety of options through which survivors express their loss. According to Kalish and Reynolds (1981), there is also evidence that in the United States certain aspects of mourning vary from one ethnic group to another (see table 13.2).

The funeral industry has been charged with taking advantage of the bereaved at a time when they are most vulnerable. Undertakers have offered expensive but needless rituals, services, and goods to those who can ill-afford such luxuries (Baird, 1976; Mitford, 1963). Many states now require "truth in services" at the time funeral arrangements are being made. The bereaved must be informed in writing of the exact charges for each specific funeral expense (see table 13.3 for examples). It is hoped that by providing charges in writing, the bereaved may choose desired options appropriately, avoid unnecessary funeral costs, and understand more completely the charges incurred (Federal Trade Commission, 1978). An average funeral now costs more than $3,000 according to the American Association of Retired Persons (1988). Annual increases are projected to be 4 to 5 percent.

Because it is difficult for the bereaved to make funeral decisions, some elderly individuals are deciding *in advance* exactly what funeral arrangements they wish to have. Funeral homes have adopted **prior-to-need** or **pre-need** (Rowse, 1988)

Table 13.2

RESPONSES OF 434 PERSONS IN THE GREATER LOS ANGELES AREA REGARDING THE LENGTH OF TIME FOLLOWING THE DEATH OF SPOUSE BEFORE IT WOULD BE APPROPRIATE FOR A PERSON OF RESPONDENT'S AGE, SEX, AND ETHNICITY TO DO EACH OF THE INDICATED ACTIONS.

	Percent of Black Americans	*Percent of Japanese Americans*	*Percent of Mexican Americans*	*Percent of "Anglo" Americans*
To remarry				
Unimportant to wait	34	14	22	26
1 week–6 months	15	3	1	23
1 year	25	30	38	34
2 years	11	26	20	11
Other (including never; depends)	16	28	19	7
To stop wearing black				
Unimportant to wait	62	42	52	53
1 day—4 months	24	26	11	31
6 months +	11	21	35	6
Other/depends	4	11	3	11
To return to his/her place of employment				
Unimportant to wait	39	22	27	47
1 day–1 week	39	28	37	35
1 month +	17	35	27	9
Other/depends	6	16	9	10
To start going out with other men/women				
Unimportant to wait	30	17	17	25
1 week–1 month	14	8	4	9
6 months	24	22	22	29
1 year +	11	34	40	21
Other/depends	21	19	18	17
What do you feel is the fewest number of times he/she should visit his/her spouse's grave during the first year— not counting the burial service?				
Unimportant to do	39	7	11	35
1–2 times	32	18	19	11
3–5 times	16	18	12	18
6 + times	13	58	59	35
(Don't know, etc.)	(11)	(6)	(3)	(19)
What do you feel is the fewest number of times he/she should visit his/her spouse's grave during the fifth year after the death?				
Unimportant to do	52	8	20	43
1–2 times	30	17	39	35
3–5 times	9	16	22	15
6 + times	10	30	18	6
(Don't know, etc.)	(14)	(6)	(4)	(22)

From R. A. Kalish and D. K. Reynolds, "An Overview of Death and Ethnicity" in *Death and Ethnicity: A Psychocultural Study.* Copyright © Baywood Publishing Company, Inc., Farmingdale, NY. Reprinted by permission.

Table 13.3

Itemization of funeral services and merchandise (January, 1990)
Services and Merchandise Provided and Price Range

Funeral Home Expenses and Mortician Charges

1. *Direct Cremation* $850–950   This charge includes transfer of remains to funeral home, required authorizations, services of funeral director and staff, unfinished wooden box or heavy cardboard container, transportation of the body to local crematory, and return of the remains to the funeral home. The direct cremation charges do not include the crematory charge.

2. *Direct Burial Costs* $800–1,395   This charge includes an immediate burial, transfer of remains to funeral home, required authorizations, funeral services and staff, transportation of the body to local area cemetery. This charge includes the least expensive casket (cloth-covered hardwood) but does not reflect cemetery charges or preparation-of-remains charges.

3. *Preparation of Remains* $660   Charges for embalming ($395), use of preparation room ($95), topical disinfectant ($85), custodial care ($45), dressing/casketing ($22), and cosmetology ($18).

4. *Arrangements* $495   Funeral director, staff, equipment, and facilities needed to respond to initial request for service, arrangement conference, coordination of service plans and final disposition of the deceased.

5. *Supervision* $285   Services provided by funeral director and staff during visitation (two days), funeral service, and graveside ceremony.

6. *Charge for Facilities* $335   Use of funeral home for visitation (two days) and funeral service.

7. *Livery Charge* $143   Hearse and flower vehicle within ten miles with $1.10 per mile charge for each mile beyond ten miles.

8. *Merchandise* Charge for casket ($695–4,995) and charge for outer interment receptacle ($645–1,895).

9. *Additional Services and Merchandise* $155   Charges for memorial cards, acknowledgment cards, register book, death notices, and cemetery equipment.

10. *Copies of Death Certificate* $10 per copy.

Cemetery Expenses

1. *Internment Costs* $300   Opening and closing of grave, rental and setting up chairs, replacement of grass, administrative fees.

2. *Cemetery Plot* $600–1,500   Costs vary by location and size (e.g., individual, couple, or family plot).

3. *Perpetual Maintenance* $400   Costs to maintain the cemetery and gravesite (lawnmowing, road upkeep, etc.).

4. *Tombstone* $500–10,000   Costs vary depending on size, material, and artwork.

burial plans so that survivors may be spared the difficulty of making and paying for such services at a time when they are intensely grieving. More and more people have opted for prior-to-need arrangements. In one study, 700,000 people over 65 years of age purchased such arrangements for themselves each year in the United States (American Association of Retired Persons, 1988).

Most bodies in the United States are placed in caskets in the ground or in mausoleums. About 9 percent are cremated. Individuals who are cremated typically have their ashes spread in the crematorium's garden; others wish their ashes taken to specific locations. A viewing of the body occurs in about 75 percent of deaths, a practice that many experts concur helps avoid denial (Swanson and Bennett, 1982–1983). Obviously, having an open casket is a personal choice for families and raises additional costs as funeral directors must perform such services as embalming, applying facial makeup, and preparing the body. While the funeral industry has been charged with exploiting the bereaved in the purchase of unnecessary services and merchandise, other factors may also come into play, including a sense of guilt on the part of survivors, their reluctance to ask about various options, and their desire to bury their loved one in style.

Grief

Researchers have identified several phases of grief. However, validation of each phase has been controversial (Kalish, 1985). One view suggests there are three phases of grief: *shock, despair,* and *recovery* (Averill, 1968). Another identifies four phases: *numbness*—downplaying the significance of the loss; *yearning*—attempting to recover or search for the person we have lost; *disorganization and despair*—accepting and no longer pining over the loss; *reorganization*—recovery from the loss (Parkes, 1970, 1972).

Drawing from Parkes's approach as well as the work of Pincus (1976) and Pollack (1961), it appears that the first phase is marked by feelings of shock, disbelief, numbness, and considerable weeping and agitation. This stage occurs very soon after the death and usually lasts no more than three days. Survivors may experience panic, faint, and even shriek or moan.

During the second phase, survivors feel a painful longing for the dead and memories and visual images of the deceased are often on their minds. People actually experience hallucinations and report seeing, hearing, being held, kissing, touching, and even talking to the deceased. Survivors feel intense psychological pain. The desire to recover the dead is very strong, and some may even contemplate suicide as a way to rejoin their loved one. Insomnia, compulsive pacing or walking, intense sadness, irritability, and restlessness are common. Private conversations, fantasies, and dreams of the deceased are also characteristic of this phase. If such responses persist and survivors continue to ignore reality, the grief process may be

Grief is an overwhelming emotion experienced as a sense of loss and despair.

difficult to complete. This phase emerges soon after death, peaks two to four weeks later, and may subside after several months but can persist for as long as one or two years.

The third phase is the realistic appraisal of what the loss means. It is characterized by the *separation reaction* of survivors, which produces both disorganization and despair as it becomes clear that the deceased is no longer physically close and will never return. Common responses include heightened anxiety and fear for one's safety and protection. Survivors may even express anger toward the deceased for leaving them and making them experience such sorrow, or they may channel their anger (displaced aggression) toward health professionals who cared for the dead. Finally, in this phase, the experience of guilt occurs (Pincus, 1976; Pollack, 1978; Stephenson, 1985). Survivors may regret what they did not do for or say to the deceased. They may even feel that if they had acted more quickly, recognized the signs of serious illness earlier, or found a better physician or hospital then the death would not have happened. Guilt may also appear in a form of *idealization* or *sanctification* (Lopata, 1979) in which a spouse identifies only the most positive image of a mate who has died. The dead spouse's faults are ignored and their strengths overdramatized. The deceased is remembered without flaws or human weaknesses; they are recalled with only positive emotion and wonderful memories.

The last phase (reorganization and recovery) usually occurs within a year after the death. It is marked by a resumption of ordinary activities, a greater likelihood that the deceased will be recalled with pleasant but realistic memories, and the resumption of social relationships—maintaining ongoing friendships as well as establishing new ones. One component of this phase is the survivor's identification with the deceased. Identification involves adopting the personal traits, behaviors, speech, mannerisms, gestures, habits, and concerns of the deceased (Stephenson, 1985). Pincus (1976) notes that through such identification the dead person becomes a part of the mourner, internalized so that the dead is still a part of the living. This too is a necessary part of grieving and helps to pave the way for continuing life. At this point, survivors realize that they can continue to live without the dead. They recognize the sources of pleasure, love, and support derived from relatives, friends, and community.

Grief is one of the most powerful emotions ever experienced. Therapists and counselors recognize the immense energy and commitment which those who are grieving must expend to arrive at some resolution of their loss. The term **grief work** is an apt description of the intensity and duration of this process. It is difficult, all-consuming, and pervasive work for those who mourn.

Outcomes of the Mourning Process

Grief can be experienced in many ways—as anger, guilt, or idealization. One of the most common is through **grief pangs.** These feelings include somatic distress occurring in waves and lasting twenty minutes to an hour, a tight feeling in the throat, shortness of breath, the need to sigh, an empty feeling in the stomach, lack of physical strength, tension, sobbing, or crying (Lindmann, 1944; Parkes, 1964; Frederick, 1983–1984; Stephenson, 1985). The sadness and deep sorrow that grieving people experience are sufficient to meet the criteria for clinical depression or physical illness (Frederick, 1983–1984). Frederick notes, for example that the experience of intense grief produces heightened levels of corticosteroids (hormones), which may account, in part, for the psychological and physical symptoms of grief. It has also been reported that among the recently bereaved, the rate of death and the incidence of serious illness are dramatically higher (Stephenson, 1985). Kalish (1985) speculates that this may be the result of psychological stress, grief, and the impact of the loss as well as the physical stress of caretaking and visiting the hospital, which may lead to inadequate sleep, exercise, and poor nutrition.

Resolution of grief leads to a renewal of interest in living and in the self. Often after a year or so, people come to terms with the death and begin to make major decisions affecting their lives. They may repaint a room, buy new furniture, or travel to emphasize that life must continue. Regression may also be a consequence of mourning; some people need to return to an earlier stage to gather their resources and try to cope with loss (Pincus, 1976). In addition, grief work may be arrested and remain incomplete as individuals deny their loss, their feelings, and their need to bring resolution to their grief. Experts have reported the existence of **delayed grief reactions** in some personal histories. Delayed grief emerges long after the deaths of those we love. It may emerge as a heightened reaction to the death of someone we barely know, of a relative with whom we were not very close, or even of the loss of a family pet (see box 13.6).

Finally, at special times that remind us of a loss, we may experience **anniversary reactions.** We may feel particularly lonely and yearn for the relationship we have lost on birthdays, at family gatherings, on holidays, or on the anniversary date of the person's death. One form of grief, **anticipatory grief,** actually begins prior to death. This form is the anticipation of a death which is virtually guaranteed to occur. The grief work may begin weeks or months in advance of the actual death. As yet, there is no evidence that anticipatory grief makes adapting to the actual loss easier (Marshall, 1980; Stephenson, 1985).

Making Sense Out of the World

One of the most important aspects of grieving is that it stimulates many people to strive to make sense of their world. Richard Kalish (1981) describes this process:

> A common occurrence during the grieving period is to go over, again and again, all the events that led up to the death. This can become a virtual preoccupation with some individuals, but almost all of us partake of it to some extent. In the days and weeks after the death, the closest family members will share experiences with each other—sometimes providing new information and insights into the person who died, sometimes reminiscing over familiar experiences. . . .

BOX 13.6

THE DELAYED GRIEF REACTION

Dr. John Dacy, psychologist, professor at Boston College, and author has allowed us to share a particularly tragic encounter with delayed grief reaction from his own life. In a discussion of grief, he related the following story:

I would like to relate an experience of mine that seems relevant to this question about the role of grief. In April, 1957, I joined the United States Navy and sailed to the Mediterranean for a six-month tour of duty on an oil supply ship. In early November I returned home to a joyful reunion with my family. After this wonderful weekend at home, I returned to my ship. Two days later I received a telegram informing me of a tragedy: my mother, two younger brothers and two younger sisters had been killed in a fire that had destroyed our house. My father and four other brothers and sisters had escaped with burns.

On the long train ride home from the naval port, I recall thinking that, as the oldest, I should be especially helpful to my father in the terrible time ahead. I was also aware of a curious absence of dismay in myself. In our upstate New York town, the catastrophe was unprecedented, and expressions of grief and condolence were myriad. People kept saying to me, "Don't try to be so brave, it's good for you to let yourself cry." And I tried to, but it just wouldn't come.

At the funeral, the caskets were closed, and I can remember thinking that maybe, just maybe, this was all just a horrible dream. I distinctly remember one fantasy about my brother Mike, who was born on my first birthday and with whom I had recently become especially close. I imagined that he had actually hit his head trying to escape, and wandered off to Chicago with a case of amnesia, and no one was willing to admit that they didn't know where he was. I knew this wasn't true, but I secretly clung to the possibility. After a very difficult period of time, our family gradually began a new life. Many people generously helped us, and eventually the memories faded.

Several times in the years that followed, I went to doctors because of a stomach ache, a painful stiff neck, or some other malady, which couldn't be diagnosed physically. One doctor suggested that I might be suffering from an unresolved subconscious problem, but I doubted it.

Then one night in 1972, fifteen years after the fire, I was watching the original version of *The Waltons* on TV, the episode in which the father is lost at Christmas. Although dissimilar from my own experience, this tragedy triggered an incredible response in me. Suddenly it occurred to me, "My God, half my family is really gone forever!" I began sobbing and could not stop for over three hours. When I finally stopped, I felt weak and empty, relieved of an awful burden. In the days that followed I believe I went through a clear-cut "delayed grief" reaction.

Therefore, the answer to the question above, at least in my experience, is clear: grief work really is essential, and we avoid it only at the cost of even greater pain. My father died recently, and my reaction was immediate and intense. I cannot help but feel that my emotional response this time was considerably more appropriate and healthy.

When a death is caused by an accident or a disaster, the effort to make sense of it is pursued more vigorously. As added pieces of news come trickling in, they are integrated into the puzzle. The bereaved want to put the death into a perspective that they can understand—divine intervention, a curse from a neighboring tribe, a logical sequence of cause and effect, or whatever it may be. . . .

Eventually each of us finds an adequate "story of the dying and death"—of John Kennedy or of our father or of a friend. Versions of the death may differ—whether the physician really did all she could to save the patient, whether Aunt Bella showed up frequently at the hospital or not, whether the operation succeeded or didn't quite succeed, whether father was ready to die or would have lived longer if possible—but each person's version satisfies him and that version, with slight modifications, becomes the official version for the teller. (pp. 227–228)

Types of Death that are Difficult to Resolve

Coping with death is never easy. However, some deaths prove to be more problematic than others. According to Richard Kalish (1981, 1985), some of the most troublesome types of death include:

1. Suicides or deaths due to self-neglect or carelessness
2. Unexpected deaths, such as deaths of young people, those recently married, or those close to achieving significant goals
3. Deaths that forced the bereaved to care for the dying person in a manner that proved to be distressing
4. Deaths in which the bereaved believes he or she was partly or fully responsible, such as a child's drowning in a swimming pool
5. Homicides
6. Unconfirmed deaths with no body found
7. Deaths so drawn out over time that the survivors become impatient for death to occur

In the remainder of this section, we will briefly describe some of the types of deaths that place the greatest burden on our coping skills.

Death of a Child

The death of a child produces such intense grief and is such a devastating loss that parents may not ever recover. The unexpected death of a child is even more difficult. If the death is due to an accident, parents experience enormous guilt, accepting responsibility far in excess of what is appropriate. If the death is anticipated, parents are encouraged to be honest and open with their child rather than engaging in mutual pretense (Stephenson, 1985). Parents may alleviate the child's fears of loneliness, separation, and pain rather than dealing with the concept of death itself (Stillion and Wass, 1979), and parents are encouraged to themselves begin the process of anticipatory grief work (Sahler, 1978).

Death of a Sibling

The death of a sibling is difficult to resolve for brothers and sisters, especially while still in childhood. Not only do they feel the loss deeply, there may be cognitive distortions as to the meaning of the loss. Younger children, as we described earlier in this chapter, may not fully comprehend death, may not have the language to express their own concerns, and may not have ready listeners in parents, who themselves are intensely grieving. Various experts (Pollack, 1978; Stephenson, 1985) suggest that with the death of a sibling, young children simply do not have much chance to deal with the guilt they experience. The rivalry and ambivalence expressed normally by all siblings heightens the guilt in the surviving siblings not only in childhood but also throughout adulthood.

Death of a Parent

The death of a parent shows persistent long-term effects whether it occurs in childhood, adolescence, or adulthood. Children are faced with separation and loss as well as a reduction in the love, affection, and attention they have received. Parental death often means other significant life changes such as moving, reduction in standard of living, changes in friends, and stepparenting. Even for adults, the death of a parent demands enormous grief work. The loss is intense and the loss of attachment bonds and emotional security are irreplaceable. Regardless of circumstances, most adult children believe that a parent who has died did not live long enough (Moss and Moss, 1983–1984). The death of a parent signifies that all humans are mortal and that our turn will also come; we realize that there is no other older generation standing between us and death.

Death of a Spouse

Usually the most difficult loss is the death of a spouse. There are more than 12 million widowed people in the United States; widows outnumber widowers by a 5:1 ratio (Campbell and Silverman, 1987). At age sixty-five, roughly 50 percent of the women in the United States are already widowed, while only 20 percent of males are widowers at the same age (Campbell and Silverman, 1987; Kalish, 1985). The death of a spouse is usually unpreventable, may shatter a long-standing attachment bond, require the pursuit of new roles and status, lead to financial hardship, and leave the survivor without a major support system (Osterweis, Solomon, and Green, 1984). A young surviving spouse is more likely to experience serious adjustment problems than an older spouse. Adjustment problems include depression, increasing physician consultations, hospitalization, increases in smoking and drinking, pathological grief reactions, and higher mortality rates (Kaprio, Kosenvuo, and Rita, 1987; Zisook, 1987; Zisook, Shuchter, and Lyons, 1987).

The experience of widowhood changes dramatically depending on sociohistorical circumstances (Lopata, 1987a). The modernization of societies has enabled many widows to live independently, free from the control of the patriarchal family, and able to maintain themselves economically through paid employment and/or

Many widows eventually create social support systems for themselves.

the Social Security system in the United States. Some widows are unable to reengage in social relations and roles after a past tie is broken through death. Yet many widows have or create support systems and eventually reimmerse themselves in their families, their neighborhoods, friendship networks, occupations, or organizations.

Lopata (1987b) also suggests that widowhood may be experienced in many different ways. Some widows are passive, accepting changes produced by the death of a husband. Others display personal abilities, long dormant, that may blossom in widowhood. Some stay in pockets of comfortable social support, while others expand, seeking new resources, new friendships, and new social roles.

Summary

Although death is inevitable, it remains an uncomfortable topic in our culture. It may seem easy to identify when an individual has died, but recent medical advances have made the determination complex. For example, brain death can occur even though critical organs like the heart and lungs continue to function. Today we are faced with ethical questions concerning the practice of euthanasia and when we should prolong a person's life. Several states are enacting laws to determine when a dying person may not be resuscitated.

It is important to consider the sociohistorical context of death. Our culture shows more avoidance and denial of death than most cultures. Furthermore, in many cultures death occurs frequently in all periods of the life span. In our culture, however, death is most likely to occur in old age.

Because of the limitations of Piagetian preoperational thought, it is difficult for the preschool child to comprehend death. Early in the elementary school years, children may still not understand the universality of death, although they do begin to understand its permanence. At some point before adolescence, most children grasp both the finality and universality of death. Adolescents often react to death in a superficial way, possibly because of the self-preoccupation that characterizes many adolescents. Young adults also show little concern for death, but during middle adulthood people begin to show considerably more interest. Studies suggest middle-aged people are often as concerned, or in some cases more concerned, about death than people in late adulthood.

Elisabeth Kubler-Ross has suggested five psychological stages of dying: denial and isolation, anger, bargaining, depression, and acceptance. Researchers have been unable to verify that dying people go through the stages in the sequence prescribed; however, Kubler-Ross's main contribution is the humanization of the dying process. E. Mansell Pattison has suggested three phases of what he calls the living-dying interval: acute, chronic, and terminal. The dying process is multifaceted and involves much more than descriptive stages or phases. For example, denial is an important aspect of the coping process for the dying person. By itself, denial is neither good nor bad. For many dying people, adaptive denial may be helpful.

An open system of communication with the dying is often an optimal strategy. Above all we should avoid stereotypes about dying and the aged. The dying person is a unique individual, with strengths and ongoing challenges to face. For those people near death and with limited ability to participate in their environment, it may be best to stress inner personal growth. The contexts in which people die are also important. Hospitals insure medical expertise and sophisticated equipment, but more intimacy and autonomy is usually possible at home. An alternative to home or hospital is the hospice, a humanizing institution that many experts believe offers the best blend of home and hospital benefits. The hospice movement began in the 1960s and continues to expand. It stresses patient control and management of pain as well as a philosophy based on open communication, family involvement, and extensive support services.

The loss of someone we are attached to is among the most stressful life events. Coping with the death of a loved one has been described in terms of bereavement—the state of loss—and mourning—the overt, behavioral expression of bereavement and grief. Mourning takes many forms, depending on the culture. In the United States, the mourning process usually involves a funeral, which is followed by burial or cremation. In recent years controversy has arisen about the funeral industry. Grief may be seen as a series of phases—shock, despair, and recovery. However, people do not have to go through each phase to cope adaptively with grief. One of the most common ways of experiencing grief is through grief pangs. Denial is also part of grief, just as it is part of dying. One aspect of the grief process involves making sense out of the world and trying to solve the puzzle of death. One of the most intense losses we can suffer is the death of a spouse. Widowed individuals may incur illness and are even more likely to die themselves.

Review Questions

1. At present, what is the biological definition of death?
2. Explain the difference between *death* and the *process of dying*.
3. Do you believe that euthanasia should be practiced? Explain.
4. Discuss the sociohistorical contexts of death.
5. What are common attitudes about death in young childhood, adolescence, and early, middle, and late adulthood?
6. Describe and critically evaluate Kubler-Ross's five psychological stages of dying.
7. Describe how denial can affect the dying person.
8. What are some of the best strategies for communicating with a dying person?
9. Describe the contexts in which people die—in hospitals, hospices, and at home—including the benefits and disadvantages of each.
10. Outline the phases of grief that people go through, how they try to make sense out of the world when someone close to them dies, and how grief may be particularly intense in the case of a widow or widower.
11. What kinds of death make it particularly difficult to resolve the grief process?
12. Discuss various forms of mourning and the controversy over the funeral industry.

For Further Reading

Garfield, C. (Ed.) (1978). *Psychological care of the dying person*. New York: McGraw-Hill.
    A range of contributors provide important psychological insights and guidelines to professionals and family who interact with the dying. Easy reading.
Kalish, R. A. (1981). *Death, grief, and caring relationships*. Monterey, CA: Brooks/Cole.
    An excellent, detailed overview of many facets of death and the dying process. One of the most thorough, comprehensive sources available. Moderate reading level.

Kastenbaum, R. (1985). Dying and death: A life-span approach. In J. E. Birren & K. W. Schaie (Eds.), *The handbook of the psychology of aging.* (2d ed.). New York: Van Nostrand Reinhold.

A very good review of theory and research regarding (1) the social context of death and dying, (2) death orientations throughout the life span, and (3) the problems associated with terminal care in later life. Moderate reading level.

Siegel, R. K. (1980). The psychology of life after death. *American Psychologist, 35,* 911–931.

The full text of Siegel's critical evaluation of the psychology of near-death experiences. Reasonably easy reading.

Shneidman, E. S. (1980). *Voices of death.* New York: Harper and Row.

A sharp contrast to the stage theory of death and dying. Individual reports of stage mixtures, stage co-occurrence, and stage regression from dying individuals lead to scientific skepticism of the validity of stages of dying. Easy reading.

Stephenson, J. S. (1985). *Death, grief, and mourning: Individual and social realities.* New York: Free Press.

A comprehensive and broadly based interdisciplinary examination of the approaches adopted to death and dying. Historical material and important philosophical traditions are presented. Reasonably easy reading.

GLOSSARY

A

ABORTIVE COPING A form of adjustment to life events which is predominantly negative, nonproductive, and limiting to human growth. (p. 445)

ACCEPTANCE The fifth and final stage of Kubler-Ross's psychological stages of dying. In this stage, said to be characterized by peace, acceptance of one's fate, and desire to be left alone, dying patients end their struggle against death. (p. 512)

ACCOMMODATION The process of eye muscle adjustments that allows the eye to have the greatest clarity of image (resolution); the ability to focus and maintain an image on the retina. (p. 102)

ACETYLCHOLINE (ACH) A neurotransmitter necessary for brain activation, responsiveness, and communication. Comprised essentially from choline, it travels from the axon across the synaptic cleft and to the dendrites of another cell. (p. 126)

ACETYLCHOLINESTERASE (ACHE) The substance responsible for the deactivation of acetylcholine and limits the length of time a neuron is stimulated. (p. 126)

ACHIEVEMENT MOTIVE The need to maintain or increase one's competence in activities in which a standard of excellence is involved. (p. 368)

ACTION POTENTIAL A brief electrical impulse that travels down the axon of a neuron. (p. 125)

ACTIVE EUTHANASIA Inducing death in an incurably ill person by some positive action, such as injecting a lethal dose of a drug. (p. 504)

ACTIVE MASTERY A style of relating to the environment that changes with age in different ways for men and women. It allows the adult more direct control over the environment. (pp. 342, 430)

ACTIVITY THEORY A theory of aging which states that activity and involvement in late adulthood are often associated with life satisfaction. (p. 345)

ACUTE BRAIN SYNDROME A form of organic brain disorder which has a sudden onset and is potentially reversible. (p. 462)

AFFIRMATIVE COPING A form of adjustment to life events which is positive, productive, and enhancing to human growth. (p. 445)

AGEISM The unwarranted assumption that chronological age is the primary determinant of human traits, abilities, and characteristics and that one age is superior to another. (p. 334)

AGE STRUCTURE The percentage of males and females within various age intervals in a given society. (p. 64)

AGNOSIA The inability to visually recognize familiar objects. (p. 120)

AIDS Acquired immune deficiency syndrome. The failure of the body's immune system which leaves afflicted individuals vulnerable to a variety of diseases and ultimately leads to death. (p. 467)

AIDS DEMENTIA COMPLEX A set of cognitive dysfunctions associated with brain infection caused by the HIV virus. (p. 467)

ALPHA RHYTHM Brain wave patterns detected by using an electroencephalogram that has a frequency of 8–12 cycles per second. (p. 121)

ALZHEIMER'S DISEASE (AD) Irreversible dementia characterized by progressive deterioration in memory, awareness, and body functions, eventually leading to death. (p. 130)

AMYLOID The chemical substance that is found in the senile plaques associated with Alzheimer's disease. (p. 130)

ANDROGYNY Acceptance of both male and female characteristics in oneself. (p. 337)

ANGER The second of Kubler-Ross's stages of dying. In this stage dying persons realize that denial of death cannot be maintained, causing them to become angry, resentful, and envious. (p. 511)

ANNIVERSARY REACTIONS Feelings of loneliness that occur on holidays, birthdays, etc., following the death of a loved one. (p. 526)

ANTICIPATORY GRIEF Feelings of grief, loneliness, and despair that precede the death of a loved one. (p. 526)

APPARENT MEMORY DEFICITS Memory losses that can be attributed to faulty encoding and retrieval processes; these are potentially reversible through intervention or instruction. (p. 219)

APPROPRIATE DEATH A mode of coping with death that approximates the wishes and ideals of the dying person. (p. 512)

ASCENDING RETICULAR ACTIVATING SYSTEM A brain system that controls levels of awareness or consciousness. (p. 117)

ATTENTION A process that controls both the content and the amount of information that is encoded. (p. 187)

AUTOBIOGRAPHICAL MEMORY TASK A task in which a person is asked to recall a personal life experience. (p. 212)

AUTOIMMUNE THEORY The idea that biological aging is the result of the diminishing capacity of the body's autoimmune system to identify foreign material. (p. 75)

AUTOIMMUNITY A condition that is caused by a failure of immune mechanisms to detect normal cells or by mistakes in the formation of antibodies that make them react to normal cells as well as foreign ones. (p. 75)

AUTOMATIC INFORMATION PROCESSING Information processing that does not draw on limited attentional capacity. (p. 196)

AXON The part of the neuron that transmits information. (p. 125)

B

BARGAINING The third of Kubler-Ross's stages of dying. In this stage dying patients hope that death may be postponed by negotiating with God. (p. 511)

BASAL METABOLISM RATE A biological mechanism defined as the minimum amount of energy a person uses in a state of rest. (p. 80)

BEHAVIORAL RESEARCH Research that obtains the direct observation and recording of behavior, including experimental approaches. (p. 36)

BENIGN SENESCENT FORGETFULNESS The normal, non-pathological memory loss associated with aging. (p. 217)

BEREAVED The status of a person or family who has survived the death of a loved one. (p. 520)

BEREAVEMENT OVERLOAD The inability to work through the deaths of loved ones which occur close to one another in time. (p. 509)

BETA RHYTHM Fast brain rhythm that characterizes an attentive, alert state. (p. 121)

BETWEEN SUBJECTS MANIPULATIONS The random assignment of subjects to groups in an experiment. (p. 46)

BIOLOGICAL AGE The relative condition of an individual's organ and body system. (p. 17)

BIOLOGICAL PERSPECTIVE The point of view that suggests that deficits in memory are caused by specific biological deterioration in the brain. (pp. 214, 215)

BONA FIDE OCCUPATIONAL QUALIFICATIONS (BFOQ) Legislation that mandates that workers in selective job classifications retire at a specific age due to the abilities or traits demanded for successful performance, e.g., police or airline traffic controllers. (p. 385)

BRAIN DEATH That point in which all electrical activity has ceased in the brain as determined by an EEG. (p. 496)

BRAIN STEM The primitive part of the lower brain that controls the basic biological processes associated with respiration and heartbeat. (p. 117)

BUSY ETHIC A theory of retirement that suggests that people need to channel their work ethic into productive, useful leisure activities in old age. (p. 393)

C

CATARACTS Opacity in the lens of the eye that can cause blindness if not corrected. (p. 104)

CENTRAL PROCESSES Psychological processes that occur within the central nervous system, e.g., the brain. (p. 116)

CENTRAL TENDENCY The manipulation of a given set of scores to determine the mean, median, or mode. (p. 41)

CEREBELLUM A primitive part of the brain that controls balance and motor programming, and simple conditioning. (p. 117)

CEREBRUM The largest and evolutionarily most recent part of the brain. (p. 119)

CHANGE A measurable alteration in a particular skill, ability, or function. (p. 4)

CHRONIC BRAIN SYNDROME Forms of organic disorders that are nonreversible and which may produce a variety of emotional and cognitive symptoms. (p. 462)

CHRONOLOGICAL AGE The number of years since a person's birth. (p. 16)

COCHLEA The primary neural receptor for hearing. (p. 108)

COHORT A group of people born in the same time period; a generation one is born into. (p. 161)

COHORT EFFECTS Differences in behaviors that are found among people born at different times in history. (pp. 13, 50)

COHORT SEQUENTIAL DESIGN A complex research design which allows a research investigator to distinguish between age effects and cohort effects. (p. 51)

COLLAGEN The stiff protein which comprises one-third of the body's protein and accumulates with age. (p. 85)

CONCRETE OPERATIONAL STYLE The third stage of Piaget's theory of mental development which highlights a type of thinking limited to concrete ideas and experiences. (p. 232)

CONSTRUCT VALIDITY The extent to which a psychological test or assessment measures a hypothetical entity, e.g., intelligence. (p. 34)

CONTEXTUAL MODEL The model that suggests that adults, like historical events, are ongoing, dynamic, and not directed towards an ideal or end-state. (pp. 20, 21)

CONTEXTUAL PERSPECTIVE The viewpoint that suggests that the effectiveness of a person's memory depends on the context or setting within which the person is required to learn and remember information. (pp. 214, 216)

CONTINUITY OF FUNCTIONING The notion that the same processes control psychological functioning throughout the life span. (p. 8)

CONTRAST The difference in brightness between adjacent parts of a visual stimulus. (pp. 105, 106)

CONTRAST SENSITIVITY An individual's ability to perceive visual stimuli that differ in terms of both contrast and spatial frequency. (pp. 105, 106)

CONTRAST THRESHOLD The minimal amount of contrast needed to perceive spacial frequency differences in gratings. (p. 106)

CONVENTIONAL LEVEL The third and fourth stages of Kohlberg's theory of moral development in which moral thought is based on the desire to preserve good interpersonal relations (stage 3) and to comply with formalized rules that exist in society (stage 4). (p. 435)

CONVERGENT THINKING A type of thinking that is designed to reveal a single correct answer for a problem. (p. 172)

CORONARY ARTERIES Those arteries that supply blood to the heart and which when blocked produce a heart attack. (p. 84)

CORPUS CALLOSUM A band of nerve fibers that connects the brain's two hemispheres. (p. 119)

CORRELATION A relationship or association between two variables that can be either positive or negative and vary from weak to strong. (p. 42)

CORRELATIONAL STUDY A type of research in which associations between variables are merely observed. (p. 44)

CORTEX The outer covering of the cerebrum. (p. 119)

CROSS-SECTIONAL STUDY A study in which individuals of different ages are observed at different times to obtain information about some variable, usually contaminated by cohort effects. (p. 49)

CROSS-SEQUENTIAL DESIGN A complex research design that allows an investigator to distinguish time of testing effects from cohort effects. (p. 53)

CRYSTALLIZED INTELLIGENCE The type of intelligence that involves skills, abilities, and understanding gained through instruction and observation. (p. 151)

CT SCAN An advanced, noninvasive technique used to determine a two- or three-dimensional representation of the human brain. (p. 120)

CURVILINEAR The reflection of the association of variables that is represented by a curved line when plotted on a graph. (p. 43)

D

DAILY HASSLES The little irritating annoyances that punctuate our daily existence. (p. 453)

DARK ADAPTATION The visual adjustment required when one enters environments of different illumination; particularly difficult for the elderly when going from a brightly lit to a dimly lit environment. (p. 103)

DECREMENT WITH COMPENSATION MODEL The notion that intellectual declines that occur during adulthood may be reversed by appropriate intervention. (p. 182)

DELAYED GRIEF REACTION A delayed and heightened reaction to the death of a loved one that is elicited in response to the death of someone to whom the individual is not emotionally attached. (p. 526)

DELIRIUM A form of acute brain syndrome marked by minimal awareness of self and environment and the presence of hallucinations, delusions, and distortions. (p. 462)

DELTA RHYTHMS The brain waves associated with deep sleep. (p. 121)

DEMENTIA An organically-based disorder of late adulthood characterized by a deterioration of intelligence and behavior. (pp. 130, 463)

DENDRITES The component of a neuron that receives information. (p. 124)

DENIAL/ISOLATION The first of Kubler-Ross's psychological stages of dying. In this stage dying persons react to terminal illness with shock, denial, and withdrawal. (p. 511)

DEPENDENT VARIABLES The values that are measured as a result of experimental manipulations. (p. 45)

DEPRESSION The fourth of Kubler-Ross's stages of dying. In this stage dying person's become silent, spend much time crying, and want to be alone in an effort to disconnect themselves from objects of love. (p. 511)

DEPRESSIVE PSEUDODEMENTIA Depression that mimics dementia. (p. 467)

DEVELOPMENT Refers to a form of change that is organized and adaptive (positive) in nature. (p. 4)

DIAGNOSTIC RELATED GROUP (DRG) National health care definitions of specific medical conditions to permit construction of average costs and lengths of treatment in a hospital for insurance reimbursement purposes. (p. 486)

DIALECTICAL VIEW The belief that individuals are constantly changing organisms in a constantly changing world. (p. 22)

DISCONTINUITY OF FUNCTIONING The belief among stage theorists that development is abrupt, with different processes controlling psychological functioning across the life span. (p. 8)

DISENGAGEMENT THEORY A theory of aging that argues that with increasing age, older individuals withdraw from society and society withdraws from individuals. (p. 345)

DISTANCING STRATEGIES Coping strategies that protect us from deeply experiencing our own emotions. (p. 494)

DIVERGENT THINKING A type of thinking closely related to creativity that produces many different answers to a single question. (p. 172)

DIVIDED ATTENTION The ability to simultaneously attend to two different pieces of environmental information. (p. 192)

DO NOT RESUSCITATE ACT Specific orders that direct physicians to not initiate heroic measures (e.g., electric shock) when breathing or heartbeat has stopped. (p. 499)

DOPAMINE (DA) A neurotransmitter implicated in Parkinson's Disease and schizophrenia. (pp. 126, 473)

DUAL-TASK PERFORMANCE A person's ability to perform two tasks at once. (p. 193)

E

EARLY-ONSET ALCOHOLISM The development of alcoholism through adolescence to middle age. (p. 479)

EFFORTFUL INFORMATION PROCESSING Information processing that draws on limited attentional resources. (p. 196)

EGO MASTERY STYLES The style adopted in coping with self and others that reflects the underlying organization of values and beliefs that govern external behavior. (p. 341)

ELASTIN Large protein molecules that comprise the elastic fibers of the body, similar to collagen but more flexible. (p. 85)

ELECTROENCEPHALOGRAM (EEG) A machine used to measure the electrical activity of the cortex. (p. 121)

EMOTION-FOCUSED COPING Behavioral and cognitive strategies designed to help manage the emotional tensions produced by stressful life situations. (p. 456)

EMPTY NEST SYNDROME A group of symptoms typified by anxiety and depression thought to be experienced by parents associated with their children's leaving home. (p. 277)

ENCAPSULATION MODEL A model of adult cognitive development designed to explain age-related changes in processing, knowing, and thinking. (p. 249)

ENCODING DEFICIT A memory failure that may be traced to the inability to acquire to-be-remembered information. (p. 215)

EPIGENIC PRINCIPLE In Erikson's theory, the belief that all growth has an underlying structure that determines the occasions during which specific psychosocial crises may occur. (p. 405)

ERAS Major portions of the life span according to Daniel Levinson. (p. 417)

ERROR CATASTROPHE THEORY The theory that errors occur in the RNA responsible for the production of enzymes that are essential to metabolism, resulting in a reduction of cell functioning and possible death. (p. 75)

ESTROGEN The primary female sex hormone, the depletion of which is associated with menopause. (p. 298)

EUTHANASIA The act of painlessly putting to death people who are suffering from incurable diseases or severe disability. (p. 504)

EVENT-RELATED RESPONSES (ERPs) A pattern of brain waves displayed within the context of sensory discrimination and decision-making. (p. 123)

EXCEPTIONAL CREATIVITY Another term for creative genius. (p. 171)

EXISTENTIAL PHASE The term Gibbs uses to describe that last two stages in Kohlberg's theory of moral development. (p. 444)

EXPERIMENTAL STUDY A study in which an independent variable is manipulated and a dependent variable is observed. (pp. 44, 45)

EXPLICIT MEMORY TASK A task in which a subject is directly instructed to consciously remember a previous event or experience. (p. 210)

EXTERNAL VALIDITY The extent to which one may generalize the results of an experiment. (p. 58)

EXTRANEOUS VARIABLES Variables that are not measured nor manipulated but are suspected to be important. (p. 46)

EXTROVERSION One of the dimensions of Costa and McCrae's five-factor model of personality. (p. 431)

F

FACTOR ANALYSIS A statistical technique that produces a summary of many correlations. (pp. 43, 154)

FACTORS The identification through factor analysis of a set of variables that may be grouped together. (p. 43)

FALSE EMOTIONAL ASSUMPTIONS Adults' erroneous beliefs about the basis of their security, satisfaction, and life-goals which, according to Gould, must be discarded throughout adulthood. (p. 416)

FILIAL MATURITY Adults' growing ability to view their parents as separate persons and personalities. (pp. 277, 480)

FILIAL PIETY The cultural belief in eastern society that the elderly possess a higher status and command a higher respect than younger people. (p. 335)

FIVE-FACTOR MODEL Costa and McCrae's belief that adult personality consists of five stable and independent personality traits: neuroticism, extroversion, openness-to-experience, agreeableness, and conscientiousness. (p. 431)

FLASHBULB MEMORIES Vivid, detailed, and long-lasting mental representations of personally experienced events. (p. 212)

FLUID INTELLIGENCE The basic information-processing abilities of the mind independent of life-experience and education; measured by relational thinking tasks such as block design and digit-symbol substitution. (p. 151)

FORMAL OPERATIONS The fourth stage in Piaget's theory of intellectual development in which individuals are capable of abstract, hypothetical thinking. (p. 233)

FREE RADICAL THEORY A theory that suggests that aging is due to deleterious and short-lived chemical changes occurring within the cells of the body. (p. 75)

FREE RECALL A test of long-term memory in which an individual is asked to recall as many items as possible from a given list. (p. 197)

FRONTAL LOBE A portion of the cortex. (p. 119)

FUNCTIONAL AGE An individual's level of capacity relative to other people of the same age for functioning in a given environment. (p. 18)

FUNCTIONAL ASSESSMENT STAGING SYSTEM (FAST) Reisberg's conceptualization of the predictable, progressive declines in patients with AD. (p. 136)

FUNCTIONAL DISORDERS Maladaptive behavior caused by psychological rather than biological factors. (p. 402)

G

GENERALIZED SLOWING HYPOTHESIS Birren's claim that all behavioral abilities slow at the same progressive rate during the course of aging. (p. 116)

GENETIC THEORY A theory that suggests that aging occurs because certain genes are programmed to "switch off" and stop producing DNA. (p. 75)

GENUINE MEMORY DEFICITS Memory impairment that is due to the brain's inability to store new information. (p. 219)

g FACTOR Spearman's term for general intelligence. (p. 150)

GLARE The reflection of light that has the capacity to limit vision; begins to limit vision in middle-age. (p. 102)

GLAUCOMA An increase in pressure within the eye that may lead to blindness if left untreated. (p. 104)

GOVERNMENT NURSING HOME Nursing homes that are subsidized by the federal, state, or local governments. (p. 484)

GRANULOVACULAR PARTICLES Small particles of matter in the soma and dendrites in deteriorating neurons. (p. 127)

GRATINGS Visual stimuli that differ in contrast and spatial frequency. (p. 106)

GRIEF The sorrow, anger, guilt, and confusion that usually accompany a significant loss. (p. 520)

GRIEF PANGS The somatic experience of grief, which includes tightness in the throat, nausea, difficulty in breathing, and sobbing. (p. 525)

GRIEF WORK The process of arriving at resolution of the loss of a loved one. (pp. 281, 525)

H

HARDWARE The physical components of a computer. (p. 188)

HEMISPHERES The division of the cerebrum into two halves. (p. 119)

HIDDEN POOR Those individuals who could be classified as poor on the basis of their own income but who reside with friends or relatives who are not poor. (p. 321)

HIERARCHICAL INTEGRATION One of the criteria used to identify cognitive stages; current stages incorporate (and extend) the characteristics of preceding stages. (p. 230)

HIPPOCAMPUS A portion of the limbic system involved with memory processes. (p. 119)

HISTORICAL TIME The socio-historical context within which a life-event occurs. (p. 425)

HISTORY A potential threat to the internal validity of a quasi-experiment; it is most likely to occur when the same individuals are tested at different times. (p. 48)

HOMEOSTATIC IMBALANCE THEORY The theory that aging is the result of the almost linear decline of the body's organ reserves and their ability to maintain homeostasis. (p. 76)

HORMONAL THEORY The theory that aging pacemakers in control centers in the brain stimulate a series of hormonal changes that cause one to age. (p. 75)

HOSPICE An institution characterized by a philosophy of caring and counseling for the terminally ill and their families. (p. 519)

I

IMAGERY The formation of picture-like representations; a process known to aid memory. (p. 205)

IMPLICIT MEMORY TASK A memory task that does not require a subject to consciously remember a previous event. (p. 210)

INDEPENDENT VARIABLES The variables that are manipulated within an experimental study. (p. 45)

INDIVIDUAL TIME The time in an individual's life at which an event occurs. (p. 425)

INFORMATION-PROCESSING APPROACH A perspective in cognitive psychology that suggests that the human mind functions in a manner similar to that of a computer. (p. 187)

INTERINDIVIDUAL VARIABILITY The different patterns of developmental change that may be observed between different adults. (p. 9)

INTERIORITY Neugarten's description of the increased sensitivity of older adults to their inner experiences. (p. 430)

INTER-ITEM RELIABILITY The extent to which measurements on one-half of the items on a test are predictable from the measurements from the other half. (p. 33)

INTERMEDIATE (ORDINARY) NURSING CARE A level of nursing care which is less intensive than that which is provided in a skilled nursing facility. (p. 484)

INTERNAL VALIDITY The extent to which an independent variable determines the outcome of an experiment. (p. 47)

INTER-RATER RELIABILITY The assessed amount of agreement between two or more observers who make independent observations in behavioral studies. (p. 32)

INTRAINDIVIDUAL CHANGE Different patterns of developmental change observed within individual adults. (p. 9)

INVARIANT MOVEMENT A criteria of developmental stages; suggests that individuals must progress through developmental stages in an unchangeable manner. (p. 230)

K

KINESTHETIC The ability to sense the position of one's body parts in space. (p. 111)

KORSAKOFF'S SYNDROME A disorder, typified by severe memory loss, manifested by chronic alcoholics. (p. 479)

KUGELBERG-WELANDER'S DISEASE A progressive spinal muscular atrophy that does not affect cognitive functioning. (p. 505)

L

LATE-ONSET ALCOHOLISM Emerges in middle to late life, usually in response to multiple stressors such as loss of loved ones; currently underdiagnosed. (p. 480)

L-DOPA A drug used in the treatment of Parkinson's Disease. (p. 126)

LEISURE Descriptive account of a person's activities during free time and may include work for some people, recreation for others, or a state of mind for others. (p. 377)

LIFE EVENTS FRAMEWORK A view that suggests that life events produce taxing circumstances for individuals, forcing the individuals to change their personality; it is important to consider the sociohistorical circumstances in which those events are occurring. (p. 420)

LIFE EXPECTANCY How long, on the average, one is expected to live. (p. 64)

LIFE REVIEW A looking-back process that is set in motion by nearness to death and that potentially proceeds toward personality reorganization; the attempt to make sense of one's own life and experiences through reflection. (p. 413)

LIFE SATISFACTION An individual's general perception or feeling about the quality of their life. (p. 345)

LIFE SPAN APPROACH The orientation that suggests development continues throughout the entire course of human development. (p. 3)

LIFE STRUCTURE Levinson's theoretical construct that defines the context in which adult development occurs, including the people, the places, the work, and the situations through which people choose to define themselves. (p. 417)

LIMBIC SYSTEM A part of the brain that controls memory and emotional responsiveness. (p. 118)

LIMITED ATTENTIONAL CAPACITY A type of psychological energy needed to perform mental work and the capacity of which varies depending on one's level of arousal, age, and other factors. (p. 196)

LIPOFUSCIN A pigment that accumulates in progressive fashion with age in specific organ systems of the body. (p. 127)

LIVING WILL A document in which an individual identifies for a physician and/or family members the specific conditions under which life-sustaining measures may be implemented or withdrawn. (p. 498)

LOBES A name used to describe different areas of the cortex of the brain. (p. 119)

LONGEVITY The theoretical upper limits of the life span that is genetically fixed and species-specific. (p. 64)

LONGEVITY DIFFERENCE The difference between the number of years individuals live when compared to the number of years they are expected to live based on their age, race, and sex. (p. 68)

LONGITUDINAL STUDY A research design in which data is collected from the same group of individuals on multiple occasions. (p. 49)

LONG-TERM MEMORY The processes involved in the storage, retrieval, and access of information over a lengthy period of time (e.g., hours, months, and years). (p. 195)

M

MAGNETIC RESONANCE IMAGING (MRI) A noninvasive procedure used to study the structure of the brain. (p. 121)

MALE CLIMACTERIC The decline of sexual potency that usually begins when men are in their sixties and seventies and progresses at a much slower rate than female menopause. (p. 301)

MASKING TECHNIQUES The use of a visual stimulus to interfere with the perception of a previously presented visual stimulus. (p. 189)

MEAN The statistical procedure use to determine the arithmetic average. (p. 41)

MECHANISTIC MODEL The model that suggests that adults are passive machines that merely react to environmental events. (pp. 20, 21)

MEDIAN The value in the exact middle of a distribution of scores. (p. 41)

MEDICAID A national medical assistance program administered by states to meet the costs of health care for those lower income individuals over the age of 65. (p. 487)

MEDICARE A national health care insurance plan provided to any individual over the age of 65 to help meet the costs of health care, regardless of income. (p. 487)

MEMORY A function that involves processes associated with the storage, retrieval, and encoding of information. (p. 187)

MENOPAUSE The permanent cessation of menstruation and the ability to bear children. (p. 298)

MENTAL ROTATION The representational process of transforming mental images. (p. 200)

MENTOR An adult who guides or advises another, typically younger, adult about personal, social, or occupational goals. (p. 373)

MODE The most frequently appearing score in a distribution of scores. (p. 41)

MODEL A metaphorical representation of some aspect of reality. (p. 19)

MOST EFFICIENT DESIGN The complex design that allows investigators to separate out the specific effects of age, time of testing, and cohort. (p. 54)

MOTOR DEVELOPMENT The ways in which physical movements and actions change throughout life. (p. 102)

MOURNING The overt, behavioral expression of grief and bereavement that is heavily influenced by cultural patterns. (p. 520)

MULTIDIRECTIONAL VERSUS UNIDIRECTIONAL CHANGE The notion that developmental changes in a given type of functioning may decline, stabilize, or improve within or between individuals; versus the notion that developmental change in a given function follows the same trajectory in all individuals. (p. 9)

MUTATION THEORY The theory that aging is due to changes in the DNA of the cells in vital organs of the body. (p. 74)

MUTUAL PRETENSE The strategy of coping in which friends, family, and medical personnel avoid coming to terms with the dying individual by pretending that the individual's disease may improve. (p. 514)

MYELIN SHEATH The fatty covering surrounding the axons. (p. 125)

N

NATURALISM VS. CONTROL DIMENSION Data collection strategies which employ naturally occurring events in environments (naturalism) compared to those artificially constructed situations such as experiments which investigators employ (control). (p. 37)

NEGATIVE CORRELATION A pattern of association between two variables in which higher scores on one variable are related to lower scores on another. (p. 42)

NEUROFIBRILLARY TANGLES Intertwined fibers that interfere with normal neuronal functioning. (p. 128)

NEURON Nerve cell; the basic building block of the nervous system.

NEUROTICISM One of the personality traits in Costa and McCrae's Five-Factor Model of adult personality. (p. 431)

NEUROTRANSMITTER A chemical substance used to send messages across a synapse. (p. 126)

NONNORMATIVE LIFE-EVENTS Influences on development that are related to chance-like factors. (p. 10)

NORMATIVE AGE-GRADED FACTORS Influences on developmental change that are closely related to an individual's chronological age. (p. 10)

NORMATIVE HISTORY-GRADED FACTORS Influences on development that are closely related to societal events. (p. 11)

O

OBESITY A condition in which an individual weighs more than 20 percent over normal skeletal and physical requirements. (p. 80)

OCCIPITAL LOBE The portion of the cortex involved in visual perception. (p. 119)

OLD-AGE DEPENDENCY RATIO The ratio of the number of retired individuals 65 years-of-age and older to every 100 of working age. (p. 72)

OPENNESS-TO-EXPERIENCE One of the personality traits that comprises Costa and McCrae's Five-Factor Model of adult personality. (p. 431)

ORDINARY CREATIVITY Creativity exhibited by "ordinary adults" in everyday situations. (p. 172)

ORGANIC DISORDERS Psychological dysfunction caused by biological factors. (p. 462)

ORGANISMIC The model that views development as genetically programmed and following a set progression of qualitatively discontinuous stages. (p. 20)

ORGANIZATION A strategy useful in enhancing memory performance. (p. 203)

ORGAN OF CORTI The organ in the inner ear that transforms sound vibrations into nerve impulses. (p. 105)

OSTEOPOROSIS The thinning and weakening of the bones due to difficulty in calcium in older people, especially women. (p. 115)

P

PALLIATIVE TREATMENT A treatment that focuses on the symptoms rather than the cause of a disease. (p. 143)

PARENTAL IMPERATIVE According to Guttman, the tendency of the birth of a child to trigger heightened sex-role differentiation between mother and father in order to assist with the division of labor. (p. 342)

PARIETAL LOBE A portion of the cortex involved in short-term memory and the representation of spatial relationships. (p. 119)

PARKINSON'S DISEASE A neurological disorder caused by decreased levels of dopamine that results in involuntary muscle tremors and rigid movements. (pp. 126, 474)

PASSIVE ACCOMMODATIVE MASTERY
STYLE (PASSIVE MASTERY) According to
Guttman, a style of coping that varies by age
and sex in which individuals fit themselves
to the environment rather than try to change
the external environment. (pp. 342, 430)

PASSIVE EUTHANASIA Inducing a natural
death by withdrawing some life-sustaining
therapeutic effort such as turning off a
respirator or heart-lung machine. (p. 504)

PEARSON PRODUCT MOMENT
CORRELATION Abbreviated as *r* this
computes the quantitative strength of a
correlation on a scale of −1.00 to +1.00.
(p. 42)

PERCEPTION The process of experiencing
incoming sensory information in a coherent,
organized, and meaningful fashion.
(pp. 101, 187)

PERIPHERAL PROCESSES The flow of
information from the senses to the brain and
from the brain to the muscles. (p. 116)

PERSONALITY The distinctive patterns of
behavior, thought, and emotion that
characterize each person's adaptation to the
situations of his/her life. (p. 404)

PLASTICITY The idea that cognitive training
programs may have beneficial effects on
older individuals due to the presence of a
cognitive reserve capacity. (p. 164)

POSITIVE CORRELATION An association
between variables such that high scores on
one variable are related to high scores on
another variable. (p. 42)

POSITRON EMISSION TOMOGRAPHY
(PETT SCAN) A noninvasive method of
measuring the metabolic activity of the
brain. (p. 121)

POSTCONVENTIONAL LEVEL The last two
stages within Kohlberg's theory of moral
development; at this level, individuals are
capable of generating moral rules that are
based on universal principles of justice.
(p. 436)

POSTFORMAL OPERATIONS The generic
term used to describe qualitative changes in
thinking beyond Piaget's stage of formal
operations; characterized by an acceptance
of relativity, dialectic thinking, and problem-
finding. (p. 241)

POTENTIAL LIFE-SPAN The maximum age
that could be attained if an individual were
able to avoid or be successfully treated for
all illnesses and accidents. (p. 65)

PRECONVENTIONAL LEVEL The first two
stages in Kohlberg's theory of moral
development; characterized by the
construction of moral rules that are based
on the fear of punishment and the desire for
pleasure. (p. 435)

PREOPERATIONAL STAGE The second stage
in Piaget's theory of cognitive development;
characterized by illogical thinking that is
marked by irreversibility as well as the
inability to distinguish fantasy from reality.
(p. 232)

PRESBYCUSIS The general term used to
describe age-related problems in hearing,
especially high-pitched sounds. (p. 108)

PRESBYOPIA The reduction in the efficacy of
near vision; usually first observed during
middle-adulthood. (p. 102)

PRESBYSTASIS Loss of balance and
equilibrium. (p. 114)

PRIMARY APPRAISAL The process of choosing
whether an event is stressful and requires
the implementation of coping strategies.
(p. 452)

PRIMARY MENTAL ABILITIES Thurstone's
belief that intelligence consisted of the
following mental abilities: verbal
comprehension, word fluency, number,
space, associative memory, perceptual
speed, and induction. (p. 150)

PRIOR-TO-NEED (OR PRE-NEED) BURIAL
The practice of arranging funeral expenses
well before the need arises, when the
individual is healthy and well. (p. 520)

PROBLEM-FINDING Arlin's description of a
fundamental feature of adult cognition, the
identification and construction of
sophisticated problems to resolve. (p. 241)

PROBLEM-FOCUSED COPING The
determination that a stressful life event
requires changing the event or obtaining
additional information about the event in
order to cope successfully. (p. 456)

PROCESSING PERSPECTIVE The idea that
memory impairment is due to the inability
to effectively encode, store, and/or retrieve
information. (p. 215)

PROPRIETARY HOMES A type of nursing home, operated by a private company, designed to make a profit. (p. 483)

PSYCHOLOGICAL AGE An individual's ability to adapt to changing environmental demands in comparison to the adaptability of other individuals of identical chronological age. (p. 17)

PSYCHOMETRIC APPROACH An approach to adult intellectual development that involves the administration of standardized adult intelligence tests such as the WAIS and PMA. (p. 149)

PSYCHOMOTOR SLOWING The age-related slowing of behavior. (p. 113)

P300 BRAIN WAVE A unique pattern of brain activity associated with the identification of novel stimuli. (p. 123)

Q

QUALITATIVE CHANGE The unique change in the type or quality of thinking that occurs as individuals move from one specific stage to another. (pp. 6, 230)

QUANTITATIVE CHANGE The differences in amount rather than kind that occur in development. (p. 6)

QUASI-EXPERIMENTS Studies that resemble true experiments in design and analysis but contain an independent variable that cannot be manipulated. (p. 47)

R

RANDOM ASSIGNMENT The technique of assigning individuals to exposure conditions on a random basis in order to evenly distribute extraneous factors. (p. 46)

RANGE The simplest measure of variability; revealed by the lowest and the highest score in a set. (p. 41)

REACTION TIME TASKS Experimental assessments of the time elapsed between the appearance of a signal and a person's responding movement. (p. 113)

REACTIVITY The way in which an individual reacts to being tested/observed within a psychological study; a threat to the internal validity of an experiment or quasi-experiment. (p. 37)

RECOGNITION TEST A basic strategy for assessing memory ability. (p. 206)

RECTANGULARIZATION OF THE LIFE SPAN The emerging demographic pattern that finds more and more individuals living to reach the maximum end of their life span. (p. 67)

RELATIVISTIC THINKING A basic feature of postformal thought which allows adults the freedom to see knowledge as contextual. (p. 242)

RELIABILITY The consistency of the results of a test in the same person(s) from one time to another. (p. 32)

REMINISCENCE The review of one's past life in old age; an important part of the life-review process and Erikson's stage of ego integrity and despair. (p. 413)

REPRESENTATIVE SAMPLE A sample of a population that has the same characteristics as the entire population. (p. 57)

RESIDENTIAL CARE FACILITY A nursing home that provides routine care and personal assistance in providing routine care for day-to-day needs. (p. 484)

RESOURCE ALLOCATION Ways in which people trade off one task against another. (p. 193)

RETRIEVAL DEFICIT Memory impairment due to the inability to successfully access stored information. (p. 216)

S

SATI The ancient Hindu practice of burning a dead man's widow to increase his family's prestige and establish her image as a goddess in his memory. (p. 520)

SCHAIE-THURSTONE ADULT MENTAL ABILITIES TEST A standardized test of adult intelligence which is adapted from Thurstone's Primary Mental Abilities Test. (p. 150)

SECONDARY APPRAISAL The person's assessment of available resources and the "cost" of such resources when facing with a stressful live event. (p. 452)

SELECTION A threat to internal validity when the procedures used to select individuals for research result in extraneous or unintended differences in the groups selected for study, e.g., young vs. old subjects may differ not only on education but also in terms of health. (p. 48)

SELECTIVE ATTENTION A type of attention in which we ignore irrelevant information while focusing on relevant information (for example, ignoring a television program while listening to a friend). (p. 192)

SELECTIVE DROPOUT The tendency for particular individuals to drop out of longitudinal studies, e.g., the infirm, the less able, those who move from the area, and thus skew the results in a biased fashion. (pp. 50, 162)

SELF-REPORT INVENTORIES The use of specific questionnaires in which participants are required to report their opinions, feelings, or activities on a wide range of topics. (p. 430)

SEMANTIC ELABORATION A strategy used to enhance memory. (p. 204)

SENESCENCE All of the changes that are associated with the normal process of aging. (p. 463)

SENILE DEMENTIA OF THE ALZHEIMER'S TYPE (SDAT) Another term used for Alzheimer's Disease. (p. 130)

SENILE PLAQUES The accumulation of spherical masses of amyloid surrounded by degenerating axons and dendrites; senile plaques prevent normal communication between neurons. (p. 130)

SENILITY An outdated term referring to abnormal deterioration of mental functions in old people. (pp. 130, 464)

SENSATION The reception of physical stimuli at a sense organ and the translation of this stimulation to the brain. (p. 101)

SENSORIMOTOR DEVELOPMENT The growth and coordination of sensory and motor processes. (p. 102)

SENSORIMOTOR STAGE The first stage in Piaget's theory of cognitive development in which the child discovers the world using the senses and motor activity. (p. 232)

SEX ROLE The behaviors that are expected of individuals because they are either male or female. (p. 337)

SHORT-TERM MEMORY Information that is stored and retained for a brief period, usually less than sixty seconds. (p. 198)

SINGLE-TASK PERFORMANCE Performance that does not entail dividing one's attention. (p. 193)

SKILLED NURSING FACILITY The most highly intensive form of nursing-home care. (p. 484)

SOCIAL AGE Refers to the social roles and social expectations people have for themselves and as well as those imposed by others in society. (p. 18)

SOCIAL CLOCK The internalized sense of timing that tells people whether they are progressing too fast or too slow in terms of social events. (p. 423)

SOCIAL COGNITION Cognitive development that is focused on the individual's reasoning about social and interpersonal matters. (p. 248)

SOFTWARE The programs and routines a computer uses to process information it has stored or accessed. (p. 188)

SOMA The cell body of a neuron. (p. 124)

SPATIAL FREQUENCY The number of cycles of bars of light imaged within a specific area of the retina. (p. 106)

SPENDING DOWN The disposition of personal assets to qualify for subsidized care in long-term health care facilities. (p. 322)

STAGE THEORIES Theories that suggest that development consists of a series of abrupt changes in psychological functions and processes, marked by qualitative change at each stage. (p. 8)

STANDARD DEVIATION A common measure of variability that reveals the extent to which the individual scores deviate from the mean of a distribution. (p. 41)

STANDARDIZATION The establishment of fixed procedures for administration, scoring, and norms for age, grade, race, sex and so on. (p. 38)

STANDARD PHASE Gibbs' term that refers to the first four stages in Kohlberg's theory of moral development. (p. 444)

STATISTICAL SIGNIFICANCE A mathematical procedure to determine the extent to which differences in performance between groups of subjects are due to chance factors or the independent variable. (p. 44)

STRUCTURED WHOLENESS A criteria for determining developmental stages; implies that individuals' cognitions are consistent with their current stage of development. (p. 230)

SUBSTANTIA NIGRA A structure in the base of the brain responsible for the production of dopamine. (p. 126)

SYNAPSE The gap or distance between nerve cells. (p. 126)

T

TEMPORAL LOBE The portion of the cortex involved in audition, language, and long-term memory. (p. 119)

TERMINAL DROP A decline in psychological functioning, revealed in standardized tests, that precedes death by about five years. (p. 164)

TESTING A threat to internal validity that is based on the readministration of the same instrument on more than one occasion. (p. 48)

TEST-RETEST RELIABILITY The degree of predictability that measurements taken on one test on one occasion will be similar to those taken on another occasion. (p. 33)

THEMATIC APPERCEPTION TEST (TAT) A standardized projective test, consisting of a series of ambiguous pictures, developed by Henry Murray used to assess personality and individual character traits. (p. 369)

TIME SEQUENTIAL DESIGN A complex research design that allows an investigator to disentangle age effects from time-of-testing effects. (p. 52)

TINNITUS A constant high-pitched or ringing sound in the ears reported in about 10 percent of older adults. (p. 108)

TRAIT THEORISTS Personality theorists who believe that there is some consistency and stability to human personality over time. (p. 427)

TRAJECTORY OF LIFE According to Pattison, our anticipated life span and the plan we make for the way we will live out our life. (p. 513)

TRANSIENT ISCHEMIC ATTACK (TIA) A temporary, reversible minor stroke. (p. 465)

TRANSITIONS According to Levinson, the periods that overlap one era with another; transitions last for approximately five years. (p. 417)

TYPE A BEHAVIOR STYLE Behavior reflecting excessive competiveness, accelerated pace of normal activities, time-urgency, hostility, and aggressiveness. (p. 85)

TYPE B BEHAVIOR STYLE Behavior reflective of the absence of Type A Behavior Style; behavior indicative of a relaxed, less-hurried, and less-preoccupied life-style. (p. 85)

U

UNDERAROUSAL The idea that age-related cognitive slowing is caused by progressively diminishing activity in the central nervous system. (p. 122)

UNFINISHED BUSINESS Completing and resolving, where possible, the interpersonal problems created in personal relationships; the desire for a dying person to bring closure to the different dimension of their life. (p. 509)

UNIVERSAL PROGRESSION A criteria for the presence of developmental stages; the belief that all individuals in all cultures progress through all stages in the same invariant sequence. (p. 230)

UPLIFTS Those small, positive experiences we encounter in daily living that counterbalance the hassles that occur in everyday life. (p. 454)

UPSWING HYPOTHESIS The contention that there is an increase in marital satisfaction when children leave home. (p. 278)

V

VALIDITY The soundness of measurements in terms of measuring what they are intended to measure. (p. 34)

VARIABILITY The statistical description of distribution scores; includes range and standard deviation. (p. 41)

VARIABLE Anything that may change and influence behavior. (p. 42)

VISUAL ACUITY The ability to accurately see small details in the visual field under maximal amounts of contrast. (pp. 105, 106)

VOLUNTARY NONPROFIT NURSING
HOMES Nursing homes that establish rates
that do not generate excess capital (i.e., a
profit); are usually designed for individuals
with a specific religious, fraternal, or union
affiliation. (p. 484)

W

WECHSLER ADULT INTELLIGENCE SCALE
(WAIS) A standard test of adult intelligence
that provides both a verbal IQ and
performance IQ as well as an overall IQ
score. (p. 153)

WIDOWER'S SYNDROME The tendency for
men, after a long period of time following
the loss of a spouse, to develop incomplete
penile erection when presented with the
opportunity for sexual intercourse. (p. 304)

WITHIN-SUBJECTS MANIPULATIONS
Experimental design in which each subject
is administered each level of an
independent variable. (p. 46)

WORKING MEMORY According to Baddeley,
the active manipulation of information in
short-term memory. (p. 199)

Y

YOUNG-AGE DEPENDENCY RATIO The
number of individuals seventeen years-of-
age and younger for every one hundred
people of working age. (p. 72)

REFERENCES

Achete, K., & Karha, E. (1986). Some psychodynamic aspects of the presuicidal syndrome with special reference to older persons. *Crisis, 1,* 24–32.

Adams, G. M., & de Vries, H. A. (1973). Physiological effects of an exercise training regimen among women aged fifty-two to seventy-nine. *Journal of Gerontology, 27,* 50–55.

Ad hoc committee of the Harvard Medical School to examine the definition of brain death: A definition of irreversible coma. (1968). *Journal of the American Medical Association, 205,* 337.

Adler, W. (1974). An autoimmune theory of aging. In M. Rockstein (Ed.), *Proceedings of a symposium on the theoretical aspects of aging.* New York: Academic Press.

Adrain, M. J. (1981). Flexibility in the aging adult. In E. L. Smith & R. C. Serfass (Eds.), *Exercise and aging: The scientific basis.* Hillsdale, NJ: Enslow.

Aging Health Policy Center. (1985). *Fiscal crisis: Impact on aging services.* Berkeley, CA: University of California, Berkeley, School of Nursing.

Ahrons, C. R., & Rodgers, R. H. (1987). *Divorced families: A multidisciplinary view.* New York: Norton.

Albert, M. (1984). Assessment of memory loss. *Psychosomatics, 25,* (Suppl. 12), 18–20.

Albert, M., Duffy, F. H., & Naeser, M. (1987). Nonlinear changes in cognition with age and their neuropsychological correlates. *Canadian Journal of Psychology, 41,* 141–157.

Albert, M. S., & Kaplan, E. (1980). Organic implications of neuropsychological deficits in the elderly. In L. W. Poon, J. L. Fozard, L. S. Cremack, D. Arenberg, & L. W. Thompson (Eds.), *New directions in memory and aging: Proceedings of the George A. Talland Memorial Conference.* Hillsdale, NJ: Erlbaum.

Aldous, J. (1978a). *Family careers: Developmental change in families.* New York: John Wiley.

Aldous, J. (1978b). *Family careers over time.* Address given at Department of Sociology, University of Notre Dame, South Bend, Indiana.

Aldwin, C. M., Levenson, M. R., Spiro, A., & Bosse, R. (1989). Does emotionality predict stress? Findings from the normative aging study. *Journal of Personality and Social Psychology, 56,* 618–624.

Aldwin, C. M., Spiro, A., Bosse, R., & Levenson, M. R. (1989). Longitudinal findings from the normative aging study: 1. Does mental health change with age? *Psychology and Aging, 4,* (3), 295–306.

Alexander, T., Roodin, P. A., & Gorman, B. (1980). *Developmental psychology.* New York: Van Nostrand Reinhold.

Allport, G. W. (1961). *Pattern and growth in personality.* New York: Holt, Rinehart & Winston.

Alpaugh, P., & Birren, J. E. (1977). Variables affecting creative contributions across the life span. *Human Development, 20,* 240–248.

American Association of Retired Persons. (1986). *A profile of older Americans.* Washington, DC: American Association of Retired Persons, Brochure.

American Association of Retired Persons. (1989). *Prepaying your funeral? Product Report, 1,* (2). Washington, DC.

American Health Care Association (1984). *Facts in brief on long-term health care.* Washington, DC: American Health Care Association, Pamphlet.

Ames, C., & Ames, R. (1989). *Research on motivation in education, Vol. 3: Goals and cognitions.* New York: Academic Press.

Anders, T. R., Fozard, J. L., & Lillyquist, T. D. (1972). The effects of age upon retrieval from short-term memory. *Developmental Psychology, 6,* 214–217.

Anderson, J. M., Hubbard, B. M., Coghill, G. R., & Slidders, W. (1983). The effect of advanced old age on the neuron content of the cerebral cortex. *Journal of the Neurological Sciences, 58,* 233–244.

Anderson, S. A., Russell, C. S., & Schumm, W. R. (1983). Perceived marital quality and family life-cycle categories: A further analysis. *Journal of Marriage and the Family, 45,* 127–139.

Anthony-Bergstone, C. R., Zarit, S. H., & Gatz, M. (1988). Symptoms of psychological distress among caregivers of dementia patients. *Psychology and Aging, 3,* 245–248.

Antonucci, T. C. (1981, August). *Attachment from adolescence to adulthood.* Paper presented at meeting of the American Psychological Association, Los Angeles.

Antonucci, T. C., & Akiyama, H. (1987). An examination of sex differences in social support in mid- and late life. *Sex Roles, 17,* 737–749.

Argyle, M., & Beit-Hallahmi, B. (1975). *The social psychology of religion.* London: Routledge and Kegan Paul.

Arlin, P. K. (1975). Cognitive development in adulthood: A fifth stage. *Developmental Psychology, 11,* 602–606.

Arlin, P. K. (1977). Piagetian operations in problem finding. *Developmental Psychology, 13,* 297–298.

Arlin, P. K. (1984). Adolescent and adult thought: A structural interpretation. In M. L. Commons, F. A. Richards, & C. Armon (Eds.), *Beyond formal operations: Late adolescent and adult cognitive development.* New York: Praeger.

Arlin, P. K. (1989). Problem solving and problem finding in young artists and young scientists. In M. L. Commons, J. D. Sinnott, F. A. Richards, & C. Armon (Eds.), *Adult development, Vol. 1: Comparisons and applications of developmental models.* New York: Praeger.

Aslanian, C. B., & Brickwell, H. M. (1980). *Americans in transition: Life changes as reasons for adult learning.* Princeton, NJ: College Board Publications.

Atchley, R. C. (1976). *The sociology of retirement.* Cambridge, MA: Schenkman.

Atchley, R. C. (1983). *Aging: Continuity and change.* Belmont, CA: Wadsworth.

Athanasion, R., & Yoshioka, G. A. (1973). The spatial character of friendship formation. *Environment and Behavior, 5,* 143–165.

Athelstan, G. T. (1981). Psychosocial adjustment to chronic disease and disability. In W. C. Stolov & M. R. Clowers (Eds.), *Handbook of Severe Disabilities.* Washington, DC: U.S. Department of Education.

Atkinson, J. H., & Shuckit, M. A. (1981). Alcoholism and over-the-counter and prescription drug misuse in the elderly. In C. Eisdorfer (Ed.), *Annual Review of Gerontology and Geriatrics, Vol. 2.* New York: Springer.

Attig, M., & Hasher, L. (1980). The processing of frequency-of-occurrence information. *Journal of Gerontology, 35,* 66–69.

Ausubel, D. P. (1968). *Educational psychology.* New York: Holt, Rinehart & Winston.

Averill, J. R. (1968). Grief: Its nature and significance. *Psychological Bulletin, 6,* 721–748.

Bachman, J., O'Malley, P., & Johnson, J. (1978). *Youth in transition (Vol. VI): Adolescence to adulthood—Change and stability of the lives of young men.* Ann Arbor: Institute for Social Research, University of Michigan.

Baddeley, A. (1986). *Working memory.* New York: Oxford University Press.

Baer, D. N. (1970). An age-irrelevant concept of development. *Merrill Palmer Quarterly, 16,* 238–245.

Bahrick, H. P., Bahrick, P. O., & Wittlinger, R. P. (1975). Fifty years of memory for names and faces: A cross-sectional approach. *Journal of Experimental Psychology: General, 104,* 54–75.

Bailey, K. D. (1987). *Methods of social research.* New York: Free Press.

Baird, J. (1976). The funeral industry in Boston. In E. Shneidman (Ed.), *Death: Current perspectives.* Palo Alto: Mayfield Press.

Ball, S. J. (1981). *Beachside comprehensive.* Cambridge, MA: Cambridge University Press.

Baltes, P. B. (1973). Prototypical paradigms and questions in life-span research on development and aging. *The Gerontologist, 13,* 458–467.

Baltes, P. B. (1987). Theoretical propositions of life-span developmental psychology: On the dynamics between growth and decline. *Developmental Psychology, 23,* 611–626.

Baltes, P. B. (1990, March). *Wisdom.* Paper presented at Third Annual Conference on Cognitive Aging, Atlanta, GA.

Baltes, P B., & Goulet, L. R. (1971). Exploration of the developmental parameters by manipulation and simulation of age differences in behavior. *Human Development, 14,* 149–170.

Baltes, P. B., & Kliegel, R. (1986). On the dynamics between growth and decline in the aging of intelligence and memory. In K. Poeck, H. J. Freund, & H. Ganshirt (Eds.), *Neurology.* Heidelberg, West Germany: Springer-Verlag.

Baltes, P. B., Reese, H. W., & Lipsitt, L. P. (1980). Life-span developmental psychology. *Annual Review of Psychology, 31,* 65–110.

Baltes, P B., Sowarka, D., & Kliegel, R. (1989). Cognitive training research on fluid intelligence in old age: What can older adults achieve by themselves? *Psychology and Aging, 4,* 217.

Bandura, A. (1982). Self-efficacy in human agency. *American Psychologist, 37,* 122–137.

Bandura, A. L. (1989). Human agency in social cognitive theory. *American Psychologist, 44,* 1175–1184.

Banzinger, G., & Roush, S. (1983). Nursing homes for the birds: A control-relevant intervention with bird feeders. *The Gerontologist, 23,* 527–531.

Barrett, T. R., & Wright, M. (1981). Age-related facilitation in recall following semantic processing. *Journal of Gerontology, 36,* 194–199.

Barron, S. A., Jacobs, L., & Kirkei, W. R. (1976). Changes in size of normal lateral ventricles during aging determined by computerized tomography. *Neurology, 26,* 1011–1013.

Bart, P. (1971). Depression in middle-aged women. In V. Gornick & B. K. Moran (Eds.), *Women in sexist society.* New York: New American Library.

Bart, P. (1973). Portnoy's mother's complaint. In H. Z. Lopata (Ed.), *Marriages and families.* New York: Van Nostrand Reinhold.

Bart, W. M. (1971). The factor structure of formal operations. *British Journal of Educational Psychology, 41,* 40–77.

Bartell, G. (1972). *Group sex.* New York: Peter H. Wyden.

Bartoshuk, L. M., Rifkin, B., Marks, L. E., & Bars, P. (1986). Taste and aging. *Journal of Gerontology, 41,* 51–57.

Baruch, G., Barrett, R., & Rivers, G. (1983). *Lifeprints: New patterns of love and work for today's women.* New York: McGraw-Hill.

Bashore, T. R., Osman, A., & Heffley, E. F. (1989). Mental slowing in elderly persons: A cognitive psychophysiological analysis. *Psychology and Aging, 4,* 235–244.

Basseches, M. (1980). Dialectic schemata: A framework for the empirical study of dialectic thinking. *Human Development, 23,* 400–421.

Basseches, M. (1984a). *Dialectic thinking.* Norwood, NJ: Ablex.

Basseches, M. (1984b). Dialectic thinking as a metasystematic form of cognitive organization. In M. L. Commons, F. A. Richards, & C. Armon (Eds.), *Beyond formal operations: Late adolescent and adult cognitive development.* New York: Praeger.

Basseches, M. A. (1989). Dialectical thinking as an organized whole: Comments on Irwin and Kramer. In M. L. Commons, J. D. Sinnott, F. A. Richards, & C. Armon (Eds.), *Adult development, Vol. 1: Comparisons and applications of developmental models.* New York: Praeger.

Bastida, E. (1987). Sex-typed norms among older Hispanics. *The Gerontologist, 27,* 59–65.

Bekker, L., DeMoyne, L., & Taylor, C. (1966). Attitudes toward the aged in a multigenerational sample. *Journal of Gerontology, 21,* 115–118.

Beland, F. (1984). The decision of elderly persons to leave their homes. *The Gerontologist, 24,* 179–185.

Beland, F. (1987). Living arrangement preferences among elderly people. *The Gerontologist, 27,* 797–803.

Belbin, R. M. (1983). The implications of gerontology for new work roles in later life. In J. E. Birren et al. (Eds.), *Aging: A challenge to science and society.* New York: Oxford University Press.

Bell, A. P., & Weinberg, M. S. (1978). *Homosexualities.* New York: Simon & Schuster.

Bell, A. P., Weinberg, M. S., & Mannersmith, S. K. (1981). *Sexual preference: Its development in men and women.* New York: Simon & Schuster.

Bell, R. R., & Bell, P. L. (1972). Sexual satisfaction among married women. *Medical Aspects of Human Sexuality, 6,* 136–144.

Bell, R. R., & Lobsenz, N. (1979, September). Married sex: How uninhibited can a woman dare to be? *Redbook,* 75–78.

Belloc, N. B., & Breslow, L. (1972). Relationship between physical health status and health practices. *Preventive Medicine, 1,* 409–421.

Belmont, J. M., & Butterfield, E. S. (1971). Learning strategies as determinants of memory deficiencies. *Cognitive psychology, 2,* 411–420.

Belsky, J. (1981, November). Early human experience: A family perspective. *Developmental Psychology, 17,* 3–23.

Belsky, J. (1986). Infant day care: A cause for concern. *Zero to Three, 7,* 1–7.

Belsky, J. (1987a, August). *Mother care, not together care, other care, and infant-parent attachment security.* Paper presented at the annual meeting of the American Psychological Association, New York.

Belsky, J. (1987b). Risks remain. *Zero to Three, 7,* 22–24.

Belsky, J. (1987c, April). *Science, social policy, and day care: A personal odyssey.* Paper presented at the annual meeting of the Society for Research in Child Development, Baltimore, MD.

Bem, S. L. (1974). The measurement of psychological androgyny. *Journal of Consulting and Clinical Psychology, 42,* 155–162.

Bem, S. L. (1977). On the utility of alternative procedures for assessing psychological androgyny. *Journal of Consulting and Clinical Psychology, 45,* 196–205.

Benet, S. (1976). *How to live to be 100.* New York: The Dial Press.

Bengston, V. L. (1985). Diversity and symbolism in grandparental roles. In V. L. Bengston & J. Robertson (Eds.), *Grandparenthood.* Beverly Hills, CA: Sage.

Bengston, V. L., Mangen, D. G., & Landry, T. J., Jr. (1984). Multigenerational family: Concepts and findings. In V. Garmsholova, E. M. Horning, & D. Schaffer (Eds.), *Intergenerational relationships.* Lewiston, NY: Hogrefe.

Bengston, V. L., Reedy, M. N., & Gordon, C. E. (1985). Aging and self-conceptions: Personality processes and social contexts. In J. E. Birren & K. W. Schaie (Eds.), *Handbook of the psychology of aging, (2nd ed.).* New York: Van Nostrand Reinhold.

Bennett, N. G., Blanc, A. K., & Bloom, D. E. (1988). Commitment and the modern union: Assessing the link between premarital cohabitation and subsequent marital stability. *American Sociological Review, 53,* 127–138.

Ben-Sira, Z. (1985). Primary medical care and coping with stress and disease: The inclination of primary care practitioners to demonstrate affective behavior. *Social Science and Medicine, 21,* 485–498.

Beresford, T. P., Blow, F. C., Brower, K. J., Adams, K. M., & Hall, R. C. (1988). Alcoholism and aging in the general hospital. *Psychosomatics, 29,* 61–72.

Bernard, J. (1975). Notes on changing life-styles: 1970–1974. *Journal of Marriage and the Family, 37,* 582–593.

Berndt, T. J. (1982). The features and effects of friendship in early adolescence. *Child Development, 53,* 1447–1460.

Berry, J. M., Geiger, H., Visocan, K., & Siebert, J. (1987, November). *Age differences on subjective and objective measures of memory.* Paper presented at the meeting of the Gerontological Society of America, Washington, DC.

Berry, J. W., & Dasen, P. R. (1974). (Eds.), *Culture and cognition: Readings in cross-cultural psychology.* New York: Methuen.

Berscheid, E. (1982). Attraction and emotion in interpersonal relations. In M. S. Clark & S. T. Fisk (Eds.), *Affect and cognition.* Hillsdale, NJ: Lawrence Erlbaum.

Berscheid, E. (1983). Emotions. In H. H. Kelley, E. Berscheid, A. Cristensen, J. Harvey, T. L. Harvey, T. L. Huston, G. Levenger, E. McClintock, A. Peplau, & D. R. Peterson (Eds.), *Close relationships.* San Francisco: W H. Freeman.

Berscheid, E. (1985). Interpersonal attraction. In G. Lindzey & E. Aronson (Eds.), *Handbook of social psychology: Vol. 2* (3rd ed.). New York: Random House.

Berscheid, E. (1988). Some comments on love's anatomy: Or whatever happened to old-fashioned lust? In R. J. Sternberg & M. L. Barnes (Eds.), *Anatomy of love.* New Haven: Yale University Press.

Berscheid, E., & Fei, J. (1977). Sexual jealousy and romantic love. In G. Clinton and G. Smith (Eds.), *Sexual jealousy.* Englewood Cliffs, NJ: Prentice-Hall.

Berscheid, E., & Snyder, M. (in press). *The measurement of relationship closeness.* Minneapolis, MN: University of Minnesota.

Berscheid, E., and Walster, E. (1974a). A little bit about love. In T. L. Huston (Ed.), *Foundations of interpersonal attraction.* New York: Academic Press.

Berscheid, E., & Walster, E. (1974b). Physical attractiveness. In L. Berkowitz (Ed.), *Advances in experimental social psychology, Vol. 7.* New York: Academic Press.

Berzonsky, M. D. (1978). Formal reasoning in adolescence: An alternative view. *Adolescence, 13,* 279–290.

Biederman, I. (1987). Recognition-by-components: A theory of human image understanding. *Psychological Review, 94,* 115–147.

Bielby, D., & Papalia, D. (1975). Moral development and perceptual role taking: Their development and interrelationship across the life span. *International Journal of Aging and Human Development, 6,* 293–308.

Birren, J. E. (1960). Behavioral theories of aging. In N. W. Shock (Ed.), *Aging: Some social and biological aspects.* Washington, DC: American Association for the Advancement of Science.

Birren, J. E. (1974). Translations in gerontology—From lab to life: Psychophysiology and speed of response. *American Psychologist, 29,* 808–815.

Birren, J. E., Munnichs, J. M. A., Thomae, H., & Marois, M. (1983). *Aging: A challenge to science and society* (Vol. 3). New York: Oxford University Press.

Birren, J. E., & Renner, J. V. (1977). Research on the psychology of aging: Principles and experimentation. In J. E. Birren & K. W. Schaie (Eds.), *Handbook of the psychology of aging.* New York: Van Nostrand Reinhold.

Birren, J. E., & Sloane, R. B. (Eds.). (1980). *Handbook of mental health and aging.* Englewood Cliffs, NJ: Prentice-Hall.

Birren, J. E., Woods, A. M., & Williams, M. V. (1980). Behavioral slowing with age. In L. W. Poon and K. W. Schaie (Eds.), *Aging in the 1980's.* Washington, DC: American Psychological Association.

Black, J. E. , Greenough, W. T., Anderson, B. J., & Isaacs, K. R. (1987). Environment and the aging brain. *Canadian Journal of Psychology, 41,* 111–130.

Black, P. M. (1983a). Clinical problems in the brain death standards. *Archives of Internal Medicine, 143,* 121–123.

Black, P. M. (1983b). Guidelines for the diagnosis of brain death. In A. H. Ropper, S. K. Kennedy, and N. T. Zervas (Eds.), *Neurological and neurosurgical intensive care.* Baltimore: University Park Press.

Blanchard-Fields, F. (1986). Attributional processes in adult development. *Educational Gerontology, 12,* 291–300.

Blanchard-Fields, F., & Irion, J. C. (1988). The relation between locus of control and coping in two contexts: Age as a moderator variable. *Psychology and Aging, 3,* 197–203.

Blanchard-Fields, F., and Robinson, S. L. (1987). Age differences in the relation between controllability and coping. *Journal of Gerontology, 42,* 497–501.

Blazer, D. (1982). *Depression in late life.* St. Louis: Mosby.

Blazer, D. G., Bacher, J. R., & Manton, K. G. (1986). Suicide in later life: Review and commentary. *Journal of the American Geriatrics Society, 34,* 519–525.

Bleecker, M. L., Bolla-Wilson, K., Agnew, J., & Meyers, D. A. (1987). Simple visual reaction time: Sex and age differences. *Developmental Neuropsychology, 3,* 93–99.

Blenkner, M. (1965). Social work and family relationships in later life with some thoughts on filial maturity. In E. Shanas & G. Streib (Eds.), *Social structure and the family.* Englewood Cliffs, NJ: Prentice-Hall.

Blieszner, R., Willis, S. L., & Baltes, P. B. (1981). Training research in aging on the fluid ability of induction. *Journal of Applied Developmental Psychology, 2,* 247–265.

Block, M. R., Davidson, J. L., & Grambs, J. D. (1981). *Women over forty.* New York: Springer.

Block, M., & Sinnott, J. (1979). *The battered elder syndrome.* College Park, MD: Center on Aging, unpublished manuscript.

Blood, R. O., & Wolfe, D. M. (1969). *Husbands and wives: The dynamics of married lives.* New York: Free Press.

Bloom, F. E., Lazerson, A., & Hofstadter, L. (1985). *Brain, mind, and behavior.* New York: W. H. Freeman.

Blueband-Langner, M. (1977). *The meanings of death to children.* In H. Feifel (Ed.), *New meanings of death.* New York: McGraw-Hill.

Blumenthal, H. (1983). Diabetes mellitus as a disorder of blood flow. In H. Blumenthal (Ed.), *Handbook of the diseases of aging.* New York: Van Nostrand Reinhold.

Bock, R. D., & Moore, E. G. J. (1986). *Advantage and disadvantage: A profile of American youth.* Hillsdale, NJ: Erlbaum.

Boland, J. P., & Follingstad, D. R. (1987). The relationship between communication and marital satisfaction: A review. *Journal of Sex and Marital Therapy, 13,* 286–313.

Bondareff, W. (1977). The neural basis of aging. In J. E. Birren & K. W. Schaie (Eds.), *Handbook of the psychology of aging.* New York: Van Nostrand Reinhold.

Bondareff, W. (1985). The neural basis of aging. In J. E. Birren & K. W. Schaie (Eds.), *Handbook of the psychology of aging* (2nd ed.). New York: Van Nostrand Reinhold.

Booth-Kewley, S., & Friedman, H. (1987). Psychological predictors of heart disease: A quantitative review. *Psychological Bulletin, 101,* 343–362.

Bortz, W. M. (1980). Effects of exercise on aging—effects of aging on exercise. *Journal of the American Geriatric Society, 28(2),* 49–51.

Borup, J. H. (1983). Relocation mortality research: Assessment, reply, and the need to refocus on the issues. *The Gerontologist, 23,* 235–242.

Boston Women's Health Book Collective. (1976). *Our bodies, ourselves* (2nd ed.). New York: Simon & Schuster.

Botwinick, J. (1977). Intellectual abilities. In J. E. Birren & K. W. Schaie (Eds.), *Handbook of the psychology of aging.* New York: Van Nostrand Reinhold.

Botwinick, J. (1978). *Aging and behavior* (2nd ed.). New York: Springer.

Botwinick, J., Robbin, J. S., & Brinley, J. F. (1959). Reorganization of perceptions with age. *Journal of Gerontology, 14,* 85–88.

Botwinick, J., & Storandt, M. (1974). *Memory, related functions, and age.* Springfield, IL: Charles C. Thomas.

Bould, S., Sanborn, B., & Reif, L. (1989). *Eighty-five plus: The oldest old.* Belmont, CA: Wadsworth.

Bowlby, J. (1969). *Attachment and loss,* (Vol. 1.) London: Hogarth (New York: Basic Books).

Bowlby, J. (1980). Loss: Sadness and depression. In J. Bowlby (Ed.), *Attachment and loss* (Vol. 6). New York: Basic Books.

Boyd, J. H., & Weissman, M. M. (1981). Epidemiology of affective disorders: A reexamination and future directions. *Archives of General Psychiatry, 38,* 1039–1046.

Boyd, J. H., & Weissman, M. M. (1982). Epidemiology. In E. S. Paykel (Ed.), *Handbook of the affective disorder.* New York: Guilford.

Boyd, P. (1969). The valued grandparent: A changing social role. In W. Donahue, J. Kornbluth, & B. Powers (Eds.), *Living in the multigenerational family.* Ann Arbor: MI: Institute of Gerontology.

Brainerd, C. J. (1978). The stage question in cognitive developmental theory. *Behavioral and Brain Sciences, 1,* 173–214.

Braithwaite, V. A., Gibson, D. M., and Bosly-Craft, R. (1986). An exploratory study of poor adjustment styles among retirees. *Social Science and Medicine, 23,* 493–499.

Bram, S. (1985–1987). Parenthood or nonparenthood: A comparison of intentional families. *Lifestyles, 8,* 69–84.

Branch, L. G. (1987). Continuing care retirement communities: Self-insuring for long-term care. *The Gerontologist, 27,* 4–8.

Branch, L. G., Friedman, D. J., Cohen, M. A., Smith, N., & Socholitzky, E. (1988). Impoverishing the elderly: A case study of the financial risk of spending down among Massachusetts elderly. *The Gerontologist, 28,* 648–658.

Braune, R., & Wickens, C. D. (1985). The functional age profile: An objective decision criterion for the assessment of pilot performance capacities and capabilities. *Human Factors, 27,* 549–554.

Brecher, W. J. (Ed.). (1984). *Love, sex, and aging: A consumer's union report.* Boston: Little, Brown.

Brent, G., Smith, D., Michaelewski, H., & Thompson, L. (1976). Differences in evoked potentials in young and old subjects during habituation and dishabituation procedures. *Psychophysiology, 14,* 96–97.

Brickel, C. M. (1980–1981). A review of the roles of pet animals in psychotherapy and with the elderly. *International Journal of Aging and Human Development, 12,* 119–128.

Brickel, C. M. (1982). Pet-facilitated psychotherapy: A theoretical explanation via attention shifts. *Psychological Reports, 50,* 71–74.

Brickel, C. M. (1985). Initiation and maintenance of the human-animal bond: Familial roles from a learning perspective. *Marriage and the Family Review, 8,* 31–48.

Brickwell, H. M. (1979). *A study of the tuition refund plan of Mack Trucks, Inc., Hagerstown, MD.* New York: College Entrance Examination Board.

Brim, O. G., Jr., & Ryff, C. D. (1980). On the properties of life events. In P. B. Baltes & O. G. Brim, Jr. (Eds.), *Life-span development and behavior* (Vol. 3). New York: Academic Press.

Broderick, C. (1982). Adult sexual development. In B. J. Wolman (Ed.), *Handbook of developmental psychology.* Englewood Cliffs, NJ: Prentice-Hall.

Brody, E. M. (1985). Parent care as a normative family stress. *The Gerontologist, 25,* 19–29.

Brooks, J. B. (1981). Social maturity in middle age and its developmental antecedents. In D. Eichorn, N. Haan, J. A. Clausen, M. Honzik, & P. Mussen (Eds.), *Present and past in middle life.* New York: Academic Press.

Bruckner, R. (1967). Longitudinal research on the eye. *Clinical Gerontology, 9,* 87–95.

Budget Standard Service. (1986). *Annual price survey—Family budget costs* (30th ed.). New York: City Planning Information Department.

Bureau of Justice Department Statistics. (1987). Special report: Elderly victims. Washington, DC: Bureau of Justice.

Burger, J. M. (1989). Negative reactions in increases in perceived personal control. *Journal of Personality and Social Psychology, 56,* 246–256.

Burnet, S. F. M. (1974). *Intrinsic mutagenesis: A genetic approach to aging.* New York: Wiley.

Burrus-Bammel, L. L., & Bammel, G. (1985). Leisure and recreation. In J. E. Birren & K. W. Schaie (Eds.), *Handbook of the psychology of aging,* (2nd ed.). New York: Van Nostrand Reinhold.

Burt, J. J., & Meeks, L. B. (1985). *Education for sexuality: Concepts and programs for teaching* (3rd ed.). Philadelphia: Saunders College.

Business Publishers, Inc. (1989). *Aging research and training news.* (Sample Issue, p. 3). Silver Springs, MD: Business Publishers.

Buss, T., & Redburn, F. S. (1983). Unpublished and untitled manuscript. Center for Urban Studies, Youngstown State University, Youngstown, Ohio.

Busse, E. W. & Maddox, G. L. (1985). *The Duke longitudinal studies of normal aging: 1955–1980.* New York: Springer.

Butcher, L. L. & Woolf, N. J. (1986). Central cholinergic systems: Synopsis of anatomy and overview of physiology and pathology. In A. B. Scheibel, A. F. Wechsler, and M. A. B. Brazier (Eds.). *The biological substrates of Alzheimer's disease.* New York: Academic Press.

Butler, R. N. (1963). The life review: An interpretation of reminiscence in the aged. *Psychiatry, 26,* 65–76.

Butler, R. N. (1975). *Why survive? Being old in America.* New York: Harper & Row.

Butler, R. N. (1987). Ageism. In G. L. Maddox (Ed.), *The encyclopedia of aging.* New York: Springer.

Butler, R. N., & Lewis, M. (1977). *Aging and mental health.* St. Louis: Mosby.

Butters, N. (1987). Procedural learning and dementia: A double dissociation between Alzheimer's and Huntington's disease patients on verbal planning and motor skill learning. *Journal of Clinical and Experimental Neuropsychology, 9,* 68–69.

Byrd, M., & Moscovitch, M. (1984). Lateralization of peripherally and centrally masked words in young and elderly subjects. *Journal of Gerontology, 39,* 699–703.

Calasanti, T. M. (1988). Participation in a dual economy and adjustment to retirement. *International Journal of Aging and Human Development, 26,* 13–27.

Callan, V. J. (1984). Childlessness and marital adjustment. *Australian Journal of Sex, Marriage, and the Family, 5,* 210–214.

Callan, V. J. (1987). Personal and marital adjustment of voluntary and nonvoluntary childless wives. *Journal of Marriage and the Family, 49,* 847–856.

Campbell, B. A., & Gaddy, J. R. (1987). Rate of aging and dietary restriction: Sensory and motor function in the Fischer 344 rat. *Journal of Gerontology, 42,* 154–159.

Campbell, D. T., & Stanley, J. C. (1963). *Experimental and quasi-experimental designs for research.* Chicago: Rand McNally.

Campbell, S., & Silverman, P. R. (1987). *Widower.* Englewood Cliffs, NJ: Prentice-Hall.

Carey, R. G. (1977). The widowed: A year later. *Journal of Counseling Psychology, 24,* 125–131.

Carp, F. M. (1976). Housing and living environments of older people. In R. H. Binstock & E. Shanas (Eds.), *Handbook of aging and the social sciences.* New York: Van Nostrand Reinhold.

Carskadon, M. A. (1982). Sleep fragmentation, sleep loss, and sleep need in the elderly. *The Gerontologist, 22,* 187.

Cartwright, A., Hockey, L., & Anderson, J. L. (1973). *Life before death.* London: Routledge and Kegan Paul.

Cartwright, W., Huang, L. F., & Hu, T. (1988). Social science index: The economic costs of senile dementia in the United States. In Public Health Reports (Vol. 1 (1)) (pp. 3–7). Washington, DC: U.S. Government Printing Office.

Carver, C. S., Scheier, M. F., & Weintraub, J. K. (1989). Assessing coping strategies: A theoretically based approach. *Journal of Personality and Social Psychology, 56,* 267–283.

Catania, J. A., Turner, H., Kegeles, S. M., Stall, R., Pollack, L., & Coates, T. J. (1989). Older Americans and AIDs transmission risks and primary prevention research needs. *The Gerontologist, 29,* 373–381.

Cattell, R. B. (1971). *Abilities: Their structure, growth, and action.* Champaign, IL: IPAT.

Cavanaugh, J. C., Grady, J. G., & Perlmutter, M. (1983). Forgetting and the use of memory aids in twenty- and seventy-year-olds' everyday lives. *International Journal of Aging and Human Development, 17,* 113–122.

Ceci, S. J., & Liker, J. K. (1986). A day at the races: A study of IQ, expertise, and cognitive complexity. *Journal of Experimental Psychology: General, 115,* 255–266.

Cerella, J. (1985). Information-processing rate in the elderly. *Psychological Bulletin, 98,* 67–83.

Cerella, J. (1989). Aging and information-processing rate. In J. E. Birren and K. W. Schaie (Eds.), *Handbook of the psychology of aging,* (3rd ed.). New York: Academic Press.

Cerella, J. (1990, March). *The aging of information processing.* Paper presented at the Third Annual Conference on Cognitive Aging, Atlanta, GA.

Cerella, J., Poon, L. W., & Fozard, J. L. (1981). Mental rotation and age reconsidered. *Journal of Gerontology, 36,* 604–624.

Chalke, H. D., Dewhurst, J. R., & Ward, C. W. (1958). Loss of sense of smell in old people. *Public Health, 72,* 223–230.

Chapman, M. (1984). Intentional action as a paradigm for developmental psychology: Conclusion, action, intention, and intersubjectivity. *Human Development, 27,* 139–144.

Charness, N. (1981). Search in chess: Age and skill differences. *Journal of Experimental Psychology: Human Perception and Performance, 7,* 467–76.

Charness, N. (1985). *Age and expertise: Responding to Talland's challenge.* Paper presented at the George A. Talland Memorial Conference on Aging and Memory, Cape Cod, MA.

Charness, N. (1988). Expertise in chess, music, and physics: A cognitive perspective. In L. K. Obler & D. A. Fein (Eds.), *The neuropsychology of talent and special abilities.* New York: Guilford Press.

Chase, W. G., & Simon, H. A. (1973). Perception in chess. *Cognitive Psychology, 4,* 55–81.

Chen, Y. P. (1987). Making assets out of tomorrow's elderly. *The Gerontologist, 27,* 410–416.

Cherlin, A., & Furstenberg, F. (1985). Styles and strategies of grandparenting. In V. L. Bengston & J. Robertson (Eds.), *Granparenthood.* Beverly Hills, CA: Sage.

Cherlin, A., & Furstenberg, F. (1986). Grandparents and family crisis. *Generations, 10,* 26–28.

Chi, M. T. H. (1985). Changing conceptions of sources of memory development. *Human Development, 28,* 50–56.

Chiarello, C., & Hoyer, W. J. (1988). Adult age differences in implicit and explicit memory: Time course and encoding effects. *Psychology and Aging, 3,* 358–366.

Chiriboga, D. A. (1982a). Adaptations to marital separation in later and earlier life. *Journal of Gerontology, 37,* 109–114. (9–13).

Chiriboga, D. A. (1982b). An examination of life events as possible antecedents to change. *Journal of Gerontology, 37,* 595–601.

Chiriboga, D. A., & Cutler, L. (1980). Stress and adaptation: Life-span perspectives. In L. W. Poon (Ed.), *Aging in the 1980s: Psychological issues.* Washington, DC: American Psychological Association.

Chiriboga, D. A., & Pierce, R. (1978). *Of time and transitions.* Unpublished manuscript. San Francisco: University of California.

Chiriboga, D. A., & Turnher, M. (1975). Concept of self. In M. F. Lowenthal, M. Turnher, & D. A. Chiriboga & Associates (Eds.), *Four stages of life: A comparative study of women and men facing transitions.* San Francisco: Jossey-Bass.

Church, D. K., Siegel, M. A., and Foster, C. D. (1988). *Growing old in America.* Wylie, TX: Information Aids.

Churchland, P. M., & Churchland, P. S. (1990). Could a machine think? *Scientific American, 262,* 32–39.

Cicirelli, V. G. (1981). *Helping elderly parents: The role of adult children.* Boston: Auburn House.

Clancy, S. & Hoyer, W. J. (1988, August). Effects of age and skill on domain-specific search. In V. L. Patel and G. J. Groen (Eds.), *Proceedings of the tenth conference of the Cognitive Science Society.* Hillsdale, NJ: Erlbaum.

Clancy, S. M., & Hoyer, W. J. (1990, March). *Costs and benefits of priming during visual search: Age and skill level differences.* Paper presented at the Third Annual Conference on Cognitive Aging, Atlanta, GA.

Clark, J. E., Lamphear, A. K., & Riddick, C. C. (1987). The effects of videogame playing of the response selection processing of elderly adults. *Journal of Gerontology, 42,* 82–85.

Clarkson-Smith, L., & Hartley, A. A. (1989). Relationships between physical exercise and cognitive abilities in older adults. *Psychology and Aging, 4,* 183–189.

Clausen, J. A. (1981). Men's occupational careers in the middle years. In D. H. Eichorn, J. A. Clausen, N. Haan, M. Honzik, & P. Mussen (Eds.), *Present and past in middle life.* New York: Academic Press.

Clayton, V. & Birren, J. E. Age and wisdom across the life-span: Theoretical perspectives. In P. B. Baltes and O. G. Brim, Jr. (Eds.), *Life-span development and behavior: Vol. 3.* New York: Academic Press.

Coalition for the Homeless (1984). *Crowded out: Homelessness and the elderly poor in New York City.* New York: Coalition for the Homeless.

Cogan, D. G. (1979). Summary and conclusion. In S. S. Hain & D. H. Coons (Eds.), *Special senses and aging.* Ann Arbor: Institute of Gerontology, University of Michigan.

Cogwill, D. O. (1974). Aging and modernization: A revision of theory. In J. F. Gubrium (Ed.), *Late life,* Springfield, IL: Charles C. Thomas.

Cogwill, D. O., & Holmes, L. (1972). *Aging and modernization.* New York: Appleton-Century-Crofts.

Cohen, C. I., Teresi, J. A., & Holmes, D. (1988). The physical well-being of older homeless men. *Journal of Gerontology, 43,* S121–S128.

Cohen, C. I., Teresi, J. A., Holmes, D., & Roth, E. (1988). Survival strategies of older homeless men. *The Gerontologist, 28,* 58–65.

Cohen, F., Bearison, D. J., & Muller, C. (1987). Interpersonal understanding in the elderly: The influence of age-integrated and age-segregated housing. *Research on Aging, 9,* 79–100.

Cohen, G. D. (1988). *The brain in human aging.* New York: Springer.

Cohen, G. D. (1989). The interface of mental and physical health phenomena in later life: New directions in geriatric psychiatry. *Gerontology and Geriatrics Education, 9,* 27–38.

Cohen, J. (1957). The factorial structure of the WAIS between early adulthood and old age. *Journal of Consulting Psychology, 21,* 283–290.

Cohen, M. A., Tell, E. J., Batten, H. L., & Larson, M. J. (1988). Attitudes toward joining continuing care retirement communities. *The Gerontologist, 28,* 637–643.

Cohler, B. J., & Grunebaum, H. V. (1981). *Mothers, grandmothers, and daughters: Personality and child-care in three-generation families.* New York: John Wiley.

Colby, A., & Kohlberg, L. (1984). Invariant sequence and internal consistency in moral judgment stages. In W. M. Kurtines & J. L. Gewirtz (Eds.), *Morality, moral behavior, and moral development.* New York: Wiley.

Colby, A., Kohlberg, L., Gibbs, J. C., & Lieberman, M. (1983). A longitudinal study of moral development. *Monographs of the Society for Research in Child Development, 48,* 4, 1–124.

Coleman, L., & Antonucci, T. (1983). Impact of working women at midlife. *Developmental Psychology, 19,* 290–294.

Coles, M. G. H., Gratton, G., Bashore, T. R., Eriksen, C. W., & Donchin, E. (1985). A psychophysiological investigation of the continuous flow model of human information processing. *Journal of Experimental Psychology: Perception and Performance, 11,* 529–553.

Collaborative Study. (1977). An appraisal of the criteria of cerebral death: A summary statement. *Journal of the American Medical Association, 237,* 982–986.

Colletta, N. D. (1978). *Divorced mothers at two income levels: Stress, support, and childrearing practices.* Unpublished Master's Thesis. Ithaca, NY: Cornell University.

Comfort, A. (1976). *A good age.* New York: Crown.

Comfort, A. (1980). Sexuality in later life. In J. E. Birren & R. B. Sloane (Eds.), *Handbook of mental health and aging.* New York: Van Nostrand Reinhold.

Commons, M. L., Richards, F. A., & Armon, C. (1982). Systematic, metasystematic, and cross-paradigmatic reasoning: A case for stages of reasoning beyond Piaget's stage of formal operations. *Child Development, 53,* 1058–1068.

Commons, M. L., Richards, F. A., & Armon, C. (1984a). Applying the general stage model. In M. L. Commons, F. A. Richards, & C. Armon (Eds.), *Beyond formal operations: Late adolescent and adult cognitive development.* New York: Praeger.

Commons, M. L., Richards, F. A., & Armon, C. (Eds.). (1984b). *Beyond formal operations: Late adolescent and adult cognitive development.* New York: Praeger.

Commons, M. L., Sinnott, J. D., Richards, F. A., & Armon, C. (1989). *Adult development, Vol. 1: Comparisons and applications of developmental models.* New York: Praeger.

Commonwealth Fund Commission. (1987). Old, alone, and poor. *Report of the Commonwealth Fund Commission: Elderly people living alone.* Baltimore: Commonwealth Fund Commission.

Community Council of Greater New York (1986). *Annual price survey of family budget costs.* As cited in D. K. Church, M. A. Siegel, & C. D. Foster (Eds.), *Aging in America,* (1988). Wylie, TX: Information Aids.

Congressional Caucus for Women's Issues (1987). *The American woman: 1987–1988.* Washington, DC: Report.

Connell, J. P., & Bridges, L. J. (1987). The life-span perspective: Promise of a prototype. *Contemporary Psychology, 32,* 727–728.

Constantinople, A. (1976). Masculinity-femininity: An exception to a famous dictum. In F. Denmark (Ed.), *Women: A PDI research reference work.* (Vol. I.) New York: Psychological Dimensions.

Cool, L., & McCabe, J. (1983). The "scheming hag" and the "dear old thing": The anthropology of aging women in J. Sokolovsky (Ed.), *Growing old in different societies: Cross-cultural perspectives.* Belmont, CA: Wadsworth.

Cooney, T. M., Schaie, K. W., & Willis, S. L. (1988). The relationship between prior functioning on cognitive and personality dimensions and subject attrition in longitudinal research. *Journal of Gerontology, 43,* P12–P17.

Corbin, J. N. (1974). *The effects of counselor-assisted exploratory activity on career development.* Unpublished doctoral dissertation. New York: Columbia University.

Corby, N., & Solnick, R. (1980). Psychosocial and physiological influences on sexuality in the older adult. In J. E. Birren & R. B. Sloane (Eds.), *Handbook of mental health and aging.* Englewood Cliffs, NJ: Prentice-Hall.

Cornelius, S. W., & Capsi, A. (1987). Everyday problem solving in adulthood and old age. *Psychology and aging, 2,* 144–153.

Corso, J. F. (1977). Auditory perception and communication. In J. E. Birren & K. W. Schaie (Eds.), *Handbook of the psychology of aging.* New York: Van Nostrand Reinhold.

Corso, J. F. (1981). *Aging, sensory systems, and perception.* New York: Praeger.

Costa, P. T., Jr. (1986, August). *The scope of individuality.* Paper presented at the meeting of the American Psychological Association, Washington, DC.

Costa, P. T., Jr. (1988, August). Personality continuity and the changes of adult life. Paper presented at the meeting of the American Psychological Association, Atlanta.

Costa, P. T., Jr., & McCrae, R. R. (1977). Age differences in personality structure revisited: Studies in validity, stability, and change. *Aging and Human Development, 8,* 261–275.

Costa, P. T., Jr., & McCrae, R. R. (1978). Objective personality assessment. In M. Storandt, I. C. Siegler, & M. P. Elias (Eds.), *The clinical psychology of aging.* New York: Plenum.

Costa, P. T., Jr., & McCrae, R. R. (1980). Still stable after all these years: Personality as a key to some issues of adulthood and old age. In P. B. Baltes & O. G. Brim, Jr. (Eds.), *Life-span development and behavior* (Vol. 3). New York: Academic Press.

Costa, P. T., Jr., & McCrae, R. R. (1982). An approach to the attribution of aging: Period and cohort effects. *Psychological Bulletin, 92,* 238–250.

Costa, P. T., Jr., & McCrae, R. R. (1985). Personality as a lifelong determinant of well-being. In C. Malatesta & C. Izard (Eds.), *Affective processes in adult development and aging.* New York: Sage.

Costa, P. T., Jr., & McCrae, R. R. (1986). Cross-sectional studies of personality in a national sample: I. Development and validation of survey measures. *Psychology and Aging, 1,* 140–143.

Costa, P. T., McCrae, R. R., Zonderman, A. B., Barbano, H. E., Lebowitz, B., & Larson, D. M. (1986). Cross-sectional studies of personality in a national sample: Stability in neuroticism, extraversion, and openness. *Psychology and Aging, 1,* 144–150.

Costa, P. T., Zonderman, A. B., McCrae, R. R., Cornon-Huntley, J., & Barbano, H. E. (1987). Longitudinal analyses of psychological well-being in a national sample: Stability and mean levels. *Journal of Gerontology, 42,* 50–55.

Cote, L. (1981). Aging of the brain and dementia. In E. R. Kandel & J. H. Schwartz (Eds.), *Principles of neural science*. New York: Elsevier-North Holland.

Council on Scientific Affairs. (1988). Magnetic resonance imaging of the central nervous system. *Journal of the American Medical Association, 259,* 1211–1222.

Covey, H. C. (1988). Historical terminology used to represent older people. *The Gerontologist, 28,* 291–297.

Coyle, J. T., Price, D. L., & DeLong, M. R. (1983). Alzheimer's disease: A disorder of cortical cholinergic innervation. *Science, 219,* 1184–1190.

Craik, F. I. M. (1977). Age differences in human memory. In J. E. Birren & K. W. Schaie (Eds.), *Handbook of the psychology of aging*. New York: Van Nostrand Reinhold.

Craik, F. I. M. (1983). On the transfer of information from temporary to permanent memory. *Philosophical Transactions of the Royal Society, B302,* 341–359.

Craik, F. I. M., Byrd, M., & Swanson, J. M. (1987). Patterns of memory loss in three elderly samples. *Psychology and Aging, 2,* 79–86.

Craik, F. I. M., & Simon, E. (1980). Age differences in memory: A framework for memory research. *Journal of Verbal Learning and Verbal Behavior, 11,* 671–684.

Cristofalo, V. J. (1986). The biology of aging: An Overview. In M. J. Horan, G. M. Steinberg, J. B. Dunbar, & E. C. Hadley (Eds.), *NIH, Blood pressure regulation and aging: Proceedings from a symposium*. New York: Biomedical Information Corporation.

Crook, M. N., Alexander, E. A., Anderson, E. M. S., Coules, J., Hanson, J. A., & Jerreries, N. T. (1962). Age and form perception. *U.S. Air Force School of Aviation Medicine Report,* No. 57–124.

Cross, K. P. (1978). A critical review of state and national studies of the needs and interests of adult learners. In C. B. Stalford (Ed.), *Conference report: Adult learning needs and the demand for lifelong learning*. Washington, DC: National Institute of Education, U.S. Department of Health, Education, and Welfare.

Cumming, E., & Henry, W. (1961). *Growing old*. New York: Basic Books.

Cunningham, D. A., Rechnitzer, P. A., Howard, J. H., & Donner, A. P. (1987). Exercise training of men at retirement: A clinical trial. *Journal of Gerontology, 42,* 17–23.

Cunningham, W. R., & Owens, W. A., Jr. (1983). The Iowa study of the adult development of intellectual abilities. In K. W. Schaie (Ed.), *Longitudinal studies of adult psychological development*. New York: Guilford Press.

Curran, J., Jaffe, H., Hardy, A., Morgan, W., Selik, R., & Dondero, T. (1988). Epidemiology of HIV infection and AIDS in the United States. *Science, 239,* 610–616.

Cutler, S. J., & Grams, A. E. (1987). Correlates of self-reported everyday memory problems. *Journal of Gerontology, 43,* S82–S90.

Cytrynbaum, S., Blum, L., Patrick, R., Stein, J., Wadner, D., & Wilk, C. (1980). Midlife development: A personality and social systems perspective. In L. W. Poon (Ed.), *Aging in the 1980s*. Washington, DC: American Psychological Association.

Dacy, J. (1978). *Adult development*. New York: Scott Foresman.

Damasio, A. R. (1985). Disorders of complex visual processing: Agnosias, achromatopsia, Balint's syndrome, and related difficulties of orientation and construction. In M. Mesulam (Ed.), *Principles of behavioral neurology*. Philadelphia: Davis Co.

Damasio, A. R., & Van Hoesen, G. W. (1986). Neuroanatomical correlates of amnesia in Alzheimer's disease. In A. B. Scheibel & A. F. Wechsler (Eds.), *The biological substrates of Alzheimer's disease*. New York: Academic Press.

Daniel, D. E., Templin, R. G., & Shearon, R. W. (1977). The value orientation of older adults towards education. *Educational Gerontology, 2,* 33–42.

Danish, S. J., & D'Augelli, A. R. (1980). Promoting competence and enhancing development through life-development intervention. In L. A. Bond & J. C. Rosen (Eds.), *Competence and coping during adulthood*. Hanover, NH: University Press of New England.

Davies, P. A. (1941). The electroencephalogram in old age. *Diseases of the Nervous System, 2,* 77.

Davis, K. E. (1985). Near and dear: Friendship and love compared. *Psychology Today, 19,* 22–30.

DeAngelis, T. (1989, January). Mania, depression, and genius: Concert, talks inform public about manic-depressive illness. *American Psychological Association Monitor, 20* (1), 1, 24.

Deci, E. (1975). *Intrinsic motivation.* New York: Plenum Press.

Deci, E. L., and Ryan, R. M. (1985). *Intrinsic motivation and self-determination.* New York: Plenum Press.

Deci, E. L., and Ryan, R. M. (1987). The support of autonomy and the control of behavior. *Journal of Personality and Social Psychology, 51,* 1024–1037.

de Groot, A. (1965). *Thought and choice in chess.* The Hague: Mouton.

DeLongis, A., Coyne, J. C., Dakof, S., Folkman, S., & Lazarus, R. S. (1982). Relationship of daily hassles, uplifts, and major life events to health status. *Health Psychology, 1,* 119–136.

Demaris, A. (1984). A comparison of remarriages with first marriages on satisfaction in marriage and its relationship to prior cohabitation. Special Issue: Remarriage and stepparenting. *Family Relations Journal of Applied Family and Child Studies, 33,* 443–449.

Denckla, W. D. (1974). Role of the pituitary and the thyroid gland in the decline of minimal oxygen consumption with age. *Journal of Clinical Investigation, 53,* 572–581.

Denney, N. W. (1982). Aging and cognitive change. In B. B. Wolman (Ed.), *Handbook of developmental psychology.* Englewood Cliffs, NJ: Prentice-Hall.

Denney, N. W. (1984). A model of cognitive development across the life span. *Developmental Review, 4,* 171–191.

Dennis, W. (1966). Creative productivity between the ages of twenty and eighty years. *Journal of Gerontology, 21,* 1–18.

Dennis, W. (1968). Creative productivity between the ages of twenty and eighty years. In B. L. Neugarten (Ed.), *Middle age and aging.* Chicago: University of Chicago Press.

Department of Health and Human Services (1990). *Program announcement: Research on the prevention of alcohol abuse in the older population (RFP).* Catalog of Federal Domestic Assistance No. 13, 273, p. 2, Washington, DC: U.S. Superintendent of Documents.

Derogatis, L. R., Meyer, J., & King, K. M. (1981). Psychopathology in individuals with sexual dysfunction. *American Journal of Psychiatry, 138,* 757–763.

de Vries, H. A. (1970). Physiological effects of an exercise training regimen upon men aged fifty-two to eighty-eight. *Journal of Gerontology, 25,* 1–18.

Diagnostic and statistical manual of mental disorders. (1987). (3rd ed. revised). Washington, DC: American Psychiatric Association.

DiLollo, V., Arnett, J. L., & Kruk, R. V., (1982). Age-related changes in the rate of visual information processing. *Journal of Experimental Psychology: Human Perception and Performance, 8,* 225–237.

Dittmann-Kohli, F., & Baltes, P. B. (1988). Toward a neofunctionalist conception of adult intellectual development: Wisdom as a prototypical case of intellectual growth. In C. Alexander, E. Langer, & R. Oetzel (Eds.), *Higher stages of human development.* New York: Oxford University Press.

Dixon, R. A., & Baltes, P. B. (1986). Toward life-span research on the functions and pragmatics of intelligence. In R. J. Sternberg & R. K. Wagner (Eds.), *Practical intelligence: Origins of competence in the everyday world.* New York: Cambridge University Press.

Dobbs, A. R., & Rule, B. G. (1989). Adult age differences in working memory. *Psychology and Aging, 4,* 500–503.

Doddridge, R., Schumm, W. R., & Bergen, M. B. (1987). Factors related to decline in preferred frequency of sexual intercourse among young couples. *Psychological Reports, 60,* 391–395.

Doherty, W. S., & Jacobson, N. S. (1982). Marriage and the family. In B. J. Wolman (Ed.), *Handbook of developmental psychology.* Englewood Cliffs, NJ: Prentice-Hall.

Dohrenwend, B. S., & Dohrenwend, B. P. (1978). Some issues in research on stressful life events. *Journal of Nervous and Mental Disease, 166,* 7–15.

Dohrenwend, B. S., Krasnoff, L., Askensay, A., & Dohrenwend, B. P. (1978). Exemplification of a method of scaling life events: The PERI life-events scale. *Journal of Health and Social Behavior, 19,* 205–229.

Doka, K. J., & Mertz, M. E. (1988). The meaning and significance of great-grandparenthood. *Gerontologist, 28,* 192–197.

Donaldson, G. (1981). Letter to the editor. *Journal of Gerontology, 36,* 634–636.

Douglas, K. W., & Arenberg, D. (1978). Age changes, cohort differences, and cultural change on the Guilford-Zimmerman temperament survey. *Journal of Gerontology, 33,* 737–747.

Douvan, D. (1983). Listening to a different drummer. *Contemporary Psychology, 28,* 261–262.

Douvan, E., and Adelson, J. (1966). *The adolescent experience.* New York: John Wiley.

Duncan, G. J., Hill, M. S., & Rogers, W. (1986, May). *The changing economic status of the young and old.* Paper presented at the annual meeting of the American Academy for the Advancement of Science, Philadelphia, PA.

Ebbinghaus, H. (1964). *Memory* (H. A. Ruger and C. E. Bussenius, trans.). (Original work published 1885). Mineola, NY: Dover.

Eckert, H. M., & Espenschade, A. S. (1980). *Motor development* (2d ed.). Columbus, OH: Charles E. Merrill.

Edwards, J. N., & Booth, A. (1976). The cessation of marital intercourse. *American Journal of Psychiatry, 133,* 1333–1336.

Edwards, M. (1977). Coupling and uncoupling vs. the challenge of being single. *Personnel and Guidance Journal, 55,* 542–545.

Eichorn, D., Clausen, J., Haan, N., Honzik, M., & Mussen, P. (1981). (Eds.), *Past and present in middle life.* New York: Academic Press.

Eisdorfer, C., Nowlin, J., & Wilkie, F. (1970). Improvement of learning in the aged by modification of the autonomic nervous system. *Science, 170,* 1327–1329.

Eisdorfer, C., & Wilkie, F. (1973). Intellectual changes with advancing age. In L. F. Jarvik, C. Eisdorfer, & J. E. Blum (Eds.), *Intellectual functioning in adults.* New York: Springer.

Ekerdt, D. J. (1986). The busy ethic: Moral continuity between work and retirement. *The Gerontologist, 26,* 239–244.

Ekerdt, D. J., Bosse, R., & Levkoff, S. (1985). An empirical test for phases of retirement: Findings from the normative aging study. *Journal of Gerontology, 40,* 95–101.

Ekstrom, R. B., French, J. W., & Harman, M. H. (1979). Cognitive factors: Their identification and replication. *Multivariate Behavior Research Monographs* (No. 79.2).

Elder, G. H., Jr. (1974). *Children of the great depression.* Chicago: University of Chicago Press.

Elder, G. H., Jr. (1981). Social history and life experience. In D. Eichorn, J. Clausen, N. Haan, M. Honzik, & P. Mussen (Eds.), *Past and present in middle life.* New York: Academic Press.

Elder, G. H., Jr. (1986). Military times and turning points in men's lives. *Developmental Psychology, 22,* 233–246.

Elder, G. H., Jr., Liker, J. K., & Cross, C. E. (1984). Parent-child behavior in the Great Depression: Life course and intergenerational influences. In P. B. Baltes and O. G. Brim, Jr. (Eds.), *Life-span development and behavior, Vol. 6.* New York: Academic Press.

Elder, G. H., Jr., Liker, J. K., & Jaworski, B. J. (1984). Hardship in lives: Depression influences from the 1930s to old age in postwar America. In K. A. McCluskey & H. W. Reese, (Eds.), *Life-span developmental psychology: Historical and generational effects.* New York: Academic Press.

Elkind, D. (1961). Quantity conceptions in junior and senior high school students. *Child Development, 32,* 551–560.

Emanuel, L. L., & Emanuel, E. J. (1989). The medical directive—A new comprehensive advance care document. *Journal of the American Medical Association, 261* (22), 3288–3293.

Embree, A. T. (1972). *The Hindu tradition.* New York: Random House.

Engen, T. (1977). Taste and smell. In J. E. Birren & K. W. Schaie (Eds.), *Handbook of the psychology of aging.* New York: Van Nostrand Reinhold.

Epstein, L. H., & Wing, R. R. (1987). Behavioral treatment of childhood obesity. *Psychological Bulletin, 101,* 331–343.

Ericsson, K. A. (in press). Peak performance and age: An examination of peak performance in sports. In P. B. Baltes & M. M. Baltes (Eds.), *Successful aging: perspectives from the behavioral sciences.* New York: Cambridge University Press.

Ericsson, K. A., & Simon, H. A. (1984). *Protocol analysis.* Cambridge, MA: Harvard University Press.

Erikson, E. H. (1962). *Young man Luther.* New York: Norton.

Erikson, E. H. (1963). *Childhood and society.* (2nd ed.). New York: Norton.

Erikson, E. H. (1968). *Identity, youth and crisis.* New York: Norton.

Erikson, E. H. (1969). *Gandhi's truth.* New York: Norton.

Erikson, E. H. (1982). *The life cycle completed: A review.* New York: Norton.

Espinoza, R., & Newman, Y. (1979). *Step-parenting.* Department of Health, Education, and Welfare Publication N (ADM): 78–579. Washington, DC: U.S. Government Printing Office.

Essex, M. J., & Nam, S. (1987). Marital status and loneliness among older women: The differential importance of close family and friends. *Journal of Marriage and the Family, 49,* 93–106.

Eysenck, M. W. (1974). Age differences in incidental learning. *Developmental Psychology, 10,* 936–941.

Farnsworth, P. R., McNemar, O., & McNemar, Q. (Eds.). (1965). *Annual review of psychology.* Vol. 16. Palo Alto, CA: Annual Reviews.

Farrel, M. P., & Rosenberg, S. D. (1981). *Men at midlife.* Boston: Auburn House.

Fassinger, R. E. (1985). A causal model of college women's career choice. *Journal of Vocational Behavior, 27,* 123–153.

Federal Trade Commission, Bureau of Consumer Protection. (1978). *Funeral industry practices.* Washington, DC: U.S. Superintendent of Documents.

Feifel, H. and Nagy, T. (1981). Another look at fear of death. *Journal of Consulting and Clinical Psychology, 49,* 278–286.

Feldman, S. S., Biringen, Z. C., & Nash, S. C. (1981). Fluctuations of sex-related self-attributions as a function of stage of family life cycle. *Developmental Psychology, 17,* 24–35.

Ferraro, K. F. (1987). Double jeopardy to health in black older adults. *Journal of Gerontology, 42,* 528–533.

Finch, C. E. (1976). The regulation of physiological changes during mammalian aging. *The Quarterly Review of Biology, 51,* 49–83.

Finch, C. E. (1988). The neural and endocrine approaches to the resolution of time as a dependent variable in the aging processes of mammals. *The Gerontologist, 28,* 29–42.

Fischer, K. W. (1980). A theory of cognitive development: The control and construction of hierarchies of skills. *Psychological Review, 87,* 477–531.

Fiske, M. L. (1980). Changing hierarchies of commitment in adulthood. In N. J. Smelser and E. Erikson (Eds.), *Theories of Love and Work in Adulthood.* Cambridge, MA: Harvard University.

Fitzgerald, J. M. (1984). Autobiographical memory across the life span. *Journal of Gerontology, 39,* 692–699.

Fitzgerald, J. M. (1988). Vivid memories and the reminiscence phenomenon: The role of a self-narrative. *Human Development, 31,* 260–270.

Fitzgerald, J. M. & Lawrence, R. (1984). Autobiographical memory across the life-span. *Journal of Gerontology, 39,* 692–699.

Fitzgerald, L. F. & Betz, N. E. (1983). Issues in the vocational psychology of women. In W. B. Walsh & S. H. Osipow (Eds.), *Handbook of vocational psychology, Vol. I: Foundations.* Hillsdale, NJ: Erlbaum.

Flavell, J. H. (1977). *Cognitive development.* Englewood Cliffs, NJ: Prentice-Hall.

Flavell, J. H. (1985). *Cognitive development.* (2nd ed.). Englewood Cliffs, NJ: Prentice-Hall.

Flavell, J. H., & Wellman, H. M. (1977). Metamemory. In R. V. Kail, Jr. & J. W. Hagen (Eds.), *Perspectives on the development of memory and cognition.* Hillsdale, NJ: Erlbaum.

Folkman, S., & Lazarus, R. S. (1980). An analysis of coping in a middle-aged community sample. *Journal of Health and Social Behavior, 21,* 219–239.

Folkman, S. L., Lazarus, R. S., Dunkel-Schetter, C., DeLongis, A., & Gruen, R. J. (1986). The dynamics of a stressful encounter: Cognitive appraisal, coping, and encounter outcomes. *Journal of Personality and Social Psychology, 50,* 992–1003.

Folkman, S., Lazarus, R. S., Gruen, R., & DeLongis, A. (1986). Appraisal, coping, health status, and psychological symptoms. *Journal of Personality and Social Psychology, 50,* 571–579.

Folkman, S., Lazarus, R. S., Pimley, S., & Novacek, J. (1987). Age differences in stress and coping processes. *Psychology and Aging. 2,* 171–184.

Ford, J. M., Hink, R. F., Hopkins, W. F., Roth, W. T., Pfefferbaum, A., & Kopell, B. S. (1979). Age effects on event-related potentials in a selective attention task. *Journal of Gerontology, 34,* 388–395.

Ford, J. M., Roth, W. T., Mohs, R. C., Hopkins, W. F., & Kopell, B. S. (1979). Event-related potentials recorded from young and old adults during a memory retrieval task. *Electroencephalography and Clinical Neurophysiology, 47,* 450–459.

Foster, G. M., and Anderson, B. G. (1978). *Medical anthropology.* New York: John Wiley.

Fredrick, J. E. (1983–1984). The biochemistry of bereavement: Possible bias for chemotherapy. *Omega, 13,* 295–303.

Freed, W. J., deMedinaceli, L., & Wyatt, R. J. (1985). Promoting functional plasticity in the damaged nervous system. *Science, 227,* 1544–1552.

Freed, W. J., Morihisa, J. M., Spoor, E., Hoffer, B. J., Oldson, L., Seiger, A., & Wyatt, R. J. (1981). Transplanted adrenal chromaffin cells in rat brain reduce lesion-induced rotational behavior. *Nature, 292,* 351–352.

Freeman, J. (1982). The old, old, very old Charlie Smith. *The Gerontologist, 22,* 532.

Freuchen, P. (1961). *Book of the Eskimos.* Cleveland: World Press.

Friedman, M., & Rosenman, R. M. (1974). *Type A behavior and your heart.* New York: Knopf.

Friedmann, E., & Havighurst, R. J. (1954). *The meaning of work and retirement.* Chicago: University of Chicago Press.

Friedmann, E., Katcher, A. H., Lynch, J. J., & Thomas, S. A. (1980). Animal companions and one-year survival of patients after discharge from a coronary care unit. *Public Health Reports, 95,* 307–312.

Fromm, E. (1947). *Man for himself: An inquiry into the psychology of ethics.* New York: Holt, Rinehart & Winston.

Fromm, E. (1955). *The sane society.* New York: Fawcett Books.

Furstenberg, F. F. (1982). Conjugal succession: Reentering marriage after divorce. In P. B. Baltes & O. G. Brim, Jr. (Eds.), *Life-span development and behavior, Vol, 4.* New York: Academic Press.

Gallagher, D., & Thompson, L. W. (1983). Depression. In P. Lewinsohn & L. Teri (Eds.), *Clinical geropsychology: New directions in assessment and treatment.* New York: Pergamon Press.

Gallagher, D., Thompson, L. W., & Breckenridge, J. S. (1986). Efficacy of three modalities of individual psychotherapy: One-year follow-up results. *The Gerontologist, 26,* 214.

Gambert, S. R. (Ed.). (1987). *Handbook of geriatrics.* New York: Plenum Medical Book Company.

Gardner, H. (1972). *The shattered mind: The person after brain damage.* New York: Knopf.

Gardner, H. (1983). *Frames of mind: The theory of multiple intelligences.* New York: Basic Books.

Gardner, H. (1985). *The mind's new science.* New York: Basic Books.

Garret, H. E. (1957). *Great experiments in psychology* (3rd ed.). New York: Appleton-Century-Crofts.

Gatz, M., Smyer, M. A., & Lawton, M. P. (1980). The mental health system and the older adult. In L. W. Poon (Ed.), *Aging in the 1980's: Psychological issues.* Washington, DC: American Psychological Association.

Geer, J. T., O'Donohue, W. T., & Schorman, R. H. (1986). Sexuality. In M. G. H. Coles, F. Donchin, & S. Porges (Eds.), *Psychophysiology: Systems, processes, applications.* New York: Guilford Press.

Gelman, R. (1979). Preschool thought. *American Psychologist, 34,* 900–904.

George, L. K. (1980). *Role transition in later life.* Belmont, CA: Wadsworth.

George, L. K., & Gwyther, L. P. (1986). Caregiver well-being: A multidimensional examination of family caregivers of demented adults. *The Gerontologist, 26,* 253–259.

Getzel, J. W. (1975). Problem finding and inventiveness of solutions. *Journal of Creative Behaviors, 9,* 12–18.

Gibbs, J. C. (1977). Kohlberg's stages of moral development: A constructive critique. *Harvard Educational Review, 47,* 43–61.

Gibbs, J. C. (1979). Kohlberg's moral stage theory: A Piagetian revision. *Human Development, 22,* 89–112.

Gibbs, J. C., Arnold, K. D., & Burkhart, J. E. (1984). Sex differences in the expression of moral judgment. *Child Development, 55,* 1040–1044.

Gilford, R. (1984). Contrasts in marital satisfaction throughout old age: An exchange theory analysis. *Journal of Gerontology, 39,* 325–333.

Gilhooly, M. L. M. (1984). The impact of caregiving on caregivers: Factors associated with the psychological well-being of people supporting a demented relative in the community. *British Journal of Medical Psychology, 57,* 544–547.

Gilhooly, M. L. M., Zarit, S., & Birren, J. E. (1986). *The dementias: Policy and management.* Englewood Cliffs, NJ: Prentice-Hall.

Gilligan, C. (1977). In a different voice: Women's conceptions of self and morality. *Harvard Educational Review, 47,* 481–517.

Gilligan, C. (1982). *In a different voice: Psychological theory and women's development.* Cambridge, MA: Harvard University Press.

Gilligan, C. (1985, April). *Response to critics.* Paper presented at the Biennial Meeting of the Society for Research in Child Development, Toronto.

Gilligan, C., & Belenky, M. F. (1980). A naturalistic study of abortion decisions. *New Directions for Child Development* (No. 7). San Francisco: Jossey-Bass, 69–90.

Ginzberg, E. (1971). *Career guidance.* New York: McGraw-Hill.

Ginzberg, E. (1972). Toward a theory of occupational choice: A restatement. *Vocational Guidance Quarterly, 20,* 169–176.

Glaser, B. G., and Strauss, A. L. (1965). *Awareness of dying.* Chicago: Aldine.

Glass, S. P., & Wright, T. L. (1985). Sex differences in type of extramarital involvement and marital dissatisfaction. *Sex-roles, 12,* 1101–1120.

Glenn, N. (1975). Psychological well-being in the post-parental stage: Some evidence from national surveys. *Journal of Marriage and the Family, 37,* 105–111.

Glick, P. C. (1980). Remarriage: Some recent changes and variations. *Journal of Family Issues, 1,* 455–479.

Glick, P. C. (1984). How American families are changing. *American Demographics, 6,* 20–25.

Glick, P. C., & Carter, H. (1976). *Marriage and divorce: A social and economic study* (2nd ed.). Cambridge, MA: Harvard University Press.

Glick, P. C., & Ling-Lin, S. (1986). Recent changes in divorce and remarriage. *Journal of Marriage and the Family, 48,* 737–747.

Golan, N. (1986). *The perilous bridge: Helping clients through midlife transitions.* New York: Free Press.

Goldgaber, D., Lerman, M. I., McBride, O. W., Saffiotti, V., & Gajdusek, D. C. (1987). Characterization and chromosomal localization of a cDNA encoding brain amyloid of Alzheimer's disease. *Science, 235,* 877–880.

Goldsmith, S. (1984). Hospitals and the elderly in Japan. *Pacific Affairs, 57,* 74–77.

Goleman, D. (1988, June 14). Erickson, in his own old age, expands his view of life. *New York Times,* pp. C1, C14.

Gould, R. L. (1975). Adult life stages: Growth toward self-tolerance. *Psychology Today, 8,* 74–78.

Gould, R. L. (1978). *Transformations: Growth and change in adult life.* New York: Simon & Schuster.

Gould, R. L. (1980a). Transformation tasks in adulthood. In *The course of life, Vol. 3: Adulthood and aging process.* Bethesda, MD: National Institute of Mental Health.

Gould, R. L. (1980b). Transformations during early and middle adult years. In N. J. Smelser & E. H. Erikson (Eds.), *Themes of work and love in adulthood.* Cambridge, MA: Harvard University Press.

Graf, P., & Mandler, G. (1984). Activation makes words more accessible, but not necessarily more retrievable. *Journal of Verbal Learning and Verbal Behavior, 23,* 553–568.

Graf, P., Mandler, G., & Haden, P. E. (1982). Simulating amnesiac symptoms in normal subjects. *Science, 218,* 1243–1244.

Greene, M. G., Hoffman, S., Charon, R., & Adelman, R. (1987). Psychosocial concerns in the medical encounter: A comparison of the interaction of doctors with their old and young patients. *The Gerontologist, 27,* 164–168.

Grober, E., & Buschke, H. (1987). Genuine memory deficits in dementia. *Developmental Neuropsychology, 3,* 13–36.

Gruman, G. (1978). Cultural origins of present day "ageism:" The modernization of the life cycle. In S. F. Spicker, K. M. Woodward, & D. D. Van Tassel (Eds.), *Aging and the elderly: Human perspectiveness in gerontology.* Atlantic Highlands, NJ: Humanities Press.

Gubrium, J. F. (1975). *Living and dying at Murray Manor.* New York: St. Martin's Press.

Guidelines for the determination of death: Report of the medical consultants on the diagnosis of death to the President's Commission for the Study of Ethical Problems in Medicine and Biomedical and Behavioral Research. (1981). *Journal of the American Medical Association, 246,* 2184–2186.

Guilford, J. P. (1959a). *Personality.* New York: McGraw-Hill.

Guilford, J. P. (1959b). Three faces of intellect. *American Psychologist, 14,* 469–479.

Guilford, J. P. (1967). *The nature of human intelligence.* New York: McGraw-Hill.

Gurin, P., & Brim, O, G., Jr. (1984). Change in self in adulthood: The example of sense of control. In P. B. Baltes & O. G. Brim, Jr. (Eds.), *Life-span development and behavior, Vol. 6.* New York: Academic Press.

Gurland, B. J. (1976). The comparative frequency of depression in various adult age groups. *Journal of Gerontology, 31,* 283–292.

Gurland, B. J. (1980). The assessment of the mental status of older adults. In J. E. Birren and R. B. Sloane (Eds.), *Handbook of mental health and aging.* Englewood Cliffs, NJ: Prentice-Hall.

Gurland, B. J., & Cross, P. S. (1982). Epidemiology of psychopathology in old age. In L. F. Jarvik & G. W. Small (Eds.), *Psychiatric clinics of North America.* Philadelphia: W. B. Saunders.

Gutmann, D. L. (1974). The country of old men: Cross-cultural studies in the psychology of later life. In R. L. LeVine (Ed.), *Culture and personality: Contemporary readings.* Chicago: Aldine.

Gutmann, D. L. (1975). Parenthood, key to the comparative study of the life cycle. In N. Datan & L. Ginsberg (Eds.), *Life-span developmental psychology: Normative life crises.* New York: Academic Press.

Gutmann, D. L. (1977). The cross-cultural perspective: Notes toward a comparative psychology of aging. In J. E. Birren and K. W. Schaie (Eds.), *Handbook of the psychology of aging.* (1st ed.) New York: Van Nostrand Reinhold.

Haan, N. (1981). Common dimensions of personality development: Early adolescence to middle life. In D. M. Eichorn, J. Clausen, N. Haan, M. Honzik, & P. Mussen (Eds.), *Present and past in middle life.* New York: Academic Press.

Haan, N., Milsap, R., & Hartka, E. (1986). As time goes by: Change and stability in personality over fifty years. *Psychology and Aging, 1,* 220–232.

Haber, P. A. L. (1987). Nursing homes. In G. L. Maddox (Ed.), *Encyclopedia of aging.* New York: Springer.

Hagberg, J. M. (1987). Effects of training on the decline of VO2max with aging. *Federation Proceedings, 46,* 1830–1833.

Hagestad, G. O. (1982). Divorce: The family ripple effect. *Generations: Journal of the Western Gerontological Society, Winter,* 24–31.

Hagestad, G. O. (1985). Continuity and connectedness. In V. Bengston & J. Robertson (Eds.), *Grandparenthood.* Beverly Hills, CA: Sage.

Hall, G. S. (1922). *Senescence: The last half of life.* New York: Appleton.

Hallihan, M. T. (1979). Structural effects on children's friendships and cliques. *Social Psychology Quarterly, 42,* 43–54.

Hamdani, R. J. (1974). *Exploratory behavior and vocational development among disadvantaged inner-city adolescents.* Unpublished doctoral dissertation. New York: Columbia University.

Hammer, B. J. (1974). *Effects of two treatments designed to foster vocational development in disadvantaged inner-city adolescents.* Unpublished doctoral dissertation. New York: Columbia University.

Harkins, S. W., & Chapman, R. (1976). Detection and decision factors in pain perception in young and elderly men. *Pain, 2,* 253–264.

Harkins, S. W., Price, D. D., & Martelli, M. (1986). Effects of age on pain perception: Thermonociception. *Journal of Gerontology, 41,* 58–63.

Harkness, S., Edwards, C. P., & Super, C. (1981). Social roles and moral reasoning: A case study in a rural African village. *Developmental Psychology, 17,* 595–603.

Harris, C. S. (1978). *Factbook on aging: A profile of America's older population.* Washington, DC: National Council on Aging.

Harris, L. (1976). *The myth and reality of aging in America.* Washington, DC: National Council on Aging.

Hart, R. P., Kwentus, J. A., Hamer, R. M., & Taylor, J. R. (1987). Selective reminding procedures in depression and dementia. *Psychology and Aging, 2,* 111–115.

Hartley, A. A., & Hartley, J. T. (1984). Performance changes in champion swimmers aged thirty to eighty-four. *Experimental Aging Research, 10,* 141–147.

Hartley, A. A., & Hartley, J. T. (1986). Age differences and changes in sprint swimming performances in master athletes, *Experimental Aging Research, 12,* 65–70.

Hartup, W. W., & Lempers, J. (1973). A problem in life-span development: The interactional analysis of family attachment. In P. B. Baltes and K. W. Schaie (Eds.), *Life-span development psychology.* New York: Academic Press.

Harvard Medical School Health Letter Staff. (1989, December). I. W. Bennet (Ed.). All fall down. *Harvard Medical School Health Letter,* pp. 4–6.

Hasher, L., & Zacks, R. T. (1979). Automatic and effortful processes in memory. *Journal of Experimental Psychology: General, 108,* 356–380.

Haung, L., Cartwright, W. S., & Hu, T. (1988). The economic costs of senile dementia in the United States. *Public Health Reports, 103,* 3–7.

Havighurst, R. J. (1972). *Developmental tasks and education* (3rd ed.). New York: David McKay.

Havighurst, R. J. (1973). History of developmental psychology: Socialization and personality development through the life span. In P. B. Baltes & K. W. Schaie (Eds.), *Life-span developmental psychology.* New York: Academic Press.

Havighurst, R. J. (1982). The world of work. In B. J. Wolman (Ed.), *Handbook of developmental psychology.* Englewood Cliffs, NJ: Prentice-Hall.

Havighurst, R. J., McDonald, W. J., Perun, P. J., & Snow, R. B. (1976). *Social scientists and educators: Lives after sixty.* Chicago: Committee on Human Development, University of Chicago.

Hayflick, L. (1977). The cellular basis for biological aging. In C. E. Finch & L. Hayflick (Eds.), *Handbook of the biology of aging.* New York: Van Nostrand Reinhold.

Hayflick, L. (1980). The cell biology of human aging. *Scientific American, 242,* 58–65.

Hayslip, B., Jr., & Leon, J. (1988). Geriatric case practice in hospice settings. Beverly Hills, CA: Sage.

Hayslip, B., Jr., & Panek, P. E. (1989). *Adult development and aging.* New York: Harper & Row.

Heald, J. E. (1977). Midlife career influence. *Vocational Guidance Quarterly, 25,* 309–312.

Heath, H. A., & Orbach, J. (1963). Reversibility of the Necker cube IV: Responses of elderly people. *Perceptual and Motor Skills, 17,* 625–626.

Henderson, G., Tomlinson, B. E., & Gibson, P. H. (1980). Cell counts in human cerebral cortex in normal adults throughout life using an image analyzing computer. *Journal of the Neurological Sciences, 46,* 113–136.

Hendricks, C. D. & Hendricks, S. (1983). *Living, loving, and relating.* Monterey, CA: Brooks/Cole.

Herrmann, D. J., & Neisser, U. (1978). An inventory of everyday memory experiences. In M. M. Gruneberg, P. E. Morris, & R. N. Sykes (Eds.), *Practice aspects of memory.* London: Academic Press.

Hertzog, C., & Schaie, K. W. (1988). Stability and change in adult intelligence: 2. Simultaneous analysis of longitudinal means and covariance structures. *Psychology and Aging, 3,* 122–130.

Herz, D. E. (1988). Employment characteristics of older women. *Monthly Labor Review, 111,* 3–9 (September).

Hess, B. (1971). *Amicability.* Unpublished doctoral dissertation. New Brunswick, NJ: Rutgers University.

Hess, B. (1972). Friendship. In M. W. Riley, M. E. Johnson, & A. Foner (Eds.), *Aging and society, Vol. 3: A sociology of age stratification.* New York: Russell Sage Foundation.

Hess, L. A. (1988). *The depiction of grandparents and their relationships with grandchildren in recent children's literature: Content analysis.* Unpublished master's thesis. State College, PA: Penn State University.

Heston, L. L., & White, J. A. (1983). *Dementia: A practical guide to Alzheimer's disease and related illnesses.* New York: W. H. Freeman.

Hetherington, E. M. (1979). Divorce: A child's perspective. *American Psychologist, 34,* 851–858.

Hetherington, E. M., Cox, M., & Cox, R. (1978). The aftermath of divorce. In J. H. Stevens & M. Mathews (Eds.), *Mother-child/father-child relations.* Washington, DC: National Association for the Education of Young Children.

Hetherington, E. M., Stanley-Hagan, M., & Anderson, E. R. (1989). Marital transitions: A child's perspective. *American Psychologist, 44,* 303–312.

Hickey, T. L., Hickey, L. A., & Kalish, R. A. (1968). Children's perception of the elderly. *Journal of Genetic Psychology, 112,* 227–235.

Hicks, M. W., & Platt, M. (1970). Marital happiness and stability: A review of the research in the sixties. *Journal of Marriage and the Family, 27,* 677–689.

Hillman, D. (1985). Artificial intelligence. *Human Factors, 27,* 21–31.

Hinton, J. M. (1972). *Death* (2nd ed.). Baltimore: Penguin Books.

Hinton, J. M. (1979). Comparison of places and policies for terminal care. *Lancet, 8106 (Jan. 6),* 29–32.

Hoffman, L. W. (1979). Maternal employment. *American Psychologist, 34,* 859–865.

Hoffman, L. W. (1982, April). Social change and its effects on parents and children: Limitations to knowledge. In P. W. Berman & E. R. Ramey (Eds.), *Women: A developmental perspective.* Washington, DC: U.S. Department of Health and Human Services, Public Health Services, National Institute of Health Publication No. 82–2298.

Hoffman, L. W. (1986). Work, family, and the child. In M. S. Pallak & R. O. Perloff (Eds.), *Psychology and work: Productivity, change, and unemployment.* Washington, DC: American Psychological Association.

Holland, J. L. (1973). *Making vocational choices.* Englewood Cliffs, NJ: Prentice-Hall.

Holland, J. L. (1985). *Making vocational choices: A theory of vocational personalities and work environments* (2nd ed.). Englewood Cliffs, NJ: Prentice-Hall.

Holmes, T. H., & Rahe, R. H. (1967). The social readjustment rating scale. *Journal of Psychosomatic Research, 11,* 213–218.

Holte, A. (1978, July). *The interaction of social-cognitive and physiological determinants of peri-menopausal "symptoms."* Paper presented at workshop on sociological, psychological, and anthropological aspects of the menopause. Second international Congress on the Menopause, Jerusalem, Israel.

Holtzmann, W. H. (1981). Cross-cultural comparisons of personality development in Mexico and the United States. In D. A. Wagner & H. W. Stevenson (Eds.), *Cultural perspectives on child development.* San Francisco: Jossey-Bass.

Hooker, K., & Ventis, G. (1984). Work ethic, daily activities and retirement satisfaction. *Journal of Gerontology, 39,* 478–484.

Horn, J. C., & Meer, J. (1987). The vintage years. *Psychology Today, 21,* 76–84.

Horn, J. L. (1970). Organization of data on life-span development of human abilities. In L. R. Goulet & P. B. Baltes (Eds.), *Life-span developmental psychology: Research and theory.* New York: Academic Press.

Horn, J. L. (1982a). The aging of human abilities. In B. B. Wolman (Ed.), *Handbook of developmental psychology.* Englewood Cliffs, NJ: Prentice-Hall.

Horn, J. L. (1982b). The theory of fluid and crystallized intelligence in relation to concepts of cognitive psychology and aging in adulthood. In F. I. M. Craik & S. Trehub (Eds.), *Aging and cognitive processes* (Vol. 8). New York: Plenum.

Horn, J. L., & Donaldson, G. (1976). On the myth of intellectual decline in adulthood. *American Psychologist, 31,* 701–709.

Hornstein, G. A., & Wapner, S. (1985). Modes of experiencing and adapting to retirement. *International Journal of Aging and Human Development, 21,* 291–315.

Hospital Law Manual, 2. (1982). Dying, death, and dead bodies (pp. 39–41). Gaithersburg: Aspen Systems Corporation.

Howard, J. H., Rechnitzer, P. A., Cunningham, D. A., & Donner, A. P. (1986). A change in Type A behavior after retirement. *The Gerontologist, 26,* 643–649.

Hoyer, W. J. (1985). Aging and the development of expert cognition. In T. M. Shlechter & M. P. Toglia (Eds.), *New directions in cognitive science.* Norwood, NJ: Ablex.

Hoyer, W. J. (1986). Toward a knowledge-based conceptualization of adult intellectual development. In C. Schooler & K. W. Schaie (Eds.), *Cognitive functioning and social structures over the life course.* Norwood, NJ: Ablex.

Hoyer, W. J., & Clancy, S. (1987, October). *Age and skill level differences in medical technologists' domain-specific and domain-general visual search conditions.* Paper presented at the meeting of the Human Factors Society, New York.

Hoyer, W. J., Labouvie-Vief, G., & Baltes, P. B. (1973). Modification of response speed deficits and intellectual performance in the elderly. *Human Development, 16,* 233–242.

Hoyer, W. J., & Plude, D. J. (1980). Attentional and perceptual processes in the study of cognitive aging. In L. W. Poon (Ed.), *Aging in the 1980s: Psychological issues.* Washington, DC: American Psychological Association.

Hoyer, W. J., Rebok, G. W., & Sved, S. M. (1979). Effects of varying irrelevant information on adult age differences in problem solving. *Journal of Gerontology, 34,* 553–560.

Hoyer, W. J., Rybash, J. M., & Roodin, P. A. (1989). Cognitive change as a function of knowledge access. In M. L. Commons, J. Sinnott, F. A. Richards, & C. Armon (Eds.), *Beyond formal operations: Comparisons and applications of adolescent and adult models.* New York: Praeger.

Hultsch, D. F. (1971). Adult age differences in free classification and free recall. *Developmental Psychology, 4,* 338–342.

Hultsch, D. F., & Deutsch, F. (1981). *Adult development and aging: A life-span perspective.* New York: McGraw-Hill.

Hultsch, D. F., & Dixon, R. A. (1983). The role of pre-experimental knowledge in text processing. *Experimental Aging Research, 9,* 17–22.

Hultsch, D. F., Hertzog, C., & Dixon, R. A. (1987). Age differences in metamemory: Resolving the inconsistencies. *Canadian Journal of Psychology, 41,* 193–208.

Hultsch, D. F., & Pentz, C. A. (1980). Encoding, storage and retrieval in adult memory: The role of model assumptions. In L. W. Poon, J. L. Fozard, L. S. Cremack, D. Arenberg, & L. W. Thompson (Eds.), *New directions in memory and aging: Proceedings of the George A. Talland memorial conference.* Hillsdale, NJ: Erlbaum.

Hultsch, D. F. & Plemons, J. K. (1979). Life events and life-span development. In P. B. Baltes and O. G. Brim, Jr. (Eds.), *Life-span development and behavior, Vol. 2.* New York: Academic Press.

Hunt, M. (1974). *Sexual behavior in the seventies.* Chicago: Playboy Press.

Hunt, M. & Hunt, B. (1977). *The divorce experience.* New York: McGraw-Hill.

Huston, T. L. & Burgess, R. L. (1979). Social exchange in developing relationships: An overview. In T. L. Huston & R. L. Burgess (Eds.), *Social exchange in developing relationships.* New York: Academic Press.

Huyck, M. H., & Hoyer, W. J. (1982). *Adult development and aging.* Belmont, CA: Wadsworth.

Iaffaldano, M. T., & Muchinsky, P. M. (1985). Job satisfaction and job performance: A meta-analysis. *Psychological Bulletin, 97,* 251–271.

Ingersoll-Dayton, B., & Antonucci, T. C. (1988). Reciprocal and nonreciprocal social support: Contrasting sides of intimate relationships. *Journal of Gerontology, 43,* S65–S73.

Ingram, D. K., Weindruch, R., Spangler, E. L., Freeman, J. R., & Walford, R. L. (1987). Dietary restriction benefits learning and motor performance of aged mice. *Journal of Gerontology, 42,* 78–81.

Inhelder, B., & Piaget, J. (1958). *The growth of logical thinking from childhood to adolescence.* New York: Basic Books.

Jacewicz, M. M., & Hartley, A. A. (1979). Rotation of mental images by young and old college students: The effects of familiarity. *Journal of Gerontology, 34,* 396–403.

Jackson, J. J. (1985). Race, national origin, ethnicity, and aging. In R. H. Binstock & E. Shanas (Eds.), *Handbook of aging and the social sciences* (2nd ed.). New York: Van Nostrand Reinhold.

Jackson, J. S. (1988). *The black American elderly.* New York: Springer.

Jacobs, J. A. (1989). *Revolving doors: Sex segregation in women's careers.* Stanford, CA: Stanford University Press.

James, A., James, W. L., & Smith, H. L. (1984). Reciprocity as a coping strategy of the elderly: A rural Irish perspective. *The Gerontologist, 24,* 483–489.

James, W. (1890). *The principles of psychology* (Vol. 1). New York: Holt, Rinehart & Winston.

Jarvik, L. (1987, November). *The aging of the brain: How to prevent it.* Paper presented at the annual meeting of the Gerontological Society of America, Washington, DC.

Jarvik, L. (1988). Aging of the brain: How can we prevent it? *The Gerontologist, 28,* 739–747.

Jenkins, J. J. (1979). Four points to remember: A tetrahedral model of memory experiments. In L. S. Cremack & F. I. M. Craik (Eds.), *Levels of processing in human memory.* Hillsdale, NJ: Erlbaum.

Johnson, C. L. (1985). Grandparenting options in divorcing families: An anthropological perspective. In V. L. Bengston & J. Robertson (Eds.), *Grandparenthood.* Beverly Hills, CA: Sage.

Johnson, C. L. (1988). Active and latent functions of grandparenting during the divorce process. *The Gerontologist, 28,* 185–191.

Johnson, S. H. (1987, May). *Originality, creativity, and the finding of problems.* Paper presented at the annual meeting of the Jean Piaget Society, Philadelphia.

Johnson, S. H. (1990, March). *Quantitative and qualitative age differences in speed of performance.* Paper presented at the third Biennial Conference on cognitive aging, Atlanta, GA.

Johnson, S. H. (in press). Creativity, originality, and the finding of problems. *Genetic Epistemologist.*

Johnson, S. H. & Rybash, J. M. (1989, June). *Toward a computational approach to senescent visual cognition: Generalized slowing reconsidered.* Paper presented at the annual conference of the Society for Adult Development, Cambridge, MA: Harvard University.

Jones, H. E., & Conrad, H. S. (1933). The growth and decline of intelligence: A study of a homogeneous group between the ages of ten and sixty. *Genetic Psychology Monographs, 13,* 223–294.

Jones, W., Chernovetz, M. E., & Hansson, R. O. (1978). The enigma of androgyny: Differential implications for males and females? *Journal of Consulting and Clinical Psychology, 46,* 278–313.

Jung, C. C. (1933). *Modern man in search of a soul.* New York: Harcourt, Brace, and World.

Jung, C. C. (1960). The stages of life. In *Collected works, Vol. 8.* Princeton, NJ: Princeton University Press.

Kacerguis, M. A. & Adams, G. R. (1978). *Erikson stage resolution: The relationship between identity and intimacy.* Unpublished manuscript, Utah State University, Provo.

Kagan, J. (1979). Family experience and the child's development. *American Psychologist, 34,* 886–891.

Kagan, J. (1980). Perspectives on continuity. In O. G. Brim, Jr. & J. Kagan (Eds.), *Constancy and change in human development.* Cambridge, MA: Harvard University Press.

Kagan, J. & Madsen, M. C. (1972). Experimental analysis of cooperation and competition of Anglo-American and Mexican children. *Developmental Psychology, 6,* 49–59.

Kahana, B., & Kahana, E. (1970). Grandparenting from the perspective of the developing grandchild. *Developmental Psychology, 3,* 98–105.

Kahneman, D. (1973). *Attention and effort.* Englewood Cliffs, NJ: Prentice-Hall.

Kalbfleisch, J., & Lawless, J. (1988). *A comment on estimation of incubation periods and epidemic parameters based on data on AIDS patients infected by blood transfusions.* (Technical Report Series Stat-87–24). Canada: University of Waterloo, Department of Statistics and Actuarial Science.

Kalish, R. A. (1981). *Death, grief, and caring relationships.* Monterey, CA: Brooks-Cole.

Kalish, R. A. (1985). The social context of death and dying. In R. H. Binstock and E. Shanas (Eds.), *Handbook of aging and the social sciences* (2nd ed.). New York: Van Nostrand Reinhold.

Kalish, R. A. (1987). Death. In G. L. Maddox (Ed.), *Encyclopedia of aging.* New York: Springer.

Kalish, R. A. & Reynolds, D. K. (1981). *Death and ethnicity: A psychosocial study.* (Original work published 1976) Farmingdale, NY: Baywood.

Kanner, A. D., Coyne, J. C., Schaefer, C., & Lazarus, R. S. (1981). Comparison of two modes of stress measurement: Daily hassles and uplifts versus major life events. *Journal of Behavioral Medicine, 4,* 1–39.

Kaplan, H. S. (1974). *The new sex therapy.* New York: Brunner/Mazel.

Kaprio, J., Kosenvuo, M., & Rita, H. (1987). Mortality after bereavement: A prospective study of 95,647 widowed persons. *American Journal of Public Health, 77,* 283.

Karuza, J., Calkins, E., Duffey, J., & Feather, J. (1988). Networking in aging: A challenge, model, and evaluation. *The Gerontologist, 28,* 147–156.

Kaslow, F. W., & Schwartz, L. I. (1987). *The dynamics of divorce: A life cycle perspective.* New York: Brunner/Mazel.

Kasper, J. D. (1988). Aging alone: Profiles and projections. *Report of the Commonwealth Fund Commission: Elderly People Living Alone.* Baltimore: Commonwealth Fund Commission.

Kastenbaum, R. (1969). Death and bereavement in later life. In A. H. Kutscher (Ed.), *Death and bereavement.* Springfield, IL: Charles C. Thomas.

Kastenbaum, R. (1981). *Death, society, and human experience* (2nd ed.). Palo Alto, CA: Mayfield.

Kastenbaum, R. (1985). Death and dying: A life-span approach. In J. E. Birren and K. W. Schaie (Eds.), *Handbook of the psychology of aging* (2nd ed.). New York: Van Nostrand Reinhold.

Katchadourian H. (1985). *Fundamentals of human sexuality* (4th ed.). New York: Holt, Rinehart & Winston.

Katchadourian, H. (1987). *Fifty: Midlife in perspective.* New York: W. H. Freeman.

Katzman, R. (1986). Alzheimer's disease. *New England Journal of Medicine, 314,* 964–973.

Kaufman, H. H., and Lynn, J. (1986). Brain death: Perspectives on neurological practice. *Neurosurgery 19,* 850–855.

Kay, D. W. K., & Bergmann, K. (1980). Epidemiology of mental disorders among the aged in the community. In J. E. Birren & R. B. Sloane (Eds.), *Handbook of mental health and aging.* Englewood Cliffs, NJ: Prentice-Hall.

Keating, D. P. (1980). Adolescent thinking. In J. Adleson (Ed.), *Handbook of adolescent psychology.* New York: Wiley.

Keith, P. M. (1981–1982). Perceptions of time remaining and distance from death. *Omega, 12,* 307–318.

Kelley, J. B. (1982). Divorce: The adult perspective. In B. J. Wolman (Ed.), *Handbook of developmental psychology.* New York: Van Nostrand Reinhold.

Kelley, J. B. (1987, August). Children of divorce: Long-term effects and clinical implications. Paper presented at the annual meetings of the American Psychological Association, New York.

Kemp, B. (1985). Rehabilitation and the older adult. In J. E. Birren and K. W. Schaie (Eds.), *Handbook of the psychology of aging* (2nd ed.). New York: Van Nostrand Reinhold.

Kenshalo, D. R. (1977). Age changes in touch, vibration, temperature, kinesthesis, and pain sensitivity. In J. E. Birren & K. W. Schaie (Eds.), *Handbook of the psychology of aging.* New York: Van Nostrand Reinhold.

Kephart, W. M. (1967). Some correlates of romantic love. *Journal of Marriage and the Family, 29,* 470–474.

Kernberg, O. (1980). Love, the couple, and the group: A psychoanalytic frame. *The Psychoanalytic Quarterly, 69,* 78–108.

Kety, S. (1980). Foreword: Bringing knowledge to bear on the mental dysfunctions associated with aging. In J. E. Birren & R. B. Sloane (Eds.), *Handbook of mental health and aging.* Englewood Cliffs, NJ: Prentice-Hall.

Kidd, A. H. & Feldman, B. M. (1981). Pet ownership and self-perceptions of older people. *Psychological Reports, 48,* 867–875.

Kiloh, L. G. (1961). Pseudodementia. *Acta Psychiatrica Scandanavica, 37,* 336–351.

King, P. M., Kitchener, K. S., Davison, M. L., Parker, C. A., & Wood, P. K. (1983). The justification of beliefs in young adults: A longitudinal study. *Human Development, 26,* 106–116.

Kinsbourne, M. (1980). Attentional dysfunctions in the elderly: Theoretical models and research perspectives. In L. W. Poon, J. L. Fozard, L. S. Cremack, D. Arenberg, & L. W. Thompson (Eds.), *New directions in memory and aging: Proceedings of the George A. Talland memorial conference.* Hillsdale, NJ: Erlbaum.

Kinsey, A. C., Pomeroy, W. B., & Martin, C. (1948). *Sexual behavior in the human male.* Philadelphia: W. B. Saunders.

Kinsey, A. C., Pomeroy, W. B., & Martin, C. (1953). *Sexual behavior in the human female.* Philadelphia: W. B. Saunders.

Kitch, D. L. (1987). Hospice. In R. J. Corsini (Ed.), *Concise encyclopedia of psychology.* New York: Wiley.

Kitchener, K. S., & King, P. M. (1981). Reflective judgment: Concepts of justification and their relationship to age and education. *Journal of Applied Developmental Psychology, 2,* 89–111.

Kitchener, K. S., & Wood, P. K. (1987). Development of concepts of justification in German university students. *International Journal of Behavioral Development, 10,* 171–186.

Kivela, S. L. (1985). Relationship between suicide, homicide, and accidental death among the aged in Finland in 1951–1979. *Acta Psychiatrica Scandinavica, 72,* 155–160.

Kivnick, H. Q. (1983). Dimensions of grandparental meaning: Deductive conceptualization and empirical derivation. *Journal of Personality and Social Psychology, 44,* 1056–1068.

Kivnick, H. Q. (1985). Grandparenthood and mental health: Meaning behavior and satisfaction. In V. L. Bengston & J. Robertson (Eds.), *Grandparenthood.* Beverly Hills, CA: Sage.

Klagsbrun, F. (1985). *Married people staying together in the age of divorce.* New York: Bantam Books.

Klahr, D., & Wallace, J. G. (1975). *Cognitive development: An information-processing view.* Hillsdale, NJ: Erlbaum.

Klar, V. A. (1962). Senescent forgetfulness: Benign and malignant. *Canadian Medical Association Journal, 86,* 257–260.

Kleemeier, R. W. (1972). Intellectual change in the senium. *Proceedings of the Social Statistics Section of the American Statistical Association, 1,* 290–295.

Kliegel, R. (1990, April). *On the triangulation of adult age differences in developmental reserve capacity.* Paper presented at the annual meetings of the Cognitive Aging Society, Atlanta.

Kline, D. W., & Schieber, F. (1985). Vision and aging. In J. E. Birren & K. W. Schaie (Eds.), *Handbook of the psychology of aging* (2nd ed.). New York: Van Nostrand Reinhold.

Kline, D. W., & Szafran, J. (1975). Age differences in backward monoptic visual noise masking. *Journal of Gerontology, 30,* 307–311.

Knox, D. (1985). *Choices in relationships.* St. Paul, MN: West.

Kobasa, S. C. (1979). Stressful life events, personality, and health: An inquiry into hardiness. *Journal of Personality and Social Psychology, 37,* 1–11.

Koff, T. H. (1981). *Hospice: A caring community.* Cambridge, MA: Winthrop.

Kohlberg, L. (1958). *The development of mode of moral thinking and choice in the years ten to sixteen.* Unpublished doctoral dissertation, University of Chicago.

Kohlberg, L. (1964). Development of moral character and moral ideology. In L. W. Hoffman and M. L. Hoffman (Eds.), *Review of child development research, Vol. 1.* New York: Russell Sage Foundation.

Kohlberg, L. (1969). Stage and sequence: The cognitive-developmental approach to socialization. In D. Goslin (Ed.), *Handbook of socialization theory and research.* Chicago: Rand McNally.

Kohlberg, L. (1973). Continuities in childhood and adult moral development revisited. In P. B. Baltes & K. W. Schaie (Eds.), *Life-span developmental psychology: Personality and socialization.* New York: Academic Press.

Kohlberg, L. (1976). Moral stages and moralization: The cognitive-developmental approach. In T. Lickona (Ed.), *Moral development and behavior: Theory, research, and social issues.* New York: Holt, Rinehart & Winston.

Kohlberg, L. (1984). *Essays on moral development: The psychology of moral development* (Vol. 2). San Francisco: Harper & Row.

Kohlberg, L. (1987). The development of moral judgment and moral action. In L. Kohlberg (Ed.), *Child development and childhood education: A cognitive-developmental view.* New York: Longman Press.

Kohlberg, L., & Candee, D. (1984). The relationship of moral judgment to moral action. In W. M. Kurtines & J. L. Gewirtz (Eds.), *Morality, moral behavior, and moral development.* New York: Wiley.

Kohlberg, L., & Kramer, R. B. (1969). Continuities and discontinuities in childhood and adult moral development. *Human development, 12,* 93–120.

Kolata, G. (1985). Down's syndrome—Alzheimer's disease linked. *Science, 230,* 1152–1153.

Kolb, B. & Whishaw, I. Q. (1985). *Fundamentals of human neuropsychology* (2nd ed.). New York: W. H. Freeman.

Koplowitz, H. (1984). A projection beyond Piaget's formal operations stage: A general system stage and a unitary stage. In M. L. Commons, F. A. Richards, & C. Armon (Eds.), *Beyond formal operations: Late adolescent and adult cognitive development.* New York: Praeger.

Kosnik, W., Winslow, L., Kline, D., Rasinski, K., & Sekuler, R. (1988). Visual changes in daily life throughout adulthood. *Journal of Gerontology, 43,* P63–P70.

Kosslyn, S. M. (1988). Aspects of a cognitive neuroscience of mental imagery. *Science, 240,* 1621–1626.

Kozol, J. (1988). *Rachel and her children: Homeless families in America.* New York: Fawcett.

Kral, K. (1962). Senescent forgetfulness: Benign and malignant. *Canadian Medical Association Journal, 86,* 257–260.

Kramer, D. A. (1983). Postformal operations: A need for further conceptualization. *Human Development, 26,* 91–105.

Kramer, D. A., & Woodruff, D. A. (1986). Relativistic and dialectic thought in three adult age-groups. *Human Development, 29,* 280–290.

Kraus, N. (1987). Understanding the stress process linking social support with locus-of-control beliefs. *Journal of Gerontology, 42,* 589–593.

Kraus, R. (1978). *Recreation and leisure in modern society* (2nd ed.). Santa Monica, CA: Goodyear.

Krauskopf, J. M., & Burnett, J. M. (1983). When protection becomes abuse. *Trial, December,* 61–76.

Kubler-Ross, E. (1969). *On death and dying.* New York: MacMillan.

Kubler-Ross, E. (1974). *Questions and answers on death and dying.* New York: MacMillan.

Kubler-Ross, E. (1981). Living with dying. New York: MacMillan.

Kuhn, D., & Angelev, J. (1976). An experimental study of the development of formal-operational thought. *Child Development, 47,* 697–706.

Kuhn, D., & Bannock, J. (1977). Development of the isolation-of-variables scheme in experimental and "natural experiment" contexts. *Developmental Psychology, 13,* 9–14.

Kuhn, D., Langer, J., Kohlberg, L., & Haan, N. (1977). The development of formal operations in logical and moral thought. *Genetic Psychology Monographs, 95,* 97–188.

Kuhn, T. S. (1970). *The structure of scientific revolutions* (2nd ed.). Chicago: University of Chicago Press.

Kurdek, L. A. (1981). An integrative perspective on children's divorce adjustment. *American Psychologist, 36,* 856–866.

Kurdek, L. A., & Schmitt, J. P. (1985–1986). Relationship quality of gay men in closed or open relationships. *Journal of Homosexuality, 12,* 85–99.

Kuwabara, T. (1979). Age-related changes in the eye. In S. S. Hain & D. H. Coons (Eds.), *Special senses and aging.* Ann Arbor, MI: Institute of Gerontology, University of Michigan.

Kuypers, J. A. (1981). Ego functioning in old age: Early adult life antecedents. In J. Hendricks (Ed.), *Being and becoming old.* Farmingdale, NY: Baywood.

Labouvie-Vief, G. (1982). Dynamic development and mature autonomy. *Human Development, 25,* 161–191.

Labouvie-Vief, G. (1984). Logic and self-regulation from youth to maturity. In M. L. Commons, F. A. Richards, & C. Armon (Eds.), *Beyond formal operations: Late adolescent and adult cognitive development.* New York: Praeger.

Labouvie-Vief, G. (1985). Intelligence and cognition. In J. E. Birren & K. W. Schaie (Eds.), *Handbook of the psychology of aging* (2nd ed.), New York: Van Nostrand Reinhold.

Labouvie-Vief, G., DeVoe, M., & Bulka, D. (1989). Speaking about feelings: Conceptions of emotions across the life-span. *Psychology and Aging, 4,* 425–437.

Labouvie-Vief, G., & Schell, D. A. (1982). Learning and memory in later life. In B. B. Wolman (Ed.), *Handbook of developmental psychology.* Englewood Cliffs, NJ: Prentice-Hall.

Lachman, J. L., & Lachman, R. (1980). Age and the actualization of world knowledge. In L. W. Poon, J. L. Fozard, L. S. Cremack, D. Arenberg, & L. W. Thompson (Eds.), *New directions in memory and aging: Proceedings of the George A. Talland memorial conference.* Hillsdale, NJ: Erlbaum.

Lachman, M. E. (1986). Personal control in later life: Stability change, and cognitive correlates. In M. M. Baltes and P. B. Baltes (Eds.), *Aging and the psychology of control.* Hillsdale, NJ: Erlbaum.

Lachman, M. E., Steinberg, E. S., & Trotter, S. D. (1987). Effects of controlling beliefs and attributions on memory self-assessments and performance. *Psychology and Aging, 2,* 266–271.

Lack, S., and Buckingham, R. W. (1978). *First American hospice:Three years of home care.* New Haven, CT: Hospice, Inc.

Lamberson, S. D., & Fischer, K. W. (1988). Optimal and functional levels in cognitive development: The individual's developmental range. *Newsletter of the International Society for the Study of Behavioral Development, 2,* 1–4.

Langer, E. J., & Rodin, J. (1976). The effects of choice and enhanced personal responsibility for the aged: A field experiment in an institutionalized setting. *Journal of Personality and Social Psychology, 34,* 191–198.

Langer, E. J., Rodin, J., Beck, P., Weinman, C., & Spitzer, L. (1979). Environmental determinants of memory improvement in late adulthood. *Journal of Personality and Social Psychology, 37,* 2003–2013.

Langer, J. (1969). *Theories of development.* New York: Holt, Rinehart & Winston.

Larsen, M. E. (1973). Humbling cases for career counselors. *Phi Delta Kappan, 54,* 374.

Larson, R. (1978). Thirty years of research on the subjective well-being of older Americans. *Journal of Gerontology, 33,* 109–125.

Larson, R., Zuzanek, J. & Mannel, R. (1985). Being alone versus being with people: Disengagement in the daily experience of older adults. *Journal of Gerontology, 40,* 375–381.

LaRue, A., Dessonville, C., & Jarvik, L. F. (1985). Aging and mental disorders. In J. E. Birren & K. W. Schaie (Eds.), *Handbook of the psychology of aging* (2nd ed.). New York: Van Nostrand Reinhold.

LaRue, A., & Jarvik, L. F. (1982). Old age and behavioral change. In B. B. Wolman (Ed.), *Handbook of developmental psychology.* Englewood Cliffs, NJ: Prentice-Hall.

Lau, E. E., & Kosberg, J. I. (1979). Abuse of the elderly by informal care providers. *Aging* (Sept: Oct.), 11–15.

Lauer, J., & Lauer, R. (1985). Marriages made to last. *Psychology Today, 19,* 22–26.

Lawton, M. P. (1977). The impact of the environment on aging and behavior. *Handbook of the psychology of aging.* New York: Van Nostrand Reinhold.

Lawton, M. P. (1980a). *Environment and aging.* Monterey, CA: Brooks/Cole.

Lawton, M. P. (1980b). Housing and the elderly: Residential quality and residential satisfaction. *Research on Aging, 2,* 309–329.

Lazarus, R. S., & DeLongis, A. (1983). Psychological stress and coping in aging. *American Psychologist, 38,* 245–254.

Lazarus, R. S., & Folkman, S. (1984). *Stress, appraisal, and coping.* New York: Springer.

Lebra, T. (1979). The dilemma and strategies of aging among contemporary Japanese women. *Ethnology, 18,* 336–353.

Lee, G. R. (1978). Marriage and morale in late life. *Journal of Marriage and the Family, 40,* 131–139.

Lefebvre-Pinard, M. (1984). Taking charge of one's cognitive activity: A moderator of competence. In E. Neimark (Ed.), *Moderators of competence.* Hillsdale, NJ: Erlbaum.

Lehman, H. C. (1953). *Age and achievement.* Princeton, NJ: Princeton University Press.

Lehman, H. C. (1960). The age decrement in outstanding scientific creativity. *American Psychologist, 15,* 128–134.

Lepper, M. R., & Greene, D. (1975). Training play into work: Effects of adult surveillance and extrinsic rewards on children's intrinsic motivation. *Journal of Personality and Social Psychology, 31,* 479–486.

Lerner, M. (1970). When, why, and where people die. In O. G. Brim, H. E. Freeman, S. Levine, and N. A. Scotch (Eds.), *The dying patient.* New York: Russell Sage Foundation.

LeShan, O. L. (1969). Psychotherapy and the dying patient. In L. Pearson (Ed.), *Death and the dying.* Cleveland: Case Western Reserve University Press.

Letzeller, M., Jungerman, C., & Freitage, W. (1986). Swimming performance in old age. *Zeitschrift fur Gerontologie, 19,* 389–395.

Levine, P., Janda, J. K., Joseph, J. A., Ingram, D. K., & Roth, G. S. (1981). Dietary restriction retards the age-associated loss of rat striatal dopaminergic receptors. *Science, 214,* 516–562.

Levinger, G. (1970). Husbands' and wives' estimates of coital frequency. *Medical Aspects of Human Sexuality, 4,* 42–57.

Levinger, G. (1974). A three-level approach to attraction: Toward an understanding of pair relatedness. In T. L. Huston (Ed.), *Foundations of interpersonal attraction.* New York: Academic Press.

Levinger, G. (1978, August). *Models of close relationships: Some new directions.* Invited address, annual meeting of the American Psychological Association, Toronto.

Levinson, D. J. (1978). *The seasons of a man's life.* New York: Knopf.

Levinson, D. J. (1980). Toward a conception of the adult life course. In N. J. Smelser & E. H. Erikson (Eds.), *Themes of work and love in adulthood.* Cambridge, MA: Harvard University Press.

Levinson, D. J. (1986). A conception of adult development. *American Psychologist, 41,* 3–13.

Levinson, D. J. (1987, August). *The seasons of a woman's life.* Paper presented at the annual meeting of the American Psychological Association, New York.

Levinson, R. J. (1987). Euthanasia. In G. L. Maddox (Ed.), *The encyclopedia of aging.* New York: Springer.

Lewin, R. (1987). Dramatic results with brain grafts. *Science, 237,* 245–247.

Libby, R. W. & Whitehurst, R. N. (1977). *Marriage and alternatives: Exploring intimate relationships.* Glenview, IL: Scott Foresman.

Lichtenberg, P. A., & Strzepek, D. M. (1990). Assessments of institutionalized dementia patients' competencies to participate in intimate relationships. *The Gerontologist, 30,* 117–120.

Lifson, A. (1988). Do alternative models for transmission of HIV exist? *Journal of the American Medical Association, 259,* 1353–1356.

Lifton, R. J. (1977). The sense of immortality: On death and the continuity of life. In H. Feifel (Ed.), *New meanings of death.* New York: McGraw-Hill.

Light, L. L., & Singh, A. (1987). Implicit and explicit memory in young and older adults. *Journal of Experimental Psychology: Learning, Memory, and Cognition, 13,* 531–541.

Lindmann, E. (1944). Symptomatology and management of acute grief. *American Journal of Psychiatry, 101,* 141–148.

Lindvall, O., Brundin, P., Widner, H., Rehnorona, S., Gustavii, B., Frackowiak, R., Leenders, K., Sawle, G., Rothwell, J., Marsden, C., & Bjorklund, A. (1990). Grafts of fetal dopamine survive and improve motor function in Parkinson's disease. *Science, 247,* 574–577.

Lipowski, Z. J. (1980). *Delerium.* Springfield, IL: Charles C. Thomas.

Litz, B. T., Zeiss, A. M., Davies, H. T. (1990). Sexual concerns of male spouses of female Alzheimer's disease patients. *The Gerontologist, 30,* 113–116.

Liu, K., Doty, P., & Manton, K. (1990). Medicaid spend-down in nursing homes. *The Gerontologist, 30,* 7–16.

Livson, F. B. (1976). Patterns of development in middle-aged women: A longitudinal study. *International Journal of Aging and Human Development, 7,* 107–115.

Livson, N., & Peskin, H. (1981). Psychological health at age forty: Prediction from adolescent personality. In D. M. Eichorn, J. Clausen, H. Haan, M. Honzik, & P. Mussen (Eds.), *Present and past in middle life.* New York: Academic Press.

Locksley, A., & Colten, M. E. (1979). Psychological androgyny: A case of mistaken identity. *Journal of Personality and Social Psychology, 37,* 1017–1031.

Longino, C. F. (1988). Who are the oldest Americans? *The Gerontologist, 28,* 515–523.

Lonky, E., Kaus, C., & Roodin, P. A. (1984). Life experience and mode of coping: Relation to moral judgment in adulthood. *Developmental Psychology, 20,* 1159–1167.

Lopata, H. Z. (1979). *Widowhood in an American city.* Cambridge, MA: Schenkman.

Lopata, H. Z. (1987a). Widowhood. In G. L. Maddox (Ed.), *Encyclopedia of aging.* New York: Springer.

Lopata, H. Z. (1987b). *Widows: The Middle East, Asia, and the Pacific.* Durham, NC: Duke University Press.

Loveridge-Sanbonmatsu, J. (1989, April). *Personal communication.* Oswego, NY: SUNY College at Oswego, Department of Communication.

Lowenthal, M. (1964). *Lives in distress.* New York: Basic Books.

Lowenthal, M. F., & Robinson, B. (1976). Social networks and isolation. In R. H. Binstock & E. Shanas (Eds.), *Handbook of aging and the social sciences.* New York: Van Nostrand Reinhold.

Lowenthal, M., Turnher, M., & Chiriboga, D. (1975). *Four stages of life: A comparative study of women and men facing transitions.* San Francisco: Jossey-Bass.

Lowman, C., & Kirchener, C. (1979). Elderly blind and visually impaired persons: Projected numbers in the year 2000. *Journal of Visual Impairment and Blindness, 73,* 73–74.

Lubomudrov, S. (1988). Congressional perceptions of the elderly: The use of stereotypes in the legislative process. *The Gerontologist, 27,* 77–81.

Ludeman, K. (1981). The sexuality of the older person: Review of the literature. *The Gerontologist, 21,* 203–208.

Luria, Z., & Rose, M. D. (1981). *Psychology of human sexuality.* New York: Wiley.

Lyons, N. (1983). Two perspectives: On self, relationships, and morality. *Harvard Educational Review, 53,* 125–145.

Lyons, R. D. (1983, October). Sex in America: Conservative attitudes prevail. *New York Times,* pp. 17 and 19.

Maas, H. S., & Kuypers, J. A. (1974). *From thirty to seventy.* San Francisco: Jossey-Bass.

Macklin, E. (1980). Nontraditional family forms: A decade of research. *Journal of Marriage and the Family, 42,* 905–922.

Mackworth, N. H. (1965). Originality. *American Psychologist, 20,* 51–66.

Madden, D. J. (1986). Adult age differences in attentional capacity demands of visual search. *Cognitive Development, 1,* 335–363.

Madden, D. J. (1987). Aging, attention, and the use of meaning during visual search. *Cognitive Development, 2,* 201–216.

Madden, D. J., & Nebes, R. D. (1981, November). *Age effects in selective attention during visual search.* Paper presented at the meeting of the Gerontological Society of America, Toronto.

Maddi, S. (1986, August). *The great stress-illness controversy.* Paper presented at the meeting of the American Psychological Association, Washington, DC.

Maddox, G. L. (1964a). Disengagement theory: A critical evaluation. *The Gerontologist, 4,* 80–83.

Maddox, G. L. (1964b). Persistence of life-style among the elderly. In B. Neugarten (Ed.), *Middle age and aging.* Chicago: University of Chicago Press.

Madrazo, I., Drucker-Colin, R., Diaz, V., Martinez-Matu, J., Torres, C., & Becerril, J. (1987). Open microsurgical autograft of adrenal medulla to the right caudate nucleus in two patients with intractable Parkinson's disease. *The New England Journal of Medicine, 316,* 831–834.

Mages, N. L., and Mendelsohn, G. A. (1979). Effects of cancer on patients' lives: A personological approach. In G. C. Stone, F. Cohen, & N. E. Adler (Eds.), *Health Psychology.* San Francisco: Jossey-Bass.

Mancini, J. A., & Orthner, D. K. (1978). Recreational sexuality preference among middle-class husbands and wives. *The Journal of Sex Research, 14,* 96–106.

Mandler, G. (1967). Organization and memory. In K. W. Spence & J. T. Spence (Eds.), *The psychology of learning and motivation 1.* New York: Academic Press.

Mannarino, A. P. (1979). The relationship between friendship and altruism in preadolescent girls. *Psychiatry, 42,* 280–284.

Marshall, V. W. (1980). *Last chapters: A sociology of aging and dying.* Monterey, CA: Brooks/Cole.

Marshall, W. A. (1973). The body. In R. R. Sears & S. S. Feldman (Eds.), *The seven ages of man.* Los Angeles, CA: William Kaufmann.

Marx, J. (1990). Fetal grafts show promise in Parkinson's disease. *Science, 247,* 529.

Mason, S. E., & Smith, A. D. (1977). Imagery and the aged. *Experimental Aging Research, 3,* 17–32.

Masoro, E. J. (1984). Food restriction and the aging process. *Journal of the American Geriatrics Society, 32,* 296–300.

Masoro, E. J. (1988). Food restriction in rodents: An evaluation of its role in the study of aging. *Journal of Gerontology, 43,* B59–B64.

Masters, W. H., & Johnson, V. E. (1966). *Human sexual response.* Boston: Little, Brown.

Masters, W. H., & Johnson, V. E. (1970). *Human sexual inadequacy.* Boston: Little, Brown.

Mayes, A. R. (1986). Learning and memory disorders and their assessment. *Neuropsychologia, 24,* 25–39.

Maymi, C. R. (1982). Women in the labor force. In P. W. Berman & E. R. Ramey (Eds.), *Women: A developmental perspective* (National Institute of Health Publication #82–2298). Washington, DC: Department of Health and Human Services.

McAvoy, L. (1979). The leisure preferences, problems, and needs of the elderly. *Journal of Leisure Research, 11,* 40–47.

McCain, G. & Segal, E. M. (1988). *The game of science* (5th ed.). Pacific Grove, CA: Brooks/Cole.

McCartney, J., Izemen, H., Rogers, D., & Cohen, N. (1987). Sexuality in the institutionalized elderly. *Journal of the American Geriatrics Society, 35,* 331–333.

McCay, C. M., & Crowell, M. F. (1934). Prolonging the life span. *Scientific Monthly, 39,* 405–414.

McClelland, D. C. (1951). *Personality.* New York: McGraw-Hill.

McClelland, D. C., Atkinson, J. W., Clark, R. W., & Lowell, E. L. (1953). *The achievement motive.* New York: Appleton-Century-Crofts.

McClelland, D., Constanian, C., Regaldo, D., and Stone, C. (1978). Making it to maturity. *Psychology Today, 12,* 42–53, 114.

McCormack, P. D. (1981). Temporal coding by young and elderly adults: A test of the Hasher-Zacks model. *Developmental Psychology, 17,* 509–517.

McCrae, R. R., Arenberg, D., & Costa, P. T., Jr. (1987). Declines in divergent thinking with age: Cross-sectional, longitudinal, and cross-sequential analyses. *Psychology and Aging, 2,* 130–137.

McCrae, R. R., & Costa, P. T., Jr. (1982). The self-concept and stability of personality: Cross-sectional comparisons of self-reports and ratings. *Journal of Personality and Social Psychology, 43,* 1282–1292.

McCrae, R. R., & Costa, P. T., Jr. (1984). *Emerging lives and enduring dispositions: Personality in adulthood.* Boston: Little, Brown.

McCrae, R. R., & Costa, P. T., Jr. (1987). Validation of the five-factor model of personality across instruments and observers. *Journal of Personality and Social Psychology, 52,* 81–90.

McDonald, R. T. (1981). The effect of death education on specific attitudes toward death in college students. *Death Education, 3,* 59–66.

McDowd, J. M., & Craik, F. I. M. (1988). The effects of aging and task difficulty on divided attention performance. *Journal of Experimental Psychology: Human Performance and Aging, 14,* 267–280.

McFarland, R. A., Domey, R. G., Warren, A. B., & Ward, D. C. (1960). Dark adaptation as a function of age. I: A statistical analysis. *Journal of Gerontology, 15,* 149–154.

McFarland, R. A., & Fischer, M. B. (1955). Alterations in dark adaptation as a function of age. *Journal of Gerontology, 10,* 424–428.

McGee, R., & Wells, K. (1982). Gender typing and androgyny in later life: New directions for theory and research. *Human Development, 25,* 116–139.

McKain, W. C. (1972). A new look at older marriages. *The Family Coordinator, 21,* 61–69.

McLachlan, D. R. C. (1982). Cellular mechanisms of Alzheimer's disease. In F. I. M. Craik & S. Trehub (Eds.), *Cognitive processes and aging* (Vol. 8). New York: Plenum.

Medical consultants on the diagnosis of death for the study of ethical problems in medicine and biomedical research: President's commission. (1981). *Journal of the American Medical Association, 246,* 2184–2186.

Medvedev, Z. A. (1974). The nucleic acids in development and aging. In B. L. Strehler (Ed.), *Advances in gerontological research* (Vol. 1). New York: Academic Press.

Messinger, L., Walker, K., & Freeman, J. (1978). Preparation for remarriage following divorce: The use of group techniques. *American Journal of Orthopsychiatry, 42,* 264–272.

Metropolitan Insurance Company (1983). 1983 Metropolitan height and weight tables. *Statistical Bulletin, 64,* 2–9.

Metzger, A. M. (1979). A Q-methodological study of the Kubler-Ross stage theory. *Omega, 10,* 291–302.

Meyers, J. (1985). *Hemingway.* New York: Harper & Row.

Miles, L. E., & Dement, W. C. (1980). Sleep and aging. *Sleep, 3,* 119–220.

Miller, G. A., Bashore, T. R., Farwell, L. A., & Donchin, E. (1987). Research in geriatric psychophysiology. In K. W. Schaie, (Ed.), *Advances in geriatrics and gerontology.* New York: Springer-Verlag.

Miller, P. H. (1983). *Theories of developmental psychology.* San Francisco: Freeman Press.

Mischel, W. (1981). *Introduction to personality* (3rd ed.). New York: Holt, Rinehart & Winston.

Mitford, J. A. (1963). *The American way of death.* New York: Simon & Schuster.

Mohs, R. C., Breitner, J. C. S., Silverman, J. M., & Davis, K. I. (1987). Alzheimer's disease: Morbid risk among first-degree relatives approximates 50 percent by ninety years of age. *Archives of General Psychiatry, 44,* 405–408.

Monat, A., & Lazarus, R. S. (Eds.). (1985). *Stress and coping* (2nd ed.). New York: Columbia University.

Mor, V. (1982). The national hospice study: Progress reports. Providence, RI: School of Medicine, Brown University.

Morgan, S. (1978). *Hysterectomy*. New York: Healthright.

Moritz, D. J., Kasl, V., & Berkman, L. F. (1989). The health impact of living with a cognitively impaired elderly spouse: Depressive symptoms and social functioning. *Journal of Gerontology, 44*, S17–S27.

Morris, J. (1982). *Technical reports: National hospice study*. Boston, MA: Hebrew Home for the Rehabilitation of the Aged: Social Gerontology Research Unit.

Morse, W. C., & Weiss, R. S. (1968). The function and meaning of work and the job. In D. G. Zytowski (Ed.), *Vocational behavior*. New York: Holt, Rinehart & Winston.

Moscovitch, M.(1982). A neuropsychological approach to perception and memory in normal and pathological aging. In F. I. M. Craik & S. Trehub (Eds.), *Aging and cognitive processes* (Vol. 8). New York: Plenum.

Moscovitch, M., Winocur, G., & McLachlan, D. (1986). Memory as assessed by recognition and by reading time of normal and transformed script: Evidence from normal young and old people and from patients with severe memory impairments due to Alzheimer's disease and other neurological disorders. *Journal of Experimental Psychology: General, 115*, 331–347.

Moss, M., & Lawton, M. P. (1982). Time budgets of older people: A window on four life-styles. *Journal of Gerontology, 37*, 115–123.

Moss, M. S. and Moss, S. Z. (1983–1984). The impact of parental death on middle-aged children. *Omega*, 74–80.

Mumford, M. D., & Gustafson, S. B. (1988). Creativity syndrome: Integration, application, and innovation. *Psychological Bulletin, 103*, 27–43.

Murdock, B. B. (1967). Recent developments in short-term memory. *British Journal of Psychology, 58,* 421–433.

Murrell, F. H. (1970). The effect of extensive practice on age differences in reaction time. *Journal of Gerontology, 25,* 268–274.

Murstein, B. I. (1982). Marital choice. In B. B. Wolman (Ed.), *Handbook of developmental psychology*. Englewood Cliffs, NJ: Prentice-Hall.

Muschel, I. J. (1984). Pet therapy with terminal cancer patients. *Social Casework, 65,* 451–458.

Mussen, P., Honzik, M., & Eichorn, D. (1982). Early adult antecedents of life satisfaction at age seventy. *Journal of Gerontology, 37*, 316–322.

Myers, D. G. (1986). *Psychology*. New York: Worth.

Myers, G. C., & Manton, K. G. (1984). Recent changes in the U.S. age-at-death distributions: Further observations. *The Gerontologist, 24,* 571–575.

Myers, J. E., & Shelton, B. (1987). Abuse and older persons: Issues and implications for counselors. *Journal of Counseling and Development, 65,* 376–380.

Nagy, M. (1948). The child's theories concerning death. *Journal of Genetic Psychology, 73,* 3–27.

Nahemow, N. R. (1984). Grandparenthood in transition. In K. A. McCluskey & H. W. Reese (Eds.), *Life-span developmental psychology: Historical and generational effects*. New York: Academic Press.

Nahemow, N. R. (1985). The changing nature of grandparenthood. *Medical Aspects of Human Sexuality, 19,* 81–92.

National Center for Health Statistics. (1987a). *Characteristics of the populations below the poverty level*. (Current Population Reports, Series P–60, No. 152). Washington, DC: U.S. Government Printing Office.

National Center for Health Statistics. (1987b). *Health statistics for older persons: United States 1986*. U.S. Department of Health and Human Services, Public Health Services (PHS 87–1409). Washington, DC: U.S. Government Printing Office.

National Center for Health Statistics. (1989). *National nursing home survey: 1989 Summary for the United States.* U.S. Department of Health and Human Services, Centers for Disease Control (DHHS 89–1758). Washington, DC: U.S. Government Printing Office.

National Funeral Directors Association. (1989). *Funeral costs.* Milwaukee, WI: National Funeral Directors Association Resource Center.

National Institute of Aging Task Force. (1980). Senility reconsidered. *Journal of the American Medical Association, 244,* 259–263.

National Institute on Aging (1982). Toward an independent old age: A national plan for research on aging: Report of the National Research on Aging Planning Panel. U.S. Department of Health and Human Services. Public Health Services, National Institutes of Health, National Institute on Aging. Washington, DC: U.S. Government Printing Office, #447-H-1.

National Institutes of Health (1987). Differential diagnosis of dementing diseases. *Census development conference statement.* Washington, DC: U.S. Government Printing Office.

National Institutes of Health (1988, September). Health benefits of pets. National Institutes of Health Technology Assessment Workshop. U.S. Department of Health and Human Services, Washington, DC: U.S. Government Printing Office.

Naveh-Benjamin, M. (1987). Coding of spatial information: An automatic process? *Journal of Experimental Psychology: Learning, Memory, and Cognition, 13,* 595–605.

Neimark, E. D. (1975a). Intellectual development during adolescence. In F. D. Horowitz (Ed.), *Review of child development research* (Vol. 4). Chicago: University of Chicago Press.

Neimark, E. D. (1975b). Longitudinal development of formal operations. *Genetic Psychology Monographs, 91,* 171–225.

Neimark, E. D. (1982). Adolescent thought: Transition to formal operations. In B. B. Wolman (Ed.), *Handbook of developmental psychology.* Englewood Cliffs, NJ: Prentice-Hall.

Nelson, L. D., and Nelson, C. C. (1973). *Religion and death anxiety.* Presentation to the annual joint meeting, Society for the Scientific Study of Religion and Religious Research Association, San Francisco. As cited in Kalish, R. A., (1985). The social context of death and dying. In J. E. Birren and K. W. Schaie, (Eds.), *Handbook of the psychology of aging* (2nd ed.). New York: Van Nostrand Reinhold.

Nesselroade, J. R., Schaie, K. W., & Baltes, P. B. (1972). Ontogenetic and generational components of structural and quantitative change in adult behavior. *Journal of Gerontology, 27,* 222–228.

Neugarten, B. L. (1964). *Personality in middle and late life.* New York: Atherton Press.

Neugarten, B. L. (1968). *Personality in middle and late life* (2nd ed.). New York: Atherton Press.

Neugarten, B. L. (1973). Personality change in late life: A developmental perspective. In C. Eisdorfer & M. P. Lawton (Eds.), *The psychology of adult development and aging.* Washington, DC: American Psychological Association.

Neugarten, B. L. (1975). The future and the young-old. *The Gerontologist, 15,* 4–9.

Neugarten, B. L. (1977). Personality and aging. In J. E. Birren & K. W. Schaie (Eds.), *Handbook of the psychology of aging.* New York: Van Nostrand Reinhold.

Neugarten, B. L. (1980a). Act your age: Must everything be a midlife crisis? In *Annual editions: Human development, 1980/1981,* pp. 289–290. Guilford, CT: Dushkin Publishers.

Neugarten, B. L. (1980b, February). Must everything be a midlife crisis? *Prime Time.*

Neugarten, B. L. (1986). The aging society. In A. Pifer & L. Bronte (Eds.), *Our aging society: Paradox and promise.* New York: Norton.

Neugarten, B. L. (1989). Policy issues for an aging society. *The psychology of aging.* Washington, DC: American Psychological Association.

Neugarten, B. L., & Datan, N. (1973). Sociological perspectives on the life cycle. In P. B. Baltes, & K. W. Schaie (Eds.), *Life-span developmental psychology.* New York: Academic Press.

Neugarten, B. L., & Gutmann, D. L. (1968). Age-sex roles and personality in middle age. In B. L. Neugarten (Ed.), *Middle age and aging.* Chicago: University of Chicago Press.

Neugarten, B. L., Havighurst, R. J., & Tobin, S. S. (1968). Personality and patterns of aging. In B. L. Neugarten (Ed.), *Middle age and aging.* Chicago: University of Chicago Press.

Neugarten, B. L., & Neugarten, D. A. (1987). The changing meanings of age. *Psychology Today, 21*(5), 29–33.

Neugarten, B. L., & Weinstein, K. K. (1964). The changing American grandparent. *Journal of Marriage and the Family, 26,* 199–204.

Neulinger, J. (1981). *The psychology of leisure.* Springfield, IL: Charles C. Thomas.

Newell, A., & Simon, H. A. (1972). *Human problem solving.* Englewood Cliffs, NJ: Prentice-Hall.

Newman, B. M. (1982). Midlife development: In B. B. Wolman (Ed.), *Handbook of developmental psychology.* Englewood Cliffs, NJ: Prentice-Hall.

New York State Department of Health. (1988). *Do-not-resuscitate orders: A guide for patients and families.* Albany, NY: New York State Department of Health.

Niederehe, G., & Burt, D. B. (1986, November). *Depression and memory dysfunction in the aged.* Paper presented at the meeting of the Gerontological Society of America, Chicago, IL.

Nisan, M., & Kohlberg, L. (1982). Universality and cross-cultural variation in moral development: A longitudinal and cross-sectional study in Turkey. *Child Development, 53,* 856–876.

Nord, W. R. (1977). Job satisfaction reconsidered. *American Psychologist, 32,* 1026–1036.

Nowak, C. A. (1977). Does youthfulness equal attractiveness? In L. E. Troll & J. Israel (Eds.), *Looking ahead: A woman's guide to the problems and joys of growing older.* Englewood Cliffs, NJ: Prentice-Hall.

Nydegger, C. (1983). Family ties of the aged in cross-cultural perspective. *The Gerontologist, 23,* 26–31.

Nystrom, E. P. (1974). Activity patterns and leisure concepts among the elderly. *American Journal of Occupational Therapy, 28,* 337–345.

Obrist, W. D., & Bissell, L. F. (1955). The electroencephalogram of aged patients with cardiac and cerebral vascular disease. *Journal of Gerontology, 10,* 315–330.

Ochs, A. L., Newberry, J., Lenhardt, M. L., & Harkins, S. W. (1985). Neural and vestibular aging associated with falls. In J. E. Birren & K. W. Schaie (Eds.), *Handbook of the psychology of aging* (2d ed.). New York: Van Nostrand Reinhold.

Okun, B. F., & Rappaport, L. J. (1980). *Working with other families: An introduction to family therapy.* North Scituate, MA: Duxbury.

Oleshansky, M. E., Gamsky, N. R., & Ramseyer, G. C. (in press). Activity level, purpose in life and repression as predictions of death anxiety in the aged. *Omega.*

Olson, L. W., Harkins, S. W., & Lenhardt, M. (1985). Aging and the auditory system. In J. E. Birren & K. W. Schaie (Eds.), *Handbook of the psychology of aging* (2nd ed.). New York: Van Nostrand Reinhold.

Orgel, L. E. (1973). Aging of clones of mammalian cells. *Nature, 243,* 441–445.

Orlofsky, J. (1976). Intimacy status: Relationship to interpersonal perception. *Journal of Youth and Adolescence, 5,* 73–88.

Orlofsky, J., Marcia, J., & Lesser, I. (1973). Ego identity status and the intimacy versus isolation crisis of young adulthood. *Journal of Personality and Social Psychology, 27,* 211–219.

Ornstein, R., & Thompson, R. F. (1984). *The amazing brain.* Boston: Houghton Mifflin.

Ory, M. G., & Goldberg, E. L. (1983). Pet possession and well-being in elderly women. *Research on Aging, 5,* 389–409.

Osipow, S. H. (1983). *Theories of career development.* Englewood Cliffs, NJ: Prentice-Hall.

Osipow, S. H. (1987). Counseling psychology: Theory, research, and practice in career counseling. *Annual Review of Psychology, 38,* 257–278.

Osterweis, M., Solomon, F., & Green, M. (1984). *Bereavement reactions, consequences, care.* Washington, DC: National Academy of Sciences.

Ostrow, A. C. (1980). Physical activity as it relates to the health of the aged. In N. Data & N. Lohmann (Eds.), *Transitions of aging.* New York: Academic Press.

Over, R. (1989). Age and scholar impact. *Psychology and Aging, 4,* 222–225.

Owens, W. A., Jr. (1966). Age and mental abilities: A second adult follow-up. *Journal of Educational Psychology, 51,* 311–325.

Owsley, C., Sekuler, R., & Siemsen, D. (1983). Contrast sensitivity throughout adulthood. *Vision Research, 23,* 689–699.

Palmore, E. (1969). Predicting longevity: A follow-up controlling for age. *The Gerontologist, 9,* 247–250.

Palmore, E. (Ed.). (1970). *Normal aging.* Durham, NC: Duke University Press.

Palmore, E. (1975). *The honorable elders: A cross-cultural analysis of aging in Japan.* Durham, NC: Duke University Press.

Palmore, E. (1979). Predictors of successful aging. *The Gerontologist, 19,* 427–431.

Palmore, E. (1980). Predictors of longevity. In S. Haynes & M. Feinleib (Eds.), *Epidemiology of aging.* Washington, DC: U.S. Government Printing Office.

Palmore, E. (1982). Predictors of the longevity difference: A twenty-five-year follow-up. *The Gerontologist, 22,* 513–518.

Palmore, E. B. (1984). Consequences of retirement. *Journal of Gerontology, 39,* 109–116.

Palmore, E. B., Burchett, B. M., Fillenbaum, G. C., George, L. K., & Wallman, L. M. (1985). *Retirement: Causes and consequences.* New York: Springer.

Palmore, E. B., George, L. K., & Fillenbaum, G. G. (1982). Predictors of retirement. *Journal of Gerontology, 37,* 733–742.

Palmore, E. B., & Jefferies, F. C. (1971). *Prediction of the life span.* Lexington, MA: Heath.

Palmore, E., & Maeda, D. (1985). *The honorable elders revisited.* Durham, NC: Duke University Press.

Paloma, M., Pendelton, B. F., & Garland, T. N. (1982). Reconsidering the dual-career marriage: A longitudinal approach. In J. Aldous (Ed.), *Two paychecks: Life in dual-earner families.* Beverly Hills, CA: Sage.

Panek, P. E. (1982). Relationship between field-dependence/independence and personality in older adult females. *Perceptual and Motor Skills, 54,* 811–814.

Papalia, D. E. (1972). The status of several conservation abilities across the life span. *Human Development, 15,* 229–243.

Papalia, D., & Bielby, P. (1974). Cognitive functioning in middle and old age adults: A review of research on Piaget's theory. *Human Development, 17,* 424–443.

Parkes, C. M. (1964). The effects of bereavement on physical and mental health—A study of the medical records of widows. *British Medical Journal, 2,* 274–279.

Parkes, C. M. (1970). "Seeking" and "finding" a lost object. *Social Science and Medicine, 4,* 187–201.

Parkes, C. M. (1972). *Bereavement: Studies of grief in adult life.* New York: International University Press.

Parnes, H. W., Crowley, J. E., Haurin, R. J., Less, L. J., Morgan, W. R., Mott, F. L., & Nestel, G. (1985). *Retirement among American men.* Lexington, KY: Lexington Books.

Pattison, E. M. (1977). *The experience of dying.* Englewood Cliffs, NJ: Prentice-Hall.

Pavio, A. (1979). *Imagery and verbal processes.* Hillsdale, NJ: Erlbaum. (Original work published 1971)

Pearlin, L. I. (1985). Life strains and psychological distress among adults. In A. Monat & R. S. Lazarus (Eds.), *Stress and coping: An anthology* (2nd ed.). New York: Columbia University Press.

Pearlin, L. I., & Lieberman, M. A. (1977). Social sources of emotional distress. In R. Simmons (Ed.), *Research in community mental health.* Greenwich, CT: J. A. I. Press.

Pearlman, R. A., & Uhlman, R. F. (1988). Quality of life in chronic diseases: Perceptions of elderly patients. *Journal of Gerontology, 43,* M25–M30.

Pepper, L. G. (1976). Patterns of leisure and adjustment to retirement. *The Gerontologist, 16,* 441–446.

Pepper, S. C. (1942). *World hypotheses.* Berkeley, CA: University of California Press.

Perlmutter, M. (1978). What is memory aging the aging of? *Developmental Psychology, 14,* 330–345.

Perlmutter, M. (1980). An apparent paradox about memory aging. In L. W. Poon, J. L. Fozard, L. S. Cremack, D. Arenberg, & L. W. Thompson (Eds.), *New directions in memory and aging: Proceedings of the George A. Talland Memorial Conference.* Hillsdale, NJ: Erlbaum.

Perlmutter, M. (1986). A life-span view of memory. In P. B. Baltes, D. Featherman, & R. Lerner (Eds.), *Advances in life-span development and behavior* (Vol. 7). Hillsdale, NJ: Erlbaum.

Perlmutter, M., Metzger, R., Nezworski, T., & Miller, K. (1981). Spatial and temporal memory in twenty- and sixty-year-olds. *Journal of Gerontology, 36,* 59–65.

Perlmutter, M., & Mitchell, D. B. (1982). The appearance and disappearance of age differences in adult memory. In F. I. M. Craik & S. Trehub (Eds.), *Aging and cognitive processes* (Vol. 8). New York: Plenum.

Perlow, M. F., Freed, W. J., Hoffer, B. J., Seiger, A., Olson, L., & Wyatt, R. J. (1979). Brain grafts reduce motor abnormalities produced by destruction of nigrostriatal dopamine system. *Science, 204,* 643–647.

Perry, W. B. (1968). *Forms of intellectual and ethical development in the college years: A scheme.* New York: Holt, Rinehart & Winston.

Person, D. C., & Wellman, H. M. (1987, November). *Implicit theories of memory beliefs.* Paper presented at the meeting of Gerontological Society of America, Washington, DC.

Peskin, H., & Livson, N. (1981). Uses of the past in adult psychological health. In D. M. Eichorn, J. Clausen, N. Haan, M. Honzik, & P. Mussen (Eds.), *Present and past in middle life.* New York: Academic Press.

Peterman, T., Stoneburner, R., Allen, J., Jaffe, H., & Curran, J. (1988). Risk of HIV transmission from heterosexual adults with transfusion-associated infections. *Journal of the American Medical Association, 259,* 55–58.

Peterson, J. A. (1980). Social-psychological aspects of death and dying and mental health. In J. E. Birren and R. B. Sloane (Eds.), *Handbook of mental health and aging.* Englewood Cliffs, NJ: Prentice-Hall.

Petit, T. L. (1982). Neuroanatomical and clinical neuropsychological changes in aging and senile dementia. In F. I. M. Craik & S. Trehub (Eds.), *Aging and cognitive processes* (Vol. 8). New York: Plenum.

Pfeiffer, E. (1983). Health, sexuality, and aging. In J. E. Birren et al. (Eds.), *Aging: A challenge to science and society, Vol. 3.* New York: Oxford University Press.

Pfeiffer, E., & Davis, G. (1974). Determinants of sexual behavior in middle life and old age. In E. Palmore (Ed.), *Normal aging III: Reports from the Duke longitudinal studies, 1970–1973.* Durham, NC: Duke University Press.

Pfeiffer, E., Verwoerdt, A., & Davis, G. C. (1974). Sexual behavior in midlife. In E. Palmore (Ed.), *Normal aging II: Reports from the Duke longitudinal studies, 1970–1973.* Durham, NC: Duke University Press.

Phillips, D., McCartney, K., & Scarr, S. (1987). Child-care quality and children's social development. *Developmental Psychology, 23,* 537–543.

Piaget, J. (1954). *The construction of reality in the child.* New York: Basic Books.

Piaget, J. (1970). Piaget's theory. In P. H. Mussen (Ed.), *Carmichael's manual of child psychology* (3rd ed., Vol. 1). New York: Wiley.

Piaget, J. (1971). *Biology and knowledge* (B. Walsh, trans.). Chicago: University of Chicago Press.

Piaget, J. (1972). Intellectual evolution from adolescence to adulthood. *Human Development, 15,* 1–12.

Piaget, J., & Inhelder, B. (1969). *The psychology of the child.* (H. Weaver, trans.). New York: Basic Books. (Original work published 1932)

Picton, T. W., Stuss, D. T., Champagne, C., & Nelson, R. F. (1984). The effects of age on human event-related potentials. *Psychophysiology, 21,* 312–325.

Pietromonaco, P. R., Manis, J., & Frohardt-Lane, K. (1986). Psychological consequences of multiple social roles. *Psychology of Women Quarterly, 10,* 373–381.

Pillemer, K. A. (1986). The dangers of dependency: New findings on domestic violence against the elderly. *Social Problems, 33,* 147–156.

Pillemer, K. A., & Finkelhor, D. (1988). The prevalence of elder abuse: A random sample survey. *The Gerontologist, 28,* 51–57.

Pillemer, K. A., & Moore, D. W. (1989). Abuse of patients in nursing homes: Findings from a survey of staff. *The Gerontologist, 29,* 314–320.

Pillemer, K. A., & Wolf, R. S. (1986). *Elder abuse.* Dover, MA: Auburn House.

Pincus, L. (1976). *Death and the family: The importance of mourning.* New York: Pantheon Books.

Pineo, P. C. (1961). Disenchantment in the later years of marriage. *Marriage and Family Living, 23,* 3–11.

Pinkus, R. L. (1984). Families, brain death, and traditional medical excellence. *Journal of Neurosurgery, 60,* 1192–1194.

Placa, J. (1990). Insights from broken brains. *Science, 248,* 812–814.

Plesser, D. R., Siegel, M. A., & Jacobs, N. R. (1986). *Growing old in America.* Plano, TX: Information Aids.

Plude, D. J., & Hoyer, W. J. (1981). Adult age differences in visual search as a function of stimulus mapping and processing load. *Journal of Gerontology, 36,* 598–604.

Plude, D. J., & Hoyer, W. J. (1986). Aging and the selectivity of visual information processing. *Psychology and Aging, 1,* 1–9.

Plude, D. J., & Murphy, L. J. (in press). Aging, selective attention, and everyday memory. In R. L. West & J. D. Sinnott (Eds.), *Everyday memory and aging: Current research and methodology.* New York: Springer-Verlag.

Pollack, G. (1961). Mourning and adaptation. *International Journal of Psychoanalysis, 42,* 341–361.

Pollack, G. (1978). Processes and affect: Mourning and grief. *International Journal of Psychoanalysis, 59,* 255–276.

Pollack, R. H. (1978). A theoretical note on the aging of the visual system. *Perception and Psychophysics, 23,* 94–95.

Ponds, R., Brouwer, W. H., & Van Walffelaar, P. C. (1988) Age differences in divided attention in a simulated driving task. *Journal of Gerontology, 43,* P151–P156.

Poon, L. W. (1985). Differences in human memory with aging: Nature, causes, and clinical implications. In J. E. Birren, & K. W. Schaie (Eds.), *Handbook of the psychology of aging* (2nd ed.). New York: Van Nostrand Reinhold.

Porcino, J. (1985). Psychological aspects of aging in women. *Women and Health, 10,* 115–122.

Powell, H. A., Eisdorfer, C., & Bogdonoff, M. D. (1964). Physiological response patterns observed in a learning task. *Archives of General Psychiatry, 10,* 192–195.

Pratt, M. W., Golding, G., & Kerig, P. (1987). Life-span differences in adult thinking about hypothetical and personal moral issues: Reflection or regression? *International Journal of Behavioral Development, 10,* 359–376.

Price, R. W., Sidtis, J., & Rosenblum, M. (1988). The AIDS dementia complex: Some current questions. *Annals of Neurology, 23* (Supplement), S27–S33.

Prosen, S., & Farmer, J. (1982). Understanding stepfamilies: Issues and importance for counselors. *Personnel and Guidance Journal, 60,* 393–397.

Protinsky, H., & Hughston, G. (1978). Conservation in elderly males: An empirical investigation. *Developmental Psychology, 14,* 114.

Quinn, M., & Tomita, S. (1986). *Elder abuse and neglect: Causes, diagnosis, and intervention strategies.* New York: Springer.

Rabkin, J. G., & Struening, E. L. (1976). Life events, stress, and illness. *Science, 194,* 1013–1020.

Rakfeldt, S., Rybash, J. M., & Roodin, P. A. (in press). Affirmative coping as a marker of adult therapeutic intervention. In M. L. Commons, F. A. Richards, & C. Armon (Eds.), *Adult development. Vol. 4: Longitudinal and case approaches.* New York: Praeger.

Ratner, H. H., Schell, D. A., Crimmins, A., Mittleman, D., & Baldinelli, L. (1987). Changes in adults' prose recall: Aging or cognitive demands. *Developmental Psychology, 23,* 521–525.

Ray, D. C., McKinney, K. A., & Ford, C. V. (1987). Differences in psychologists' ratings of older and younger clients. *The Gerontologist, 27,* 77–81.

Read, D. E. (1987). Neuropsychological assessment of memory in the elderly. *Canadian Journal of Psychology, 41,* 158–174.

Rebok, G. W. (1987). *Life-span cognitive development.* New York: Holt, Rinehart & Winston.

Reedy, M. N., Birren, J. E., & Schaie, K. W. (1981). Age and sex differences in satisfying love relationships across the adult life span. *Human Development, 24,* 52–66.

Reese, H. W. (1973). Models of memory and models of development. *Human Development, 16,* 397–416.

Reese, H. W., & Overton, W. F. (1970). Models of development and theories of development. In L. R. Goulet & P. B. Baltes (Eds.), *Life-span developmental psychology: Research and theory.* New York: Academic Press.

Reichard, S., Livson, F., & Peterson, P. (1962). *Aging and personality: A study of eighty-seven older men.* New York: John Wiley.

Reisberg, B. (1981). *Brain failure.* New York: Free Press.

Reisberg, B. (1983). *Alzheimer's disease: The standard reference.* New York: Free Press.

Reisberg, B. (1986). Dementia: A systematic approach to identifying reversible causes. *Geriatrics, 41,* 30–46.

Reisberg, B. (1987, October). *Classification of the various stages of Alzheimer's disease.* Paper presented at the conference on Alzheimer's Update: Translating Theory into Practice, Utica, NY.

Reisberg, B., & Bornstein, J. (1986). Clinical diagnosis and assessment. *Drug Therapy, 16,* 43–59.

Reisberg, B., Ferris, S. H., deLeon, M. J., & Crook, T. (1985). Age associated cognitive decline and Alzheimer's disease: Implications for assessment and treatment. In M. Berganer, M. Ermini, & H. B. Stahelin (Eds.), *Thresholds in aging.* London: Academic Press.

Reisberg, B., Ferris, S. H., & Franssen, E. (1985). An ordinal functional assessment toll for Alzheimer's-type dementia. *Hospital and Community Psychiatry, 36,* 593–595.

Reisberg, B., Shulman E., Steinberg, G., Rabinowitz, E., Kahn, R., & Harris, S. H. (1986). Patient and care giver management. *Drug Therapy, 16,* 65–93.

Remafedi, G. (1987a). Adolescent homosexuality: Psychosocial and medical implications. *Pediatrics, 79,* 331–337.

Remafedi, G. (1987b). Male homosexuality: The adolescent's perspective. *Pediatrics, 79,* 326–330.

Reskin, B. F. & Roos, P. A. (1990). *Job queues, gender queues: Explaining women's inroads into male occupations.* Philadelphia, PA: Temple University Press.

Retherford, R. D. (1975). *The changing sex differential in mortality.* Westport, CT: Greenwood Press.

Revenson, T. A. (1989). Compassionate stereotyping of elderly patients by physicians: Revision of the social contract hypothesis. *Psychology and Aging, 4,* 230–234.

Reveron, D. (1982, February). Aged are a mystery to most psychologists. *American Psychological Association Monitor,* p. 9.

Reynolds, D. K., & Kalish, R. A. (1974). Anticipation of futurity as a function of ethnicity and age. *Journal of Gerontology, 29,* 224–231.

Rhodes, S. L. (1977). A developmental approach to the life cycle of the family. *Social Casework, 58,* 301–311.

Rhodes, S. R. (1983). Age-related differences in work attitudes and behavior: A review and conceptual analysis. *Psychological Bulletin, 93,* 328–367.

Richards, F. A., & Commons, M. L. (1984). Systematic, metasystematic and cross-paradigmatic reasoning: A case for stages of reasoning beyond formal operations. In M. L. Commons, F. A. Richards, & C. Armon (Eds.), *Beyond formal operations: Late adolescent and adult cognitive development.* New York: Praeger.

Richards, R. A. (1976). A comparison of selected Guilford and Wallach-Kogan creative-thinking tests in conjunction with measures of intelligence. *Journal of Creative Behavior, 10,* 151–164.

Richmond-Abbott, M. (1983). *Masculine and feminine.* Reading, MA: Addison-Wesley.

Riddick, C. C. (1985). Health, aquariums, and the noninstitutionalized elderly. *Marriage and the Family Review, 8,* 163–173.

Riegel, K. F. (1973). Dialectical operations: The final period of cognitive development. *Human Development, 16,* 346–370.

Riegel, K. F. (1976). The dialectics of human development. *American Psychologist, 31,* 689–700.

Riegel, K. F., & Riegel, R. M. (1972). Development, drop, and death. *Developmental Psychology, 6,* 306–319.

Rikli, R., & Busch, S. (1986). Motor performance of women as a function of age and physical activity level. *Journal of Gerontology, 41,* 645–649.

Riley, M. W., & Foner, A. (1968). *Aging and society (Vol. 1): An inventory of research findings.* New York: Russell Sage Foundation.

Riley, M. W., Johnson, M. E., & Foner, A. (1972). *Aging and society: A sociology of age stratification.* New York: Russell Sage Foundation.

Rissenberg, M., & Glanzer, M. (1987). Free recall and word finding ability in normal aging and senile dementia of the Alzheimer's type: The effect of item concreteness. *Journal of Gerontology, 42,* 318–322.

Rivlin, A. M., & Weiner, J. M. (1988). *Caring for the elderly: Who will pay?* Washington, DC: Brookings Institution.

Roadberg, A. (1981). Perceptions of work and leisure among the elderly. *The Gerontologist, 21,* 142–145.

Roberts, P., & Newton, P. M. (1987). Levinsonian studies of women's adult development. *Psychology and Aging, 2,* 154–163.

Robertson, J. (1976). Significance of grandparents: Perceptions of young adult grandchildren. *The Gerontologist, 16,* 137–140.

Robertson, J. (1977). Grandmotherhood: A study of role conceptions. *Journal of Marriage and the Family, 39,* 165–174.

Rockstein, M. & Sussman, M. (1979). *Biology of aging.* Belmont, CA: Wadsworth.

Rodin, J. (1986). Aging and health: Effects of the sense of control. *Science, 233,* 1271–1276.

Rollins, B. C. & Feldman, H. (1970). Marital satisfaction over the life cycle. *Journal of Marriage and the Family, 32,* 20–28.

Rollins, B. C. & Gallagher, R. (1978). The developing child and marital satisfaction. In R. Lerner & G. Spanier (Eds.), *Child influences on marital interaction: A life-span perspective.* New York: Academic Press.

Romaniuk, J. G., & Romaniuk, M. (1981). Creativity across the life span: A measurement perspective. *Human Development, 24,* 366–381.

Romaniuk, J. G., & Romaniuk, M. (1982). Participation motivates older adults in higher education: The elderhostel experience. *The Gerontologist, 22,* 364–368.

Romaniuk, M. (1981). Reminiscence and the second half of life. *Experimental Aging Research, 7,* 315–336.

Roodin, P. A., Rybash, J. M., & Hoyer, W. J. (1984). Affect in adult cognition: A constructivist view of moral thought and action. In C. Malatesta & C. Izard (Eds.), *The role of affect in adult development and aging.* Beverly Hills, CA: Sage.

Roodin, P. A., Rybash, J. M., and Hoyer, W. J. (1985, November). *Qualitative dimensions of social cognition in adulthood.* Paper presented at meetings of Gerontological Society of America, New Orleans.

Rook, K. S. (1987). Reciprocity of social exchange and social satisfaction among older women. *Journal of Personality and Social Psychology, 52,* 145–154.

Rose, C., & Bell, B. (1971). *Predicting longevity.* Lexington, MA: Heath.

Rosen, J. L., & Neugarten, B. L. (1964). Ego functions in the middle and later years: A thematic apperception study. In B. L. Neugarten (Ed.), *Personality in middle and late life.* New York: Atherton.

Rosenfeld, A. (1976). *Prolongevity.* New York: Avon.

Rosenwaike, L., & Dolinsky, A. (1987). The changing demographic determinants of the growth of the extreme aged. *The Gerontologist, 27,* 275–280.

Rossi, A. (1977). A biosocial perspective on parenting. *Daedalus, 106,* 1–31.

Rossi, A. (1984). Gender and parenthood. *American Sociological Review, 49,* 1–19.

Roth, S., & Cohen, L. J. (1986). Approach, avoidance, and coping with stress. *American Psychologist, 41,* 813–819.

Rovee, C. K., Cohen, R.Y., & Shlapack, W. (1975). Life-span stability in olfactory sensitivity. *Developmental Psychology, 11,* 311–318.

Rowe, J. W., & Kahn, R. L. (1987). Human aging: Usual and successful. *Science, 237,* 143–149.

Rowse, T. (1988). *Cemetery goods and services.* Washington, DC: American Association of Retired Persons #PF4087 (488). D13162.

Roy, D. J., Verret, S., & Roberge, C. (1986). Brain death—1986. *Critical Care Clinics, 2,* 161–172.

Rozin, P. (1976). The evolution of intelligence and access to the cognitive unconscious. *Progress in Psychobiology and Physiological Psychology, 6,* 46–53.

Rubenstein, C., & Shaver, P. (1981). The experience of loneliness. In L. A. Peplau & D. Perlman (Eds.), *Loneliness: A source book of current theory, research, and therapy.* New York: Wiley Interscience.

Rubin, Z. (1970). Measurement of romantic love. *Journal of Personality and Social Psychology, 16,* 265–273.

Rubin, Z. (1973). *Liking and loving: An invitation to social psychology.* New York: Holt, Rinehart & Winston.

Rubin, Z. (1979, October). Seeking a cure for loneliness. *Psychology Today, 13,* 82–91.

Rubinstein, R. L. (1986). *Singular paths: Old men living alone.* New York: Columbia University Press.

Ruble, D. N., Fleming, A. S., Hackel, L. S., & Stagnor, C. (1988). Changes in the marital relationship during the transition to first-time motherhood: Effects of violated expectations concerning division of household labor. *Journal of Personality and Social Psychology, 55,* 78–87.

Ruth, J. E., & Birren, J. E. (1985). Creativity in adulthood and old age: Relations to intelligence, sex, and mode of testing. *International Journal of Behavioral Development, 8,* 99–109.

Rybash, J. M. (1990, March). *Multiple memory systems and aging: Let's be explicit about what we think is implicit.* Paper presented at Third Biennial Conference on Cognitive Aging, Atlanta, GA.

Rybash, J. M., Hoyer, W. J., & Roodin, P. A. (1986). *Adult cognition and aging: Developmental changes in processing, knowing, and thinking.* New York: Pergamon.

Rybash, J. M., Hoyer, W. J., & Roodin, P. A. (1987, September). *Adult cognitive development: Universal themes and individual variations.* Paper presented at the meeting of the Jean Piaget Archives Foundation, Geneva, Switzerland.

Rybash, J. M., & Roodin, P. A. (1989). A comparison of formal and postformal modes of health-care decision-making competence. In M. L. Commons, J. D. Sinnott, F. A. Richards, & C. Armon (Eds.), *Beyond formal operations: Comparisons and applications of adolescent and adult developmental models.* New York: Praeger.

Rybash, J. M., Roodin, P. A., & Hoyer, W. J. (1983). Expressions of moral thought in later adulthood. *The Gerontologist, 23,* 254–260.

Rybash, J. M., Roodin, P. A., & Hoyer, W. J. (1984). Adult morality: A neo-Piagetian perspective on cognition and affect. *The Genetic Epistemologist, 14,* 24–29.

Sacks, O. (1985). *The man who mistook his wife for a hat.* New York: Summit Books.

Sahler, O. J. (1978). *The child and death.* St. Louis: Mosby.

Salthouse, T. A. (1984). Effects of age and skill in typing. *Journal of Experimental Psychology: General, 113,* 345–371.

Salthouse, T. A. (1985). Spread of behavior and its implications for cognition. In J. E. Birren & K. W. Schaie (Eds.), *Handbook of the psychology for aging* (2nd ed.). New York: Van Nostrand Reinhold.

Salthouse, T. A., Mitchell, D., & Palmon, R. (1989). Memory and age differences in spatial manipulation ability. *Psychology and Aging, 4,* 480–486.

Salthouse, T. A. & Somberg, B. L. (1982). Skilled performance: Effects of adult age and experience on elementary processes. *Journal of Experimental Psychology: General, 111,* 176–207.

Sameroff, A. J., & Chandler, M. J. (1975). Reproductive risk and the continuum of caretaking casualty. In F. D. Horowitz (Ed.), *Review of child development research* (Vol. 4). Chicago: University of Chicago Press.

Sande, M. A. (1986). Transmission of AIDS: The case against casual contagion. *New England Journal of Medicine, 314,* 380–382.

Santrock, J. W., & Warshak, R. A. (1979). Father custody and social development in boys and girls. *Journal of Social Issues, 35,* 112–125.

Sarason, I. G. (1980). Life stress, self-preoccupation, and social supports. In I. G. Sarason & C. D. Speilberger (Eds.), *Stress and anxiety* (Vol. 7). Washington, DC: Hemisphere.

Sarason, I. G. and Speilberger, C. D. (1980). *Stress and anxiety* (Vol. 7). Washington, DC: Hemisphere.

Sarrell, L., & Sarrell, P. (1974). The college subculture. In M. S. Calderone (Ed.), *Sexuality and human values.* New York: Association Press.

Sati: A pagan sacrifice. (1987, October). *India Today,* pp. 58–61.

Sauber, M. & Corrigan, E. M. (1970). *The six-year experience of unwed mothers as parents.* New York: Community Council of Greater New York.

Saunders, C. (1977). Dying to live: St. Christopher's Hospice. In H. Feifel (Ed.), *New meanings of death.* New York: McGraw-Hill.

Schacter, D. L. (1987). Implicit memory: History and current status. *Journal of Experimental Psychology: Learning, Memory, and Cognition, 12,* 432–444.

Schacter, D. L. (1989). On the relationship between memory and consciousness: Dissociable interactions and conscious experience. In H. L. Roediger and F. I. M. Craik (Eds.), *Varieties of memory and consciousness: Essays in honor of Endel Tulving.* Hillsdale, NJ: Erlbaum.

Schaie, K. W. (1965). A general model for the study of developmental problems. *Psychological Bulletin, 64,* 92–107.

Schaie, K. W. (1977a). Quasi-experimental research designs in the psychology of aging. In J. E. Birren & K. W. Schaie (Eds.), *Handbook of the psychology of aging.* New York: Van Nostrand Reinhold.

Schaie, K. W. (1977b). Toward a stage theory of adult cognitive development. *International Journal of Aging and Human Development, 8,* 129–138.

Schaie, K. W. (1979). The primary mental abilities in adulthood: An exploration in the development of psychometric intelligence. In P. B. Baltes & O. G. Brim, Jr. (Eds.), *Life-span development and behavior* (Vol. 2). New York: Academic Press.

Schaie, K. W. (1983). Consistency and changes in cognitive functioning of the young-old and old-old. In M. Bergner, U. Lehr, E. Lang, & R. Schmidt-Scherzer (Eds.), *Aging in the eighties and beyond.* New York: Springer.

Schaie, K. W. (1985). *Manual for the Schaie-Thurstone Adult Mental Abilities Test (STAMAT).* Palo Alto, CA: Consulting Psychologists Press.

Schaie, K. W. (1989). The hazards of cognitive aging. *The Gerontologist, 29,* 484–493.

Schaie, K. W. (in press). The optimization of cognitive functioning in old age: Predictions based on cohort-sequential and longitudinal data. In P. B. Baltes & M. M. Baltes (Eds.), *Longitudinal research and the study of successful aging.* New York: Cambridge University Press.

Schaie, K. W., & Hertzog, C. (1983). Fourteen-year cohort-sequential studies of adult intelligence. *Developmental Psychology, 19,* 531–543.

Schaie, K. W., & Hertzog, C. (1985). Toward a comprehensive model of adult intellectual development: Contributions of the Seattle longitudinal study. In R. J. Sternberg (Ed.), *Advances in human intelligence* (Vol. 3). New York: Academic Press.

Schaie, K. W., & Labouvie-Vief, G. (1974). Generational versus ontogenetic components of change in adult cognitive behavior: A fourteen-year cross-sequential study. *Developmental Psychology, 10,* 305–320.

Schaie, K. W., & Parham, I. A. (1976). Stability of adult personality traits: Fact or fable? *Journal of Personality and Social Psychology, 34,* 146–158.

Schaie, K. W., & Willis, S. L. (1986a). *Adult development and aging* (2nd ed.). Boston: Little, Brown.

Schaie, K. W. & Willis, S. L. (1986b). Can adult intellectual decline be reversed? *Developmental Psychology, 22,* 223–232.

Schaie, K. W., Willis, S. L., Hertzog, C., & Schulenberg, J. E. (1987). Effects of cognitive training on primary mental ability structure. *Psychology and Aging, 2,* 233–242.

Scheibel, A. B., & Wechsler, A. F. (Eds.). (1986). *The biological substrates of Alzheimer's disease.* New York: Academic Press.

Scheidt, R. J. (1985). The mental health of the aged in rural environments. In R. T. Coward & G. R. Lee (Eds.), *The elderly in rural society.* New York: Springer.

Schiffman, S. (1977). Food recognition by the elderly. *Journal of Gerontology, 32,* 586–592.

Schiffman, S., & Pasternak, M. (1979). Decreased discrimination of food odors in the elderly. *Journal of Gerontology, 34,* 73–79.

Schmitz-Secherzer, R. (1976). Longitudinal change in leisure behavior of the elderly. *Contributions to Human Development, 3,* 127–136.

Schmitz-Secherzer, R. (1979). Aging and leisure. *Society and leisure, 2,* 377–396.

Schneider, W. & Shiffrin, R. M. (1977). Controlled and automatic human information processing. *Psychological Review, 84,* 1–66.

Schonfield, D. (1982). Who is stereotyping whom and why? *The Gerontologist, 22,* 267–272.

Schonfield, D. & Robertson, B. A. (1966). Memory storage and aging. *Canadian Journal of Psychology, 20,* 228–236.

Schuckitt, M. A., Morrissey, E. R., & O'Leary, M. R. (1979). Alcohol problems in elderly men and women. In D. M. Peterson (Ed.), *Drug use among the aged.* New York: Spectrum.

Schultz, J. H. (1985). *The economics of aging* (3rd ed.). New York: Van Nostrand Reinhold.

Schultz, N. C., & Schultz, C. L. (1987). Affection and intimacy as special strengths of couples in blended families. *Australian Journal of Sex, Marriage, and the Family, 8,* 66–72.

Schultz, N. R., Jr., Elias, M. F., Robbins, M. A., Streeten, D. P. H., & Blakeman, N. (1986). A longitudinal comparison of hypertensives and normotensives on the Wechsler Adult Intelligence Scale: Initial findings. *Journal of Gerontology, 41,* 169–175.

Schulz, R. (1985). Emotion and affect. In J. E. Birren and K. W. Schaie (Eds.), *Handbook of the psychology of aging* (2nd ed.). New York: Van Nostrand Reinhold.

Schulz, R., and Alderman, D. (1974). Clinical research and the stages of dying. *Omega, 5,* 137–143.

Schulz, R., Tompkins, A., and Rau, M. T. (1988). A longitudinal study of the psychosocial impact of stroke on primary support systems. *Psychology and Aging, 3,* 131–141.

Schwartzman, A. E., Gold, D., Andres, D., Arbuckle, T. Y., & Chiakelson, J. (1987). Stability of intelligence: A forty-year follow-up. *Canadian Journal of Psychology, 41,* 244–256.

Seals, D. R., Hagberg, J. M., Hurley, B. F., Ehsani, A. A., & Hooszy, J. O. (1984). Endurance training in older men and women: I. Cardiovascular responses to exercise. *Journal of Applied Physiology, 57,* 1024–1029.

Sears, R. R. (1977). Sources of satisfaction of the Terman gifted men. *American Psychologist, 32,* 119–128.

Segerberg, O. (1982). *Living to be 100: 1,200 who did and how they did it.* New York: Charles Scribner's Sons.

Selkoe, D. J., Bell, D. S., Podlisny, M. B., Price, D. L., & Cork, L. C. (1987). Conservation of brain amyloid proteins in aged mammals and humans with Alzheimer's disease. *Science, 235,* 873–877.

Sharps, M. J., & Gollin, E. S. (1987). Speed and accuracy of mental image rotation in young and elderly adults. *Journal of Gerontology, 42,* 342–344.

Shaughnessy, J. J., & Zechmeister, E. B. (1990). *Research methods in psychology* (2nd ed.). New York: McGraw-Hill.

Shaver, P. (1986, August). Being lonely, falling in love: Perspectives from attachment theory. Paper presented at the annual meeting of the American Psychological Association, Washington, DC.

Shaw, R. J., Salthouse, T. A., & Babcock, R. (1990, March). Age and working memory: Effects of number and type of processing. Paper presented at the Third Annual Conference on Cognitive Aging, Atlanta, GA.

Sheehy, G. (1976). *Passages: The predictable crises of adult life.* New York: Dutton.

Sheehy, G. (1981). *Pathfinders.* New York: Dutton.

Shepard, R. N., & Metzler, J. (1971). Mental rotation of three-dimensional objects. *Science, 171,* 701–703.

Shields, S. A. (1973). *Personality trait attribution and reproductive role.* Unpublished master's thesis, Pennsylvania State University, University Park.

Shimamura, A. P. (1986). Priming effects in amnesia: Evidence for a dissociable memory function. *Quarterly Journal of Experimental Psychology, 38A,* 619–644.

Shimamura, A. P., Salmon, D. P., Squire, L. R., & Butters, N. (1987). Memory dysfunction unique to Alzheimer's disease: Impairment in word priming. *Journal of Clinical and Experimental Neuropsychology, 9,* 70.

Shneidman, E. (1973). *Deaths of man.* New York: Quadrangle/New York Times.

Shneidman, E. (1977). *Death: Current perspectives.* Palo Alto, CA: Mayfield.

Shneidman, E. (1980). *Voices of death.* New York: Harper & Row.

Shock, N. W. (1960). Mortality and measurement of aging. In B. L. Strehler, J. B. Ebert, H. B. Glass, & N. W. Shock (Eds.), *The biology of aging.* Washington, DC: American Institute of Biological Sciences.

Shock, N. W. (1977). The cellular basis for biological aging. In C. E. Finch & L. Hayflick (Eds.), *Handbook of the biology of aging.* New York: Van Nostrand Reinhold.

Shock, N. W. (1986). Biology of aging: Comment. In M. J. Horan, G. M. Steinberg, J. B. Dunbar, & E. C. Hadley (Eds.), *NIH, Blood pressure regulation and aging: Proceedings from a symposium.* New York: Biomedical Information Corporation.

Shupe, D. R. (1985). In J. E. Birren and J. Livingston (Eds.), *Cognition, stress, and aging.* Englewood Cliffs, NJ: Prentice-Hall.

Siakotos, A. N., Armstrong, D., Koppang, N., & Muller, J. (1977). Biochemical significance of age pigment in neurons. In K. Nandy & I. Sherwin (Eds.), *The aging brain and senile dementia: Advances in behavioral biology,* (Vol. 23). New York: Plenum.

Siegler, I. C. (1983). Psychological aspects of the Duke longitudinal studies. In K. W. Schaie (Ed.), *Longitudinal studies of adult psychological development.* New York: Guilford Press.

Siegler, I. C., & Costa, P. T., Jr. (1985). Health behavior relationships. In J. E. Birren & K. W. Schaie (Eds.), *Handbook of the psychology of aging* (2nd ed.). New York: Van Nostrand Reinhold.

Siegler, R. S. (1982). Information-processing approaches to development. In W. Kessen (Ed.), *Carmichael's manual of child psychology* (Vol. 1, 4th ed.). New York: Wiley.

Simms, L. M., Jones, S. J., & Yoder, K. K. (1982). Adjustment of older persons in nursing homes. *Journal of Gerontological Nursing, 8,* 383–386.

Simon, H. A. (1980). Information-processing explanations of understanding. In T. W. Jusczy & R. M. Klien (Eds.), *The nature of thought: Essays in honor of D O. Hebb.* Hillsdale, NJ: Erlbaum.

Simon, J. L., & Burstein, P. (1985). *Basic research methods in social science* (3rd ed.). New York: Random House.

Simon, S. (1980). The neuroses, personality disorders, alcoholism, drug use and misuse, and crime in the aged. In J. E. Birren & R. B. Sloane (Eds.), *Handbook of mental health and aging.* Englewood Cliffs, NJ: Prentice-Hall.

Simon, W., & Gagnon, J. H. (1969). On psychosexual development. In D. Goslin (Ed.), *Handbook of socialization theory and research.* Chicago: Rand McNally.

Simonton, D. K. (1988). Age and outstanding achievement: What do we know after a century of research? *Psychological Bulletin, 104,* 251–267.

Simonton, D. K. (1989). The swan-song phenomenon: Last-works effects for 172 classical composers. *Psychology and Aging, 4,* 42–47.

Simpson, J. A., Campbell, B., & Berscheid, E. (1986). The association between love and marriage: Kephart (1967) twice revisited. *Personality and Social Psychology Bulletin, 12,* 363–372.

Sinnott, J. D. (1981). The theory of relativity: A metatheory for development? *Human Development, 24,* 293–311.

Sinnott, J. D. (1984). Postformal reasoning: The relativistic stage. In M. L. Commons, F. A. Richards, & C. Armon (Eds.), *Beyond formal operations: Late adolescent and adult cognitive development.* New York: Praeger.

Sinnott, J. D. (1989). Life-span relativistic postformal thought: Methodology and data from everyday problem-solving studies. In M. L. Commons, J. D. Sinnott, F. A. Richards, & C. Armon (Eds.), *Adult Development, Vol. 1: Comparisons and applications of developmental models.* New York: Praeger.

Sinnott, J. D., & Gutmann, D. (1978). Dialectics of decision making in older adults. *Human Development, 21,* 190–200.

Skolnick, E. (1986). *The intimate environment: Exploring marriage and family* (4th ed.). Boston: Little, Brown.

Small, G. W., & Jarvik, L. F. (1982). The dementia syndrome. *The Lancet, 2,* 1443–1446.

Smith, A. D. (1977). Adult age differences in cued recall. *Developmental Psychology, 13,* 326–331.

Smith, G. T., Snyder, D. K., Trull, T. S., & Monsma, B. R. (1988). Predicting relationship satisfaction from couples' uses of leisure time. *American Journal of Family Therapy, 16,* 3–13.

Smith, J. L., Dixon, R. A., & Baltes, P. B. (1989). Expertise in life planning: A new research approach to investigating aspects of wisdom. In M. L. Commons, J. D. Sinnott, F. A. Richards, & C. Armon (Eds.), *Adult development, Vol. 1: Comparisons and applications of developmental models.* New York: Praeger.

Smith, J. S., & Kiloh, I. G. (1981). The investigation of dementia: Results in 200 consecutive admissions. *The Lancet, 1,* 824–827.

Soares, C. J. (1985). The companion animal in the context of the family system. *Marriage and the Family Review, 8,* 49–62.

Society for the Right to Die. (1987). *A living will.* New York: Society for the Right to Die.

Sokolovsky, J. (1983). *Growing old in different societies: Cross-cultural perspectives.* Belmont, CA: Wadsworth.

Sokolovsky, J. (1985). Ethnicity, culture, and aging: Do differences really make a difference? *Journal of Applied Gerontology, 37,* 609–615.

Solnick, R. E., & Corby, N. (1983). Human sexuality and aging. In D. S. Woodruff and J. E. Birren (Eds.), *Aging: Scientific perspectives and social issues* (2nd ed.). Monterey, CA: Brooks-Cole.

Somberg, B. L., & Salthouse, T. A. (1982). Skilled performance: Effects of adult age and experience on elementary processes. *Journal of Experimental Psychology: General, 111,* 176–207.

Sorensen, T., Nielsen, G. G., Andersen, P., & Teasdale, T. (1988). Genetic and environmental influences on premature death in adult adoptees. *The New England Journal of Medicine, 318,* 727–732.

Spanier, G., & Glick, P. (1981). Marital instability in the United States: Some correlates and recent changes. *Family Relations, 31,* 329–338.

Spanier, G. B. & Margolis, R. L. (1983). Marital separation and extramarital sexual behavior. *Journal of Sex Research, 19,* 23–48.

Spearman, C. (1927). *The abilities of man.* New York: MacMillan.

Speece, M. W. & Brent, S. B. (1984). Children's understanding of death: A review of three components of a death concept. *Child Development, 55,* 1671–1686.

Spence, J. T. (1979, August). *Achievement and achievement-related motives.* Paper presented at the meeting of the American Psychological Association, New York.

Spence, J. T., & Helmreich, R. L. (1978). *Masculinity and femininity: Their psychological dimensions.* Austin, TX: University of Texas Press.

Spence, J. T., Helmreich, R. L., & Stapp, J. (1974). Personal attributes questionnaire: A measure of sex-role stereotypes and masculinity-femininity. *JSAS Catalog of Selective Documents in Psychology, 4,* 43.

Spencer, G., Goldstein, A. A., & Taeuber, C. M. (1987). *America's centenarians.* Washington, DC: U.S. Government Printing Office.

Spicer, J., & Hampe, G. (1975). Kinship interaction after divorce. *Journal of Marriage and the Family, 28,* 113–119.

Spiegel, P. M. (1977). Theories of aging. In P. S. Timiras (Ed.), *Developmental physiology and aging.* New York: MacMillan.

Spitz, R. A. (1945). Hospitalism: An inquiry into the genesis of psychiatric conditions in early childhood. In D. Fenschel (Ed.), *Psychoanalytic study of the child,* (Vol. 1). New York: International University Press.

Spitzer, M. E. (1988). Taste acuity in institutionalized and noninstitutionalized elderly men. *Journal of Gerontology, 43,* P71–P74.

Springer, K. J., & Dietzmann, H. E. (1970). *Correlational studies of diesel exhaust odor measured by instrumental methods to human odor panel ratings.* Paper presented at the Odor Conference at the Korslinska Institute, Stockholm, Sweden.

Springer, S. P., & Deutsch, G. (1985). *Left brain, right brain* (2nd ed.). New York: W. H. Freeman.

Squire, L. R. (1986). Mechanisms of memory. *Science, 232,* 1612–1619.

Squire, L. (1987). *Memory and brain.* New York: Oxford University Press.

Stagner, R. (1985). Aging in industry. In J. E. Birren & K. W. Schaie (Eds.), *Handbook of the psychology of aging* (2nd ed.). New York: Van Nostrand Reinhold.

Stall, R., Catania, J., & Pollack, L. (1988). AIDS as an age-defined epidemic. The social epidemiology of HIV infection among older Americans. *Report to the National Institute of Aging.* Unpublished document.

Stall, R., Catania, J., & Pollack, L. (1990). AIDS as an age-defined epidemic. In M. Riley, M. Ory, & D. Zablotsky (Eds.), *AIDS in an aging society: What we need to know.* New York: Springer.

Stankov, L. (1988). Aging, attention, and intelligence. *Psychology and Aging, 3,* 59–74.

Stearns, H. L., Barrett, G. V., and Alexander, R. A. (1985). Accidents and the aging individual. In J. E. Birren and K. W. Schaie (Eds.), *Handbook of the psychology of aging* (2nd ed.). New York: Van Nostrand Reinhold.

Steenland, S. (1987). *Prime time women: An analysis of older women on entertainment television.* Washington, DC: National Commission on Working Women.

Steger, H. G. (1976). Understanding the psychological factors in rehabilitation. *Geriatrics, 31,* 68–73.

Stein, S., Linn, M. W., & Stein, E. M. (1985). Patient's anticipation of stress in nursing home care. *The Gerontologist, 25,* 88–94.

Stein, S., Linn, M. W., & Stein, E. M. (1986). *Patient's perceptions of nursing home stress related to quality of care.* Unpublished report, VA Health Services Research Grant (# 547). Miami, FL: University of Miami Medical School.

Steinmetz, S. (1978). Battered parents. *Society, 15,* 54–55.

Steinmetz, S. (1981, January-February). Elder abuse. *Aging,* pp. 6–10.

Stephens, J. (1976). *Loners, losers, and lovers: Elderly tenants in a slum hotel.* Seattle: University of Washington Press.

Stephens, M. A. P., Norris, V. K., Kinney, J. M., Ritchie, S. W., & Grotz, R. C. (1988). Stressful situations in caregiving: Relations between caregiver coping and well-being. *Psychology and Aging, 3,* 208–209.

Stephenson, J. S. (1985). *Death, grief, and mourning: Individual and social realities.* New York: Free Press.

Sternberg, R. J. (1985). *Beyond IQ: A triarchic theory of human intelligence.* New York: Cambridge University Press.

Sternberg, R. J. (1986a). *Intelligence applied: Understanding and increasing your intellectual skills.* New York: Harcourt Brace Jovanovich.

Sternberg, R. J. (1986b). A triangular theory of love. *Psychological Review, 93,* 119–135.

Sternberg, R., & Grajek, S. (1984). The nature of love. *Journal of Personality and Social Psychology, 47,* 312–329.

Sternberg, S. (1969). Memory scanning: Mental processes revealed by reaction time processes. *American Scientist, 57,* 421–457.

Stevens-Long, J. (1988). *Adult life: Developmental processes.* (3d ed.). Palo Alto, CA: Mayfield.

St. George-Hyslop, P. H., Tanzi, R. E., Polinsky, R. J., Haines, J. L., Nee, L., Watkins, P. C., Myers, R. H., Feldman, R. G., Pollen, D., Drachman, D., Growdon, J., Bruni, A., Foncin, J. F., Salmon, D., Frommelt, P., Amaducci, L., Sorbi, S., Piacentini, S., Steward, G. D., Hobbs, W. J., Conneally, P. M., & Gusella, J. F. (1987). The genetic defect causing familial Alzheimer's disease maps on chromosome 21. *Science, 235,* 885–889.

Stillings, N. A., Feinstein, M. H., Garfield, J. L., Rissland, E. L., Rosenbaum, D. A., Weisler, S. E., Baker-Ward, L. (1987). *Cognitive science: An introduction.* Boston: MIT Press.

Stillion, J., and Wass, H. (1979). Children and death. In H. Wass (Ed.), *Dying: Facing the facts.* New York: McGraw-Hill.

Stinnett, N., Carter, L. M., & Montgomery, J. E. (1972). Older persons' perceptions of their marriages. *Journal of Marriage and the Family, 34,* 665–670.

Stones, M. J., & Kozma, A. (1982). Cross-sectional, longitudinal, and secular age trends in athletic performance. *Experimental Aging Research, 8,* 185–188.

Stones, M. J., & Kozma, A. (1989). Age, exercise, and coding performance. *Psychology and Aging, 4,* 190–194.

Strayer, D. L., Wickens, C. D., & Braune, R. (1987). Adult age differences in the speed and capacity of information processing: 2. An electrophysiological approach. *Psychology and Aging, 2,* 99–110.

Strehler, B. L. (1973, February). A new age of aging. *Natural History, 82,* 9–19.

Stroebe, W., Stroebe, M. S. Gergen, K. J., & Gergen, M. (1985). The effects of bereavement on mortality: A social psychological analysis. In A. Monat & R. S. Lazarus (Eds.), *Stress and coping: An anthology.* New York: Columbia University Press.

Stueve, A. & O'Donnell, L. (1984). The daughter of aging parents. In G. Baruch and J. Brooks-Gunn (Eds.), *Women in midlife.* New York: Plenum Press.

Stull, D. E., & Hatch, L. R. (1984). Unraveling the effects of multiple life changes. *Research on Aging. 6,* 560–571.

Sturr, J. F., Church, K. L., Nuding, S. C., Van Orden, K., & Taub, H. A. (1986). Older observers have attenuated increment thresholds upon transient backgrounds. *Journal of Gerontology, 41,* 743–747.

Sturr, J. F., Church, K. L., & Taub, H. A. (1985). Early light adaptation in young, middle-aged, and older observers. *Perception and Psychophysics, 37,* 455–458.

Sturr, J. F., Church, K. L., & Taub, H. A. (1986). Temporal summation functions for detection of sine-wave gratings in young and older adults. *Visual Science* (Supplement) *27,* 111.

Sturr, J. F., Van Orden, K., & Taub, H. A. (1988). Selective attenuation in brightness for brief stimuli at low intensities supports age-related transient channel losses. *Experimental Aging Research, 13,* 145–149.

Summers, R., et al., (1986). Oral tetrahydroaminoacridine in long-term treatment of senile dementia, Alzheimer's type. *New England Journal of Medicine, 315,* 1241–1245.

Super, D. E. (1969). Vocational developmental theory: Persons, positions, and processes. *The Counseling Psychologist, 1,* 2–8.

Super, D. E. (1975). *The psychology of careers.* New York: Harper & Row.

Super, D. E. (1980). A life-span, life-space approach to career development. *Journal of Vocational Behavior, 16,* 282–298.

Super, D. E., Kowalski, R., & Gotkin, E. (1967). *Floundering and trial after high school.* Unpublished manuscript, Columbia University, New York.

Surwillo, W. W. (1960). Central nervous system factors in simple reaction time. *American Psychologist, 15,* 419.

Surwillo, W. W. (1961). Frequency of the "alpha" rhythm, reaction time and age. *Nature, 191,* 823–824.

Sussman, M. B. (1978, March-April). The family today—Is it an endangered species? *Children Today, 32*–37 and 45.

Sussman, M. B. (1985). Family life of old people. In R. H. Binstock & E. Shanas (Eds.), *Handbook of aging and the social sciences* (2nd ed.). New York: Van Nostrand Reinhold.

Sussman, M. B., Romeis, J., & Maeda, D. (1980). Age bias in Japan: Implications for normative conflict. *International Review of Modern Sociology, 10,* 243–254.

Swanson, E. A., & Bennett, T. F. (1982–1983). Degree of closeness: Does it affect the bereaved's attitudes toward selected funeral practices? *Omega, 13,* 43–50.

Taeuber, C. (1987, November). *New census data on the oldest old.* Paper presented at the annual meeting of the Gerontological Society of America, Washington, DC.

Tanner, J. M. (1961). *Educational and physical growth.* London: University Press.

Tanner, J. M. (1966). Growth and physique in different populations of mankind. In P. T. Baker & J. S. Weiner (Eds.), *The biology of human adaptability.* Oxford: Clarendon.

Tanner, J. M. (1973). Growing up. *Scientific American, 229,* 35–43.

Tanzi, R. E., et al. (1987). Amyloid B protein gene: cDNA, mRNA distribution, and genetic linkage near the Alzheimer locus. *Science, 219,* 1184–1190.

Taylor, E. (1974). Creativity and aging. In E. Pfeiffer (Ed.), *Successful aging.* Durham, NC: Center for the Study of Aging and Human Development.

Taylor, R. J., & Chatters, L. M. (1988). Correlates of education, income, and poverty among aged blacks. *The Gerontologist, 28,* 435–441.

Taylor, S. E. (1983). Adjustment to threatening events: A theory of cognitive adaptation. *American Psychologist, 38,* 1161–1173.

Taylor, S. E. (1990). Health psychology: The science and the field. *American Psychologist, 45,* 40–50.

Taylor, W. (1988). Real problems, real answers. *Boston Magazine, 80,* 176–228.

Tell, E. J., Cohen, M. A., Larson, M. J., & Batten, H. L. (1987). Assessing the elderly's preferences for life-care retirement options. *The Gerontologist, 27,* 503–509.

Tesch, S. A. (1983). Review of friendship development across the life span. *Human Development, 6,* 266–276.

Tesch, S., Whitbourne, S. K., & Nehrke, M. F. (1981). Friendship, social interaction, and subjective well-being of older men in an institutional setting. *International Journal of Aging and Human Development, 13,* 317–327.

Thomas, J. (1986a). Gender differences in satisfaction with grandparenting. *Psychology and Aging, 1,* 215–219.

Thomas, J. (1986b). Age and sex differences in perceptions of grandparenting. *Journal of Gerontology, 41,* 417–423.

Thomas, L. E. (1977). Midlife career changes: Self-selected or externally mandated? *Vocational Guidance Quarterly, 25,* 320–328.

Thomas, L. W., & Gallagher, D. (1985). Depression and its treatment in the elderly. *Aging, 348,* 14–18.

Thompson, L., & Spanier, G. (1983). The end of marriage and acceptance of marital termination. *Journal of Marriage and the Family, 45,* 103–114.

Thompson, L. W. (1980). Testing and mnemonic strategies. In L. W. Poon, J. L. Fozard, L. S. Cremack, D. Arenberg, & L. W. Thompson (Eds.), *New directions in memory and aging: Proceedings of the George A. Talland Memorial Conference.* Hillsdale, NJ: Erlbaum.

Thompson, R. A., Tinsley, B. R., Scalora, M. J., & Parke, R. D. (1989). Grandparents' visitation rights. *American Psychologist, 44,* 1217–1222.

Thompson, R. F. (1985). *The brain: An introduction to neuroscience.* New York: W. H. Freeman.

Thurstone, L. L. (1938). *Primary mental abilities.* Chicago: University of Chicago Press.

Tibbits, C. (1979). Can we invalidate negative stereotypes of aging? *The Gerontologist, 19,* 10–20.

Tietjen, A. M., & Walker, L. J. (1983). Social roles and moral reasoning: A case study in a rural African community. *Developmental Psychology, 17,* 595–603.

Tietjen, A. M., & Walker, L. J. (1985). Moral reasoning and leadership among men in a Papua, New Guinea society. *Developmental Psychology, 21,* 982–992.

Tilak, S. (1989). *Religion and aging in the Indian tradition.* Albany, NY: SUNY Press.

Tinsley, B. J., & Parke, R. D. (1987). Grandparents as interactive and socialization agents. In M. Lewis (Ed.), *Beyond the dyad.* New York: Plenum.

Tobin, J. J. (1987). The American idealization of old age in Japan. *The Gerontologist, 27,* 53–58.

Tobin, S. S. (1978). Old people. In H. Mass (Ed.), *Review of research in the social services.* New York: National Association of Social Workers.

Tobin, S. S., & Lieberman, M. (1976). *Last home for the aged.* San Francisco: Jossey-Bass.

Tobin, S. S., & Lieberman, M. (1983). *The experience of old age.* New York: Basic Books.

Tomlinson-Keasey, C. (1972). Formal operations in females from eleven to fifty-four years of age. *Developmental Psychology, 6,* 364.

Tomlinson-Keasey, C., & Keasey, C. B. (1974). The mediating role of cognitive development in moral judgment. *Child Development, 45,* 291–298.

Tomlinson, P. S. (1987). Spousal differences in marital satisfaction during transition to marriage. *Nursing Research, 36,* 239–243.

Torrance, E. P. (1966). *Torrance test of creative thinking.* Lexington, MA: Personnel Press.

Traupmann, J., Eckels, E., & Hatfield, E. (1982). Intimacy in older women's lives. *The Gerontologist, 22,* 493–498.

Troll, L. E. (1971). The family of later life: A decade review. *Journal of Marriage and the Family, 33,* 263–290.

Troll, L. E. (1975). *Early and middle adulthood.* Monterey, CA: Brooks-Cole.

Troll, L. E. (1983). Grandparents: The family watchdogs. In T. Brubaker (Ed.), *Family relationships in later life.* Beverly Hills, CA: Sage.

Troll, L. E. (1985). *Early and middle adulthood* (2nd ed.). Monterey, CA: Brooks-Cole.

Troll, L. E., & Smith, J. (1976). Attachment through the life span: Some questions about dyadic bonds among adults. *Human Development, 19,* 156–170.

Trunzo, C. E. (1982). Solving the age-old problem. *Money, 11,* 70–80.

Tryban, G. M. (1985). Effects of work and retirement within long-term marital relationships. *Lifestyles, 7,* 207–223.

Tulving, E., Schacter, D. L., & Stark, H. A. (1982). Priming effects in word-fragment completion are independent of recognition memory. *Journal of Experimental Psychology: Learning, Memory and Cognition, 8,* 336–342.

Turner, B F. (1982). Sex-related differences in aging. In B. B. Wolman (Ed.), *Handbook of developmental psychology.* Englewood Cliffs, NJ: Prentice-Hall.

Turner, B. F. & Turner, C. B. (1974). Evaluations of women and men among black and white college students. *Sociological Quarterly, 15,* 442–456.

Udry, J. R. (1974). *The social context of marriage.* Philadelphia: Lippincott.

Uhlenberg, P. (1980). Death and the family. *Journal of Family History, 5,* 313–320.

Uhlenberg, P., Cooney, T., & Boyd, R. (1990). Divorce for women after midlife. *Journal of Gerontology, 45,* S3–S11.

Upton, A. C. (1977). Pathology. In L. E. Finch & L. Hayflick (Eds.), *Handbook of the biology of aging.* New York: Van Nostrand Reinhold.

U.S. Bureau of the Census. (1977). *Household and family characteristics* (Current population reports, special studies, Series P–20, No. 326). Washington, DC: U.S. Government Printing Office.

U.S. Bureau of the Census. (1982). *Projections of the population of the United States* (Current population reports, Series P–25, No. 922). Washington, DC: U.S. Government Printing Office.

U.S. Bureau of the Census. (1983). *U.S. Census of population and housing, 1980: Summary* (Vol. 2). Washington, DC: U.S. Government Printing Office.

U.S. Bureau of the Census. (1984). *Marital status and living arrangements, March 1983.* (Current population reports: Population characteristics series, P–20, No. 389). Washington, DC: U.S. Government Printing Office.

U.S. Bureau of the Census. (1985). *Statistics.* Washington, DC: U.S. Government Printing Office.

U.S. Bureau of the Census. (1986). *Statistics.* Washington, DC: U.S. Government Printing Office.

U.S. Bureau of the Census. (1987a). *Statistics.* Washington, DC: U.S. Government Printing Office.

U.S. Bureau of the Census. (1987b). *Who's minding the kids? Child care arrangements: Winter 1984–1985.* (Current population reports: Household economic studies, Series P–70, No. 9). Washington, DC: U.S. Government Printing Office.

U.S. Census Projections. (1984). *Projections of the population of the United States by age, sex, and race: 1983 to 2080.* (Series P–25). Washington, DC: U.S. Government Printing Office.

U.S. Decennial Life Tables for 1979–81. (1985). *National center for health statistics.* Washington, DC: U.S. Government Printing Office.

U.S. Department of Health, Education, & Welfare. (1976). *The condition of education in the United States.* Washington, DC: U.S. Government Printing Office.

U.S. Department of Health, Education, & Welfare. (1979). *Monthly vital statistics report: Advanced report, final mortality, 1977.* Hyattsville, MD: National Center for Health Statistics.

U.S. Department of Labor. (1987, August). *United States Department of Labor News,* 87–345.

U.S. Department of Labor, Bureau of Labor Statistics. (1988). *Employment of older women.* Report No. 758. Washington, DC: United States Department of Labor.

U.S. Department of Labor. (1989, January). *Labor market problems of older women.* Report of the Secretary. Washington, DC: United States Department of Labor.

U.S. Senate Special Committee on Aging. (1985, June 14). *The pension gamble: Who wins? Who loses?* (Hearings). Washington, DC: U.S. Government Printing Office.

Valliant, G. (1977). *Adaptation to life.* Boston: Little, Brown.

Valliant, G. E., & Valliant, C. O. (1981). Natural history of male psychological health, X: Work as a predictor of positive mental health. *American Journal of Psychiatry, 138,* 1433–1440.

Van Hoose, W. H., & Worth, M. (1982). *Adulthood in the life cycle.* Dubuque, IA: Wm. C. Brown.

Vatican Congregation for the Doctrine of the Faith. (1980). Vatican declaration on euthanasia. *Origins, 10,* 154–157.

Veatch, R. M. (1981). *A theory of medical ethics.* New York: Basic Books.

Veevers, J. E. (1980). *Children by choice.* Toronto, Canada: Butterworth.

Verillo, R. T. (1980). Age-related changes in sensitivity to vibration. *Journal of Gerontology, 35,* 185–193.

Verwoerdt, A., Pfeiffer, E., & Wang, H. S. (1969). Sexual behavior in senescence—Changes in sexual activity and interest aging men and women. *Journal of Ger tric 'sychiatry, 2,* 163–180.

Visher, E. B., & Visher, J. S. 78). Common problems of stepparents and the r spouses. *American Journal of Orthopsychiatry, 48,* 252–262.

Visher, E. B., & Visher, J. S. (1 . Stepparenting: Blending families. In H. I. McCubbin and C. R. Figley (Eds.), *Stress and the family, Vol. 1: Coping with normative transitions.* New York: Brunner/ Mazel.

Visher, J. S., & Visher, E. B. (1979). Stepfamilies and stepchildren. In J. D. Noshpitz (Ed.), *Handbook of child psychiatry.* New York: Basic Books.

Vondareck, F. W., Lerner, R. M., & Schulenberg, J. E. (1986). *Career development: A life-span developmental approach.* Hillsdale, NJ: Erlbaum.

Waddell, K. J., & Rogoff, B. (1981). Effects of contextual organization on spatial memory of middle-aged and older women. *Developmental Psychology, 17,* 878–885.

Wagenwoord, J., & Bailey, J. (1978). *Men: A book for women.* New York: Avon Books.

Waldron, I. (1976). Why do women live longer than men? *Social Science and Medicine, 10,* 349–362.

Waldrop, M. M. (1984). The necessity of knowledge. *Science, 223,* 1279–1283.

Walford, R. L. (1969). *The immunological theory of aging.* Baltimore: Williams & Wilkins.

Walker, L. J. (1984). Sex differences in the development of moral reasoning: A critical review. *Child Development, 55,* 1040–1044.

Walker, L. J. (1986). Experiential and cognitive sources of moral development in adulthood. *Human Development, 29,* 113–124.

Walker, L. J., de Vries, B., & Bichard, S. L. (1984). The hierarchical nature of stages of moral development. *Developmental Psychology, 20,* 960–966.

Walker, L. J., de Vries, B., & Trevethan, S. D. (1987). Moral stages and moral orientations in real-life and hypothetical dilemmas. *Child Development, 58,* 842–858.

Wallace, J. G. (1977). The course of cognitive growth. In V. P. Varma, & P. Williams (Eds.), *Piaget, psychology, and education.* Itasca, IL: Peacock.

Wallach, M. A. (1973). Ideology, evidence, and creative research. *Contemporary Psychology, 18,* 162–164.

Wallach, M. A., & Kogan, N. (1965). *Modes of thinking in young children.* New York: Holt, Rinehart & Winston.

Wallerstein, J. S. (1986). Women after divorce: Preliminary report from a ten-year follow-up. *American Journal of Orthopsychiatry, 56,* 65–77.

Wallerstein, J. S., & Blakeslee, S. (1988). *Second chances: Men, women, and children a decade after divorce.* Boston: Ticknor & Fields.

Walsh, D. A. (1976). Age differences in central perceptual processing: A dichoptic backwards masking investigation. *Journal of Gerontology, 31,* 178–185.

Wang, H. S., Obrist, W. D., & Busse, E. W. (1970). Neurophysiological correlates of the intellectual function of elderly persons living in the community. *American Journal of Psychiatry, 126,* 1205–1212.

Ward, J., Holmberg, S., Allen, J., Cohn, D., Critchley, S., Kleinman, S., Lenes, B., Ravenholt, D., Davis, J., Quinn, M., & Jaffe, H. (1988). Transmission of HIV by blood transfusions screened as negative for HIV antibody. *New England Journal of Medicine, 312,* 473–478.

Ward, R. A. (1984). *The aging experience: An introduction to social gerontology* (2nd ed.). New York: Harper & Row.

Warner, L. & Lunt, P. (1941). *The social life of a modern community.* New Haven, CT: Yale University Press.

Waterman, A. S. (1982). Identity development from adolescence to adulthood: An extension of theory and a review of the literature. *Developmental Psychology, 18,* 341–359.

Weale, R. A. (1985). What is normal aging: Part XI: The eyes of the elderly. *Geriatric Medicine Today, 4* (3), 29–37.

Wechsler, D. (1939). *Measurement of adult intelligence.* Baltimore: Williams & Wilkins.

Wechsler, D. (1958). *The measurement and appraisal of adult intelligence.* Baltimore: Williams & Wilkins.

Wechsler, D. (1972). "Hold" and "don't hold" tests. In S. M. Chown (Ed.), *Human aging.* New York: Penguin.

Weg, R. B. (1983). Changing physiology of aging: Normal and pathological. In D. W. Woodruff & J. E. Birren (Eds.), *Scientific perspectives and social issues* (2nd ed.). Monterey, CA: Brooks/Cole.

Weiffenbach, J. M., Cowart, B. J., & Baum, B. J. (1986). Taste insensitivity and aging. *Journal of Gerontology, 41,* 460–468.

Weigly, E. S. (1984). Average? Ideal? Desirable? A brief overview of height-weight tables in the United States. *Journal of the American Dietetic Association, 84,* 417–423.

Weinraub, M., Brooks, J., & Lewis, M. (1977). The social network: A reconsideration of the concept of attachment. *Human Development, 20,* 31–47.

Weir, R. F. (Ed.). (1986). *Ethical issues in death and dying.* New York: Columbia University Press.

Weisberg, R. W. (1986). *Creativity.* New York: W. H. Freeman.

Weisfeldt, M. L. (1981). Left ventricular function. In M. L. Weisfeldt (Ed.), *The aging heart: Its function and response to stress.* New York: Raven Press.

Weisman, A. T. (1972). *On dying and denying: A psychiatric study of terminality.* New York: Behavioral Publications.

Weiss, L., & Lowenthal, M. (1975). Life course perspectives on friendship. In M. Lowenthal, M. Turnher, & D. Chiriboga (Eds.), *Four stages of life.* San Francisco: Jossey-Bass.

Weiss, P. A. (1973). *The science of life: The living system—A system for living.* Mount Kisco, NY: Futura.

Weiss, R. S.(1975). *Marital separation.* New York: Basic Books.

Welford, A. T. (1980). Sensory, perceptual, and motor processes in older adults. In J. E. Birren & R. B. Sloane (Eds.), *Handbook of mental health and aging.* Englewood Cliffs, NJ: Prentice-Hall.

Wentowski, G. (1985). Older women's perceptions of great-grandparenthood: A research note. *The Gerontologist, 25,* 593–596.

Wertheimer, M. (1945). *Productive thinking.* New York: Harper & Row.

Whitbourne, S. K. (1985a). *The aging body.* New York: Springer-Verlag.

Whitbourne, S. K. (1985b). The psychological construction of the life span. In J. E. Birren and K.W. Schaie (Eds.), *The handbook of the psychology of aging* (2nd ed.). New York: Van Nostrand Reinhold.

White, C. B. (1981, August). *Sexual interest, attitudes, knowledge and sexual history in relation to sexual behavior in the institutionalized aged.* Paper presented at the meeting of the American Psychological Association, Los Angeles, CA.

White, C. B., & Catania, J. (1982). Psychoeducational intervention for sexuality with aged, family members of the aged, and people who work with the aged. *International Journal of Aging and Human Development,* 121–138.

White, N., & Cunningham, W. R. (1988). Is terminal drop pervasive or specific? *Journal of Gerontology, 44,* P141–P144.

Wickens, C. D., Braune, R., & Stokes, A. (1987). Age differences in the speed and capacity of information processing: 1. A dual-task approach. *Psychology and Aging, 2,* 70–78.

Wiggins, J. D., & Lederer, D. A. (1984). Differential antecedents of infidelity in marriage. *American Mental Health Counselors Association Journal, 6,* 152–161.

Wilkie, F., & Eisdorfer, C. (1971). Intelligence and blood pressure in the aged. *Science, 172,* 959–962.

Wilkie, F., & Eisdorfer, C. (1973, November). *Intellectual change: A fifteen-year follow-up of the Duke sample.* Paper presented at the meeting of the Gerontological Society of America.

Williamson, J. B., Munley, A., & Evans, I. (1980). *Aging and society: An introduction to social gerontology.* New York: Holt, Rinehart and Winston.

Willis, S. L. (1985). Towards an educational psychology of the adult learner. In J. E. Birren & K. W. Schaie (Eds.), *Handbook of the psychology of aging* (2nd ed.). New York: Van Nostrand Reinhold.

Willis, S. L., Blieszner, R., & Baltes, P. B. (1981). Intellectual training research in aging: Modification of performance on the fluid ability of figural relations. *Journal of Educational Psychology, 73,* 41–50.

Willis, S. L., & Schaie, K. W. (1985). Practical intelligence in later adulthood. In R. J. Sternberg & R. K. Wagner (Eds.), *Intelligence in the everyday world.* New York: Cambridge University Press.

Willis, S. L., & Schaie, K. W. (1986). Training the elderly on the ability factors of spatial orientation and inductive reasoning. *Psychology and Aging, 2,* 239–247.

Wilson, R. W., & White, E. L. (1977). Changes in morbidity, disability, and utilization differentials between the poor and nonpoor: Data from the Health Interview Survey, 1964 and 1973. *Medical Care, 15,* 636–646.

Winch, R. F. (1974). Complementary needs and related notions about voluntary mate selection. In R. F. Winch and G. B. Spanier (Eds.), *Selected studies in marriage and the family.* New York: Holt, Rinehart and Winston.

Winocur, G. (1985). The hippocampus and thalamus: Their roles in short- and long-term memory and the effects of interference. *Behavioral Brain Research, 16,* 135–152.

Winocur, G. (1986). Memory decline in aged rats: A neuropsychological interpretation. *Journal of Gerontology, 41,* 758–763.

Wohlwill, J. F. (1973). *The study of behavioral development.* New York: Academic Press.

Wolf, E. (1960). Glare and aging. *Archives of Ophthalmology, 60,* 502–514.

Women's Bureau, U.S. Bureau of the Census. (1979). *Marital Status and living arrangements: March 1978.* (Current population reports, Series P–20, No. 338). Washington, DC: U.S. Government Printing Office.

Women's Medical Center. (1977). *Menopause.* Washington, DC: Women's Medical Center.

Wood, J. V., Taylor, S. E., & Lichtman, R. R. (1985). Social comparison in adjustment to breast cancer. *Journal of Personality and Social Psychology, 49,* 1169–1183.

Woodruff, D. S. (1975). Relationships among EEG alpha frequency, reaction time, and age: A biofeedback study. *Psychophysiology, 12,* 673–681.

Woodruff, D. S. (1983a). Physiology and behavioral relationships in aging. In D. S. Woodruff & J. E. Birren (Eds.), *Aging ended.* Monterey, CA: Brooks-Cole.

Woodruff, D. S. (1983b). The role of memory in personality continuity: A twenty-five-year follow-up. *Experimental Aging Research, 9,* 31–34.

Woodruff, D. S. (1985). Arousal, sleep, and aging. In J. E. Birren & K. W. Schaie (Eds.), *Handbook of the psychology of aging* (2nd ed.). New York: Van Nostrand Reinhold.

Woodruff, D. S., & Birren, J. E. (1972). Age changes and cohort differences in personality. *Developmental Psychology, 6,* 252–259.

Woodruff-Pak, D. S., & Thompson, R. F. (1988). Classical conditioning of the eyeblink response in delay paradigm in adults aged nineteen to eighty-three years. *Psychology and Aging, 3,* 219–229.

Woodward, N. J., & Wallston, B. S. (1987). Age and health-care beliefs: Self-efficacy as a mediator of low desire for control. *Psychology and Aging, 2,* 3–8.

Wright, J. W. (1982). *The American almanac of jobs and salaries.* New York: Avon.

Wright, L. (1988). The Type A behavior pattern and coronary artery disease: Quest for the active ingredients and the elusive mechanism. *American Psychologist, 43,* 2–14.

Wurtman, R. J. (1985). Alzheimer's disease. *Scientific American, 252,* 62–74.

Yankelovich, D. (1982). New rules in American life: Searching for self-fulfillment in a world turned upside down. *Psychology Today, April,* 35–91.

Yin, P. (1985). *Victimization and the aged.* Springfield, IL: Charles C. Thomas.

Yu, B. P., Masoro, E. J., Murata, I., Bertrand, H. A., & Lynd, F. T. (1982). Life-span study of SPF Fischer 344 male rats fed Ad Libitum or restricted diets: Longevity, growth, lean body mass, and disease. *Journal of Gerontology, 37,* 130–141.

Zarit, S. H. (1980). *Aging and mental disorder.* New York: Free Press.

Zarit, S. H., & Zarit, J. M. (1983). Cognitive impairment. In P. M. Lewinsohn & L. Teri (Eds.), *Clinical geropsychology: New directions in assessment and treatment.* New York: Pergamon Press.

Zarit, S. H., Anthony, C. R., & Boutselis, M. (1987). Intervention with caregivers of dementia patients: Comparison of two approaches. *Psychology and Aging, 2,* 225–232.

Zarit, S. H., Cole, K. D., & Guider, R. L. (1981). Memory-training strategies and subjective memory complaints in the aged. *The Gerontologist, 21,* 158–164.

Zarit, S. H., Eiler, J., & Hassinger, M. (1985). Clinical assessments. In J. E. Birren & K. W. Schaie (Eds.), *Handbook of the psychology of aging* (2nd ed.). New York: Van Nostrand Reinhold.

Zarit, S. H., Orr, N. K., & Zarit, J. M. (1985). *The hidden victims of Alzheimer's disease: Families under stress.* New York: New York University Press.

Zarit, S. H., Todd, P. A., & Zarit, J. M. (1986). Subjective burden of husbands and wives as caregivers: A longitudinal study. *The Gerontologist, 26,* 260–266.

Zarit, S. H., & Zarit, J. M. (1983b). Cognitive impairment. In P. M. Lewinsohn & L. Teri (Eds.), *Clinical geropsychology: New directions in assessment and treatment.* New York: Pergamon Press.

Zisook, S. (1987). Adjustment to widowhood. In S. Zisook (Ed.), *Biopsychosocial aspects of grief and bereavement.* Washington, DC: American Psychiatric Press.

Zisook, S., Shuchter, S. R., & Lyons, L. E. (1987). Predictors of psychological reactions during the early stages of widowhood. *Psychiatric Clinics of North America, 10,* 355–368.

Zivian, M. T., & Darjes, R. W. (1983). Free recall by in-school and out-of-school adults: Performance and metamemory. *Developmental Psychology, 19,* 513–520.

Zola-Morgan, S., & Squire, L. (1986). Memory impairments in monkeys following lesions limited to the hippocampus. *Behavioral Neuroscience, 100,* 155–160.

Photo Credits

Photo Research by Toni Michaels.

CHAPTER 1
Opener © Ulrike Welsch
11   UPI/Bettmann Newsphotos
12   The Bettmann Archive
18   *(left)* © Mike Rizza/The Picture Cube, Inc.
18   *(right)* © Robert Kalman/The Image Works

CHAPTER 2
Opener © Katrina Thomas/Photo Researchers, Inc.
29   *(left)* © Gretje Ferguson
29   *(right)* © Jack Spratt/The Image Works

CHAPTER 3
Opener © Jaye R. Phillips/The Picture Cube, Inc.
71   © Toni Michaels
80   © Dion Ogust/The Image Works
91   courtesy of Patricia M. Peterson

CHAPTER 4
Opener © Dion Ogust/The Image Works
104   *(both)* © Toni Michaels
109   National Archives
132, 133   *(both)* © Dr. Robert Terry, Department of Neurosciences Education and Research Foundation, University of California, San Diego, School of Medicine
137   © David Witbeck/The Picture Cube, Inc.

CHAPTER 5
Opener © Meyer Rangell/The Image Works
165   AP/Wide World Photos
179   © Spencer Grant/Photo Researchers, Inc.

CHAPTER 6
Opener, 188 © Annie Hunter
190   *(fig. 6.1d)* Courtesy of Illusion, Park Ridge, Ill.
194   © Frank Siteman/The Picture Cube, Inc.

CHAPTER 7
Opener © Ulrike Welsch
231   courtesy of Dr. Andrew Schwebel
235   © Leslie Starobin/The Picture Cube, Inc.
253   © F. Grunsweig/Photo Researchers, Inc.

CHAPTER 8
Opener © Ursula Markus/Photo Researchers, Inc.
271   © Annie Hunter
272   © James Carroll
280   © Toni Michaels
287   © Ulrike Welsch
302   © Annie Hunter

CHAPTER 9
Opener © Annie Hunter
314   © Bettye Lane/Photo Researchers, Inc.
330   © Ulrike Welsch
347   *(top)* © Jim Goodwin/Photo Researchers, Inc.
347   *(bottom)* © David Wells/The Image Works

CHAPTER 10

Opener © Ulrike Welsch

357   © David M. Grossman/Photo Researchers, Inc.
362   © John Griffin/The Image Works
373   © Annie Hunter
374   © Lynn McLaren/Photo Researchers, Inc.
379   © Julie O'Neil/The Picture Cube, Inc.
388   © David M. Grossman/Photo Researchers, Inc.

CHAPTER 11

Opener © Toni Michaels

412   AP/Wide World Photos
429   *(all)* UPI/Bettmann Newsphotos
442   © Mark Antman/The Image Works

CHAPTER 12

Opener © J. Berndt/The Picture Cube, Inc.

454   © Nancy Bates/The Picture Cube, Inc.
459   © Blair Seitz/Photo Researchers, Inc.
476   © Michael Hayman/Photo Researchers, Inc.
485   © David Strickler/The Picture Cube, Inc.
489   © Michael McGovern/The Picture Cube, Inc.

CHAPTER 13

Opener © Jim Mahoney/The Image Works

499   © Harriet Gans/The Image Works
518   *(top)* © Annie Hunter
518   *(bottom)* © Joseph Nettis/Photo Researchers, Inc.
524   © David Strickler/The Picture Cube, Inc.
530   © Marianne Gontary/The Picture Cube, Inc.

Figure and Excerpt Credits

CHAPTER 3
Figure 3.4 From L. L. Langley, *Physiology of Man.* Copyright © 1971 Van Nostrand Reinhold Company, New York, NY.

CHAPTER 4
Figure 4.2 From R. Ornstein and R. F. Thompon, *The Amazing Brain.* Copyright © Houghton Mifflin Company.

Box 4.2 © Alzheimer's Disease and Related Disorders Association, Inc.

CHAPTER 5
Figure 5.1 From J. L. Horn, et al., *Research on Aging,* 3:40. Copyright © Sage Publications, Newbury Park, CA.

Figure 5.6 Data from K. W. Schaie, *The Seattle Longitudinal Studies of Adult Psychological Development.* Copyright © 1983 Guilford Press, New York, NY.

Figure 5.9 From J. Botwinick, *Cognitive Process in Maturity and Old Age.* Copyright © 1967 Jack Botwinick. Reprinted by permission.

CHAPTER 6
Figure 6.1b © Gerald F. Fisher, University of Newcastle upon Tyne, United Kingdom.

Figure 6.1e,f Bernstein, Douglas, Edward J. Roy, Thomas K. Srull, and Christopher D. Wickens, *Psychology.* Copyright © 1988 by Houghton Mifflin Company. Used with permission.

Figure 6.2 From T. A. Salthouse and B. L. Somberg, "Effects of Adult Age and Experiences on Elementary Processes" in *Journal of Experimental Psychology: General,* III:176–207. Copyright 1982 by the American Psychological Association. Reprinted by permission.

Box figure 6.1 From G. G. Murdock, Jr., "Recent Developments in Short-Term Memory" in *British Journal of Psychology,* 58:421–433. Copyright © 1967 The British Psychological Society, Leicester, England. Reprinted by permission.

Figure 6.3 Copyright (1966) Canadian Psychological Association. Reprinted by permission.

Figure 6.4 From T. R. Anders, et al., "The Effects of Age Upon Retrieval from Short-Term Memory" in *Developmental Psychology,* 6:214–217. Copyright © 1972 by the American Psychological Association. Reprinted by permission of the author.

Figure 6.6 Reprinted by permission of the *Journal of Gerontology,* 36:620–624, 1981.

Figure 6.7 D. L. Hultsch, "Adult Age Differences in Free Classification and Free Recall" in *Developmental Psychology,* 4:338–342. Copyright © 1971 by the American Psychological Association. Reprinted by permission of the author.

Figure 6.8 From H. P. Bahrick, et al., "Fifty Years of Memory for Names and Faces: A Cross-Sectional Approach" in *Journal of Experimental Psychology,* 104:54–75. Copyright © 1975 by the American Psychological Association. Reprinted by permission of the author.

Figure 6.9 From F. I. M. Craik, et al., *Psychology and Aging,* 2:79–86. Copyright © 1987 by the American Psychological Association.

Box figure 6.2 From J. M. Fitzgerald, "Vivid Memories and the Reminiscence Phenomena: The Role of a Self-Narrative" in *Human Development,* 31:265. Copyright © 1988 S. Karger AG, Basel, Switzerland. Reprinted by permission.

CHAPTER 7

Figure 7.1 From M. D. Berzonsky, "Formal Reasoning in Adolescence: An Alternative View" in *Adolescence,* 13:279–290. Copyright © 1978 Libra Publishers, Inc., San Diego, CA.

CHAPTER 8

Figure 8.2 From M. N. Reedy, J. E. Birren, and K. W. Schaie, "Age and Sex Differences in the Life Span" in *Human Development,* 24:52–66. Copyright © 1981 S. Karger AG, Basel, Switzerland. Reprinted by permission.

excerpt, page 285 From G. O. Hagestad, "Continuity and Connectedness" in *Grandparenthood,* V. Bengston and J. Robertson (eds.). Copyright © 1985 Sage Publications, Inc., Newbury Park, CA.

CHAPTER 9

Figure 9.1 © The Commonwealth Fund Commission, 1987.

CHAPTER 10

Figure 10.3 From *The Social Forces in Later Life: An Introduction to Social Gerontology,* Second Edition, by Robert C. Atchley. © 1977 by Wadsworth Publishing Company, Inc. Reprinted by permission of Wadsworth Publishing Company, Belmont, California 94002.

CHAPTER 11

Figure 11.1 Reprinted by permission of the publishers from *Themes of Work and Love in Adulthood,* edited by Neil J. Smelser and Erik H. Erikson, Cambridge, Mass.: Harvard University Press. Copyright © 1980 by the President and Fellows of Harvard College.

Figure 11.3 From D. F. Hultsch and J. K. Plemons, "Life Events and Life Span Development" in *Life Span Development and Behavior,* P. B. Baltes and O. G. Brim (eds.). Copyright © 1979 Academic Press, Orlando, FL. Reprinted by permission.

excerpt, pages 427 and 428 From P. T. Costa, Jr. and R. R. McCrae, "Still Stable After All These Years: Personality as a Key to Some Issues of Adulthood and Old Age" in *Life Span Development and Behavior,* Vol. 3, P. B. Baltes and O. G. Brim (eds.). Copyright © 1980 Academic Press, Orlando, FL.

Figure 11.4 From P. T. Costa, Jr. and R. R. McCrae, "Still Stable After All These Years: Personality as a Key to Some Issues in Adulthood and Old Age" in *Life Span Development and Behavior,* Vol. 3, P. B. Baltes and O. G. Brim (eds.). Copyright © 1980 Academic Press, Orlando, FL. Reprinted by permission of the publisher and the author.

CHAPTER 12

Figure 12.1 From S. K. Whitbourne, "The Psychological Construction of the Life Span" in *Handbook of the Psychology of Aging,* 2d ed., J. E. Birren and K. W. Schaie (eds.). Copyright © 1985 Van Nostrand Reinhold Company, New York, NY. Reprinted by permission.

Figure 12.2 From S. K. Whitbourne, "The Psychological Construction of the Life Span" in *Handbook of the Psychology of Aging,* 2d ed., J. E. Birren and K. W. Schaie (eds.). Copyright © 1985 Van Nostrand Reinhold Company, New York, NY. Reprinted by permission.

excerpt, page 464 From A. LaRue, et al., "Aging and Mental Disorders" in *Handbook of the Psychology of Aging,* 2d ed., J. E. Birren and K. W. Schaie (eds.). Copyright © 1985 Van Nostrand Reinhold Company, New York, NY.

Figure 12.3 Copyright © 1988 by The New York Times Company. Reprinted by permission.

CHAPTER 13

Figure 13.1 © Society for the Right to Die, 250 West 57 Street, New York, NY. Reprinted with permission.

NAME INDEX

SUBJECT INDEX

P